Street by Street

GLOUCESTERSHIRE

PLUS BRISTOL, CHEPSTOW, CRICKLADE, LEDBURY, MALMESBURY, SHIPSTON-ON-STOUR

Enlarged Areas Cheltenham, Gloucester

1st edition May 2001

© Automobile Association Developments Limited 2001

This product includes map data licensed from Ordnance Survey® with the permission of the Controller of Her Majesty's Stationery Office. © Crown copyright 2000. All rights reserved. Licence No: 399221.

Published by AA Publishing (a trading name of Automobile Association Developments Limited, whose registered office is Norfolk House, Priestley Road, Basingstoke, Hampshire, RG24 9NY. Registered number 1878835).

Mapping produced by the Cartographic Department of The Automobile Association.

A CIP Catalogue record for this book is available from the British Library.

Printed by in Italy by Printer Trento srl

The contents of this atlas are believed to be correct at the time of the latest revision. However, the publishers cannot be held responsible for loss occasioned to any person acting or refraining from action as a result of any material in this atlas, nor for any errors, omissions or changes in such material. The publishers would welcome information to correct any errors or omissions and to keep this atlas up to date. Please write to Publishing, The Automobile Association, Fanum House, Basing View, Basingstoke, Hampshire, RG21 4EA.

Ref: MX079

Key to map pages	ii-iii
Key to map symbols	iv-1
Enlarged scale pages	2-7
Street by Street	8-353
Index – towns & villages	354-356
Index – streets	356-385
Index – featured places	385-390

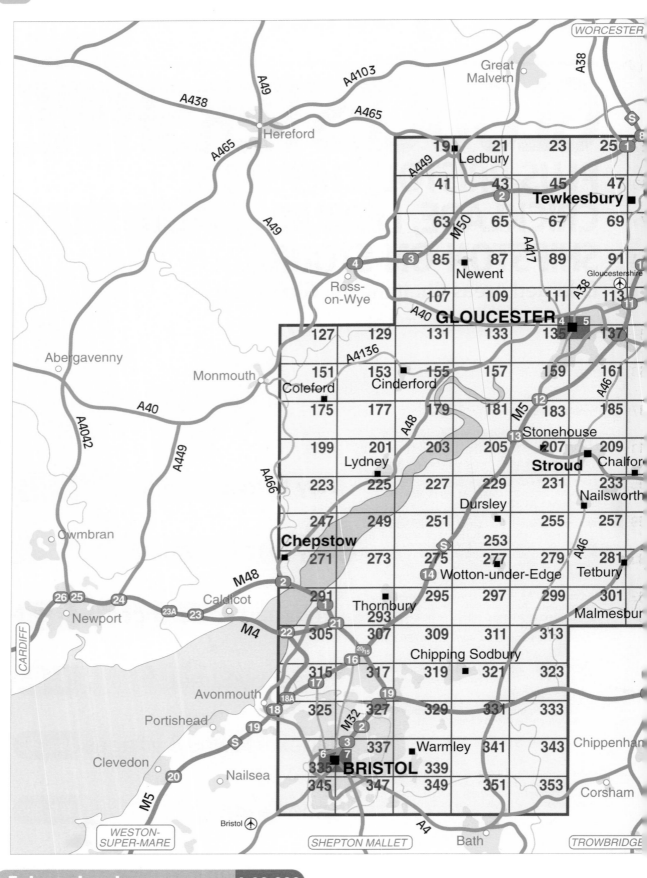

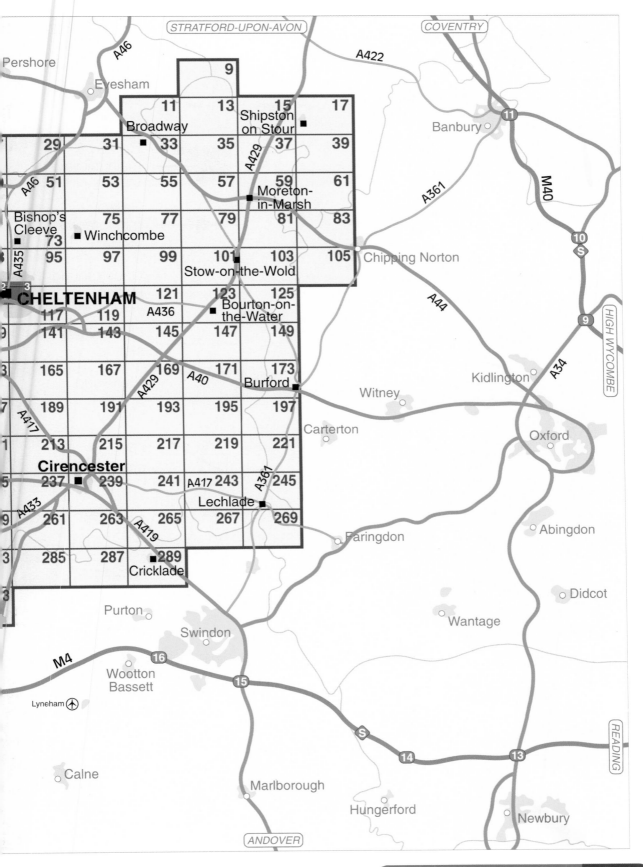

STRATFORD-UPON-AVON

COVENTRY

Pershore

A46

A422

Evesham

Banbury

9

11 13 15 17
Broadway Shipston
on Stour

29 31 33 35 37 39
A429

51 53 55 57 59 61
A46 Moreton-
in-Marsh

Bishop's 75 77 79 81 83
Cleeve
73 Winchcombe

95 97 99 101 103 105
A435 Stow-on-the-Wold Chipping Norton

CHELTENHAM 121 123 125
A436 Bourton-on-
117 119 the-Water

141 143 145 147 149

165 167 169 171 173
A429 A40 Burford

189 191 193 195 197
A417 Carterton

213 215 217 219 221
Cirencester

237 239 241 243 245
A417 A361
A433 Lechlade

261 263 265 267 269
A419

285 287 289
Cricklade

A361

A44

A34

A361

M40

11

10
S

9 HIGH WYCOMBE

Kidlington

Witney

Oxford

Abingdon

Faringdon

Didcot

Purton

Swindon

Wantage

M4

16

Wootton
Bassett

15

Lyneham

S

14

13 READING

Calne

Marlborough

Hungerford

Newbury

ANDOVER

3.6 inches to 1 mile **Scale of main map pages** 1:17,500

0   1/2   miles   1

0   1/2   1   kilometres   1 1/2   2

Junction 9	Motorway & junction			Park & Ride
Services	Motorway service area			Bus/coach station
	Primary road single/dual carriageway			Railway & main railway station
Services	Primary road service area			Railway & minor railway station
	A road single/dual carriageway			Underground station
	B road single/dual carriageway			Light railway & station
	Other road single/dual carriageway			Preserved private railway
	Restricted road		*LC*	Level crossing
	Private road			Tramway
←	One way street			Ferry route
	Pedestrian street			Airport runway
	Track/ footpath			Boundaries- borough/ district
	Road under construction			Mounds
	Road tunnel		**93**	Page continuation 1:17,500
P	Parking		7	Page continuation to enlarged scale 1:10,000

River/canal
lake, pier

Toilet with
disabled facilities

Aqueduct
lock, weir

Petrol station

465
▲
Winter Hill

Peak (with
height in
metres)

PH   Public house

Beach

PO   Post Office

Coniferous
woodland

Public library

Broadleaved
woodland

ℓ   Tourist Information
Centre

Mixed
woodland

Castle

Park

Historic house/
building

Cemetery

Wakehurst
Place NT

National Trust
property

Built-up
area

Ⓜ   Museum/
art gallery

Featured building

✝   Church/chapel

City wall

Country park

A&E   Accident &
Emergency
hospital

Theatre/
performing arts

Toilet

Cinema

Pittville Comprehensive School

G9 1 Sandford Mill Cl
H9 1 Knightsbridge Crs
K3 1 Evenlode Av

Albert Road

Lakebridge Rd
Hemount

Welland Rd
Welland Drive

PRESTBURY ROAD
B4632

Prescott Walk
Prescott

Coronation Road

PRIORS ROAD

B4075

Chiltern Road

Bouncer's Lane
Bouncer's Lane

Studland Drive
Fawley Drive
Core Road
Court Road

G H J K **94** L M

Cheviot Road

Pennine Road

Fir Tree Close
Bowen Close

Lynworth Primary School

Cotswold Road

Police Station

Honeysuckle Drive
Ivy Bank
Whitethorn
Willowherb Close
Briar Walk

1 Nov

Bramble Rise

Black Berry Fld

Temple Industrial Estate

Cleevemount Close
Lt Cleevemount

Overbrook Drive

Oakland Avenue

B4632

Mendip Close
Mendip Road

Lynworth Place

Cromwell Road

Cam Road
Chett Road

Priors Road

2 Cemetery †

Pittville Crs Lane
Windsor Street
Pittville Crs
PRESTBURY ROAD

Temple Industrial Est

Cakebridge Place

Cheltenham Town Association Football Club

Cromwell Road

Lynworth

Clyde Crescent

Dart Road

Isbourne Road

Burma Avenue

Somme Road

Oakley Road

3 **Oakley**

Pittville Circ
Pittville

Selkirk Gdns
Selkirk Close
Whaddon Drive

Whaddon Road

Wyman's Road
Colne Av

Thames Road

Severn Road

Tamar Road

Clyde Road

Whaddon

Whaddon Primary School

Ladysmith Road

Kimberley Walk

Salamanca Road

Imjin Road

Fairview

Moor Ct Dr
Hotel

Hayes Road

Cleeve View Road

Whaddon Avenue

Robins Cl

PO

† 1

Whaddon Road

Windsor Road

Mersey Road

Avon Rd
Churn Av

Humber Road

Whaddon Road

Whaddon Road

Hill Vw Rd

Wessex Dr

Burma Avenue

St Anne's Cl
N Hall Ms
Hotel
St Hall St

Winstonian Road

All Saints Vis

Jersey Av

Ariel Log Rd

Berkhampstead School

Hewlett Road

Teme Rd

GL52

Oak Mnr Dr

Richmond Md
Battledown Md

Harp Hill

4

Victoria Pl
All Saints Road

Hewlett Road

All Saints' Terrace

Eldon Road

Beechurst Av

Eldon Av

B4075

Hales Close

Foxgrove Dr

5

116

Westdown Gardens
Brighton Road
Leighton Road

PO

Cheltenham Cricket Club

ROAD

The Grove

Battledown Close

Harp Hill

Camp Road

6

Duke Street

Carlton Street

PO

King's Road

Cranham Rd

Prince's Victoria Terrace

Holy Apostles C of E School

Oakley Road

Stanley Road

Ashley Road

Beechwood Close

Priory Ter
Priory

Sydenham Road

HALES

Battledown

Battledown **7**

Sydenham Villas
Sydenham Rd

Athelney Way

King Alfred Way

Saxon Way

Haywards Lane

Approach

Battledown Dr

Battledown Industrial Estate

Birchley Road

Ashley Road

Greenway Lane

Keynsham Bank
Keynsham Street

Coltham Fields

PO

Rosehill Street

Strickland Road

Coltham Road

8

A40
Avenall Parade

Upper Park Street

Ewens Road

Pine Cl

Oakhurst Rise

Greenway Lane

SANDFORD MILL ROAD

Chelsea Cl
1

A40

Westminster Rd
Southgate Drive

Haywards Road

Churchill Dr

Roosevelt Av

Beaufort Road

Charlton Court Rd

Oak Av

St Edwards School

St Edwards Junior School

Ashley Road

9

King Arthur Close

Charlton Drive

LONDON ROAD

CIRENCESTER

†

Langton Gv
Oakland Street
Hamilton Street

The Charlton Kings Clinic

116

Sixway Clinic

Greenway Lane

Ashley Close

Ryeworth Drive

Ryeworth Road

Ham Close

Ch **G** **lton Park**

H **J** Cudnall Street **K** **L** **M**

Ryeworth Road

Briarpa

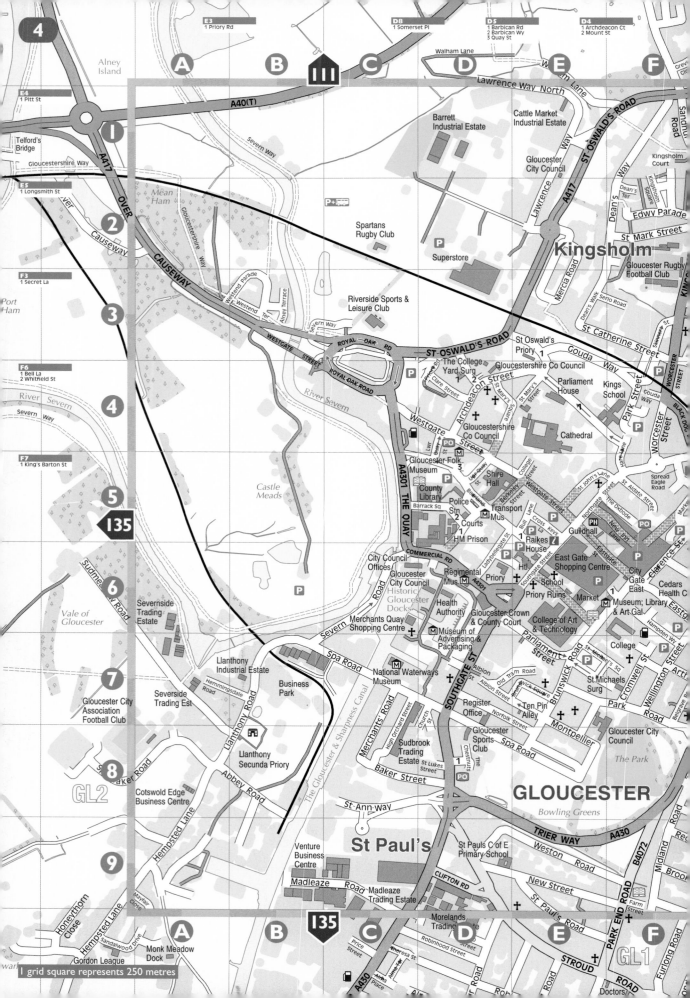

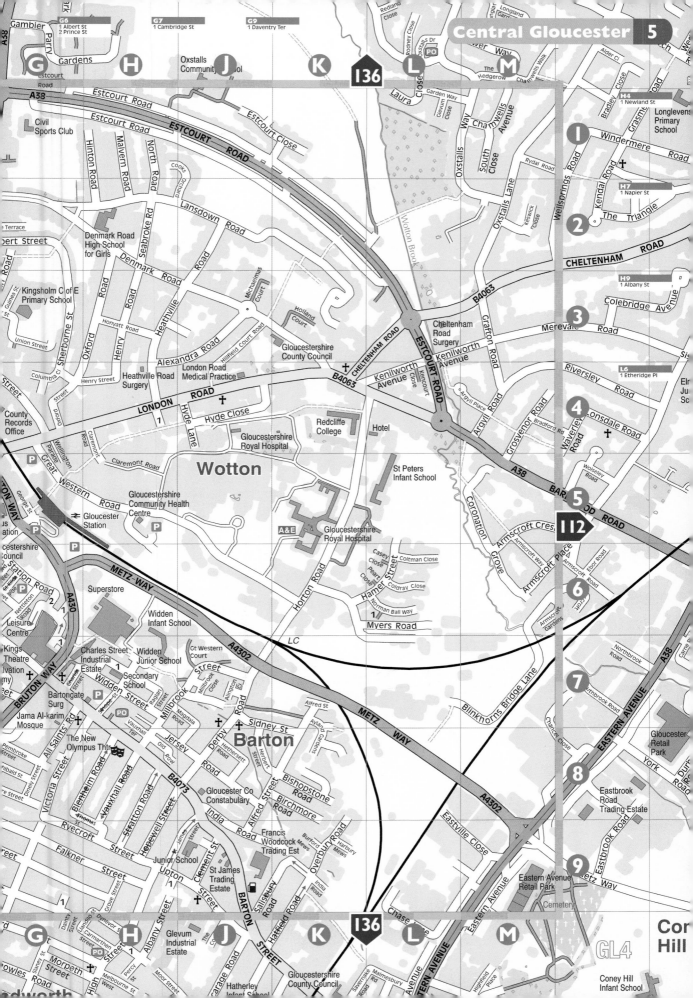

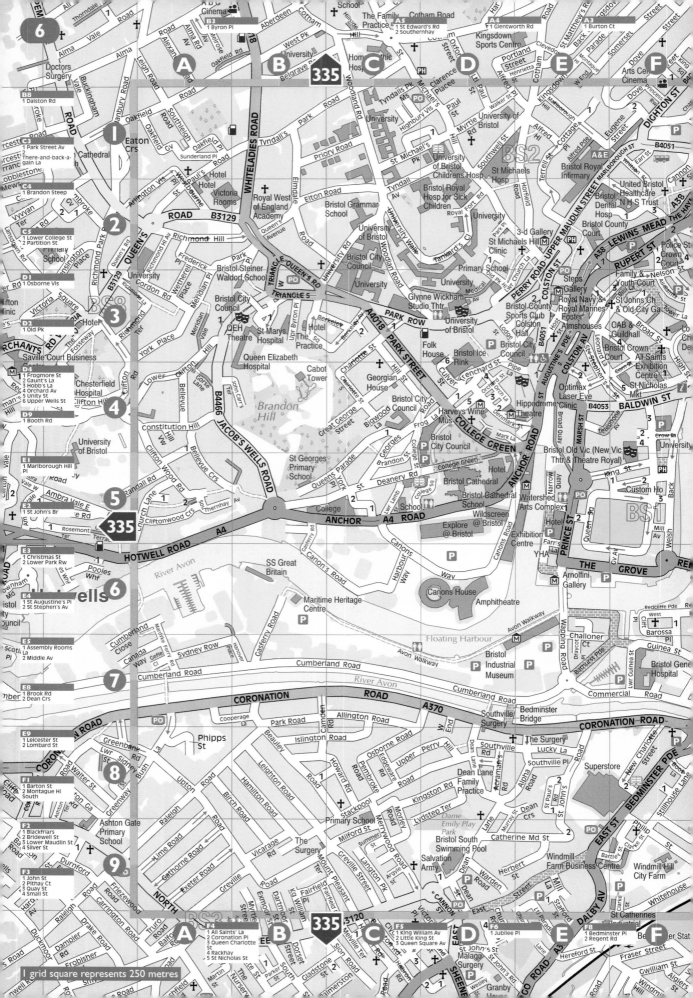

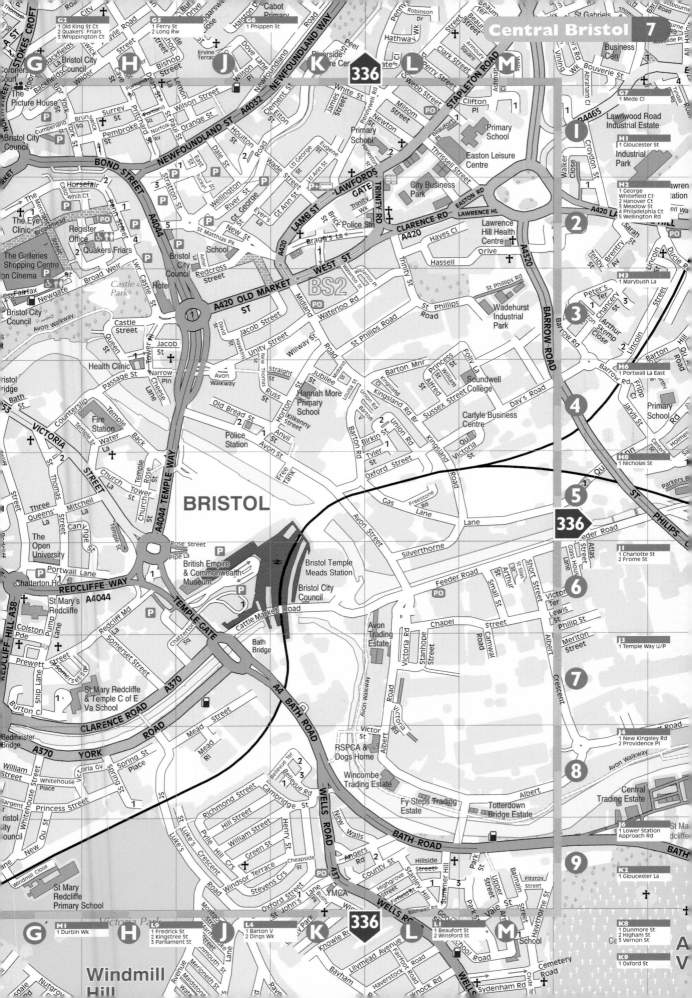

G H J K L M

1

Lower Quinton

2

3

4

5

6

7

8

1 Orchard Cl

Sharry Lane

B4632

Tailor's Lane

Edmonds Lane

Dobbe Rd

Hill Lane

Meon Close

Goose Lane

The Surgery

Magdale Cl

Infant School

Mistone Cl

St John's Cl

St Swithin's Dr

Main Road

The Close

Friday St

The Firs

Thackera Cl

Stileman Cl

Bastyan Av

**Upper
Quinton**

**Lower
Clopton**

CAMPDEN ROAD

ROAD

Meon House

Heart of England Way

Heart of England Way

Monarch's Way

Lower Meon

Meon Hall

Monarch's Way

Adming Farm

Admington Lane

B4632

Meon Road

Nursery

Granbrook Lane

Cedar Road

GRANBROOK LANE

B4632

Old Mnr Gdns

Mickleton

Cemetery

Baker's Hill

Lane

Upper Clopton

Warwickshire County
Gloucestershire County

Coleman's Hill

Monarch's Way

Mickleton Wood Farm

Hidcote Combe

Gloucestershire County
Warwickshire County

Kiftsgate Gardens

Hidcote Garden (NT)

13

**Hidcote
Bartrim**

G H J K L M

10

The Lankets
Brewers Lane
The Lane
Badsey Fields
Badsey Lane
Chapel Street
High Street
Mill Lane
PO
The Knapp

A · **B** · **C** · **D** · **E** · **F**

B4035

School La
Fields Close
Binyon Cl
Willersey Road
Badsey First School
Badsey

Stoneford Lane

1

Sands Lane

2
Golden Lane
Cemetery

Penelon
Washington Rd
Sally Close
Manor
Dale

Bowers Hill

3

Worcestershire County
Gloucestershire County

Willersey Road
Badsey Lane

Wickhamford

4
PO
PITCHERS
Pitchers Hl
Sandy's Avenue

Whitfurrows Farm

Bond Industrial Estate

HILL

5

Downrip Farm

A44

Gallipot House

6

Hayway Farm

Murcot Road

EVESHAM ROAD

7

Old Well Farm

Collin Lane

A44

8

Hotel

Evesham Road

A Broadway Road **B** **Child Bickham** **C** **32** **D** **E** A44 **F**
Green Cl
PO
Childswickham School
Atkinson St
Pennylands Bank
Smallbrook Road

1 grid square represents 500 metres

G7
1 Frampton Dr

G8
1 Jordans Cl

H7
1 Church St

G   H   J   K   L   M

WESTON ROAD

Weston Road

1

Larkborough
Farm

B4035

2

Honeybourne Airfield
Industrial Estate

Worcestershire County
Gloucestershire County

3

Saintbury
Grounds

Honeybourne Road

Weston-
sub-Edge

4

Buckle Street

PO
Cider Mill
Barn

Dover's Vw

Parsons Lane

Chapel Lane

B4632

12

5

Top Farm

6

Willersey
Industrial
Estate

B4632

Saintbury

7

Timms Green

Leys Orchard

PO

Willersey
School

Willersey

Park Farm

Collin Close

Hays Close

MAIN STREET

B4632

Fields Lane

Willow Road

BROADWAY ROAD

Campden Lane

Buckle Street

Weston
Park

8

G   H   J   K   L   M

Gloucestershire County
Worcestershire County

Foxhill Manor

The Narrow

A B C **8** D E F

1

Norton
Grounds Farm

Poden Lane

B4632

2

Aston
Subedge

Niveveh
Farm

B4632

B4035

3

Manor
House

Burnt
Norton

Middle Norton
Farm

CAMPDEN ROAD

B4081

4

II

ASTON

5

The
Lynches

Attlepin
Farm

ROAD

B4081

6

Kingcomb

The
Bratches

Monarch's Way

7

Cotswold Way

Kingcomb

Cotswold Way

Lane

Cotswold Way

Hoo

The Hoo

Chipping
Campden

ASTON ROAD

Grevel Lane

Chipping
Campden
School

Monarch's Way

Haydons Cl

Woods End
Close

Griggs
Close

Rolling
Stones

B4035

CIDERMILL
LANE
PH

CHURCH
STREET

STATION

8

Dyer's
Lane

Littleworth

Littleworth

The
Medical Centre

Primary
School
Hotel

Back
Ends

The
Town
Hall

Hotel

HIGH ST

LEYSBOURNE

High St

B4081

County
Police Court

Police
Stn

Calf's Lane

Bangers

Station Rd

Weston
Park

LWR HIGH ST

PO
PH

Lwr High St

Coldicotts

SHEEP
STREET

Haysum

34

Park
Road

Blind Lane

Littleworth
Road

Shepherd's
Close

Federated Primary Schools of
Ebrington & St James

Cherry
Orchard
Close

A B **C** D **E** F

Westington

G H J **9** K L M

I

Baker's Hill

Kiftsgate Gardens

Hidcote Manor Garden (NT)

Hidcote Bartrim

Gloucestershire / Warwickshire

Monarch's Way

Nebsworth Lane 2

Heart Of England Way

Hidcote Boyce

3

Longlands Farm

4

Furze Lane

GL55 **14**

Hidcote Road

Mickleton Hills Farm

5

Nash's Lane

Ebrington 6

Elm Grove Road

Nash's Lane

Campden Road

New Road

Battledene Farm

May Lane

7

LC

Station Road

Castle Gardens

Close

Road

THE CAM B4035

8

G H J **35** K L M

B4035 PULPIT LANE

B5
1 High St
2 Horsefair
3 Husbandmans Cl
4 Market Pl
5 Norluck Ct
6 Pound Cl

B4
1 Badgers Crs

A6
1 Costard Av
2 Hanson Av

A5
1 Farm Cl

A B C D E F

Hill Clumps

1

River Stour

Honington

Granby Road

2

Fell Mill Lane

Centenary Way

3

Fell Mill Lane

Fell Mill Farm

Mayo Rd

4

Shipston Medical Cen

Shipston Industrial Estate

Station

Donnington Rd

STRATFORD ROAD

A3400

Centenary Way

River Way

15

Tilemans La

Junior & Infant School

Watery La / 5

The Ellen Badger Hospital

Shipston-on-Stour

Hay Meadow

Darlingscote Rd

Birdhill Rd

Greenway Road

Manor La

Oxway Cl

Telegraph St

Stour Valley Community School

Warwick Pl

Berry Cl

Glen Cl

Berry Avenue

Sheep St

PO

PH

CHURCH ST

5

Pittway Av

Queens Av

Saltens Av

WEST ST

Campden Rd

Clark Cl

Green Lane

Gerrards Rd

Old Rd

NEW STREET

CAMPDEN ROAD

Oldbutt Rd

Hanson Av

Marshall Av

PH

River Stour

B4035

6

The Maldens

Pettora Rd

Greenfields Cl

Simpson Rd

Callaways Rd

Springfield

The Hobbins

Bosley Cl

Bannister Rd

Keeley Rd

Furze Hill Road

Burford Meadow

Barcheston

7

Hawthorn Way

Holly Rd

Elm Rd

Ashgrove

LONDON ROAD

Cemetery

8

Pig Brook

Willington

Horseleys Farm

River Stour

CV36

1 grid square represents 500 metres

G H J K L M

Centenary Way

Centenary Way

Littleworth Farm

Aylesmore Farm

St Dennis

Tus Brook

Tusbrook Farm

Knolland's Farm

B4035

Barcheston Ground Farm

Roundhill Farm

FANT HILL

Castle Hill

Bells Lane

Hill Lane

Gillett's Lane

Upper Brailes

Brailes C of E Primary School

Castle Hill Lane

Henbrook Lane

Grove End

Jeff's Close

Famington Farm

Highwall Spinney

Sutton Lane

Tom Tun Lane

1 2 3 4 5 6 7 8

G H J K L M

41
20

Map labels

L2
1 Abercrombie Cl
2 Drinkwater Cl
3 Northdown Cl
4 Sunshine Cl

L3
1 Massey Rd

M1
1 Challen Cl
2 The Garth
3 Plaister's End

M5
1 Furlong Ct
2 Miller Craddock Wy

M2
1 Kempley Brook Dr

Grid letters (top)
G H J K L M

Grid numbers (right)
I 2 3 4 5 6 7 8

Grid letters (bottom)
G H J K L M

Place names and features

New Mills
Grovesend
Wallhills
LEDBURY
Saxon Way
Yeoman
Viking Wy
BUSH PITCH
HEREFORD ROAD
Gosling Wy
Callow End
Northmead
The Langland
Ridley
Newbury Park
Cooke
Gibson Rd
Target
Frome Brook Road
Preston Brook Close
Ledbury Station
Station Industrial Estate
THE HOMEND
B4214
Knapp Rd
Upperfields
Hillfield Drive
Crescent
Homend
John Lee
Pl
Rupert Rd
New Mills Way
Austin
Frost Rd
The Mews
Orchard La
Belle Orch
Primary School
Margaret Rd
Long Acres
Station Industrial Est
Shell Ho
Gallery
PO
Queen's Wy
Lawnside Rd
Bye St
St Katherine's
Market St
Upr Hall
Church
STREET
Bridge Street
Barrett
Chapel
Woodleigh Close
Oatleys Ter
Woodleigh Rd
Ledbury Market Surg
Queen's Ct
Mkt Theatre
B4216
Hotel
PH
PH
Victoria Road
Oatleys Crts
Oatleys Road
Lower Road
Albert Road
Churchill Mew
Pound Meadow
Pound
Souths Pde
THE SOUTH END
A449
THE SOUTHEND
Little Marcle Road
NEW STREET
Elmsdale Rd
Birch Close
John Masefield High School
A449
Bankside Industrial Estate
Egar St
Chestnut Cl
Oakland Drive
Oakland Dr
Cemetery
Ledbury Town Football Club
Martins Wy
Aston Cl
Villa Wy
Russet
Bramley
Oakham
Old Wharf
Biddulph
Blenheim Dr
Orchard Pl
Spring Gv
WAY
LEADON
Hazle Cl
Woodfield
Shepherds
Old Wharf Industrial Estate
B4216
Hazel Farm
River Leadon
Rowland's Green
Falcon Lane
Flights Farm
Old Lilly Hall
Lilly Hall Lane
Hill House
Robinscroft
A449
Orlham Lane
Ludstock
A449
Orlham Farm
Siddington Farm
Oldfields
Poets Path
County of Herefordshire
Gloucestershire County
Argus Farm
B4216
Dinchall
A438
A417 LEADON WAY
A438
Orchard Business Park
The Hops Business Park

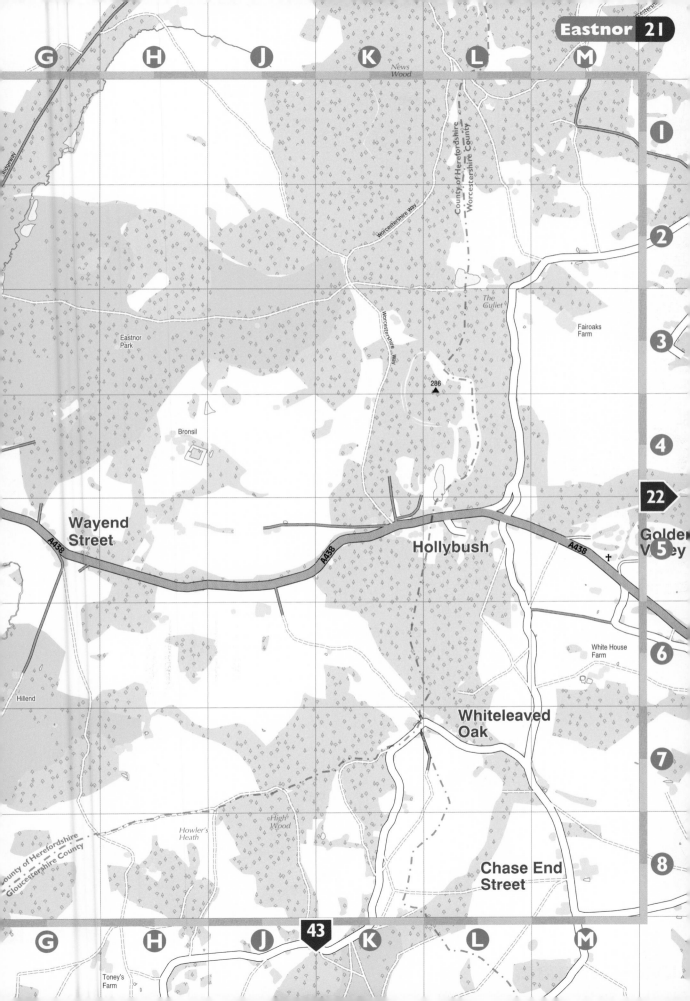

G H J K L M

News Wood

I

2

3

4

22

5

6

7

8

Worcestershire Way

County of Herefordshire
Worcestershire County

The Gullet

Fairoaks Farm

Eastnor Park

286

Bronsil

Wayend Street

A438

Hollybush

A438

Golden Valley

White House Farm

Hillend

Whiteleaved Oak

Chase End Street

Howler's Heath

High Wood

County of Herefordshire
Gloucestershire County

G H J **43** K L M

Toney's Farm

A   B   C   D   E   F

1

Eight Oaks Farm

New Road

2

Chandler's Cross

Druggers End

Drugger's End Lane

B4208

Biddle's Farm

3

Rough Chase

Castlemorto

Hollybed Common

Mill Farm

B4208

Castlemorton School

4

†

21

Golden Valley

Miller's Court

Coombegreen Common

Miller's Court Road

5

†

Birts Street

White Farm

PH

6

A4438

B4208

7

Rye Court

Rye Street

8

B4208

Camer's Green

A4438

A4434

A   B   C   D   E   F

Whiting Farms

I grid square represents 500 metres

G H J K L M

I

2

3

4

24

5

6 L

7

8

Cutler's
Farm

Welland
Stone

Longdon
Hill End

Little
Welland

Walk
Farm

Worcestershire Way Link

Drinkwater's
Farm

Hillend
Court

Worcestershire Way Link

Longdon
Marsh

er's Court Road

Birtsmorton

Longdon Brook

Marsh
End

The
Hill

Red
House

G H J K L M

45

A438

Pendock
Moor

A   B   C   D   E   F

Green

B4211

Wheatley Lane

Longdon Heath

Stanks Lane

Avenue

Road

Ham Court

1

2

Holdfast

B4211

3

Worcestershire Way

4

Hillworth

Green Farm

Heath Hill Farm

5

Queenhill

Bushley Brook

Longdon

School

6

Orchard Ridge

The Badhams

Moat Bank

Worcestershire Way Link

Bear Lane

Gunnice

M50

7

B4211

Chambers Court

Guller's End

Hill House

Rectory Farm

8

M50

Worcestershire Way

A   B   C   D   E   F

per's End

Slades Green

B4211

1 grid square represents 500 metres

H5
1 Bricknell Av
2 The Croftlands
3 Glebeland Dr
4 Gravel Pits Cl
5 Homestead Cl
6 Plantation Crs
7 Russet Cl

G H J K L M

I
2
3
28
4
5
6
7
8

Bredon's
Norton

Rectory
Farm

Westmancote

Chapel Lane
Farm Lane

Wing Lane
Bayliss Road

Lower
Westmancote

Hill Cl

Kemerton Road

Kemerton

PO
Job's Lane
• The Priory

Kinsham Lane

MORETON LANE

Mill End

Severn
Sailing Club

Dock Lane
Avon

First School
PH
PO
Back La
Church St
HIGH ST

B4080

Rosenose Rd

Cherry Rd

Bredon

KEMERTON ROAD

Farm La
Oak La

Station Dr
Blenheim Drive
Jubilee Dr
Cotswold

4
6
5
1
2
3

Pippins Rd

Waterloo Wy
Orchard Cl

Queensmead

CHELTENHAM ROAD

Chapel Lane
Kinsham
B4079

Kinsham Lane

Carrant Brook

Worcestershi
Gloucester

A B C D E F

1

2

Bell's Castle

3

✝

ving Lane

Overbury Park

Court

Overbury

✝

Pigeon Lane

merton

riory

4

School Lane

Overbury First School

Watergrip Lane

Conderton

Manor House

27

5

6

Crashmore Lane

7

Silk Mill

✝

Main Street

PO

Ashton Road

Station

Manor House

Back Lane

8

Carrant Brook

Little Beckford

A46(T) CHELTENHAM

Worcester County
Gloucestershire County

A B C D E F

50

Cheltenham Road

Blacksmiths La

Back Cl

Western

sweden

1 grid square represents 500 metres

A   B   C   D   E   F

DI
1 Millfield

I

Sandfield
Farm

Sandfield
Lane

The Hollows

Cheltenham   Road

Sedgeberrow

The
Yd

CHELTENHAM ROAD

Bridge Meadow
Close

Bridewell Dr

Churchill Road

Ca...brook
Fa...

2

C of E
First
School

Barn

Main   Street

PO

Blacksmiths
Close

1

A46(T)

WINCHCOMBE

Asto
Som

3

Worcestershire Coun...
Gloucestershire County

B4078

River Isbourne

4

29

5

Cullabine
Farm

Bank
Farm

6

Dumbleton

B4078

Blacksmiths
Lane

Dairy Lane

Mill Farm

7

B4078

Leyfield Farm

8

Cotton's Farm

A   B   C   **52**   D   E   F

Raymeadow
Farm

G2
1 Old Hall Cl

H2
1 Woodland Cl

G H J K L M

Hinto L d

1

2

ille

3

Glebe Rd

School Rd

PO

Broadway Road

Church Rd

✝

Buckland Fields

4

32

Worcestershire County

Gloucestershire County

5

6

Wormington

Leasow House

B4632

7

Stanton Fields

8

G H J 53 K L M

Wormington Grange

G H J K L M

1 Willow
Fields Lane
1 Bridgemans Cl

G2
G3
1 Bredon Vw
2 Daston Cl
3 High St

BR... WAY ROAD

Gloucestershire County
Worcestershire County

Foxhill Manor

Golf Course

Bibsworth Farm

A44

Farncombe House

Hotel

Buckle Street

Cotswold Way

Ten Lane

Buckle Street

Weston Park

1

2

3

4

34

Cotswold

Tilbury Hollow

Coombe Farm

5

Bibsworth Lane

Anderson Gallery
Cotswold Teddy Bear Mus
Kirtlands Preparatory School

FISH HILL

Cotswold Way

Cotswold Way

Peter's Farm

A44

Broadway Tower

Broadway Tower Country Park

Buckle Street

Springhill Industrial Estate

6

7

Dor Knap

Kite's Nest

Middle Hill House

Buckle Street

Worcestershire County

Heath Farm

8

Dull... Wo...

G H J K 55 L M

Seven Wells

THE CAM B4035

B4035 PUDLICOTT LANE

B4479

Paxford

PH

B4479

Brookside

Knee Brook

Greystone Farm

Briar Hill Farm

LC

36 Farm

Northwick Business Centre

Wellacres Farm

John Woofe Court

B4479 STATION ROAD

Northwick Park

Monarch's Way

Draycott

Wydelands

Northcot Lane

Post Office Lane

Dorn Hill

STATION ROAD B4479

Winterway

Springfield

Summerfield Cl

Cem

C of E School

Police Station

Sleepy Hollow Farm Park

kley

PO

Hotel

Chapel Lane

Bell

PH

School Lane

Lower St

Millview

Pasture Lane

B4479

Pasture Farm

36

A B4035
B
C 1035
14
D
E
Gloucestershire County
Warwickshire County
F

Charingworth
Grange G7
1 Church Farm La

Braxfield
House

1
Marfurlong
Farm
B4479

Cottage
Farm
Tankards Hill

2
B4479

Blackdowns

**Stretton
on-Foss**

Paxford
3

Middle
Ditchford

4

Knee Brook

35
Stapenhill
Farm

Ditchford
Hill

5
Neighbrook

Knee Brook

6

7
Church vw
†

**Aston
Magna**

Aston
Hale
A429

8

Dorn
Hill
A
B
C **58**
D
E
F

I grid square represents 500 metres

Pig

G   H   J   **15**   K   L   M

Rowborough

Horseleys
Farm

I

Carson
Cl
Belcony
Chapel
Corr

2

A429

Paddle Brook

High Furze

3

Ditchford
Frary Village

4

38

Lower Ditchford
Village

Lower Farm

5

Becket
Cl

6

Stone
Br

Todenham

7

Gloucestershire County
Warwickshire County

Oldborough
Farm

8

Wolford Road

G   H   J   **59**   K   L   M

Geat
Wolf

Mount
Sorrell

The
Green

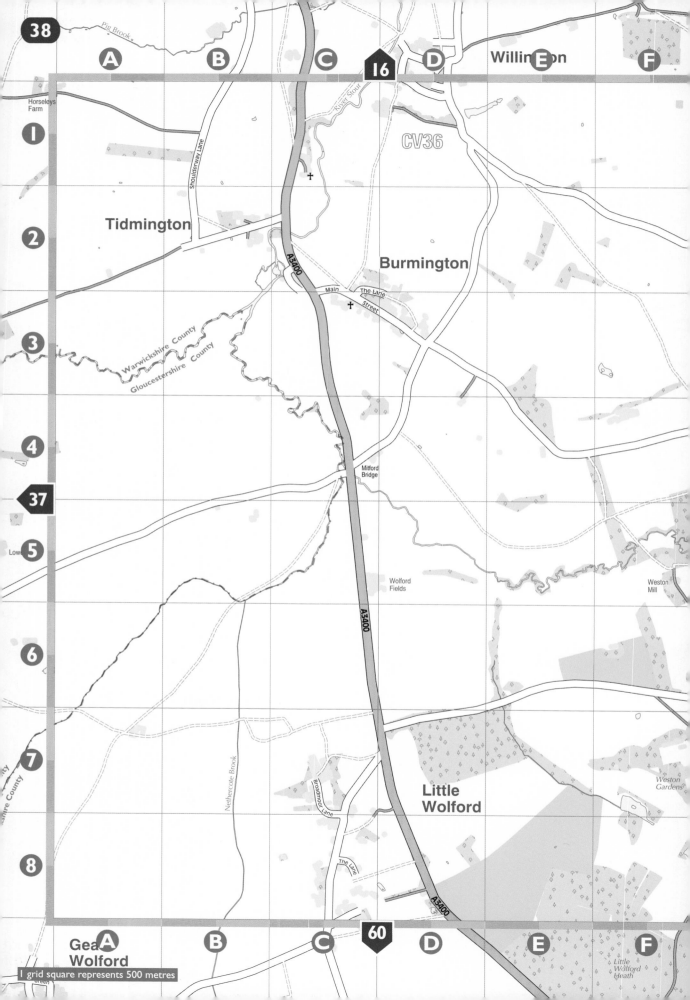

Farnington Farm

G H J **17** K L M

I

North Farm

2

New House Farm

Brailes Golf Club

Sutton Lane

Tommy's Turn Lane

Sutton Lane

Jeff's Close

Highwall Spinney

3

Rmington Range

Cherington Butts

Church Farm

Sutton Lane

4

Sutton-under-Brailes

† **Stourton**

5

St John's Road

St John's Cl

Feathered Lane

Sutton Mill

Cherington

Wood Lane

Berrills Lane

Street Ln

6

Lanes End Farm

7

Stourton Hill

8

Margett's Hill

Weston Park

County of Herefordshire
Gloucestershire County

G H Oldfields J **19** K L M

I

Henberrow

Leddington

Dinchall Farm

†

2

Mirabels Farm

Donnir

3

Poets Path

Poets Path

B4216

Tillputsend Cott

Donnington Hall

Greenway
PO

4

42

Rosehill

Poets Path

Tillers' Green

5

Great Netherton

Ockington Farm

B4215

Preston Brook

Poets Path

6

B4024

Windcross Farm

Wilton Place

B4216

Poets Path No 2

7

Hill Ash

Poets Path

Shakesfield

Poets' Path No 1

B4215

Poets Path No 1

8

Allums

Dymock

Poets Path No 2

†

Daffodil Way

Poets Path No 1

PO

Lane

Crowfield

The Pound

Daffodil Way

Western Way

†

The Old Rock

G H J **63** K L M

B4215

B4215

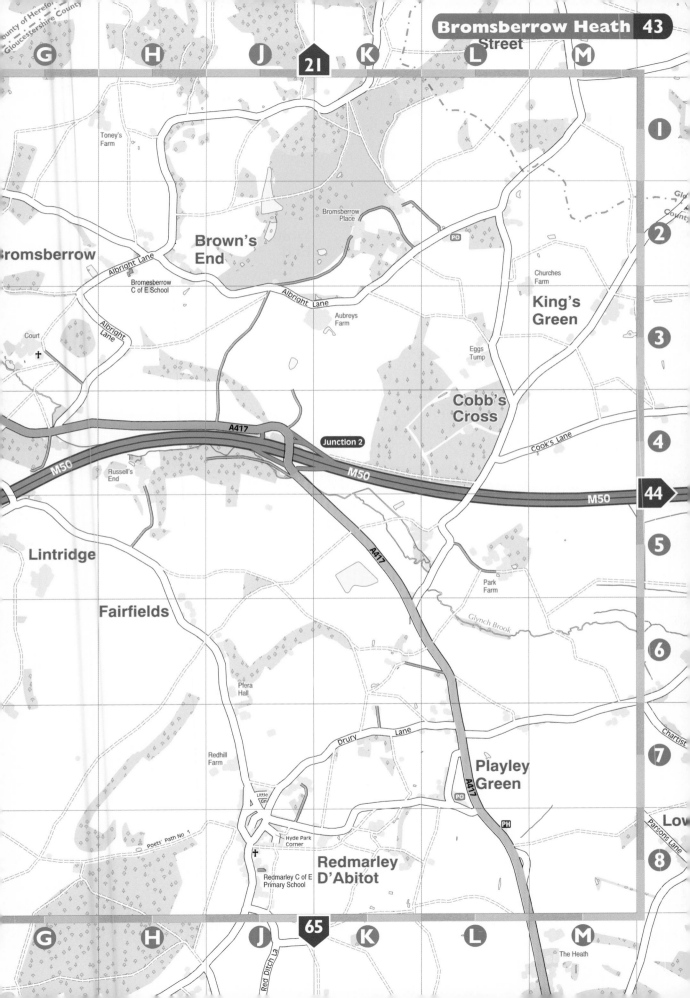

Street

G   H   J   21   K   L   M

I

2

Toney's
Farm

Bromsberrow
Place

**Brown's
End**

Bromsberrow

Albright Lane

Churches
Farm

Bromesberrow
C of E School

PO

**King's
Green**

Albright Lane

Court

✝

Albright
Lane

Aubreys
Farm

Eggs
Tump

3

**Cobb's
Cross**

Cook's Lane

A417

4

M50

Junction 2

M50

44

Russell's
End

A417

44

5

Lintridge

Park
Farm

Fairfields

Glynch Brook

6

Chartist

7

Drury   Lane

**Playley
Green**

Redhill
Farm

Pfera
Hall

A417

PO

Little
Gn

PH

Lo

Poets' Path No 1

Hyde Park
Corner

✝

Parsons Lane

8

**Redmarley
D'Abitot**

Redmarley C of E
Primary School

Red Ditch La

The Heath

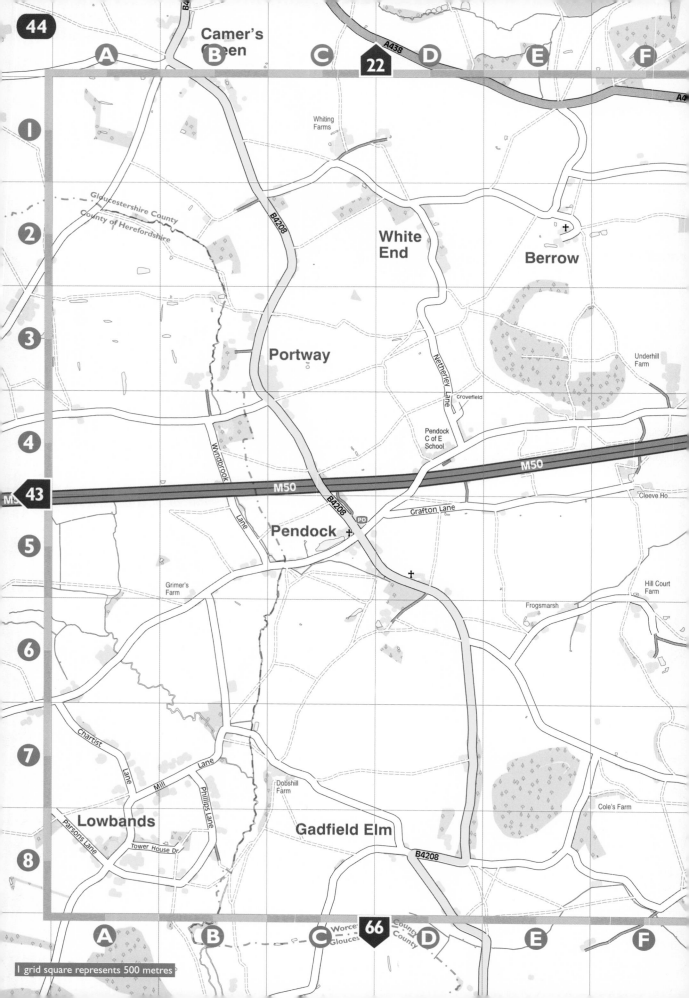

44

A B C 22 D E F

I

Whiting
Farms

Gloucestershire County
County of Herefordshire

White
End

Berrow

2

3

Portway

Underhill
Farm

Netherley Lane

Grovefield

Wyndbrook

Pendock
C of E
School

4

M50

M50

43

M50

B4208

Cleeve Ho

PO

Grafton Lane

Pendock

5

Grimer's
Farm

Hill Court
Farm

Lane

Frogsmarsh

6

Chartist

7

Lane

Mill

Dobshill
Farm

Lane

Phillips Lane

Cole's Farm

Lowbands

Gadfield Elm

8

Parsons Lane

Tower House Dr

B4208

A B C 66 D E F

Worce
Glouces

Coun
Glouces

County
County

1 grid square represents 500 metres

Bushley Green

Bushley

Upper Lode

TEWKESBURY

Lower Lode

Worcestershire County
Gloucestershire County

River Severn

Golf Course

G1
1 Tug Wilson Close!

G2
1 The Apple Orch
2 Bevan Gdns
3 Cromers Cl
4 George Dowty Dr
5 Monkey Meadow
6 The Pear Orch
7 Redwood Ct
8 Wheatstone Cl

G H J 27 K L M

Worcester

I

Carrant Brook

Aston on Carra

2

Gould Dr
Sinderberry Dr
Bowler Rd
4
Carrant Brook
Junior School
le Downs
6
1
2
7
3
5
8
The Sandfield
Well Cl
Grange Ct
Northway Lane
LC
Grange   Road

Northway

Aston
Cross

3

A46(T)

stfield
Avenue
gston Rd
Howard
Cl
ward
Rd
anford
Infant School
Cedar Rd
Virginia Rd
Elm Rd
Steward Rd
Ash Rd
Lee Rd
Fairway
Northway
Trading Est
North Av
Austin Road
St Davids
Road
St Georges
Road
South Av

ndra

Northway
Trading
Estate

Ashchurch for
Tewkesbury
Station
A46(T)
St Davids
Road
St Andrews
Cl
St Patricks Rd
Ashchurch
County
Primary School
Fitznamon Pk
St Barbara's Cl
Twinbrook Cra

Tirle Brook

Pamington

Ellendene
Dr

B4079

4

50

Ashchurch

Natton

LC

5

Homedowns
Business
Park

nedowns

6

B4079

edowns

7

A435

Monks
Lane

Claydon

8

iddington

G H J 71 K L M

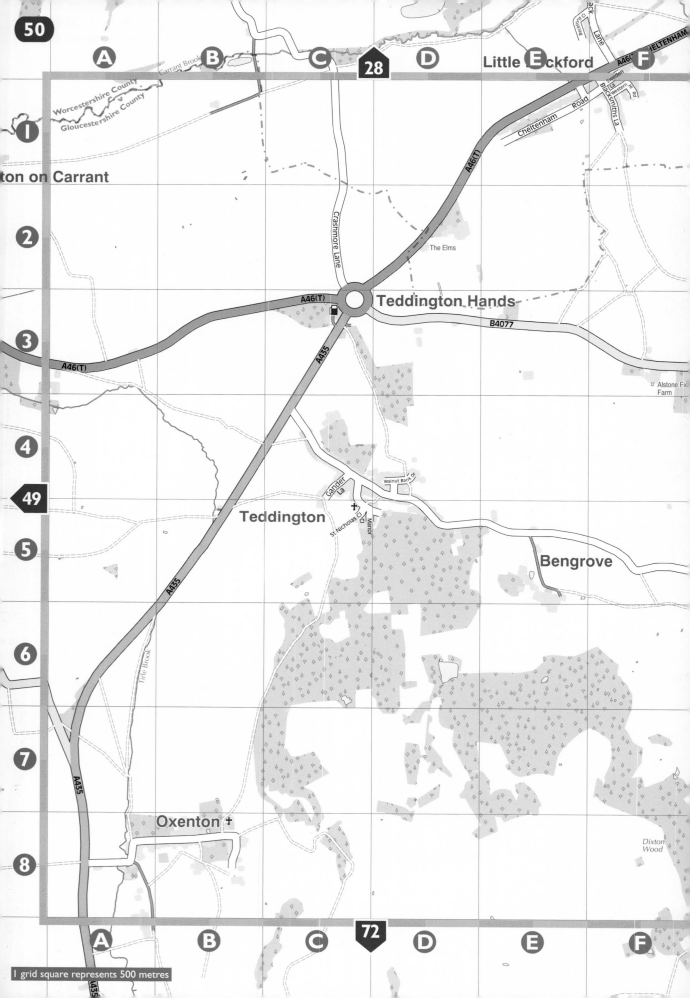

A **B** **C** **D** Little **E**ckford **F**

28

I

Worcestershire County
Gloucestershire County

ton on Carrant

Cheltenham Road

A46(T)

Blacksmiths La

2

The Elms

Crashmore Lane

A46(T)
A46(T)

A435

3

A46(T)

Teddington Hands

B4077

Alstone Fie
Farm

4

Walnut Bank Dr

49

Gander La

Teddington

St Nicholas Cl

Manor

5

Bengrove

A435

Title Brook

6

7

A435

Oxenton †

Dixton
Wood

8

A **B** **C** **D** **E** **F**

72

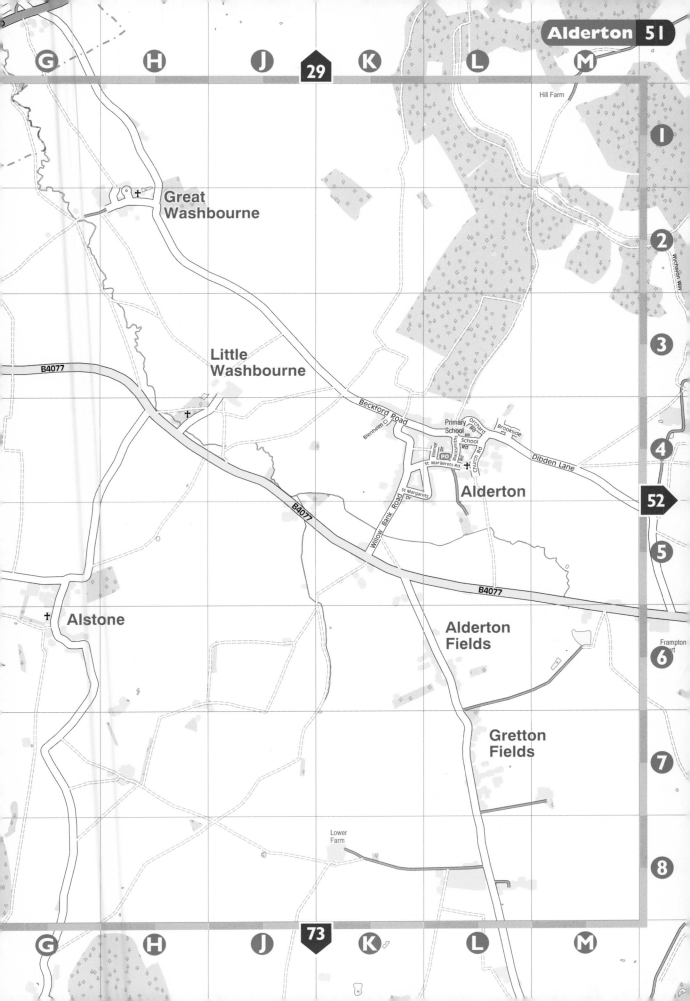

G   H   J   **29**   K   L   M

1

2

3

Hill Farm

Wychavon Way

✝ Great
Washbourne

Little
Washbourne

B4077

Beckford Road

Primary
School

Orchard Rd

School Rd

Brookside

Dibden Lane

4

52

Blenheim Cl

Eleanor Dr

PO

Blacksmiths Rd

St Margarets Rd

Church Rd

Alderton

5

B4077

Willow Bank Road

St Margarets Dr

B4077

✝ **Alstone**

**Alderton
Fields**

Frampton
Court

6

**Gretton
Fields**

7

Lower
Farm

8

G H J K L M

Nest

Middle
Hill House

Gloucest
Worcestershire County

Dulverton
Wood

Broadway
Wood

Seven
Wells

Buckle Street

I

2

Spring Hill

3

Hill Barn
Farm

Buckle Street

4

Snowshill
Hill

56

5

Upper
Slatepits

Buckle Street

6

Hornsleasow
Farm

7

Half Moon
Plantation

8

Scarborough
Farm

G H J K L M

A B 34 C D E F

Dovedale Farm

1

Campden
Ashes

2

3

Upton Wold
Farm

FIVE MILE DRIVE

A44

4

55

Far Upton
Wold Farm

5

Highland
Lodge

A424

Bourton
Far Hill Farm

Kildanes
Bottom

6

Bourton
Hill House

7

Wavert
Stud

8

Sezincote
Warren

A B 78 C D E F

Hinchwick
Hill Barn

1 grid square represents 500 metres

G **H** **J** 35 **K** **L** **M**

1 Chantry Gdns

C of E School

Police Station

PO

Bell Bank

Hotel

PH

Chapel Lane

High St

School Lane

Brook La

Donkey La

Dovedale

B4479

Winc...

Summerfie...

Moor Hille

Millview

LOWER ST

Sleepy Hollow Farm Park •

Pasture Lane

Pasture Farm

Park Farm

Monarch's Way

Downs Farm

Dorn Hill

I

2

† **Batsford**

3

Hailstone Farm

Bourton Woods

B4479

• Arboretum

Monarch's Way

Batsford Park

Falconry Centre

4

58

Monarch's Way

5

A44

Bourton-on-the-Hill

1

†

Fernhill Close

A44

6

Hill Top House

7

8

Sezincote

G **H** **J** 79 **K** **L** **M**

Sezincote House & Ga...

Icehouse Lane

Monarch's Way

A B 36 C D E F

D5
1 The Green

C7
1 Bowes Lyon Cl
2 St Edwards Ct
3 St James Ct
4 St Pauls Ct
5 St Peters Ct

C6
1 Jameson Ct
2 University Farm

C5
1 Bowling Green Ct
2 High St

Hale

Dorn
Hill

1

2

Dorn

Lower
Lemington

A429

Batsford

3

Lemington
Grange

4

57

Boram Home
Farm

MORETON-
IN-MARSH

A429

Nursery Ct

5

Fosse Way
Business
Cen

Moreton-
in-Marsh
Hospital

Police
Station

Dormer House
PNEU School

Moreton-in-Marsh
Station

Hospital Road

High St

New Road

PO

1

Monarch's Way

Corder's La

Council
Offices

1

Doctors
Surg

OXFORD
ST

Davies
Road
Errington

Mosedale

Cemetery

LONDON ROAD

Duvecote

Primrose Court

Stockwells

2

1

A44

St Davids
Primary School

Croft Holm

Cotsmore Close

Evenlode

Cemetery

6

A44

BOURTON ROAD

A429

East St

Hotel

Church St

Gray's
La

St George's

Gdns

Warneford

Moreton Wanderers
Football Club

GL56

Swan
Close

2

Parkers La

Cotswold

Wellington
Rd

Evenlode
Gdns

Way

STOW ROAD

1

Tinker's

Fosseway Dr

Oriel

Monarch's

Redesdale
Place
Hotel

3

2

1

Sankey
Rd

Keble

7

Upper Fields
Farm

1

4

Fosseway
Avenue

Fosseway
Farm

Monarch's Way

8

Coldicote
Farm

Lower
Rye Farm

A429

Frogmore
Farm

1 grid square represents 500 metres

G   H   J   **37**   K   Wolford Road   L   M

Geat
Wolfe

1

Mount
Sorrell

The Green

PO

PH

2

Woodhills
Farm

Upper Lemington
Village

3

*Wolford
Wood*

4

*Old
Covert*

60

Fire Service
Technical College

*Gravels
Coppice*

5

6

The Four
Shire Stone

A44

7

Wells
Folly

Gloucestershire County
Oxfordshire County

Kitebrook

A44

8

Brookend
House

G   H   J   **81**   K   L   M

Middle Brookend

Ⓐ   Ⓑ   Ⓒ   **38**   Ⓓ   Ⓔ   Ⓕ

Geat Wolford

Little Wolford Heath

Ⓘ

PO

PH

100

A3400

Nethercote

② ②

Pepperwell Farm

Kings Brake Farm

③ Rectory Farm

Mill Far

Stanford Brook

④ Barton Road

◀ **59**

Coates Barn

⑤

Barton-on-the-Heath

Camden Cl
PO

⑥

⑦

⑧

Salter's Well Farm

Ⓐ   Ⓑ   Ⓒ   **82**   Ⓓ   Ⓔ   Ⓕ

Hawton Farm

Slade Farm

G H J 39 K L M

I

2

3

4

5

6

7

8

Whichford

Ascot

Roman Rw

Margett's Hill

Weston Park

Hack Lane

Whichford Wood

Macmillan Way

Long Compton Woods

Macmillan Way

SHIPSTON ROAD

Compton

Crockwell St

Long Compton

Burnway Lane

Malthouse La

Vicarage Lane

PO

Broad Street

East street

Weston Ct

School Cl

Butlers Cl

Long Compton Junior & Infant School

Butlers La

A3400

Barn Cl

Butlers Road

Clarks Lane

Coombe Farm

Oxfordshire County
Warwickshire County

Butlers Road Farm

Butlers Road

Butlers Hill Farm

Macmillan Way

The Hollows

South Hill Farm

A3400

G H J 83 K L M

Kings Men

Whispering Knights

Warwickshire County
Oxfordshire County

Dymock

The Pound

Crowfield Lane

The Old Rock

New Rock

Haind Park Wood

Normans Land Farm

Boyce Court

Boyce Way

The New Grange

Daffodil Way

Timber Hill Farm

Dymock Wood

M50

Four Oaks

Hillend Green

Oxenhall Wood

Holder's Lane

Holder's Farm

Gloucestershire County

County of Herefordshire

M50

Shaw Common

Peter's Farm

Hilter Farm

Hay Wood

White House

Hawthorn Hill

Allums

Daffodil Way

Poets Path No 1

Poets Path No 1

Western Way

PO

B4215

B4215

Daffodil Way

1 2 3 4 64 5 6 7 8

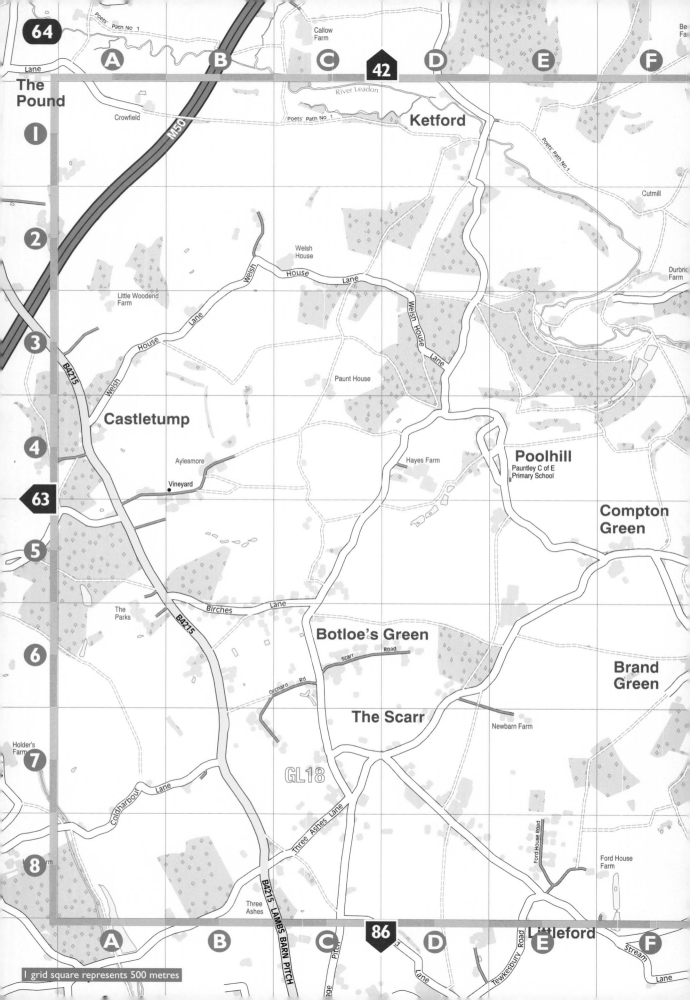

G H J K L M

I

Redmarley D'Abitot

† Redmarley C of E Primary School

Hyde Park Corner

43

The Heath

The Down House

2

A417

Red Ditch La

Chapel Lane

Scar Farm

Hawcross

Roundbush

Durbridge Road

Murrell's End

3

A417

Payford Bridge

River Leadon

Innerstone Lane

Innerstone La

Chapel Farm

Sacksfield Farm

Chapel Lane

4

Pauntley Court Drive

† Pauntley Court

66

Everess Farm

5

Sladbrook

6

Collinpark Wood

7

8

Forge Lane

Poets Path

Eden's Hill

Gloucester

bury Road

Carswalls Manor

87

G H J K L M

Upleadon

Upleadon Court

A B C D E F

B4208

D5
1 Johnstone Cl

I

The Down
House

2

Roundbush

A417

3

Mill Lane

Mill
Lane

Mill

Hethelpit Cross

The Hill

Worcestershire County
Gloucestershire County

The Moat

Moat Lane

B4208

MALVERN ROAD

Pillows Green Road

**Pillows
Green**

Staunton

A417

Ledbury Road Crescent

B4213 **STRAIGHT LANE**

PO

Staunton & Corse C of E
Aided School

4

Staunton Court Business Park

Cullingham
Cooper
Kover
Collins

Chartist Way
Chartist Piece
Hadfield
Close

Sovereign
Cha

GLOUCESTER RD

Staunton
Court

Prince
Crescent

Crescent

Corse
Surgery

5

Sladbrook

Brierley Grange

The Stone Rd

Jubilee Pl

1
Boundary Pl

Police Station

Compton

Corse

School Crescent

**Snig's
End**

6

Pitt's Mill

Stanbrook Farm

Lawn Farm

Corse House
Farm

Oridge Street

A417

7

Grove
Farm

Oridge Street

Oridge Street

Old Field
Top

WORCESTER ROAD

8

The
Tailors

Crosshands
Farm

A B C D E F

1 grid square represents 500 metres

Linkend

A   B   C   D   E   F

Linkend Rd

B4211

Eldersfield Lawn School

Corse Lawn

1 Cotswold Vw

I

Hotel

Chaceley Hole

Hillend

Rock Street

Ch

B4211

2

Rye Court Farm

Hawker's Farm

3

Sandpits

Cumberwood Farm

4

River Severn

Town Street

Josend Crescent

5

Tirley

Tirley St

B4213

Cabb Lane

6

7

Great House

B4213

Haw Bridge

Court

Ham Road

The Haw

Apperley Court

8

B4213

A   B   C   D   E   F

Wainlode Lane

Greyhill Farm

I grid square represents 500 metres

Claydon

M7
1 Ashlea Mdw
2 Beechurst Wy
3 Farriers Reach
4 Harvesters Vw
5 Nortenham Cl
6 Vilverie Mead

G

iddington

Monks Lane

H

J

49

K

L

M

1

A435

2

3

4

72

5

6

7

8

LC

Bozard's Farm

Gothic Farm

Gotherington Fields

Gotherington Field Farm

Stoke Orchard

Dean Brook

Dean Lane

Banady Lane

Stoke Road

Glebe Farm

Court Farm

Hayfield Way

Acacia Rd

Wheatsheaf Dr

The Cornfields

Lt. Acorns

4

1

5

Malvern View Business Park

Stella Way

Whitefields

Cutsdean Cl

Minster St

Stoke Road

Hurley Wy

Lyndley Chta

3

6

9

Sweetbriar

Kingscote

7

Cheltenham North Rugby Club

Bishop's Cleeve

4

8

ll Lane

The Park

Wingmoor Farm

G

H

J

93

K

L

M

A435

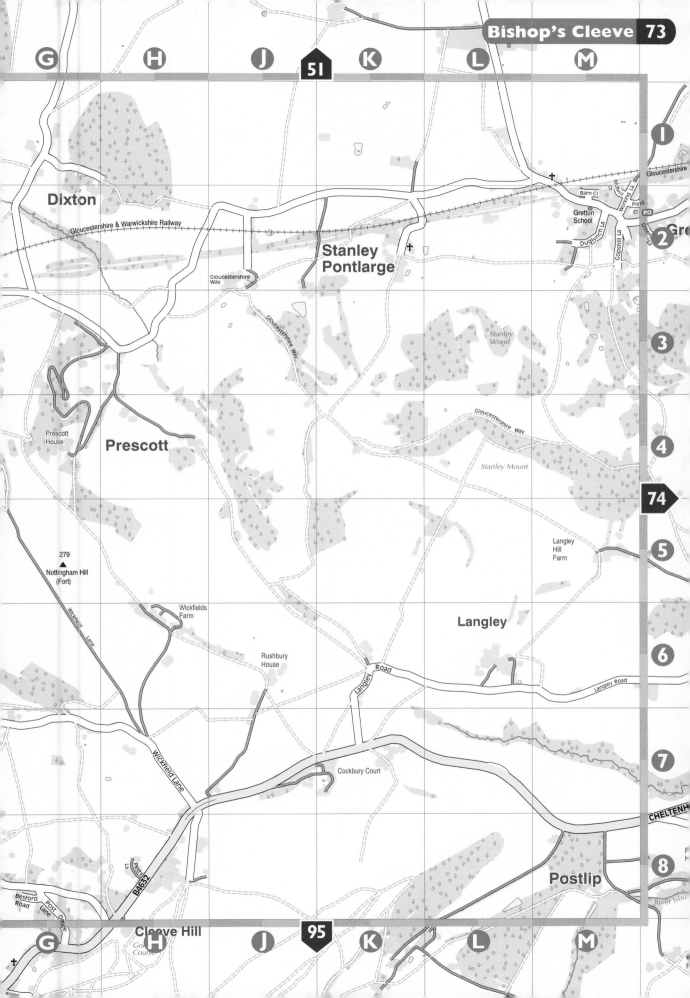

G H J **53** K L M

Millhampost Farm

B4632

Lower Coscom

1

Salter's Lane

Hailes

†
Hailes
Abbey (NT)

Hailes
Wood

2

3

Cotswold Way

4

Farmcote

76

Salter's
Lane

Little
Farmcote

5

Gloucestershire Way

6

Lynes Barn
Farm

7

Sudeley
Lodge

8

Farmcote Wood
Farm

A **B** **C** **D** **E** **F**

Taddington

54

I

Lower
Coscombe

B4077

2

Stumps
Cross

Upper
Coscombe

PO

Cutsdean

+

3

Jackdaws Castle

B4077

4

PH

Ford

75

Gloucestershire Way

B4077

5

Slade Barn
Farm

Hyde

Temple
Guiting

6

Pinnock
Farm

Manor
Farm

The sherry

PO

7

Temple Guiting
School

+

8

A **B** **C** **D** **E** **F**

98

I grid square represents 500 metres

G   H   J   55   K   L   M

I

2

Scarborough Farm

Ford Hill Farm

Gloucestershire Way

Gloucestershire Way

Gloucestershire

3

Trafalgar Farm

4

78

B4077

5

B4077

6

7

Leigh Wood

Kinetonhill Farm

8

Bemborough Farm

Cotswold Farm Park

G   H   J   99   K   L   M

A B C **56** D E F

E6
1 Church Vw
2 Close Gdns

I

Hinchwick
Hill Barn

2

Gloucestershire way

3

4

Guitinghill
Farm

77

The Warren

Hinchwick

Hinchwick
Manor Farm

5

Condicote

6

Condicote Lane

7

Fox Farm

B4077

8

Kinetonhill
Farm

A B **100** C D E F

I grid square represents 500 metres

G H J K L M

K3
1 Orchard Ri

K4
1 Old Rectory Gdns

Sezincote
House & Gardens

Icehouse Lane

Monarch's Way

I

2

3

Bean Hl

Charleswal

PO

Ganborough   Road

Longborough C of E
Primary School

1

High Street

Longborough

4

80

Banks Fee La

PH

Ganborough

Luckley
Farm

Banks Fee

5

Banks Fee
Farm

Monarch's Way

Donning n   6

A424

Duncombe House

7

stone Farm

8

B4077

G H J 101 K **Upper Swe** L M

PO

80

A   B   C   58   D   E   F   Coldicote Farm

1   Lower Rye Farm   Frogmore Farm

A429

2

3   River Evenlode

4   Little Barrow

79   Heath Barn

5   North Rye House   Cownham Farm

Donington   6

7   Monarch's Way   Kennel   Lane   Quinmoor Farm

Manor House   Foxes Row   Millbrook Ley   Chapel Street   Broadwell

8

A   B   C   102   D   E   F

1 grid square represents 500 metres

G   H   J   **59**   K   L   M

1

Middle Brookend
Farm

2

Grove Farm

Chasleton
Glebe

3

Oxfordshire County
Gloucestershire County

The
Lane

⌂ Chastleton
House (NT)

✝

82

Chastleton

4

PO   Green Lane

Church Lane

Horn   Lane

Horn   Lane

Horn Farm

Macmillan Way

Peasewell
Wood

5

Evenlode

6

Fern Farm

Coomb
Wood

7

Hillside
Farm

Evenlode Grounds
Farm

Macmillan Way

8

Sydenham
Farm

River Evenlode

Back Rw
Schooler's
Lane

Main Street

PO

Adlestrop

A B C 60 D E F

I

Salter's Well Farm

Hawton Farm

Slade Farm

Cemetery

Oakham Road

Oakham

A44

Willow End

Little Compton

PO Pill La
Pool Cl
Deerhurst Cl

Drivers Lane

New Town

A44

Macmillan Way

Chastleton House (NT)

81

Hill Farm

Greygoose Lane

Warwickshire County
Oxfordshire County

A436

A44

Peasewell Wood

Chastleton Barrow

Coomb Wood

A436

Park Farm

A436

Glebe Farm

Cornwell

Cornwell Manor

A B C 104 D E F

1 grid square represents 500 metres

Daylesford Hill Farm

G H J 61 K L M

I

2

3

Choicehill
Farm

4

Choicehill

5

Ove
Nor

6

7

8

Little
Rollright

Kings Men

Whispering
Knights

Warwickshire County

Oxfordshire County

South Hill
Farm

Hirons
Hill Farm

Springhill
Farm

Golden Lane

The
Green

Chapel Lane

Cooks Lane

Roses Lane

Lower End

Orchard
Close

Salford

A44

WORCESTER ROAD

105

Kennel Lane

Cox Lane

Toy Lane

Common Lane

A44

Primsdown
Industrial
Estate

Cemetery

WORCESTER ROAD

NEW STREET

Dixton's La

Station Rd

Lewis Road

Webb Crescent

Dunstan Avenue

Withers Wy

William Bliss
Parade

The
Leys

Cross Leys

Leys

B4450

G H J K L M

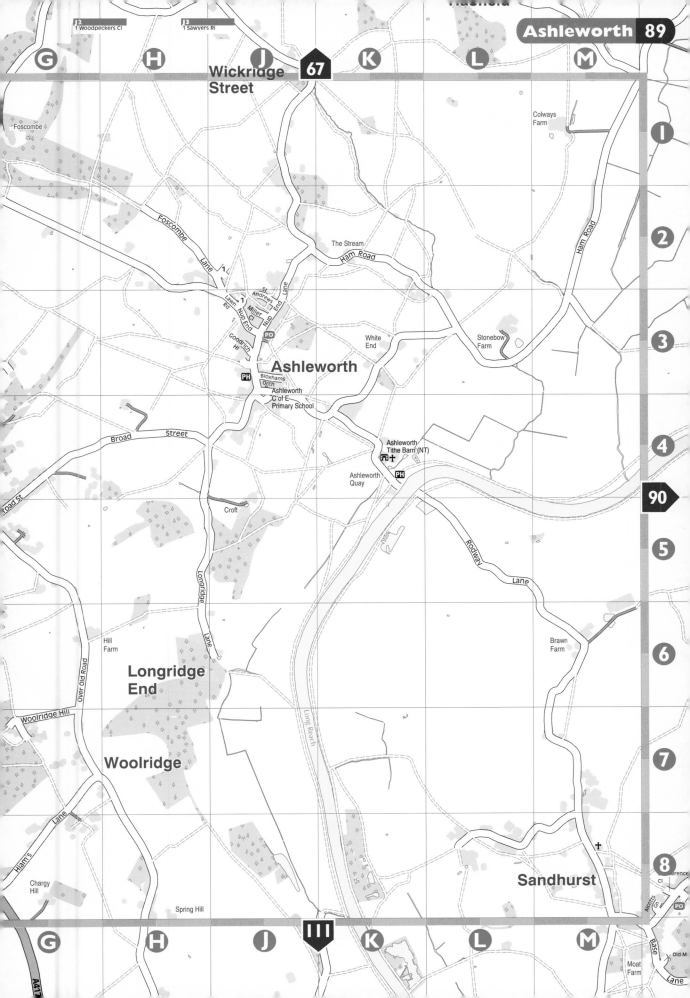

G   H   J   **67**   K   L   M   I

Wickridge Street

Colways Farm

Foscombe

Ham Road

2

Foscombe Lane

The Stream

Ham Road

St Andrews

Nup End Lane

Miller Cl

Lawn Rd   Nup End

PO

White End

Stonebow Farm

3

Goodrich HI

Ashleworth

PH

Bloxhams Orchn

Ashleworth C of E Primary School

Broad   Street

Ashleworth Tithe Barn (NT)

4

Road St

Ashleworth Quay

PH

90

Croft

Rodway Lane

5

Longridge Lane

Hill Farm

Brawn Farm

6

Longridge End

Over Old Road

Long Reach

Woolridge

Woolridge Hill

7

Hiam's Lane

Chargy Hill

Sandhurst †

8

Alcotts Gn   PO

Spring Hill

Base Ln

G   H   J   **III**   K   L   M

Moat Farm

Old M

A417

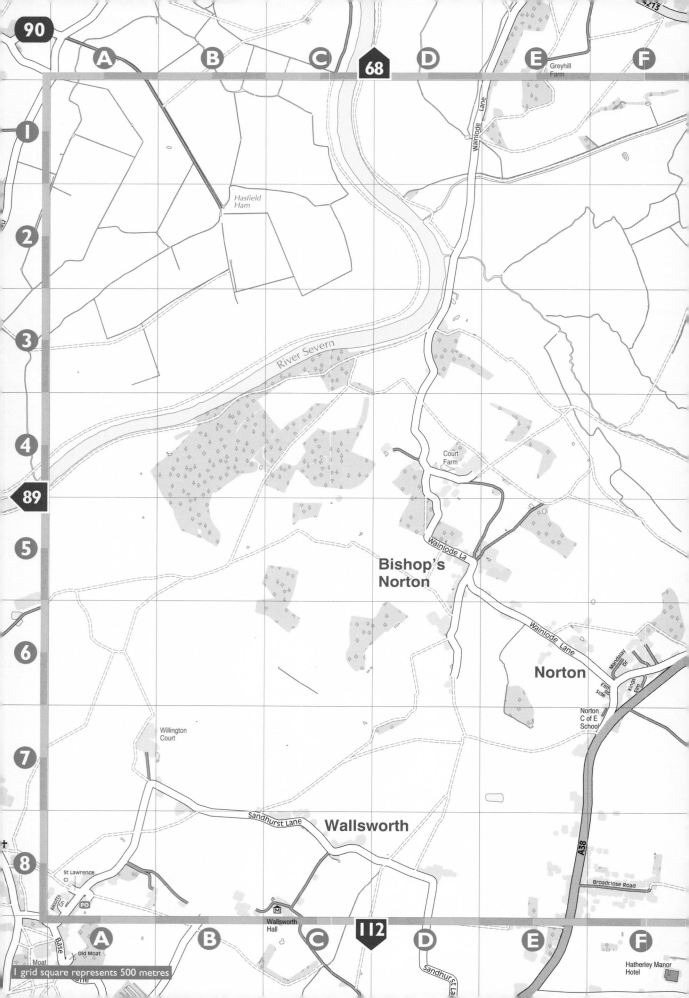

F8
1 Beale Rd
2 Dunster Cl
3 Oldbury Cl
4 Stanley Pl
5 Tiverton Cl
6 Wentworth Cl

F7
1 Carlyle Gv
2 Hazledean Rd
3 Maythorn Dr
4 Thistledown Cl
5 Watermoor Cl
6 Wheatland Dr
7 Whitemarsh Cl

F6
1 Cornmeadow Dr
2 Fulbrook Cl
3 Hallmead Cl
4 Harvest Gv
5 Rye Av
6 William Gough Cl

E8
1 Ettington Cl

70

Knightsbridge
Business Centre

Knightsbridge

Piff's
Elm

Barn Farm

Colman's Farm

Villa Farm

Manor

Boddington

Junction 10

Withybridge Gardens

91

Butler's
Court

Moat Lane

Ucking

TEWKESBUR

Withy
Bridge

Pilgrove
Farm

OLD GLOUCESTER ROAD

B4634

The Cherry Orch

Staverton

Hayden
Lane

Hope Farm

Arthur Dye
CP School

Springbank

Hester's

B4634 ROAD

Whitehall
Farm

Hayden

Springbank

St Helens
Cl

GLOUCESTER ROAD

114

Fiddler's
Glen

GL51

Golden

Primary
School

G
H
J
73
K
L
M

Cleeve Hill

Golf Course

I

The Ring

Besford Road

Cotswold Way

2

Cleeve Cloud

Cleeve Common

3

utterswood

4

96

5

Wontley Farm

Cotswold Way

Upper Hill Farm

6

West Down

Lower Hill Farm

7

Cotswold Way

Drypool Farm

8

Piccadilly Farm

G
H
J
117
K
L
M

The Hewletts

B4632

Corn Farm

Postl House

River Isbourne

Puckham

Postlip
House

A   B   C   74   D   E   F

River Isb

I

Corndean
Farm

Corndean Lane

Wadfield
Farm

Cotswold Way

2

Corndean
Hall

3

Waterhatch

Cotswold Way

4

95

Cotswold Way

• Belas Knap

Humblebee

5

ntley
Farm

Goldwell
Farm

Holt
Farm

6

West
Down

West
Wood

**Charlton
Abbots**

†

7

8

Whitehall
Farm

A   B   C   118   D   E   F

Cotehay

Brockhampton
Park

Puckham

I grid square represents 500 metres

Breesmoor Brook

G H J **75** K L M

I

Guiting Wood

2

3

4

98

5

6

7

8

G H **119** J K L M

Farmcote Wood Farm

Parks Farm

Wardens' Way

Deadmanbury Gate

Campden La

Wardens' Way

Spoonley Farm

Roel Hill Farm

Campden Lane

Roel Gate

Windrush Way

Whitehill Farm

Hawling

G H J **77** K L M

I
2
3
4
100
5
6
7
8

Bemborough
Farm

Cotswold
Farm Park

Guiting
Stud

Summerhill

Wardens' Way

Wardens' Way

Grange Hill
Farm

Wardens' Way

Naunton

Village Av

PO PH

Wardens' Way

Dale St

Brockhill
Barn

B4068

Naunton Downs
Golf Club

G H J **121** K L M B4068

Lower

100

78

A B C D E F

I

Swell Wold
Farm

2

Swell Hill
Farm

3

4

Eyford Hill
Farm

99

5

Eyford
Park

Rockcliffe

Wardens' Way

6

Wardens' Way

Wardens' Way

Eyford
Knoll

Swiss Farm
House

B4068

7

Upper
Slaughter

River Eye

8

Bro
Ba

Wardens' Way

Hotel

ridge

Lower

A B C D E F

122

ecky Hill

Manor Farm

Wagborough

Condicote

G   H   J   K   L   M

J3
1 Whittlestone Cl

J4
1 Stonehouse Ct

B4077

79

Upper Swell

Gloucestershire Wy

B4077 TEWKESBURY ROAD

Abbotswood

Bowl Farm

B4068

STOW-ON-THE-WOLD

well Buildings
arm

EVESHAM ROAD

A424

High St

Well

Talbot
Sq

Hotel

Hotel

Hotel

PO

John E

Church Street Gallery

Walton Ho Gallery

SHEEP S

Back

St Mary's
Close

Whittlestone
Hollow

Cemetery

Lower Swell

Swell
Primary School

Rectory
Cl

Mill Lane

Nether Swell
Manor

Monarch's Way

A429

102

Fir Farm

Monarch's Way

Macmillan Way

Monarch's Way

Hyde Mill

Hotel

A424

Kirkham
Farm

Monarch's Way

River Dikler

Copse Hill

Meadow Farm

A429

Stow Bridge

123

G   H   J   K   L   M

Copsehill Road

Macmillan Way

Mill
La

The Old
Mill Museum

**Lower
Slaughter**

Heath
Hill

I

2

3

4

5

6

7

8

B3
1 Mount Pleasant
Cl

A4
1 Fisher Cl

A3
1 Church St
2 Digbeth St
3 Glebe Cl
4 Market Sq

A2
1 Fosse Folly
2 Fosse La

A   B   C   **80**   D   E   F

I

Broadwell
Hill

Blac
Pit

B429

EVESHAM ROAD

2

Monarch's Way

Stow
Well

A424

2
1

Well

High St
Talbot
Sq

Hotel

3

Hotel

Church Street Gallery

Walton Ho Gallery

SHEEP ST

Lane

White Hart
La

Chapel St

Doctors Surgery

Camp Gdns

Shepherds Wy

Primary
School

St Edwards
Drive

Sterling

Kg

Georges
Field

Griffin Cl

Griffin Cl

John Blockley Gal

Union St

Back Walls

Htl

A436

ODDINGTON RD   A436

A436

Cemetery

The Park

Bartletts
Park

Chamberlayne
Cl

Maugersbury Pk

Lower Pk

1

Chapel
Street

Maugersbury
Manor

B4450

Martin's
Hill

4

A429

101

Macmillan Way

Cotswold Crest
Farm

5

6

Hotel

Oxleaze
Farm

Ash
Farm

A424

7

Smenham
Farm

8

Wyckhill
Farm

A   B   C   **124**   D   E   F

A424

I grid square represents 500 metres

G3
1 Embrook

G Syden Farm

H

J

81

K

L PO

Back Rw
Scholers Lane
Street

M

Adlestrop

✝

Macmillan Way

Adlestrop Park

1

2

Broadwell Road

A436

Sawpits
La
PH

Home Cl

Church Place

PO

✝

Lower Oddington

Church Road

✝

Upper Oddington

Back Lane

Brans Lane

✝

Daylesford

New Farm

River Evenlode

3

104

4

5

Bledington Heath

B4450

6

Bledington Grounds

B4450

Jay Farm

7

Mickland's Hill

B4450

8

G

H

Pebbly Hill Farm

J

125

K

L

STOW ROAD

PH
CHAPEL ST
PO

Chapel Street

CHAPEL
Church St
MAIN STREET

New Rd

Old Forge Close

M

Bledington County

Lower Farm

A436

I

River Evenlode

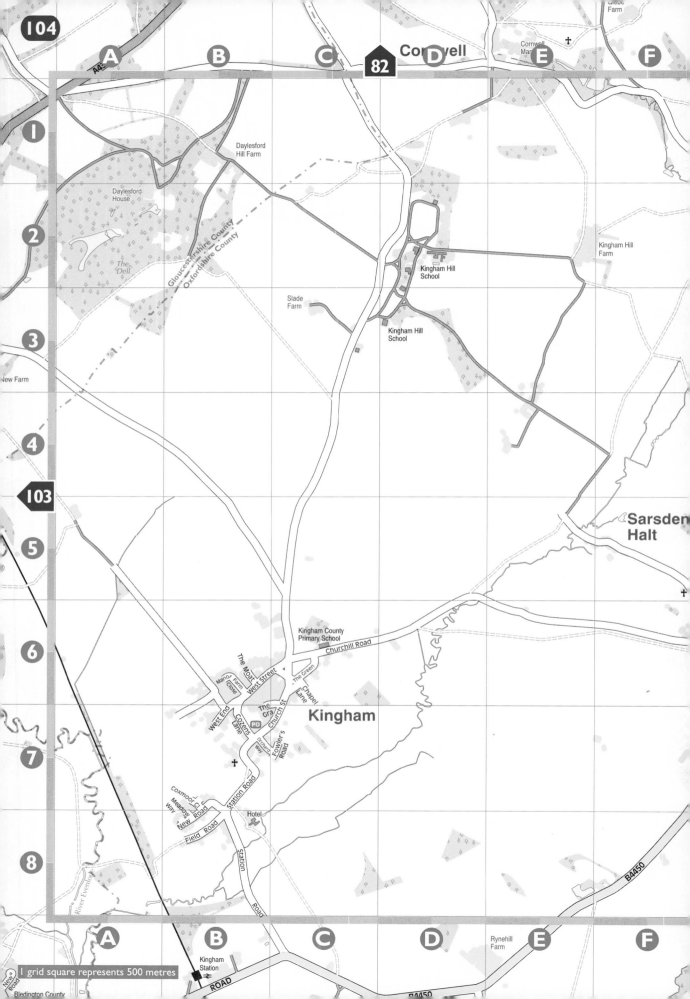

A45

A

B

82

C

D

Cornwell

Cornwell
Manor

E

✝

Glebe
Farm

F

1

Daylesford
Hill Farm

2

Daylesford
House

Gloucestershire County
Oxfordshire County

The
Dell

Slade
Farm

Kingham Hill
School

Kingham Hill
School

Kingham Hill
Farm

3

New Farm

4

Sarsden
Halt

5

✝

6

Kingham County
Primary School

Churchill Road

The Moat

Manor Farm
Close

West Street

West End

The
Green

Chapel
Lane

The
Cra

Cozens
Lane

Church St

PO

Kingham

Fowler's
Road

Orchard
Way

7

✝

Coxmoor Cl

Meadow
Way

New Road

Field Road

Station Road

Hotel

B4450

8

River Evenlode

Station
Road

A

Bledington County

B

Kingham
Station

ROAD

Rynehill
Farm

C

D

E

B4450

F

G H J **87** K L M

Tipton Court

Lower Farm

1

2
Bovone

Old Ct Dr
Orchard Rise
Phelps Way
Tibberton Primary School
3
Muzzle Patch
Bovone Lane

Court Farm †
Tibberton

The Grove
Court Farm

Meredith

4
Whitehall Farm
Whitehall Lane

110

Birdsend

Morse's Farm

5

Rundlesshill

errimans

Collier's Elm

6

Woodgreen

7
†
Bulley

Bulley Lane

Churcham House

Bulley Lane

8

Lake Lane

Bulley Lane

Spring Dale
†
G H J **133** K L M
†
A40(T)
Churcham School
A40(T)
Halfway

B4215

A **B** **C** **D** **E** **F**

90

St Lawrence Cl

Moat Farm
Old Moat

Base Lane

I

Bengrove Farm

Wallsworth Hall

Hatherley Manor Hotel

Sandhurst Lane

A38

Twigworth

Ash Lane

Brook Lane

2

Base Lane

Abbot's Lodge

3

Abloads Court

4

Twigworth C of E School

Drymeadow Farm

Dry Meadow La

Innsworth Lane

III

Austin Dr

Lewis Av

TEWKESBURY ROAD

A38

Horsbere Brook

Innsworth Technology Park

Finch Rd
Wren Ter
Rookery
Blackswan
Crescent

5

Sandhurst

Longford

Sherwood Cl

Police Station
Victoria Rd

Longford La

Crescentdale

Fircroft

A40(T)

Brionne Way
Fleming Way
Lacy Cl
Crispin Cl

Avenue
Grisedale
Ennerdale Av

Innsworth County Primary School

A40(T)

6

Winfield Hospital

Plock Ct
Fairmile Gdns

Westfield Ter
Orchard Cl

Rivermead Close
Gambier
Parry Gdns
Greville

Highbank Pk

Beechcroft Road

The Milestone School
Longford Special School
Longlevens RFC

Simon Rd
Montfort Rd
Beaumont Rd
Little Normans

Chaffon Wy
Kenton Wy

Brooklands Park
Paddock Gdns
Hurst Av
Westmead Road
Breinton Wy

7

Lawrence Way North
Cattle Market Ind Est
Gloucester City Council

ST OSWALDS ROAD

Dean's Way

KINGSHOLM ROAD

A430

ESTCOURT ROAD

Estcourt Road

Estcourt Road

Estcourt Close

Oxstalls Community School

Oxstalls Drive

Rodney
Redland Cl
Longland Gdns

Flower Way

Oxstalls Lane

Wellsprings Road

Church Road

The Avenue

Alder Cl
Bradley
Craemere Rd

Primary School
Leven Cl

Windermere Road

Longlevens Primary Sch

B4063

Civil Sports Club

Hinton Road
Malvern Road

North Road

Lansdown Road

Denmark Road High Sch for Girls

Estcourt Road

A38

Laura

Keswick Rd
Rydal Rd

South Cl

Kendal Rd

The Triangle

CHELTENHAM

Colebridge Avenue

Elmleaze
Meadowleaze

8

Gloucester City Council

Mercia Road
Serlo Rd
Parade

Swan Rd

Rugby Football Club

St Mark St

Vine Terrace

Sebert St

Kingsholm

Primary School

Denmark Road

Alexandra Road

Cheltenham Road Surg

Grafton Road

Merevale Road

Riverside

Sandyleaze
Willowleaze

Elmbridge Rugby Sch

The College Yard Surg

Co Council

St Oswald's Priory

Parliament House

St Catherine
Worcester St

Oxford Road
Henry Road

Heathville Road

Co Council

Redcliffe College

Cheltenham Road Hotel

A38

BARN

Grove Rd

Sisson Road

Gram School

136

Gloucestershire Royal Hosp

Infant School

Wotton

A **B** **C** **D** **E** **F**

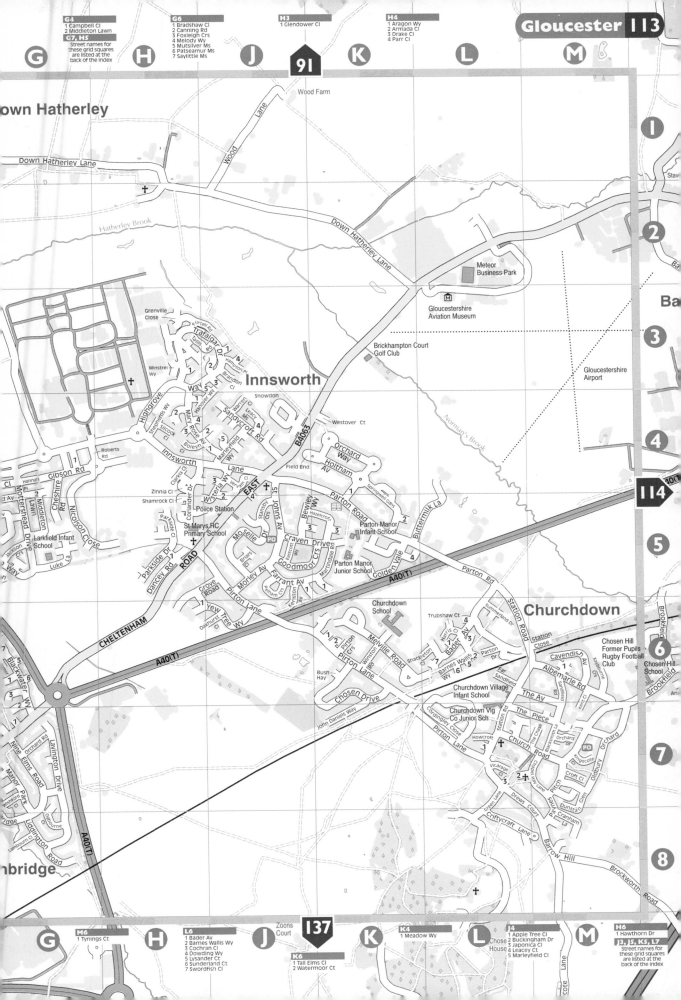

G4
1 Campbell Cl
2 Middleton Lawn
G7, H5
Street names for these grid squares are listed at the back of the index

G6
1 Bradshaw Cl
2 Canning Rd
3 Foxleigh Crs
4 Melody Wy
5 Mutsilver Ms
6 Patseamur Ms
7 Saylittle Ms

H3
1 Glendower Cl

H4
1 Aragon Wy
2 Armada Cl
3 Drake Cl
4 Parr Cl

G   H   J   **91**   K   L   M

I
2
3
114
5
6
7
8

Wood Farm

Down Hatherley Lane

Down Hatherley

Down Hatherley Lane

Hatherley Brook

Meteor Business Park

Gloucestershire Aviation Museum

Brickhampton Court Golf Club

Gloucestershire Airport

Grenville Close

Trafalgar Dr

Minstrel Wy

Innsworth

Snowdon

Westover Ct

Norman's Brook

Highgrove

Shepherds Wy

Silcock Cl

Man Rose Av

Boleyn Cl

Sandycroft Rd

Warren Cl

Marleyfield Wy

Legacy Ms

BAO63

Orchard Way

Holtham Av

Roberts Rd

Innsworth Lane

Field End

EAST

Gibson Rd

Hannah Cl

Cheshire Rd

Nicolson Close

Mottershead Drive

Larkfield Infant School

Jackson Crs

Luke La

Zinnia Cl

Shamrock Cl

Coriander Dr

Clarks Wy

Wisteria Wy

Verc Pl

St Johns Av

Stansby

St Johns Rd

Bewley Wy

Hazelcroft

Parton Road

Springwell Gdns

Parton Manor Infant School

Buttermilk La

Parkside Cl

Police Station

St Marys RC Primary School

Moselle

Brans

Goodmoor Crs

Craven Drive

Barcott

Bartonal Rd

Marldale Rd

Parton Manor Junior School

Golden Vale

Parton Rd

A40(T)

Parton Rd

Parkside Rd

Dancey Rd

ROAD

Morley Av

Farrant Av

Keyston

Behsm

Churchdown School

Trubshaw Ct

Summerland Dr

Churchdown

Station Road

Chosen Hill Former Pupils Rugby Football Club

Chosen Hill School

Brookfield

CHELTENHAM

A40(T)

Grove Road

Pirton Lane

Yew Tree Wy

Oakhurst Wy

Pirton Crs

Melville Road

Winston

Shackleton

Bush Hay

Chosen Drive

Pirton Lane

Hart's Cl

Bader

Barnes Wallis Wy

Parton Dr

Far Sandfield

Station Rd

Station Close

Cavendish Av

Albemarle Rd

Chosen Hill

The Av

The Piece

Howcroft

Church Road

The Chase

Orchard Dr

Kingscote

Oldbury Orchard

John Daniels Way

Churchdown Village Infant School

Churchdown Vlg Co Junior Sch

Coraingley Close

Pirton Lane

Vicarage Cl

Green Lane

Drews Court

Criftycraft Lane

Blackacre La

Chapel Hay Lane

Dunsta Dr

Croft Cl

Cranham

Glen

Barrow Hill

Brockworth Road

A40(T)

Nine Elms Road

Lavington Drive

Manor Park

Wisford Av

Blackwater Wy

Orchard Rd

Lambrook Road

Iddington Road

ridge

nbridge

G   **M6**
1 Tynings Ct

H   **L6**
1 Bader Av
2 Barnes Wallis Wy
3 Cochran Cl
4 Dowding Wy
5 Lysander Ct
6 Sunderland Ct
7 Swordfish Cl

J   Zoons Court   **137**
K6
1 Tall Elms Cl
2 Watermoor Ct

K   **K4**
1 Meadow Wy

L   Chose House
J4
1 Apple Tree Cl
2 Buckingham Dr
3 Japonica Ct
4 Leacey Ct
5 Marleyfield Cl

M   **H6**
1 Hawthorn Dr
J3, J5, K5, L7
Street names for these grid squares are listed at the back of the index

G   H   J   K   L   M

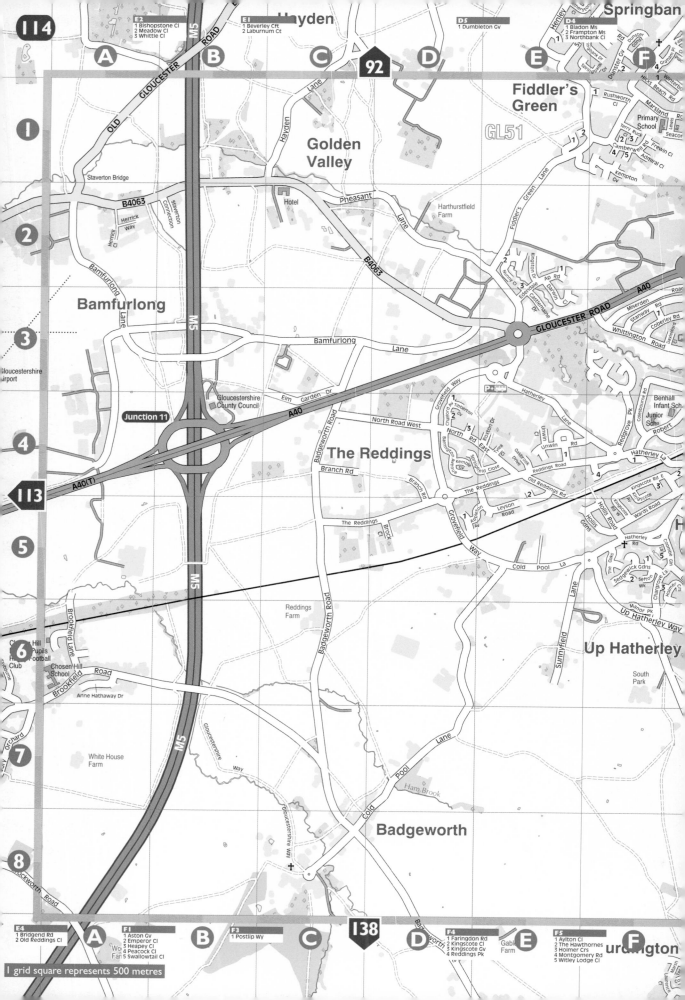

A B C 96 D E F

1

2

3

4

117

5

6

7

8

A B C 142 D E F

Whitehall
Farm

Cotehay

Brockhampton
Park

Brockl

PO

Park Lane

Nash
Barn

† Church Lane

Sevenhampt

Whittington

†

Syreford

Sandywell
Park

Hunter's
Way
PO
Station
A40

Waterside
Close

A436

Andoversford

A436

Ossage

Primary
School
PH
†
Sports
Club
Templefields
7
GLOUCESTER ROAD
A436

Andoversford
Industrial Estate

Andoversford
Link

Andoversford
Industrial Estate

Shipton
Solers

1 grid square represents 500 metres

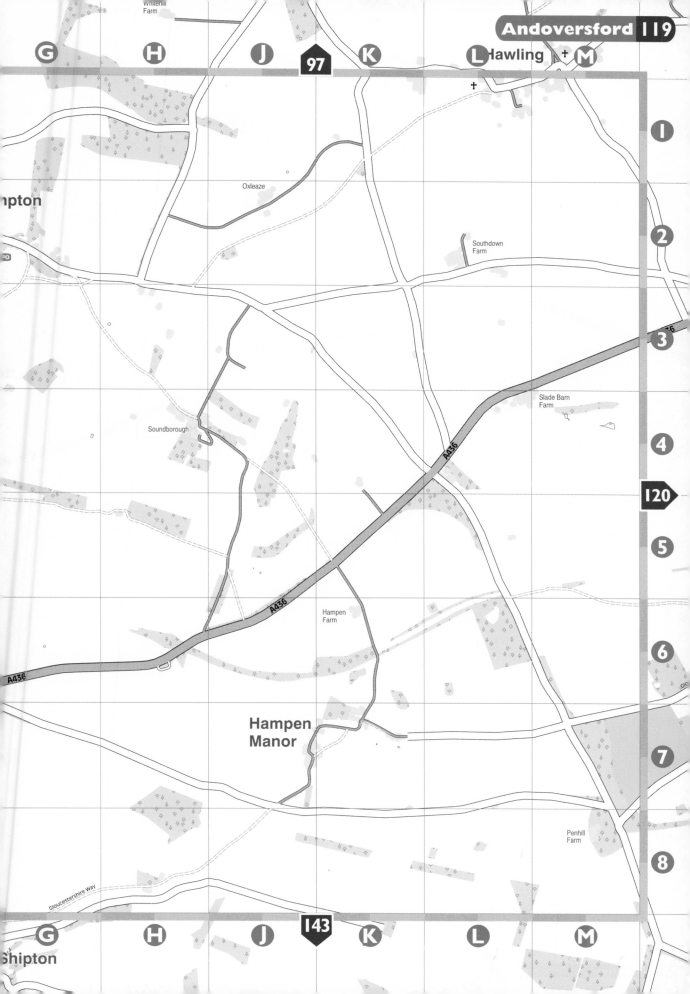

G H J **97** K L Hawling + M

I

Whitehill Farm

Oxleaze

Southdown Farm

2

3

Slade Barn Farm

A436

Soundborough

4

120

5

A436

Hampen Farm

6

A436

Hampen Manor

7

Penhill Farm

8

Gloucestershire Way

G H J **143** K L M

Shipton

B4068

G   H   J   K   L   M

99

B4068   Harford Bridge

1
Lower
Harford Farm

Windrush Way   Windrush Way

2

Roundhill Farm

3

Aylworth

Windrush Way

4

Hill Farm

Upper
Harford   A436

122

A436

5

Folly
Farm

6

Notgrove

PO   **Cold Aston**
Cold Aston C of E
Primary School

7

PH

Gloucestershire   Way

Chapel La
Aston Gro

Way   Macmillan   Way

Gloucestershire

Lane

Bangup
Barn   Bangup

8
Grove
Farm

G   H   J   K   L   M

145

Pountwell

Aston
Grove

A   B   C   **100**   D   E   F

Becky Hill

I

Lower
Harford Farm

Harfordhill
Farm

Wagborough
Bush

Manor Farm

2

River Windrush

Windrush Way

3

Windrush   Way

Slaughter
Farm

Aston
Farm

Gloucestershire
Way

Windrush Way

4

A436

Windrush
Farm

A436   OLD GLOUCESTER ROAD

5

Camp Farm

B
th

A429

6

Gloucestershire Way

Cold Aston C of E
Primary School

7

Aston

millan Way

A429

Grove

8

Tagm
Farm

A   B   **146**   D Fox Hill   E   F
Farm

1 grid square represents 500 metres

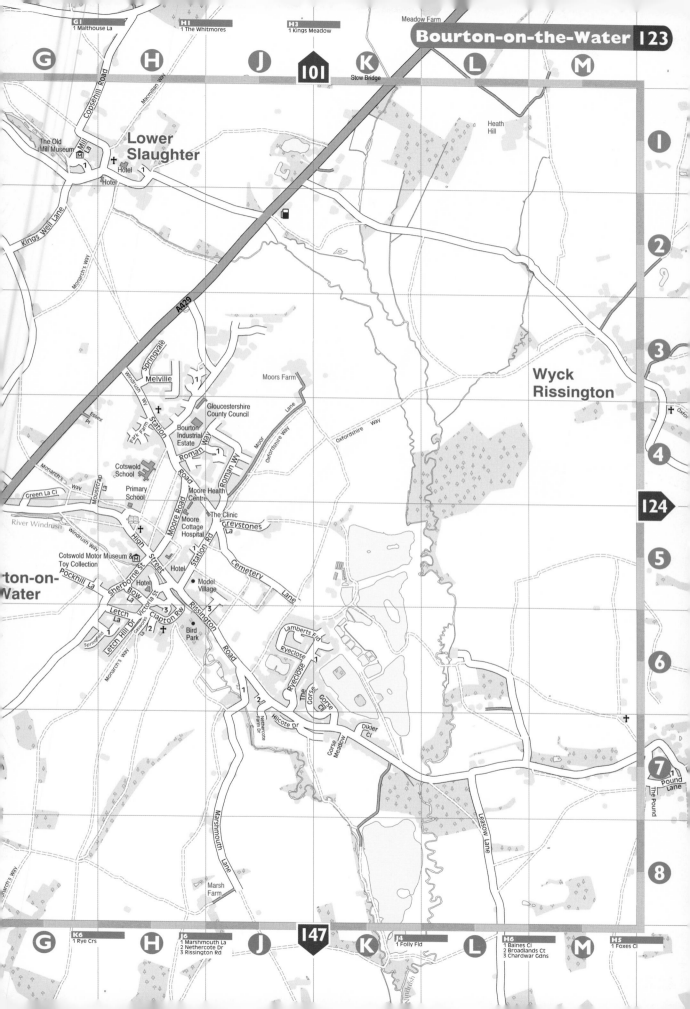

A B C 102 D E F

1

Wyck
Farm

Hill Farm

Icomb

2

Hotel

A424

3

Oxfordshire Way

Oxfordshire Way

Gawcombe

4

123

Wyck
Beacon

A424

Oxfordshire Way

5

Ceme

6

Bobble
Barn

Sopwith Rd
Siskin Road
Vickers Rd
Bristol Road
Wright Cl
Wright Road
Folland Dr
Avro Road
Hawker Sq

Upper
Rissington

7

Sandy Lane

Farman Road
Bleriot Road
Grebe Square
Hawker Sq
Dodd Drive
Smith Barry Crescent
Smith Barry Cres
Smith Barry Rd

The Pound
Pound Lane

Little Rissington

Wellington Rd
Gerrard Rd
Longmore Rd
Fulton Road
Longmore Av
Kirby Road
Road

8

A P Ellis Rd
Lichfield Rd
Randall Road
Linlithgow Road

Little Rissington
Airfield

A B C 148 D E F

G H J **103** K B4450 L M 1

Mickland's Hill

Pebbly Hill Farm

STOW ROAD

Chapel Street

CHAPEL ST

MAIN STREET

PO

PH

Old Forge Close

Church Street

Church Lane

Firs Cl

Jackson Road

New Road

Bledington County Primary School

Lower Farm

Oxfordshire Way

Bledington

OLD BURFORD ROAD

River Evenlode

B4450

2

Westcote Brook

Oxfordshire Way

Gloucestershire County

Oxfordshire County

Oxfordshire

3

Foscot

4

Nature Reserve

Bould

5

Church Westcote

6

ether Westcote

†

Church St

†

Spring Lane

Church

Idbury

Herbert's Heath

7

A424

8

Gloucestershire County

Oxfordshire County

G H J A424 **149** K **Fifield** L M

High St

†

†

Church Street

rrymouth Road

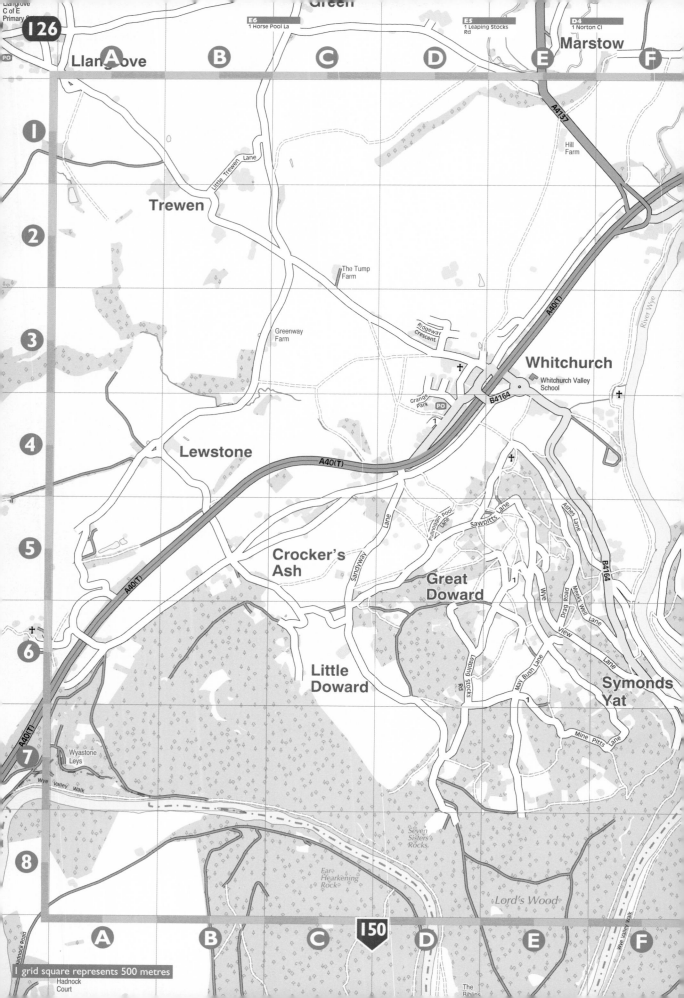

Llangrove
C of E
Primary Sc

PO

Llangrove

Green

E6 1 Horse Pool La

E5 1 Leaping Stocks Rd

D4 1 Norton Cl

Marstow

1

Hill Farm

A4137

Little Trewen Lane

Trewen

2

The Tump Farm

Ridgeway Crescent

A40(T)

3

Greenway Farm

Whitchurch

Whitchurch Valley School

Grange Park

PO

1

B4164

4

Lewstone

A40(T)

5

Crocker's Ash

Pulrossjon Pool Lane

Sawpitts Lane

Lane

Sandyway Lane

Asher Lane

Great Doward

1

Wye

Meak Well Lane

B4164

6

†

Little Doward

Leaping Stocks Rd

May Bush Lane

View

Lane

Symonds Yat

1

Mine Pitts Lane

7

A40(T)

Wyastone Leys

Wye Valley Walk

8

Seven Sisters Rocks

Far Hearkening Rock

Lord's Wood

Wye Valley Walk

Hadnock Road

I grid square represents 500 metres

Hadnock Court

The Biblins

K8
1 Redhouse La

PO
Cas
Lane
B4229

G H J K L M

K ne Bridge

B4234

**Goodrich
Cross**

A40(T)
Old Forge
Newmills Hill
B4229

River Wye
Wye Valle

homas
Wood

Rocklands
Farm

Mainoaks

Baynhams

Wye Valley Walk

upper Stowfield
Road

Huntsham
Court

The Green

County of Herefordshire

Gloucestershire County

128

Probertsbarn

Wye Valley Walk

Wye Valley Walk

Common Grove

Symond's Yat
Rock

PH
Hotel

Hotel

Coldwell
Rocks

English Bicknor
C of E
Primary School

Bicknor
Court

Redinhorne

orchard
Cl

**English
Bicknor**

Redhouse Lane

Holly
Barn

Murrells
Road
Smithy
Close

Eastbach
Court

Ancient Road

Hill
Dryslade
Farm

G3
1 Belle Vue Rd
2 Boxtree Cl

H3
1 Crooked End Pl

H5
1 Roebuck Mdw

G   H   J   K   L   M

I

2

3

4

I30

Harrow
H5

6

7

8

Cowles
House

Hom Grove
Farm

Puddlebrook

County of Herefordshire

Vain
Farm

Hawthorns Road

Hillside Road

Woodland Road

Mannings Rd

Morgan Close

West End

Hazel Road

High Street

North La

Peck Lane

Drybrook
Rugby Football
Club

PO

St Margaret's
Road

Varnister Road

Park Vw

Varnister

Morse Lane

Morse Lane

Whitehill Lane

Drybrook

St John's Rd

Highfield Road

Crooked
End

Ruardean

Turner's
Tump

croft

Meend Lane

Morse Road

Well Lane

Swish Lane

Quabbs Lane

Drybrook
Surgery

Drybrook
Primary
School

Dean's Walk

Ruardean
Hill

Spout Lane

Spout
Lane

The Hollow

Morse Road

Drybrook Road

Mount Cl

Trinity

Larksfield

Woodend Rd

Ruardean
Woodside

Bakers Piece Road

Farm Road

PO

Millers Gr

Highview

Morgans Lane

Ashfield Rd

Baptist Way

Road

Greenbank Cl

Bridge Road

Sycamore Road

Eastwood Road

2

1

Barn Lane

Ruardean Road

Webley Rd

The Patches

Duttons La

Forest Road

Denehurst Road

A4136

Brierley Road

Woodside
CP School

A4136

Nailbridge

A4151

The Branch

STEAM

Steam Mills
School

Steam Mills
Road

MILLS

Steam
Mills

ROAD A4151

Gloucestershire Way

A4136

Newtown Road

Broadmoor Road

Brierley

Brierley Banks

A4136

High Street

HIGH STREET

BROADMOOR ROAD

Corinium
Business
Park

Pavilion
Business Park

Whimsey Rd

Forest Rd

Speculation

Whimsey
Industrial
Estate

Estate

FOREST

G   H   J   K   L   M

M5
1 Eastwood Rd
2 Oakland Rd

M3
1 Sunnymead Cl

Serridge
Green

Birch
Wood

A   B   C **106** D   E   F

I

Mitcheldean

CROSS ROAD
CARISBRC RD
Hollywell Rd
Old Dean Rd
Deans Rd
BRADLEY C
TOWNSEND
Police Stn
Court Farm
Lower Farm
Brook St
Ash Grove
The Crescent

Churchill Way
St Michael
Close
PO
HIGH ST
Mitcheldean Surgery
Eastern Avenue
Parks Road
Ladygrove Business Park

Stenders Business Park
Orchard Rd
Stenders Rd
Mary Meadow
Meadow
Deane
GLOUCESTER RD – A4136
BARTON HILL
Brimp Hill

Stenders Business Cen NEW Street
Witley
Colchester Cl
Primary School
The Stenders
Baynham Rd
Warden Close
NEW ROAD
Silver Street
Anns Wk

2

GL17

Folly Farm

Dene Magna Community School

3

Rugby Football Club
Street
Mannings Rd
Norman Close

The Wilderness

A4136
Jubilee Road

Gloucestershire Way

†

4

Plump Hill

Abenhall

Walk
Road

Glencoe Lane
Docturn Hill Way

129

Gloucestershire Way

5

Harrow Hill

Eastwood Road
Road
Blackfield
A4136

Plump Hill County Primary School

A4136

6

Nailbridge

The Rookery

Jubilee Road

Shapridge

Mills
Steam Mills Road

7

MILLS ROAD

The Mills
ROAD A4151
Newtown Road
Broadmoor Park

Green Bottom

8

Broadmoor

Pavilion Business Park
Whimsey Rd

†

Whimsey Industrial Estate
Boey's Pike

A   B   C **154** D   E   F

Collafield

Heywood Sports Centre

CI
1 Oakhill Rd

1 grid square represents 500 metres

G H J **107** K L M

Chessgrc
H1
1 The Bramleys
2 Latchen Orch
3 Nupend Gdns

Chessgrove Lane

Hobbs Lane

Road

Hope Est

Station Rd

PO

Napping Lane

The Nappin

Wend The Willows

Longhope

I

Nupend Lane

Gloucestershire Way

Latchen

Bathams

Old Monmouth Rd

The Temple

Old Hill

Velthouse Lane

Mill Lane

A4136

A4136

Hopes Hill Primary School

Royal Spring

Chapel Lane

A4136

Chapel Lane

Little London

Hinders Lane

Blaisdon Lane

2

Hope Wood

Longhope Brook

Nottwood Hill

Stanley House

3

Velthouse

Blaisdon Wood

†

4

†

132

Blaisdon

5

Gaulet

Flaxley Woods

6

Monk Hill Farm

Welshbury Wood

Boseley Court

7

Flaxley

†

8

Grove Farm

G H J **155** K L M

Broughtons

Bere's

G   H   J   **109**   K   L   M

A40(T)   I

Birdwood

Spring Dale

A40(T)   A40(T)

Halfway Bridge

Churcham School

Church Lane

Churcha

Hill Farm

Church La

2

Sainthill

Court

Old Ley Court

Oakle Street

3

Ley Brook

Gloucestershire Way

4

A4

134

Duni Farm

River Severn   Severn Way

5

LC

Ley Road

A48(T)

Gloucestershire Wy

Ley Court

Hooks Farm

severn Way

Lake Street

6

Ley Road

A48(T)

severn Way

Lower Ley

7

Ley Road

The Flat

Lake Street

PO

Severn Way

Farleys End   8

Walmore Common

Bridgemacote

G   H   J   **157**   K   Severn Way   L   M

Walmore Hill Primary School

Broadway Lane

A48(T)

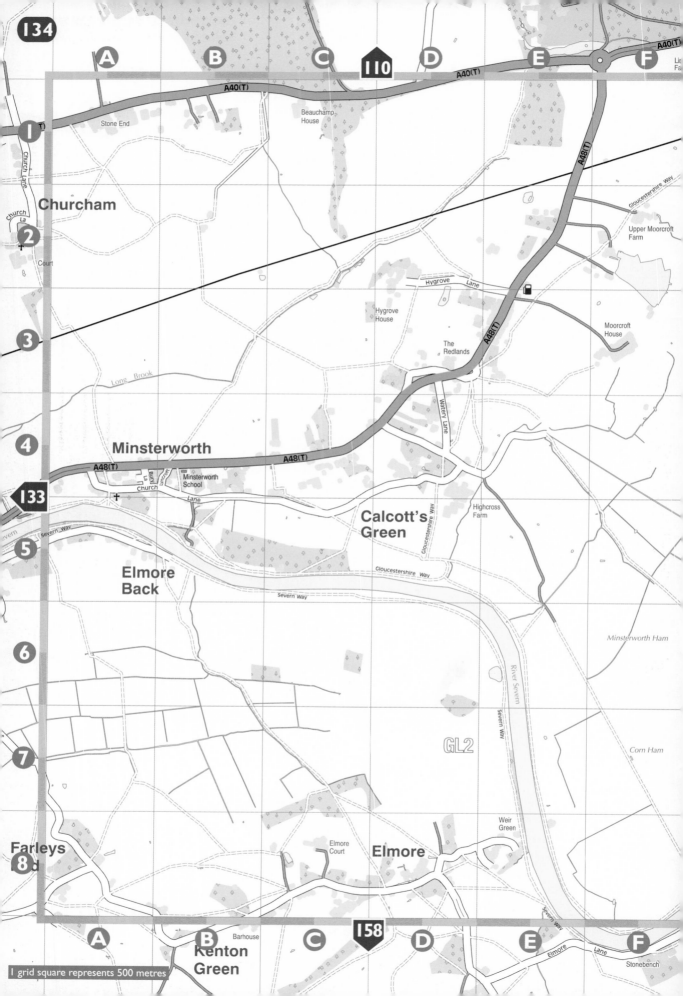

G   H   J   K   L   M

Rugby Club

River Severn

Port Ham

Lower Parting

Sports & Leisure Ctr

ROYAL OAK RD
ROYAL OAK ROAD

THE QUAY

River Severn

St Oswald's
The College
Yard Surg
Priory
St Oswald's
St John's
Co Council
Co Cath
Parliament House
City Ga
P
Gloucester Folk Mus
Transport Mus
County Library County Co
Police St
HM Prison
Castle Meads
Shire Hall
New Inn PH
Guild
Sch
City Gt
Courts
Regimental Mus
Crown & Co Court
Hlth Authority
City Council
Register Office
Sports Club
Priory Ruins
Mkt
Norfolk St
Montpellier
Albion St
Register Office
SLMk Surg
GLOUCES

Severn Way

Vale of Gloucester

Sudmeadow Road

Severnside Trading Est
Business Park
Llanthony Industrial Est
National Waterways Museum
Mus of Advertising & Packaging

Llanthony Road
Spinnaker Road
Abbey Road

Gloucester City Association Football Club
Cotswold Edge Business Cen

Llanthony Secunda Priory
Sudbrook Trading Est
Baker Street

Venture Business Cen

St Ann Way

Weston Rd
New Street
Primary Sch

TRIER WAY

GLOUCES **3**

Madleaze Road
Madleaze Trading Est
Newark
Hempsted Lane
Hornethorn Cl
Sanda Wood

Gordon League Rugby Football Club
Monk Meadow Dock

Madleaze Trading Est
Moreland's Trading Est

St Paul's
BRISTOL ROAD
Robinhood St
Clearam Cl
Alma Pl
Robinson
Doctors Surgery

Glearam Road
Frampton Road
Lysons Avenue
Linden Road
Cecil Road
Granville Street
Seymour Rd
Bloomfield Rd
Churchill
Balfour Avenue
Lanner

Hempsted School

Rectory La
St Swithuns Rd
Chartwell
Bridge
Hilton Cl
Court Gdns

Hempsted Lane
Ladywell Cl

Hempsted

Linden Primary Sch
Linden

Tudor St
Harrington
Gladstone Road
Newark Road
Tuffley Avenue
Wilton Road
Raikes Rd
Rowhy Rd
The Oval
Henley
Roseberry Avenue
Kitchener Av
Lewisham
Ribston Girls

136

Rea Lane

Severn Way

Netheridge Close

Gloucester & Sharpness Canal

BRISTOL ROAD A430

Ashville Rd
Centurion Ind Est
Byard Rd
Empire Way
Caesar Rd
St Albans Rd
Trading Est
Ashville Industrial Estate

Tuffley Crescent
Mansel Cl
Woodpecker
Partridge Rd
Chaucer Cl
Podsmead Pl
Podsmead Road
Laburnum Rd
Sycamore
Redwood
Poplar Cl

Ribston Cl
Romney Cl

Linden **6**

Rea

Riversmead Farm

Sims Lane
Ind Est

Tuffley Trading Est
Pearce Way

Milton Avenue
Harvey Cl
Bijeman
Shelley Av
Mayfield Dr
Pennyson Av
Scott Avenue
Epping

Podsmead

The Crypt School

Lower Tuffley Lane
Byron Avenue

COLE AVENUE A38
SOUTHERN A

7

Lower Rea

Woolslop Av
Goodridge Av
Goodridge Trading Est
Bristol

Woodrow Way
North Star Business Park
Ramdale Rd
Corlola Rd
Lwr Tuffley La

Shakespeare Avenue
Keats Avenue
Burns Avenue
Hathaway

Tuffley Lane
Silver
Emerald
Shepherd Rd
Central Trading Estate
Russell St
Holmleigh Road
St George's Rd
Grange Road
Junior School
Nympsfield Rd
Coral St
St David's
Ryelands
Arlingham Road
Fretherne Rd
Longney Road
Falfield Road
Simbrook Av
Flaxley Rd
Tuffley

Westbury Rd
Birchwood
Cedarwood
Frywood Dr
Larchwm
Tintern
Cheltworth Rd

8

Pegasus Gdns
Elmore

Shepherd Rd
Gloucestershire County Council
Hendingham Close
Trading Estate

Lower Tuffley

Beaufort Community School

STROUD

A38

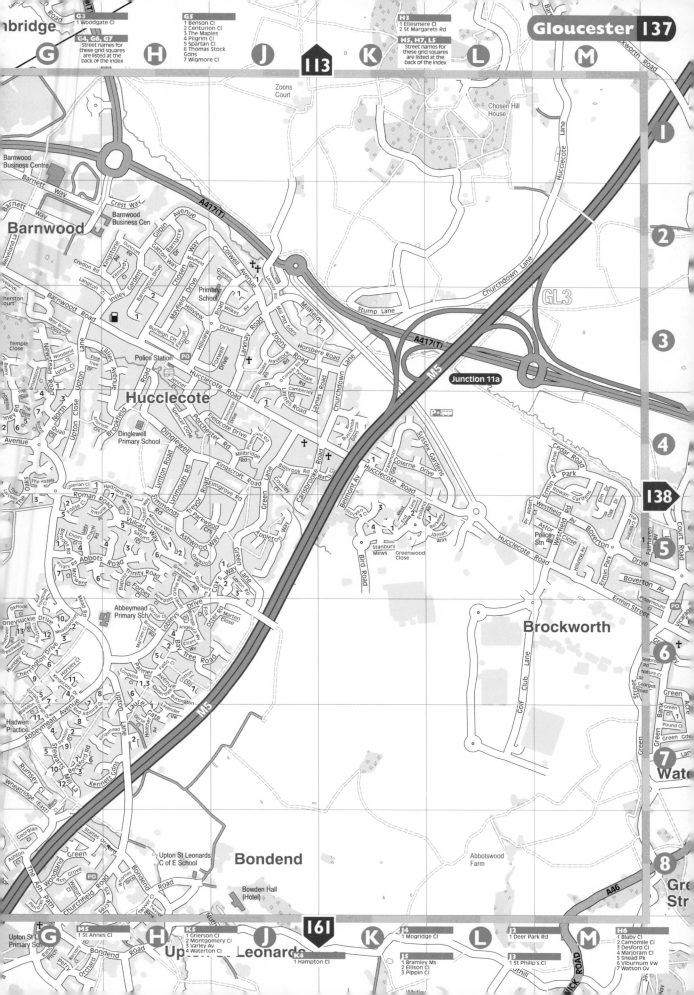

G H J 115 K L M

I

2

3

4

140

5

6

7

8

G H 163 J K L M

The Tynings

Shurdington Road

A46

Church Lane

Bishop Road

School Lane

Vicarage

Blenheim

Orch

PH

Close

Lawn Crs

Police Station

Gwinnette Court

Lane

Little Shurdington

Crippets

Leckhampton

Greenway Lane

Leckhampton Hill

Salterley Grange

Cotswold Way

Gloucestershire Way

Cotswold Way

Dryhill Farm

Ullenwood

National Star Centre College

Golf

Gloucestershire Way

Cold Slad

Crickley Hill Country Park

cotswold Way

A436

A417(T)

Gloucestershire Way

A417(T)

Dog Lane

A417(T)

Cotswold Way

A417(T)

Barrow Wake (Viewpoint)

Gloucestershire Way

Cuckoopen Barn Farm

Shab Hill

Cotswold Way

116

139

164

A   B   C   D   E   F

I
2
3
4
5
6
7
8

Lampton Hill
Undercliff
Daisybank Road
Sandy Lane
Manor
Golf Course
Cirencester Road
Cladehill Road
be Lane

Cotswold Way
Charlton Kings Common
Cotswold Way
Vineyards Farm

Hartley Farm

Salterley Grange

A436
Cotswold
Chatcombe Wood

Hartley Bottom

Seven Springs

A435

A436

Cotswold Way

Golf Course

A436

New Farm

Dowman's Farm

Coberley School
PO

Coberley

Close Farm

Gloucestershire Way

A435

Gloucestershire Way

Coldwell Bottom

Cowley

GD3

A435

I grid square represents 500 metres

142

A   B   C   D   E   F

GLOUCESTER ROAD

Templefields Club

118

Andover Industrial Estate

I

PH

A40

Shipton Solers

School Lane

Kilham Lane

Shi
Oli

A436

2

Foxcote

PH

A40(T)

3

Cleevely Wood

4

Northfield Farm

Thorndale

141

5

6

Upcote Farm

7

Withington C of E School

Withington Primary School

Harnham Lane

Withington

High Street

PH

The Farmings

Brassing Gdns

Kings Head Lane

8

A   B   C   D   E   F

166

Woodbridge Lane

Staple

1 grid square represents 500 metres

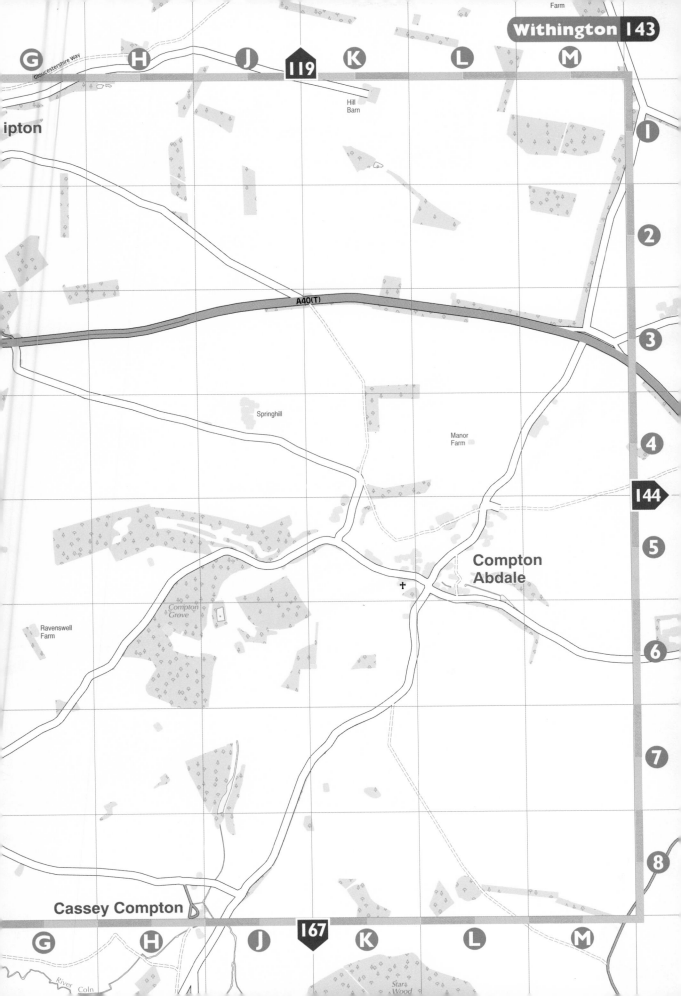

G   H   J   119   K   L   M

Gloucestershire Way

ipton

Farm

Hill
Barn

1

2

A40(T)

3

Springhill

Manor
Farm

4

144

5

Compton
Abdale

Ravenswell
Farm

Compton
Grove

6

7

8

Cassey Compton

G   H   J   167   K   L   M

River
Coln

Star
Wood

144

A   B   Canon's Barn   C   120   D   E   F

1

2   ✝ Hazleton

Hazleton Grove

Milkwell Covert

3   A40 (T)

The Downs Brake

4

143

Hill Barn

5

Compton Farm

6   A40 (T)

7   Hampnett

Macmillan Way

8   Hangman's Stone

Oaks Bottom   B   C   168   D   Macmillan Way   E   F

A

1 grid square represents 500 metres

146

Grove

A   B   C   **122**   D   E   F

Tagr
Farm

1
Ash
Grove

Fox Hill
Farm

Bourton Hill
Farm

2
Sweetslade
Farm

Monar

Monarch's Way
Goms
Hole

3

A429

Monarch's Way

Broadwater
Bottom

4

145

Furzehill
Wood

Monarch's Way

5

Starvall

Farmington
Grove

6

Haycroft
Bottom

Camp
Farm

Monarch's Way

7

Haycroft
House

Farmington
Lodge

8
†

arch's Way

Monarch's Way

Farmington

A   B   C   **170**   D   E   F

Empshill
Farm

Folly

1 grid square represents 500 metres

G H J **123** K L M

I

2

3

Clapton-on-
the-Hill

Leasow Lane

4 at
Rissi

148

5

Broadmoor
Farm

The Fork

Upper
Broadmoor

6

Sandy Hill
Farm

Sherborne
Common

7

Crookmoor
Ash

Northfield
Barn

8

G H **171** J K L M

Sherborne Br

Cemetery

River Windrush

Marsh
Farm

Lane

Sherborne

148

A   B   C   **124**   D   Little Rissington Airfield   E   **B4** 1 Orchard Bank   F

A P Ellis Rd
Littlenow Road
Randall
Idderdale
Road

1

Leasow Lane

2

The Barn Business Centre

3

Lane End

Green's Cl

1

PH

4   Great Rissington

†

The Follies

147

Sherborne Lane

Great Rissington CP School

5

Barrington Bushes

6

7

Miletree Clump

8

A   B   Horseclo Copse   **172**   C   D   E   F

1 grid square represents 500 metres

A B C D E F

1 Hadnock Court

2

3

STAUNTON ROAD

4

5

Duke Of York Road

A4136 STAUNTON ROAD

6

Monmouthshire
Gloucestershire County

7

Offa's Dyke Path

8

Suck Stone

Near
Hearkening
Rock

Redding's
Inclosure

Highmeadow
Woods

Buck
Stone

Bunjups
Wood

Knockalls Inclosure

Far
Hearkening
Rock

Lady
Park
Wood

Monmouthshire
Gloucestershire County

Wellmeadow

Staunton

Forest
Close

A4136 STAUNTON ROAD

Tillis
VW

Birchen
Wood

Lord's Wood

The
Biblins

The
Slaughter

Mai
Wo

Braceland

Wye Valley Walk

A B C D E F

REDBRO
ROAD

Lane

1 grid square represents 500 metres

A   B   Church Lane   C   132   Morwents Farm   D   E   F

I

Brook Farm

Adsett

Hunthill

A48(T)

2

HIGH ST   Westbury-On-Severn C of E Primary School   Adsett Court   Hunt Hill

A48

Colchester Cl   PO   Westbury Surgery

Westbury-on-Severn   Medical Surgery   A48(T)   WINTLE'S HILL   A48(T)   Stantway   Rock Lane   Rock And Fountain Lane

3   Westbury Court Garden (NT)   Stantway Lane

Gatwick

Strand   Lane   Upper

4   Strand

Moys Hill Farm

155   Cleeve

5   Arlingham Warth

Gravel Farm

6   Severn Way

Hayden Farm

7   Warth Lane   Lower Dumball

River Severn

Slowwe House

8   Silver Street   Street   Woolthorpe La   Friday   Severn Way

High   Vale Bank

A   B   Milton End   C   180   D   E   F

The ct Gdns   PO

1 grid square represents 500 metres

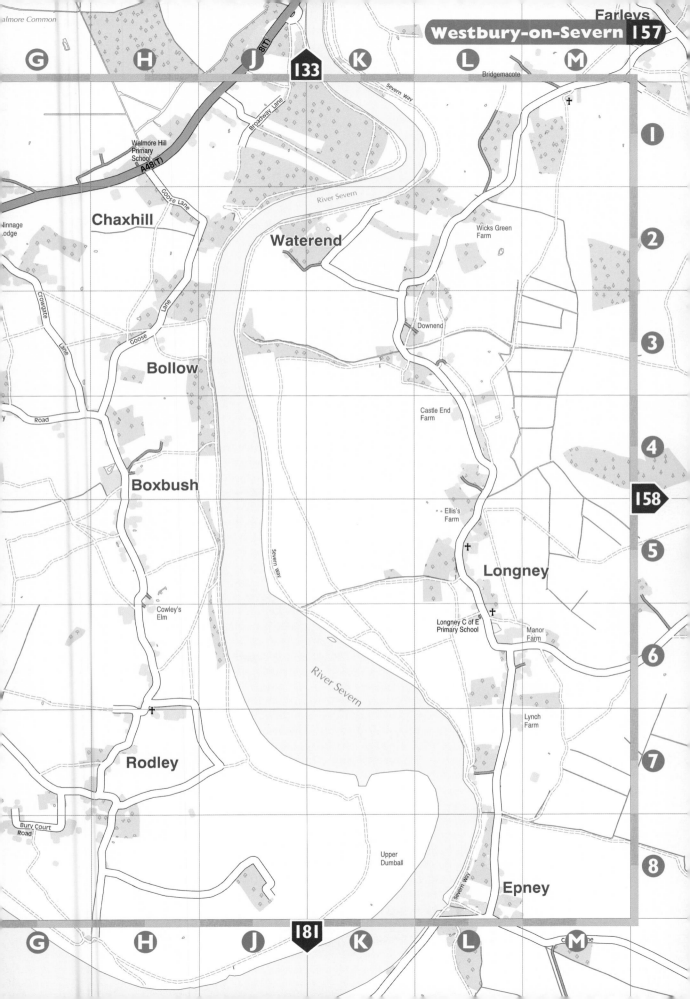

G   H   J   **133**   K   L   M

almore Common

Walmore Hill Primary School
A48(T)
Broadway Lane
Goose Lane
Chaxhill
linnage Lodge

Severn Way

River Severn

Waterend

Wicks Green Farm

I

2

Crowgate Lane
Goose Lane
Bollow

Downend

Goose Lane

3

Road

Castle End Farm

Boxbush

4

158

Ellis's Farm

5

Severn Way

Longney

Cowley's Elm

Longney C of E Primary School

Manor Farm

6

Lynch Farm

River Severn

Rodley

7

Bury Court Road

Upper Dumball

Severn Way

Epney

8

Elmore
Court

Elmore

F3 1 Bekdale Cl
    2 Waterdaie Cl

F2 1 Ferry Gdns
    2 Kingfisher Ri
    3 Merchants Mead
    4 Millers Dyke
    5 Sandpiper Cl
    6 Watermans Ct
    7 Waterside Cl

A B C 134 D E F

Barhouse

Kenton Green

Stonebench

Severn Way

Elmore Lane

1

Velthouse Farm

Hollow Farm

Moorhen Ct
Durlin Cl
Pochard Cl
Whimbrel Rd
Road
Shelduck Rd
Ardea
Pintail Close
The Causeway
Mallard
Millers Dyke
Turnstone Dr

2

3

Hardwicke Farm

Springdale Cl
Wharfdale Wy
Arkendale Dr
School La
Sud Rd
West

Clarke's Farm

4

157

Madam's End Farm

School Farm

Sellars Road
Orchard Close
West

5

Stank Lane

Church Lane

Laynes Farm

+

6

Southfield Farm

Pound Lane

Hardwicke Court

7

A38

Road Farm

8

Oakey Farm

Gloucester and Sharpness Canal

A B C 182 D E F

le Lane

Hiltmead

Parkend Bridge

Lower Rea

G H J 135 K L M

I

Lower Tuffley

Quedgeley

Severn Vale Secondary School

Manor Farm

Naas Lane

Hunts Grove View

160

Needham Av

Waterwells Farm

Naas Farm

Hardwicke

Naas Lane

Sticky Lane

Four Mile Elm

M5

Broc

Haresfield Lane

Colethrop Farm

Quedgeley Trading Estate West

Brook

M5

Pool Farm

Chambers' Farm

Naas Lane

Junction 12

G H J 183 K L M

Colethrop

2 3 4 5 6 7 8

Bondend

Green Street

G
H
J
K
L
M A46

137

1 Sanatorium Rd

Upton St Leonards C of E School

Upton St Leonards Primary Sch

Upton St Leonards

Bondend Road

The Stanley

Stanley Walk

Portway

Valley Lane

Moorend

GL4

Watery Lane

Prinknash Abbey

Bird Park

Whitley Court

Pincott Farm

PAINSWICK ROAD

Nuthill

Cotswold Way

Nature Reserve

1

Brockworth Wood

High

High E3 the

Nature Reserve

Cotswold Way

Buckholt Road

Simmond's Hall Farm

162

Pope's Wood

Kimsbury House

Castle End

WAY

B4073

Fort

A46

Cotswold Way

Beacon Close

Portway

Cotswold Way

Mill Lane

Mill Lane

Olivers

Painswick Stream

Batch Farm

Castle Godwyn

Paradise

Golf Course

Rococo

B4073

Cotswold Way

A46

Cem

Nurse Road

185

Damsells Cross

G
H
J
K
L
M

1
2
3
4
5
6
7
8

A46

Green Street

A

B

C

138

D

E

F

1

Green Street

Droys Court

Witcombe Reservoir

Great Witcombe

†

Witcombe Park

Cotswold Way

Nature Reserve

2

Cotswold Way

Brockworth Wood

Woodland Farm

3 **High Brotheridge**

The Buckholt

Buckholt Road

Cotswold Way

Cotswold Way

Witcombe Wood

Buckholt Wood

Buckholt Road

Buckholt Road

4

Buckle Wood

B4070

PO

PH

†

Cranham

Cranham Wood

Hazel Hang Wood

5

Cranham Common

Mill Lane

Simmond's Hall Farm

†

6

Overtown

Climperwell Farm

B4070

Batch Farm

7

8

B4070

Calf Way

Wateredge Farm

A

B

C

186

Way

D

E

F

1 grid square represents 500 metres

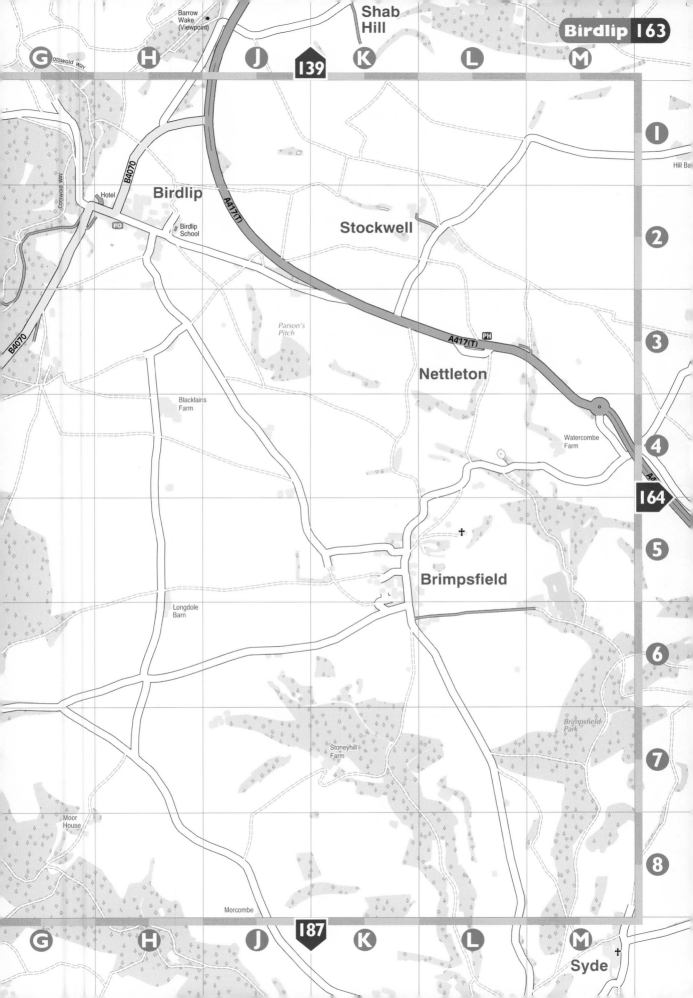

G H J **141** K L M

I

2

3

4

166

5

6

M

7

8

Pinswell
Plantation

The Forest

Chescombe
Bottom

Lyde
Bank

Barncombe
Bottom

Colesbourne
Park

Little
Colesbourne

A435

Southbury
Farm

River Churn

A435 PO PH

Colesbourne

Penhill
Farm

Slutswell

Penhill
Plantation

A435

Hall's
Grove

Combend
Manor

Rapsgate
Park

Eycot
Wood

Shewel
Wood

G H J **189** K L M

A   B   C   142   D   E   F

1

2

3

4

165

5

6

7

8

A   B   190   C   D   E   F

Staple
Farm

Withington
Woods

The Gulf
Scrubs

Boy's
Grove

Woodlands

Pinswell

Monkham
Wood

Iticomb
Wood

Marsden

Shawswell

Clifferdine
Wood

River Churn

Woodbridge Lane

Kings Head L

Woo

Woo

lesbourne

A435

C
L

Chittlegrove

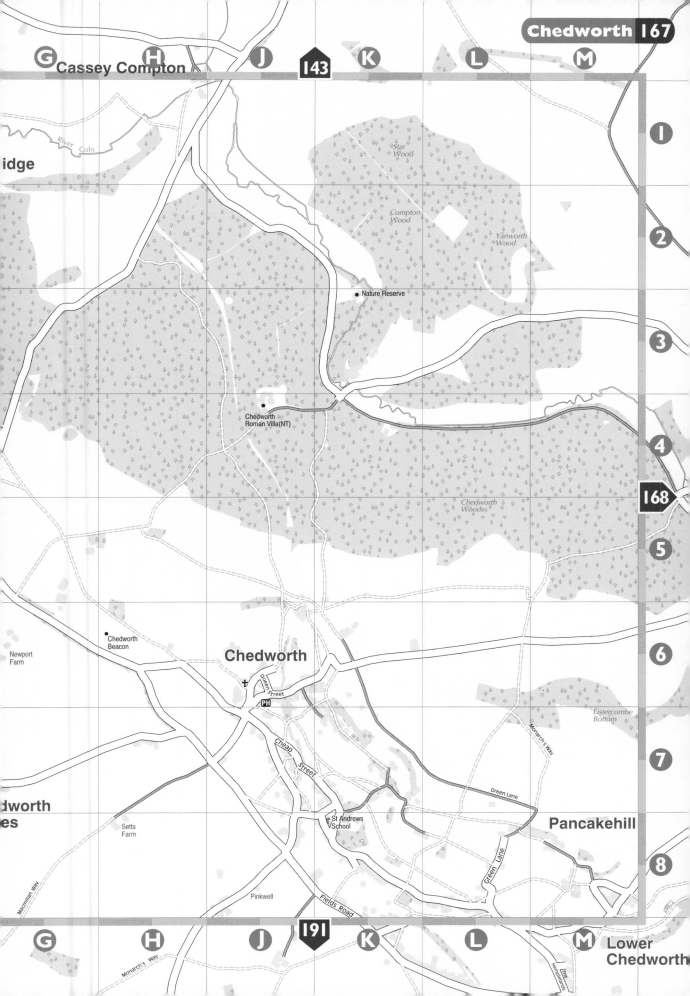

G Cassey Compton

H

J 143

K

L

M

I

2

3

4

168

5

6

7

8

River Coln

idge

Star Wood

Compton Wood

Yanworth Wood

Nature Reserve

Chedworth Roman Villa(NT)

Chedworth Woods

Newport Farm

Chedworth Beacon

Chedworth

Queen Street

PH

Listercombe Bottom

Cheap Street

Monarch's Way

Green Lane

dworth es

Setts Farm

St Andrews School

Pancakehill

Macmillan Way

Pinkwell

Fields Road

Green Lane

G

H

J 191

K

L

M Lower Chedworth

Monarch's Way

The Hemplands

Ⓐ   Ⓑ   Ⓒ   **144**   Ⓓ   Ⓔ   Ⓕ

Hangman's
Stone

1

*Oaks
Bottom*

*Cowlease
Grove*

2

Oxpens
Farm

Monarch's Way

3

✝

Yanworth

*Stowell
Grove*

4

A429

◄167

Stowell

Monarch's Way

✝

*Stowell
Park*

5

6

Raybrook
Barn

A429

*Listercombe
Bottom*

7

8

A429

Hotel
PH

Fossebridge

G H J **145** K L M

1 Barnett Wy
2 Bettenson Ri
3 Hammond Dr

Prison Copse **K1**
1 Farmington Ri

K2
1 Short Hedges Cl

rch's Way

I

Heritage Centre

Old Coalyard Farm Est.

3 Tayler Rd

Grace Dr

Gravenel Rd

Jessop Dr

Minchin Rd

Guggle La

West End

Shepherds Wy

2

Police Stn

Antelope Paddock

PO

Mill View

Ward Pl

May's C

Hotel

High St

Fortey Road

MacArthur Rd

Farmington Road

Northleach

1

Walkers Garden

East End

South End

Crap Vw

Leys

Dixton

Eastington Rd

Brook

Ashway

Nostle Rd

1

Fallows Rd

Bassett Road

A40(T)

A40(T)

I

2

Oldhill Barn

A429

Mill End

All Alone

A429

Upper End

3

Winterwell Barn

Cats Abbey Farm

Winterwell Farm

4

Easti

170

5

Trinder's Barn

6

Crickley Barrow Farm

Broadfield Covert

Trowel Covert

7

Sheep House Farm

Broadfield Farm

8

G H J **193** K L M

Saltway Farm

Calcot Peak Farm

G H J 147 K L M

I

River Windrush

2

3

4

Windrush

172

5

6

7

8

Barn

Sherborne Brook

Cemetery

Sherborne

PO

Sherborne Park

Home Farm

A40(T)

A40(T)

A40(T)

Snowbottom Belt

Camp Barn

Budgehill Wood

Blackpits

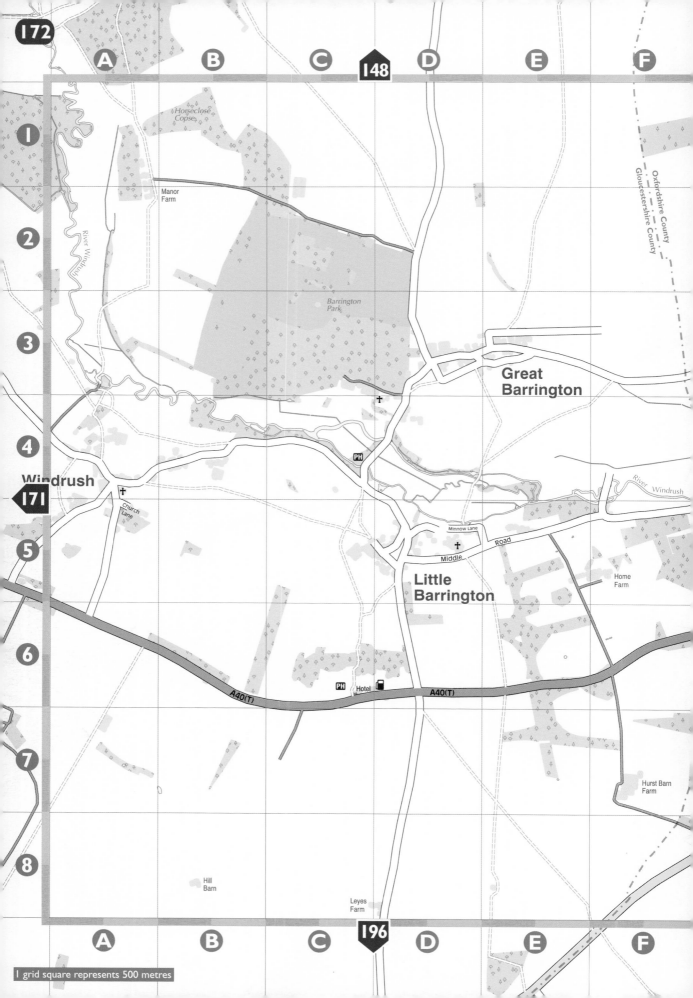

148

196

Horseclose
Copses

Manor
Farm

River Windrush

Barrington
Park

Great
Barrington

Oxfordshire County
Gloucestershire County

Windrush

Church
Lane

PH

River Windrush

Minnow Lane

Middle

Road

Little
Barrington

Home
Farm

A40(T)

PH

Hotel

A40(T)

Hurst Barn
Farm

Hill
Barn

Leyes
Farm

G H J **149** K L M

I

2

A424

3

4

Taynton

5 We
Hill

River Windrush

Upton

Burford
Primary
School

Burford Surgery
Sheep Street
Hotel
Priory
Lane Stone
Gal

A424

A40(T)

Burford Cottage
Hospital
The Brian
Sinfield Gal

6
M
PH

M

Oxfordshire County
Oxfordshire County

Lane
Barn La
Place
Sweeps Lane
Swan
Barns Lane
HIGH STR

Hunts Close

Tanner's

B4425

A40(T)

Upton
Down

Hotel

7

Burford School

Burford
Golf
Club

8

Signet
Hill

A361

G H J **197** K L M

Baker's Hill

Broad

Scowles

COLEFORD

High Nash

Whitecliff

Palmer's Flat

Tufthorn Industrial Estate

Millend

Puzzle Wood

Pingry Farm

Scatterford Farm

Milkwall

Clearwell Caves

Clearwell

The Rocks

Ellwood County Primary School

Marsh Lane

Sling

Orepool

Clements End

Stowe Green

Trow Green

K1
1 The Crescent
2 Kings Meade
3 Market Pl
4 Poolway Ct
5 Prospect Pl
6 Vicarage Ct

151

176

199

M2
1 Crown Meadow

M1
1 Wynols Rd

L7
1 Michaels Wy

L6
1 Gorse La

K2
1 Bessemer Cl
2 Centurions Wk
3 Copley Dr
4 Fairfield Cl
5 Fairways Av
6 Nash Wy
7 Tufthorn Av

G H J K L M

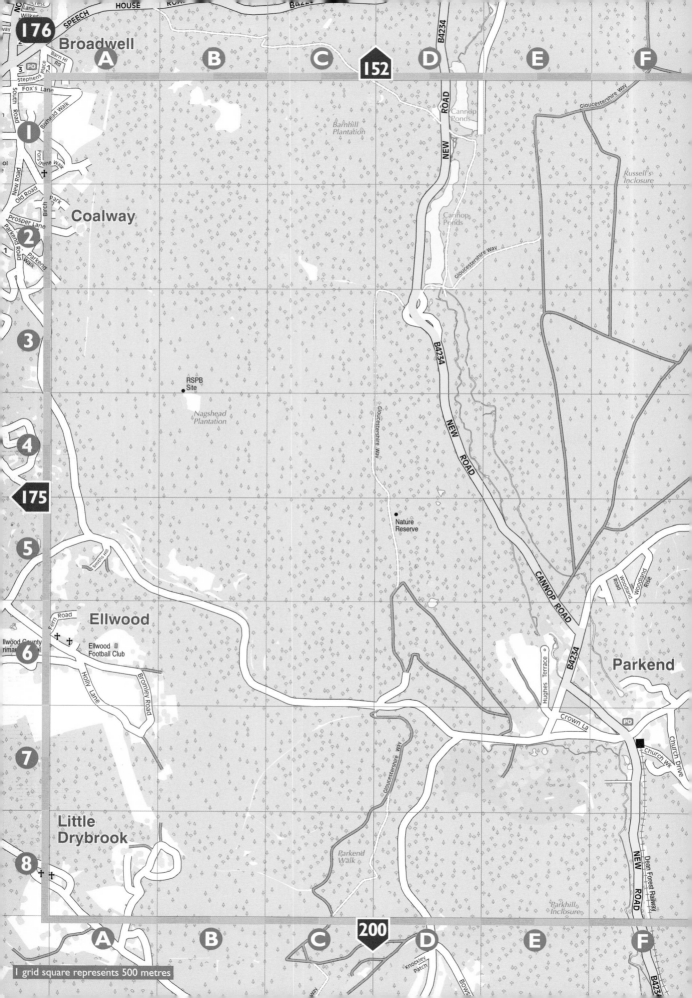

176

Broadwell

A **B** **C** 152 **D** **E** **F**

1

Coalway

2

3

RSPB
Site

Nagshead
Plantation

4

175

Nature
Reserve

5

Ellwood

6

Parkend

7

Little
Drybrook

8

A **B** **C** 200 **D** **E** **F**

1 grid square represents 500 metres

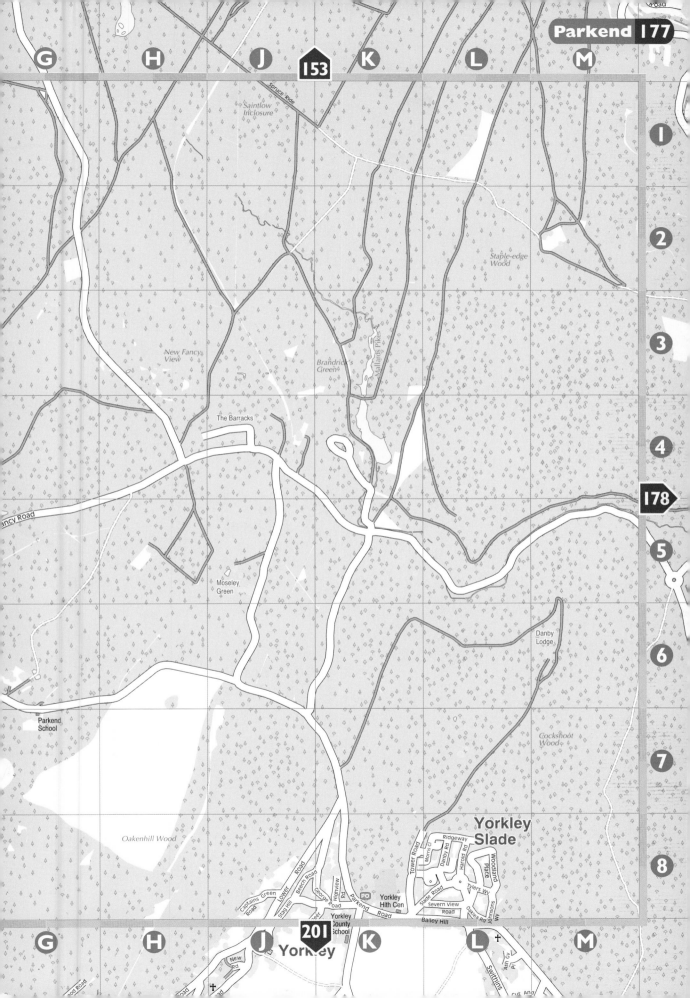

G H J **153** K L M

I
2
3
4
178
5
6
7
8

Spruce Ride

Saintlow Inclosure

Staple-edge Wood

New Fancy View

Brandrick's Green

Mallards Pikes

The Barracks

Fancy Road

Moseley Green

Danby Lodge

Parkend School

Cockshoot Wood

Oakenhill Wood

Yorkley Slade

Ridgeway
Morris Cl
Danby Rd
Harold Rd
Woodland Place
Tower Road
Tylers Wy
Slade Road
Oakea Rd
Johnsons
severn View Road
Captains Green Road
Lower
Stag Hill
Beech Road
cedge Road
Highview Rd
Parkend Road
PO
Yorkley Hith Cen
Bailey Hill
Swithins
Cut Ang
Yorkley County School

Yorkley

New Rd

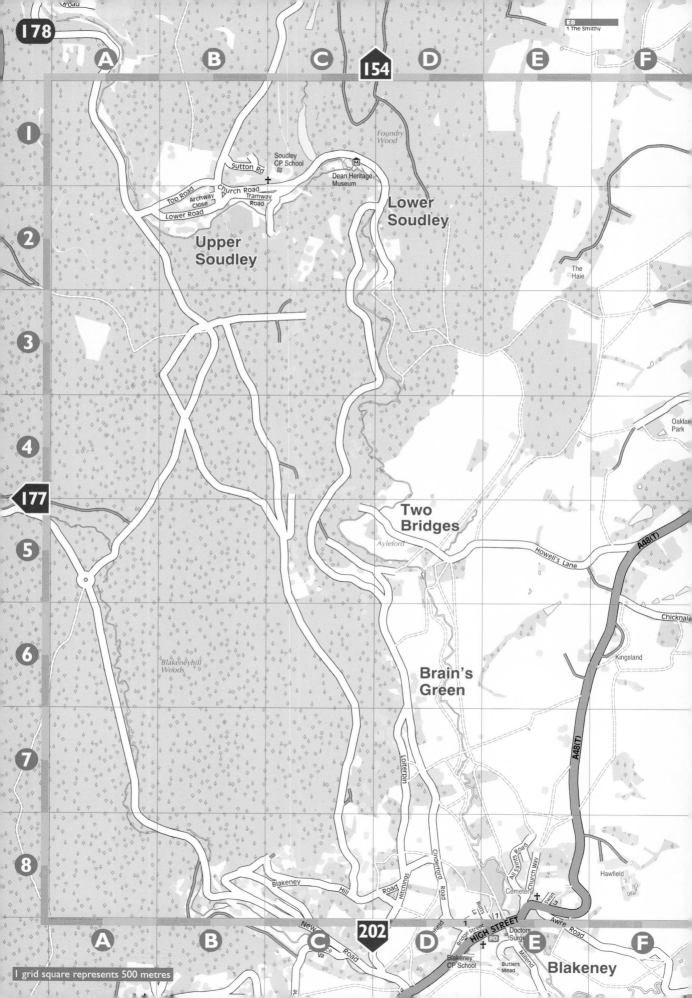

156

Milton End

Overton

Overton Lane

Overton Farm

Fretherne

The Reddings

Hock Cliff

179

Severn Way

Severn Way

Severn Way

River Severn

204

A B C D E F

I grid square represents 500 metres

G H J **157** K L M

Epney

Upper
Dumball

Castle Lane

I

River Severn

Lea Court
Farm

2

Moor
Farm

Framilode

Severn Way

Upper Framilode

Moor Street

3

Packthorne
Farm

Passage Road

Park View

Saul

Saul C of E
Primary School

HIGH STREET

4

182

Whitminster
House

Wheatenhurst

Church Lane

B4071

Gloucester and Sharpness Canal

Stroudwater Canal

5

Highfield
House

Oatfield

Whitminster Lane

Whitminster
Endowed
Primary School

Lake Lane

Primrose Gdns

Oatfield Rd

Frampton on Severn
C of E School

Lake Lane

Oval

Ann Wicks Road

Whitminster
ts Cl

6

Whitminster

Severn Way

The Oval

BRIDGE ROAD

Frampton on Severn

Stroudwater Canal

PO

Saul
Warth

B4071

7

Frampton
Court

PERRY WAY

Whitlies Lane

The Street

Watery Lane

8

Fromebridge

Vicarage Lane

Glebe Circus

G H J **205** K L M A38

Splatt
Bridge

Nastfield
Farm

B4071

G Junction 12
H
J 159
K
L
M

I

Colethrop

2

3

Cotswold Way

4

184

Cotswold Way

5

6

7

Standish Wood

Rus

8

Cotswold Way

Haresfield ✝

Haresfield C of E
Primary School

Haresfield
Court

The College

**Little
Haresfield**

B4008

B4008

Haresfield Beacon
Hill Fort (NT)

✝ **Standish**

Quedgeley Trading
Estate East

Arlebrook

Oxlynch

Standish Park
Farm

B4008

**Stroud
Green**

G
H
J 207
K
L
M

Standish
Hospital

Randwick

The Stocks
The Lane
Ocker Hill

Robbers Road

✝ Randwick C of E
Primary School

Lighty

Penn

Cl

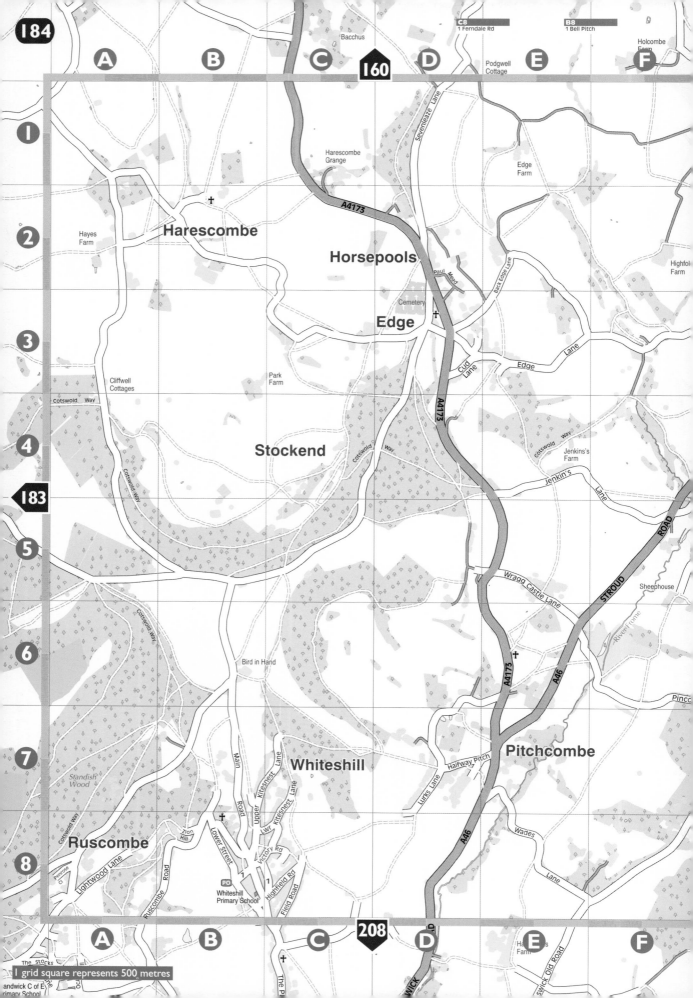

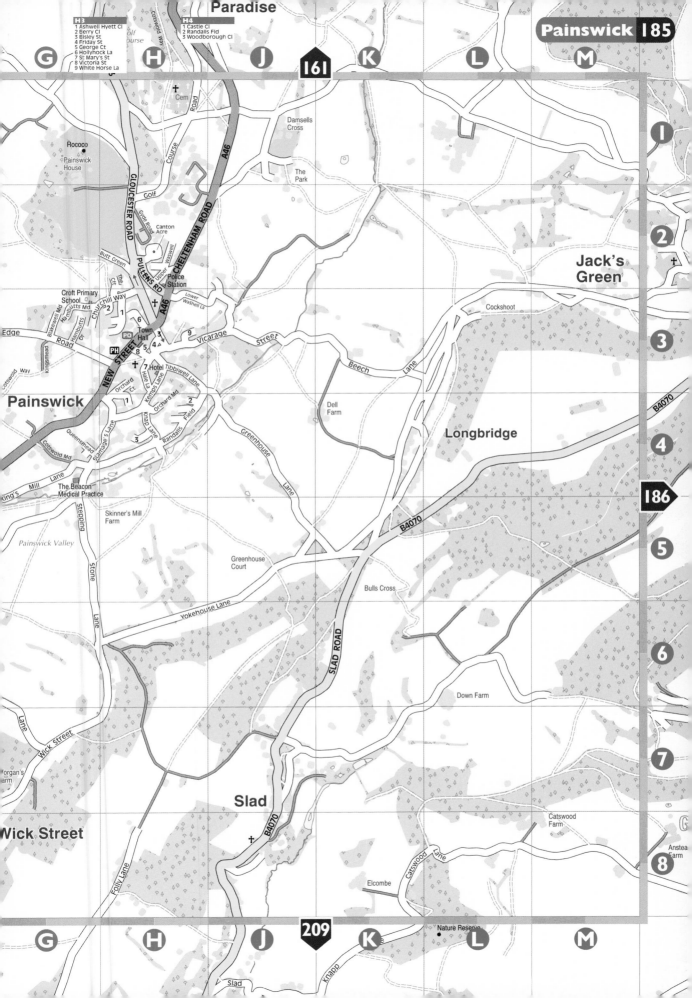

Paradise

H3
1 Ashwell Hyett Cl
2 Berry Cl
3 Bisley St
4 Friday St
5 George Ct
6 Hollyhock La
7 St Mary's St
8 Victoria St
9 White Horse La

H4
1 Castle Cl
2 Randalls Fld
3 Woodborough Cl

G H J **161** K L M

Cem

Course Road

A46

Damsells Cross

The Park

GLOUCESTER ROAD

Rococo

Painswick House

CHELTENHAM ROAD

Golf

Canton Acre

Clyde Road

Butt Green

PULLENS RD

Upper Washell

Jack's Green

Cockshoot

Croft Primary School

Churchill Way

Police Station

Lower Washell La

Blakewell Md

Hamburts Md

Hamburts Dr

A46

Town Hall

Vicarage Street

Beech Lane

Longbridge

Edge Road

Cotswold Way

Kingsmead

PO

NEW STREET

PH

Hotel

Tibbiwell Lane

Dell Farm

B4070

Cotswold Way

Orchard Ct

Hale La

Kemps Lane

Orchard Md

Randalls Field

Greenhouse Lane

Painswick

Queensmead

Sumage Lane

Knap Lane

The Beacon Medical Practice

King's Mill Lane

Stepping

Painswick Valley

Skinner's Mill Farm

Greenhouse Court

B4070

Stone

Bulls Cross

186

Yokehouse Lane

SLAD ROAD

Down Farm

Lane

Wick Street

Morgan's Farm

Folly Lane

Slad

B4070

Catswood Lane

Catswood Farm

Anstea Farm

Wick Street

Elcombe

Nature Reserve

G H J **209** K L M

Slad

Knapp

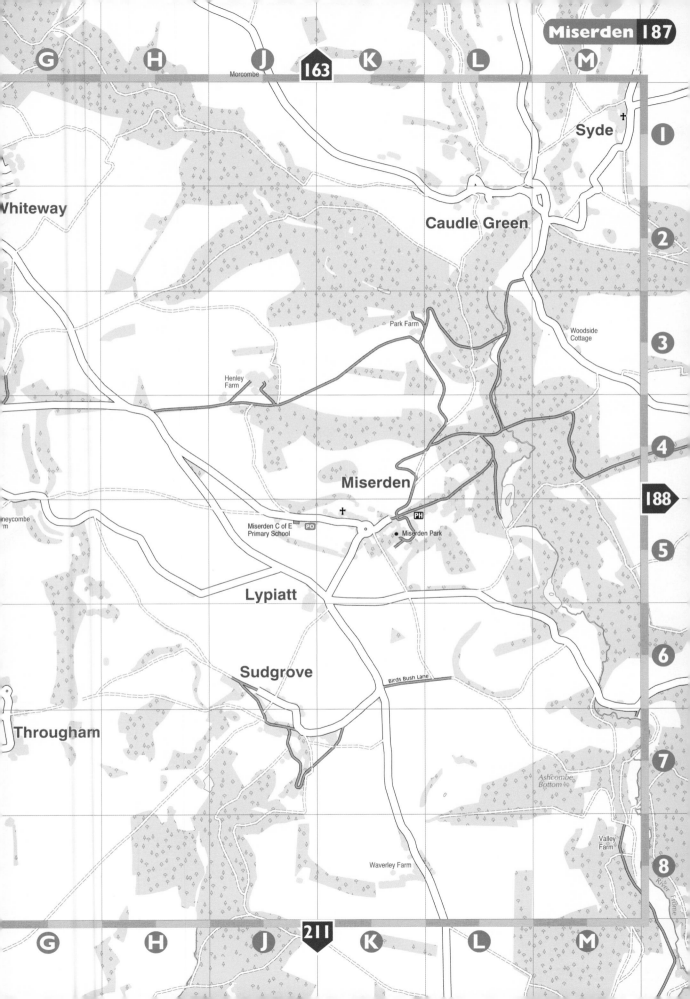

G H J 163 K L M

Morcombe

Syde † 1

Whiteway

Caudle Green 2

Park Farm

Woodside
Cottage 3

Henley
Farm

4

Miserden 188

neycombe
m

† PH

Miserden C of E PO
Primary School

Miserden Park 5

Lypiatt

6

Sudgrove

Birds Bush Lane

Througham

7

Ashcombe
Bottom

Valley
Farm

Waverley Farm 8

River Frome

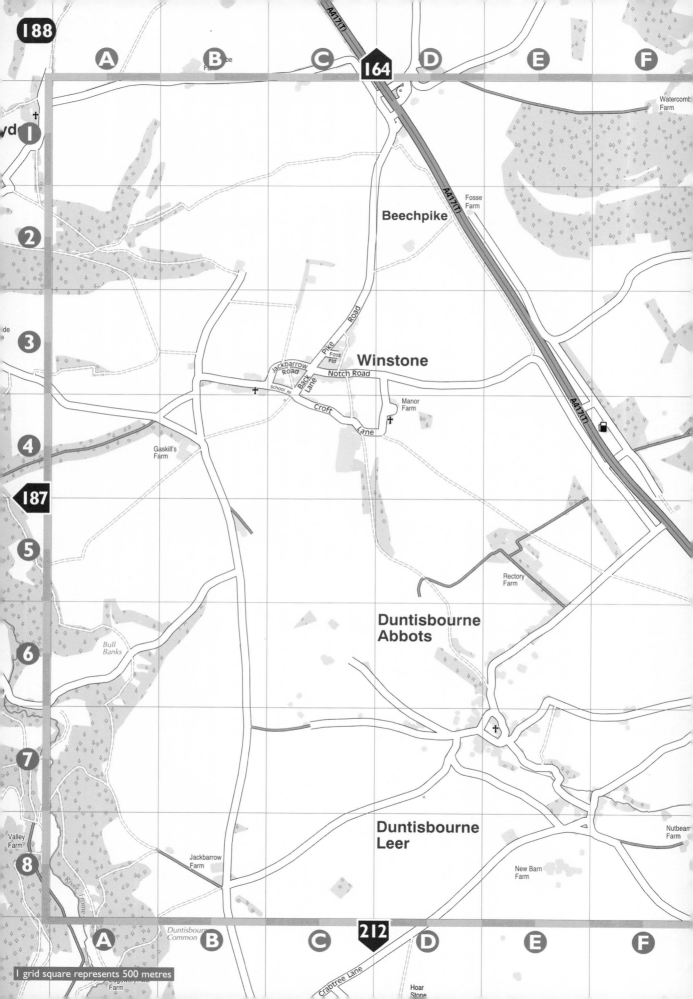

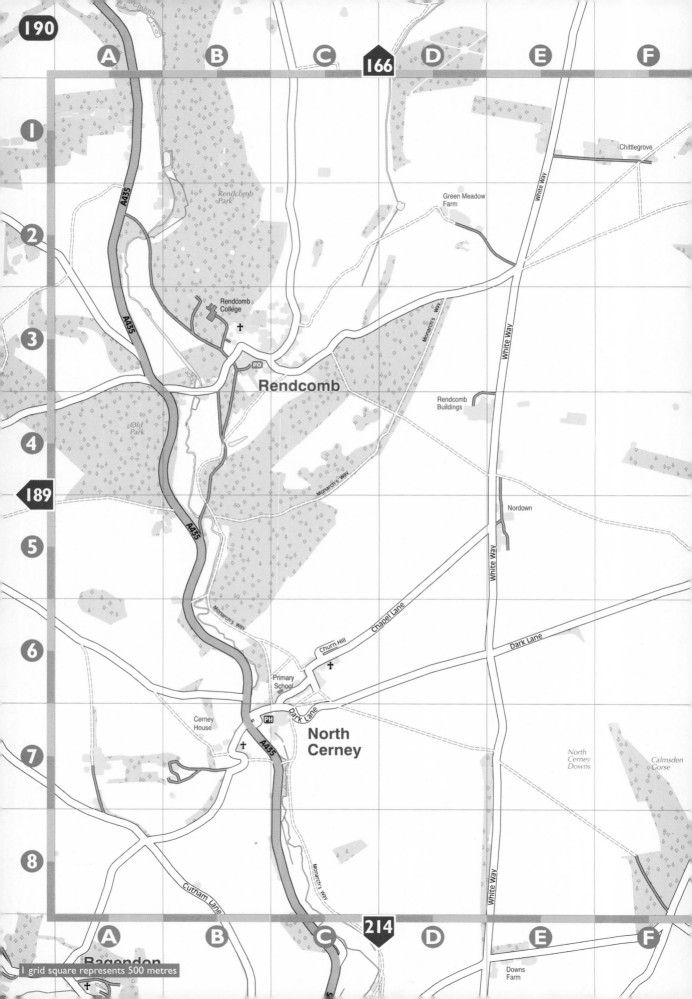

G   H   J   **167**   K   L   M

1 Lower
Chedworth

Macmillan Way

Monarch's Way

's Road

Green Lane

The
Hempelands

Denfurlong Farm
(Farm Trail)

2

Ashwell
Lodge

A429

3

Fosse Cross **PH**

4

Fosse Cross
Industrial
Estate

192

STOW ROAD

5

Dark Lane

Calmsden

A429

6

Hollow Fosse
Farm

Colnp
Copse

7

STOW ROAD
A429

Barnsley
Wold

8

G   H   J   **215**   K   L   M

ney Down
m

G   H   J   169   K   L   M

Broad
Farm

I

2

3

4

194

5

6

7

8

Saltway
Farm

Calcot Peak
Farm

Oldwalls
Farm

● Prehistoric
Monument

Ablington

Potlicker's Lane

Meadowlands
Farm

Bibury
Farm

B4425

G   H   J   217   K   L   M

Arlington

Police
Station

Arlington Mill
Museum
PO
B4425

Hawkers Hill

PH

Awkward

The Diane
Breen Gallery

M

Horse Lane

Bibury

A   B   C   170   D   E   F

1

2   Cocklebarrow
    Farm

3

4   Kilkenny
    Farm

193

5

6

7

8

A   B   C   218   D   E   F

Wall
Farm

Al

PO
Shable Cl

B4425   Swyre
        Farm

Bratch
Copse

Johnmans
Barn

River Leach

Kilkenny
Cottages

Knoll
Barn

G H J K L M

171

1
2
3
4
196
5
6
7
8

Blackpits Copse

orth

B4425

B4425

Barrington Downs Farm

Ladbarrow Farm

Dean Farm

Macaroni Downs Farm

River Leach

Lappingwell Wood

Coltsmoor Farm

G H J K L M

219

Tyning Wood

Ⓐ   Ⓑ   Ⓒ   **172**   Ⓓ   Ⓔ   Ⓕ

Hill

I

2

B4425

...gton Downs

3

Downs
Farm

4

195

No Man's Land
Plantation

Westwell
Copse

Holwell Downs
Farm

5

6

Eastleach
Downs Farm

Oxfordshire County
Gloucestershire County

7

8

Broughtondowns
Plantation

Ⓐ   Ⓑ   Ⓒ   **220**   Ⓓ   Ⓔ   Ⓕ

I grid square represents 500 metres

L5
1 Clissard Wy

Signet

Westwell

Job's Lane

A361

Holwell

Hawthorn Dr
Birch Dr
Acer Cl
Woodside Drive
1

A361

Woodside Farm

Bradwell Grove

Wildlife Park

Home Farm

Bradwell Grove Wood

A361

Filkins Down Farm

Furze Ground

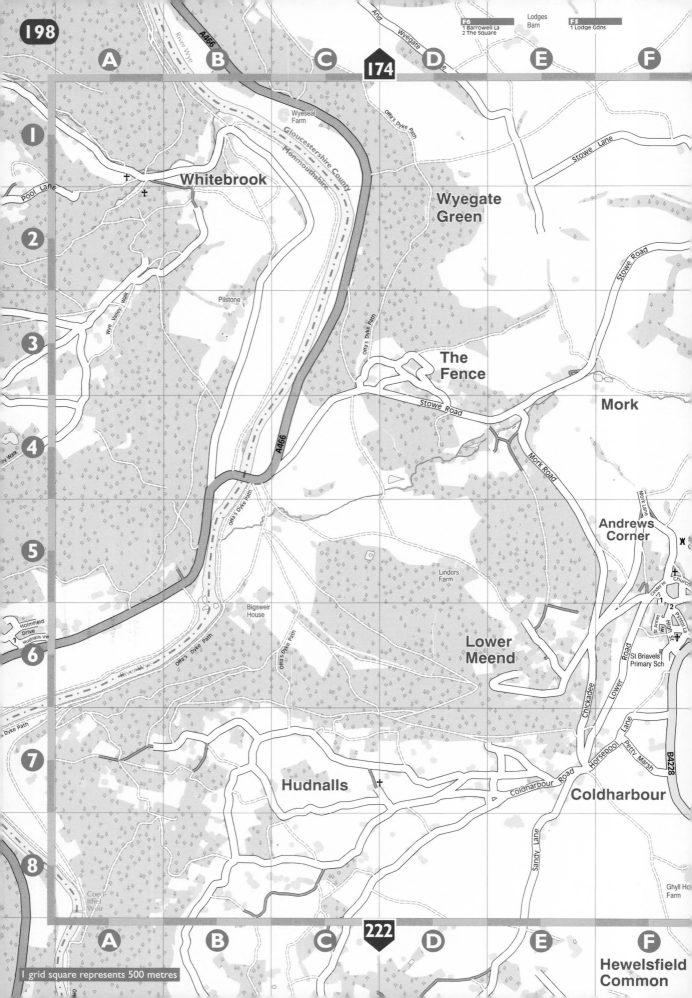

A   B   C   174   D   E   F

1 Barrowell La
2 The Square

F6   Lodges
Barn

F5
1 Lodge Gdns

River Wye

A466

Wyeseal
Farm

Offa's Dyke Path

Stowe Lane

† Whitebrook

†

Gloucestershire County

Monmouthshire

Wyegate
Green

Stowe Road

1

2

Pool Lane

Wye Valley Walk

Pilstone

3

Offa's Dyke Path

The
Fence

Stowe Road

Mork

y Walk

4

A466

Mork Road

5

Offa's Dyke Path

Lindors
Farm

Andrews
Corner

Mork Lane

Church

Holmfield
Drive

Bigsweir
House

Lower
Meend

St Briavels
Primary Sch

Hudnalls Vw

6

Offa's Dyke Path

River Wye

St Annes
Wy

High St

Cinder Hl

Pistol La

Dyke Path

7

Hudnalls

†

Chickadee

Horsepool Lane

Lower Road

Coldharbour

Petty Marsh

B4228

Coldharbour Road

Sandy Lane

Ghyll Ho
Farm

Coed
Ithel
Weir

8

A   B   C   222   D   E   F

Hewelsfield
Common

1 grid square represents 500 metres

G6
1 St Bruel's Cl

G H J **175** K L M

Clements End

I

Stowe Green

Trow
Green

Stowe

B4228

2

Longley
Farm

Noxon
Farm

Nexon
Park

B4228

BREAM

3
231

Bearse
Common

AVENUE

B4228

Slade Bottom

4

B
C

Bearse
Farm

Roads
Farm

200

Close Turf
Farm

Gloucestershire Way

t Briavels

B4228

The Great
Hoggins Farm

Bream Road

5

Willsbury
Farm

Smithville
Place

Smithville
Close

St Briavels
Surg

ROWELL LANE

6

ark
Cl

Townsend
Close

Bream Road

The Warren

Gloucestershire Way

field Lane

Severn View
Farm

7

Park
Farm

Great
Dunkilns

Rodmore
Farm

8

Aylesmore
Court

Highgrove
Farm

G H J **223** K L M

Clanna
Lodge

G2
1 Morcroft Pl

J8
1 The Springs

G H J **177** K L M

Lydney 201

Slade

1 Charnwood Ct
Woodland Place

Yorkley Hlth Cen
Severn View Road

Bailey Hill

I

Yorkley

Yorkley County School

Crown

New Rd

Main Road

School Road

Lower Road

Beech Road

Castle Road

Highview Rd

Parkend Road

Slade Road

Harold Rd

Oakfield Rd

St Swithins

Ash Gv

Ash Pl

K6

2

Herberts Way

Holly Tree

Cut Ang
Fry Rd

Aisne Rd

Swithine Road

Church

Oldc

High Delf Wy
Bath Crs

Wye Road
Pillowell

Chestnut Wood Road

Westley Road

Pillowell CP School

Kidnalls

Upper

Blimeshire

Yorkley Wood Road

Corner Rd
James Wk

Pillowell

LC

7

Yorkley Court

Yorkley Lane

Philip's Cl

Brierley Wy
St

Berkeley Wy

3

B4234

Kidnalls

Soilwell

Old Dam Road

Soilwell

4

202

Dean Forest Railway

B4234

NEW ROAD

Allaston Windsor

Grove Lane Road

5

New Mills

Allaston

Oak Meadow

Court Road

Hill

Lancaster Drive

Lancaster Crs

School Crs

Dean Ct

Berkeley Crs

Allaston

6

Highbury

Lynwood Rd

PO

Primrose Way

Willow Hts

Primrose

Lime Way

Ash Cl

Almond Wk

Woodland Rise

Livia Wy

1

Augustus Wy

Minerva Wk

Sabrina Wy

Octavia Cl

Highfield Lane

Drifield

Highfield Road

Beaucrame Meadow

Cross Hands

A48(T)

7

Hurst Farm

Lydney & District Hospital

Stonebury Day Hospital

Grove Road

FOREST ROAD

Springfield Rd

Spring Meadow Rd

Cherry Tree

Tibenus Av

Harnan Cl

Queen St

Albert

Claudius Wy

1

Centurion Road

Nodens Wy

Highfield

8

Watery Lane

Temple Way

Stamford

Lydney C of E School

The Ormerds

B4234

Newerne St

Lydney Hlth Cen

1

Hams Road

The Hawthorns

Kimberley Dr

Bracken Close

Bracken Dr

Manor Rd

Meadowbank

Severn Banks Primary School

Newerne

Bath Pl

Fairfield

Jubilee Road

Klondyke Av

Steel Av

Rodley Sq

St Mary's Cl

Shepherdine Cl

Severn Cl

HIGH ST

B4231

Oxford

Town Hall
Old Town Ms

Church St

Whitecross School

Whitecross Business Park

B4231 CHURCH RD

Hill St

VW

Police Station

PO

Victoria

Lydney Rugby Football Club

Pylers Way

1 Caesars Cl

Severn St

Orchard Rd

Mount Pleasant

PO

Summerleaze Rd

K6

Harrison Way

Pur

1 The Folders

Naas Lane

K7

1 Alderdale

A48(T)

A B C **178** D E F

I

2

201

3

4

5

6

7

8

Blakeney

Nibley

Viney Hill

Oldcroft

Etloe

Oatfield Farm

Gatcombe

The Purlieu

A48(T)

Lensbrook

Hill Farm

Purton

Gurshill Farm

The Wards

Wellhouse Bay

River Severn

Hurst Farm

Sharpness

Severn Way

Chapel Rd

Pine Tree Way

Meadow Walk

Swithin's Road

Church Walk

Holly Tree Pl

Brierly Wy

PO

Hayes

Viney

New Road

Furnace Va

Blakeney

Hill

Clark's Lane

Hitchings

Cinderford Road

Butts

Bridge Street

HIGH STREET

Blakeney CP School

Doctors Surgery

PO

Butlers Mead

Highfield

All Saints Road

Cemet

Church Way

Awre Road

Swan La

Millend

1 Orchard Ga

Hawfield

Pollards Lane

Cliff Farm

A B C **226** D E F

grid square represents 500 metres

G H J K L M

I
2
3
4
204
5
6
7
8

Little Box

LC

179

Poulton Court

Hagloe

Hagloe House

Tites Point

Purton

Severn Way

severn Way

Gloucester and Sharpness Canal

Kingshill Farm

Hinton

Red Wood

G H J K L M

227

A　　B　　C　　D　　E　　F

R Cr Severn

180

1

2

3

Middle
Point

New
Grounds

4

The
Dumbles

203

The Wildfowl
Trust

5

Newgrounds Lane

Severn Way

6

The
Warth

Shepherd's Patch

Longast

Kingston Road

Longaston Close Lane

Churchend

7

Gloucester and Sharpness Canal

Lane

Lightenbrook

Merrett's Orch

8

Vale of
Berkeley

The
Moors

Moorend Lane

Berkeley

228

Lane

Moorend

A　　B　　C　　D　　E　　F

Hurst
Farm

1 grid square represents 500 metres

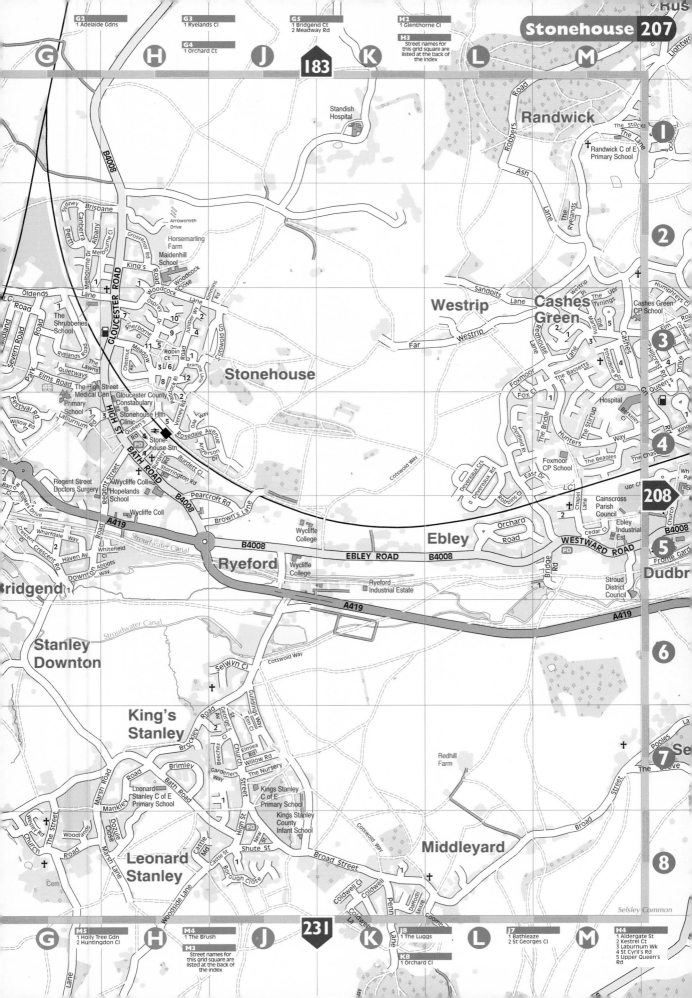

183

G   H   J   K   L   M

Rus

Randwick

The Stocks

The Lane

Ryelands Road
Robbers Road

Standish Hospital

Randwick C of E Primary School

Ash Lane

The Lane

Ock

1

2

Sydney
Brisbane
Canberra
Perth
Albany
Melbourne Dr
Menlow Cl

Grosvenor Rd
King's Road

Arrowsmith Drive

Horsemarling Farm
Maidenhill School

Woodcock Close

sandpits

Westrip Lane

Upr Tynings
The Martins

Cashes Green
CP School

Humphreys Rd

Cashes Green

Elm
Hillcrest Rd
Cotswold

3

B4008
GLOUCESTER ROAD

Woodcock Lane

Osprey

King's
Woodcock Close

Kimmins Rd

Cotswold Rd

Westrip

Cashes Green

Rednose Lane

The Bassetts

Etheldene Rd
PO

Queen's Rd

Berkeley Rd
King

4

Oldends
Moreland Road
Severn Road

LC

The Shrubberies School

Ryelands Rd
The Lawns

Sherborne Close

10
9
5
11

Chestnut
Meadow

Robin Ct

3 6 1

Juniper Way
4

Osprey Rd

12
Bramble Lane

Paddock Rd

Stonehouse

Far

Westrip

Foxmoor Lane

Fox Cl
1

Hospital

The Bridle

The Stirrup

Hunters Way

The Beagles
The Chas

Wh Pat

Park Road
Festival Rd
Willow Rd
Elms Road
Quietways

The High Street
Laburnum Rd

Medical Cen
Primary School
Gloucester County Constabulary
Stonehouse Hlth Clinic

Verney Rd
Oak Way

Rosedale Avenue
Anderson Dr

Cotswold Way

Chidfield Rd

Devereaux Crs
Devereaux Rd

East Dr

Foxmoor CP School

Robins Cl
LC

Upr Ch

5

208

Bari Cl
Boakes Drive
Crescent Crescent Rd
Wharfdale Way
Haven Av
Downfield Rd
Abbots Way

HIGH ST

Regent Street
Queen's Rd

BATH ROAD

PO

Stonehouse Stn
Burdett Cl
Storrington Rd
Burdett Rd

Regent Street Doctors Surgery
Wycliffe Coll
Hopelands School

Pearcroft Rd

Brown's Lane

B4008

Wycliffe Coll

Wycliffe College

Ryeford
Industrial Estate

Ebley

Orchard Road

Chapel Lane
Cedar Rd

Cainscross Parish Council

Ebley Industrial Est

WESTWARD ROAD

Bridge Rd
PO

Stroud District Council

B4008

Frome Gard

Dudbr

Bridgend

Stroudwater Canal

A419

Whitefield Cl

Downt

EBLEY ROAD   B4008

A419

6

Stanley Downton

Stroudwater Canal

Selwyn Cl

Cotswold Way

Redhill Farm

The Grove
Pooles La

Se

7

King's Stanley

Brockley Road
George's
Road

Buildings Way
Elm Cl
St Georges Church
Willow Rd
Beeches

The Nursery

Se

Marsh Road
Bath Road
Mankley Road

Brimley

Gardeners Way

Elmlea Rd

Leonard Stanley C of E Primary School

Kings Stanley C of E Primary School

Kings Stanley County Infant School

High St
PO

Redhill Farm

Broad Road

8

Wesley Rd
The Street
Church Road
Woodlands
Marsh Lane
Cem

Castle Rd
Castle St
Borough Close
Shute St

New St

Broad Street

Coldwell Cl
Coldwell

Coombe
Lane

Penn

Middleyard

Selsley Common

Leonard Stanley

Woodside Lane

231

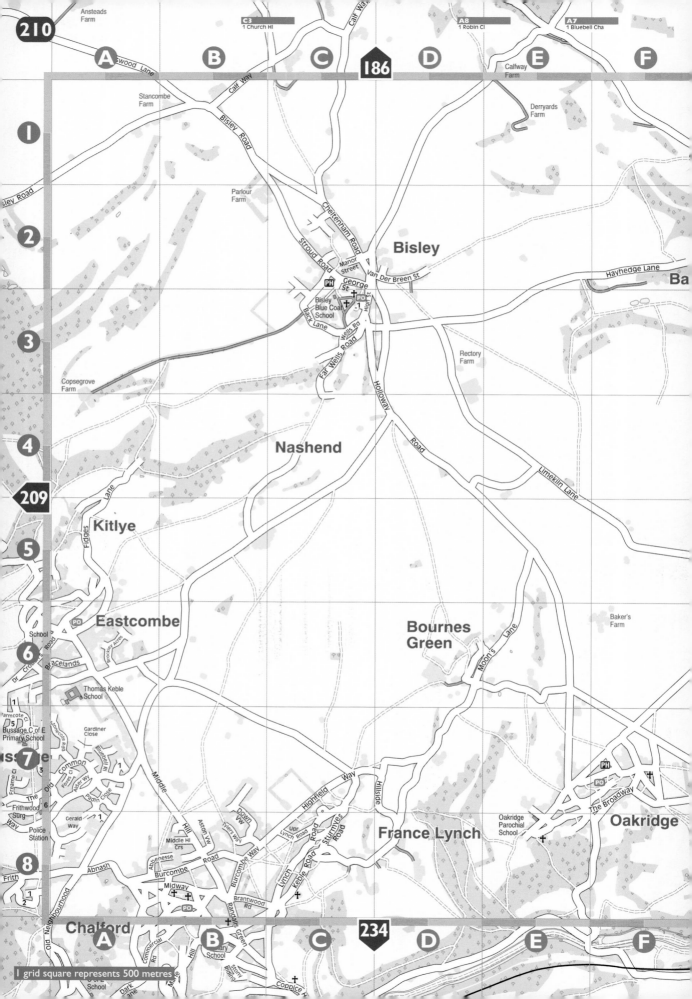

G H J **189** K L M

I 3a

Welsh Way

Middle Duntisbourne

Upper End

Merchants' Downs

Bagendon Downs

2

Welsh Way

Macmillan Way

~~untisbourne~~
~~ouse~~

3

Itlay

A417(T)

Dowers' Lane

Lane

Dowers' Lane

~~onghill Road~~

Daglingworth

4

214

Overley Farm

Lower End

5

6

Cemetery

7

Wellhill Plantation

Hill

Stratto

Barn

8

G H J **237** K L M

Cirencester Park

G H J 191 K L M

STOW ROAD

Ampney Down Farm

The Dillies Farm

Field Barn

The Warren

Welsh Way

STOW ROAD

A419

Smith's Covert

216

Wiggold

Ampney Sheephouse

Barnfields

Glebe Farm

Ampneyfield

B4425

Bown's Farm

Yellow School Copse

B4425

239

Park Farm

G H J K L M

1 2 3 4 5 6 7 8

A B C 192 D E F

1

Oxwold
House

Barn

Hay
Lane

Cadmoor
Copse

2

3

B4425

4

B4425

Barnsley

Welsh Way

Poultmoor
Farm

PH

Welsh Way

5

Barnsley House
Gardens

Welsh Way

6

Ampney
Knowle

7

Ampney
Riding

Lower Field
Farm

Brookfield
Farm

8

Long Furlong

A B C 240 D E GL7 F

1 grid square represents 500 metres

G　　H　　J　　193　　K　　L　　M

Arlington

Arlington Mill
Museum
PO　B4425

Police
Station

PH

Hotel

Packhorse Lane

The Diane
Breen Gallery

Bibury

Hawkers Hill

Awkward Hill

M

Church Road

Cemetery Lane
Bibury C of E
Primary School

Hotel

Meadowlands
Farm

The Quarry

The Grove

River Coln

I

2

3

Quarry Hill
Farm

Furzey
Barn Farm

218

**Ready
Token**

Coneygar
Wood

4

5

Welsh Way

Hartwell
Farm

6

Poulton
Grange

7

8

G　　H　　J　　241　　K　　L　　M

Welsh Way

Poulton
Fields

Sunhill

G H J **195** K L M

I

Coltsmoor Farm

Williamstrip Farm

Tyning Wood

East Leach Folly

2

eer Furl Buildings

3

Macaroni Farm

4

220

op

Macaroni Wood

5

6

Barrow Elm Farm

Homeleaze Farm

Hammersmith Bottom

7

Tiltup

8

Farhill Farm

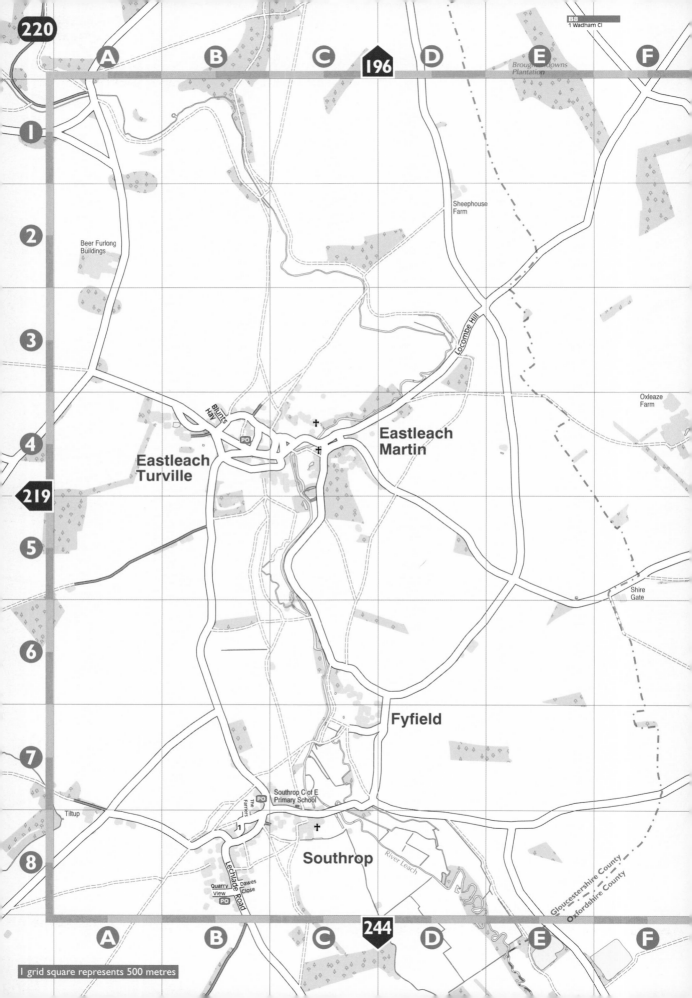

A B C **196** D E F

1

Brough Downs
Plantation

B8
1 Wadham Cl

I

Sheephouse
Farm

2

Beer Furlong
Buildings

Locombe Hill

3

Oxleaze
Farm

Blums Hay

PO

4

**Eastleach
Turville**

**Eastleach
Martin**

219

5

Shire
Gate

6

Fyfield

7

Tiltup

Southrop C of E
Primary School

The Farriers

PO

8

Lechlade Road

Quarry
View

PO

Dawes
Close

Southrop

River Leach

Gloucestershire County
Oxfordshire County

A B C **244** D E F

G H J 197 K L M

1

Filkins Down Farm

College Farm

Kencot Hill Farm

2

Furzey Hall Farm

3

A361

Filkins Farm

4

The Pills

5

Cross Tree La

Woollen Mill

Rouses La

PO

Filkins

Manor Farm

6

Hazells La

PH

Kings Lane

7

Manor Farm

Broughton Poggs

Broadwell

Colston House Tennis Club

8

Langford Downs Farm

A361

Broadwell Brook

Filkins Road

Broadwell Road

ade Road

Lang

A   B   C   D   E   F

1

2

3

4

5

6

7

8

A   B   C   D   E   F

Hewelsfield
Common

St Briavels
Common

Belmont Road

PO

Triangle

Bailey Lane

Mill Hill

Wye Va Wk

Offa's Dyke Path

Wye Valley Walk

River Wye

Coed
Beddick

Wye Valley Walk

Underhill

Quayside

Mill Hill

PO

Brockweir

Sylvan View

Trelleck

Park Gate

Road

Parva Spring

Wye Valley Wk

MAIN ROAD

A466

Monmouthshire

Gloucestershire County

Old
Station

Wye Valley Walk

Caswell
Wood

Madgetts
Farm

Tintern Police
Station

Tintern Surgery

Abbey House
Studio & Gallery

Offa's Dyke Path

Offa's Dyke Path

Chase
House

PARK HILL

Wye Valley Walk

Miss Grace's
Lane

Sheepcot

Miss Grace's Lane

The
Park

Nature
Reserve

B4228

Reddings
Farm

Devil's
Pulpit

Shorn
Cliff

High
Wood

Offa's Dyke Path

Ghyll H
Farm

Catchmays Court

Offa's Dyke Path

Chase
Farm

Tidenham

1 grid square represents 500 metres

G   H   J   199   K   L   M

1

2   Clanna

Clanna
Lodge

3

Royle
Reddings

**Woolaston
Common** 4

224

5

Hewelsfield

Church Road

B4228

Barnage Lane

Gloucestershire Way

Poolfield Court
Farm

Woolaston Common

Ring Fence

Birchwood Road
Elm Ct
Oak Crs
Pinedale
Reddings
Close
Road

Oakhill Pitch

Little
Meend

**Woolaston
Woodside**

Woodside

Sandtumps

Severn   View

6   eth

East
Wood

Gloucestershire Way

**Woolaston
Slade**

Keynsham

Keynsham   Lane   Woodside

Road

7

Brookend

Park Hill Common

Park   Hill   Road

**Park
Hill**

Gloucestershire Way

Park   Hill   Road

High Woolaston

Ashwell
Grove

acon
h

Keynsham Lane

St

Braivels

Road

Church Lane

Woolaston

A48(T)

8

G   H   J   247   K   L   M

Ashwell

D2
1 Great Western Rd

A B C 202 D E Way F

I

A(A?)

Cliff
Farm

LC

2
Naas
Court

3
as House

Lydney
Yacht Club

4

5

6

The
Paddock

7

8

Naas Lane

Sharpness

Bridge Road

Dock Road
PO

Bridge

Severn Road

Severn Way

Oldminster Road

Oakfield Way

Road

Newtown

The
Crescent

Baylands

Bays Hill

Jubilee
New St
Gloucester
Rd
PO
Sharpness
Primary
School

B4066

Saniger Lane

Saniger
Farm

Wa

Oakhunger
Farm

Westfield
Brake

Severn Way

Severn Way

Berkeley Pill

Hook Street

Oakhunger La

Lynch

Park View

Road

Hamfield Farm

Severn Way

Hamfield Lane

A B C 250 D E F

Severn Way

Ham

Flood
Farm

Hinton

G7
1 Berrycroft
2 The Brambles
3 Gilbert Hl

G8
1 Church La
2 Coach Cl
3 Jenner Ct
4 Lantern Cl

G **H** **J** 203 **K** **L** **M**

I

rookend

Church La

Halmore

Acton Hall

Pool Farm

Slimbridge Lane

Red

2

Stambourne Lane

Hainses

Halmore Lane

Oldlands Farm

3

Pitbrook

Rookery La

Berkeley Vale Community School

well

Berkeley Leisure Centre

Wanswell Court Farm

4

228

Bushy Grove

Breadstone

5

Station Road

Rigestate Industrial Estate

Whitehall

6

Wickselm

Howhead

Forest View

Fishers Rd

Leland Rd

Berkeley Association Football Club

Canon Park

Crawless Farm

Station Road

B4066

Cemetery

Severn Dr

Fitzhardinge Way

The Leys

Hillcrest

Marybrook Medical Centre

Ironmonger's La

7

A38

Lorridge Farm

Berkeley Primary School

Marybrook Street

Lwr Berrycroft

Trevisa Crs

Berkeley

Berkeley Heath

Berkeley Hospital

PO

Lease Cl

Town Hall

Police Station

B4066

B4066

The Common

8

Salter St

High Street

Stock Lane

Lantern Cl

Canonbury St

Cemetery

Mobley

Jumpers Lane

G **H** **J** 251 **K** **L** **M**

Berkeley Castle

Coldelm Farm

Kitts Green Farm

209

234

257

G H J K L M

H1
1 Brimscombe La

H2
1 The
Roundabouts
2 Spinney Ct

H4, H5
Street names for
these grid squares
are listed at the
back of the index

J2
1 Claire's Cl

I

2

3

4

5

6

7

8

Kingfisher
Business Park

Phoenix
Trading Est

The Ropes

Middle
Wall The

Veal The

Primary
School

Far
Thrup

Brewery Lane

PO

Delaway

Thrupp Lane

LONDON ROAD

Hope
Mill
Lane

River Frome

Swells

Brimscombe
Mills Estate

PO

Brimscombe Port
Business Park

Port
La

Albert Road

Victoria Road

Water Lane

Brimscombe Hill

Hill

Burleigh

Dean's
Quarry

Lane

Burleigh

Cirencester Road

Everest Cl

Tooke
Rd

Olinet Rd

Hart Rd

Sheppard Way

Ricardo Road

Dr Browns Road

Cambridge Way

Grange Cl

Manor Cl

Dr Brown's Cl

School Rd

Windmill Road

West End

Box Cl

Cuckoo Row

Box

Box

Road

Lane

Forwood

New
Rd

New Rd

Chapel
Lane

Well Hill

**Ball's
Green**

Tetbury Lane

Tetbury Lane

ROAD

Hazel
Wood

Box
House

Gatcombe
Wood

AVE

Quarhouse

Brimscombe

Bourne
Lane

Quarhouse Lane

Bourne
Lane

Lewiston Rd

Youngs
Orch

Golden Va

Churchill Road

Toadsmoor Road

Valley Cl

A419

LONDON ROAD

Cemetery

Knapp Lane

Primary
School

Hotel

Brownshill
Road

The
Pitch

Browns Hill

Browns Hill

Police Station

Stroudwater Canal

Golden Valley

A419

LC

Belvedere M

Hyde

Besbury
Park

Cirencester Road

Old Common

Summersfield Rd

Burt
Street

Trinity Drive

Glebe
Road

Summersfield Cl

Police
Station

The
Bulwarks

Friday St

Minchinhampton

Tobacconist
Rd

PO

Tetbury Street

Woefuldane

Bottom

Bubblewell

**Burnt
Ash**

PH
Brickwell
Swimming
Pools

Crackstone

Crackstone

**Hampton
Fields**

Gatcombe
Park

The Tingle
Stone

Step's Lane

Field House

Minchinhampton
Golf Club

PH

Chal

Christ
C of
Sch

Cowswel

Ashley

Drive

Station

The

Old Neighbourhood

G H J K L M

M1
1 Srnythe Meadow

K5
1 Eastfield Rd
2 Glebe Rd
3 Syon Rd

K2
1 Cotswold Cl

K4
Street names for
this grid square
are listed at the
back of the index

J5
1 Bell La
2 High St
3 Kings St
4 Parsons Ct

M
1 Blue Boys' Pk

Longman's

B4014

Trillis
Cottage

Daneway

G   H   J   211   K   L   M

Cemetery

Broad Ride

1

River Frome

Frampton
Mansell

2

Beacon
Farm

Chapman's
Cross

A419   A419

3

Hailey
Farm

4

Cranhill
Barn

236

Emmerson Lane

5

Hargrove
Barn

6

Macmillan   Way

Tarlton
Down

Lowesmoor
Farm

7

Macmillan Way

8

Hazelton
Covert

G   H   J   259   K   L   M

G H J **213** K L M

I

2

Cirencester Park

Ivy Lodge

Ewe Pens

Pope's Seat

A419 STROUD ROAD A419

3

Cirencester Comprehensive School Cirenc

A419

4

Cire FC

238

Bledisloe

Monarch's Way

est 5

Monarch's Way Field Barn

TETBURY ROAD

A429

6

A429

Swallow Copse

7

rton ion

A433

A429

Source of the River Thames

Thames Head

Thames Path

8

Field Farm

Barn

G8
1 Hambledon Cl

M2
1 The Pleydells

B4425

I

2

3

4

240

5

6

7

8

Park
Farm

Norcote

Ampney
Park

LONDON ROAD

Ampney
Crucis

School Lane

Allotment Lane

A417

PH Hotel

A417

Witpit Lane

A417(T)

Waterton
House

Witpit Lane

Kingsway

Preston

St Augustine
Farm

Church
Lane

Harnhill

Manor
House

A417(T)

Siddington House

A419

Gray Rd

Thompson
Rd

Hannah
Rd

CRS

Jackson Road

Aaron
Road

Mottershead
Road

CIRENCESTER ROAD

Ermin
Farm

A417(T)

Trenchard
Gardens

Airfield

Driffield
Cross Roads

Cirencester Road

A B C 216 D E F

GL7

I

2 Ampney
Crucis

Hilcot
End

Ampney
St Mary

Allotment Lane

School Lane

The Domey Field

Hotel

3 A417

Ampney Brook

Eastington
House

A417

4

239

Ampney
St Peter

Stoney Pool

5

Edwards Cl

Cricklade

Str

Church Lane

6 Manor House

Priory Farm

Poulton Priory

7 Driffield

8

A B 264 C D E F

Manor Farm

1 grid square represents 500 metres

G H J **217** K L M

1

2

3

4

242

5

6

7

8

G H J **265** K L M

Welsh Way

Sunhill

Welsh Way

Honeycomb
Leaze Farm

Poulton
Fields

Betty's
Grave

Bell Lane

mbrook La

Elf Meadow

PO

LONDON ROAD

Poulton

A417

Verge
Farm

Manor
Farm

Gloucest

Gloucest
shire

A417

Hampton
Grove

Elizabeth
Gardens

St. Marys
Fld

High Street

Meysey
Close

Beech Lea

School PO

Hamilton Croft

Church Street

School La

Strawberry
La

PH

High Street

**Meysey
Hampton**

Wiltshire County

Gloucestershire County

Ma
Hi

A B C D E F

218

1

2

3

4

241

5

6

7

8

A B C D E F

266

F5
1 Beaumoor Pl

F4
1 Barker Pl
2 Beauchamp Cl
3 Keble Lawns
4 Manor Cl

E5
1 Little Horcott La

E4
1 Market Pl
2 The Orchard

Lea Wood

comb Farm

Welsh Way

Toms Copse

Milton End

Welsh Way

Mill Lane

Broad Water

Farmors School

Fairford C of E Primary School

Crabtree Pk

St Marys Dr

FAIRFORD

Leafield Road

Queens Pig

Park Cl

Hatherop

Churchill Pl

Park Street

Coln Gallery

Police Station

Hotel

Fairford Hospital

The Cft

Lower Cft

LONDON RO

Coronation St

Bettertons Close

The Green

Milton Pl

MILTON STREET

BRIDGE STREET

Back Lane

Waterloo

Coln House Special School

The Plies

Moor La

Lygon Ct

Eas End

CIRENCESTER ROAD

A417

Horcott Road

Horcott

Courtbrook

Horcott Road Industrial Estate

Gloucestershire County

Wiltshire County

Lakeside

Horcott Industrial Estate

Faulkner's Cl

Totterdown Lane

Florida Blvd

Kansas Drive

Furzey Hill

Marston Hill

Wiltshire County

cestershire Cou

Ash Copse

Totterdown Lane

1 grid square represents 500 metres

G　H　J　**219**　K　L　M

1

2

Stanford Hall

3

Snowstorm Gorse

4

244

5

Claydon Fields

South Farm

The Aldsworth Cl

Homeground

Cinder Lane

Fairford FC

A417

Thornhill Farm

6

Cotsworld Water Park

7

Cotswold Water Park

8

G　H　✝　J　**267**　K　L　M

Whelford

River

Southrop

F5
1 Swansfield

E7
1 Chancel Wy

E6
1 The Close

D7
1 Orchard Cl

A B C D E F

Gloucestershire Co.
Oxfordshire County

River Leach

I

2
Stanford
Hall

3
Great Lemhill
Farm

243

4
Little Lemhill
Farm

Bryworth Lane

5
Claydon
Fields

Briary
Road

Kingsmead
The Cursus
Hambridge
Kingsmead
Wy
West
Wy
Roman
Way

6
Claydon
House

Butler's
Field

Cuthwine
Place

Cassons Rd

STATION ROAD

Cemetery

A417

Warren's Cross
Farm

Bryworth Lane

Butler's
Court

Cemetery

The Spinney

Spring
Gardens

Medical
Centre

Lechlade
on Than

7
A417

Moorgate

Lodersfield

Bridge House
Gallery

Greystones
Gallery

Seeba
Gallery

Sherborne Street

Pleasant

BURFORD ST

OAK ST

St Lawrence Road

Catherine's
Walk

abbots Walk

Swan
Close

St
Lawrence
Walk

HIGH ST A417

Bell La

THAMES STREET / A361

Police Stn
PO

St Lawrence
C of E School

ST JOHN'S STREET A4

Wharf
Lane

Cotswold
Water Park

8

Thames Path

River Thames or Isis

F6
1 Keble Cl

I grid square represents 500 metres

G H J **221** K L M

Farm

non Barn

A361

Hulse Grounds
Farm

Filkins Road

Lechlade Road

The Elms

St Christophers
C of E School

Rectory
Farm

Church La

I
Lang

Hooks
Close

2

**Little
Faringdon**

Langford
House

Langford Brook

3

4

Horseshoe
Lake

5

6

7

Mill Lane

River Leach

Paradise Farm

Oxfordshire County
Gloucestershire County

Kelmscot

PH

8

PH

High Woolaston

Woolaston

St Briavels Road

Church La

Ashwell Grove

Gloucestershire Way

Kellys Lane

Beacon Ash

G H J **223** K L M

Ashwell Grange

Woolaston Grange

A48(T)

Stroat

Rosemary Lane

Wibdon

A48(T)

Hanley House

Philpots Court

Tidenham

Pill House

G H J **271** K L M

I

2

3

4

248

5

6

7

8

248

Plusterwine

Road

A B **LC** C **224** D E F

1

Woolaston
Grange

2

River Severn

3

4

247

Gloucestershire County
South Gloucestershire

5

Chapel House

6

†

7

Shepperdine

8

A B C **272** D E **Jobsgreen
Farm** F

I grid square represents 500 metres

G H J K L M

225

1
2
3
4
250
5
6
7
8

Severn Way

Sever

Worlds

Worlds

Severn House Farm

County of Gloucestershire
South Gloucestershire

Severn Way

Dayhouse Farm

Nupdown Road

The Laurels

Nupdown

Tranton Lane

ne Road

Hill Lane

Nupdown Road

Scotlands Farm

Hill Court

Hill

Woodend Lane

Chur
Woga

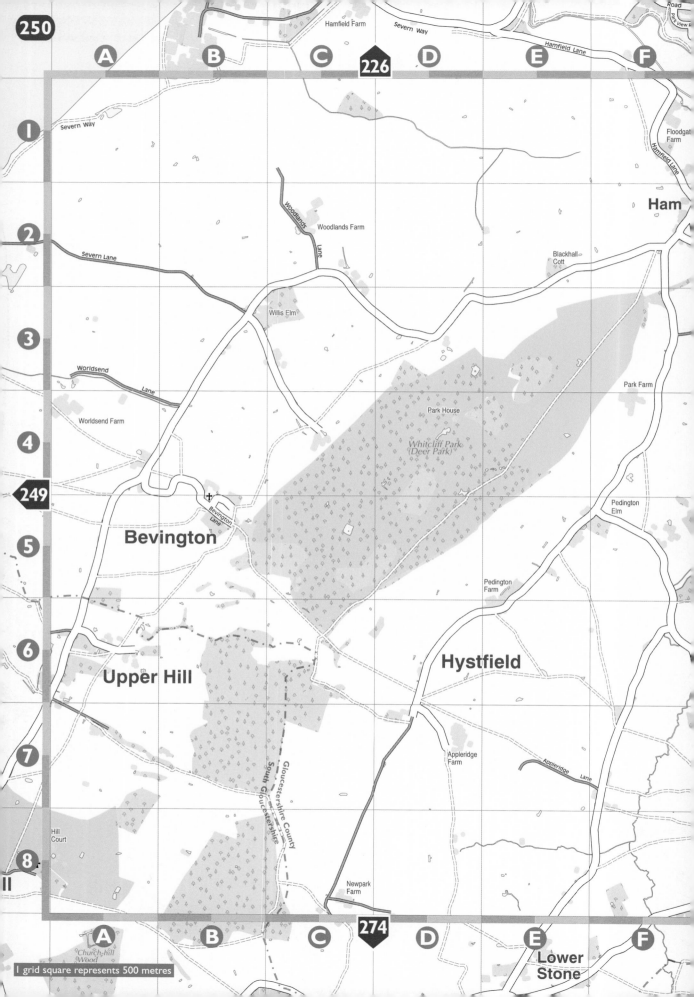

A B C D E F

226

I

Severn Way

Ham

2

Severn Lane

Woodlands Lane

Woodlands Farm

Blackhall
Cott

3

Worldsend

Lane

Willis Elm

Park Farm

Worldsend Farm

4

Whitcliff Park
(Deer Park)

Park House

249

Pedington
Elm

Bevington

5

Bevington Lane

6

Upper Hill

Pedington
Farm

Hystfield

7

South Gloucestershire

Gloucestershire County

Appleridge
Farm

Appleridge Lane

Hill
Court

8

II

Newpark
Farm

A B C D E F

274

Church hill
Wood

Lower
Stone

G H J 229 K L M

Kingshill

DURSLEY

Highfields

Woodmancote

Forthay

Millend

Pitt Court

Southend

254

G H J 277 K L M

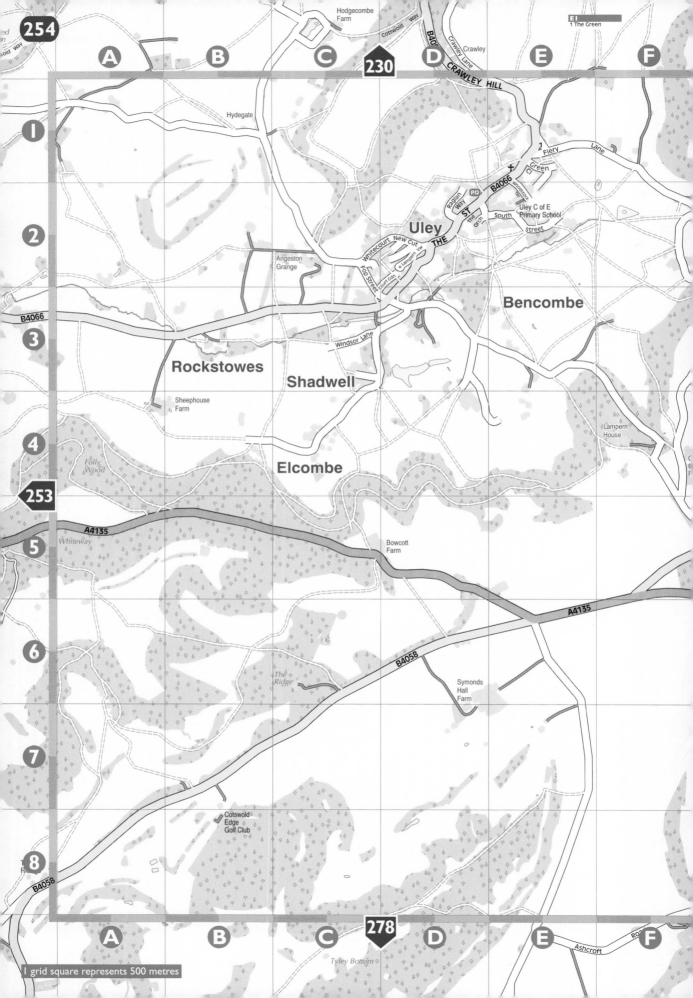

G H J K L M

231

I

Woodcock

Upper Lutheredge
Farm

Sallywood
Farm

Owlpen

2

Nu

B4058

Boscombe

Woodleaze
Farm

3

Kingscote
Wood

4

Binley
Farm

256

B4058

5

PO

A4135

Lower
Hazelcote

6

Kingscote

Ashel Barn

7

8

Barnhill
Farm

A4135

shcroft
ouse

G H J K L M

279

Bagpath

Newington

A   **B**   C   **232**   **D**   E   **F**

Wallow Green

Rockness

NAILSWORTH

I

Tickmorend

Sugley   Lane

Whiteway Downend

Harleywood

Tetbury Lane

2

Nupend

Horsley

Shipton's   Grave

THE STREET   PO

Horsley School

Bartonend   Lane

Barton End

3

Hartley Br Hl

4

Hay Lane

Tiltups End

Longlength Lane

5

Ledgemore Bottom

Hazlecote Lane

6

Lower Hazlecote

Hazlecote Farm

7

Cranmore Farm

8

Union Gorse Covert

Calcot Farm

Hotel

A   **B**   C   **280**   D   E   **F**

A4135

G   H   J   **233**   K   L   M

Park

K2
1 Woodstock Cl

L2
1 Church St

L3
1 Orchard Fld
2 Pound Hi

Gatcombe Wood

AVENING ROAD

B4014

Hazel Wood

Longman's Barn Farm

I

Minchinhampton Golf Club
PH

Hill Farm

Nag's H2d

Brandhouse Farm

Avening House

Hampton Hill

The Sunground

Lawrence Rd

Old Hill

Macmillan

Woodstock Lane

HIGH ST

Rectory Lane

Avening School

Sandford
PO

Leaze

Powis Lane

Macmillan Way

Avening Co

Westfield Barn

New Inn La

B4014

Mill La

3

Farm Hi

Point Rd

The Grove

Mays Lane

Avening Park

TETBURY HILL

Avening

West End

Macmillan Way

B4014

Star Lane

4

258

Star Farm

5

Longtree Bottom

6

Macmillan Way

7

Chavenage Green

B4014

Chavenage House

Lodge Farm

Tetbury Upton

8

Lowfield Farm

Macmillan Way

Upton Grove

G H J **235** K L M

I

Macmillan Way

Hocberry

2

Hazelton
Manor Farm

PO † St. Peter's Close Rodmarton
School

Rodmarton

Monarch

3

Oathill Lane

Monarch's Way

Rodmarton
Manor

*Windmill
Tump*
Long Borrow •

Irongate
Farm

4

*Tump
Plantation*

Monarch's Way

A

260

ckfield
od

5

Trull
House

6

A433

Oxleaze

Holt
Farm

Culkerton

Road

Manor
Farm

7

Purley
Covert

New
Barn

8

Gloucestershire County
Wiltshire County

G H J **283** K L M

†
Ashley

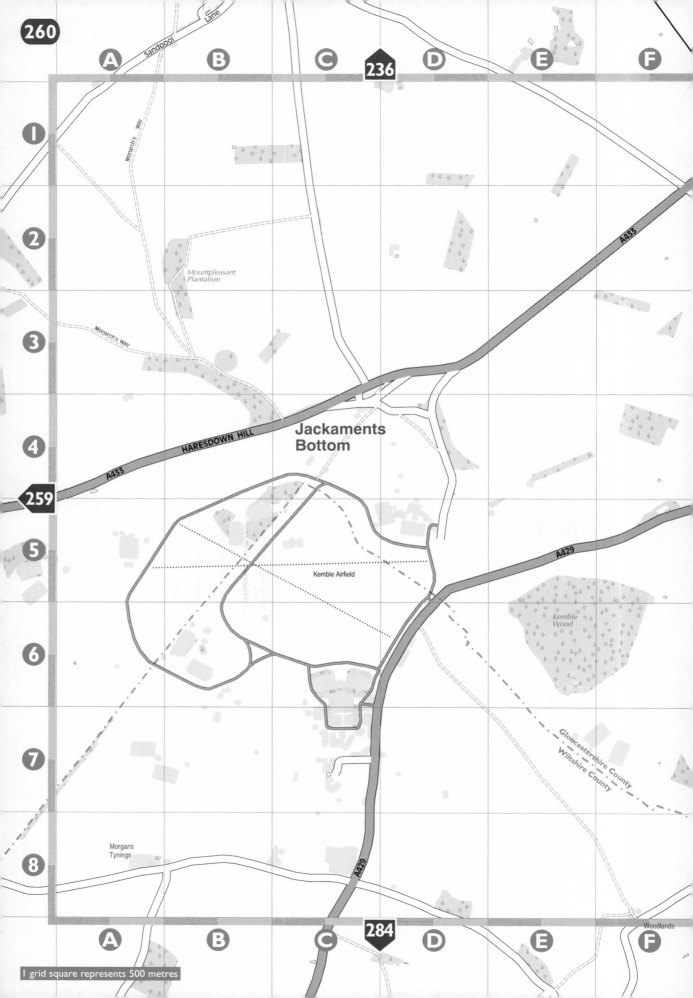

A B C **236** D E F

1

2

3

4

259

5

6

7

8

A B C **284** D E F

Sandpool Lane

Monarch's Way

Mountpleasant
Plantation

Monarch's Way

HARESDOWN HILL

A433

A433

**Jackaments
Bottom**

A429

Kemble Airfield

Kemble
Wood

A429

Gloucestershire County
Wiltshire County

Morgans
Tynings

Woodlands

1 grid square represents 500 metres

H4
1 The Oaks
2 Tamesis Dr

Thames
Head
ames

G H J **237** K L M

I

2

Field Farm

3

Thames Path

Thames Path Hotel

Ewen

PH

4

262

Kemble Station

Windmill Road

A429

Clayfurlong Farm

Clay furlong Gv

PO

Glebe La

W Hall Gv

Station Road

Kemble

Kemble County Primary School

West Lane

Limes Road

School Road

Church Road

1 2

Old Vicarage La

Kemble House

†

†

†

Thames Path

River Thames Or Isis

5

6

Glebe Farm

7

Kemble Wick

Thames Path

8

†

Poole Keynes

G ion H J **285** K L M

Thames Path

A   B   C   D   E   F

238

I

2

3
Hotel

H

wen

4

261

5

6

7

8

A   B   C   D   E   F

286

Furzen Leaze
Farm

Ashton Road

Dryleaze
Farm

Ashton Road

South Leaze
Farm

River Thames Or Isis

Thames Path

Shorncote

Gloucestershire County
Wiltshire County

Upper Mill
Farm

Keynes
Country
Park

Thames Path

Cotswold
Communi

Elm
View

Somerford
Keynes

Neigh Bridge
Country Park

Spine Road

West

Clark's
Clark's Lane
Nursery View
Ashton

Spratsgate Lane

G H J **239** K L M

I

Airfield

Driffield
Cross Roads

Cirencester Road

A419(T)

Northmoor Lane

Northmoor

2

Cirencester K

Sisters
Farm

3

Northmoor Lane

Silver Street

**South
Cerney**

Timbrells Cl

School Lane

Church La

Bow

WOW

River Churn

The Close

Boxbush Road

Field Cl

Lakeside

Robert Franklin Way

Wildmoorway Lane

4

264

River Way

Phoenix
Surgery

Meadow Way

Church

PO

Police
Station

Willow Gv

Station Road

The Lennards

Huxley

Station Road

Langet

Jubilee Gdns

High Street

Ham Lane

Station Road

5

Upper Up

Berkeley Cl

Sudeley Drive

Broadway Lane

OakWay

Beaverstone Cl

Ann Edwards
School

The Leaze

Beaverstone Rd

Spine Road (East)

Cerney Wick Lane

Evergreen
Industrial
Estate

B4696

6

Broadway Lane

Broadway
Trading Estate

Cotswold
Water
Park

7

Broadway Lane

Wickwater Lane

Whitefriars Lane

B4696

SPINE ROAD (EAST)

Fridays Lane

8

G H **287** J K L M

North End

Ham Lane

Cleveland
Farm

Clayhill

A B C 240 D E F

I

2

3

263

4

5

6

7

8

A B 288 C D E F

Manor Farm

Poulton Hill Farm

The Folly

Vines Brake

Ampney Brook

Fosse Farm

Cirencester Road

Dukes Brake

Chestnut Cl Suffolk Pl

Down Ampney Road

Manor Farm

Cirencester Road

Down Ampney Road

Cerney Wick Lane

Westfield Farm

Cirencester Road

Lane

Croft

Cerney Wick

Riding School

The Street

Gosditch

Upcott

Latton

A419(T)

A419(T)

Thames Path

North Meadow

Gloucestershire County
Wiltshire County

F4
1 Charlham La

A4
1 Cirencester Rd

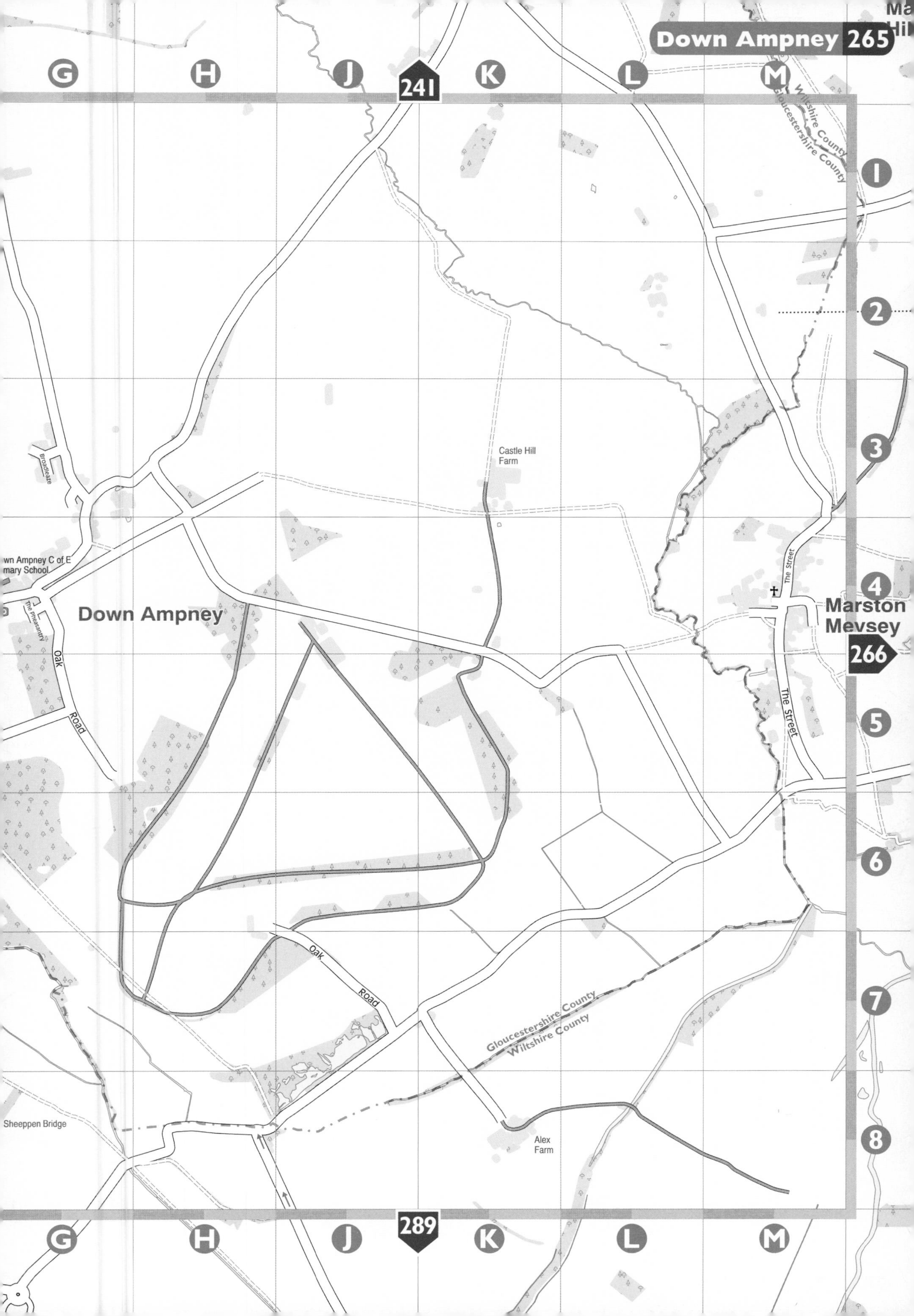

G   H   J   241   K   L   M

I

2

3

Castle Hill
Farm

wn Ampney C of E
mary School

Down Ampney

The Pheasantry

Oak

Road

Sheeppen Bridge

Oak

Road

Gloucestershire County
Wiltshire County

Alex
Farm

Wiltshire County
Gloucestershire County

The Street

**Marston
Mevsey**

266

4

5

6

7

8

G   H   J   K   L   M

243

I

2

3

4

268

5

6

7

8

Whelford

River Coln

Ham
Barn

Lancaster
Holford Cres
Brickwell Rd
Northen
St Mary's
Close

Ham Lane

River Thames or Isis

Gloucestershire County
Swindon

Hannington
Bridge

Thames Path

Thames Path

Blackford
Farm

Manor
Farm

**Hannington
Wick**

North L
Farm

G   H   J   K   L   M

Box Hedge
Farm

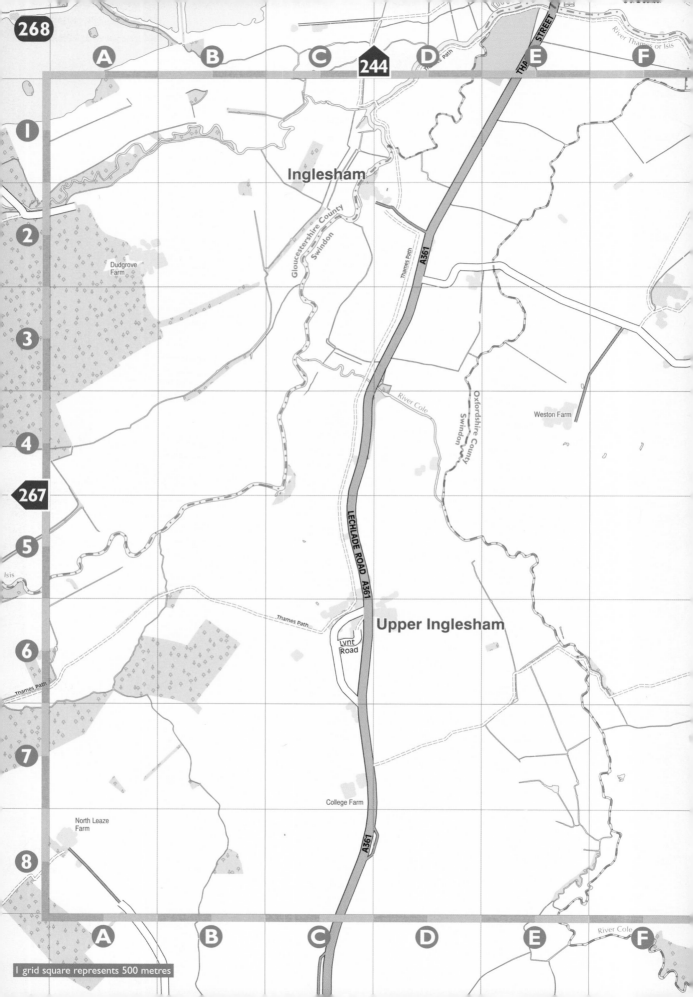

244

267

Inglesham

Dudgrove
Farm

Gloucestershire County
Swindon

Thames Path

A361

THP STREET

River Thames or Isis

River Cole

Oxfordshire County
Swindon

Weston Farm

Isis

LECHLADE ROAD A361

Thames Path

Upper Inglesham

Lynt
Road

Thames Path

College Farm

North Leaze
Farm

A361

River Cole

A B C D E F

I grid square represents 500 metres

G H J 245 K L M

PH

1
2
3
4
5
6
7
8

Oxfordshire County
Gloucestershire County

River Leach

LECHLADE ROAD

A417

Thames Path

†

Snowswick Lane

Buscot

PO

River Thames or Isis

Kilmester's Farm

LECHLADE ROAD A417

Buscot Park (NT)

Broadleaze Farm

Bushy Heath

Heath Farm

Oldfield F

Snowswick Farm

Pennyswick Farm

Brimstone Farm

G H J K L M

Middle Leaze Farm

G H J **247** K L M

I

2

3

4

272

5

6

7

8

Gloucestershire County
South Gloucestershire

edbury
liffs

River Severn

Severn Way

Littleton
Warth

G H J **291** K L M

A   B   C   **248**   D   E   F

1

2

3

4

271

5

6

7

8

A   B   C   **292**   D   E   F

Jobsgreen
Farm

Oldbury Power Station
Visitors Centre

Knight's
Farm

Sheperdine Road

**Oldbury
Naite**

Ham Lane

Oldbury
House

The Naite

Westend Lane

W End

Westend

Camp Road

Featherbed Lane

PO

+

PH

Chapel Road

Oldbury-on-Severn

Pickedmoor

Westmarsh Lane

**Pullens
Green**

Kington Road

Oldbury-on-Severn
C of E School

+

Church Road

Severn Way

Severn Way

Pillhead
Gout

Cowhill

Churchme
Farm

Littleton
Warth

Lower Corston
Farm

St Arild's House

1 grid square represents 500 metres

K8
1 Kempton Cl

L8
1 Pittville Cl

G   H   J   249   K   L   M

249

Nubdown Road

Scotla
Farm

Woodend Lane

Church
Wood

I

2

3

Rockhampton Rhine

Lodge Farm

Gully Lane

Hill Lane

Foss Lane

4

274

5

Duckhole

PO   Newton

Lane

6

Horse Lane

Lower
Morton

Parkmill
Farm

Morton Street

7

Oldbury Lane

U
M

Kington Road

Butt Lane

GLOUCESTER RO

Kington
House

Park Farm

8

Park Road

Queens Wk
Manor Wk
Parkland Way
1

Dyrham Cl
Rosslyn Wk
1

Charles Cl

Swallow Park

Morton Way

Osprey Park

Victoria
Cl
Alexandra
Wy
Hyde Av
Regents Cl
2

Manor
Brook
School

Emsworth Ct

Park
Dean Av
Millfield
North Road

GLOUCESTER ROAD

Finch Cl
Nightingale
Park
3

Severn View Road
Squires
Leaze
Eastland Av
Park La

Falcon Wy

Morton

G   H   J   293   K   L   M

293

The Cas
Scho

Hotel

Park Road

Chantry

Ring Rd
Drive

B4061

6
3
Mallow

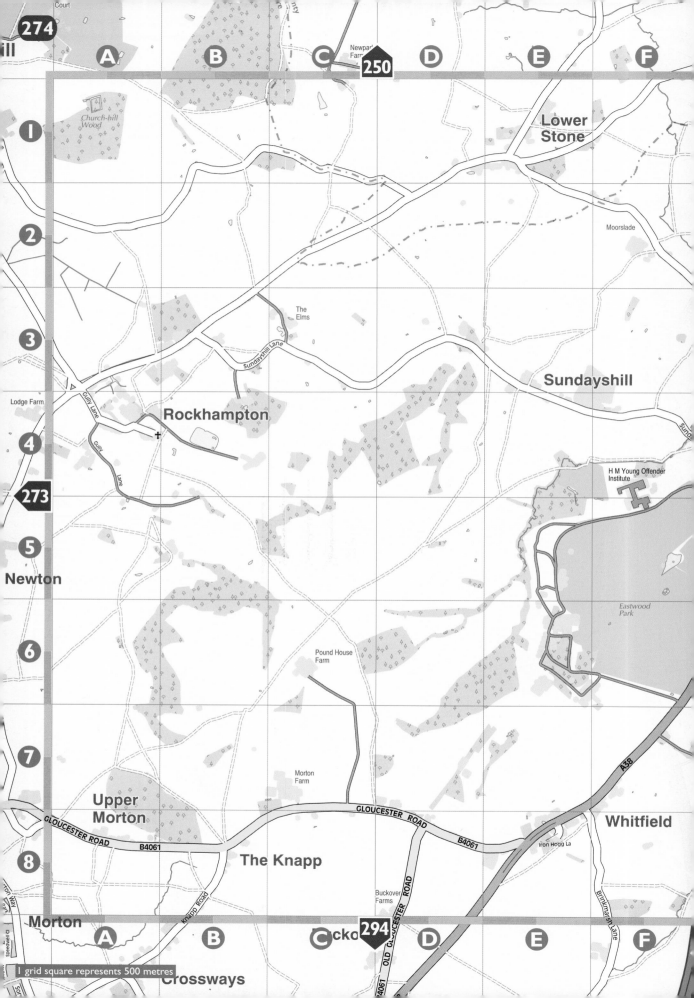

G **Stone**

H

J

251

K

L

M

I

Damer

2

A...nin Green

3

Tortworth

4

276

5

6

7

8

Falfield

Green Farm

Middle Mill Farm

1 Watermill Cl

G4

Damery Lane

Damery Lane

Little Avon River

Heneage Ct

Heneage La

Old Court Farm

M5

Brook Farm

B4509

Junction 14

Tortworth VC Primary School

Elmtree Farm

B4509

Mill La

Church Av

Eastley Cl

Lane

PO

A38

Gambril Lane

Leyhill

Court Road

Forest Road

Park Road

Woodland Road

Meadow Rd

Hammerley Down

Bloody Acre

Parkend

B4058

Bibstone

Abbotside Farm

Sodam Mill

G

H

J

295

K

B4058

Fareigh Lane

L

M

The Burford

PO

Talbot's End

252

296

A   B   C   D   E   F

1

2

3

4

275

5

6

7

8

D6
1 Cotswold Vw
2 The Sidings

C7
1 Hawthorn Cl
2 Severn Cl
3 Thames Cl

C6
1 Katherine Dr

Damery

Michaelwood
Lodge Farm

Katherine's
Farm

Daisy Green Lane

Kites Nest
Farm

Swinhay Lane

Huntingford

Gloucestershire County
South Gloucestershire

Swinhay
Farm

Vernals Lane

Avening
Green

Burrough
Hill
Farm

Swinhay Lane

Little Avon River

Little Avon River

Elmtree
Farm

B4058

CHARFIELD RD

New Farm Lees

Longs View

Street

Charfield
Hill

Charfield

Charfield
Green

Grange
Farm

Charfield
CP School

WOTTON

ROAD

2

Hereford Rd

B4058

Durham Road

PO

Newtown

Station Road

1

Underhill Road

Old Mill

Willow Cl

Berkeley

Little Bristol Lane

Avon Rd

Orchard

2

Manor

3

Lane

Hammerley
Down

Hawthorn
Close

1

Woodlands Rd

GL12

Churchend Lane

Little
Bristol

South Gloucestershire
Gloucestershire County

Charfield Hall
Farm

LC

Neathwood
Farm

B4060

Churchend

A   B   C   D   E   F

B4509

Devil's

Lane

B4509

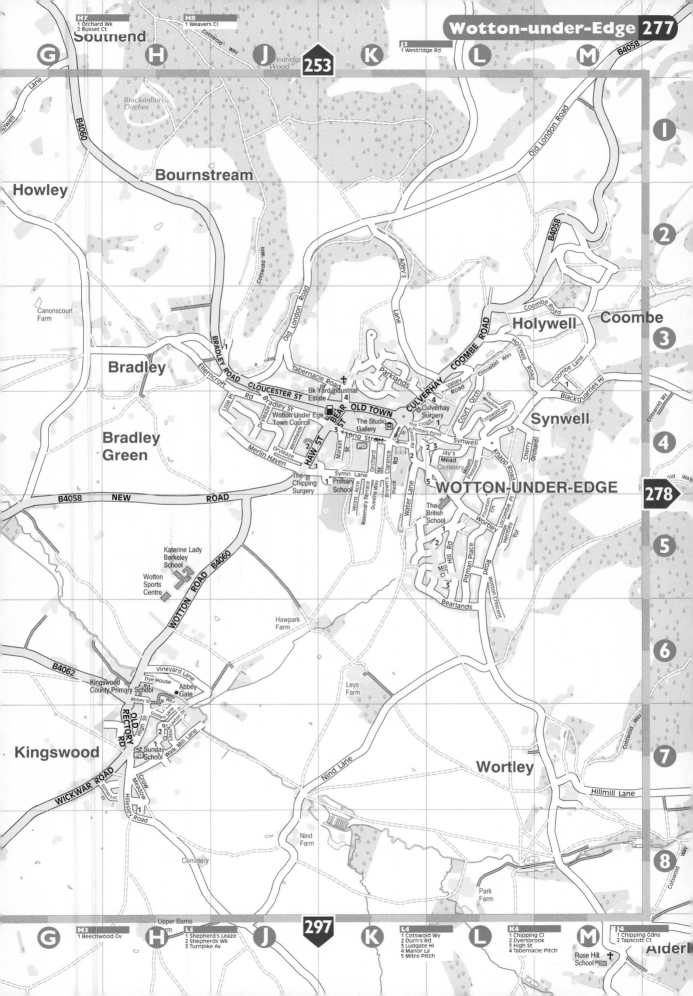

253
278
297

Southend

G H J K L M

I
2
3
4
5
6
7
8

Howley

Bournstream

Brackenbury
Ditches

Westridge
Wood

Cotswold Way

Canonscourt
Farm

Bradley

Bradley
Green

Holywell

Coombe

BRADLEY ROAD

Ellerncroft

GLOUCESTER ST

Lisle Pl
Rd

Bradley St

Dryleaze

Westfield

Tabernacle Road

Bk Yard Industrial
Estate

OLD TOWN

Wotton Under Ege
Town Council

HAW ST

BEAR ST

Market St

Long Street

The Studio
Gallery

PO

Orchard

Clarence Rd

Brown's Piece

Water Lane

Parklands

CULVERHAY

Culverhay
Surgery

The Cloud
& Potter's Pond

Synwell

COOMBE ROAD

Valley
Road

Court Orch

Mount
Pleasant

Jay's
Mead
Cemetery

Holywell
Road

Cotswold Way

Meadow Gdns

Cotswold Gdns

Knapp Road

Cherry
Orchard

Blackquarries Hl

Cotswold Wy

Synwell

WOTTON-UNDER-EDGE

Dryleaze

Merlin Haven

The Chipping
Surgery

Symn Lane

Primary
School

Venns Acre

Rosemary Terrace

Queens Way

The British
School

Wortley Rd

Fountain

Locombe Rd

Hentley
Tor

Hill Rd

Mill
Cl

Pitman Place

Wotton Crescent

Bearlands

B4058   NEW   ROAD

Katerine Lady
Berkeley
School

Wotton
Sports
Centre

WOTTON ROAD B4060

Hawpark
Farm

Leys
Farm

B4062

Vineyard Lane

Dye House
Rd

Abbey
Gate

Kingswood
County Primary School

Abbey St

Golden Lane

High St

OLD
RECTORY
RD

Bramley

Braxton Ct

Sunday
School

PO

Crow
Meadow

Mill Lane

Kingswood

WICKWAR ROAD

Somerset

Hillesley
Road

Cemetery

Nind Lane

Nind
Farm

Wortley

Hillmill Lane

Park
Farm

Rose Hill
School

Alder[...]

B4058

A B C 254 D E F

1

2

Coombe

3

Tyley Bottom

Ashcroft Road

Sawcombe Farm

Fernley Farm

Ozleworth

Park Lane

Blackquarries Hill

Cotswold WY

es HI

Newark Park

Cotswold Way

4

277

Blacksmith Hill

Ozleworth Park

5

Ozleworth Bottom

Holwell Farm

6

Hillmill Lane

Hen's Cliff

Monarch's Way

7

Cotswold Way

Hillmill Lane

8

Winterspring Lane

Cotswold Way

Alderley Wood

Tresham

Burdon Court Farm

A Alderley B C 298 D E F

1 grid square represents 500 metres

G   H   J   255   K   L   M

I

2

3

4

280

5

6

7

8

Ashcroft
House

Bagpath

Scrubbett's Lane

Scrubbett's
Farm

Newington
Bagpath

Lasborough

Lasborough
Park

Long
Covert

Goss

Boxdown Road

A46

West Wood

Monarch's Way

Boxwell

Boxwell
Road

Cross Roads
Lodge

A46

Haymead
Lane

Whitewater
Farm

Whitewater Road

Stonehill
Wood

Boxwell Road

Leighterton
County
Primary
School

Leighterton

Back Lane

Farm Ln

Tetbury Lane

The Meads

Cem

PO

G   H   J   299   K   L   M

Glentworth
Farm

Bath Road

Monarch's Way

280

A B C 256 D E F

Calcot Farm

Hotel

A4135

1

Babdown
Farm

2

3 Bowldown Road

Tump
Covert

Goss
Covert

Park
Bottom

4

279

5

Bowldown
Farm

Bowldown Road

Nesley
Farm

6

Lane

7

Bowldown
Wood

Charltondown
Covert

8

Monarch's Way

A B C 300 D E F

Down
Farm

1 grid square represents 500 metres

Colly Farm
A4
1 Chantry Ct
2 Gumstool Hl
3 Long St
4 Market Pl
5 Silver St

A3
1 Cherry Orchard Rd
2 Cookspool
3 Cotswold Cl

A2
1 Jacobs Cl
2 Suffolk Cl

A   B   258   C   D   E   F

I

2   Sir William Romneys School   Highfield Farm   Ilsom   Great Larkhill Farm

Upton Gdns
Rd
Ryland Close
Berkeley Wk
Northlands
Clarrie Rd
Shepherds Md
Conygar Road
Bartier Cft
St Mary's Road

Newnton Hill

3   St Marys of E Prima   Magdalen Road   A433   Priory Industrial Estate   Tetbury Industrial Estate   Northfield Rd   Northgate   Cirencester   Road   Springfield
Field Ct
B4014
LONG LANE
Priory Way
Park Close
Hotel
The Damsels

4   CHURCH ST   Chipping Street   Connoisseur Gal   **TETBURY**   Monarch's Way   Monarch's Way
Close Gdns
Htl
Htl
Tetbury Gal
The Hlth Clinic
PO
Eight Bells Gal
West Stn
Romney Ho
The Green
Herd Lane

281   FOX HILL   Monarch's Way   The Folly Farm   Church Farm   Crudwell Lane

5   The Berrells   Old Quarries Industrial Estate   B4014   NEWNTON ROAD
Rd

6   Slads Farm   B4014   Long Newnton   The Priory   Pump La

7   Thorn Covert   Oak Covert   Powells Way   B4014   Newnton House

8   Shipton Wood   Merchants Farm

A   B   302   C   D   E   F

G H J 259 K L M

I

Gloucestershire County
Wiltshire County

Manor
Farm

✝ **Ashley**

Monarch's Way

Fosse
Gate

2

Stadborough
Copse

3

**West
Crudwell**

ch's Way

Boldridge
Farm

4

Chedglow

284

Crudwell Lane

5

The Dawneys
Lane

Tetbury

The Butts

THE STR

The
Ridg

PO

Gooselands

Hodge Meadow

THE

6

A429

7

Mur

Marsh
Farm

8

Bishoper
Farm

Poole
Keynes

G   H   J   261   K   L   M

I

Dean
Plantation

Dean
Farm

Lowfield
Farm

2

Oaksey Moor
Farm

Lower Moor
Farm

3

Wick Road

The Street

Chapel La
PO
Eyrs Cnr
Court Farm
The Street
Oaksey
Bendy Bow
The Green

Clattinger

4

Flintham
House

286

Park
Farm

Stert
Farm

5

Minety Lane

6

Lyngrove
Farm

7

Oaksey
Nursery

Braydon Brook
Farm

Oaksey Road

Flisteridge
Wood

Upper
Minety

8

Flisteridge Road

St Leonard's

PO

G   H   J   K   L   M

**Cloatley
End**

Cloatley

Hankerton Road

A   B   Somerford
Keynes
C   262   D   E   F

Neigh Bridge
Country Park

West

Spine   Road

I

2

Thames Path

3

Swill Brook

Clattinger
Farm

4

285

Swillbrook
Farm

Pike
Corner

5

Cooles
Farm

6

Rigsby's
Lane

LC

Brandier

7

Flower's
Farm

Field
Farm

8

Lower Moor

A   B   C   D   E   SAMBOURNE   F
ROAD

Sawyers
Hill

Sawyers
Cl

Minety C of E
School

Chapel La

Sawyer's Hill

Silver   Oakleaze

Hill

G H J 263 K L M

FRIARS
1 Milling Cl
2 Park End
B4696

1 Ashfield
SPINE ROAD (EAST)

Fridays Ham Lane

I

Clayhill Copse

North End

Cleveland Farm

Cox's Hill

Ashton Keynes

Kent End

2

Street
The Leaze
Back

Fridays Ham Lane

Church Wk

Richmond Ct

PO

Fore Street

Kent End

Harris La

Ashton Keynes C of E School

High

1

Eastfield

1

Dairy Farm

Gosditch

Park Pl

Thames

Birch Cld

The Lotts

Four Acre Cl

3

Derry Fields

The Md

The

Thames Path

River Thames or Isis

Manor Farm

4

Derry

High Bridge

Waterhay Bridge

Waterhay

288

B4696 ASHTON

Archer's Farm

5

Glebe Farm

Derry Brook

Grove Farm

Cove House Farm

ROAD

Swan Lane

MALMESBURY ROAD

6

Leigh

Leigh C of E School

Swan Lane

Hillside

B4040

7

B4696

B4040 MALMESBURY ROAD

8

Greenacres

G H J K L M

sheeppen Bridge

G3
1 Hammonds

G **H** **J** 265 **K** **L** **M**

I

Alex Farm

Eysey

River Thames or Isis

2

Thames Path

Thames Path

3

Water Eaton House

Wall

Red Rectory Lion Lane

Abingdon Ct

Thames Path

Thames Lane

Manor Orch

High Street

Home Farm Lane

Thames Lane

B4040

CALCUTT ST

Spiral La

The Surg

Prior Park Preparatory School

SWINDON ROAD

Calcutt

CRICKLADE

Wayland

Pauls

A419(T)

A419(T)

4

Dance Common

5

Seven Bridges Farm

Kingshill Farm

Ox House Farm

6

Farfield Farm

Headlands Farm

Farfield Lane

Farfield Lane

Wiltshire County Swindon

7

Lower Widhill Farm

A419(T)

River Ray

Chapel Farm

8

udgemore arm

Hayes Oak Farm

G **H** **J** **K** **L** **M**

Hayes

270

Beachley

College

M48

Beachley Road

Old Coach Road

Pavilion Road

Wyern Rd

Beachley
Point

Monmouthshire
Gloucestershire County

Gloucestershire County
South Gloucestershire

Monmouthshire
South Gloucestershire

River Severn

Severn Way

A403

Warth Lane

Aust Rd

Severn Way

Redwick &
Northwick
C of E School

304

A B C D E F

1 2 3 4 5 6 7 8

Littleton Warth

I

Littleto
upon-S

2

Rusholme   Jubilee Way

Severn Way

Jubilee Way

Severn Way

3

Cote Farm

Severn View Service Area

Toll

Severn Way

M48

Manor Farm

B4461

4

Junction 1

A403

Sandy Lane

The Rw

PH

292

Old Passage

severn Way

Aust

B4461

5

Red Hill

REDHIL

Aust Ro

A403

6

Ingst

Old Splott Rhine

Valley Farm

Ingst Road

Ingst

7

Cake Pill Gout

M48

Rhine Ingst

8

Bilsham Farm

Bilsham Lane

H7
1 Hazel Gdns
2 Olive Gdns

K1
Street names for this grid square are listed at the back of the index

J6
1 Beanhill Crs
2 Bodyce Rd
3 Down Leaze
4 Downs Cl
5 Orchard Lea

K2
1 Crispin La
2 Quaker La
3 Saw Mill La

K3
1 Dart Cl
2 St Mary St
3 Tyndale Vw
4 Upper Bath Rd

Kington House

G H J 273 K L M

Morton

I

Kington

Manor Brook School

The Castle School

Hotel

St Marys C of E School

Park Road

Chantry Road

Church Road

GLOUCESTER ROAD B4061

North Road

THORNBURY

Sheilding Schools

St Gloucester Co

Castle Business Cen

The Elms Day Hospital

Thornbury Hospital

Thornbury Health Cen

Christ the King RC School

New Siblands School

Hacket

2

Cem

HIGH ST

Infant School

Westwing School

Kington Lane

Castle Lane

St John St

Gillingstool

Oakleaze

Ashgrove

Sibland Way

The Paddocks

Jubilee Dr

Cheviot Dr

3

BRISTOL ROAD

B4061

The Surgery

Chapel St

Rock Street

Bath Road

Prim School

Streamleaze

Grovesend

Midland Way Business Park

Midland Way

Mead Way

Short Way

Walker Way

Cooper Road

Brunel Way

Vilner Lane

Hopkin Close

Avon Way

4

Club House

ALVESTON HILL

Thornbury Leisure Centre

Jubilee Way

Vilner Farm

294

Golf Course

Gate Farm

Marlwood Grange

The Chalet

A38

Abbey Lane

5

Mumbleys Lane

Jubilee Way

6

VATTINGSTONE LANE

own

Marlwood School

Quarry Road

Quarry Md

DOWN ROAD

THORNBURY RD

Old Gloucester Rd

Hotel

New Lane

Alveston

Strode Gdns

Strode Common

Rosewood Av

Greenwood Drive

Wolfridge Lane

West View

Beech Leaze

Greenhill Road

Paddock Gdns

Hotel

The Street

Grove Farm

7

Stroud Common

Bridle Way

Underwood Close

Greenhill Lane

Primary School

Greenhill Road

Green Hill

Davids Close

Davids Lane

Shellards Lane

Owlsnest Farm

8

Hazel Lane

A38

GLOUCESTER ROAD

The Loans

Hayward's Farm

Lower Hazel

G

M3, M4
Street names for these grid squares are listed at the back of the index

H

M1
1 Campion Cl
2 Foxglove Cl
3 Fulmar Cl
4 Kestrel Cl
5 Kingfisher Cl
6 Nightingale Cl

J 307 K

L3
1 Ladden Ct
2 Springfield

L4
1 Cherwell Cl
2 Medina Cl

L

L2
1 Chestnut Dr
2 Sycamore Dr
3 Thicket Wk

M

L1
1 Cossham Cl
2 Hawthorn Crs
3 Howard Rd
4 North East Rd
5 Whitfield Rd

A B C 276 D E F

Churchend

Bristol

1

2

3

295

4

5

6

7

8

A B 310 D E F

Devil's Lane

Newhouse Farm

Southwood Farm

The Downs

B4509

Church Lane

The Cliffs

West End Road

West End

Cowship Lane

Lane

's Court

Arnoldsfield Trading Estate

Wickwar

PO

Westend Road

Frith Farm

Frith Lane

Hillhouse

Charfield Hall Farm

LC

B4060

Wickwar Trading Estate

Chase Lane

Station Road

Turnpike Gate

Avon Crescent

North St

High Street

Back Lane

Arrells Court

Inglestone Road

Wickwar Primary School

Amberley Way

Canters Leaze

Poplar Lane

Poplar Farm

Horwood

Sodbury Road

Pincots

Pincots Farm

Lane

1 Honeyborne Wy

D6

D5

1 Cotswold Vw

Gloucestershire

Neathwood Farm

B4060

Highwood Farm

Cherryrock Farm

Kites Farm

Chase Hill

Upper Wetmoor

Bishop's Hill Wood

Bays Wood

M3
1 St Giles Barton
2 Vicarage La

Cemetery

Farm

G

H

J

277

K

L

M

Alderle

I

Upper Barns
Farm

2

Rose Hill
School

Folly
Farm

Alderley Road

New

Haroldsfield
Farm

Lower Witheymore
Farm

Farmcote

Kingswood Road

3

Killcott Road

Primary Sch

Day   House   Lane

Day House
Farm

2

Hillesley

High Street

Chapel Lane

1

Mounteney's
Farm

Gloucestershire County

South Gloucestershire

4

298

ey's

Assley
Common

Splatt's

5

Inglestone
Farm

South Moon
Ridings

Lovetts Wood
Farm

Lance
Coppice

Oxleaze
Farm

Hawkesbury Road

6

Lower Woods
Lodge

Inglestone
Common

7

Lower
Wetmoor

Littley
Wood

Hawkesbury
Knott

8

Newhouse
Farm

Burnt
Wood

Hawkesbury
Common

G

H

J

311

K

L

M

Hawkesbury

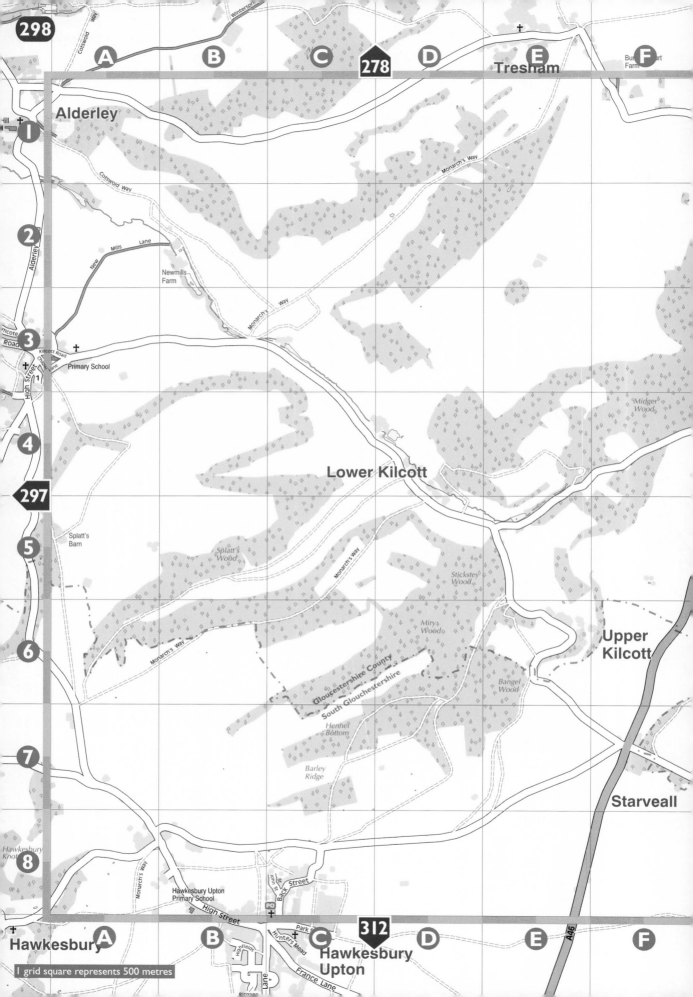

298

A   B   C   **278**   D   E   Tresham   F

Burnt Part Farm

Cotswold Way

Wintersoll

Alderley

† Hill

1

Cotswold Way

Monarch's Way

Alderley Road

2

New Mills Lane

Newmills Farm

Midger Wood

Kilcott Road

Chapel Lane

Incote Road

3

† Primary School

High Street

[1]

Monarch's Way

4

Lower Kilcott

297

Splatt's Barn

5

Splatt's Wood

Sticksley Wood

Monarch's Way

Upper Kilcott

Miry Wood

6

Monarch's Way

Gloucestershire County
South Glouchestershire

Bangel Wood

Hennel Bottom

Starveall

7

Barley Ridge

Hawkesbury Knoll

8

Monarch's Way

Hawkesbury Upton Primary School

Back Street

PO †

Hawkesbury   A

High Street

Park Lane

Hunters Mead

France Lane

St John St

Highfields Lane

A46

312

Hawkesbury
Upton

A   B   C   **312**   D   E   F

†

I grid square represents 500 metres

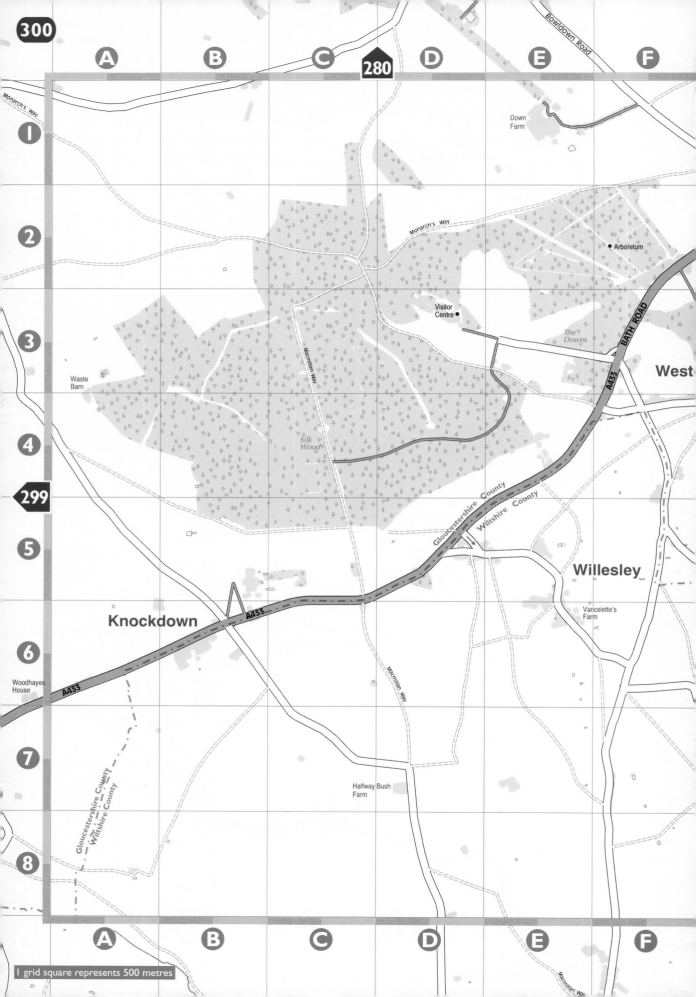

280

299

A B C D E F

1
2
3
4
5
6
7
8

Bowldown Road

Down Farm

Monarch's Way

Arboretum

Visitor Centre

The Downs

BATH ROAD

West

A433

Monarch's Way

Macmillan Way

Waste Barn

Silk Woods

Gloucestershire County

Wiltshire County

Willesley

Vancelette's Farm

Knockdown

A433

A433

Woodhayes House

Macmillan Way

Gloucestershire County
Wiltshire County

Halfway Bush Farm

Macmillan Way

A B C D E F

1 grid square represents 500 metres

302

A　B　C　282　D　E　F

I

Estcourt House

Eagle Lodge

2

Whitehouse Lane

Manor Farm

River Avon (Tetbury Branch)

B4014

Bell Farm

3

The Street

Hodges Farm

Fosse Tilery Farm

✝ Shipton Moyne
PO

Gloucestershire County
Wiltshire County

Church Lane

✝

Brokenborough

4

301

5

Cranmore Farm

Fosse Farm

Boakley Farm

...cestershire County
...iltsh... ...ounty

6

7

B4040

B4040

B4040

Park

Twatley Manor Farm

8

Hyam Wood

Hyam Farm

River Avon (Sherston Branch)

A　B　C　D　E　F

Shipton Wood

G7
1 Corn Gastons

H7
1 The Rowans
2 Willow View Cl

J6
1 John Betjeman Cl
2 Michael Pym's Rd
3 Orwell Cl

G　**H**　**J**　283　**K**　Bishoper Farm　**L**　**M**

1

Gilboa Farm

Five Lanes

2

3

Quobwell Farm

B4014

A429

Griffins Barn Farm

4

Cha
Par

5

B4014

Filands

Filand School

The Old Orchard

CHARLTON

6

Backbridge Farm

Malmesbury Business Park

Leland Close
Aubrey Rise
Webbs Way
Lacemakers Rd
Golding Close

B4040

Milbourne Lane

SN16

Back Bridge

Cemetery

Malmesbury C of E Primary School

Redd Farm Road

North Wilts District Council

Town Council

MALMESBURY

A429

B4040

Milbourne Lane

Monks Pk

7

Milbourne

White Lion Pk
Parklands
Malmesbury Swimming Pool
Old Alexander Rd
Park Mead
Park Road
St Aldhelms Rd
Hobbes Close
Gloucester Road Industrial Est
Malmesbury Cricket Club

SHERSTON ROAD

Corn Gastons
Alexander Rd
Athelstan Road
Hodge La
Foundry Road
Gloucester Rd
Burnham Rd
Lover's La
Holloway
Blicks Hill

Malmesbury School

Bremilham Rise

BRISTOL STREET
Dark Lane

Foxley Road

ABBEY ROW
Burnivale
Malmesbury Abbey
Mill
Abbotts Gdn
HOLLOWAY

8

River Avon

OXFORD St
ABBEY ROW
Town Hall
King's Wall
HIGH STREET
Gable House Surg
St John's St

G　**H**　**J**　**K**　River A　**L**　**M**

Haddo Close

Common Road

Arches Farm

Barley Cl

Cowbridge

J8
1 Cross Hayes La
2 High St
3 Katifer La
4 Oliver's La
5 St Dennis La
6 St Mary's St
7 Silver St

J7
1 Gloucester Rd
2 Old Railway Cl
3 St Marys La
4 Shipton Hl

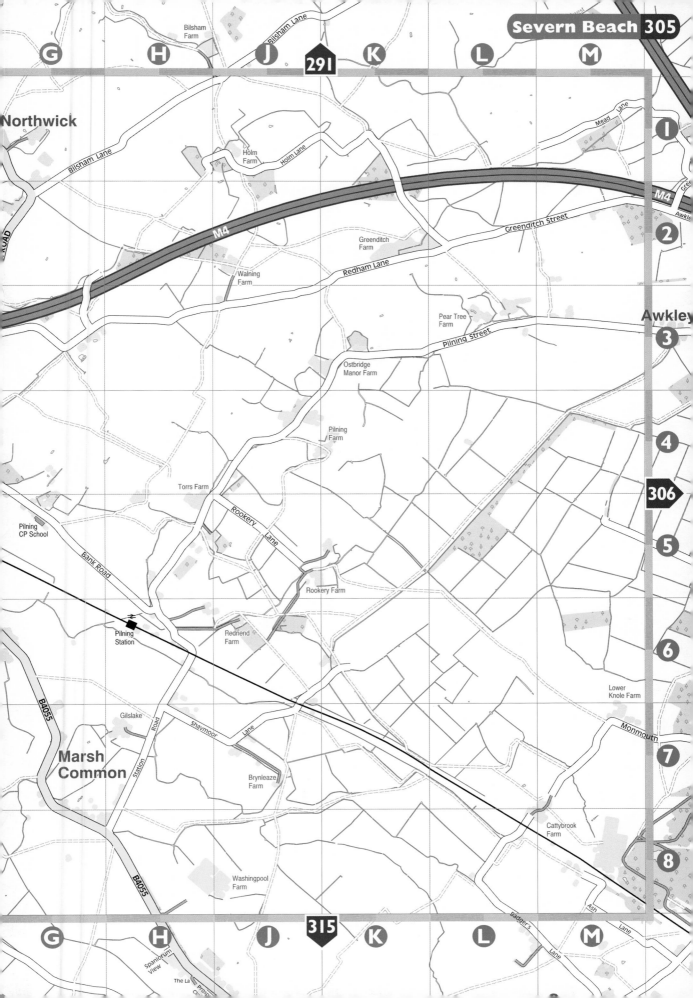

G H J **291** K L M

1

Northwick

Mead Lane

Bilsham Farm

Bilsham Lane

Holm Farm

Holm Lane

Bilsham Lane

M4

Greenditch Street

2

Greenditch Farm

Redham Lane

Walning Farm

Pear Tree Farm

Awkley

Pilning Street

3

Ostbridge Manor Farm

Pilning Farm

4

306

Torrs Farm

Rookery Lane

5

Pilning CP School

Bank Road

Rookery Farm

6

Pilning Station

Rednend Farm

Lower Knole Farm

B4055

Gilslake

Station Road

Shaymoor Lane

Monmouth

7

Marsh Common

Brynleaze Farm

Cattybrook Farm

8

B4055

Washingpool Farm

Badger's Lane

Ash Lane

G H **315** J K L M

Spaniorum View

The La Prospe Cla

A   B   C   D   E   F

296

B7
1 Barkers Mead
2 Carmarthen Cl
3 Hampshire Wy
4 Harts Cft

B6
1 The Knapp
2 Tylers Wy

A8
1 Piper Rd
2 Warren Wy

A6
1 Dryleaze
2 Pear Tree Hey

Cots
m

1

Hillhouse
Farm

Bays
Wood

2

Birdsbush
Farm

WICKWAR ROAD

Oxwick
Farm

Lady's
Wood

3

Bury   Hill   Lane

The
Chase

Tan House
Farm

Tanhouse Lane

Mapleridge Lane

4

Bury Hill

Yate   Rocks

Jubilee Way

309

5

Yate Rocks

Brinsham   Lane

Road

6

Meadow
Mead

Eastfield Drive

Coopers
Dr

**The
Rocks**

Jubilee Way

Gravel

Clayfield

Hill

B4060

Long
Croft

Leechpool Wy

Barkers

Summers Mead

Eastfield Drive

Lane

7

Randolph Avenue

Lower
Moor
Road

LOVE LANE

Love Lane

Lime
Croft

Jubilee Way

York Cl

Wellington

Sturmer
Close

Argyle Dr

Goose Gn

Greenways Road

Gravel Hl Rd

Golf Course

Mead Riding

Halifax

Doctors
Surgery

**Goose
Green**

BS37

HomeField

Lancaster
Road

Church Road

Ullswater Cl

Cornwall
Crs

Kent Av

Wiltshire

**Stub
Riding**

8

Mountbatten

Cambrian Drive

Cheshire Cl

Crowthers
Av

Canterbury

Church
Close

Somerset Avenue

Dorset Way

Avenue

WICKWA

Bank
School

Lyndale Avenue

Poole Cl
Drive

A   B   C   D   E   F

Yate
Town
Council

St Marys C of E
Primary School

B4059

GOOSE GREEN W

Mercer Cl

Firgrove Crs

Meirose Cl

BB
1 Rectory Cl

Avenue

Horton Road

Jubilee Way

Johns

Portway Lane

The Ridge
Junior School

Lawns

Tree Leaze

Broadway County

St

Horton

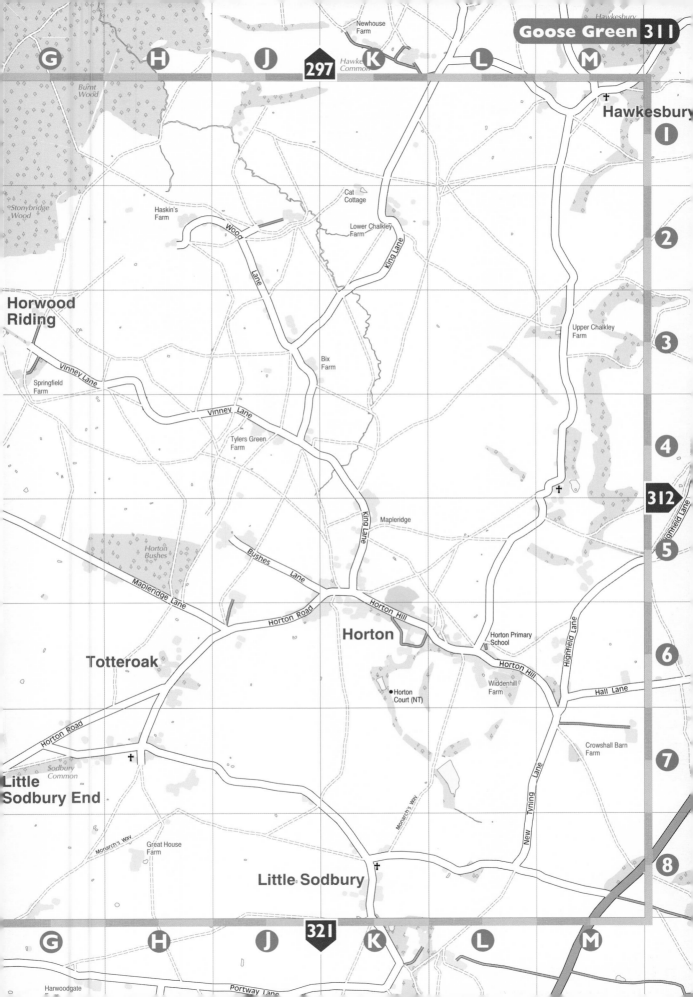

G H J 297 K L M

Newhouse
Farm

Hawkesbury
Common

Hawkesbury

1

Burnt
Wood

Stonybridge
Wood

Haskin's
Farm

Wood Lane

Cat
Cottage

Lower Chalkley
Farm

King Lane

2

Horwood
Riding

Upper Chalkley
Farm

3

Springfield
Farm

Vinney Lane

Vinney Lane

Bix
Farm

Tylers Green
Farm

4

312

Highfield Lane

5

King Lane

Mapleridge

Horton
Bushes

Bushes Lane

Mapleridge Lane

Horton Road

Horton Hill

Horton

Horton Primary
School

Highfield Lane

6

Totteroak

Horton Hill

Horton
Court (NT)

Widdenhill
Farm

Hall Lane

Horton Road

Sodbury
Common

Little
Sodbury End

Crowshall Barn
Farm

7

Monarch's Way

New Tyning Lane

8

Monarch's Way

Great House
Farm

Little Sodbury

G H J 321 K L M

Harwoodgate

Portway Lane

A B C **298** D E F

Hawkesbury

Hawkesbury Primary Sc

High Street

Jubil St

Back Street

PO

Park Street

France Lane

Hunter's Mead

High

field

Lane

**Hawkesbury
Upton**

Birgage Road

Monarch's Way

Monarch's Way

Highfield Lane

Highfield Farm

**Britain
Bottom**

Dunkirk Farm

A46

A433

Swangrov

Dunkirk

halkley

**Petty
France**

Hotel

Hotel

Bodkin Wood

GL9

Highfield Lane

Bodkin Hazel Wood

A46

Hall Lane

wshall Barn

A46

American Barn

Grickstone Farm

Seven Mile Plantation

A B C **322** D E F

Castle Barn

Tyning, The

1 grid square represents 500 metres

1 2 3 4 5 6 7 8

G H J 299 K L M

I

Folly Farm

Hinnegar

Bullpark Wood

2 **Sopworth**

PO

Church La

3

Badminton Down

4

Luckley Farm

South Gloucestershire
Wiltshire County

Wick Farm

5

Little
Badminton

North End Farm

Church La

6

Well Lane

Cherry Orchard

Cherry Orchard Lane

Cherry Orchard Lane

Prima
Schoo

Hermit's Cell

Luckingto

7

Allengrove Farm

Allengrove Lane

Badminton Park

Badminton
Show Jumping
Circuit

Allengrove Lane

8

Giant's Cave

OL ROAD

G H J 323 K L M

Kennel D

Shop La

PO
High Street

Haye's

**Great
Badminton**

A   **B**   **C**   **D**   **E**   **F**

306

I
2
3
4

315

5
6
7
8

Aztec
West

PATCHWAY

Little
Stoke

Stoke
Gifford

BS34

GIPSY PATCH LA

The Mall

Patchway
Trading Estate

Patchway
Station

Filton

Northway

326

A   **B**   **C**   **D**   **E**   **F**

1 grid square represents 500 metres

G

H

J

307

K

L

M

BRADLEY STOKE

St Marys Rugby Club

Water Park

North Woods

Gloucester Road Farm

Trench Lane

Hotel

Swan Lane

Bradley Brook

Old Gloucester Road

B4427

Green Lane

318

Silverhill Sch

Winterbou

St Michaels C of E
VC Primary School

Church Lane

BEACON LANE B4057

Flower Gallery

Flaxpits

Winterbourne Hl

Dragon Rd

Great Stoke

WINTERBOURNE ROAD B4057

Primary School

St Michaels Primary School

Stoke Gifford Medical Centre

Bristol Parkway Station

The Green

Hambrook Lane

Curtis Lane

Junction 19

Old Gloucester Road

Player's Close

Whiteshill

Pye Corner

Hambrook Sports Club

Quarry Barton

Hambrook CP School

Camp View

Harry Stoke Road

G

H

J

327

K

L

M

Junction

Hambrook

I

2

3

4

5

6

7

8

Green

L4
1 Cranham
2 Pitchcombe

M1
1 Cranleigh Ct Rd
2 Folly Bridge Cl
3 Longs Dr
4 Mow Barton
5 Staples Rd
6 The Willows

G H J **309** K L M

IRON ACTON WAY

Pool Farm

Dyer's Lane

Wade Rd

Armstrong Way

North Road

Great Western Business P

Northavon Business Ce

Northridge Business Centre

Frome Bank School

Cheshire Cl

Yate Town Council

I

Lavenham Rd

Beeches Trading Estate

Waverley Road

Lawrence Drive

Stover Road

B4059

Millbrook Rd

North Road

Yate Station

BADMINTON ROAD   STATION ROAD

STATION

Hope Road

Bridge Road

Nibley Lane

Frome valley walkway

River Frome

Frome valley walkway

Nibley

Stover Trading Est

South Av

Badminton Road Trading Estate

Westerleigh Cl

Sunnyvale La

Moorland Avenue

Moorpark Avenue

Moordell Close

2

Mayshill

BADMINTON ROAD

A432

Cemetery

Westerleigh Common

Westerleigh Road

Stanshawes Dr

YATE

King Edmund Community School

Birkdale

3

Tubb's Bottom

Says Court Farm

Brookthorpe

Quedgeley

Longford

St Briavels

Primary School

Drive

Frog Lane

Westerleigh Road

Deerhurst

Barnwood Road

Prestbury

Erisley Infant School

Rodford CP School

Glenfall

Rodford

4

Chedworth

Rodford Way

Abbotswood Surg

PO

Witcombe

Culverhill School

320

Road

Westerleigh Rd

Rodborough

Brockworth

Abbotswood Infant School

Maisemore

5

Shire Way

Edgeworth

Badgeworth

Kingscote

Kelston

Cherington

Shire Wa

6

Wapley Common

Besom Lane

7

Westerleigh Road

Westerleigh

Newman Close

Jorrocks Estate

The Quadrangle

PO

Beanwood Farm

Wapley

Broad Lane

Mill Crs

Old Mill Close

Shorthill Road

8

Boxhedge Farm Lane

nfield

Hill

Westerleigh Road

Cliff Farm

Westerleigh Hill

G H J **329** K L M

M4
1 Abbotswood

M3
1 Elmore
2 Lydbrook Cl
3 Prescott
4 Sandhurst

M2
1 Blakeney Mills
2 Village Cl

322

A B C 312 D E F

1

Beech
Copse

2

Grickst
Farm

Lyegrove
House

3

Lyegrove
Farm

Castle
Barn

Tyning The

Lime Av

Roach's Lane

Lime Avenue

Old Down Road

4

321 040 B4040

Newhouse
Farm

5

Oakes

Lane

6

Warre
Barn

7

Old Warren

Sheepcot
Barn

Parks
Farm

8

A B C 332 D E F

1 grid square represents 500 metres

313

G H J K L M

I
2
3
4
5
6
7
8

Great
Badminton

Shop La

Kennel Drive

High Street

PO

School La

The Limes

Haye's La

Cape
Farm

Hebden
Farm

Macmillan Way

B4040

B4040

Allengrove Lane

Station Road

Station Approach
Industrial Estate

B4040

B4040

Wiltshire County
South Gloucestershire

Alderton Road

Acton Turville

B4039

Chapel La

Hollybush Cl

Trinity
C of E
School

Police
Station

BURTON ROAD

Tormarton   Road

B4039

Viner's La

Macmillan Way

Littleton Drew

Marsh Lane

M4

M4

M4

B4039

Marsh   Lane

B4039

South Gloucestershire
Wiltshire County

Tog Down
Way

PH

Burton

The
Meads

Horsedown

Edgecorner Lane

Nettleton   Road

Macmillan Way

G H J K L M

333

Westfield
Farm

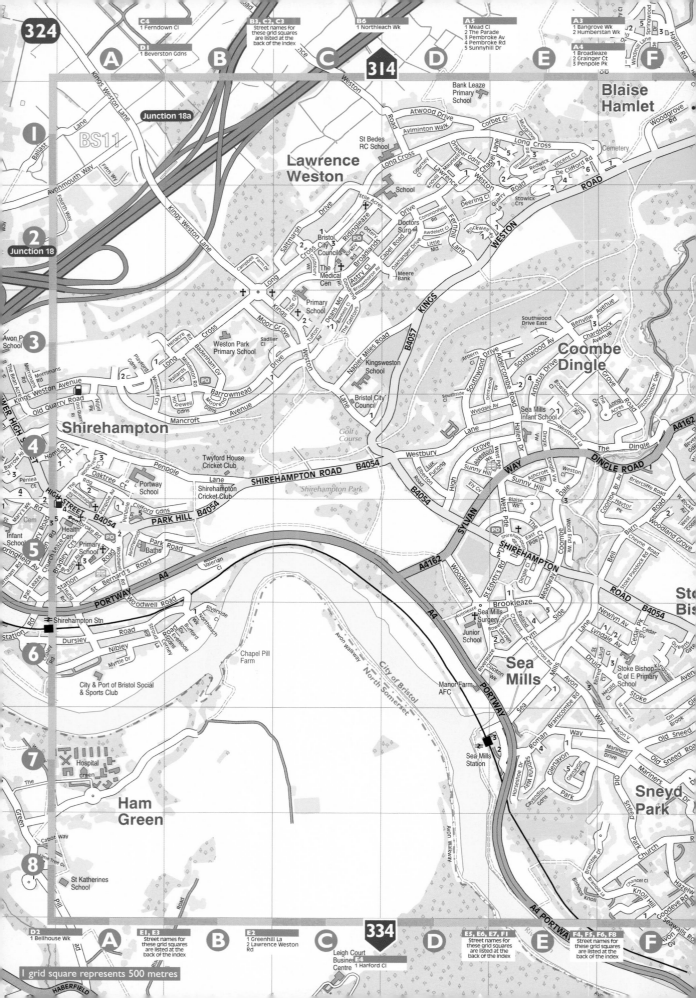

Westerleigh Hill

G H J K6 1 Dennisworth L6 1 Cherrytree Ct L7 1 Goldfinch Wy 2 Merlin Rdg 3 Woodpecker Crs L M

`319`

Westerleigh Road

Cliff Farm

Leigh Lane

Leigh Lane

Leigh Farm

WESTERLEIGH ROAD

B4465

Batchfield Lane

M4

M4

Lyde Green

Parkfield Road

Parkfield

St Aldam's Ash Farm

`330`

Parkfield Road

The Vale

Pucklechurch C of E Primary School

Cranford Farm

The Surgery

WESTERLEIGH ROAD

Edmund Court

Lansdown Rd

Castle Road

Feltham Road

Marsh Farm

Pucklechurch

Shortwood Lodge

Queen's Rd

Homefield Rd

PO

Abson Rd

Hill Vw Rd

Hill View Road

Orchard Rd

Poplar Dr

B4465

St Aldams Drive

Becket Court

Birch Dr

Maple Wk

Cedar Wy

Holly Cl

Dennisworth Farm

Hawthorne Cl

Kestrel Dr

Oak Tree Av

Partridge Rd

Eagle Crs

Hoddon Lane

Hoddon Lane

Becket Court

Oak Tree Av

Cossham Rd

Back Lane

Cossham Rd

Redford Lane

WOOD HILL

SHORTWOOD ROAD

SHORTWOOD

Siston Lane

Northmead Farm

Siston

G H J `339` K L M

Abson

1 2 3 4 5 6 7 8

G H J K L M

321

331

Sands
Court

Old
Farm

PH

Hotel

Dodington Ash

B4465

I rn

Lapdown Lane

Marshfield

2 A4

Springs
Farm

Lower Lapdown
Farm

Junction 18

3

Cotswold Way

West Littleton
Down

4

332

A46(T)

5

Field

Lane

Wallsend Lane

Dunsdown Lane

6

7

Dyrham Park (NT)

Butt's Lane

Camp Lane

Sands Hill

A46(T)

West
Littleton

8

Sands
Farm

G H J K L M

341

West Littleton Road

332

A   B   C   **322**   D   E   F

†

I Tormarton

Lapdown Lane

2 M4

Marshfield Road

Lower Lapdown Farm

South Gloucestershire

Wiltshire County

Kington Down Farm

3

Shire Hill

West Down

4 Down Farm

331

Rownham Farm

5

Broadmead Brook

Broadmead Brook

Shirehill Farm

6

Tormarton Road

7 Harcombe Farm

8 Downthorns Farm

A   B   C   **342**   D   E   F

West Littleton Road

Marshmead Lane

Marton Industrial Est

Culverslade

Down Road

South Gloucestershire Wiltshire County

I grid square represents 500 metres

G   H   J   **323**   K   L   M

I

Westfield
Farm

**Nettleton
Green**   PO

2

Lugbury
Farm

Wood Lane

3

Holloway Hill

**Nettleton
Shrub**

Drifton Hill

Broadhead Brook

Smith Street

4

**West
Kington**

**West Kington
Wick**

5

6

7

Fosse
Farm

**Mountain
Bower**

8

G   H   J   **343**   K   L   M

North Wraxall   Old Coach Road   **A420**

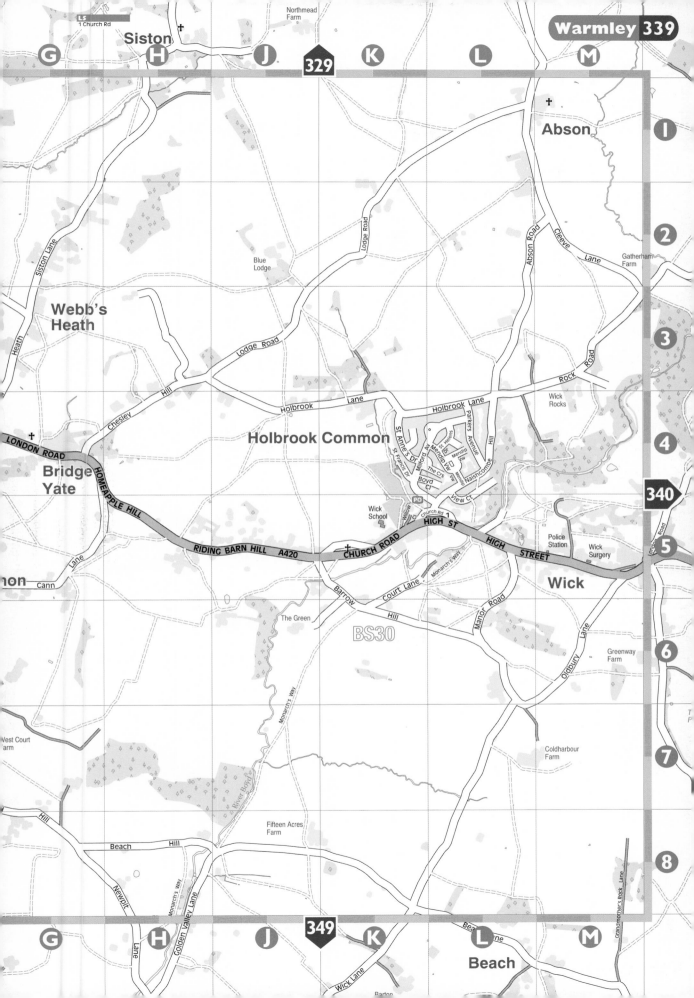

G H J **329** K L M

1

2

3

340

4

5

6

7

8

Siston

1 Church Rd

Northmead Farm

Abson

Gatherham Farm

Blue Lodge

Lodge Road

Webb's Heath

Siston Lane

Heath

Lodge Road

Abson Road

Cleeve Lane

Rock Road

Wick Rocks

Holbrook Lane

Holbrook Common

Holbrook Lane

Chesley Hill

Holbrook Lane

Parkers Avenue

St Annes Dr

St Francis Dr

Milford Av

Mendip Vw

St Helens

The Crs

Mendip Vw

Naishcombe Hill

LONDON ROAD

Bridge Yate

HOMEAPPLE HILL

Boyd Cl

View Ct

PO

Wick School

Church Rd 1

RIDING BARN HILL A420

CHURCH ROAD

HIGH ST

HIGH STREET

Police Station

Wick Surgery

Wick

Lane

Cann

London Road

Barrow Hill

Court Lane

Monarch's Way

Manor Road

Oldbury Lane

Greenway Farm

The Green

BS30

Coldharbour Farm

West Court Farm

River Boyd

Monarch's Way

Fifteen Acres Farm

Hill

Beach Hill

Newpit

Monarch's Way

Golden Valley Lane

Wick Lane

Bea Lane

Grandmother's Rock Lane

Beach

Lane

Barton

G H J **349** K L M

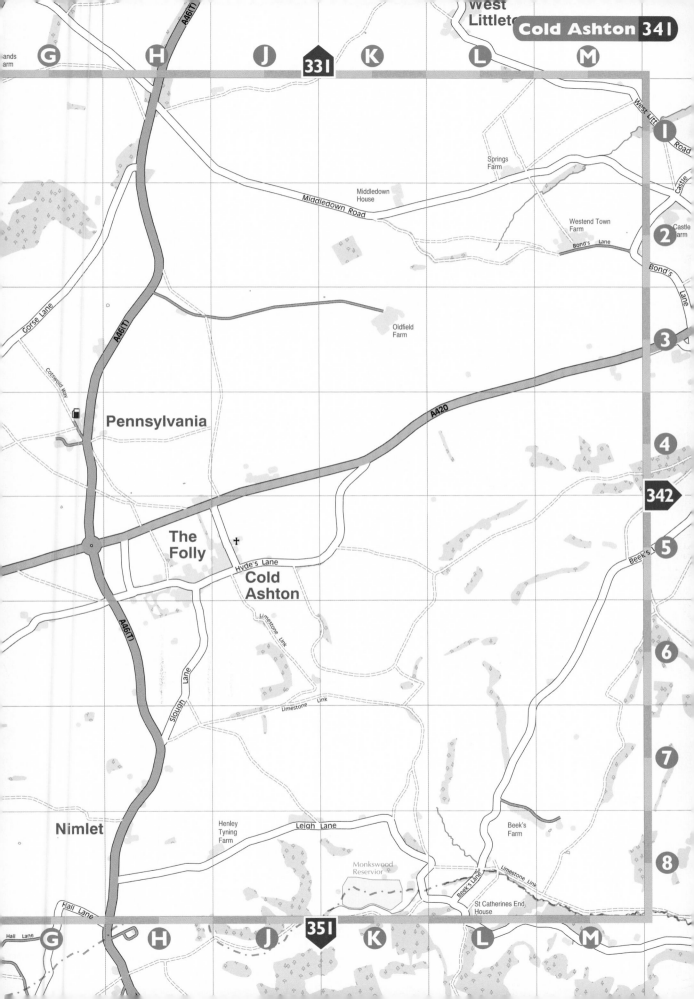

H5
1 Holly Dr

J6
1 Ash Rd
2 Cherry Rd
3 Rowan Cl

J8
1 Green La
2 Nursery Rd

G H J K L M

333

I

Old Coach Road

A420

North Wraxall

2

Upper Wraxall

A420

The Shoe

Bury Camp

3

Doncombe Hill

4

Pinewood Way

Doncombe Lane

Ha Fa

Hotel

Luckham Park

5

Walnut Drive
Linden Close
Cypress Walk
Larch Road
Laurel Drive

Hillcrest
Fairview
Valley Way
Woodlea
Thickwood Lane

Thickwood

Oak Road
Palm Rd
Lime Close
Elm Road
Hazel Way
Poplar Way
Redwood Way
Beech Rd

PO

6

Eastrip

7

Barracks

Doncombe Lane

Airfield

Colerne C of E Primary School

Malcms Croft

8

Colerne Rugby Football Club

Totts La
Quarry Lane
Forrest Green
Silver Street
Fosseway
Round Barrow Close
Rickfield
High St
Trimnells
Vicarage
Market Pl
Chapel
Tutton Hill
The Bank
Watergates
Eastrip Lane

Colerne

The Firs Surgery

Clares Av
Box View

PO

Washmead

Bath Rd

353

K8
1 Grocyn Cl
2 Hitchings Skilling
3 Mulling Cl

A **B** **C** **D** **E** **F**

334

D1
1 Ridgeview
2 Westward Gdns

C2
1 Providence Vw

B3
1 Paulman Gdns

B2
1 Birdwell La
2 Lovelinch Gdns

School
B3128
CLARKEN

Pill Grove

B5128
ASHTON ROAD
B312
A370

1

Golf Course

Long Ashton Road

Providence Lane

Monarch's Way

Warren Lane

Cherry Rd
Orchard Road
Keedwell Hl
Cedar Cl
Willow Cl

Heath Ridge
Kempe's Cl
Estune Wy
Highlands Rd
Short Lane

Ridgeway
Chestnut Rd
North Leaze

Folleigh Cl
Folleigh Dr
Folleigh Lane
Lodge Dr

Glebe Rd
Parsonage Rd
Hillside Rd

Long Ashton Road

Church Lane

Primary School

2

Cross Road
Ravens

Fenswood Md
Fenswood Rd
Weston Road

Surgery
PO
Yeomeads
Lynbrook

Birdwell
Bradville Gdns
Raymore Rd
NK
Lampton
Fenshurst Gdns

Hollis Cl

LONG ASHTON

Trevnes Croft
Well Cl
Copford La
Brook Cl
Cattey CV
Ryecroft
Liveson Wy

Yanley Lane

Birdwell Primary School

3

Road

Warren La

Wildcountry Lane

A370

Yanley

Yanley Lane

4

A370
A370

Monarch's Way

Barrow Hospital

A38
A370

Yanley Lane

5

Barrow Wood

Bridgwater Road
Yanleigh Cl

Colliter's Brook

6

Barrow Gurney

Wildcountry Lane

Hern Lane

STREET
ool La
PO

BS41

7

Barns Close

B3130

Hobbs Lane

Reservoir

Bridgwater Road

Dundry Lane

Monarch's Wy

Barrow Common

Highridge Road

Highridge

8

A38

Reservoir

Reservoir

Dundry Lane

Monarch's Way

Ham Lane

Glen Farm
B3130
ROAD
Lane

Castle Farm
Castle Farm

Dundry Primary School
PO

The Md
Church Road
Andrus Rd

Dundry

1 grid square represents 500 metres

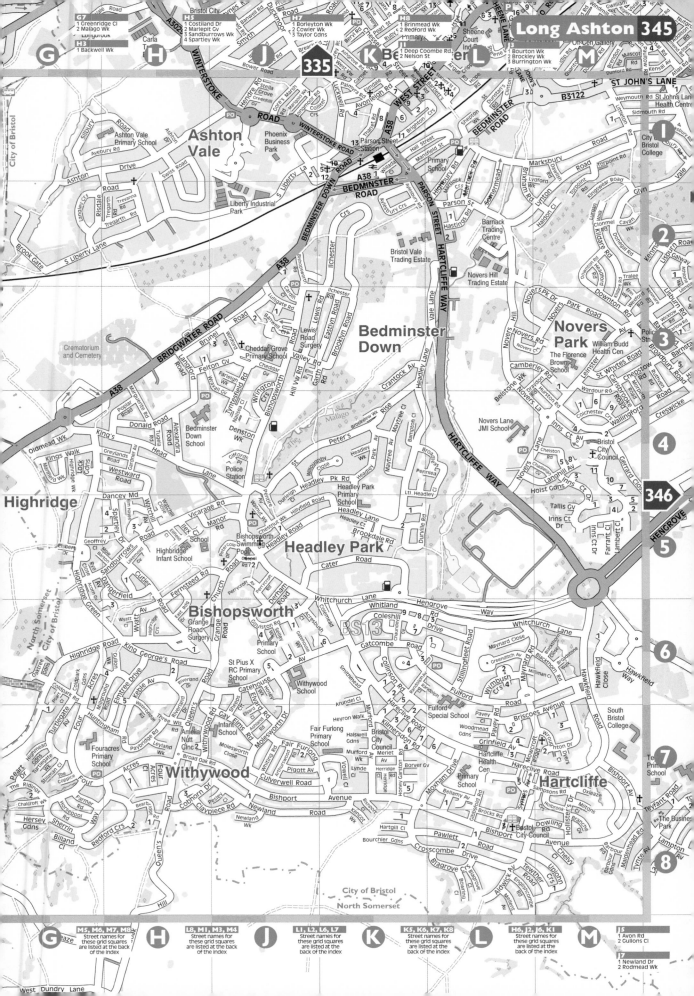

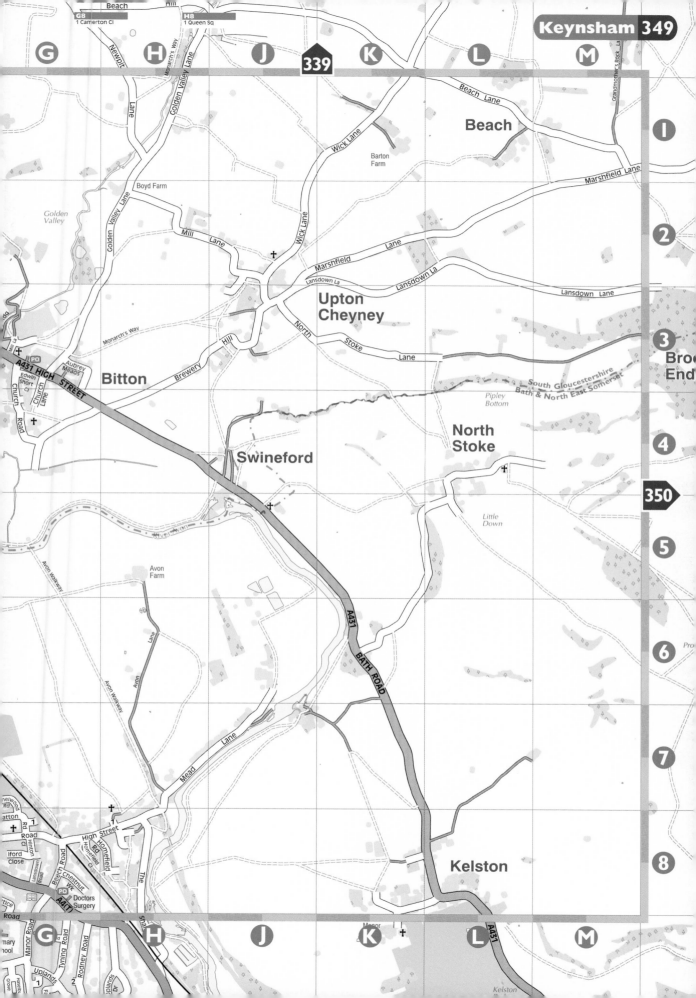

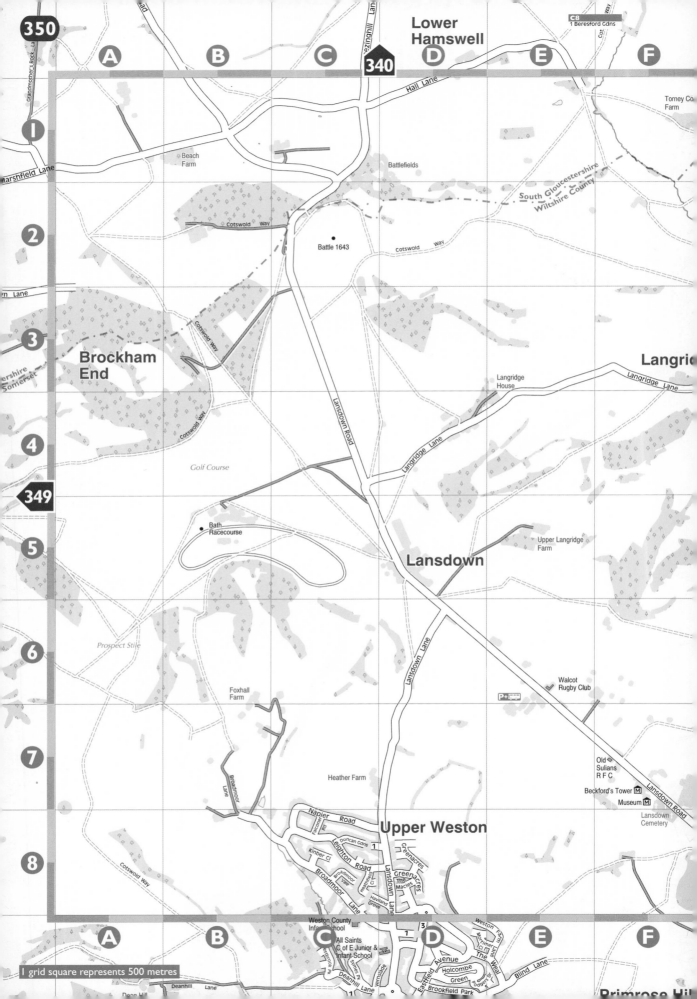

A   **B**   **C**   **D**   **E**   **F**

Lower Hamswell

340

C8
1 Beresford Gdns

Grandmother's Rock La

Marshfield Lane

I

Beach Farm

Battlefields

Torney Co Farm

South Gloucestershire
Wiltshire County

2

Cotswold Way

Battle 1643

Cotswold Way

Lane

3

Brockham End

Cotswold Way

Langridge House

Langrid

Langridge Lane

Somerset

Cotswold Way

Golf Course

Langridge Lane

4

349

Bath Racecourse

5

Lansdown

Upper Langridge Farm

Prospect Stile

6

Foxhall Farm

Lansdown Lane

Walcot Rugby Club

P+

7

Broadmoor Lane

Heather Farm

Old Sulians R F C

Lansdown Road

Beckford's Tower 🅼
Museum 🅼

Lansdown Cemetery

Napier Road

Upper Weston

Falconer Rd

Duncan Gdns

Leighton Road

Greenacres

Kinber Cl

Broadmoor Vale

Lansdown Lane

The Macies

Greenacres

8

Cotswold Way

Broadmoor Lane

Haviland Grove

1

Weston County Infant School

All Saints C of E Junior & Infant School

Weston Farm

Mortimer Lane

The Weal

Blind Lane

A   **B**   **C**   **D**   **E**   **F**

Deanhill Lane

Dean Hill

Vernslade

Deanhill Lane

Eastfield Avenue

Holcombe

Brookfield Park

Holcombe Green

Primrose Hil

A B C 342 D E F

Nailey Farm

D7
1 Whitefield Cl

B8
1 Avondale Pl

A8
1 The Willowfalls

Ayford Farm

South Gloucestershire
Wiltshire County

1

The Rocks

Oakford Lane

Hunters Hall

St Catherine

2

Limestone Link

Oakford Farm

Three Shire Stones

Road Hill

3

Oakford Lane

Holtsdown

Holts Down

Limestone Link

South Gloucestershire
Bath and North East Somerset

Rodney Farm

Steway Lane

Bailey's Wood

4

Bannerdown Road

Charmy Farm

Ramscombe Lane

Hollies Lane

5

Chilcombe Bottom

Limestone Link

Banner Down

Shockerwick Lane

6

Eagle Park Lane

Seven Acres Lane

Eagle Road

Brookside Cl

Steway Lane

Northend

The Mount

Prospect Gdns

Lwr Northend

Catherine Way

Hill Fort

Church La

School La

High Bannerdown

Bannerdown Road

7

Solsbury Lane

Limestone Link

Batheaston Primary Sch

Wayfield Gdns

Coalpit Road

Avon Ct

Fosse Lane

Banner Lane

Bannerdown Drive

Bannerdown Cl

Eden park Dr

Bannerfield Wy

Shockerwick Lane

Batheaston

Solsbury Lane

Brow Hill

Eden park Dr

Court Gdns

Morris Lane

Meadow Park

Swainswick Lane

Laburnum Ter

High Street

Vale Vw

PO

Medical Centre

London Road

West View Rd

Marsh Dr

Westwood

8

Bailbrook Lane

Victoria Gdns

London Road East

Hotel

BOX ROAD A4

London Road West

Mill Lane

Toll Br Rd

Hotel

Toll

A B A4 C D Bathford Hill E Ashley Road F

Kings Lane

Church Street

Manor Dr

PO

Manor Dr Primary School

Dovers Lane

High Street

Main Wood

Park

New Rd

The Garstons

A365

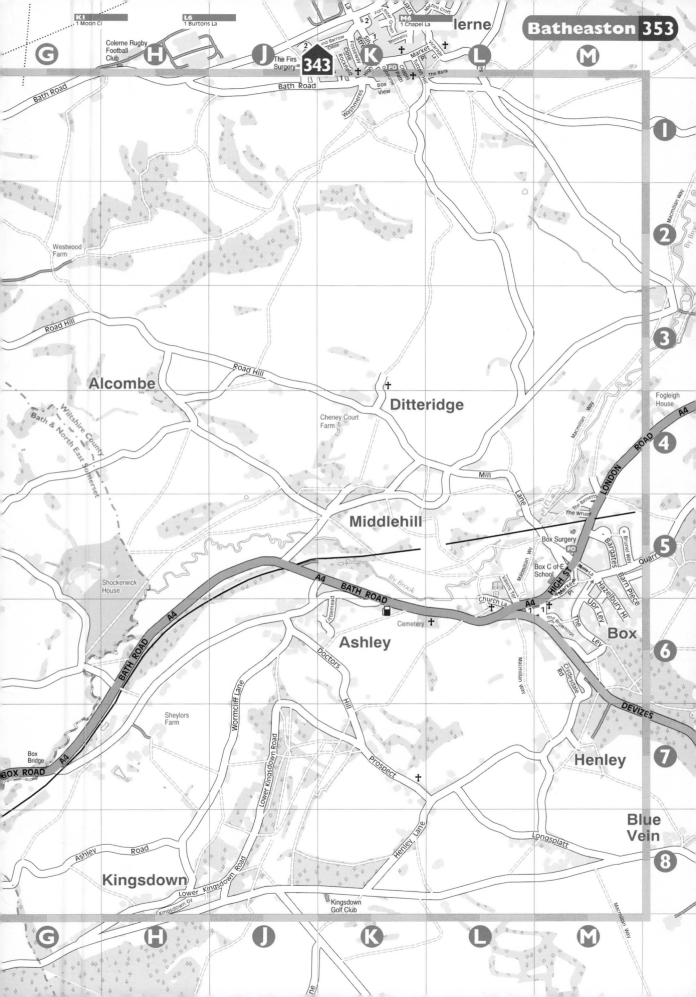

G H J 343 K L M

I
2
3
4
5
6
7
8

ierne

K1
1 Moon Cl

L6
1 Burtons La

Colerne Rugby
Football
Club

The Firs
Surgery

Bath Road

Bath Road

Ind Barrow
Close
Fosseway
Roadfield

M6
1 Chapel La

Market
Pl

Tutton Hill

The Bank

PO

Box
View

Washmeres

Macmillan Way

By Brook

Westwood
Farm

Road Hill

Road Hill

Alcombe

Ditteridge

Cheney Court
Farm

Mill
Lane

Wiltshire County
Bath & North East Somerset

Fogleigh
House

A4

LONDON ROAD

Macmillan Way

The Bassetts

The Wharf

Box Surgery

PO

Middlehill

By Brook

Shockerwick
House

A4

A4

BATH ROAD

Valens Ter

Macmillan Wy

Box C of E
School

HIGH ST

Bargates

Brunel Way

Quarr

Hazelbury Hl

Barn Piece

Cemetery

Church La

A4

Market
Pl

The
Brownings

Upr Ley

Box

The
Ley

Ashley

Doctors Hill

Clydesdale
Rd

Sheylors
Farm

Wormcliff Lane

Lower Kingsdown Road

Prospect

Henley Lane

Macmillan Way

Henley

Box
Bridge

A4

BOX ROAD

Longsplatt

Blue
Vein

Ashley Road

Kingsdown

Lower Kingsdown Road

Kingsdown Gv

Kingsdown
Golf Club

Macmillan Way

G H J K L M

Abbeydale	136 E7	Bollow	157 H3	Chedglow	283 K4	Dursley	253 K1	Grovesend	294 B4
Abbots Leigh	334 C3	Bondend	137 J8	Chedworth	167 J6	Dursley Cross	107 J5	Guiting Power	98 F5
Abenhall	130 E4	Botloe's Green	64 C6	Chedworth Laines	166 F7	Dyer's Common	304 E8	Guller's End	24 C5
Ablington	193 H7	Boughspring	246 E4	Cheltenham	2	Dymock	41 K8	The Hacket	294 B3
Abson	339 M1	Bould	125 L5	Chelworth	284 E2	Dyrham	330 E7	Hagloe	203 H1
Acton Turville	323 G5	Boulsdon	86 A5	Chelworth Lower Green	288 B5	Earthcott Green	308 B4	Hailes	75 J2
Adlestrop	103 M1	Bournes Green	210 D6	Chelworth Upper Green	288 D5	Eastcombe	210 A6	Hallen	314 C6
Alcombe	353 G3	Bournside	115 J4	Cherington	39 H5	Eastcourt	284 F5	Hall End	295 M8
Alderley	298 A1	Bournstream	277 H1	Cherington	258 D1	East Dean	106 A5	Halmore	227 K2
Alderton	51 L4	Bourton-on-the-Hill	57 K5	Chesterton	238 A5	East End	242 F5	Ham	116 F4
Alderton Fields	51 L6	Bourton-on-the-Water	122 F5	Childswickham	32 B1	East End	342 D3	Ham	250 F2
Aldsworth	194 F2	Bowbridge	208 F6	Chipmans Platt	206 B2	Easter Compton	315 H2	Hambrook	327 L4
Alkerton	206 A4	Bower Ashton	334 F7	Chipping Campden	12 D7	Eastfield	325 K4	Ham Green	324 A7
Allaston	201 K5	Bowling Green	238 D1	Chipping Sodbury	320 F2	Eastington	170 A4	Hampen Manor	119 J7
Almondsbury	306 E7	Box	233 C6	Christchurch	151 J5	Eastington	206 B3	Hampnett	144 E7
Alstone	51 G6	Box	353 M6	Churcham	133 M2	Eastleach Martin	220 D4	Hampton Fields	233 A5
Alstone	115 J1	Boxbush	106 F5	Church Down	113 M5	Eastleach Turville	220 A4	Hamshill	230 A5
Alveston	293 H6	Boxbush	157 H4	Churchdown	114 A7	Eastnor	20 E4	Hanham	337 L6
Alveston Down	292 F6	Boxwell	279 J6	Church End	25 M6	Easton	336 E2	Hanham Green	337 L8
Alvington	224 C5	Bradley	277 H3	Church End	205 G1	Easton Grey	301 L7	Hannington Wick	267 J8
Amberley	232 E4	Bradley Green	277 H4	Churchend	206 C3	Eastrip	343 M7	Hardwicke	70 D7
Ampney Crucis	239 M2	Bradley Stoke	317 G3	Churchend	276 B8	Eastville	326 E8	Hardwicke	158 D6
Ampney St Mary	240 D2	Bradlow	20 B1	Churchill	105 H6	The Eaves	200 E2	Hardwicke	159 G5
Ampney St Peter	240 C4	Brain's Green	178 D6	Church Westcote	125 G5	Ebley	207 L5	Hardwick Green	45 J5
Andoversford	118 D7	Brand Green	64 F6	Cinderford	154 B5	Ebrington	13 L6	Harescombe	184 B2
Andrews Corner	198 F5	Breadstone	227 M5	Cirencester	238 E4	Edge	184 D3	Haresfield	183 H2
Anthony's Cross	86 C7	Bread Street	208 B2	Clapton-on-the-Hill	147 H2	Edge End	152 A4	Harleywood	256 D5
Apperley	69 H6	Bream	200 C3	Claydon	49 J8	Edgeworth	211 M2	Harnhill	239 M6
Arle	93 J7	Bream's Meend	200 B2	Clay Hill	337 H1	Elberton	292 C6	Harrow Hill	130 A5
Arlebrook	183 H6	Bredon	27 G5	Claypits	205 M2	Elcombe	254 C4	Harry Stoke	327 G1
Arlingham	179 L1	Bredon's Hardwick	26 E8	Clearwell	175 H7	Eldersfield	45 G8	Hartcliffe	345 L6
Arlington	217 H1	Bredon's Norton	27 J1	Cleeve	156 C5	Elkstone	164 E5	Hartpury	88 E4
Arno's Vale	336 D7	Brentry	325 K1	Cleeve Hill	95 H1	Ellwood	176 A6	Hasfield	67 L8
Ashchurch	49 H4	Bridge End	45 H7	Clements End	199 M1	Elmbridge	112 F8	Hatherley	114 F5
Ashleworth	89 J3	Bridgend	207 G5	Clencher's Mill	20 E8	Elmore	134 D8	Hatherop	218 F4
Ashley	283 J1	Bridge Yate	339 G4	Clifford's Mesne	107 L1	Elmore Back	134 A5	Hawcross	65 L2
Ashley	353 K6	Brierley	129 G8	Clifton	335 H3	Elmstone Hardwicke	93 G2	Hawkesbury	311 M1
Ashley Down	326 B7	Brimpsfield	163 L5	Clingre End	253 L2	Elton	155 L2	Hawkesbury Upton	312 C1
Ashmead Green	229 M7	Brimps Hill	130 F2	Coaley	230 A3	Emerson's Green	328 E5	Hawling	97 L3
Ashton Gate	335 H7	Brimscombe	233 H1	Coaley Peak	230 D5	Engine Common	309 K6	Hayden	92 C8
Ashton Keynes	287 G2	Brislington	337 G2	Coalpit Heath	318 F5	English Bicknor	127 K8	Hazleton	144 C2
Ashton under Hill	29 H3	Bristol	7 J5	Coalway	176 A2	Epney	157 L8	Headley Park	345 J5
Ashton Vale	345 H1	Britain Bottom	312 D2	Coates	236 E5	Etloe	202 E3	Heath End	295 K3
Aston Crews	84 E8	Broad Campden	34 F3	Cobb's Cross	43 L4	Evenlode	81 G5	Heathfield	251 L2
Aston Cross	49 L3	Broad Marston	8 B2	Coberley	140 B7	Ewen	261 M4	Hempsted	135 J3
Aston Ingham	85 H7	Broad Moor	130 A8	Cockleford	164 C2	Fairfields	43 H6	Henbury	325 G1
Aston Magna	36 A7	Broadoak	155 L4	Codrington	330 C1	Fairford	242 E4	Henfield	318 F4
Aston on Carrant	49 M1	Broadrock	246 D6	Cold Ashton	341 J5	Fairview	2 F4	Hengrove	346 C5
Aston Somerville	30 F2	Broadway	32 E3	Cold Aston	121 L7	Falfield	275 G4	Hengrove Park	346 A5
Aston Subedge	12 C3	Broadwell	80 E7	Cold Elm	46 C5	Far Green	230 B6	Henleaze	325 L5
Aust	291 K5	Broadwell	152 A8	Coldharbour	198 E7	Farleys End	133 M8	Henley	138 C6
Avening	257 L2	Brockham End	350 A3	Coleford	175 H1	Farmcote	75 L4	Henley	353 M7
Avening Green	276 A3	Brockhampton	93 L2	Colerne	343 L8	Farmington	146 B8	Hester's Way	93 G8
Awkley	305 M3	Brockhampton	118 F2	Colethrop	183 L1	Far Oakridge	211 H7	Hethelpit Cross	66 A3
Awre	179 L6	Brockhollands	200 D4	Collafield	154 D1	Far Thrupp	209 H8	Hewelsfield	223 H2
Aylburton	224 F3	Brockweir	222 C4	Coln Rogers	192 C4	The Fence	198 D3	Hewelsfield Common	222 F1
Aylburton Common	224 D2	Brockworth	137 L6	Coln St Aldwyns	218 C4	Fiddington	48 F8	Hicks Gate	347 K3
Aylton	18 B3	Brokenborough	302 E4	Coln St Dennis	192 D1	Fiddler's Green	114 E1	Hidcote Bartrim	13 K1
Aylworth	121 H2	Bromley Heath	327 L1	Colt's Green	321 C3	Fifield	149 K1	Hidcote Boyce	13 K3
Aztec West	316 C1	Bromsberrow	43 G2	Compton Abdale	143 L5	Filands	303 J5	High Brotheridge	162 A3
Badgeworth	114 D8	Bromsberrow Heath	42 E5	Compton Green	64 F5	Filkins	221 L6	Highfield	201 L7
Badsey	10 A1	Brookend	223 M7	Compton Greenfield	315 G3	Filton	316 D8	Highfields	253 L2
Bagendon	214 A1	Brookend	227 G2	Conderton	28 D4	Filwood Park	346 B3	Highleadon	88 A8
Bagpath	232 E1	Brookthorpe	160 A6	Condicote	78 E5	Fishponds	327 H6	Highnam	110 D3
Bagpath	279 H1	Broomhill	327 G5	Coney Hill	136 E4	Fishpool	62 D4	Highnam Green	110 E6
Bagstone	295 H7	Broom Hill	337 J7	Conham	337 J6	Five Acres	151 L5	High Nash	175 J7
Bailbrook	351 M8	Broom's Green	42 A5	Coombe	277 M3	The Flat	133 J7	Highridge	344 F7
Baker's Hill	151 L8	Broughton Poggs	221 K7	Coombe Dingle	324 E3	Flaxley	131 J8	High Woolaston	223 H4
Ball's Green	233 H7	Brown's End	43 H2	Coombegreen Common	22 A5	The Folly	341 H5	Hilcot	141 K6
Bamfurlong	114 A3	Browns Hill	233 M1	Coomb's End	321 J5	Footbridge	74 E5	Hilcot End	240 B2
Barcheston	16 C7	Bubblewell	233 J6	Cornwell	82 D8	Ford	76 D4	Hill	249 M8
Barnsley	216 B4	Bubb's Hill	164 D4	Corse	66 D5	The Fording	84 A4	Hill End	26 C3
Barnwood	137 G2	Buckbury	46 D2	Corse Lawn	68 A1	Forest Green	232 C6	Hillend Green	63 L5
Barrow	91 L5	Buckland	32 C6	Cotham	335 L2	Forthampton	46 E5	Hillersland	151 L2
Barrow Common	344 D7	Buckover	294 C1	Cotswold Community	262 F7	Forthay	253 L5	Hillesley	297 M3
Barrow Gurney	344 A6	Bulley	109 L7	Cowhill	272 C8	Forwood	233 H6	Hillfields	327 K8
Barton	5 J8	Bullo	179 H3	Cowhorn Hill	338 E7	Foscot	125 M3	Hinchwick	78 D2
Barton	98 F3	Bulwark	270 A6	Cowley	164 C1	Fossebridge	168 A3	Hinnegar	313 H1
Barton End	256 E3	Burleigh	233 G4	Cranham	162 B5	Four Mile Elm	159 H6	Hinton	203 G8
Barton Hill	336 E5	Burmington	38 C2	Cress Green	206 C5	Four Oaks	63 K5	Hinton	330 E7
Barton-on-the-Heath	60 B5	Burnt Ash	233 M4	Crews Hill	106 E2	Foxcote	142 C2	Holbrook Common	339 J4
The Batch	338 D6	Burton	323 K8	Crew's Hole	337 H4	Frampton Cotterell	318 C4	Holdfast	24 E3
Batheaston	352 D7	Bury End	32 F4	Cribbs Causeway	315 H5	Frampton End	318 E3	Hollybed Common	22 B4
Batsford	57 M3	Buscot	269 J3	Cricklade	289 J2	Frampton Mansell	235 G1	Hollybush	21 K5
Battledown	3 L7	Bushley	47 K2	Crocker's Ash	126 C5	Frampton on Severn	181 J2	Holwell	197 J4
Battlescombe	210 F2	Bushley Green	47 G1	Cromhall	295 J2	France Lynch	210 D8	Holywell	277 L3
Baunton	214 C5	Bussage	209 M7	Cromhall Common	295 J4	Frenchay	327 K3	Homedowns	48 F3
Beach	349 L1	Butterrow	208 F7	Crooked End	129 H3	Fretherne	180 F4	Honington	16 C1
Beachley	270 D8	Cadbury Heath	338 C6	Cross Hill	246 E6	Frocester	206 D8	Hook Street	226 E7
Beavan's Hill	84 F5	Cainscross	208 B4	Crossways	151 G8	Frogland Cross	307 L7	Horcott	242 E5
Beckford	29 G7	Calcot	192 C2	Crossways	294 B1	Fromebridge	181 M8	Horfield	326 B4
Bedminster	335 K8	Calcott's Green	134 C5	Crudwell	284 A5	Fyfield	220 D7	Horsedown	323 M8
Bedminster Down	345 K3	Calcutt	289 J4	Culkerton	259 J6	Gadfield Elm	44 C8	Horsepools	184 C2
The Beeches	238 F2	Calmsden	191 H5	Cutsdean	76 D2	Ganborough	79 H4	Horsey Down	288 D3
Beechpike	188 D2	Cam	229 H7	Daglingworth	213 J4	Ganders Green	107 L6	Horsley	256 B2
Bencombe	254 E3	Cambridge	205 J7	Damery	276 A2	Gatwick	156 E3	Horton	311 K6
Bengrove	50 E5	Camer's Green	22 B8	Daneway	211 K8	Gaunt's Earthcott	307 K6	Horwood Riding	311 G3
Benhall	115 G3	The Camp	186 E4	Darlingscott	15 H2	Gawcombe	124 E4	Hotwells	335 J6
Bentham	138 F6	Cannop	152 D7	Daylesford	103 M3	Geat Wolford	60 A1	Houndscroft	232 D2
Berkeley	227 H8	Carterspiece	152 A2	Deerhurst	69 J3	Glasshouse	107 L4	Howley	277 G2
Berkeley Heath	227 J8	Cashes Green	207 M3	Deerhurst Walton	69 L6	Gloucester	4	Hucclecote	137 H4
Berkeley Road	228 B6	Cassey Compton	143 G8	Derry Fields	287 G3	Golden Hill	325 M5	Hudnalls	198 C7
Berrow	44 E2	Castle Eaton	266 D7	Didbrook	53 K8	Golden Valley	114 C1	Huntingford	276 B3
Berry Hill	151 J5	Castlemorton	22 F4	Didmarton	299 J7	Golden Valley	114 C1	Huntley	108 C8
Berwick	314 F5	Castletump	64 A4	Ditteridge	353 K4	Goodrich	127 J1	Hyde	76 D7
Beverston	281 C3	Catbrain	315 K5	Dixton	73 C2	Goose Green	309 M8	Hyde	233 M3
Bevington	250 A5	Caudle Green	187 L2	Dodington	321 C6	Goose Green	338 E2	Hystfield	250 D6
Bibstone	275 K8	Cerney Wick	264 B7	Donnington	42 A3	Gorsley	85 G3	Icomb	124 F1
Bibury	217 F1	Chaceley	68 F3	Donnington	79 M6	Gorsley Common	84 D3	Idbury	125 K7
Bilson Green	153 M2	Chaceley Hole	68 C1	Dorn	58 D2	Gossington	228 F2	Inchbrook	232 E3
Birdlip	163 H2	Chaceley Stock	69 G3	Down Ampney	265 G4	Gotherington	72 C3	Inglesham	268 C1
Birdwood	133 G1	Chalford	234 A1	Downend	256 B2	Grafton	29 G4	Ingst §	291 L7
Birtsmorton	23 G7	Chandler's Cross	22 B2	Downend	327 M4	Grange Village	154 F6	Innsworth	113 J5
Birts Street	22 C6	Chapel Hill	224 E3	Down Hatherley	113 C1	Great Badminton	323 H1	Iron Acton	308 F7
Bishop's Cleeve	71 M8	Charfield	276 B6	Doynton	340 B2	Great Barrington	172 E3	Itchington	308 B1
Bishop's Norton	90 D5	Charfield Green	276 B6	Draycott	35 L7	Great Doward	126 D5	Jackaments Bottom	260 C4
Bishopston	325 M7	Charfield Hill	276 B6	Draycott	229 H3	Great Rissington	148 A4	Jack's Green	185 M2
Bishopsworth	345 H6	Chargrove	115 H7	Driffield	240 A7	Great Stoke	317 G6	Joy's Green	128 C5
Bisley	210 D2	Charingworth	14 C7	Druggers End	22 E2	Great Washbourne	51 H2	Kelmscot	245 M8
Bitton	349 H3	Charlcombe	351 M8	Drybrook	129 M4	Great Witcombe	162 D1	Kelston	349 L8
Blackhorse	328 B4	Charlton Abbots	96 D6	Duckhole	273 L5	Green Bottom	130 D8	Kemble	261 J4
Blaisdon	131 L5	Charlton Kings	116 E5	Dumbleton	30 B6	Green Street	138 A8	Kemble Wick	261 H7
Blaise Hamlet	324 F1	Charlton Park	116 B4	Dunfield	266 C3	Green Street	229 L5	Kemerton	27 M4
Blakeney	202 E1	Chase End Street	21 L8	Dunkirk	312 D3	Greenway	41 L4	Kempley	62 E3
Bledington	125 L2	Chase Hill	296 F5	Dunkirk	261 J6	Greet	74 D2	Kempley Green	62 E5
Blockley	34 F8	Chastleton	81 L5	Duntisbourne Abbots	188 D6	Gretton	74 A2	Kempsford	266 C2
Blue Vein	353 M8	Chavenage Green	257 G7	Duntisbourne Leer	188 D8	Gretton Fields	51 L7	Kendleshire	318 C8
Boddington	92 A4	Chaxhill	157 H2	Duntisbourne Rouse	212 F2	Grove End	17 M8		

Kenton Green 158 B1
Kent's Green 87 G7
Ketford 64 D1
Keynsham 348 C6
Kilcot 85 K4
Kilkenny 141 L1
Kineton 98 E1
Kingham 104 C7
Kingscote 255 J6
Kingscourt 208 D8
Kingsditch 93 J6
Kingsdown 353 H8
King's Green 43 M3
Kings Hill 238 F3
Kingshill 253 J1
Kingsholm 4 E2
King's Stanley 207 H7
Kingswood 277 G7
Kingswood 338 A3
Kington 293 G2
Kinsham 27 J7
Kitebrook 59 M8
Kitlye 210 A5
The Knapp 274 B8
Knightsbridge 92 A1
Knockdown 300 A6
Knowle 346 C2
Langley 73 L6
Langridge 350 F3
Lansdown 115 J3
Lansdown 350 D5
Lasborough 279 L2
Latteridge 308 D5
Latton 264 F7
Laverton 32 B8
Lawrence Weston 324 C1
Lea 106 B3
Lea Line 106 E4
Leathern Bottle 228 D6
Lechlade 244 F7
Leckhampton 115 L7
Ledbury 19 L3
Leddington 41 J1
Leigh 287 L6
Leighterton 279 M8
The Leigh 91 G2
Leigh Woods 334 E5
Leonard Stanley 207 H8
Lewstone 126 B4
Leyhill 275 K6
Lightpill 208 B7
Lime Street 67 J2
Linden 135 M6
Linkend 45 M8
Linton 84 C4
Linton Hill 84 D5
Lintridge 43 G5
Little Badminton 313 G6
Little Barrington 172 D5
Little Barrow 80 C4
Little Beckford 28 E8
Little Bristol 276 D8
Little Compton 82 D2
Littledean 154 E3
Littledean Hill 154 D2
Little Doward 126 C6
Little Drybrook 176 A8
Little Faringdon 245 H3
Littleford 86 E1
Little Gorsley 85 J5
Little Haresfield 183 G4
Little Herbert's 116 E7
Little London 131 L2
Little Marcle 18 D5
Little Rissington 124 A7
Little Rollright 83 J2
Little Shurdington 139 G3
Little Sodbury 311 J8
Little Sodbury End 311 G7
Little Stoke 316 F4
Littleton Drew 323 M6
Littleton-upon-Severn 292 A2
Little Washbourne 51 J3
Little Welland 23 H2
Little Witcombe 138 E7
Little Wolford 38 D7
Littleworth 12 C8
Littleworth 232 E3
Lockleaze 326 E4
Long Ashton 344 C2
Longborough 79 L4
Long Compton 61 J4
Longdon 24 A6
Longdon Heath 24 C1
Longdon Hill End 23 L2
Longford 112 A5
Long Green 46 C4
Longhope 131 J1
Long Newnton 282 E6
Longney 157 L5
Longridge 185 L4
Longridge End 89 H6
Longwell Green 338 A8
Lowbands 44 A8
Lower Apperley 69 G7
Lower Berry Hill 151 H7
Lower Cam 229 G6
Lower Chedworth 191 M1
Lower Clopton 9 H3
Lower Dowdeswell 117 L7
Lower End 213 K5
Lower Hamswell 340 D8
Lower Hazel 293 G8
Lower Kilcott 298 C4
Lower Knowle 346 A2
Lower Lemington 58 F2
Lower Ley 133 H7
Lower Lode 47 L7
Lower Lydbrook 128 B6
Lower Meend 198 D6
Lower Moor 286 D8
Lower Morton 273 M7
Lower Oddington 103 H3
Lower Rea 135 G8
Lower Slaughter 123 H1
Lower Soudley 178 D2
Lower Stone 274 E1
Lower Swainswick 351 L8

Lower Swell 101 K4
Lower Tuffley 159 L1
Lower Westmancote 27 K4
Lower Wick 252 A5
Luckington 313 M7
Ludstock 19 H7
Luxley 107 G3
Lyde Green 329 G3
Lydney 225 K1
Lynworth 3 K2
Lynworth 94 C7
Lypiatt 187 J5
Maisemore 111 J4
Malmesbury 303 J7
Malswick 87 G4
Mangotsfield 328 B6
Marle Hill 93 M7
Marsden 166 A7
Marsh Common 305 G7
Marsh End 23 K8
Marshfield 342 A3
Marsh Lane 175 M7
Marston Hill 242 A8
Marston Meysey 265 M4
Matson 136 E8
Mayshill 319 G2
Mead Riding 310 E8
Meysey Hampton 241 L7
Mickleton 9 G7
Middle Duntisbourne 213 H1
Middlehill 353 K5
Middle Street 206 A5
Middle Wick 252 B6
Middle Yard 207 K8
Milbourne 303 M7
Milbury Heath 294 D2
Mile End 152 A7
Milkwall 175 M4
Mill End 169 H2
Millend 175 H4
Millend 206 C4
Millend 253 J6
Mill Hill 200 C7
Milton End 180 B1
Milton End 242 C4
Minchinhampton 233 J5
Minsterworth 134 A4
Miserden 187 K4
Mitcheldean 130 B1
Mitton 48 A7
Montpelier 336 A1
Moor End 116 B6
Moorend 161 G3
Moorend 228 D1
Moorend 328 A1
Moreton-in-Marsh 58 E5
Moreton Valence 182 D3
Mork 198 F4
Morton 293 M1
Mountain Bower 333 M7
Mount Hill 338 A5
Much Marcle 40 B5
Murcott 284 A7
Murrell's End 65 G2
Murrell's End 110 D2
Nag's Head 258 A2
Nailbridge 129 M6
Nailsworth 232 E8
Nashend 210 C4
Nastend 206 D2
Natton 49 H5
Naunton 99 K7
Nebsworth 14 B1
Netham 336 E5
Netherend 224 A6
Netherton 218 E5
Nether Westcote 125 G6
Nettleton 163 L3
Nettleton Green 333 J2
Nettleton Shrub 333 K3
New Cheltenham 338 B2
Newent 86 B5
Newerne 201 J8
New Grounds 204 D3
Newington Bagpath 279 K1
Newland 174 F3
Newmarket 232 B7
New Mills 19 L1
New Mills 201 J6
New Mills 238 F3
Newnham 155 J7
New Passage 304 C2
Newport 251 K3
Newton 273 M5
Newtown 48 E5
New Town 53 G6
New Town 82 C3
Newtown 206 D3
Newtown 226 F2
Nibley 202 C1
Nibley 319 J2
Nibley Green 252 B6
Nimlet 341 C8
Ninewells 151 L4
Norcote 239 H1
Norman Hill 229 J8
North Cerney 190 C7
North Common 338 F5
North Corner 318 B2
North End 287 H1
Northend 352 C6
Northington 179 K5
Northleach 169 K1
North Nibley 252 F7
North Stoke 349 L4
Northway 49 G1
Northwick 305 G1
Northwood Green 132 B6
North Wraxall 343 K1
Norton 90 E6
Notgrove 121 J4
Nottwood Hill 131 L3
Novers Park 345 M3
Noverton 94 F8
Nupdown 249 H6
Nupend 206 D1
Nupend 256 A2
Nuppend 224 C4

Nympsfield 231 G6
Oakle Street 133 K3
Oakley 116 E1
Oakridge 210 F8
Oaksey 285 H3
Okle Green 87 K3
Oldbury Naite 272 E6
Oldbury-on-Severn 272 E5
Oldbury on the Hill 299 J6
Oldcroft 202 A3
Old Down 292 E8
Oldend 206 F2
Old Forge 127 G1
Oldland 338 C8
Oldland Common 338 F8
Old Passage 291 H5
Old Sodbury 321 K4
Old Wharf 19 M5
Olveston 292 C8
Oridge Street 66 D7
Over 111 J7
Over 315 M1
Overbury 28 B3
Overton 180 D2
Owlpen 255 G2
Oxenhall 86 A1
Oxenton 50 B8
Ozleworth 278 E3
Paganhill 208 C3
Painswick 185 G4
Palmer's Flat 175 L3
Pamington 49 K4
Pancakehill 167 M8
Paradise 161 J8
Parkend 176 F6
Parkend 182 E1
Parkfield 329 J4
Park Hill 223 H7
The Park 115 K5
Parkway 20 B7
Patchway 316 C2
Paxford 35 M3
Pebworth 8 B1
Pendock 44 C5
Pennsylvania 341 H4
Perrott's Brook 214 B3
Petty France 312 C4
Picklenash 86 A2
Piff's Elm 92 C2
Pilley 116 A7
Pillowell 201 H2
Pillows Green 66 F3
Pilning 304 F4
Pinfarthings 232 D5
Piper's End 46 C1
Pitchcombe 184 E7
Pitt Court 253 J6
Pittville 2 F1
Pixley 18 C1
Playley Green 43 L7
The Pludds 128 F6
Plump Hill 130 C4
Plusterwine 224 A8
Podsmead 135 M7
Poole Keynes 261 L8
Poolhill 64 E4
Pope's Hill 155 H1
Portway 44 C3
Postlip 73 M8
Poulton 241 G5
The Pound 63 M1
Prescott 73 H4
Prestbury 94 D6
Preston 18 E8
Preston 41 G1
Preston 239 H5
Prior's Norton 91 H6
Priors Park 48 B6
Pucklechurch 329 J6
Puckrup 25 L5
Puckshole 208 A3
Pullens Green 272 E6
Purton 202 D5
Putley Green 18 A3
Putloe 182 C3
Pye Corner 317 M8
Quarhouse 233 J1
Quedgeley 159 G2
Queenhill 24 F5
Quenington 218 C6
Ram Hill 318 F7
The Rampings 46 E2
Randwick 207 L1
Rangeworthy 309 J2
Rea 135 H7
Readings 128 E6
Ready Token 217 G5
Redbrook 174 B2
The Reddings 114 C4
Redland 325 L8
Redmarley D'Abitot 43 K8
Redwick 304 D3
Reedcomb 190 B3
Ridgeway 327 H8
Ripple 25 J3
Rockhampton 274 B4
Rockness 256 C1
The Rocks 310 B6
Rockstowes 254 B3
Rodborough 208 B5
Rodley 157 H7
Rodmarton 259 L3
Rooksmoor 232 C1
Rowanfield 115 H1
Rowland's Green 19 H5
Ruardean 129 G4
Ruardean Hill 129 J4
Ruardean Woodside 129 G5
Ruddle 155 G8
Rudford 110 A4
Rudgeway 307 H2
Ruscombe 184 A8
Ruspidge 154 A6
Ryeford 207 J5
Rye Street 22 C7
Ryeworth 116 E4
Ryton 42 D6

St Anne's Park 337 G5
St Briavels 199 G5
St Briavels Common 222 C2
Saintbridge 136 D5
Saintbury 11 J7
St Catherine 352 A2
St Chloe 232 D3
St George 337 J4
St Mark's 115 H2
St Paul's 4 C9
St Paul's 135 M4
St Peter's 93 K8
Salford 83 J6
Salperton 120 B6
Salperton Park 120 B7
Sandhurst 89 L8
Sandpits 68 A3
Sapperton 211 M8
Sarsden 105 J8
Sarsden Halt 104 F5
Saul 181 H4
The Scarr 64 C7
Scowles 175 G1
Sea Mills 324 E6
Sedbury 270 D4
Sedgeberrow 30 C1
Selsley 208 A7
Sevenhampton 118 F3
Seven Springs 140 C4
Severn Beach 304 D5
Sezincote 57 J8
Shab Hill 139 K8
Shadwell 254 C3
Shakesfield 41 J7
Shapridge 130 F6
Sharpness 226 D1
Shaw Common 63 J7
Sheepscombe 186 A2
Shepherd's Patch 204 D6
Shepperdine 248 F8
Sherborne 171 J1
Shipston-on-Stour 16 B5
Shipton 142 E1
Shipton Moyne 302 A3
Shipton Oliffe 143 G1
Shipton Solers 142 E1
Shirehampton 324 A4
The Shoe 343 J2
Shorncote 262 D5
Shortstanding 151 G4
Shortwood 232 B8
Shortwood 328 F7
Shurdington 138 F1
Shuthonger 25 M7
Shutton 84 A3
Siddington 238 F7
Signet 197 M2
Signet Hill 173 K8
Silver Street 230 C4
Siston 329 H8
Siston Common 338 C2
Slad 185 J7
Sladbrook 65 M5
Slades Green 46 E1
Sledge Green 45 J2
Slimbridge 205 C2
Sling 175 L7
Smallbrook 224 B5
Sneyd Park 324 F7
Snig's End 66 E5
Snowshill 54 E3
Somerdale 348 A4
Somerford Keynes 262 C8
Sopworth 313 M2
Soundwell 328 A8
Southam 94 D3
South Cerney 263 H4
Southend 253 G8
Southmead 325 K2
Southrop 220 C8
Speedwell 337 J1
Springbank 92 F8
Standish 183 G6
Stanley Downton 207 G6
Stanley Pontlarge 73 K2
Stanton 54 A2
Stantway 156 D3
Stanway 53 K6
Staple Hill 328 A7
Stapleton 326 E6
Starveall 298 F7
Staunton 66 C4
Staunton 150 E5
Staverton 92 A7
Steam Mills 129 M7
Stinchcombe 252 D2
Stockend 184 B4
Stockwell 163 K2
Stockwood 346 F5
Stockwood Vale 347 K5
Stoke Bishop 324 F5
Stoke Gifford 316 F6
Stoke Orchard 71 G5
Stone 251 G8
Stone Hill 338 A7
Stonehouse 207 J3
Stourton 39 K5
Stourton Hill 39 L7
Stowe 199 G1
Stowe Green 199 H1
Stowell 168 G4
Stow-on-the-Wold 101 M3
Strand 156 B4
Stratford 25 L1
Stratton 214 A7
Stretton-on-Fosse 36 F2
Stroat 247 J3
Stroud 208 C2
Stroud Green 183 H7
Stub Riding 310 D8
Stumps Cross 76 B2
Sudgrove 187 J6
Sundayshill 274 E3
Sunhill 241 J7
Sutton-under-Brailes 39 L4
Swanley 251 L6
Swindon 93 M4
Swineford 349 J4

Syde 187 M1
Symonds Yat 126 F6
Synwell 277 L4
Syreford 118 D6
Taddington 54 C8
Tadwick 351 G2
Talbot's End 295 L1
Tarlton 236 B7
Taynton 108 D3
Taynton 173 K3
Teddington 50 B5
Teddington Hands 50 D3
Temple Guiting 76 E6
Tetbury 282 A4
Tetbury Upton 257 K8
Tewkesbury 47 M6
Thames Head 237 H8
The Mythe 48 A2
Thickwood 343 L6
Thornbury 293 K6
Througham 187 G7
Thrupp 209 J2
Tibberton 109 K3
Tickmorend 256 B1
Tidenham 247 G7
Tidenham Chase 246 E1
Tidmington 38 A2
Tillers' Green 41 J5
Tilsdown 229 H7
Tiltups End 256 D4
Tirley 68 B5
Tirley Knowle 67 L3
Tockington 306 C2
Toddington 52 F5
Todenham 37 L6
Tormarton 332 A1
Tortworth 275 L4
Totteroak 311 G6
Town Street 68 B4
Townwell 295 K2
Tredington 70 C3
Tredworth 136 B4
Tresham 278 C3
Trewen 126 A2
Triangle 222 D3
Trow Green 199 L1
Tuffley 136 A8
Tumpy Green 228 C3
Tunley 211 J6
Turkdean 145 H4
Tutnalls 225 L1
Tutshill 270 B2
Twigworth 112 C2
The Twittocks 25 M4
Two Bridges 178 D5
Two Mile Hill 337 K2
Twyning 26 B5
Twyning Green 26 C5
The Tynings 139 H1
Tytherington 294 E6
Uckinghall 25 H2
Uckington 92 F5
Uley 254 D2
Up Hatherley 114 F6
Uplands 209 G2
Upleadon 87 H1
Upleadon Court 87 M1
Upper Brailes 17 L7
Upper Cam 229 K7
Upper Coberley 141 G7
Upper Dowdeswell 117 L8
Upper End 169 L3
Upper End 213 M1
Upper Framilode 181 G2
Upper Hill 250 A6
Upper Inglesham 268 D6
Upper Kilcott 298 F6
Upper Ley 132 E3
Upper Lode 47 L4
Upper Lybrook 128 D7
Upper Minety 285 L8
Upper Morton 274 A7
Upper Oddington 103 G4
Upper Quinton 9 J2
Upper Rissington 124 D7
Upper Siddington 238 D7
Upper Slaughter 100 F7
Upper Soudley 178 C3
Upper Swainswick 351 J6
Upper Swell 101 K1
Upper Up 263 G5
Upper Weston 350 D8
Upper Wick 252 B5
Upper Wraxall 343 G2
Upthorpe 229 K6
Upton 173 L5
Upton Bishop 62 A8
Upton Cheyney 349 K3
Upton St Leonards 161 L7
Viney Hill 202 B2
Vinney Green 328 C4
Walham 111 M6
Wallow Green 232 B8
Wallsworth 90 C8
Walton Cardiff 48 C6
Wanswell 226 F4
Wapley 320 A2
Warden Hill 115 H6
Warmley 338 C4
Warmley Hill 338 B3
Warmley Tower 338 D3
Waterend 157 J2
Waterhay 287 L4
Waterlane 210 F5
Watermead 138 A7
Watermoor 238 D4
Watledge 232 E6
Watley's End 318 C4
Wayend Street 21 G5
Webb's Heath 339 G3
Welland Stone 23 K1
Welsh Bicknor 128 A2
Westbury-on-Severn 155 M3
Westbury on Trym 325 G5
Westbury Park 325 K7
West Crudwell 283 M4
West End 32 E5
Westend 206 B1

West End 257 K3
Westend 272 D5
West End 296 A5
Westerleigh 319 J7
Westerleigh Hill 319 M8
Westington 34 C1
West Kington 333 G4
West Kington Wick 333 K5
West Littleton 331 L8
Westmancote 27 L3
Westonbirt 300 F1
Weston-sub-Edge 11 M4
Westrip 207 L3
Westwell 197 G2
Whaddon 3 K3
Whaddon 160 B3
Wheatenhurst 181 L5
Whelford 267 J1

Whichford 61 M1
Whitchurch 126 E3
Whitchurch 346 F7
Whitebrook 198 B1
Whitecliff 175 H2
Whitecroft 200 F2
White End 44 D2
Whitehall 336 E2
Whiteleaved Oak 21 L7
Whiteshill 184 C7
Whiteshill 317 L8
Whiteway 187 G2
Whiteway 256 B1
Whitfield 274 F8
Whitminster 181 M6
Whittington 118 A4
Wibdon 247 H4
Wick 339 M5

Wickhamford 10 A4
Wickridge Street 67 J8
Wick Street 185 H7
Wickwar 296 C6
Wiggold 215 H5
Willersey 11 H7
Willesley 300 E5
Willington 16 E8
Willsbridge 348 D1
Winchcombe 74 B5
Windmill Hill 336 A8
Windrush 172 B5
Windsoredge 232 B6
Winson 192 D5
Winstone 188 C3
Winterbourne 317 M5
Winterbourne Down 318 B7
Wishanger 186 F3

Withington 142 C7
Withywood 345 H7
Woodbridge 166 F1
Woodchester 232 B1
Woodcroft 246 D7
Woodfield 229 G8
Woodford 251 J7
Woodhouse Down 306 F4
Woodmancote 72 D8
Woodmancote 189 M4
Woodmancote 253 J3
Wood Stanway 53 M8
Woolaston 223 L8
Woolaston Common 223 M4
Woolaston Slade 223 K6
Woolaston Woodside 223 L5
Woolley 351 H5
Woolridge 89 H7

Woolstone 72 C7
Worley 232 C7
Wormington 31 G6
Worrall Hill 152 C1
Wortley 277 L7
Wotton 5 J5
Wotton-under-Edge 277 L4
Wyck Rissington 123 M3
Wyegate Green 198 D2
Wymans Brook 93 L5
Yanley 344 E3
Yanworth 168 C3
Yate 319 M2
Yate Rocks 310 B5
Yorkley 201 L3
Yorkley Slade 177 L8

USING THE STREET INDEX

Street names are listed alphabetically. Each street name is followed by its postal town or area locality, the Postcode District, the page number, and the reference to the square in which the name is found.

Example: **Abbey Ct** BRSG/KWL/STAPK BS4 .... 337 H6 🔟

Some entries are followed by a number in a blue box. This number indicates the location of the street within the referenced grid square. The full street name is listed at the side of the map page.

GENERAL ABBREVIATIONS

ACC	ACCESS	CTYD	COURTYARD	HLS	HILLS	MWY	MOTORWAY
ALY	ALLEY	CUTT	CUTTINGS	HO	HOUSE	N	NORTH
AP	APPROACH	CV	COVE	HOL	HOLLOW	NE	NORTH EAST
AR	ARCADE	CYN	CANYON	HOSP	HOSPITAL	NW	NORTH WEST
ASS	ASSOCIATION	DEPT	DEPARTMENT	HRB	HARBOUR	O/P	OVERPASS
AV	AVENUE	DL	DALE	HTH	HEATH	OFF	OFFICE
BCH	BEACH	DM	DAM	HTS	HEIGHTS	ORCH	ORCHARD
BLDS	BUILDINGS	DR	DRIVE	HVN	HAVEN	OV	OVAL
BND	BEND	DRO	DROVE	HWY	HIGHWAY	PAL	PALACE
BNK	BANK	DRY	DRIVEWAY	IMP	IMPERIAL	PAS	PASSAGE
BR	BRIDGE	DWGS	DWELLINGS	IN	INLET	PAV	PAVILION
BRK	BROOK	E	EAST	IND EST	INDUSTRIAL ESTATE	PDE	PARADE
BTM	BOTTOM	EMB	EMBANKMENT	INF	INFIRMARY	PH	PUBLIC HOUSE
BUS	BUSINESS	EMBY	EMBASSY	INFO	INFORMATION	PK	PARK
BVD	BOULEVARD	ESP	ESPLANADE	INT	INTERCHANGE	PKWY	PARKWAY
BY	BYPASS	EST	ESTATE	IS	ISLAND	PL	PLACE
CATH	CATHEDRAL	EX	EXCHANGE	JCT	JUNCTION	PLN	PLAIN
CEM	CEMETERY	EXPY	EXPRESSWAY	JTY	JETTY	PLNS	PLAINS
CEN	CENTRE	EXT	EXTENSION	KG	KING	PLZ	PLAZA
CFT	CROFT	F/O	FLYOVER	KNL	KNOLL	POL	POLICE STATION
CH	CHURCH	FC	FOOTBALL CLUB	L	LAKE	PR	PRINCE
CHA	CHASE	FK	FORK	LA	LANE	PREC	PRECINCT
CHYD	CHURCHYARD	FLD	FIELD	LDG	LODGE	PREP	PREPARATORY
CIR	CIRCLE	FLDS	FIELDS	LGT	LIGHT	PRIM	PRIMARY
CIRC	CIRCUS	FLS	FALLS	LK	LOCK	PROM	PROMENADE
CL	CLOSE	FLS	FLATS	LKS	LAKES	PRS	PRINCESS
CLFS	CLIFFS	FM	FARM	LNDG	LANDING	PRT	PORT
CMP	CAMP	FT	FORT	LTL	LITTLE	PT	POINT
CNR	CORNER	FWY	FREEWAY	LWR	LOWER	PTH	PATH
CO	COUNTY	FY	FERRY	MAG	MAGISTRATE	PZ	PIAZZA
COLL	COLLEGE	GA	GATE	MAN	MANSIONS	QD	QUADRANT
COM	COMMON	GAL	GALLERY	MD	MEAD	QU	QUEEN
COMM	COMMISSION	GDN	GARDEN	MDW	MEADOWS	QY	QUAY
CON	CONVENT	GDNS	GARDENS	MEM	MEMORIAL	R	RIVER
COT	COTTAGE	GLD	GLADE	MKT	MARKET	RBT	ROUNDABOUT
COTS	COTTAGES	GLN	GLEN	MKTS	MARKETS	RD	ROAD
CP	CAPE	GN	GREEN	ML	MALL	RDG	RIDGE
CPS	COPSE	GND	GROUND	ML	MILL	REP	REPUBLIC
CR	CREEK	GRA	GRANGE	MNR	MANOR	RES	RESERVOIR
CREM	CREMATORIUM	GRG	GARAGE	MS	MEWS	RFC	RUGBY FOOTBALL CLUB
CRS	CRESCENT	GT	GREAT	MSN	MISSION	RI	RISE
CSWY	CAUSEWAY	GTWY	GATEWAY	MT	MOUNT	RP	RAMP
CT	COURT	GV	GROVE	MTN	MOUNTAIN	RW	ROW
CTRL	CENTRAL	HGR	HIGHER	MTS	MOUNTAINS	S	SOUTH
CTS	COURTS	HL	HILL	MUS	MUSEUM	SCH	SCHOOL

SE	SOUTH EAST
SER	SERVICE AREA
SH	SHORE
SHOP	SHOPPING
SKWY	SKYWAY
SMT	SUMMIT
SOC	SOCIETY
SP	SPUR
SPR	SPRING
SQ	SQUARE
ST	STREET
STN	STATION
STR	STREAM
STRD	STRAND
SW	SOUTH WEST
TDG	TRADING
TER	TERRACE
THWY	THROUGHWAY
TNL	TUNNEL
TOLL	TOLLWAY
TPK	TURNPIKE
TR	TRACK
TRL	TRAIL
TWR	TOWER
U/P	UNDERPASS
UNI	UNIVERSITY
UPR	UPPER
V	VALE
VA	VALLEY
VIAD	VIADUCT
VIL	VILLA
VIS	VISTA
VLG	VILLAGE
VLS	VILLAS
VW	VIEW
W	WEST
WD	WOOD
WHF	WHARF
WK	WALK
WKS	WALKS
WLS	WELLS
WY	WAY
YD	YARD
YHA	YOUTH HOSTEL

POSTCODE TOWNS AND AREA ABBREVIATIONS

ALMDB	Almondsbury
AVONM	Avonmouth
BAD	Badminton
BATHSE	Bath south & east
BBLUN	Broad Blunsdon
BDWAY	Broadway
BMSTR	Bedminster
BMSTRD/HC/WWD	Bedminster Down/ Hartcliffe/Withywood
BRKLY	Berkeley
BRSG/KWL/STAPK	Brislington/Knowle/ St Anne's Park
BRSTK/PCHW	Bradley Stoke/Patchway
BUR/CRTN	Burford/Carterton
BWTH/CHD	Brockworth/Churchdown
CBATH/BATHN	Central Bath/Bath north
	Central Bristol/ Floating Harbour
CBRIS/FH	

CBRISNE	Central Bristol north & east
CFTN/FAIL	Clifton/Failand
CHCAM	Chipping Campden
CHELT	Cheltenham
CHELTE/BC	Cheltenham east/ Bishop's Cleeve
CHELTS	Cheltenham south
CHELTW	Cheltenham west
CHEP	Chepstow
CHNTN	Chipping Norton
CHPMW/MSHF	Chippenham west/ Marshfield
CIND	Cinderford
CIR	Cirencester
CLFD	Coleford
COR/BOX	Corsham/Box
COTS	Cotswolds
DSLY	Dursley

EVE	Evesham
EVILLE/WHL	Eastville/Whitehall
FGDN	Faringdon
FRCTL/WBN	Frampton Cotterell/ Winterbourne
GL	Gloucester
GLE	Gloucester east
HGHW	Highworth
HGRV/WHIT	Hengrove/Whitchurch
HNBRY/STHM	Henbury/Southmead
HNLZ/SM/SNYPK/WT	Henleaze/ Sea Mills/Sneyd Park/ Westbury-on-Trym
HORF/LLZ	Horfield/Lockleaze
KEYN	Keynsham
KGWD/HNM	Kingswood/Hanham
LED	Ledbury
LGASH	Long Ashton

LYD	Lydney
MALM	Malmesbury
MANG/FISH	Mangotsfield/Fishponds
MIM	Moreton-in-Marsh
MONM	Monmouth
MTCHDN	Mitcheldean
NAIL	Nailsea
NWNT	Newent
OLD/WMLY/WICK	Oldland/ Warmley/Wick
PER	Pershore
PTSHD/EG	Portishead/ Easton-in-Gordano
RBANSW	Rural Banbury south & west
RDLND/MONT	Redland/Montpelier
RGTMLV	Rural Great Malvern
RSTROUD/NAIL	Rural Stroud/Nailsworth

RTEWK/TIB	Rural Tewkesbury/ Tibberton
RWYE	Ross-on-Wye
SHPSTR	Shipston-on-Stour
STNHO	Stonehouse
STRAT	Stratford-upon-Avon
STROUD	Stroud
SWDNW	Swindon west/Purton
TET	Tetbury
TEWK	Tewkesbury
THNB/SVB	Thornbury/Severn Beach
UUSV	Upton upon Severn
VGL	Vale of Gloucester
WUE	Wotton-under-Edge
YATE/CS	Yate/Chipping Sodbury

A

Aaron Rd CIR GL7 .... 239 H7
Abbenesse RSTROUD/NAIL GL6 ... 210 A8
Abbey Ct
  BRSG/KWL/STAPK BS4 .... 337 H6 🔟
Abbeydale FRCTL/WBN BS36 ... 318 A5
Abbey La THNB/SVB BS35 .... 293 M5
Abbeymead Av GLE GL4 .... 136 F4
Abbey Meadow TEWK GL20 ... 48 B8 🔟
Abbey Pk KEYN BS31 .... 348 B5
Abbey Rd
  HNLZ/SM/SNYPK/WT BS9 ... 325 H5
  VGL GL2 .... 4 A8
Abbey Rw MALM SN16 .... 303 J8
Abbey St CIND GL14 .... 154 B3
  WUE GL12 .... 277 H6
Abbey Wy CIR GL7 .... 238 B1
Abbeywood Dr
  HNLZ/SM/SNYPK/WT BS9 ... 324 E6 🔟
Abbots Av KGWD/HNM BS15 ... 337 L7
Abbots Cl CHELT GL50 .... 115 K6
Abbots Cl HGRV/WHIT BS14 ... 346 C8

Abbots Court Dr TEWK GL20 .... 26 A6
Abbotsford Rd
  RDLND/MONT BS6 .... 335 K2
Abbots Leigh Rd CFTN/FAIL BS8 334 D4
Abbots Leys Rd COTS GL54 ..... 74 B6
Abbots Ms CHELTE/BC GL52 .... 94 A1
Abbots Rd CIR GL7 .... 238 E3 🔟
  GLE GL4 .... 137 G5
  KGWD/HNM BS15 .... 347 L1
  TEWK GL20 .... 48 A7
Abbots Vw CIND GL14 .... 154 B6
Abbots Wk CIR GL7 .... 244 F7
Abbots Wy
  HNLZ/SM/SNYPK/WT BS9 ... 325 M5
  STNHO GL10 .... 207 G5
Abbotswood
  KGWD/HNM BS15 .... 337 M4 🔟
  YATE/CS BS37 .... 319 M4 🔟
Abbotswood Rd
  BWTH/CHD GL3 .... 138 A6
Abbott Rd THNB/SVB BS35 ..... 304 C6
Abbotts Gdn MALM SN16 .... 303 J8
Abercrombie Cl LED HR8 .... 19 L2 🔟

Aberdeen Rd
  RDLND/MONT BS6 .... 335 K2
Abingdon Court La HGHW SN6 289 G3
Abingdon Rd MANG/FISH BS16 327 J8
Ableton La HNBRY/STHM BS10 314 B3
  THNB/SVB BS35 .... 304 C5
Ableton Wk
  HNLZ/SM/SNYPK/WT BS9 ... 324 E6 🔟
Abnash RSTROUD/NAIL GL6 ... 210 A8
Abraham Cl EVILLE/WHL BS5 ... 336 D3 🔟
Abson Rd MANG/FISH BS16 .... 329 K6
  OLD/WMLY/WICK BS30 .... 339 L1
Acacia Av MANG/FISH BS16 .... 327 L7
Acacia Cl CHELTE/BC GL52 .... 94 C6
  LYD GL15 .... 200 D3 🔟
  MANG/FISH BS16 .... 327 L8 🔟
Acacia Ct KEYN BS31 .... 347 L7 🔟
Acacia Dr DSLY GL11 .... 229 J8
Acacia Pk CHELTE/BC GL52 .... 71 M6
Acacia Rd MANG/FISH BS16 .... 327 M8
Acer Cl BUR/CRTN OX18 .... 197 M4
Acer Gv VGL GL2 .... 159 G1
Acomb Crs CHELTE/BC GL52 ... 116 D5 🔟
Acorn Gv
  BMSTRD/HC/WWD BS13 ...... 345 G5

The Acorns RWYE HR9 .... 106 B4 🔟
Acraman's Rd BMSTR BS3 .... 6 D8
Acresbush Cl
  BMSTRD/HC/WWD BS13 ...... 345 J6
Acre St STROUD GL5 .... 208 E4
Acton Rd MANG/FISH BS16 .... 327 J8 🔟
Adams Hay
  BRSG/KWL/STAPK BS4 .... 346 F2 🔟
Adams Wy CLFD GL16 .... 151 J6
Adderly Ga MANG/FISH BS16 .. 328 D4
Addiscombe Rd
  HGRV/WHIT BS14 .... 346 D6
Addison Rd BMSTR BS3 .... 336 A8
Addis Rd CHELTW GL51 .... 95 K8 🔟
Addymore DSLY GL11 .... 229 H6 🔟
Adelaide Gdns STNHO GL10 ... 207 G2 🔟
Adelaide Pl EVILLE/WHL BS5 ... 336 D5 🔟
  MANG/FISH BS16 .... 327 H7 🔟
Adelaide St GL GL1 .... 136 C4
Adey's La WUE GL12 .... 277 K2
Admington La SHPSTR CV36 ...... 9 M5
Admiral Cl CHELTW GL51 .... 114 F1
Admirals Cl LYD GL15 .... 200 D2 🔟
Aesops Orch CHELTE/BC GL52 72 E8
Agate St BMSTR BS3 .... 335 K8

Aggs Hl CHELTE/BC GL52 ...... 116 F2
Aggs La CHELTE/BC GL52 .... 72 C5
Aiken St EVILLE/WHL BS5 ...... 336 D5
Aintree Dr MANG/FISH BS16 ... 328 E4
Air Balloon Rd EVILLE/WHL BS5 337 J4
Airport Rd HGRV/WHIT BS14 ... 346 C3
Aisne Rd LYD GL15 .... 201 M2
Akeman Rd CIR GL7 .... 238 E3 🔟
Akermans Orch NWNT UL18 ... 86 B3
Alard Rd BRSG/KWL/STAPK BS4 346 B4
Albany STNHO GL10 .... 207 G2
Albany Ga BRSTK/PCHW BS34 317 G6
Albany Rd CHELT GL50 .... 115 K4
  RDLND/MONT BS6 .... 336 B2 🔟
Albany St GL GL1 .... 5 H9 🔟
  GL GL1 .... 136 B4
  KGWD/HNM BS15 .... 337 L3
Albany Wy
  OLD/WMLY/WICK BS30 .... 338 D5
Albemarle Ga CHELT GL50 ..... 93 M7
Albemarle Rd BWTH/CHD GL3 113 M6
Albermarle Rw
  CFTN/FAIL BS8 .... 335 H5 🔟
Albert Crs CBRISNE BS2 .... 7 M7
Albert Dr CHELTE/BC GL52 ...... 94 A7

Albert Gv *EVILLE/WHL* BS5 ...... **337** H3
Alberton Rd *MANG/FISH* BS16 .... **328** B6
Albert Pde *EVILLE/WHL* BS5 ..... **336** E3
Albert Pk *RDLND/MONT* BS6 ..... **336** B2
Albert Park Pl
  RDLND/MONT BS6 .... **336** A2
Albert Pl *CHELTE/BC* GL52 .... **2** F3
  HNLZ/SM/SNYPK/WT BS9 .... **325** J4
Albert Rd *CBRISNE* BS2 .... **7** M8
  CBRISNE BS2 .... **336** D7
  CHELTE/BC GL52 .... **3** G2
  CHELTE/BC GL52 .... **94** A7
  CIND GL14 .... **154** A4
  CLFD GL16 .... **175** J1
  KEYN BS31 .... **348** A6
  KGWD/HNM BS15 .... **337** M6
  LED HR8 .... **19** L4
  MANG/FISH BS16 .... **328** B4
  STROUD GL5 .... **233** H2
  THNB/SVB BS35 .... **304** C5
Albert St *CHELT* GL50 .... **2** C2
  GL **5** G6
  LYD GL15 .... **201** J7
Albert Ter *MANG/FISH* BS16 .... **327** H7
Albion Cl *MANG/FISH* BS16 ..... **328** B6
Albion Pl *CHELTE/BC* GL52 ..... **2** E4
Albion Rd *CIND* GL14 .... **154** B1
  EVILLE/WHL BS5 .... **336** D2
Albion St *CHELTE/BC* GL52 ..... **2** E5
  CIR GL7 .... **214** B8
  EVILLE/WHL BS5 .... **336** E3
  GL1 .... **4** D7
Albion Wk *CHELTE/BC* GL52 .... **2** D4
Albright La *LED* HR8 .... **43** H3
Alcotts Gn *VGL* GL2 .... **90** A8
Alcove Rd *MANG/FISH* BS16 .... **327** G8
Alder Cl *VGL* GL2 .... **112** E7
Aldercombe Rd
  HNLZ/SM/SNYPK/WT BS9 ... **324** E3
Alderdale *LYD* GL15 .... **201** K7
Alderdown Cl *AVONM* BS11 .... **324** C3
Alder Dr *EVILLE/WHL* BS5 ..... **337** G2
Aldergate St *STNHO* GL10 .... **207** H4
Alderley Rd *WUE* GL12 .... **297** M2
Aldermoor Wy
  OLD/WMLY/WICK BS30 .... **338** A7
Aldernay Av
  BRSG/KWL/STAPK BS4.... **337** H7
Alders Gn *VGL* GL2 .... **112** D6
The Alders *CHELTS* GL53 ..... **115** K7
Alderton Cl *GLE* GL4 .... **137** G7
Alderton Rd *CHELTW* GL51 .... **115** C3
  HORF/LLZ BS7 .... **326** A3
Alder Wy *RSTROUD/NAIL* GL6 .. **210** A7
Aldridge Cl *CHELT* GL50 ...... **2** B1
Aldsworth Cl *CIR* GL7 .... **243** G4
Aldwick Av
  BMSTRD/HC/WWD BS13.... **345** L8
Alexander Dr *CIR* GL7 .... **238** B5
Alexander Gdns *TET* GL8 ..... **281** M3
Alexander Rd *MALM* SN16 .... **303** G7
Alexandra Cl
  MANG/FISH BS16 .... **327** M7
Alexandra Gdns
  MANG/FISH BS16 .... **327**M7
Alexandra Pk *MANG/FISH* BS16 .. **327**M7
  RDLND/MONT BS6........ **335** L1
Alexandra Rd
  BMSTRD/HC/WWD BS13.... **345** H4
  CFTN/FAIL BS8 .... **335** K3
  CHEP NP16 .... **270** B5
  FRCTL/WBN BS36........ **318** F4
  GL **5** H4
  HNBRY/STHM BS10 ...... **325** L3
  KGWD/HNM BS15 .... **337** M6
Alexandra Sq *CHNTN* 0X7 .... **105** M1
Alexandra St *CHELT* GL50 .... **115** K4
Alexandra Wy *TEWK* GL20.... **48** F4
  THNB/SVB BS35 .... **273** K8
Alford Rd
  BRSG/KWL/STAPK BS4.... **346** E1
Alfred Rd *CBRISNE* BS2 ...... **6** E1
Alfred Pde *CBRISNE* BS2 ..... **6** E1
Alfred Pl *CBRISNE* BS2 ...... **335** L3
Alfred Rd *BMSTR* BS3 .... **335**M8
  RDLND/MONT BS6 .... **325** J7
Alfred St *CBRISNE* BS2 ...... **7** L4
  EVILLE/WHL BS5 .... **336** E3
  GL1 .... **5** J9
Algiers St *BMSTR* BS3 ...... **335**M8
Alice Crs *CHEP* NP16 .... **270** C7
Alington Cl *GL* GL1 .... **5** J7
Alkerton Rd *STNHO* GL10..... **206** B4
Allanmead Rd
  HGRV/WHIT BS14 ...... **346** D3
Allaston Rd *LYD* GL15 ...... **201** K5
Allendale Cl *VGL* GL2 ...... **112** E7
Allen Dr *STROUD* GL5 ...... **208** B3
Allenfield Rd *CHELTS* GL53 .. **115** L6
Allengrove La
  CHPMW/MSHF SN14 ..... **313** L8
Allerton Crs *HGRV/WHIT* BS14.. **346** C6
Allerton Gdns *HGRV/WHIT* BS14.. **346** D6
Allerton Rd *HGRV/WHIT* BS14.. **346** C8
Allfoxton Rd *HORF/LLZ* BS7 .. **326** C8
All Hallows Rd
  EVILLE/WHL BS5 .... **336** D3
Allington Dr
  OLD/WMLY/WICK BS30 ... **338** B7
Allington Rd *BMSTR* BS3 .... **6** C7
Allison Av
  BRSG/KWL/STAPK BS4.... **337** G7
Allison Rd
  BRSG/KWL/STAPK BS4.... **337** G8
Allotment La *CIR* GL7 ...... **240** A2
All Saints' La *CBRIS/FH* BS1 .. **6** F4
All Saints' Rd *CFTN/FAIL* BS8 .. **335** J3
  CHELTE/BC GL52 .... **3** G5
  GL **5** G6
  LYD GL15 .... **178** E8
  STROUD GL5 .... **208** F3
All Saints' St *CBRIS/FH* BS1 .. **6** F3
All Saints' Ter *CHELTE/BC* GL52 .. **3** H4
All Saints' Villas Rd
  CHELTE/BC GL52 .... **3** G4
Allsopp Cl *CIND* GL14 ...... **155** H7

Alma Cl *CHELTW* GL51 .... **115** H4
  KGWD/HNM BS15 .... **338** A3
Alma Pl *GL* GL1 .... **135** M4
Alma Rd *CFTN/FAIL* BS8 ..... **335** J5
  CHELTW GL51 .... **115** H5
  KGWD/HNM BS15 .... **338** A2
Alma Road Av *CFTN/FAIL* BS8 .. **335** K3
Alma Ter *GL* GL1 .... **135** M4
Alma Vale Rd *CFTN/FAIL* BS8 .. **335** J3
Almeda Rd *EVILLE/WHL* BS5 .. **337** J3
Almond Cl *GLE* GL4 .... **136** F8
Almond Wk *LYD* GL15 ...... **201** K7
Almond Wy *MANG/FISH* BS16 .. **328** B6
Almorah Rd *BMSTR* BS3 .... **336** A8
Almshouses Rd *CLFD* GL16 .. **174** E4
Alney Ter *GL* GL1 .... **4** B1
Alpha Cl *TEWK* GL20 .... **48** E4
Alpha Rd *BMSTR* BS3 ...... **6** E8
Alpine Cl *GLE* GL4 .... **136** D5
Alpine Rd *EVILLE/WHL* BS5 .. **336** E2
Alsop Rd *KGWD/HNM* BS15 .. **337** M3
Alstone Av *CHELTW* GL51 ... **115** K1
Alstone Cft *CHELTW* GL51 ... **115** K1
Alstone La *CHELTW* GL51 ... **115** J1
Althorp Cl *GL* GL1 .... **159** K1
Alton Rd *HORF/LLZ* BS7 .... **326** C5
Altringham Rd
  EVILLE/WHL BS5 .... **336** F3
Alverstoke *HGRV/WHIT* BS14 .. **346** B4
Alverton Dr *CHELTE/BC* GL52 .. **94** A1
Alveston Gra *CHCAM* GL55 .. **8** F8
Alveston Hl *THNB/SVB* BS35 .. **293** J8
Alveston Rd *ALMDB* BS32 ... **292** E8
Alveston Wk
  HNLZ/SM/SNYPK/WT BS9 .. **324** D4
Alwin St *GL* GL1 .... **4** F4
Alwins Ct
  OLD/WMLY/WICK BS30 ... **338** B7
Amaranth Wy *CHELTW* GL51 .. **115** H6
Amberley Cl *KEYN* BS31 .... **348** A1
  MANG/FISH BS16 .... **327** M4
Amberley Rd
  BRSTK/PCHW BS34 ..... **316** D3
  CHELTW GL51 .... **115** C1
  GLE GL4 .... **136** D6
  MANG/FISH BS16 .... **327** M4
Amberley Wy *WUE* GL12 .... **296** D6
Amble Cl *KGWD/HNM* BS15 .. **338** B4
Ambleside Av
  HNBRY/STHM BS10 ..... **325** K2
Ambra V *CFTN/FAIL* BS8 .... **335** J5
Ambra V East *CFTN/FAIL* BS8 .. **335** J5
Ambra V South
  CFTN/FAIL BS8 .... **335** J5
Ambra V West *CFTN/FAIL* BS8 .. **335** J5
Ambrose Cl *CLFD* GL16 ..... **151** M8
Ambrose Pl *CHELT* GL50..... **2** C4
Ambrose Rd *CFTN/FAIL* BS8 .. **335** J5
Ambrose St *CHELT* GL50..... **2** C4
Amercombe Wk
  HGRV/WHIT BS14 ...... **346** F4
America Gdns *NWNT* GL18 .. **86** C3
Ampney La *CIND* GL14 ...... **132** B3
Anbrook Crs *GLE* GL4 ...... **137** G4
Anchor Rd *CBRIS/FH* BS1 ... **6** B5
  KGWD/HNM BS15 .... **338** C2
Ancient Rd *CLFD* GL16 ..... **151** H1
Andereach Cl *HGRV/WHIT* BS14 .. **346** D4
Anderson Dr *STNHO* GL10 .. **207** H4
Andorra Wy *BWTH/CHD* GL3 .. **113** K5
Andover Rd
  BRSG/KWL/STAPK BS4.... **346** B1
  CHELT GL50 .... **2** A8
  CHELT GL50 .... **115** K3
Andover Wk *CHELT* GL50.... **2** A9
Andrew's Cl *GLE* GL4 ...... **160** B6
Angela Wy *GLE* GL4 .... **137** H6
Angels Gnd
  BRSG/KWL/STAPK BS4.... **337** H5
Angers Rd *BRSG/KWL/STAPK* BS4 .. **7** K9
Anglesea Pl *CFTN/FAIL* BS8 .. **335** J1
Anne Hathaway Dr
  BWTH/CHD GL3 .... **114** A6
Anns Wk *MTCHDN* GL17..... **130** C3
Ann Wicks Rd *VGL* GL2 .... **181** J6
Ansdell Dr *BWTH/CHD* GL3 .. **138** A5
Ansell Cl *CHELT* GL50 ...... **115** H5
Anstey's Rd *KGWD/HNM* BS15 .. **337** K6
Anstey St *EVILLE/WHL* BS5 .. **336** D2
Antelope Paddock *COTS* GL54 .. **169** J1
Anthea Rd *EVILLE/WHL* BS5 .. **337** G1
Anthony's Cross *NWNT* GL18 .. **86** C7
Antrim Rd
  HNBRY/STHM BS10 ..... **325** L2
Anvil St *CBRISNE* BS2 ...... **7** K4
A P Ellis Rd *COTS* GL54 .... **124** D8
Apperley Ct *YATE/CS* BS37 .. **319** M3
Apperley Dr *VGL* GL2 ...... **159** G2
Apperley Pk *RTEWK/TIB* GL19 .. **69** G5
Appleby Wk
  BRSG/KWL/STAPK BS4.... **345** M4
Apple Cl *CHELTE/BC* GL52 ... **94** C6
Appledore Cl *HGRV/WHIT* BS14 .. **346** D3
Applegate *HNBRY/STHM* BS10 .. **315** K8
Apple Orch *CHELTE/BC* GL52 .. **94** C6
The Apple Orch *TEWK* GL20 .. **49** G2
Appleridge La *BRKLY* GL13 .. **250** E7
Appleton Av *CHELTW* GL51 .. **114** D5
Appleton Wy *BWTH/CHD* GL3 .. **137** J5
Apple Tree Cl *BWTH/CHD* GL3 .. **113** J4
  CHELTE/BC GL52 .... **94** E1
  GLE GL4 .... **137** G7
April Cl *DSLY* GL11 .... **253** J3
Apseleys Md *ALMDB* BS32 .. **316** E1
Apsley Cl *CIR* GL7 .... **238** B4
Apsley Rd *CFTN/FAIL* BS8 ... **335** J2
  CIR GL7 .... **238** B5
Apsley St *EVILLE/WHL* BS5 .. **336** E1
Aragon Wy *BWTH/CHD* GL3 .. **113** H4
Arbour Cl *CHCAM* GL55 .... **8** F8
Arbutus Dr
  HNLZ/SM/SNYPK/WT BS9 .. **324** E4
Archdeacon Ct *GL* GL1 ..... **4** D1
Archdeacon St *GL* GL1 ..... **4** D4

Archer Ct
  OLD/WMLY/WICK BS30 ... **338** B8
Archers La *CHELTE/BC* GL52 .. **70** F6
Archer Wk *HGRV/WHIT* BS14 .. **347** G5
Archery Rd *CIR* GL7 .... **238** E3
Archfield Rd *RDLND/MONT* BS6.. **335** L2
Archibald St *GL* GL1 .... **5** G8
Archway *CIND* GL14 .... **178** D2
Archway Gdns *STROUD* GL5 .. **208** B3
Ardea Cl *VGL* GL2 .... **158** E2
Arden Cl *ALMDB* BS32 ..... **317** G5
Arden Rd *CHELTS* GL53 .... **115** L6
Ardenton Wk
  HNBRY/STHM BS10 ..... **315** J8
Ardern Cl
  HNLZ/SM/SNYPK/WT BS9 .. **324** D3
Ardmore Cl *GLE* GL4 ...... **136** A4
Argus Rd *BMSTR* BS3 ...... **335** L8
Argyle Cl *YATE/CS* BS37 .... **310** A7
Argyle Rd *CBRISNE* BS2 .... **336** A3
  MANG/FISH BS16 ...... **337** K1
Argyle St *BMSTR* BS3 ...... **6** E9
  EVILLE/WHL BS5 .... **336** E1
Argyll Pl *VGL* GL2 .... **5** L4
Argyll Rd *CHELTS* GL53 .... **2** F8
  VGL GL2 .... **5** M4
Ariel Lodge Rd *CHELTE/BC* GL52.. **3** H4
Arkells Ct *WUE* GL12 ...... **296** C5
Arkendale Dr *VGL* GL2 ..... **158** F3
Arkle Cl *CHELT* GL50 ...... **93** L6
Arle Av *CHELTW* GL51 ..... **115** K1
Arle Cl *CHELTW* GL51 ..... **115** K1
Arle Dr *CHELTW* GL51 ..... **115** J1
Arle Gdns *CHELTW* GL51 ... **115** J1
Arle Rd *CHELTW* GL51 ..... **115** J1
Arley Cottages
  RDLND/MONT BS6 ...... **335** M2
Arley Hl *RDLND/MONT* BS6.. **335**M2
Arley Pk *RDLND/MONT* BS6 .. **335** M2
Arley Ter *EVILLE/WHL* BS5 .. **337** G2
Arlingham *CHELTW* GL51 ... **115** G6
Arlingham Rd *GL* GL1 ..... **135** M7
Arlingham Wy
  BRSTK/PCHW BS34 ..... **316** A3
Arlington Rd
  BRSG/KWL/STAPK BS4.... **336** F5
Arlington Vls *CFTN/FAIL* BS8 .. **335** J4
Armada Cl *BWTH/CHD* GL3 .. **113** H4
Armada Pl *CBRIS/FH* BS1 ... **336** A3
Armidale Av
  RDLND/MONT BS6 ...... **336** A2
Armoury Sq *EVILLE/WHL* BS5 .. **336** C2
Armscroft Ct *VGL* GL2 ..... **136** E2
Armscroft Crs *GLE* GL4 .... **5** M6
Armscroft Gdns *VGL* GL2 ... **159** G3
Armscroft Pl *VGL* GL2 ..... **5** M6
Armscroft Rd *VGL* GL2 .... **136** E2
Armscroft Wy *VGL* GL2 .... **5** M5
Armstrong Cl
  THNB/SVB BS35 .... **293** M4
Armstrong Dr
  OLD/WMLY/WICK BS30 .. **338** D6
Armstrong Wy *YATE/CS* BS37 .. **309** L8
Arnall Dr *HNBRY/STHM* BS10 .. **325** H2
Arneside Rd *HNBRY/STHM* BS10 .. **325** L2
Arnold's La
  RSTROUD/NAIL GL6 ..... **232** D8
Arnolds Wy *CIR* GL7 .... **238** E2
Arreton Av *GLE* GL4 .... **136** E5
Arrowhead Cl *GLE* GL4 .... **136** D7
Arrowsmith Dr *STNHO* GL10 .. **207** H2
Arthur Skemp Cl
  EVILLE/WHL BS5 .... **336** D4
Arthur St *CBRISNE* BS2 ..... **7** M6
  EVILLE/WHL BS5 .... **336** E3
  GL GL1 .... **4** F7
Arthurswood Rd
  BMSTRD/HC/WWD BS13.. **345** J7
Arundel Cl
  BMSTRD/HC/WWD BS13.. **345** K7
  GL GL1 .... **159** L2
Arundel Dr *STROUD* GL5 ... **208** D5
Arundell Mill La *STROUD* GL5 .. **208** F5
Arundel Rd *HORF/LLZ* BS7... **325** M8
  TEWK GL20 .... **48** C3
Ascot Cl *MANG/FISH* BS16 .. **328** B2
Ascot Rd *HNBRY/STHM* BS10 .. **325** M1
Ashbourne Cl
  OLD/WMLY/WICK BS30 .. **338** E5
Ashbrook La *CIR* GL7 ...... **241** G4
Ashburton Rd
  HNBRY/STHM BS10 ..... **325** L2
Ashchurch Rd *TEWK* GL20 .. **48** B5
Ash Cl *BRSTK/PCHW* BS34 .. **316** F4
  CHELTS GL53 .... **116** D7
  CHEP NP16 .... **270** A6
  DSLY GL11 .... **229** J7
  LYD GL15 .... **201** K7
  YATE/CS BS37 .... **309** M8
Ashcombe Cl
  OLD/WMLY/WICK BS30 .. **338** E5
Ashcombe Crs
  OLD/WMLY/WICK BS30 .. **338** F5
Ashcot Ms *CHELTW* GL51 ... **115** G6
Ashcott *HGRV/WHIT* BS14 .. **346** B5
Ashcroft Av *KEYN* BS31 .... **347** M6
Ashcroft Cl *GLE* GL4 ...... **160** F1
Ashcroft Gdns *CIR* GL7 .... **238** C3
Ashcroft Rd *CIR* GL7 ...... **238** C3
  HNLZ/SM/SNYPK/WT BS9 .. **324** E4
  WUE GL12 .... **278** C1
Ashdale Cl *COTS* GL54 ..... **194** F2
Ashdene Av *EVILLE/WHL* BS5 .. **326** F8
Ash Dene Rd *MTCHDN* GL17 .. **128** F6
Asher La *CBRISNE* BS2 ..... **7** J2
Ashes La *RWYE* HR9 .... **126** E5
Ashfield *HGHW* SN6 .... **287** J2
Ashfield Cl *CHELTE/BC* GL52 .. **72** C8
Ashfield Pl
  RDLND/MONT BS6 ...... **336** B2
Ashfield Rd *BMSTR* BS3 .... **335** K8
  MTCHDN GL17 .... **129** K5
Ashford Rd *BRSTK/PCHW* BS34 .. **316** C4
  CHELT GL50 .... **2** A9
Ash Gv *GLE* GL4 .... **137** G8
  MANG/FISH BS16 ...... **327** L8

  MTCHDN GL17 .... **106** C8
Ashgrove *CHELTS* GL53 .... **116** D7
  SHPSTR CV36 .... **16** B7
  THNB/SVB BS35 .... **293** L2
Ashgrove Av *CFTN/FAIL* BS8 .. **334** D4
  GLE GL4 .... **136** E5
  HORF/LLZ BS7 .... **326** B7
Ashgrove Cl *VGL* GL2 ..... **159** G4
Ash Grove Pl *LYD* GL15 .... **201** L1
Ashgrove Rd *BMSTR* BS3 .. **335** K8
  HORF/LLZ BS7 .... **326** B7
Ashgrove Wy *GLE* GL4 .... **136** E5
Ashland Rd
  BMSTRD/HC/WWD BS13.. **345** J5
Ashlands Cl *CHELTW* GL51 .. **93** C8
Ashlands Rd *CHELTW* GL51 .. **93** C8
Ash La *ALMDB* BS32 ...... **305** M8
  STNHO GL10 .... **207** L1
  VGL GL2 .... **112** C1
Ashlea Mdw *CHELTE/BC* GL52 .. **71** M7
Ashleigh La *CHELTE/BC* GL52 .. **94** F2
Ashletts Rd *RSTROUD/NAIL* GL6 .. **211** L3
Ashleworth Gdns *VGL* GL2 .. **159** G3
Ashley *KGWD/HNM* BS15 .. **338** B3
Ashley Cl *CHELTE/BC* GL52 .. **116** D4
  HORF/LLZ BS7 .... **326** D7
Ashley Court Rd
  RDLND/MONT BS6 ...... **336** B1
Ashley Down Rd *HORF/LLZ* BS7 .. **326** A6
Ashley Dr *RSTROUD/NAIL* GL6.. **209** L8
Ashley Grove Rd
  CBRISNE BS2 .... **336** B1
  CBRISNE BS2 .... **336** C2
Ashley Hl *RDLND/MONT* BS6.. **326** B8
Ashley Pde *CBRISNE* BS2 ... **336** B1
Ashley Pk *RDLND/MONT* BS6 .. **326** B8
Ashley Rd *CBATH/BATHN* BA1.. **353** C8
  CHELTE/BC GL52 ...... **3** L9
  RDLND/MONT BS6 ...... **336** A2
Ashley St *CBRISNE* BS2 .... **336** C2
Ashman Cl *EVILLE/WHL* BS5 .. **7** M1
Ashmead *VGL* GL2 .... **112** D6
Ashmead Dr *CHELTE/BC* GL52.. **72** C3
Ashmead Rd *CIND* GL14 ... **154** B4
  KEYN BS31 .... **348** D6
Ashmead Wy *CBRIS/FH* BS1 .. **335** H6
Ashmore Rd *GLE* GL4 ..... **136** E5
The Ash Pth *GLE* GL4 ..... **137** C8
Ash Ridge Rd *ALMDB* BS32 .. **306** C8
Ash Rd *CHPMW/MSHF* SN14 .. **343** J6
  HORF/LLZ BS7 .... **326** A6
  STROUD GL5 .... **208** C7
  TEWK GL20 .... **49** G3
Ashton Av *CBRIS/FH* BS1 ... **335** J6
Ashton Cl *GLE* GL4 .... **137** C8
Ashton Dr *BMSTR* BS3 .... **345** C2
Ashton Gate Rd *BMSTR* BS3 .. **335** J7
Ashton Gate Ter *BMSTR* BS3 .. **335** J7
Ashton Rd *BMSTR* BS3 .... **335** H8
  CIR GL7 .... **238** E8
  CIR GL7 .... **262** E1
  LGASH BS41 .... **334** E8
  MALM SN16 .... **287** H5
  TEWK GL20 .... **28** F6
Ashton Vale Rd *BMSTR* BS3 .. **335** G8
Ashton Wy *KEYN* BS31 .... **348** A5
Ash Tree Cl *NWNT* GL18 ... **86** C3
Ashville Rd *BMSTR* BS3 .... **335** J7
  VGL GL2 .... **135** K6
Ash Wk *HNBRY/STHM* BS10 .. **315** K8
Ashway *COTS* GL54 .... **169** K1
  LYD GL15 .... **224** B6
Ashwell Cl *HGRV/WHIT* BS14 .. **347** G5
Ashwell Hyett Cl
  RSTROUD/NAIL GL6 ..... **185** H3
Ashwicke *HGRV/WHIT* BS14 .. **346** B5
Ashwicke Rd
  CHPMW/MSHF SN14 .... **342** D7
Ashwood Wy *BWTH/CHD* GL3.. **137** H5
Askwith Rd *GLE* GL4 ...... **136** D5
Aspen Dr *VGL* GL2 .... **159** C1
Asquith Rd *CHELTS* GL53 ... **116** A5
Assembly Rooms La
  CBRIS/FH BS1 .... **6** E5
Aston Bank *RWYE* HR9 .... **126** C6
Aston Cl *CLFD* GL16 ...... **151** K6
  LED HR8 .... **19** M5
Aston Gv *CHELTW* GL51 ... **114** F1
  COTS GL54 .... **121** M7
Aston Rd *CHCAM* GL55 .... **12** E7
Aston Vw *RSTROUD/NAIL* GL6.. **210** B8
Astor Cl *BWTH/CHD* GL3 ... **137** M5
Astridge Rd *BWTH/CHD* GL3 .. **138** C7
Astry Cl *AVONM* BS11 ..... **324** C2
Atchley St *EVILLE/WHL* BS5 .. **336** D4
Atcombe Rd *STROUD* GL5 .. **232** B3
Athelney Wy *CHELTE/BC* GL52 .. **3** H7
Athelstan Rd *MALM* SN16 .. **303** H7
Atherstone
  OLD/WMLY/WICK BS30 .. **338** E6
Atherstone Cl *CHELTW* GL51 .. **92** E8
Atherton Cl *CHELTW* GL51 .. **138** F1
Athlone Wk
  BRSG/KWL/STAPK BS4.... **346** A2
Atkins Cl *HGRV/WHIT* BS14 .. **347** G5
Atkinson St *BDWY* WR12 ... **32** A1
Atlas Cl *EVILLE/WHL* BS5 ... **337** J1
Atlas Rd *BMSTR* BS3 ...... **336** A8
Atlas St *CBRISNE* BS2 ..... **336** B2
Attwood Cl *CHELTW* GL51 .. **93** H6
Atwell Dr *ALMDB* BS32 .... **316** D2
Atwood Dr *AVONM* BS11 ... **324** D1
Aubrey Meads
  OLD/WMLY/WICK BS30 .. **349** G3
Aubrey Ri *MALM* SN16 .... **303** J6
Aubrey Rd *BMSTR* BS3 .... **335** K8
Auburn Av
  OLD/WMLY/WICK BS30 .. **338** D3
Auburn Rd *RDLND/MONT* BS6 .. **335** K1
Auden Crs *LED* HR8 ...... **19** L3
Audley Cft *LED* HR8 ...... **19** M1
Audrey Wk
  HNLZ/SM/SNYPK/WT BS9 .. **325** J4
Augustine Wy
  BWTH/CHD GL3 .... **137** H5
Augustus Wy *LYD* GL15 .. **201** K6
Aust Crs *CHEP* NP16 ..... **270** A6

Austen Gv *HORF/LLZ* BS7 .. **326** C3
Austin Dr *VGL* GL2 .... **112** B5
Austin Rd *CIR* GL7 .... **238** C3
  TEWK GL20 .... **49** J3
Aust Rd *THNB/SVB* BS35 .. **290** F8
  THNB/SVB BS35 .... **292** A6
Avalon Rd *EVILLE/WHL* BS5 .. **337** K5
Avebury Cl *GL* GL1 ...... **159** K1
Avebury Rd *BMSTR* BS3 .. **335** G8
Avenall Pde *CHELTS* GL53 .. **3** G8
Avening Rd *GLE* GL4 ..... **136** B6
  KGWD/HNM BS15 ..... **337** J3
  RSTROUD/NAIL GL6 .... **232** F8
Avenue Rd *UUSV* WR8 ... **24** C1
The Avenue *BRSTK/PCHW* BS34 .. **316** C5
  BWTH/CHD GL3 .... **113** L6
  CFTN/FAIL BS8 .... **335** J2
  CHELTS GL53 .... **116** A6
  CIR GL7 .... **238** D3
  DSLY GL11 .... **228** F8
  EVILLE/WHL BS5 ...... **337** H4
  HNLZ/SM/SNYPK/WT BS9 .. **334** F1
  KEYN BS31 .... **348** A4
  MANG/FISH BS16 ...... **327** C2
  RDLND/MONT BS6 ...... **326** A8
  RSTROUD/NAIL GL6 .... **209** L8
  VGL GL2 .... **112** E7
  YATE/CS BS37 .... **319**M2
Averay Rd *MANG/FISH* BS16 .. **326** E7
Avon Cl *BRSG/KWL/STAPK* BS4.. **337** H5
  KEYN BS31 .... **348** B5
Avon Ct *CBATH/BATHN* BA1 .. **352** C7
Avon Crs *BWTH/CHD* GL3 .. **138** B6
  CBRIS/FH BS1 .... **335** J6
Avondale Pl
  CBATH/BATHN BA1 ..... **352** B8
Avondown Cl
  HNBRY/STHM BS10 ..... **325** M1
Avon Gv
  HNLZ/SM/SNYPK/WT BS9 .. **334** F1
Avon La *KEYN* BS31 ...... **349** H6
Avonlea *KGWD/HNM* BS15 .. **337** L6
Avonleaze
  HNLZ/SM/SNYPK/WT BS9 .. **324** D6
Avonleigh Rd *BMSTR* BS3 .. **345** K1
Avon Mill La *KEYN* BS31 ... **348** B5
Avon Pk *EVILLE/WHL* BS5 .. **336** F4
Avon Rd
  BMSTRD/HC/WWD BS13.. **345** J5
  CHELTE/BC GL52 ...... **3** K4
  KEYN BS31 .... **348** A5
  MALM SN16 .... **303** H7
  WUE GL12 .... **276** C2
Avonside Rd *CBRISNE* BS2 .. **336** E5
Avonside Wy
  BRSG/KWL/STAPK BS4.... **337** H5
Avon St *CBRISNE* BS2 ..... **7** J4
Avon V
  HNLZ/SM/SNYPK/WT BS9 .. **324** F1
Avonvale Rd *EVILLE/WHL* BS5 .. **336** E4
Avon Vw *KGWD/HNM* BS15 .. **337** K8
  VGL GL2 .... **48** C3
Avon Walkway
  OLD/WMLY/WICK BS30 .. **348** B5
Avon Wy *HNBRY/STHM* BS10 .. **325** M3
  HNLZ/SM/SNYPK/WT BS9 .. **324** E6
  THNB/SVB BS35 .... **293** L3
Avonwood Cl *AVONM* BS11 .. **324** A5
Avro Rd *COTS* GL54 ...... **124** D6
Awdelett Cl *AVONM* BS11 .. **324** C2
Awdry Wy *GLE* GL4 ...... **159** M1
Awebridge Wy *GLE* GL4 ... **136** E7
Awkley La *THNB/SVB* BS35 .. **306** A2
Awkward Hl *CIR* GL7 ..... **217** J1
Awre Rd *LYD* GL15 .... **202** E1
Axbridge Rd
  BRSG/KWL/STAPK BS4.... **346** B1
Aycote Cl *GLE* GL4 .... **136** D6
Ayford La *CHPMW/MSHF* SN14 .. **342** B6
Ayland Gdns *GL* GL1 ...... **5** K7
Aylesbury Crs *BMSTR* BS3 .. **345** K2
Aylesbury Rd *BMSTR* BS3 .. **345** K2
Aylmer Crs *HGRV/WHIT* BS14 .. **346** D5
Aylminton Wk *AVONM* BS11 .. **324** D1
Aylton Cl *CHELTW* GL51 ... **114** F5
Aysgarth Av *CHELTW* GL51 .. **115** G6
Azalea Dr *CHELTW* GL51 ... **115** H6
Azalea Gdns *VGL* GL2 ..... **159** G1

B

Back Albert Pl *CHELTE/BC* GL52 .. **2** F3
Back Br *MALM* SN16 ...... **303** G6
Back Edge La
  RSTROUD/NAIL GL6 ..... **184** E3
Back Ends *CHCAM* GL55 ... **12** D8
Backfields *CBRISNE* BS2 ... **7** G1
Backfields La *CBRISNE* BS2 .. **336** A3
Back La *BDWY* WR12 ..... **32** E3
  CHCAM GL55 .... **8** F7
  CHPMW/MSHF SN14 .... **342** B3
  CIR GL7 .... **188** C3
  CIR GL7 .... **242** E5
  COTS GL54 .... **74** B6
  KEYN BS31 .... **348** A5
  MANG/FISH BS16 ...... **329** H8
  MIM GL56 .... **103** G3
  MTCHDN GL17 .... **129** L3
  RSTROUD/NAIL GL6 ..... **210** C3
  SHPSTR CV36 .... **61** J5
  TET GL8 .... **279** L8
  TEWK GL20 .... **27** G4
  TEWK GL20 .... **28** E8
  WUE GL12 .... **296** C5
Back Montpellier La *CHELT* GL50 .. **2** B8
Back of Avon *TEWK* GL20 .. **48** A5
Back of Kingsdown Pde
  .... **335**M3
Back of Mount Pleasant
  TEWK GL20 .... **48** B5
Back Rd *BMSTR* BS3 ...... **335** J7
Back Rw *MIM* GL56 ...... **81** L8

Back Stoke La
  HNLZ/SM/SNYPK/WT BS9 .... 325 H5
Back St BAD GL9 .... 298 C8
  CIND GL14 .... 155 J7
  HGHW SN6 .... 287 H2
The Back CHEP NP16 ...... 270 B2
Back Walls COTS GL54 .... 102 A3
Backwell Wk
  BMSTRD/HC/WWD BS13 .... 345 H3
Badenham Gv AVONM BS11 .. 324 B3
Baden Hill Rd WUE GL12 .. 294 E6
Baden Rd EVILLE/WHL BS5 . 336 E4
  KGWD/HNM BS15 .... 338 C4
Bader Av BWTH/CHD GL3 ... 113 L6
Bader Cl YATE/CS BS37 ... 309 M8
Badger Cl GLE GL4 .... 136 F8
Badgers Cl ALMDB BS32 ... 306 F8
Badgers Crs SHPSTR CV36 . 16 B4
Badger's La ALMDB BS32 .. 315 L1
Badgers Wk
  BRSG/KWL/STAPK BS4 .... 346 F1
Badgers Wy LYD GL15 ..... 200 D2
Badger Vale Ct GL GL1 ... 135 L6
Badgeworth YATE/CS BS37 . 319 M5
Badgeworth La CHELTW GL51 138 E2
Badgeworth Rd CHELTW GL51 114 C6
The Badhams TEWK GL20 ... 24 B6
Badmington Rd
  MANG/FISH BS16 .... 328 B3
Badminton Cl CHELTS GL53 115 M5
Badminton Rd CBRISNE BS2 336 B2
  FRCTL/WBN BS36 .... 318 C6
  GLE GL4 .... 136 D6
  MANG/FISH BS16 .... 328 A4
  YATE/CS BS37 .... 319 K1
  YATE/CS BS37 .... 321 G3
Badsey La EVE WR11 ...... 10 E4
Bafford Ap CHELTS GL53 .. 116 B7
Bafford Gv CHELTS GL53 .. 116 B7
Bafford La CHELTS GL53 .. 116 C6
Baglyn Av KGWD/HNM BS15 . 328 B8
Bagnell Cl HGRV/WHIT BS14 347 G6
Bagnell Rd HGRV/WHIT BS14 347 G6
Bagpath La STROUD GL5 ... 232 F1
Bagstone Rd WUE GL12 .... 295 J6
Bagworth Dr
  OLD/WMLY/WICK BS30 .... 338 B8
Bailbrook Gv
  CBATH/BATHN BA1 ...... 351 L8
Bailbrook La
  CBATH/BATHN BA1 ...... 352 A8
Bailey Hl LYD GL15 ...... 201 K1
Bailey La LYD GL15 ...... 222 D3
Bailey Rd STRAT CV37 .... 8 F1
Baileys Court Rd ALMDB BS32 317 G5
Baileys Mead Rd
  MANG/FISH BS16 .... 326 E6
Bailiffe Piece HGHW SN6 . 288 F2
Baines Cl COTS GL54 ..... 123 H6
Bakehouse La CHELT GL50 . 115 K4
Bakersfield
  OLD/WMLY/WICK BS30 .... 338 C8
Bakers Gnd
  BRSTK/PCHW BS34 ...... 317 H6
Baker's Hl CHCAM GL55 ... 9 G8
  CLFD GL16 .... 151 L8
Baker's La EVE WR11 ..... 29 K2
  RTEWK/TIB GL19 .... 88 F5
Bakers Piece MTCHDN GL17 129 H5
Baker St CHELTW GL51 .... 2 B2
  GL GL1 .... 4 C8
Balaclava Rd
  MANG/FISH BS16 .... 327 H8
Bala Rd CHELTW GL51 ..... 115 H5
Balcarras CHELTS GL53 ... 116 E6
Balcarras Gdns CHELTS GL53 116 E6
Balcarras Retreat
  CHELTS GL53 .... 116 E6
Balcarras Rd CHELTS GL53 116 E6
Baldwin St CBRIS/FH BS1 . 6 F4
Balfour Rd BMSTR BS3 .... 335 K8
  GL GL1 .... 135 M4
Ballards Cl CHCAM GL55 .. 8 F8
Ballinode Cl CHELTW GL51 93 K6
Ballinska Ms VGL GL2 .... 112 F6
Balmain St BRSG/KWL/STAPK BS4 7 M9
Balmoral Cl
  BRSTK/PCHW BS34 ...... 316 F7
Balmoral Ct
  MANG/FISH BS16 .... 328 C6
Balmoral Rd KEYN BS31 ... 348 A7
  OLD/WMLY/WICK BS30 .... 348 B1
  RDLND/MONT BS6 .... 336 B1
Bamfield HGRV/WHIT BS14 . 346 B4
Bamfurlong La CHELTW GL51 114 A2
Bampton Cl
  BMSTRD/HC/WWD BS13 .... 345 K4
Bampton Dr
  MANG/FISH BS16 .... 327 M2
Banady La CHELTE/BC GL52 71 G6
Baneberry Rd GLE GL4 .... 136 C6
Banfield Cl AVONM BS11 .. 324 C3
Bangor Gv
  BRSG/KWL/STAPK BS4 .... 337 H6
Bangup La COTS GL54 ..... 121 M8
Banister Wy SHPSTR CV36 . 16 B7
Bank Crs LED HR8 .... 20 A2
Bank Rd KGWD/HNM BS15 ... 337 M3
  THNB/SVB BS35 .... 304 F4
Banks Fee La MIM CL56 ... 79 K4
Bankside MANG/FISH BS16 . 328 B7
Bankside Rd
  BRSG/KWL/STAPK BS4 .... 336 F8
Bank Sq CHEP NP16 .... 270 A3
Bank St CHEP NP16 .... 270 A3
  CLFD GL16 .... 175 J1
The Bank CHELTE/BC GL52 . 94 E7
  CHPMW/MSHF SN14 ...... 343 L8
Bannerdown Cl
  CBATH/BATHN BA1 ...... 352 D7
Bannerdown Dr
  CBATH/BATHN BA1 ...... 352 C7
Bannerdown Rd
  CBATH/BATHN BA1 ...... 352 C8
Bannerleigh La
  CFTN/FAIL BS8 .... 335 G5
Bannerleigh Rd CFTN/FAIL BS8 335 G4

Bannerman Rd
  EVILLE/WHL BS5 .... 336 D3
Banner Rd RDLND/MONT BS6 336 A2
Bannetts Tree Crs
  THNB/SVB BS35 .... 293 J6
Bantry Rd
  BRSG/KWL/STAPK BS4 .... 346 A3
Banwell Cl
  BMSTRD/HC/WWD BS13 .... 345 J3
Banwell Rd BMSTR BS3 .... 335 J8
Baptist Cl GLE GL4 ...... 137 H5
Baptist St EVILLE/WHL BS5 336 C2
Baptist Wy MTCHDN GL17 .. 129 K5
Barbican Rd GL GL1 ...... 4 D5
Barbican Wy GL GL1 ...... 4 D5
Barbour Gdns BMSTRD/HC/WWD BS13
  345 M8
Barbour Rd
  BMSTRD/HC/WWD BS13 .... 345 M8
Barbridge Rd CHELTW GL51 93 G8
Barcroft Cl KGWD/HNM BS15 337 L3
Baregains La LED HR8 .... 18 F2
Bargates COR/BOX SN13 ... 353 M5
Barker Pl CIR GL7 .... 242 F4
Barker's Leys CHELTE/BC GL52 72 C7
Barkers Md YATE/CS BS37 . 310 B7
Barker Wk EVILLE/WHL BS5 336 C2
Barksdale COTS GL54 ..... 74 B6
The Barlands CHELTE/BC GL52 117 C7
Barley Cl CHELTW GL51 ... 92 F6
  FRCTL/WBN BS36 .... 318 C3
  MANG/FISH BS16 .... 328 C5
  VGL GL2 .... 159 G5
Barley Cft
  HNLZ/SM/SNYPK/WT BS9 .. 325 H5
Barleycroft Cl GLE GL4 .. 160 F1
Barlow Cl STNHO GL10 .... 207 C4
Barlow Rd CHELTW GL51 ... 93 H7
Barnabas St CBRISNE BS2 . 336 A2
Barnaby Cl GL GL1 .... 136 B4
Barnacre Dr GLE GL4 ..... 137 H2
Barnage La LYD GL15 ..... 223 J3
Barnard Wk KEYN BS31 .... 347 M7
Barn Cl COTS GL54 .... 73 M2
  GLE GL4 .... 137 G7
  RSTROUD/NAIL GL6 ..... 232 B4
Barncroft SHPSTR CV36 ... 61 H6
Barn End CHPMW/MSHF SN14 342 C3
Barnes St EVILLE/WHL BS5 336 F4
Barnes Wallis Wy
  BWTH/CHD GL3 .... 113 L6
Barnett Av LED HR8 ...... 19 L3
Barnett Cl CHELTW GL51 .. 93 G6
Barnetts Cl LED HR8 ..... 19 L3
Barnett Wy COTS GL54 .... 169 J1
  GLE GL4 .... 137 G2
Barn Field Rd
  RSTROUD/NAIL GL6 ..... 232 C7
Barnfield Wy
  CBATH/BATHN BA1 ...... 352 D7
Barn Gnd VGL GL2 .... 110 F6
Barnhay BWTH/CHD GL3 .... 113 L7
Barn Hill Rd CLFD GL16 .. 151 M8
Barnhill Rd YATE/CS BS37 320 D2
Barn La BUR/CRTN OX18 ... 173 M6
  EVE WR11 .... 30 B2
  MTCHDN GL17 .... 129 G5
Barnmeadow Rd COTS GL54 . 74 C5
Barn Owl Wy
  BRSTK/PCHW BS34 ...... 317 H6
Barn Piece COR/BOX SN13 . 353 M5
Barns Cl NAIL BS48 ...... 344 A7
Barnstaple Rd
  BRSG/KWL/STAPK BS4 .... 346 A3
Barnstaple Wk
  BRSG/KWL/STAPK BS4 .... 346 B3
Barn Wy CIR GL7 .... 214 A3
Barnwood Av GLE GL4 ..... 136 F3
Barnwood Rd GLE GL4 ..... 137 G3
  VGL GL2 .... 5 M5
  YATE/CS BS37 .... 319 L4
Barossa Pl CBRIS/FH BS1 . 6 E5
Barrack Sq GL GL1 .... 4 C5
Barratt's Mill La CHELT GL50 2 E6
Barratt St EVILLE/WHL BS5 336 D2
Barrington Av CHELTW GL51 114 D4
Barrington Cl KGWD/HNM BS15 338 B1
Barrington Ct
  KGWD/HNM BS15 .... 338 A2
Barrington Dr GLE GL4 ... 137 H3
Barrow Cl VGL GL2 .... 159 H3
Barrowell La LYD GL15 ... 198 H6
Barrowfield Rd STROUD GL5 208 C2
Barrow Hl BWTH/CHD GL3 .. 113 M8
  OLD/WMLY/WICK BS30 .... 339 K5
Barrowmead Dr AVONM BS11 324 D3
Barrow Rd EVILLE/WHL BS5 336 D4
  EVILLE/WHL BS5 .... 336 D4
Barrs Court Av
  OLD/WMLY/WICK BS30 .... 338 C6
Barrs Court Rd
  OLD/WMLY/WICK BS30 .... 338 C6
Barrs La DSLY GL11 ...... 253 G7
Barry Cl
  OLD/WMLY/WICK BS30 .... 348 E2
Barry Rd
  OLD/WMLY/WICK BS30 .... 348 E1
Bartletts Pk COTS GL54 .. 102 A4
Bartlett's Rd BMSTR BS3 . 345 L1
Bartley Cft TET GL8 ..... 282 A3
Bartley St BMSTR BS3 .... 6 F7
Barton Cl
  BRSG/KWL/STAPK BS4 .... 337 H5
  CHELTS GL53 .... 116 C7
  FRCTL/WBN BS36 .... 318 A6
  THNB/SVB BS35 .... 293 J6
Barton Cl EVILLE/WHL BS5 336 E5
Bartonend La
  RSTROUD/NAIL GL6 ..... 256 C2
Barton Hl MTCHDN GL17 ... 130 D1
Barton Hill Rd EVILLE/WHL BS5 336 D5
Bartonia Gv
  BRSG/KWL/STAPK BS4 .... 346 F2
Barton La CIR GL7 .... 238 B2
Barton Mnr CBRISNE BS2 .. 7 L4
Barton Ms TEWK GL20 ..... 48 B5
Bean Hl MIM CL56 .... 79 L3

  SHPSTR CV36 .... 60 D4
  TEWK GL20 .... 48 A5
Barton St CBRIS/FH BS1 .. 6 F1
  GL GL1 .... 5 J9
The Barton KGWD/HNM BS15 337 K7
Barton V CBRISNE BS2 .... 7 L4
Barton Wy CHELTW GL51 ... 115 G5
Barwick Rd CHELTW GL51 .. 115 H6
Barwood
  KGWD/HNM BS15 .... 338 B3
Base La VGL GL2 .... 111 M3
Basil Cl GLE GL4 .... 136 F7
Bassett Cl CHELTS GL53 .. 74 C5
Bassett Rd COTS GL54 .... 169 K2
The Bassetts COR/BOX SN13 353 M5
  STROUD GL5 .... 207 M3
Batchfield La YATE/CS BS37 329 L3
Bateman Cl GLE GL4 ...... 159 M2
Bates Cl EVILLE/WHL BS5 . 336 C3
Bathams Cl MTCHDN GL17 .. 131 H1
Bath Br BRSG/KWL/STAPK BS4 7 J7
Bath Buildings
  RDLND/MONT BS6 .... 336 A2
Bath Crs LYD GL15 .... 201 J2
Bath Hl KEYN BS31 .... 348 B6
Bathleaze STNHO GL10 .... 207 J7
Bath Pde CHELTS GL53 .... 2 E7
Bath Pl CLFD GL16 .... 151 K5
  LYD GL15 .... 201 K8
Bath Rd BAD GL9 .... 331 L1
  BRSG/KWL/STAPK BS4 .... 7 K7
  BRSG/KWL/STAPK BS4 .... 347 H2
  CHELT GL50 .... 2 D7
  CHELTS GL53 .... 115 M4
  CHPMW/MSHF SN14 ...... 353 C1
  COR/BOX SN13 .... 353 H6
  HGHW SN6 .... 288 F3
  KEYN BS31 .... 347 K3
  OLD/WMLY/WICK BS30 .... 338 F5
  OLD/WMLY/WICK BS30 .... 340 A8
  OLD/WMLY/WICK BS30 .... 348 F3
  RSTROUD/NAIL GL6 ..... 256 D4
  STNHO GL10 .... 206 B5
  STNHO GL10 .... 207 H4
  STROUD GL5 .... 208 C5
  TET GL8 .... 299 K1
  THNB/SVB BS35 .... 293 K3
  WUE GL12 .... 299 H2
  YATE/CS BS37 .... 321 L6
Bath Road Brislington Hl
  BRSG/KWL/STAPK BS4 .... 347 G1
Bath St BMSTR BS3 .... 335 J7
  CBRIS/FH BS1 .... 7 G4
  MANG/FISH BS16 .... 328 A7
Bath Ter CHELT GL50 ..... 2 C9
Bathurst Pde CBRIS/FH BS1 6 E7
Bathurst Park Rd LYD GL15 201 J8
Bathurst Rd CIR GL7 ..... 238 B4
  GLE GL4 .... 136 B5
Bath Ville Ms CHELTS GL53 2 D8
Bathwell Rd
  BRSG/KWL/STAPK BS4 .... 336 C8
Batley Ct
  OLD/WMLY/WICK BS30 .... 338 F7
Battenburg Rd
  EVILLE/WHL BS5 .... 337 J5
Batten Cl YATE/CS BS37 .. 320 E2
Batten's La EVILLE/WHL BS5 337 J5
Battens Rd EVILLE/WHL BS5 337 K4
Battersby Wy
  HNBRY/STHM BS10 ...... 325 C1
Battersea Rd EVILLE/WHL BS5 336 E3
Battledown Ap CHELTE/BC GL52 3 J4
Battledown Cl CHELTE/BC GL52 3 J6
Battledown Dr CHELTE/BC GL52 3 K7
Battledown Md CHELTE/BC GL52 3 K5
Battle Rd TEWK GL20 ..... 47 M7
Battson Rd HGRV/WHIT BS14 347 G1
Baugh Gdns MANG/FISH BS16 328 A2
Baunton La CIR GL7 ...... 214 A6
Baxter Cl KGWD/HNM BS15 . 338 B3
Bay Gdns EVILLE/WHL BS5 . 336 E1
Bayham Rd
  BRSG/KWL/STAPK BS4 .... 336 B8
Baylands BRKLY GL13 ..... 226 F3
Bayleys Dr KGWD/HNM BS15 337 L5
Bayliss Rd TEWK GL20 .... 27 M4
Baynham Rd MTCHDN GL17 .. 130 C2
Baynham's Wk CLFD GL16 .. 151 M7
Baynham Wy CHELT GL50 ... 2 D4
Baynton Rd BMSTR BS3 .... 335 J7
Bays Hl BRKLY GL13 ...... 226 F3
Bayshill La YATE/CS BS37 2 B6
Bayshill Rd CHELT GL50 .. 2 B6
Bayswater Av
  RDLND/MONT BS6 .... 325 K7
Bayswater Rd HORF/LLZ BS7 326 B4
Bay Tree Cl BRSTK/PCHW BS34 316 B4
Bay Tree Rd GLE GL4 ..... 137 H6
Bazeley Rd GLE GL4 ...... 160 D1
Beach Av THNB/SVB BS35 .. 304 C4
Beachgrove Gdns
  MANG/FISH BS16 .... 327 L7
Beachgrove Rd
  MANG/FISH BS16 .... 327 K7
Beach Hl
  OLD/WMLY/WICK BS30 .... 339 H8
Beach La
  OLD/WMLY/WICK BS30 .... 349 L1
Beachley Rd CHEP NP16 ... 270 C4
Beach Rd THNB/SVB BS35 .. 304 B4
Beacon Cl RSTROUD/NAIL GL6 161 J6
Beacon La MANG/FISH BS16 317 K6
Beaconlea KGWD/HNM BS15 . 337 M5
Beacon Rd GLE GL4 .... 136 D8
Beaconsfield Rd
  BRSG/KWL/STAPK BS4 .... 336 D8
  CFTN/FAIL BS8 .... 335 J2
  EVILLE/WHL BS5 .... 336 E5
Beaconsfield St
  EVILLE/WHL BS5 .... 336 D5
Beacons View Rd CIND GL14 154 C2
The Beagles STROUD GL5 .. 207 M4
Beale Cl HGRV/WHIT BS14 . 347 G5
  RSTROUD/NAIL GL6 ..... 209 M7
Beale Rd CHELTW GL51 .... 92 F8
Beam St EVILLE/WHL BS5 .. 336 E4

Beanhill Crs THNB/SVB BS35 293 J6
Bean St EVILLE/WHL BS5 .. 336 C2
Bearbridge Rd
  BMSTRD/HC/WWD BS13 .... 345 H7
Bearcroft Gdn CHCAM GL55 8 F7
Beard's La STROUD GL5 ... 208 C4
Bear Hl STROUD GL5 ...... 232 C1
Bearland GL GL1 .... 4 D5
Bearlands WUE GL12 ...... 277 L6
Bear La GLE GL4 .... 136 F8
Bear St WUE GL12 .... 277 K4
Beauchamp Cl CIR GL7 .... 242 F4
Beauchamp Meadow LYD GL15 201 L7
Beauchamp Rd HORF/LLZ BS7 325 M7
Beaufort Cl EVILLE/WHL BS5 336 F4
Beaufort Ct CIR GL7 ..... 238 C4
Beaufort Crs
  BRSTK/PCHW BS34 ...... 317 G7
Beaufort Dr LYD GL15 .... 225 K1
Beaufort Pl CHEP NP16 ... 270 A3
  EVILLE/WHL BS5 .... 7 L1
  MANG/FISH BS16 .... 327 K2
  TEWK GL20 .... 48 A7
Beaufort Rd CFTN/FAIL BS8 335 J2
  CHELTE/BC GL52 .... 3 J9
  EVILLE/WHL BS5 .... 336 F4
  FRCTL/WBN BS36 .... 318 C3
  GLE GL4 .... 136 B6
  HORF/LLZ BS7 .... 326 B5
  KGWD/HNM BS15 .... 337 K2
  MANG/FISH BS16 .... 328 A7
  YATE/CS BS37 .... 319 M1
Beaufort St BMSTRD BS3 .. 345 L1
Beauley Rd BMSTR BS3 .... 6 B8
Beaumont Cl
  OLD/WMLY/WICK BS30 .... 338 C8
Beaumont Dr CHELTW GL51 . 92 F7
Beaumont Pl LYD GL15 .... 201 F7
Beaumont Rd CHELTW GL51 . 92 F7
  VGL GL2 .... 112 E6
Beaumont St
  EVILLE/WHL BS5 .... 336 C3
Beaumont Ter
  EVILLE/WHL BS5 .... 336 C3
Beaumoor Pl CIR GL7 ..... 242 F5
Beaver Cl FRCTL/WBN BS36 318 B4
Beaverstone Cl CIR GL7 .. 263 H5
Beazer Cl MANG/FISH BS16 327 M8
Becket Cl MIM CL56 ...... 37 L6
Becket Ct MANG/FISH BS16 329 K6
Becketts La COTS GL54 ... 74 D3
Beckfordcl TEWK GL20 .... 28 E8
Beckford Gdns
  HGRV/WHIT BS14 .... 346 C8
Beckford Rd EVE WR11 .... 29 K4
  GLE GL4 .... 137 L7
  TEWK GL20 .... 51 K4
Beckington Rd BMSTR BS3 346 B1
Beckington Wk BMSTR BS3 346 B1
Beckspool Rd
  MANG/FISH BS16 .... 327 L3
Becky Rd COTS GL54 ...... 122 F1
Bedford Av CHELTW GL51 .. 115 H1
Bedford Crs HORF/LLZ BS7 326 B6
Bedford St GL GL1 .... 5 G6
  STROUD GL5 .... 208 E4
Bedminster Br BMSTR BS3 . 7 G8
Bedminster Down Rd
  BMSTR BS3 .... 345 K1
  BMSTRD/HC/WWD BS13 .... 345 J2
Bedminster Pde BMSTR BS3 6 F8
Bedminster Pl BMSTR BS3 345 L1
Beech Av CLFD GL16 ...... 151 L6
  OLD/WMLY/WICK BS30 .... 338 C6
  THNB/SVB BS35 .... 293 J6
  VGL GL2 .... 110 F7
  VGL GL2 .... 159 G4
Beechcroft Rd CHELTW GL51 112 C6
Beechcroft Wk HORF/LLZ BS7 326 A2
Beechen Dr MANG/FISH BS16 337 K1
Beeches Cl STNHO GL10 ... 207 J8
Beeches Gn STROUD GL5 ... 208 D3
Beeches Gv
  BRSG/KWL/STAPK BS4 .... 346 F1
Beeches Rd CHELTS GL53 .. 116 D7
  CIND GL14 .... 155 J7
  CIR GL7 .... 238 D3
The Beeches ALMDB BS32 .. 316 F3
  BRSG/KWL/STAPK BS4 .... 337 G6
  OLD/WMLY/WICK BS30 .... 348 E1
Beechfield Cl LGASH SN41 344 E1
Beech Gv CIR GL7 .... 238 E2
  STROUD GL5 .... 232 C1
Beech La RSTROUD/NAIL GL6 185 K3
Beech Lea CIR GL7 .... 241 L6
Beech Leaze THNB/SVB BS35 293 J6
Beechmore Dr CHELTW GL51 115 G6
Beechmount Gv
  HGRV/WHIT BS14 .... 346 C8
Beech Rd CHPMW/MSHF SN14 343 J6
  HORF/LLZ BS7 .... 326 A6
  KEYN BS31 .... 349 G8
  LYD GL15 .... 177 J8
Beechurst Av CHELTE/BC GL52 3 H5
Beechurst Wy
  CHELTE/BC GL52 .... 71 M7
Beech Wy CIND GL14 ...... 154 D3
  LYD GL15 .... 200 C3
Beech Well La CLFD GL16 . 152 A4
Beechwood Av
  KGWD/HNM BS15 .... 337 M6
Beechwood Cl HGRV/WHIT BS14 347 H4
Beechwood Dr
  RSTROUD/NAIL GL6 ..... 209 M8
Beechwood Gv GLE GL4 .... 136 A8
  WUE GL12 .... 277 M3
Beechwood Ri DSLY GL11 .. 253 H1
Beechwood Rd
  MANG/FISH BS16 .... 327 H7
Beek's La CBATH/BATHN BA1 341 L8
  CHPMW/MSHF SN14 ...... 341 M5
Beesmoor Rd FRCTL/WBN BS36 318 D4

Begbrook Dr MANG/FISH BS16 327 L6
Begbrook La MANG/FISH BS16 327 H5
Begbrook Pk MANG/FISH BS16 327 J4
Beggarswell Cl CBRISNE BS2 336 B3
Bekdale Cl VGL GL2 ...... 158 F3
Belfast Ms
  BRSG/KWL/STAPK BS4 .... 346 A3
Belfry Cl GLE GL4 .... 137 G3
Belgrave Hl CFTN/FAIL BS8 335 J1
Belgrave Pl CFTN/FAIL BS8 335 L4
Belgrave Rd CFTN/FAIL BS8 335 K3
  GL GL1 .... 4 F7
Bellamy Av
  BMSTRD/HC/WWD BS13 .... 345 L7
Bellamy Cl KGWD/HNM BS15 337 L5
Belland Dr CHELTS GL53 .. 116 C7
  HGRV/WHIT BS14 .... 346 B7
Bella Vis CHELTE/BC GL52 72 D8
Bell Bank MIM CL56 ...... 57 C1
Bell Barn Rd
  HNLZ/SM/SNYPK/WT BS9 .. 324 F5
Bell Cl HNBRY/STHM BS10 . 326 A4
Belle Orch LED HR8 ...... 19 M2
Belle Orchard Cl LED HR8 19 M3
Bellevue CFTN/FAIL BS8 .. 6 A4
Bellevue Cl KGWD/HNM BS15 338 A4
Belle Vue Cl STROUD GL5 . 208 F4
Bellevue Crs CFTN/FAIL BS8 6 A4
Bellevue Pk
  BRSG/KWL/STAPK BS4 .... 346 F1
Belle Vue Rd CIND GL14 .. 154 B3
  EVILLE/WHL BS5 .... 336 F2
  MTCHDN GL17 .... 129 G3
  STROUD GL5 .... 208 F4
Bellevue Rd
  BRSG/KWL/STAPK BS4 .... 7 K8
  EVILLE/WHL BS5 .... 337 J3
  KGWD/HNM BS15 .... 338 B4
Bellevue Ter BMSTR BS3 .. 7 K8
  BRSG/KWL/STAPK BS4 .... 346 F1
Bell Hl MANG/FISH BS16 .. 326 E7
Bellhouse Wk AVONM BS11 . 324 D2
Bell La CBRIS/FH BS1 .... 6 F3
  CIR GL7 .... 241 G4
  GL GL1 .... 4 F6
  LED HR8 .... 42 F4
  RSTROUD/NAIL GL6 ..... 233 J5
  STROUD GL5 .... 208 A7
Bell Orch VGL GL2 .... 155 M8
Bell Pitch RSTROUD/NAIL GL6 184 B8
Bell Rd FRCTL/WBN BS36 .. 318 E5
Bells La RBANSW OX15 .... 17 L6
Bells Pl CIND GL14 ...... 154 A7
  CLFD GL16 .... 175 K1
Belluton Rd
  BRSG/KWL/STAPK BS4 .... 336 C8
Belmont Av BWTH/CHD GL3 . 137 K5
Belmont Dr BRSTK/PCHW BS34 317 G6
Belmont La CLFD GL16 .... 151 K5
Belmont Rd
  BRSG/KWL/STAPK BS4 .... 336 E8
  CHELTE/BC GL52 .... 71 M7
  LYD GL15 .... 222 D2
  RDLND/MONT BS6 .... 336 A1
  STROUD GL5 .... 209 G5
Belmont St EVILLE/WHL BS5 336 D2
Belmore Pl CHELT GL50 ... 2 D7
Beloe Rd HORF/LLZ BS7 ... 325 M6
Belroyal Av
  BRSG/KWL/STAPK BS4 .... 337 H8
Belsher Dr KGWD/HNM BS15 338 C5
Belstone Wk
  BRSG/KWL/STAPK BS4 .... 345 L4
Belton Rd EVILLE/WHL BS5 336 D2
Belvedere Ms
  RSTROUD/NAIL GL6 ..... 233 M2
Belvedere Rd
  RDLND/MONT BS6 .... 325 J8
Belvoir Rd RDLND/MONT BS6 336 A1
Belworth Dr CHELTW GL51 . 115 H4
Bence Ct KGWD/HNM BS15 .. 337 K6
Bendy Bow MALM SN16 ..... 285 H3
Benford Cl MANG/FISH BS16 327 L5
Benhall Av CHELTW GL51 .. 115 G3
Bennett Rd EVILLE/WHL BS5 337 G4
Bennett's Ct YATE/CS BS37 320 B2
Bennett's Rd
  CBATH/BATHN BA1 ...... 351 L8
Bennington St CHELT GL50 2 D4
Bensaunt Gv
  HNBRY/STHM BS10 ...... 315 M3
Benson Cl GLE GL4 .... 137 G5
Bentley Cl HGRV/WHIT BS14 346 B8
  VGL GL2 .... 159 H1
Bentley La CHELTE/BC GL52 94 F4
Benton Ct STNHO GL10 .... 231 G5
Benville Av
  HNLZ/SM/SNYPK/WT BS9 .. 324 E3
Berenda Dr
  OLD/WMLY/WICK BS30 .... 338 D8
Beresford Gdns
  CBATH/BATHN BA1 ...... 350 C8
Berkeley Av CFTN/FAIL BS8 6 C3
  CHELTE/BC GL52 .... 2 E4
  HORF/LLZ BS7 .... 325 M8
Berkeley Cl BWTH/CHD GL3 137 L5
  CIR GL7 .... 263 H5
  MANG/FISH BS16 .... 328 B3
  STROUD GL5 .... 207 M4
  WUE GL12 .... 276 C7
Berkeley Ct VGL GL2 ..... 204 F8
Berkeley Crs LYD GL15 ... 201 K6
Berkeley Gdns KEYN BS31 . 347 M7
Berkeley Gn EVILLE/WHL BS5 336 E1
  MANG/FISH BS16 .... 327 K2
Berkeley Gv EVILLE/WHL BS5 336 F1
Berkeley Md ALMDB BS32 .. 317 G5
Berkeley Pl CFTN/FAIL BS8 2 F6
  CIR GL7 .... 238 C6
  HORF/LLZ BS7 .... 325 M8
  KGWD/HNM BS15 .... 338 A4
  MANG/FISH BS16 .... 327 M7
  MANG/FISH BS16 .... 337 J1
  RDLND/MONT BS6 .... 325 J7
Berkeley Sq CFTN/FAIL BS8 6 B3

Berkeley St CHELTE/BC GL52 ...... 2 F6
EVILLE/WHL BS5 .... 326 E8
GL GL1 .... 4 D5
Berkeley Wy MANG/FISH BS16 ... 328 B4
TET GL8 .... 282 A2
Berkshire Rd HORF/LLZ BS7 ...... 325 M8
The Berrells TET GL8 .... 281 M5
Berrills La SHPSTR CV36 .... 39 J6
Berrington Rd CHCAM GL55 ...... 13 G8
Berrow Wk BMSTR BS3 .... 346 A1
Berry Av SHPSTR CV36 .... 16 A5
Berry Cl RSTROUD/NAIL GL6 ...... 185 H3
SHPSTR CV36 .... 16 A5
Berrycroft BRKLY GL13 .... 227 G7
Berryfield Gld
BWTH/CHD GL3 .... 113 J5
Berry Hill Ct CIR GL7 .... 214 C8
Berry Hill Rd CIR GL7 .... 214 C8
Berry Lawn GLE GL4 .... 136 F8
Berrymore Rd STROUD GL5 .... 232 B1
Bertha's Fld BAD GL9 .... 299 K7
Berwick La HNBRY/STHM BS10 ... 314 E6
Berwick Rd CHELTE/BC GL52 ..... 72 E8
EVILLE/WHL BS5 .... 336 D1
Beryl Gv HGRV/WHIT BS14 .... 346 E3
Beryl Rd BMSTR BS3 .... 335 K8
Besbury La CHLTN OX7 .... 105 H5
Besbury Pk RSTROUD/NAIL GL6 .. 233 K4
Besford Rd CHELTE/BC GL52 ...... 73 G8
Besom La YATE/CS BS37 .... 319 C8
Bessemer Cl CLFD GL16 .... 175 K2
Beta Cl TEWK GL20 .... 48 E3
Bethel Rd EVILLE/WHL BS5 .... 337 H3
Bethesda St CHELT GL50 .... 2 C9
Betjeman Cl VGL GL2 .... 135 L7
Betjeman Ct
OLD/WMLY/WICK BS30 .... 338 C6
Bettenson Ri COTS GL54 .... 169 J1
Bettertons Cl CIR GL7 .... 242 D4
Bevan Ct BRSTK/PCHW BS34 ...... 326 B1
Bevan Gdns TEWK GL20 .... 49 G2
Beverley Av MANG/FISH BS16 .... 328 B2
Beverley Cl EVILLE/WHL BS5 ...... 337 K5
Beverley Cft CHELTW GL51 .... 114 E1
Beverley Gdns CHELTE/BC GL52 .. 72 E8
HNLZ/SM/SNYPK/WT BS9 .... 324 F4
Beverstone
KGWD/HNM BS15 .... 337 L3
Beverstone Rd CIR GL7 .... 263 H6
Beverston Gdns
AVONM BS11 .... 324 D1
Bevington Cl
BRSTK/PCHW BS34 .... 316 A2
Bevington La BRKLY GL13 .... 250 B5
Bevington Wk
BRSTK/PCHW BS34 .... 316 A2
Bewley Wy BWTH/CHD GL3 .... 113 J5
Bexley Rd MANG/FISH BS16 ...... 327 K8
Beyon Dr DSLY GL11 .... 229 H5
Bibstone KGWD/HNM BS15 .... 338 C3
Bibsworth Av BDWAY WR12 .... 33 G3
Bibsworth La BDWAY WR12 .... 32 F1
Bibury Av BRSTK/PCHW BS34 ..... 316 C3
Bibury Cl
HNLZ/SM/SNYPK/WT BS9 .... 325 M4
Bibury Crs
HNLZ/SM/SNYPK/WT BS9 .... 325 M4
KGWD/HNM BS15 .... 337 L6
Bibury Rd CHELTW GL51 .... 115 C3
GLE GL4 .... 136 B5
Bickerton Cl
HNBRY/STHM BS10 .... 315 H8
Bickford Cl
OLD/WMLY/WICK BS30 .... 338 C5
Bickley Rd KGWD/HNM BS15 ..... 347 L1
Bicknor St CLFD GL16 .... 151 K4
Biddestone Rd HORF/LLZ BS7 ... 326 A5
Biddulph Wy LED HR8 .... 19 M5
Bideford Crs
BRSG/KWL/STAPK BS4 .... 346 B3
Bidwell Cl HNBRY/STHM BS10 ... 315 K8
Bifield Cl HGRV/WHIT BS14 .... 347 H6
Bifield Gdns HGRV/WHIT BS14 ... 347 G6
Bifield Rd HGRV/WHIT BS14 ...... 347 H6
Bigstone Gv CHEP NP16 .... 270 C1
Bigwood La CBRIS/FH BS1 .... 6 C4
Bilberry Cl GLE GL4 .... 137 H7
HNLZ/SM/SNYPK/WT BS9 .... 324 E3
Bilbie Cl HNBRY/STHM BS10 ..... 325 M5
Billand Cl
BMSTRD/HC/WWD BS13 .... 345 G8
Billbrook Rd BWTH/CHD GL3 ..... 137 J4
Billingham Cl GLE GL4 .... 136 D5
Billings Wy CHELT GL50 .... 115 K5
Bilsham La THNB/SVB BS35 .... 305 G1
Bindon Dr HNBRY/STHM BS10 ... 315 M7
Binley Gv HGRV/WHIT BS14 ...... 346 F6
Binmead Gdns
BMSTRD/HC/WWD BS13 .... 345 K7
Binyon Cl EVE WR11 .... 10 A1
Binyon Rd COTS GL54 .... 74 B6
Birbeck Rd
HNLZ/SM/SNYPK/WT BS9 .... 325 G6
Birchall Av GLE GL4 .... 160 E1
Birchall Rd RDLND/MONT BS6 ... 325 L7
Birch Av GLE GL4 .... 136 D5
Birch Cl BRSTK/PCHW BS34 ...... 316 A4
CHELTS GL53 .... 116 E7
LED HR8 .... 19 M4
Birch Ct KEYN BS31 .... 347 L7
Birch Cft HGRV/WHIT BS14 ...... 346 D8
Birchdale Rd HGRV/WHIT BS14 .. 346 C3
Birch Dr BUR/CRTN OX18 .... 197 L4
MANG/FISH BS16 .... 329 K6
THNB/SVB BS35 .... 293 H7
Birches Cl STROUD GL5 .... 208 E3
Birches Dr STROUD GL5 .... 208 E4
Birches La NWNT GL18 .... 64 B6
Birchfield Rd CHELTE/BC GL52 .. 72 C7
Birch Gld HGHW SN6 .... 287 H3
Birchley Rd CHELTE/BC GL52 .... 3 K7
Birchmore Rd GL GL1 .... 5 K8
Birch Pk CLFD GL16 .... 175 M2
Birch Rd BMSTR BS3 .... 6 A8
CLFD GL16 .... 151 M7
DSLY GL11 .... 229 J7

KGWD/HNM BS15 .... 328 A8
STROUD GL5 .... 208 C8
YATE/CS BS37 .... 319 M1
Birchwood Cl CIND GL14 .... 153 M2
Birchwood Flds GLE GL4 .... 135 M8
Birchwood Rd
BRSG/KWL/STAPK BS4 .... 337 G2
LYD GL15 .... 224 A5
Birdale Cl HNBRY/STHM BS10 ... 315 G8
Bird Rd BWTH/CHD GL3 .... 137 K5
Birds Bush La
RSTROUD/NAIL GL6 .... 187 K6
Birdwell La LGASH BS41 .... 344 B3
Birdwell Rd LGASH BS41 .... 344 B2
Birdwood KGWD/HNM BS15 ...... 337 M5
Birdwood Cl GLE GL4 .... 137 G7
Birgage Rd BAD GL9 .... 312 B1
Birkdale OLD/WMLY/WICK BS30 .. 338 D5
YATE/CS BS37 .... 320 A3
Birkin St CBRISNE BS2 .... 7 K4
Bishop Manor Rd
HNBRY/STHM BS10 .... 325 M4
Bishop Rd CHELTW GL51 .... 139 C1
HORF/LLZ BS7 .... 325 L7
Bishops Cl CHELTE/BC GL52 ..... 72 E6
CHEP NP16 .... 270 B7
HNLZ/SM/SNYPK/WT BS9 .... 325 G8
Bishops Cove
BMSTRD/HC/WWD BS13 .... 345 H6
Bishops Dr CHELTE/BC GL52 ..... 72 E8
Bishopsfield HGHW SN6 .... 288 E4
Bishops Ga LYD GL15 .... 225 J1
Bishops Knoll
HNLZ/SM/SNYPK/WT BS9 .... 324 E8
Bishops Meadow
CHELTE/BC GL52 .... 72 A7
Bishops Rd GLE GL4 .... 137 G5
Bishopstone Cl CHELTW GL51 ... 114 E2
Bishopstone Rd GL GL1 .... 5 K8
Bishop St CBRISNE BS2 .... 336 A3
Bishop's Wk RTEWK/TIB GL19 ... 46 D5
Bishop's Wd ALMDB BS32 .... 306 E5
Bishopsworth Rd
BMSTRD/HC/WWD BS13 .... 345 J4
Bishopthorpe Rd
HNBRY/STHM BS10 .... 325 M4
Bishport Av
BMSTRD/HC/WWD BS13 .... 345 L8
Bishport Cl
BMSTRD/HC/WWD BS13 .... 345 K7
Bishton La CHEP NP16 .... 246 C5
Bisley Cl YATE/CS BS37 .... 319 L4
Bisley Old Rd STROUD GL5 .... 208 F4
Bisley Rd CHELTW GL51 .... 115 G3
GLE GL4 .... 160 A2
RSTROUD/NAIL GL6 .... 210 B1
STROUD GL5 .... 208 F5
Bisley St RSTROUD/NAIL GL6 .... 185 H3
Bissex Md MANG/FISH BS16 ..... 328 D6
Bittern Av GLE GL4 .... 136 F5
Bitterwell Cl FRCTL/WBN BS36 .. 318 F8
Bixhead Wk CLFD GL16 .... 175 M1
Blaby Cl GLE GL4 .... 137 H6
Blackacre HGRV/WHIT BS14 ..... 346 E8
Blackberry Av
MANG/FISH BS16 .... 327 G6
Blackberry Cl GLE GL4 .... 137 G7
Black Berry Fld CHELTE/BC GL52 .. 94 E8
Blackberry Gv CHELTE/BC GL52 .. 72 A7
Blackberry Hl MANG/FISH BS16 .. 327 G6
Blackbird Av VGL GL2 .... 112 F5
Blackbird Ct STNHO GL10 .... 207 H3
Blackboys DSLY GL11 .... 229 J8
Black Dog Wy GL GL1 .... 4 F4
Blackdown Ct
HGRV/WHIT BS14 .... 346 D6
Blackford La HGHW SN6 .... 266 E7
Blackfriars CBRIS/FH BS1 .... 6 F2
Blackhorse Hl THNB/SVB BS35 ... 315 K3
Blackhorse La MANG/FISH BS16 .. 328 C3
Blackhorse Pl
MANG/FISH BS16 .... 328 C5
Blackhorse Rd
KGWD/HNM BS15 .... 337 M5
MANG/FISH BS16 .... 328 C5
Black Jack St CIR GL7 .... 238 C2
Blacklow Cl STROUD GL5 .... 232 B1
Blackmoor St CFTN/FAIL BS8 ..... 334 A1
Blackmoors La BMSTR BS3 .... 335 G8
Blackquarries Hl WUE GL12 ...... 277 M4
Blacksmith Hl WUE GL12 .... 278 E4
Blacksmith La BWTH/CHD GL3 .. 113 M7
CBATH/BATHN BA1 .... 351 K5
RTEWK/TIB GL19 .... 91 K2
Blacksmiths Cl EVE WR11 .... 30 C2
Blacksmiths Gnd VGL GL2 .... 110 F6
Blacksmiths La BDWAY WR12 .... 32 A1
CHELTE/BC GL52 .... 94 D7
EVE WR11 .... 30 B6
TEWK GL20 .... 50 F1
VGL GL2 .... 111 H4
Blacksmiths Rd TEWK GL20 ...... 51 L4
Blackswarth Rd
EVILLE/WHL BS5 .... 336 F4
Blackthorn Cl
BMSTRD/HC/WWD BS13 .... 345 M6
Blackthorn Dr ALMDB BS32 ...... 316 F4
Blackthorn Gdns VGL GL2 .... 159 G2
Blackthorn Rd
BMSTRD/HC/WWD BS13 .... 345 M6
Blackthorn Wk
KGWD/HNM BS15 .... 338 A1
Blackwater Wy VGL GL2 .... 113 G6
Black Wls DSLY GL11 .... 253 K4
Bladon Ms CHELTW GL51 .... 114 D4
Blagrove Cl
BMSTRD/HC/WWD BS13 .... 345 L8
Blagrove Crs
BMSTRD/HC/WWD BS13 .... 345 L8
Blaisdon YATE/CS BS37 .... 320 A4
Blaisdon Cl GLE GL4 .... 137 G7
HNBRY/STHM BS10 .... 325 M2
Blaisdon La MTCHDN GL17 .... 131 M2
Blaisdon Wy CHELTW GL51 .... 93 G6
Blaise Wk
HNLZ/SM/SNYPK/WT BS9 .... 324 E5
Blake Cft CHELTW GL51 .... 93 G7
Blake Hill Wy GLE GL4 .... 136 F4

Blakeney Cl GL GL1 .... 135 M8
Blakeney Hill Rd LYD GL15 .... 178 C8
Blakeney Mills YATE/CS BS37 .. 319 M2
Blakeney Rd
BRSTK/PCHW BS34 .... 316 A2
HORF/LLZ BS7 .... 326 C4
Blake Rd CIR GL7 .... 238 C2
HORF/LLZ BS7 .... 326 D5
Blakes Rd THNB/SVB BS35 .... 293 K2
Blakewell Md
RSTROUD/NAIL GL6 .... 185 G3
Blanchards YATE/CS BS37 .... 320 E3
Blandford Cl
HNLZ/SM/SNYPK/WT BS9 .... 325 K5
Blenheim Cl COTS GL54 .... 124 C7
TEWK GL20 .... 51 K4
Blenheim Ct COTS GL54 .... 74 C5
Blenheim Dr
BRSTK/PCHW BS34 .... 316 D7
LED HR8 .... 20 A5
NWNT GL18 .... 86 D3
TEWK GL20 .... 27 H5
YATE/CS BS37 .... 309 L8
Blenheim Orch CHELTW GL51 ... 139 G1
Blenheim Rd GLE GL4 .... 5 G8
RDLND/MONT BS6 .... 325 L8
Blenheim Sq CHELTW GL51 ...... 93 G8
Blenman Cl MANG/FISH BS16 ... 327 J4
Bleriot Rd COTS GL54 .... 124 C7
Blethwin Cl HNBRY/STHM BS10 .. 325 H2
Blicks Hl MALM SN16 .... 303 K8
Blimeshire LYD GL15 .... 201 H2
Blind La CHCAM GL55 .... 34 D1
Blinkhorns Bridge La VGL GL2 .. 5 M7
Bloomfield Rd
BRSG/KWL/STAPK BS4 .... 336 E7
GL GL1 .... 135 M4
Bloomfield Road Link
BRSG/KWL/STAPK BS4 .... 336 E7
Bloomfield Ter GL GL1 .... 135 M5
Bloomsbury St CHELTW GL51 .... 2 A3
Bloxham Rd BDWAY WR12 .... 32 F2
Bloxhams Orch RTEWK/TIB GL19 .. 89 J3
Bloy St EVILLE/WHL BS5 .... 336 E2
Bluebell Cha
RSTROUD/NAIL GL6 .... 210 A7
Bluebell Cl GLE GL4 .... 136 F6
THNB/SVB BS35 .... 293 M1
Bluebell Dr CHEP NP16 .... 270 B6
Bluebell Gv CHELTW GL51 .... 115 H6
Bluebell Ri RSTROUD/NAIL GL6 .. 210 A7
The Bluebells ALMDB BS32 .... 317 G4
ALMDB BS32 .... 317 H4
Blue Boys' Pk
RSTROUD/NAIL GL6 .... 233 J4
Blue La NWNT GL18 .... 85 K3
Blue Quarry Rd CIR GL7 .... 238 E2
Blue Rock Crs LYD GL15 .... 200 D2
Blunts Hay CIR GL7 .... 220 B4
Boakes Dr STNHO GL10 .... 207 C4
Bockenem Cl
THNB/SVB BS35 .... 293 M4
Bodey Cl
OLD/WMLY/WICK BS30 .... 338 C6
Bodham Rd CHELTW GL51 .... 93 G7
Bodiam Av GL GL1 .... 159 K2
Bodmin Wk
BRSG/KWL/STAPK BS4 .... 346 B3
Bodyce Rd THNB/SVB BS35 .... 293 J6
Boleyn Cl BWTH/CHD GL3 .... 113 H4
Bolton Rd HORF/LLZ BS7 .... 326 A8
Bondend Rd GLE GL4 .... 161 C1
Bond's La CHPMW/MSHF SN14 .. 341 M2
Bond St CBRIS/FH BS1 .... 7 H1
Bonners Cl MALM SN16 .... 303 J7
Bonnington Wk HORF/LLZ BS7 .. 326 D4
Bonville Rd
BRSG/KWL/STAPK BS4 .... 347 G2
Bootenhay Rd
CHELTE/BC GL52 .... 72 C7
Booth Rd BMSTR BS3 .... 6 D9
Boot La BMSTR BS3 .... 6 F8
Borage Cl BWTH/CHD GL3 .... 137 H6
Bordesley Rd HGRV/WHIT BS14 .. 346 C8
Borleyton Wk
BMSTRD/HC/WWD BS13 .... 345 H7
Borough Cl STNHO GL10 .... 207 J8
Borver Gv
BMSTRD/HC/WWD BS13 .... 345 K7
Boscombe Crs
MANG/FISH BS16 .... 328 B4
Boscombe La
RSTROUD/NAIL GL6 .... 256 A3
Bosley Cl SHPSTR CV36 .... 16 A7
Bospin La STROUD GL5 .... 232 B2
Boswell St EVILLE/WHL BS5 ...... 336 E1
Botham Dr
BRSG/KWL/STAPK BS4 .... 347 G2
Bottom Cl HGRV/WHIT BS14 ..... 346 C5
Boucher Pl CBRISNE BS2 .... 336 C1
Boulters Rd
BMSTRD/HC/WWD BS13 .... 345 L7
Boulton La DSLY GL11 .... 253 K3
Boulton Rd CHELT GL50 .... 93 M6
Boulton's Rd KGWD/HNM BS15 .. 337 M3
Bouncer's La CHELTE/BC GL52 .. 3 M2
Boundary Pl RTEWK/TIB GL19 ... 66 D5
Boundary Rd FRCTL/WBN BS36 .. 318 F4
Bourchier Gdns
BMSTRD/HC/WWD BS13 .... 345 K8
Bourne Cl FRCTL/WBN BS36 ..... 318 A4
KGWD/HNM BS15 .... 337 K3
Bourne Lake Pk HGHW SN6 ...... 288 A5
Bourne La STROUD GL5 .... 233 J2
Bourne Rd KGWD/HNM BS15 .... 337 J3
Bourneville Rd
EVILLE/WHL BS5 .... 336 F3
Bournside Cl CHELTW GL51 ...... 115 J4
Bournside Dr CHELTW GL51 ...... 115 J4
Bournside Rd CHELTW GL51 ..... 115 J4
Boursland Cl ALMDB BS32 .... 316 F1
Bourton Av BRSTK/PCHW BS34 .. 316 E3
Bourton Cl BRSTK/PCHW BS34 .. 316 E3
Bourton Rd GLE GL4 .... 160 A1
MIM SL56 .... 58 C6
Bourton Wk
BMSTRD/HC/WWD BS13 .... 345 J3

Boverton Av BWTH/CHD GL3 .... 137 M5
Boverton Dr BWTH/CHD GL3 .... 137 M5
Boverton Rd
BRSTK/PCHW BS34 .... 316 D8
Bovone La VGL GL2 .... 109 M3
Bowbridge La CHELTE/BC GL52 .. 94 D7
STROUD GL5 .... 208 F5
Bowbridge Lock STROUD GL5 .... 208 F6
Bowden Cl
HNLZ/SM/SNYPK/WT BS9 .... 324 E3
Bowden Pl MANG/FISH BS16 .... 328 B4
Bowden Rd EVILLE/WHL BS5 ..... 337 G2
CHELTE/BC GL52 .... 94 C7
Bowen's Hl CLFD GL16 .... 175 J1
Bowen's Hill Rd CLFD GL16 ...... 175 J1
Bowerleaze
HNLZ/SM/SNYPK/WT BS9 .... 324 D6
Bower Rd BMSTR BS3 .... 335 J8
Bower Wk BMSTR BS3 .... 336 A8
Bowes Lyon Cl MIM SL56 .... 58 C7
Bow La COTS GL54 .... 123 H5
TEWK GL20 .... 25 J3
Bowldown Rd TET GL8 .... 280 E8
Bowler Rd TEWK GL20 .... 49 G2
Bowl Hl STROUD GL5 .... 208 C8
Bowling Green Av CIR GL7 .... 238 C1
Bowling Green Ct MIM SL56 ..... 58 C5
Bowling Green Crs CIR GL7 ...... 238 C1
Bowling Green Gdns CIR GL7 ... 238 C2
Bowling Green Hl CIR GL7 .... 238 C1
Bowling Green La CIR GL7 .... 238 C1
Bowling Hl YATE/CS BS37 .... 320 C2
Bowling Rd YATE/CS BS37 .... 320 D3
Bowly Crs CIR GL7 .... 238 B5
Bowly Rd CIR GL7 .... 238 B5
GL GL1 .... 135 M5
Bownham Md STROUD GL5 .... 232 E1
Bownham Pk STROUD GL5 .... 232 F2
Bowring Cl
BMSTRD/HC/WWD BS13 .... 345 L8
Bowsland Wy ALMDB BS32 .... 316 F1
Bowson Rd LYD GL15 .... 200 D1
Bowstreet La THNB/SVB BS35 ... 315 J3
Bow Wow CIR GL7 .... 263 J4
Box Br CHPMW/MSHF SN14 ..... 353 G7
Boxbush Cl CIR GL7 .... 263 J4
Boxbush Rd CIR GL7 .... 263 J4
CLFD GL16 .... 175 J1
Box Crs RSTROUD/NAIL GL6 ..... 233 H5
Boxhedge Farm La
FRCTL/WBN BS36 .... 319 G8
Box La RSTROUD/NAIL GL6 .... 233 G6
Box Rd CBATH/BATHN BA1 .... 352 E8
DSLY GL11 .... 229 J3
Box Road Av DSLY GL11 .... 229 H3
Boxtree Cl MTCHDN GL17 .... 129 C3
Box Vw CHPMW/MSHF SN14 .... 353 K1
Boxwell Rd TET GL8 .... 279 L8
Boyce Dr CBRISNE BS2 .... 336 C1
Boyce's Av CFTN/FAIL BS8 .... 335 J4
Boyd Cl OLD/WMLY/WICK BS30 . 339 K4
Boyd Rd KEYN BS31 .... 348 F8
Brabazon Rd
BRSTK/PCHW BS34 .... 326 D1
Bracelands RSTROUD/NAIL GL6 .. 209 M6
Bracelands Dr CLFD GL16 .... 151 J5
Bracewell Gdns
HNBRY/STHM BS10 .... 315 L7
Bracey Dr MANG/FISH BS16 ..... 327 L5
Brackenbury Dr
BRSTK/PCHW BS34 .... 317 G6
Bracken Cl LYD GL15 .... 201 L8
Brackendene ALMDB BS32 .... 316 E2
Bracken Dr LYD GL15 .... 201 K8
Bracton Dr HGRV/WHIT BS14 ... 346 B8
Bradeston Gv MANG/FISH BS16 . 327 J4
Bradford Rd VGL GL2 .... 5 M4
Bradfords Cl NWNT GL18 .... 86 A3
Bradfords Ct NWNT GL18 .... 86 A3
Bradfords La NWNT GL18 .... 86 A3
Bradhurst St
EVILLE/WHL BS5 .... 336 D5
Bradley Av AVONM BS11 .... 324 A5
FRCTL/WBN BS36 .... 318 A6
Bradley Cl VGL GL2 .... 112 E7
Bradley Court Rd
MTCHDN GL17 .... 130 C1
Bradley Crs AVONM BS11 .... 324 A5
Bradley Rd BRSTK/PCHW BS34 .. 316 B3
CHELTS GL53 .... 116 C7
WUE GL12 .... 277 J3
Bradley Stoke Wy ALMDB BS32 .. 316 E1
Bradley St WUE GL12 .... 277 J6
Bradshaw Cl VGL GL2 .... 113 G6
Bradstone Rd
FRCTL/WBN BS36 .... 317 M6
Bradville Gdns LGASH BS41 ...... 344 B3
Bradwell Gv HNBRY/STHM BS10 .. 325 L3
Braemar Av HORF/LLZ BS7 .... 326 B2
Braemar Cr HORF/LLZ BS7 .... 326 B2
Brae Wk GLE GL4 .... 136 F7
Bragg's La CBRISNE BS2 .... 7 K2
Braikenridge Rd
BRSG/KWL/STAPK BS4 .... 336 F7
Brainsfield
HNLZ/SM/SNYPK/WT BS9 .... 325 H5
Brake Cl ALMDB BS32 .... 317 C5
KGWD/HNM BS15 .... 338 B4
The Brake FRCTL/WBN BS36 ..... 318 E6
YATE/CS BS37 .... 310 A6
Bramble Cha CHELTE/BC GL52 .. 72 A6
Bramble Dr DSLY GL11 .... 229 J8
HNLZ/SM/SNYPK/WT BS9 .... 324 E8
Bramble La
HNLZ/SM/SNYPK/WT BS9 .... 324 E8
STNHO GL10 .... 207 H3
Bramble Lawn GLE GL4 .... 136 F8
Bramble Ri CHELTE/BC GL52 .... 94 E8
Bramble Rd CLFD GL16 .... 175 L4
The Brambles BRKLY GL13 .... 227 G7
KEYN BS31 .... 347 M8
RWYE HR9 .... 106 B3
Brambling Wk
MANG/FISH BS16 .... 327 H6
Bramley Cl LED HR8 .... 19 M5
THNB/SVB BS35 .... 292 C8
WUE GL12 .... 277 H7

Bramley Ct
OLD/WMLY/WICK BS30 .... 338 B7
Bramley Dr RTEWK/TIB GL19 ... 108 D7
Bramley Ms BWTH/CHD GL3 ..... 137 J5
Bramley Rd CHELTW GL51 .... 93 G8
TEWK GL20 .... 48 B4
Branche Gv
BMSTRD/HC/WWD BS13 .... 345 M8
Branch Hill Ri CHELTS GL53 ..... 116 C7
Branch Rd CHELTW GL51 .... 114 D4
The Branch CIND GL14 .... 129 M6
Brandash Rd YATE/CS BS37 ...... 320 E2
Branders CIND GL14 .... 129 M6
Brandon Cl BWTH/CHD GL3 ..... 113 J3
Brandon Pl CHELT GL50 .... 115 L4
Brandon Steep CBRIS/FH BS1 ... 6 C4
Brandon St CBRIS/FH BS1 .... 6 C5
Brangwyn Gv HORF/LLZ BS7 .... 326 D5
Branksome Crs
BRSTK/PCHW BS34 .... 316 D8
Branksome Dr
BRSTK/PCHW BS34 .... 316 D8
FRCTL/WBN BS36 .... 318 A5
Branksome Rd
RDLND/MONT BS6 .... 325 K8
Branscombe Rd
HNLZ/SM/SNYPK/WT BS9 .... 324 E7
Bransdown Hl MALM SN16 .... 301 J8
Brans La MIM SL56 .... 103 C3
Brantwood Rd
RSTROUD/NAIL GL6 .... 210 B8
Branwhite Cl HORF/LLZ BS7 ..... 326 D4
Brasenose Rd TEWK GL20 .... 27 C5
Brassington Gdns COTS GL54 ... 142 F7
The Bratches CHCAM GL55 .... 12 E6
Bratton Rd
BRSG/KWL/STAPK BS4 .... 345 M4
Braunton Rd BMSTR BS3 .... 335 L8
Bray Av LED HR8 .... 20 A4
Braydon Av BRSTK/PCHW BS34 .. 316 F3
Braydon La HGHW SN6 .... 288 B6
Brayne Ct
OLD/WMLY/WICK BS30 .... 338 B8
Breaches Ga ALMDB BS32 .... 317 H5
Breach Rd BMSTR BS3 .... 335 J8
Bream Av CLFD GL16 .... 199 M2
Bream Rd LYD GL15 .... 199 J6
Brean Down Av
HNLZ/SM/SNYPK/WT BS9 .... 325 K6
Brecknock Rd
BRSG/KWL/STAPK BS4 .... 336 C5
Brecon Cl VGL GL2 .... 159 C3
Brecon Rd
HNLZ/SM/SNYPK/WT BS9 .... 325 J5
Brecon Wy CLFD GL16 .... 152 A4
Bredon YATE/CS BS37 .... 319 M4
Bredon Cl KGWD/HNM BS15 .... 338 B4
Bredon Nook Rd
HNBRY/STHM BS10 .... 325 L4
Bredon Ri TEWK GL20 .... 48 B4
Bredon Vw BDWAY WR12 .... 33 G3
Bregawn Cl CHELTE/BC GL52 ... 94 A7
Breinton Wy VGL GL2 .... 112 F6
Bremilham Ri MALM SN16 .... 303 G8
Bremilham Rd MALM SN16 ...... 303 H7
Brendon Cl
OLD/WMLY/WICK BS30 .... 338 E7
Brendon St EVILLE/WHL BS5 .... 336 D1
Brenner St EVILLE/WHL BS5 ..... 336 E1
Brensham Rd TEWK GL20 .... 48 D4
Brent Rd HORF/LLZ BS7 .... 326 B6
Brentry Av EVILLE/WHL BS5 ..... 336 D4
Brentry La HNBRY/STHM BS10 .. 325 J1
Brentry Rd MANG/FISH BS16 ... 327 C7
Brereton Wy
OLD/WMLY/WICK BS30 .... 338 D7
Brewerton Cl
HNBRY/STHM BS10 .... 315 L8
Brewery Hl
OLD/WMLY/WICK BS30 .... 349 H3
Brewery La RSTROUD/NAIL GL6 . 232 D4
Briarbank Ri CHELTE/BC GL52 .. 116 E4
Briar Cl STROUD GL5 .... 208 F2
Briarfield Av
KGWD/HNM BS15 .... 337 L6
Briar Lawn GLE GL4 .... 136 F8
Briarleaze THNB/SVB BS35 .... 307 H1
Briars Cl BWTH/CHD GL3 .... 113 J5
Briarside Rd
HNBRY/STHM BS10 .... 315 L8
Briar Wk CHELTE/BC GL52 .... 94 E8
MANG/FISH BS16 .... 327 L8
Briar Wy MANG/FISH BS16 .... 327 K7
Briarwood
HNLZ/SM/SNYPK/WT BS9 .... 325 H5
Briary Rd CIR GL7 .... 244 F5
Briavels Gv RDLND/MONT BS6 .. 336 B1
Brickhill Cl SHPSTR CV36 .... 16 A5
Bricknell Av TEWK GL20 .... 27 H5
Brickrow STROUD GL5 .... 208 D3
Brick St CBRISNE BS2 .... 7 K2
Bridewell Dr EVE WR11 .... 30 B2
Bridewell St CBRIS/FH BS1 .... 6 F2
Bridge Cl CIR GL7 .... 238 D5
HGRV/WHIT BS14 .... 346 E7
VGL GL2 .... 135 K5
Bridge End CIR GL7 .... 238 D4
Bridge Farm Cl VGL GL2 .... 111 K4
Bridge Farm Cl
HGRV/WHIT BS14 .... 346 C8
Bridgeleap Rd
MANG/FISH BS16 .... 328 B3
Bridgemans Cl BDWAY WR12 ... 33 G2
Bridge Meadow Cl EVE WR11 .... 30 C1
Bridgend St STNHO GL10 .... 207 C5
Bridgend Rd FRCTL/WBN BS36 .. 317 M5
Bridge Rd BRKLY GL13 .... 226 F1
CFTN/FAIL BS8 .... 334 F5
CIR GL7 .... 238 C5
EVILLE/WHL BS5 .... 326 D8
KGWD/HNM BS15 .... 328 B3
MANG/FISH BS16 .... 328 E7
MTCHDN GL17 .... 129 M5
STROUD GL5 .... 207 M5
VGL GL2 .... 181 H6
YATE/CS BS37 .... 319 J1

Bridges Ct *MANG/FISH* BS16 .... 327 K7 🅐
Bridges Dr *MANG/FISH* BS16 .... 327 L5 🅑
Bridge-side *STROUD* GL5 .... 208 B5 🅐
Bridge St *CBRIS/FH* BS1 .... 6 F4
  CHELT GL51 .... 93 K7 🅐
  CHEP NP16 .... 270 A2
  CIR GL7 .... 242 E4
  EVILLE/WHL BS5 .... 336 F1 🅑
  LED HR8 .... 19 L3
  LYD GL15 .... 202 D1
  NWNT GL18 .... 86 C2
  RSTROUD/NAIL GL6 .... 232 E7 🅑
  STROUD GL5 .... 208 B5 🅑
Bridget Dr *CHEP* NP16 .... 270 C4
Bridge Valley Rd *CFTN/FAIL* BS8.. 335 C3
Bridgman Gv
  BRSTK/PCHW BS34 .... 316 D8
Bridgwater Rd
  BMSTRD/HC/WWD BS13...... 345 H3
  NAIL BS48 .... 344 C7
The Bridle *STROUD* GL5 .... 207 M4
Bridle Wy *THNB/SVB* BS35 ...... 293 H7
Briercliffe Rd
  HNLZ/SM/SNYPK/WT BS9 ...... 324 F4
Brierley Banks *MTCHDN* GL17 .... 129 H8
Brierley Cl *GLE* GL4 .... 137 G6 🅐
Brierley Rd *MTCHDN* GL17 ...... 129 H6
Brierley Wy *LYD* GL15 .... 201 M2
Brierly Furlong
  BRSTK/PCHW BS34 .... 316 F8
Briery Leaze Rd
  HGRV/WHIT BS14 .... 346 C6
Brightlands *CIND* GL14 .... 155 J7 🅑
Brighton Crs *BMSTR* BS3 .... 345 K1
Brighton Pk *EVILLE/WHL* BS5 .. 336 D5 🅑
Brighton Pl
  KGWD/HNM BS15 .... 337 M2 🅑
Brighton Rd
  BRSTK/PCHW BS34 .... 316 B3
  CHELTE/BC GL52 .... 3 G5
  RDLND/MONT BS6 .... 335 L2
Brighton St *CBRISNE* BS2 .... 336 A2
Brighton Ter *BMSTR* BS3 .... 345 K1 🅑
Bright St *EVILLE/WHL* BS5 ...... 336 D4 🅑
  KGWD/HNM BS15 .... 337 M3
Brigstocke Rd *CBRISNE* BS2 .... 336 A2 🅑
Brimbles *HORF/LLZ* BS7 .... 326 D1
Brimley *STNHO* GL10 .... 207 H7
Brimscombe HI *STROUD* GL5 .... 233 G3
Brimscombe La *STROUD* GL5 .... 233 H1 🅐
Brimsome Meadow *VGL* GL2 .... 110 F6
Brindle Cl *GLE* GL4 .... 136 E7 🅐
Brinkmarsh La *WUE* GL12 ...... 274 F7
Brinkworthy Rd
  MANG/FISH BS16 .... 326 F5
Brinmead Wk
  BMSTRD/HC/WWD BS13 ...... 345 H8 🅐
Brins Cl *BRSTK/PCHW* BS34 ...... 317 H7
Brinsham La *YATE/CS* BS37 ...... 310 C5
Brionne Wy *VGL* GL2.. .... 112 D6
Brisbane *STNHO* GL10 .... 207 C2
Briscoes Av
  BMSTRD/HC/WWD BS13....... 345 L7
Bristol Br *CBRIS/FH* BS1................ 7 G4
Bristol HI *BRSG/KWL/STAPK* BS4.. 346 F1 🅐
Bristol Rd *CIR* GL7 .... 238 D4
  COTS GL54 .... 124 D7
  FRCTL/WBN BS36 .... 318 B3
  GL GL1 .... 135 M4
  HGRV/WHIT BS14 .... 346 E8
  KEYN BS31 .... 347 M5
  MANG/FISH BS16 .... 327 K3
  STNHO GL10 .... 206 F4
  THNB/SVB BS35 .... 293 K4
  VGL GL2 .... 159 H3
  VGL GL2 .... 205 H8
  WUE GL12 .... 295 J5
Bristol St *MALM* SN16 .... 303 C4
Britannia Crs
  BRSTK/PCHW BS34 .... 316 F6
Britannia Rd
  BRSTK/PCHW BS34 .... 315 M4
  EVILLE/WHL BS5 .... 336 D2
  KGWD/HNM BS15 .... 337 L3
Britannia V *CHELTE/BC* GL52 .... 72 D8
British Rd *BMSTR* BS3 .... 335 L4
Britten Ct
  OLD/WMLY/WICK BS30 ...... 338 B7 🅐
Brixham Rd *BMSTR* BS3 .... 345 L1
Brixton Rd *EVILLE/WHL* BS5 .... 336 D3
Brizen La *CHELTS* GL53 .... 115 J7
Broadbury Rd
  BRSG/KWL/STAPK BS4.. ...... 346 A3
Broadclose Rd *VGL* GL2 .... 90 F8
Broad Cft *ALMDB* BS32 .... 316 E1 🅐
Broadfield Av
  KGWD/HNM BS15 .... 337 L3
Broadfield Rd
  BRSG/KWL/STAPK BS4.......... 346 C2
  STNHO GL10 .... 206 B4
Broadlands Av *KEYN* BS31 ...... 347 M5
Broadlands Cl *COTS* GL54 ...... 123 H6 🅑
Broadlands Dr *AVONM* BS11 .... 324 C2
Broad La *FRCTL/WBN* BS36 ...... 318 F6
  YATE/CS BS37 .... 309 L7
  YATE/CS BS37 .... 319 L7
Broadleas
  BMSTRD/HC/WWD BS13....... 345 K4
Broadleaze *AVONM* BS11 .... 324 A4 🅐
  CIR GL7 .... 265 C3
Broadleys Av
  HNLZ/SM/SNYPK/WT BS9 ...... 325 K4
Broad Leys Rd *GLE* GL4 .... 136 F4
Broad Marston Rd *CHCAM* GL55 .... 8 E5
Broadmead La *KEYN* BS31 .... 348 C5
Broadmere Cl *DSLY* GL11 .... 229 G8
Broadmoor La
  CBATH/BATHN BA1 .... 350 B7
  SHPSTR CV36 .... 38 C7
Broadmoor Pk *CIND* GL14 .... 129 M8
Broadmoor V
  CBATH/BATHN BA1 .... 350 C8
Broad Oak Rd
  BMSTRD/HC/WWD BS13........ 345 H7

Broad Oaks *CFTN/FAIL* BS8 ...... 335 G5 🅐
Broadoak Wk *MANG/FISH* BS16.. 327 K7
Broad Oak Wy *CHELTW* GL51 .... 115 G5
Broad Quay *CBRIS/FH* BS1 .... 6 E4
Broad Rd *KGWD/HNM* BS15 ...... 337 L2
Broadstone Cl *GLE* GL4 .... 137 G4
Broadstone Rd
  BMSTRD/HC/WWD BS13....... 345 M6
Broad St *CBRIS/FH* BS1 .... 6 F3
  CIND GL14 .... 154 D3
  MANG/FISH BS16 .... 328 A4
  NWNT GL18 .... 86 C3
  RTEWK/TIB GL19 .... 89 G5
  SHPSTR CV36 .... 61 H5
  STNHO GL10 .... 207 J8
  STROUD GL5 .... 207 M8
  YATE/CS BS37 .... 320 D2
Broad Wk
  BRSG/KWL/STAPK BS4.......... 346 B1
  YATE/CS BS37 .... 320 B1 🅐
Broadway *KEYN* BS31 .... 348 F8 🅐
Broadway Av
  HNLZ/SM/SNYPK/WT BS9 ...... 325 M5
Broadway Cl *CIR* GL7 .... 266 C5
Broadway La *CIND* GL14 .... 157 J1
  CIR GL7 .... 263 H5
Broadway Rd *BDWAY* WR12 ...... 11 G8
  BDWAY WR12 .... 31 H2
  BMSTRD/HC/WWD BS13 ...... 345 H6 🅑
  CHCAM GL55 .... 8 E3
  COTS GL54 .... 53 H6
  HORF/LLZ BS7 .... 325 M8
Broadways Dr
  MANG/FISH BS16 .... 327 H4 🅐
The Broadway *DSLY* GL11 ...... 253 H3
  RSTROUD/NAIL GL6 .... 210 E7
Broad Weir *CBRIS/FH* BS1 .... 7 H3
Broadwell Cl *GLE* GL4 .... 137 G6 🅑
Broadwell Rd *CIR* GL7 .... 221 M8
  MIM GL56 .... 103 H2
Brock Cl *CHELTW* GL51 .... 114 D5
Brockeridge Cl *VGL* GL2 .... 159 G1 🅑
Brockeridge Rd *TEWK* GL20 .... 26 C5 🅑
Brockhollands Rd *LYD* GL15 .... 200 D3
Brockhurst Gdns
  KGWD/HNM BS15 .... 337 J3 🅐
Brockhurst Rd
  KGWD/HNM BS15 .... 337 J3
Brockley Acres
  RSTROUD/NAIL GL6 .... 210 A6
Brockley Cl
  BRSTK/PCHW BS34 .... 316 E4 🅐
Brockley Rd *KEYN* BS31 .... 348 F8 🅐
  STNHO GL10 .... 207 H7
Brockley Wk
  BMSTRD/HC/WWD BS13 ...... 345 J3 🅐
Brockmoor La *NWNT* GL18 ...... 85 H3
Brockridge La
  FRCTL/WBN BS36 .... 318 E4
Brocks Rd
  BMSTRD/HC/WWD BS13 ...... 345 L8
Brockworth *YATE/CS* BS37 ...... 319 L5
Brockworth Crs
  MANG/FISH BS16 .... 327 H4 🅐
Brockworth Rd *BWTH/CHD* GL3.. 113 M8
Brome Rd *GLE* GL4 .... 137 H6
Bromfield Wk
  MANG/FISH BS16 .... 328 D4 🅐
Bromley Dr *MANG/FISH* BS16 .... 327 M3
Bromley Heath Av
  MANG/FISH BS16 .... 327 M3
Bromley Heath Rd
  MANG/FISH BS16 .... 327 M3 🅐
Bromley Rd *CLFD* GL16 .... 176 A6
  HORF/LLZ BS7 .... 326 B6
Brompton Cl *KGWD/HNM* BS15 .. 338 B3 🅐
Broncksea Rd *HORF/LLZ* BS7 .... 326 B2
Bronte Cl *CHELTW* GL51 .... 115 H4 🅐
Brook Cl *COTS* GL54 .... 74 B7 🅐
  COTS GL54 .... 169 K2
  LGASH BS41 .... 344 D2
Brookcote Dr
  BRSTK/PCHW BS34 .... 316 F5
Brook Ct *CHELT* GL50 .... 115 K5
Brookdale Rd
  BMSTRD/HC/WWD BS13 ...... 345 K5
Brooke Rd *CIR* GL7 .... 238 B5
  LED HR8 .... 19 L2
Brookfield Av *HORF/LLZ* BS7 .... 325 M8 🅐
Brookfield Cl *YATE/CS* BS37 .... 320 E2
Brookfield La *BWTH/CHD* GL3 .. 114 A4
  RDLND/MONT BS6 .... 335 M1 🅐
Brookfield Rd
  BRSTK/PCHW BS34 .... 316 D3
  BWTH/CHD GL3 .... 114 A4
  GLE GL4 .... 137 H4
  RDLND/MONT BS6 .... 335 M1 🅑
Brookfield Wk
  OLD/WMLY/WICK BS30 ...... 338 E8 🅐
Brook Ga *BMSTR* BS3 .... 345 G4
Brook HI *RDLND/MONT* BS6 ...... 336 A2
Brookland Rd
  RDLND/MONT BS6 .... 325 M6 🅐
Brooklands Pk *VGL* GL2 .... 112 E6
Brook La *MANG/FISH* BS16 ...... 327 G5
  MIM GL56 .... 57 G1
  RDLND/MONT BS6 .... 336 B2 🅐
  VGL GL2 .... 112 E2
Brooklea
  OLD/WMLY/WICK BS30 ...... 338 D7
Brookleaze
  HNLZ/SM/SNYPK/WT BS9 ...... 324 E6
Brook Lintons
  BRSG/KWL/STAPK BS4.......... 336 F8 🅐
Brooklyn Cl *CHELTW* GL51 ...... 93 H8 🅐
Brooklyn Gdns *CHELTW* GL51 .... 93 J8 🅐
Brooklyn Rd
  BMSTRD/HC/WWD BS13....... 345 K3
  CHELTW GL51 .... 115 H1
Brookmead *THNB/SVB* BS35 .... 293 M4 🅐
Brook Rd *BMSTR* BS3 .... 6 E8 🅐
  CHELTW GL51 .... 93 J7 🅐
  EVILLE/WHL BS5 .... 337 G2
  KGWD/HNM BS15 .... 338 C3 🅐
  MANG/FISH BS16 .... 327 J8 🅐
  RDLND/MONT BS6 .... 336 B2

Brooksdale La *CHELTS* GL53 .... 115 L5 🅑
Brookside *MALM* SN16 .... 284 A5 🅐
  MIM GL56 .... 35 L4
  NWNT GL18 .... 86 C3
  TEWK GL20 .... 48 C3
  TEWK GL20 .... 51 L4
Brookside Dr *FRCTL/WBN* BS36 .. 318 D3
Brookside Rd
  BRSG/KWL/STAPK BS4.......... 347 G1
  CIND GL14 .... 153 M2
Brook St *EVILLE/WHL* BS5 .... 336 E4 🅐
  GL GL1 .... 4 F9
  MTCHDN GL17 .... 130 C1
  YATE/CS BS37 .... 320 C2
Brookthorpe *YATE/CS* BS37 .... 319 M3
Brookthorpe Av *AVONM* BS11 .. 324 C3
Brookthorpe Cl *GL* GL1 .... 135 M8
Brook V *CHELTE/BC* GL52 .... 3 J9
Brookview Wk
  BMSTRD/HC/WWD BS13........ 345 K4
Brook Wy *ALMDB* BS32 .... 316 E2 🅐
Brookway Dr *CHELTS* GL53 .... 116 C5
Brookway Rd *CHELTS* GL53 .... 116 C5
Broom Bungalows *GLE* GL4 .... 136 C6 🅐
Broom HI *CLFD* GL16 .... 151 H5
Broom HI *CLFD* GL16 .... 151 H5 🅐
  MANG/FISH BS16 .... 327 G6
Broomhill Rd
  BRSG/KWL/STAPK BS4.......... 337 H8
The Brooms *MANG/FISH* BS16 .. 328 C1 🅐
Brow HI *CBATH/BATHN* BA1 ...... 352 B8
Brown Cl *CHELTW* GL51 .... 93 G8 🅐
Browning Ct *HORF/LLZ* BS7 .... 326 D3 🅐
Browning Ms *CHELTW* GL51 .... 115 H4 🅐
The Brownings *COR/BOX* SN13 .. 353 M8
Browns HI *RSTROUD/NAIL* GL6 .. 233 L1
Brownshill Rd
  RSTROUD/NAIL GL6 .... 233 K2
Brown's La *STNHO* GL10 .... 207 J5
Brown's Piece *WUE* GL12 .... 277 K5
Broxholme Wk *AVONM* BS11 .... 324 B3 🅐
Bruce Av *EVILLE/WHL* BS5 .... 336 E2
Bruce Rd *EVILLE/WHL* BS5 .... 336 E2
Brummels Dr *CLFD* GL16 .... 151 J5
Brunel Cl
  OLD/WMLY/WICK BS30 ...... 338 E4
Brunel Lock Rd *CBRIS/FH* BS1 .. 335 H6
Brunel Rd
  BMSTRD/HC/WWD BS13........ 345 H3
  CHEP NP16 .... 270 A5
Brunel Wy *BMSTR* BS3 .... 335 C8
  COR/BOX SN13 .... 353 M5
  STNHO GL10 .... 206 E3
  THNB/SVB BS35 .... 293 K4
Brunswick Pl *CBRIS/FH* BS1 ..... 335 H6 🅐
Brunswick Rd *GL* GL1 .... 4 E7
Brunswick Sq *CBRISNE* BS2 ..... 7 G1 🅐
  GL GL1 .... 4 E7
Brunswick St *CBRISNE* BS2 .... 336 A3 🅑
  CHELT GL50 .... 2 C3
  EVILLE/WHL BS5 .... 336 E4 🅐
The Brush *STROUD* GL5 .... 207 M4 🅐
Bruton Cl *EVILLE/WHL* BS5 ...... 337 H3 🅐
Bruton Wy *GL* GL1 .... 5 G7
Bryansons Cl
  MANG/FISH BS16 .... 326 F5 🅐
Bryants Cl *MANG/FISH* BS16 ... 327 L2 🅐
Bryant's HI *EVILLE/WHL* BS5 .... 337 K5
Bryaston Cl *CHELTW* GL51 ...... 115 J1
Bryerland Rd *CHELTW* GL51 .... 138 C7
Brymore Av *CHELTE/BC* GL52 .... 94 C4 🅐
Brymore Cl *CHELTE/BC* GL52...... 94 C4 🅐
Brynland Av *HORF/LLZ* BS7 .... 326 A7
Bryony Bank *CHELTS* GL53 ..... 115 K7 🅑
Bryworth La *CIR* GL7 .... 244 C5
Buchanan Av *CLFD* GL16 .... 151 J8
Buchanan St *CLFD* GL16 .... 151 J8 🅐
Buckholt Rd *GLE* GL4 .... 161 M4
Buckholt Wy *BWTH/CHD* GL3 .. 138 A6 🅐
Buckingham Av *CHELTW* GL51 .. 115 J1
Buckingham Cl *STNHO* GL10 .... 206 A3
Buckingham Dr
  BRSTK/PCHW BS34 .... 316 F7
  BWTH/CHD GL3 .... 113 J4 🅐
Buckingham Gdns
  MANG/FISH BS16 .... 328 A5
Buckingham Pl
  MANG/FISH BS16 .... 328 A5 🅐
Buckingham Rd
  BRSG/KWL/STAPK BS4.......... 336 F6 🅐
Buckingham St *BMSTR* BS3 .... 345 L1 🅐
Buckingham V
  CFTN/FAIL BS8 .... 335 J3 🅐
Buckland Cl *CHELTE/BC* GL52 .. 72 B7 🅐
Buckles Cl *CHELTS* GL53 .... 116 D6
Buckle St *BDWAY* WR12 .... 33 J7
  CHCAM GL55 .... 11 L4
Buckshaft Rd *CIND* GL14 .... 154 A7
Buckstone Cl *CLFD* GL16 .... 151 M6
Budding Rd *STNHO* GL10 .... 206 A3
The Budding *STROUD* GL5 ...... 209 G2
Buddleia Cl *GLE* GL4 .... 137 H7 🅐
Bude Av *EVILLE/WHL* BS5 .... 337 J3
Bude Rd *BRSTK/PCHW* BS34 ..... 316 D8
Buettell Wy *MALM* SN16 .... 303 H6
Buller Rd *BRSG/KWL/STAPK* BS4.. 346 E1 🅐
Bulley La *VGL* GL2 .... 109 G8
Bullfinch Rd *GLE* GL4 .... 136 E5
Bullfinch Wy *VGL* GL2 .... 112 F4 🅐
Bullingham Ct *CHELTW* GL51 .... 2 A1
Bull La *COTS* GL54 .... 74 D6
  EVILLE/WHL BS5................ 337 H5
  GL GL1 .... 4 E5
Bull Pitch *DSLY* GL11 .... 253 K2
Bulls La *COR/BOX* SN13 .... 353 M5 🅐
Bully La *YATE/CS* BS37 .... 309 M3
Bulwark Av *CHEP* NP16 .... 270 B5
Bulwark Rd *CHEP* NP16 .... 270 A4
The Bulwarks
  RSTROUD/NAIL GL6 .... 233 K5
Bunting HI
  RSTROUD/NAIL GL6 .... 232 C7 🅐
Bunting Wy
  RSTROUD/NAIL GL6 .... 232 B7
Burbank Cl
  OLD/WMLY/WICK BS30 ...... 338 C8

Burchells Green Cl
  KGWD/HNM BS15 .... 337 K3
Burchells Green Rd
  KGWD/HNM BS15 .... 337 K3 🅐
Burcombe Cl *FRCTL/WBN* BS36 .. 318 F4
Burcombe La *CIR* GL7 .... 189 H6
Burcombe Rd
  RSTROUD/NAIL GL6 .... 210 A8
Burcombe Wy
  RSTROUD/NAIL GL6 .... 210 B8
Burden Cl *ALMDB* BS32 .... 317 G5
Burdett Cl *STNHO* GL10 .... 207 H4
Burdett Rd *STNHO* GL10 .... 207 H4
Burfoote Gdns
  HGRV/WHIT BS14 .... 347 G7
Burfoot Rd *HGRV/WHIT* BS14 .. 347 G7
Burford Dr *STROUD* GL5 .... 208 C4
Burford Gv *AVONM* BS11 .... 324 B6
Burford Ms *GL* GL1 .... 5 K9
Burford Rd *CIR* GL7 .... 238 E2
Burford St *CIR* GL7 .... 244 E7
Burgage Cl *YATE/CS* BS37 ...... 320 D3 🅐
The Burgage *CHELTE/BC* GL52 .. 94 C6
Burgess Green Cl
  BRSG/KWL/STAPK BS4.......... 336 C4
Burghill Rd *HNBRY/STHM* BS10.. 325 J2
Burghley Ct
  FRCTL/WBN BS36 .... 318 A6 🅐
Burghley Rd *RDLND/MONT* BS6.. 336 A1
Burgis Rd *HGRV/WHIT* BS14 .... 346 F5 🅐
Burleigh Cft *GLE* GL4 .... 137 H3
Burleigh La *STROUD* GL5 .... 233 G3
Burleigh Tor *STROUD* GL5 ...... 233 H4 🅐
Burleigh Vw
  RSTROUD/NAIL GL6 .... 209 M7
Burleigh Wy *WUE* GL12 .... 296 D6
Burley Av *MANG/FISH* BS16 .... 328 B6
Burley Crest *MANG/FISH* BS16 .. 328 B5
Burley Gv *MANG/FISH* BS16 .... 328 B5
Burlington Rd
  RDLND/MONT BS6 .... 335 L4
The Burltons *WUE* GL12 .... 295 K1
Burma *CHELTE/BC* GL52 .... 3 L3
Burma Rd *RSTROUD/NAIL* GL6 .. 232 C7
Burnbush Cl *HGRV/WHIT* BS14 .. 347 G5
Burnell Dr *CBRISNE* BS2 .... 336 B3
Burneside Cl
  HNBRY/STHM BS10 .... 325 L1 🅐
Burnet Cl *GLE* GL4 .... 136 C7
Burney Wy
  OLD/WMLY/WICK BS30 ...... 338 C5
Burnham Cl
  KGWD/HNM BS15 .... 338 B2 🅐
Burnham Dr *KGWD/HNM* BS15... 338 B2 🅑
Burnham La *MALM* SN16 .... 303 H7
Burnivale *MALM* SN16 .... 303 J8
Burns Av *VGL* GL2 .... 135 J7
Burnt Barn Rd *CHEP* NP16 ..... 270 A6
Burnt Oak *DSLY* GL11 .... 253 J2
Burrington Av
  BMSTRD/HC/WWD BS13 ...... 345 J3 🅑
Burrough Wy *FRCTL/WBN* BS36.. 318 A6
Burrups La *RWYE* HR9 .... 84 F2
Burton Cl *CBRIS/FH* BS1 .... 7 G7
Burton Ct *CFTN/FAIL* BS8 .... 6 A3 🅐
Burton Rd *BAD* GL9 .... 323 H5
Burtons La *COR/BOX* SN13 .... 353 L6 🅑
Burton St *CHELT* GL50 .... 2 B4
Burwalls Rd *CFTN/FAIL* BS8 .... 335 G5
Bury Bar La *NWNT* GL18 .... 86 C3
Burycourt Cl *AVONM* BS11 ...... 324 C2
Bury Court Rd *CIND* GL14 ...... 157 C3
Bury HI *MANG/FISH* BS16 .... 318 A4
Bury Hill La *YATE/CS* BS37 .... 310 C3
Bury La *OLD/WMLY/WICK* BS30 .. 340 B3
  VGL GL2 .... 134 A4
Buryway La *SHPSTR* CV36 .... 61 H4
Buscombe Gdns
  BWTH/CHD GL3 .... 137 K4
Bush Av *BRSTK/PCHW* BS34 .... 316 E6
Bush Cl *STNHO* GL10 .... 206 B3
Bushcombe Cl *CHELTE/BC* GL52 .. 72 E8
Bushcombe La *CHELTE/BC* GL52 .. 72 F7
Bushes La *YATE/CS* BS37 .... 311 J5
Bush Hay *BWTH/CHD* GL3 ...... 113 K6
Bush Pitch *LED* HR8 .... 19 L1
Bushy Pk *BRSG/KWL/STAPK* BS4 .. 7 K9
  BRSG/KWL/STAPK BS4.......... 336 B8
Bushy Wy *CHELTW* GL51 .... 92 F6
Bussage HI *RSTROUD/NAIL* GL6 .. 209 L7
Butcher Hill's La
  RSTROUD/NAIL GL6 .... 232 D8 🅑
Butcombe Wk
  HGRV/WHIT BS14 .... 346 D6
Butlers Cl *EVILLE/WHL* BS5 .... 337 H4
  SHPSTR CV36 .... 61 J5
Butlers Fld *CIR* GL7 .... 244 E6
Butlers La *SHPSTR* CV36 .... 61 H6
Butlers Md *LYD* GL15 .... 202 E1
Butlers Rd *SHPSTR* CV36 .... 61 J6
Buttercross La *CHELTE/BC* GL52 .. 94 B6
Buttercup Lawn *GLE* GL4 ...... 160 F1
Butterfield Cl
  HNBRY/STHM BS10 .... 325 L3
Butterfield Rd
  HNBRY/STHM BS10 .... 326 A4
Butterow West *STROUD* GL5 ... 208 D8
Butterow HI *STROUD* GL5 ...... 208 E8
Butterow La *STROUD* GL5 ...... 208 D8
Buttersend La *RTEWK/TIB* GL19.. 88 C3
Butterworth Ct
  BRSG/KWL/STAPK BS4.......... 345 M4 🅑
Butt Gn *RSTROUD/NAIL* GL6 .... 185 G2
Buttington Cl *GLE* GL4 .... 137 H6
Buttington HI *CHEP* NP16 ...... 270 D4
Buttington Rd *CHEP* NP16 ...... 270 C3 🅐
Buttington Ter *CHEP* NP16 ..... 270 D5
Butt La *THNB/SVB* BS35 .... 273 L8
Butt's La *CHELTE/BC* GL52 ...... 72 E6
  CHPMW/MSHF SN14 .... 331 K7
The Butts *GLE* GL4 .... 136 C7
  MALM SN16 .... 284 A5
  NWNT GL18 .... 86 C3
Butt St *RSTROUD/NAIL* GL6 ..... 233 J5
Buxton Wk *HORF/LLZ* BS7 .... 326 C3

Byard Rd *VGL* GL2 .... 135 K6
Bybrook Gdns *GLE* GL4 .... 159 M2
Bybrook Rd *GLE* GL4 .... 159 M2
Bye Md *MANG/FISH* BS16 .... 328 C3
Bye St *LED* HR8 .... 20 A3
Byfield Cl *CHELTE/BC* GL52 .... 94 E1
Byfords Cl *RTEWK/TIB* GL19 .... 108 C7 🅐
Byfords Rd *RTEWK/TIB* GL19 .... 108 C7 🅐
Byron Av *VGL* GL2 .... 135 L7
Byron Pl *CFTN/FAIL* BS8 .... 6 B3 🅐
  MANG/FISH BS16 .... 328 A7 🅐
Byron Rd *CHELTW* GL51 .... 115 H2
  DSLY GL11 .... 253 L4
  STROUD GL5 .... 208 B3
Byron St *CBRISNE* BS2 .... 336 C2 🅐
  EVILLE/WHL BS5 .... 336 E4 🅐

C

Cabot Cl *YATE/CS* BS37........... 320 B2
Cabot Wy *CFTN/FAIL* BS8 .... 335 H5
Cadbury Heath Rd
  OLD/WMLY/WICK BS30 ...... 338 D6
Caddick Cl *KGWD/HNM* BS15 ... 338 B1
Cade Cl *BRSTK/PCHW* BS34 ..... 317 C6
  KGWD/HNM BS15 .... 338 B5
Cadogan Rd *HGRV/WHIT* BS14 .. 346 C3
Caen Rd *BMSTR* BS3.............. 335 M4
Caernarvon Cl *CHELTW* GL51 .. 115 G5
Caernarvon Rd *CHELTW* GL51... 115 G5
  KEYN BS31 .... 347 L7
Caerwent La *CHEP* NP16 .... 270 D2
Caesar Rd *VGL* GL15 .... 135 L6
Caesars Cl *LYD* GL15 .... 201 L7 🅐
Caine Rd *HORF/LLZ* BS7 .... 326 B4 🅐
Cains Cl *KGWD/HNM* BS15 ..... 338 A5
Cainscross Rd *STROUD* GL5..... 208 B4
Caird St *CHEP* NP16 .... 270 A4
Cairn Gdns *FRCTL/WBN* BS36 .. 318 A7 🅐
Cairns' Crs *CBRISNE* BS2 ...... 336 B2 🅐
Cairns Rd *RDLND/MONT* BS6 .. 325 K6
Cakebridge Pl *CHELTE/BC* GL52 .. 3 K7
Cakebridge Rd *CHELTE/BC* GL52 .. 94 B7 🅐
Calcott Rd
  BRSG/KWL/STAPK BS4.......... 336 C8
Calcutt St *HGHW* SN6 .... 289 G3
Caldbeck Cl
  HNBRY/STHM BS10 .... 325 M1 🅐
Calder Cl *KEYN* BS31 .... 348 C7
Calderdale *GLE* GL4 .... 137 H6
Calderwood Ct *CHELT* GL50 ...... 2 C8
Caldicot Cl *AVONM* BS11 .... 324 E1 🅐
  OLD/WMLY/WICK BS30 ...... 348 D1
Caledonian Rd *GLE* GL4 .... 160 D1
Caledonia Pl *CFTN/FAIL* BS8 ..... 6 A4
Calf's La *CHCAM* GL55............. 12 E8
Calf Wy *RSTROUD/NAIL* GL6 .... 186 E2
  RSTROUD/NAIL GL6 .... 210 B1
California Rd
  OLD/WMLY/WICK BS30 ...... 338 D7 🅐
Callaways Rd *SHPSTR* CV36 ..... 16 E2
Callicroft Rd
  BRSTK/PCHW BS34 .... 316 C4
Callington Rd
  BRSG/KWL/STAPK BS4.......... 346 E2
  HGRV/WHIT BS14 .... 346 E2
Callow End *LED* HR8 .... 19 M1
Callowhill Ct *CBRIS/FH* BS1 ...... 7 G2
Calspick Wy *VGL* GL2 .... 112 F6 🅐
Calton Rd *GL* GL1 .... 136 A5
Calverley Ms *CHELTW* GL51 .... 115 G6 🅐
Calverton Rd
  EVILLE/WHL BS5 .... 336 F2 🅐
Cam Gn *DSLY* GL11 .... 229 L6
Camomile Cl *GLE* GL4 .... 137 H6 🅐
Campbell Cl *BWTH/CHD* GL3 .... 113 L4
Campbell Farm Dr
  AVONM BS11.. .... 324 C1
Campbell Rd *CLFD* GL16........ 151 M8
Campbell St *CBRISNE* BS2 ...... 336 A2
Campden Av *SHPSTR* CV36 ..... 14 A2
Campden La *BDWAY* WR12 ...... 11 J8
  COTS GL54 .... 97 K5
Campden Pitch *SHPSTR* CV36 ... 14 B1
Campden Rd *CHCAM* GL55 ..... 13 K6 🅐
  CHELTW GL51 .... 115 H5
  GLE GL4 .... 136 A8 🅐
  SHPSTR CV36 .... 15 M6
  STRAT CV37 .... 9 H3
Campion Gdns *COTS* GL54 ...... 102 A3
Campion Cl *GLE* GL4 .... 136 D7
  THNB/SVB BS35 .... 293 M1 🅐
Campion Dr *ALMDB* BS32 .... 316 F1 🅐

Campion Pk CHELTW GL51 ..... 115 H7
Cam Pitch DSLY GL11 ..... 229 H6
Camp La CHPMW/MSHF SN14 ..... 331 L7
Camp Rd CFTN/FAIL BS8 ..... 335 H4
  CHELTE/BC GL52 ..... 3 M6
  CHEP NP16 ..... 270 B5
  THNB/SVB BS35 ..... 272 D5
Camp Vw FRCTL/WBN BS36 ..... 318 A7
Cam Rd CHELTE/BC GL52 ..... 3 L2
Cams Gnd VGL GL2 ..... 110 F5
The Cam CHCAM GL55 ..... 13 H8
Camwal Rd CBRISNE BS2 ..... 7 M6
Canada Wy CBRIS/FH BS1 ..... 335 J6
Canberra STNHO GL10 ..... 207 G2
Canberra Gv BRSTK/PCHW BS34 316 D7
Canford La HNLZ/SM/SNYPK/WT BS9 325 H3
Canford Rd HNLZ/SM/SNYPK/WT BS9 325 H4
Cannans Cl FRCTL/WBN BS36 ..... 318 A4
Canning Rd VGL GL2 ..... 113 G6
Cann La OLD/WMLY/WICK BS30 ..... 339 G5
Cannon St BMSTR BS3 ..... 6 D9
  CBRIS/FH BS1 ..... 6 F7
Cannop Rd LYD GL15 ..... 176 E5
Canonbury St BRKLY GL13 ..... 227 H8
Canon Pk BRKLY GL13 ..... 227 G7
Canon's Rd CBRIS/FH BS1 ..... 6 B6
  CBRIS/FH BS1 ..... 6 B6
Canons Wy KGWD/HNM BS15 ..... 338 C7
Canowie Rd RDLND/MONT BS6 ..... 325 K8
Cantell Gv HGRV/WHIT BS14 ..... 347 H6
Canterbury Cl YATE/CS BS37 ..... 310 A8
Canterbury Leys TEWK GL20 ..... 48 C4
Canterbury St
  EVILLE/WHL BS5 ..... 336 D5
Canterbury Wk CHELTW GL51 ..... 115 J5
Canters Leaze WUE GL12 ..... 296 D7
Canton Acre
  RSTROUD/NAIL GL6 ..... 185 H2
Cantors Ct CHELTE/BC GL52 ..... 94 B1
Cantors Dr CHELTE/BC GL52 ..... 94 A1
Canvey Cl
  HNBRY/STHM BS10 ..... 326 A4
Canynge Rd CFTN/FAIL BS8 ..... 335 H3
Canynge Sq CFTN/FAIL BS8 ..... 335 H3
Canynge St CBRIS/FH BS1 ..... 7 G5
Capel Cl KGWD/HNM BS15 ..... 338 D3
Capel Ct STROUD GL5 ..... 208 F3
Capel Rd AVONM BS11 ..... 324 D2
  GLE GL4 ..... 160 E1
Capgrave Cl
  BRSG/KWL/STAPK BS4 ..... 337 J8
Capgrave Crs
  BRSG/KWL/STAPK BS4 ..... 337 J8
Captain Barton Cl STROUD GL5 ..... 209 H3
Captains Green Rd LYD GL15 ..... 177 J8
Caraway Gdns
  EVILLE/WHL BS5 ..... 336 E1
Cardigan Rd
  HNLZ/SM/SNYPK/WT BS9 ..... 325 K5
Cardill Cl
  BMSTRD/HC/WWD BS13 ..... 345 K5
Cares Cl CHELTE/BC GL52 ..... 72 C7
Carisbrooke Dr
  CHELTE/BC GL52 ..... 116 E4
Carisbrooke Rd
  BRSG/KWL/STAPK BS4 ..... 345 M3
  BWTH/CHD GL3 ..... 137 J5
Carisbrooke Rd MTCHDN GL17 ..... 106 C8
Carlow St
  BRSG/KWL/STAPK BS4 ..... 346 A3
Carlton Gdns STROUD GL5 ..... 208 E5
Carlton Pk EVILLE/WHL BS5 ..... 336 E3
Carlton Pl CHELTW GL51 ..... 2 B2
Carlton St CHELTE/BC GL52 ..... 3 G6
Carlyle Gv CHELTW GL51 ..... 92 F7
Carlyle Rd EVILLE/WHL BS5 ..... 336 E2
Carmarthen Cl YATE/CS BS37 ..... 310 A8
Carmarthen Gv
  OLD/WMLY/WICK BS30 ..... 348 D2
Carmarthen Rd CHELTW GL51 ..... 114 F5
  HNLZ/SM/SNYPK/WT BS9 ..... 325 J6
Carmarthen St GL GL1 ..... 136 B4
Carnarvon Rd
  RDLND/MONT BS6 ..... 335 L1
Carne Pl GLE GL4 ..... 136 E2
Caroline Cl KEYN BS31 ..... 347 L7
  YATE/CS BS37 ..... 320 D1
Carpenters La CIR GL7 ..... 238 D3
  KEYN BS31 ..... 348 B4
Carrant Rd TEWK GL20 ..... 48 B4
Carrington Av BMSTR BS3 ..... 335 J7
Carrol Gv CHELTW GL51 ..... 92 F7
Carson Rd MIM GL56 ..... 37 G2
Carsons Rd MANG/FISH BS16 ..... 328 D8
Carter Rd CHELTW GL51 ..... 93 H6
Carters Orch VGL GL2 ..... 159 H1
Carters Wy
  RSTROUD/NAIL GL6 ..... 232 B6
Carter Wk ALMDB BS32 ..... 316 F3
Cartledge Rd
  EVILLE/WHL BS5 ..... 336 E2
Cartway Gn CIND GL14 ..... 154 A3
Casey Cl LYD GL15 ..... 5 L6
Cashes Green Rd STROUD GL5 ..... 207 M8
Cash Hl MTCHDN GL17 ..... 128 F3
Casino Pl CHELT GL50 ..... 2 B9
Cassell Rd MANG/FISH BS16 ..... 327 L6
Cassey Bottom La
  EVILLE/WHL BS5 ..... 337 J4
Castle Cl HNBRY/STHM BS10 ..... 325 G1
  RSTROUD/NAIL GL6 ..... 185 H4
Castle Coombe THNB/SVB BS35 ..... 293 L1
Castle Ct BRSG/KWL/STAPK BS4 ..... 336 E7
  THNB/SVB BS35 ..... 293 K2
Castle Crs LYD GL15 ..... 198 F6
Castle End RSTROUD/NAIL GL6 ..... 161 L6
Castle Farm Rd
  KGWD/HNM BS15 ..... 347 L1
Castlefields Av
  CHELTE/BC GL52 ..... 116 E5
Castlefields Dr CHELTE/BC GL52 ..... 116 E5
Castlefields Rd
  CHELTE/BC GL52 ..... 116 E5
Castleford Gdns CHEP NP16 ..... 270 B1
Castleford Hl CHEP NP16 ..... 270 A1

Castle Gdns CHCAM GL55 ..... 13 G8
Castle Hl RBANSW OX15 ..... 17 M6
Castle Hill Dr BWTH/CHD GL3 ..... 138 B7
Castle Hill La RBANSW OX15 ..... 17 M7
Castle La CHPMW/MSHF SN14 ..... 342 A2
  VGL GL2 ..... 181 M1
Castlemaine Dr CHELTW GL51 ..... 114 E3
Castle Md STNHO GL10 ..... 207 H8
Castlemead Rd STROUD GL5 ..... 208 D5
Castle Ri STROUD GL5 ..... 208 E5
Castle Rd KGWD/HNM BS15 ..... 337 L1
  MANG/FISH BS16 ..... 329 L5
  OLD/WMLY/WICK BS30 ..... 338 E8
Castle St CBRISNE BS2 ..... 7 H3
  CIR GL7 ..... 238 C3
  COTS GL54 ..... 74 D6
  STNHO GL10 ..... 207 J8
  STROUD GL5 ..... 208 E5
  THNB/SVB BS35 ..... 293 J1
Castleton Rd GLE GL4 ..... 136 F4
Castlett St COTS GL54 ..... 98 E4
Castle Vw CHEP NP16 ..... 270 C2
Catbrain Hl HNBRY/STHM BS10 ..... 315 K5
Catbrain La HNBRY/STHM BS10 ..... 315 K5
Catbrook Cl CHCAM GL55 ..... 34 E2
Catchpot La YATE/CS BS37 ..... 321 J5
Cater Rd
  BMSTRD/HC/WWD BS13 ..... 345 K5
Catherine Hl HNBRY/STHM BS10 ..... 306 B1
Catherine Mead St BMSTR BS3 ..... 6 D9
Catherine Wy
  CBATH/BATHN BA1 ..... 352 B6
Catkin Cl VGL GL2 ..... 159 G4
Catley Gv LGASH BS41 ..... 344 D2
Catswood Ct STROUD GL5 ..... 209 G2
Catswood La
  RSTROUD/NAIL GL6 ..... 185 K8
Cattistock Dr EVILLE/WHL BS5 ..... 337 J5
Cattle Market Rd CBRIS/FH BS1 ..... 7 J6
Cattybrook Rd
  MANG/FISH BS16 ..... 328 F6
Cattybrook St
  EVILLE/WHL BS5 ..... 336 D3
Caudle Cl MTCHDN GL17 ..... 128 F3
Caudle La MTCHDN GL17 ..... 128 F4
Causeway Rd CIND GL14 ..... 154 B1
The Causeway
  FRCTL/WBN BS36 ..... 318 E4
  VGL GL2 ..... 158 F2
Causley Dr
  OLD/WMLY/WICK BS30 ..... 338 B6
Cavan Wk
  BRSG/KWL/STAPK BS4 ..... 345 M2
Cave Dr MANG/FISH BS16 ..... 327 M5
Cave Gv MANG/FISH BS16 ..... 328 D4
Cavendish Av BWTH/CHD GL3 ..... 113 M6
Cavendish Gdns
  HNLZ/SM/SNYPK/WT BS9 ..... 324 E7
Cavendish Rd
  BRSTK/PCHW BS34 ..... 316 B3
  HNLZ/SM/SNYPK/WT BS9 ..... 325 J6
Cave St CBRISNE BS2 ..... 336 A3
Cecil Av EVILLE/WHL BS5 ..... 337 H2
Cecil Rd CFTN/FAIL BS8 ..... 335 H3
  GL GL1 ..... 135 M4
  KGWD/HNM BS15 ..... 337 M3
Cecily Hl CIR GL7 ..... 238 B2
Cedar Cl BRSTK/PCHW BS34 ..... 316 B4
  CHELTS GL53 ..... 116 D6
  LGASH BS41 ..... 344 B2
  OLD/WMLY/WICK BS30 ..... 338 D7
  STROUD GL5 ..... 207 M5
Cedar Ct LED HR8 ..... 20 A3
Cedar Court Rd CHELT GL50 ..... 2 D7
Cedar Dr DSLY GL11 ..... 253 J2
  KEYN BS31 ..... 347 M7
Cedar Gdns STNHO GL10 ..... 207 H3
Cedar Gv COTS GL54 ..... 74 C5
  HNLZ/SM/SNYPK/WT BS9 ..... 324 F6
Cedar Pk
  HNLZ/SM/SNYPK/WT BS9 ..... 324 F6
Cedar Rd BWTH/CHD GL3 ..... 137 M4
  CHCAM GL55 ..... 9 G7
  TEWK GL20 ..... 49 G3
Cedar Wy CLFD GL16 ..... 151 M7
  FRCTL/WBN BS36 ..... 317 M6
  MANG/FISH BS16 ..... 329 K6
Cedarwood Dr GLE GL4 ..... 136 A8
Celandine Bank
  CHELTE/BC GL52 ..... 72 D7
Celandine Cl THNB/SVB BS35 ..... 293 M1
Celestine Rd YATE/CS BS37 ..... 309 L8
Celia Ter
  BRSG/KWL/STAPK BS4 ..... 337 H5
Cemetery La CIR GL7 ..... 217 K1
  COTS GL54 ..... 123 J5
Cemetery Rd
  BRSG/KWL/STAPK BS4 ..... 336 C8
  GLE GL4 ..... 136 C8
Cennick Ar KGWD/HNM BS15 ..... 338 A2
Centaurus Rd
  BRSTK/PCHW BS34 ..... 315 L4
Central Av HNBRY/STHM BS10 ..... 304 C8
  KGWD/HNM BS15 ..... 337 L6
Central Cross Dr CHELTE/BC GL52 ..... 2 F2
Central Rd GL GL1 ..... 136 A4
  STROUD GL5 ..... 208 B4
Central Wy CHELTW GL51 ..... 115 K1
Centurion Cl GLE GL4 ..... 137 G5
Centurion Rd LYD GL15 ..... 201 L7
Centurions Wk CLFD GL16 ..... 175 K2
  OLD/WMLY/WICK BS30 ..... 348 B1
Ceres Cl OLD/WMLY/WICK BS30 ..... 348 B1
Cerimon Ga
  BRSTK/PCHW BS34 ..... 317 G6
Cerney La AVONM BS11 ..... 324 A6
Cerney Wick La CIR GL7 ..... 263 M6
Cesson Ct YATE/CS BS37 ..... 320 E2
Chaceley Cl GLE GL4 ..... 137 G6
  VGL GL2 ..... 159 G3
Chadbournes
  BWTH/CHD GL3 ..... 113 K5
Chadleigh Gv
  BRSG/KWL/STAPK BS4 ..... 345 L4
Chad Rd CHELTW GL51 ..... 115 H2
Chadwick Cl GLE GL4 ..... 159 M1
Chaffinch Cl VGL GL2 ..... 112 F4
Chaffinch St STNHO GL10 ..... 207 H3
Chaingate La YATE/CS BS37 ..... 309 H5

Chakeshill Cl
  HNBRY/STHM BS10 ..... 315 L8
Chakeshill Dr
  HNBRY/STHM BS10 ..... 315 L8
Chalcombe Cl
  BRSTK/PCHW BS34 ..... 316 E3
Chalcroft Wk
  BMSTRD/HC/WWD BS13 ..... 345 G7
Chalford Av CHELTW GL51 ..... 114 D4
Chalford Cl YATE/CS BS37 ..... 319 M3
Chalford Rd GLE GL4 ..... 160 A2
Chalks Rd EVILLE/WHL BS5 ..... 336 F5
Challen Cl LED HR8 ..... 19 M1
Challender Av
  HNBRY/STHM BS10 ..... 315 H1
Challoner Ct CBRIS/FH BS1 ..... 6 E7
Chamberlayne Cl COTS GL54 ..... 102 A4
Champion Rd
  KGWD/HNM BS15 ..... 338 C1
Champneys Av
  HNBRY/STHM BS10 ..... 315 H8
Chamwells Av VGL GL2 ..... 5 M1
Chamwells Wk VGL GL2 ..... 112 D7
Chancel Cl GLE GL4 ..... 5 M7
  HNLZ/SM/SNYPK/WT BS9 ..... 324 F8
Chancel Pk CHELTS GL53 ..... 116 B5
Chancel Wy CHELTS GL53 ..... 116 B5
  CIR GL7 ..... 244 E7
Chancery St EVILLE/WHL BS5 ..... 336 D4
Chance St TEWK GL20 ..... 48 B5
Chandag Rd KEYN BS31 ..... 348 C7
Chandler Rd CHELTE/BC GL52 ..... 94 B1
Chandos Dr BWTH/CHD GL3 ..... 138 A6
Chandos Rd KEYN BS31 ..... 348 A4
  RDLND/MONT BS6 ..... 335 K2
  STROUD GL5 ..... 208 C7
Chandos St COTS GL54 ..... 74 C5
Channell's Hl
  HNLZ/SM/SNYPK/WT BS9 ..... 325 J3
Channel Vw CHEP NP16 ..... 270 A5
Channon's Hl MANG/FISH BS16 ..... 327 H7
Chantry Cl LYD GL15 ..... 225 J2
Chantry Ct TET GL8 ..... 282 A4
Chantry Gdns MIM GL56 ..... 57 J6
Chantry Ga CHELTE/BC GL52 ..... 94 A1
Chantry Gv AVONM BS11 ..... 324 A4
Chantry Lv MANG/FISH BS16 ..... 328 B2
Chantry Rd CFTN/FAIL BS8 ..... 335 K2
  THNB/SVB BS35 ..... 293 K1
Chapel Cl CIR GL7 ..... 236 E8
  CIR GL7 ..... 266 F4
Chapel Gdns
  HNBRY/STHM BS10 ..... 325 J2
  MIM GL56 ..... 37 G2
  VGL GL2 ..... 159 H4
Chapel Green La
  RDLND/MONT BS6 ..... 335 K1
Chapel Hay Cl BWTH/CHD GL3 ..... 113 L7
Chapel Hay La BWTH/CHD GL3 ..... 113 M7
Chapel Hl BRKLY GL13 ..... 251 K4
  CLFD GL16 ..... 151 K1
  LYD GL15 ..... 224 D2
Chapel La AVONM BS11 ..... 324 D1
  BAD GL9 ..... 323 J5
  BDWAY WR12 ..... 32 B1
  CHCAM GL55 ..... 8 F7
  CHCAM GL55 ..... 11 L5
  CHELT GL50 ..... 2 C9
  CHELTE/BC GL52 ..... 72 D8
  CHNTN OX7 ..... 83 H6
  CHNTN OX7 ..... 104 C6
  CHPMW/MSHF SN14 ..... 330 E6
  CIR GL7 ..... 190 C6
  COR/BOX SN13 ..... 353 M6
  COTS GL54 ..... 121 M7
  EVILLE/WHL BS5 ..... 337 G1
  KGWD/HNM BS15 ..... 338 D3
  MALM SN16 ..... 285 G3
  MANG/FISH BS16 ..... 327 L4
  MIM GL56 ..... 57 G1
  MTCHDN GL17 ..... 131 L2
  RSTROUD/NAIL GL6 ..... 233 J6
  RTEWK/TIB GL19 ..... 65 J2
  RWYE HR9 ..... 84 E3
  STROUD GL5 ..... 207 M5
  TEWK GL20 ..... 27 K3
  TEWK GL20 ..... 27 J7
  VGL GL2 ..... 133 G2
  WUE GL12 ..... 294 C2
  WUE GL12 ..... 297 M3
  YATE/CS BS37 ..... 321 J5
Chapel Pth
  CHPMW/MSHF SN14 ..... 343 K8
Chapel Pitch NWNT GL18 ..... 85 K8
Chapel Rd
  BMSTRD/HC/WWD BS13 ..... 345 G2
  CIR GL7 ..... 266 F5
  CLFD GL16 ..... 151 K6
  EVILLE/WHL BS5 ..... 336 D2
  KGWD/HNM BS15 ..... 337 L6
  LYD GL15 ..... 202 B1
  STRAT CV37 ..... 8 A1
  THNB/SVB BS35 ..... 272 E6
Chapel St CBRISNE BS2 ..... 7 L6
  CHELT GL50 ..... 2 C4
  CHNTN OX7 ..... 125 L1
  COTS GL54 ..... 102 A3
  DSLY GL11 ..... 229 H6
  MIM GL56 ..... 80 D8
  STROUD GL5 ..... 208 F4
  THNB/SVB BS35 ..... 293 K3
Chapel Wk BAD GL9 ..... 299 K8
  CHELT GL50 ..... 2 C6
  CLFD GL16 ..... 152 A4
Chapel Wy
  BRSG/KWL/STAPK BS4 ..... 337 G5
Chaplin Rd EVILLE/WHL BS5 ..... 336 D2
Chapman Wy CHELTW GL51 ..... 115 H4
Chapter St CBRISNE BS2 ..... 336 A3
Charbon Ga
  BRSTK/PCHW BS34 ..... 317 G6
Charborough Rd
  BRSTK/PCHW BS34 ..... 326 F1
Chardstock Av
  HNLZ/SM/SNYPK/WT BS9 ..... 324 C5
Chardwar Gdns COTS GL54 ..... 123 H6
Charfield KGWD/HNM BS15 ..... 338 C3

Charfield Rd
  HNBRY/STHM BS10 ..... 325 L2
  WUE GL12 ..... 276 F5
Chargrove
  OLD/WMLY/WICK BS30 ..... 338 E5
  YATE/CS BS37 ..... 319 M4
Chargrove La CHELTW GL51 ..... 114 F5
Charis Av HNBRY/STHM BS10 ..... 325 L4
Charlcombe La
  CBATH/BATHN BA1 ..... 351 H8
Charlcombe Rd
  HNLZ/SM/SNYPK/WT BS9 ..... 325 H5
Charlecote Av GL GL1 ..... 159 L3
Charlecote Cnr
  CHELTE/BC GL52 ..... 72 A8
Charles Av
  BRSTK/PCHW BS34 ..... 317 G7
Charles Cl THNB/SVB BS35 ..... 273 L8
Charles Pl CFTN/FAIL BS8 ..... 335 J5
Charles Rd BRSTK/PCHW BS34 ..... 316 D8
Charles St CBRISNE BS2 ..... 6 F1
  CHELTW GL51 ..... 2 A2
  GL GL1 ..... 5 G7
Charlesway MIM GL56 ..... 79 L3
Charleswood Rd LYD GL15 ..... 201 G1
Charlham La CIR GL7 ..... 264 F4
Charlock Cl GLE GL4 ..... 136 C7
Charlotte St CBRIS/FH BS1 ..... 6 C4
  CBRISNE BS2 ..... 7 J1
Charlotte St South CBRIS/FH BS1 ..... 6 C4
Charlton Av BRSTK/PCHW BS34 ..... 326 B1
Charlton Dr CHELTS GL53 ..... 3 H9
Charlton Gdns
  HNBRY/STHM BS10 ..... 315 M7
Charlton La CHELTS GL53 ..... 115 M6
  HNBRY/STHM BS10 ..... 315 J8
Charlton Mead Dr
  HNBRY/STHM BS10 ..... 315 M7
Charlton Pk KEYN BS31 ..... 347 M6
Charlton Park Dr CHELTS GL53 ..... 116 A4
Charlton Park Ga CHELTS GL53 ..... 116 A5
Charlton Pl
  HNBRY/STHM BS10 ..... 315 M7
Charlton Rd
  HNBRY/STHM BS10 ..... 325 L2
  KGWD/HNM BS15 ..... 337 K2
  MALM SN16 ..... 303 M6
  TET GL8 ..... 281 L4
Charlton St EVILLE/WHL BS5 ..... 336 D4
Charlton Wy VGL GL2 ..... 112 G6
Charminster Rd
  MANG/FISH BS16 ..... 327 K8
Charnell Rd MANG/FISH BS16 ..... 328 A7
Charnhill Brow
  MANG/FISH BS16 ..... 328 C7
Charnhill Crs MANG/FISH BS16 ..... 328 C7
Charnhill Dr MANG/FISH BS16 ..... 328 B7
Charnhill Rdg MANG/FISH BS16 ..... 328 C7
Charnhill V MANG/FISH BS16 ..... 328 B7
Charnwood MANG/FISH BS16 ..... 328 C7
Charnwood Cl CHELTS GL53 ..... 115 M6
Charnwood Ct LYD GL15 ..... 201 K6
Charnwood Rd CHELTS GL53 ..... 115 M6
  HGRV/WHIT BS14 ..... 346 B8
Charterhouse Rd
  EVILLE/WHL BS5 ..... 336 F3
Chartist Av RTEWK/TIB GL19 ..... 44 A7
Chartist Piece RTEWK/TIB GL19 ..... 66 E4
Chartists Wy CHEP NP16 ..... 270 A6
Chartists Wy RTEWK/TIB GL19 ..... 66 D4
Chartwell Cl VGL GL2 ..... 135 J5
Chase Av CHELTE/BC GL52 ..... 116 E5
Chasefield La
  MANG/FISH BS16 ..... 327 K7
Chase La GLE GL4 ..... 5 L9
  GLE GL4 ..... 136 D4
  WUE GL12 ..... 296 E5
Chasely Crs CHELTW GL51 ..... 115 G6
Chase Rd KGWD/HNM BS15 ..... 337 M1
The Chase BWTH/CHD GL3 ..... 113 M7
  GLE GL4 ..... 136 F6
  MANG/FISH BS16 ..... 327 L8
  STROUD GL5 ..... 207 M4
Chasewood Cnr
  RSTROUD/NAIL GL6 ..... 209 M7
Chatcombe Av YATE/CS BS37 ..... 320 A4
Chatcombe Cl CHELTS GL53 ..... 116 D7
Chatcombe Rd GLE GL4 ..... 136 D6
Chatsworth Av GL GL1 ..... 159 L2
Chatsworth Dr CHELTS GL53 ..... 115 M7
Chatsworth Pk THNB/SVB BS35 ..... 293 L1
Chatsworth Rd
  BRSG/KWL/STAPK BS4 ..... 336 E7
  MANG/FISH BS16 ..... 327 K8
Chatterton Gn
  HGRV/WHIT BS14 ..... 346 B8
Chatterton Rd YATE/CS BS37 ..... 319 M2
Chatterton Sq CBRIS/FH BS1 ..... 7 H7
Chaucer Cl GL GL1 ..... 135 M6
Chaucer Rd DSLY GL11 ..... 253 L4
Chaundey Gv
  BMSTRD/HC/WWD BS13 ..... 345 K6
Chavenage La TET GL8 ..... 281 L3
Cheapside CBRISNE BS2 ..... 336 B3
  STROUD GL5 ..... 208 D4
Cheapside St BMSTR BS3 ..... 7 K9
Cheap St COTS GL54 ..... 167 J7
Cheddar Gv
  BMSTRD/HC/WWD BS13 ..... 345 J3
Chedworth KGWD/HNM BS15 ..... 328 A8
Chedworth Rd GLE GL4 ..... 135 M8
  HORF/LLZ BS7 ..... 326 C5
Chedworth Wy
  CHELTW GL51 ..... 115 G3
Cheese La CBRISNE BS2 ..... 7 H4
Chelford Gv
  BRSTK/PCHW BS34 ..... 316 D3
Chelmer Gv KEYN BS31 ..... 348 B7
Chelmsford Av CHELTW GL51 ..... 115 J4
Chelmsford Wk
  BRSG/KWL/STAPK BS4 ..... 337 H6
Chelsea Cl CHELTS GL53 ..... 116 C5
  KEYN BS31 ..... 348 C6
Chelsea Pk EVILLE/WHL BS5 ..... 336 E3
Chelsea Rd EVILLE/WHL BS5 ..... 336 D2

Chelston Rd
  BRSG/KWL/STAPK BS4 ..... 345 M4
Cheltenham La
  RDLND/MONT BS6 ..... 336 A1
Cheltenham Rd BDWAY WR12 ..... 32 C4
  CHELTE/BC GL52 ..... 94 B2
  CIR GL7 ..... 214 B8
  COTS GL54 ..... 74 A8
  EVE WR11 ..... 30 D1
  GL GL1 ..... 5 K4
  RDLND/MONT BS6 ..... 335 M2
  RSTROUD/NAIL GL6 ..... 185 H3
  RSTROUD/NAIL GL6 ..... 210 C2
  TEWK GL20 ..... 27 J6
  VGL GL2 ..... 112 E8
Cheltenham Rd East BWTH/CHD GL3 113 H6
Chelt Rd CHELTE/BC GL52 ..... 3 L2
Chelvy Cl BMSTRD/HC/WWD BS13 345 M8
Chelwood Rd KEYN BS31 ..... 349 G7
Chelworth Rd HGHW SN6 ..... 288 D5
Chepstow Pk
  MANG/FISH BS16 ..... 328 B2
Chepstow Rd
  BRSG/KWL/STAPK BS4 ..... 345 M3
Chequers Cl
  OLD/WMLY/WICK BS30 ..... 338 E8
Chequers Rd GLE GL4 ..... 136 C4
Cherington KGWD/HNM BS15 ..... 337 K6
  YATE/CS BS37 ..... 319 M5
Cherington Rd
  HNBRY/STHM BS10 ..... 325 L4
Cheriton Cl CHELTW GL51 ..... 115 H6
Cheriton Pl
  HNLZ/SM/SNYPK/WT BS9 ..... 325 K4
  OLD/WMLY/WICK BS30 ..... 338 E5
Cherrington Dr GLE GL4 ..... 137 G6
Cherry Av CHELTS GL53 ..... 116 E7
Cherry Bank NWNT GL18 ..... 86 C4
Cherry Cl VGL GL2 ..... 159 G4
Cherry Garden La
  OLD/WMLY/WICK BS30 ..... 348 D1
Cherry Garden Rd
  OLD/WMLY/WICK BS30 ..... 348 E2
Cherry Gdns
  OLD/WMLY/WICK BS30 ..... 348 E2
Cherry Gv MANG/FISH BS16 ..... 328 C5
Cherry La CBRIS/FH BS1 ..... 6 F1
Cherry Orch TEWK GL20 ..... 27 G5
  WUE GL12 ..... 277 L4
Cherry Orchard La CHCAM GL55 ..... 34 E1
Cherry Orchard La
  CHPMW/MSHF SN14 ..... 313 K6
  TEWK GL20 ..... 25 M5
Cherry Orchard Rd TET GL8 ..... 282 A3
The Cherry Orch CHELTW GL51 ..... 92 A7
Cherry Rd
  CHPMW/MSHF SN14 ..... 343 J6
  LGASH BS41 ..... 344 B1
  YATE/CS BS37 ..... 320 C2
Cherry Tree Cl KEYN BS31 ..... 347 L7
  RSTROUD/NAIL GL6 ..... 232 C7
Cherrytree Ct
  MANG/FISH BS16 ..... 329 L6
Cherrytree Crs
  MANG/FISH BS16 ..... 337 L1
Cherrytree La CIR GL7 ..... 238 F1
Cherry Tree La CLFD GL16 ..... 152 A7
Cherry Tree Rd HGHW SN6 ..... 288 D5
Cherrytree Rd
  KGWD/HNM BS15 ..... 337 L1
Cherry Wk LYD GL15 ..... 201 J7
Cherry Wd
  OLD/WMLY/WICK BS30 ..... 348 D1
Cherrywood Gdns GLE GL4 ..... 136 A8
Cherston Ct GLE GL4 ..... 137 G3
Chertsey Rd RDLND/MONT BS6 ..... 335 K2
Chervil Cl GLE GL4 ..... 136 D7
Cherwell Cl THNB/SVB BS35 ..... 293 L4
Cherwell Rd KEYN BS31 ..... 348 C7
Chesham Wy
  KGWD/HNM BS15 ..... 337 M2
Cheshire Cl YATE/CS BS37 ..... 310 A8
Cheshire Rd BWTH/CHD GL3 ..... 113 G5
The Chesils COTS GL54 ..... 74 D1
Chesley Hl
  OLD/WMLY/WICK BS30 ..... 339 H4
Chessel Cl ALMDB BS32 ..... 316 E1
Chessell Av THNB/SVB BS35 ..... 304 E4
Chessel St BMSTR BS3 ..... 335 K8
Chessgrove La MTCHDN GL17 ..... 107 G8
Chessington Av
  HGRV/WHIT BS14 ..... 346 D6
Chestal DSLY GL11 ..... 253 K2
Chester Cl RTEWK/TIB GL19 ..... 69 G6
Chester Crs CIR GL7 ..... 238 C5
Chesterfield Av
  RDLND/MONT BS6 ..... 336 A1
Chesterfield Rd
  MANG/FISH BS16 ..... 328 A6
  RDLND/MONT BS6 ..... 336 A1
Chestermaster Cl
  ALMDB BS32 ..... 306 C6
Chester Park Rd
  MANG/FISH BS16 ..... 337 K1
Chester Rd EVILLE/WHL BS5 ..... 337 G2
  GLE GL4 ..... 136 E3
Chesters
  OLD/WMLY/WICK BS30 ..... 338 C7
Chester St CIR GL7 ..... 238 D3
  EVILLE/WHL BS5 ..... 336 D1
Chesterton Gv CIR GL7 ..... 238 C5
Chesterton La CIR GL7 ..... 238 A4
Chester Wk CHELT GL50 ..... 2 C4
Chestnut Av STNHO GL10 ..... 207 H3
Chestnut Cl CIR GL7 ..... 264 F4
  CLFD GL16 ..... 151 M7
  HGRV/WHIT BS14 ..... 347 G6
  LED HR8 ..... 19 M4
  RSTROUD/NAIL GL6 ..... 232 D7
  TET GL8 ..... 281 M3
  VGL GL2 ..... 159 G4
Chestnut Ct MANG/FISH BS16 ..... 328 C6
Chestnut Dr THNB/SVB BS35 ..... 293 L2
  YATE/CS BS37 ..... 320 C2
Chestnut Hl RSTROUD/NAIL GL6 ..... 232 D7
Chestnut La STROUD GL5 ..... 208 C5

Chestnut Pl CHELTS GL53 .... 115 K7 [2]
Chestnut Rd GLE GL4 .... 137 G6
  KGWD/HNM BS15 .... 328 B8 [1]
  LGASH BS41 .... 344 D1
  MANG/FISH BS16 .... 327 M5 [1]
The Chestnuts GL GL1 .... 4 D8
Chestnut Wk
  BMSTRD/HC/WWD BS13 .... 345 J5
  KEYN BS31 .... 349 G8
Chetwode Cl
  HNBRY/STHM BS10 .... 315 M8
Chevening Cl
  BRSTK/PCHW BS34 .... 316 F7 [2]
Cheviot Cl VGL GL2 .... 159 G3 [3]
Cheviot Dr THNB/SVB BS35 .... 294 A3
Cheviot Rd CHELTE/BC GL52 .... 94 D7 [1]
Cheviot Wy
  OLD/WMLY/WICK BS30 .... 338 E6
Chewton Cl MANG/FISH BS16 .... 327 K8
Cheyne Rd
  HNLZ/SM/SNYPK/WT BS9 .... 324 F5
Cheyney Cl GL4 .... 136 D5
Chichester Wy
  YATE/CS BS37 .... 309 M8 [1]
Chickadee LYD GL15 .... 198 E7
Chicknalls La LYD GL15 .... 178 F6
Childswickham Rd
  BDWAY WR12 .... 32 D3
Chillington Ct
  BRSTK/PCHW BS34 .... 316 A2
Chillwood Cl YATE/CS BS37 .... 309 G8
Chiltern Av CHELTE/BC GL52 .... 72 A7
Chiltern Cl HGRV/WHIT BS14 .... 346 D7
  OLD/WMLY/WICK BS30 .... 338 D7
Chiltern Pk THNB/SVB BS35 .... 294 A3
  VGL GL2 .... 159 G3
Chilton Rd
  BRSG/KWL/STAPK BS4 .... 346 E3
The Chine MANG/FISH BS16 .... 326 F6
Chine Vw MANG/FISH BS16 .... 328 B3
Chiphouse Rd
  KGWD/HNM BS15 .... 338 A1
Chippenham Rd
  CHPMW/MSHF SN14 .... 342 C3
Chipperfield Dr
  KGWD/HNM BS15 .... 338 B2
Chipping Cl WUE GL12 .... 277 K4 [1]
Chipping Gdns WUE GL12 .... 277 J4 [1]
The Chippings
  MANG/FISH BS16 .... 326 F6
Chipping St TET GL8 .... 282 A4
Chisbury St EVILLE/WHL BS5 .... 326 E8 [1]
Chislet Wy GLE GL4 .... 159 M2
Chittening Rd AVONM BS11 .... 314 A1
Chock La
  HNLZ/SM/SNYPK/WT BS9 .... 325 J4
Choirs Cl GLE GL4 .... 137 G5
Chosen Dr BWTH/CHD GL3 .... 113 K6
Chosen View Rd CHELTW GL51 .... 93 K7
Chosen Wy GLE GL4 .... 137 H3
Christchurch Av
  MANG/FISH BS16 .... 327 M6 [1]
Christchurch La
  MANG/FISH BS16 .... 327 M6 [1]
Christchurch Rd CFTN/FAIL BS8.. 335 J4
Christ Church Rd CHELT GL50 .... 115 K3
Christmas St CBRIS/FH BS1 .... 6 E3 [1]
Christowe La CHELTS GL53 .... 116 A4
Chubb Cl MALM SN16 .... 303 J6
  OLD/WMLY/WICK BS30 .... 338 B6
Church Av CIR GL7 .... 238 E6
  EVILLE/WHL BS5 .... 336 D2 [1]
  HNLZ/SM/SNYPK/WT BS9 .... 325 G7
  OLD/WMLY/WICK BS30 .... 338 E6
  WUE GL12 .... 275 G4
Church Cl BDWAY WR12 .... 32 E4
  FRCTL/WBN BS36 .... 318 D3
Churchdown La BWTH/CHD GL3 .. 137 K4
Church Dr LYD GL15 .... 176 F7
  VGL GL2 .... 159 H2
Churchend GL2 .... 204 F7
Churchend La WUE GL12 .... 276 B7
Churchfarm Cl YATE/CS BS37 .... 310 B8
Church Farm La MIM SN16 .... 36 C7 [1]
Church Farm Rd
  MANG/FISH BS16 .... 328 C5
Churchfield Rd GLE GL4 .... 161 G1
  STROUD GL5 .... 208 F5 [1]
Churchfields CHELTE/BC GL52 .... 72 C7
Church Gdns LYD GL15 .... 225 J1
Church Hl
  BRSG/KWL/STAPK BS4 .... 347 G1
  MTCHDN GL17 .... 128 C7
  RSTROUD/NAIL GL6 .... 210 C3 [1]
  THNB/SVB BS35 .... 292 B8
Churchill Rd CHNTN OX7 .... 105 M2
  RSTROUD/NAIL GL6 .... 233 K2
Churchill Cl
  OLD/WMLY/WICK BS30 .... 338 C6 [2]
  RSTROUD/NAIL GL6 .... 232 D7 [2]
Churchill Dr CHELTE/BC GL52 .... 3 J8
  HNLZ/SM/SNYPK/WT BS9 .... 324 F4
Churchill Gv TEWK GL20 .... 48 D5
Churchill Meadow LED HR8 .... 19 L4
Churchill Pl CIR GL7 .... 242 F1
Churchill Rd
  BRSG/KWL/STAPK BS4 .... 336 E7
  CHELTS GL53 .... 115 M6
  CHNTN OX7 .... 104 C6
  CIR GL7 .... 238 E2 [1]
  GL GL1 .... 136 A4
  EVE WR11 .... 30 B2
  RSTROUD/NAIL GL6 .... 232 D7
Churchill Wy MTCHDN GL17 .... 130 C1
  RSTROUD/NAIL GL6 .... 185 G3
Church La BAD GL9 .... 313 G6
  BDWAY WR12 .... 53 M2
  BMSTR BS3 .... 335 M8 [1]
  BRKLY GL13 .... 227 G2
  BRKLY GL13 .... 227 G8 [1]
  BUR/CRTN OX18 .... 172 A5
  CBATH/BATHN BA1 .... 352 B7
  CBRIS/FH BS1 .... 7 H5
  CFTN/FAIL BS8 .... 6 A5
  CHELTW GL51 .... 139 G1
  CHNTN OX7 .... 125 M1

  CHPMW/MSHF SN14 .... 313 M2
  CHPMW/MSHF SN14 .... 342 C3
  CIND GL14 .... 132 B7
  CIR GL7 .... 211 M8
  CIR GL7 .... 239 M6
  CIR GL7 .... 245 M1
  CIR GL7 .... 263 H4
  COR/BOX SN13 .... 353 L6
  COTS GL54 .... 52 F5
  COTS GL54 .... 118 E3
  FRCTL/WBN BS36 .... 317 L5
  FRCTL/WBN BS36 .... 318 E5 [3]
  GLE GL4 .... 136 F3
  GLE GL4 .... 160 A3
  HNBRY/STHM BS10 .... 325 C1
  LYD GL15 .... 223 M8
  LYD GL15 .... 224 C6
  MALM SN16 .... 302 F4
  MANG/FISH BS16 .... 328 A1
  MIM GL56 .... 81 G5
  OLD/WMLY/WICK BS30 .... 349 G4
  RTEWK/TIB GL19 .... 46 F5
  RTEWK/TIB GL19 .... 91 H3
  STNHO GL10 .... 207 G4
  VGL GL2 .... 133 M1
  VGL GL2 .... 134 A4
  VGL GL2 .... 158 E5
  VGL GL2 .... 182 B3
  WUE GL12 .... 295 J2
  WUE GL12 .... 296 C5
  YATE/CS BS37 .... 309 H2
  YATE/CS BS37 .... 321 K4
Church Pde
  BRSG/KWL/STAPK BS4 .... 347 G1 [1]
Church Piece CHELTS GL53 .... 116 D6 [3]
Church Pl MIM GL56 .... 103 J3
Church Ri VGL GL2 .... 111 J4
Church Rd ALMDB BS32 .... 306 C6
  BDWAY WR12 .... 31 H2
  BMSTR BS3 .... 6 D9
  BMSTRD/HC/WWD BS13 .... 345 J6
  BRSTK/PCHW BS34 .... 316 J6
  BRSTK/PCHW BS34 .... 317 G8
  BWTH/CHD GL3 .... 113 L7
  CFTN/FAIL BS8 .... 334 F5
  CFTN/FAIL BS8 .... 334 C3
  CHELTE/BC GL52 .... 72 B7
  CHELTS GL53 .... 115 L7
  CHELTW GL51 .... 93 J5
  CHELTW GL51 .... 115 H3 [1]
  CHEP NP16 .... 270 B3
  CIND GL14 .... 154 A4
  CIND GL14 .... 155 J7
  CIND GL14 .... 178 B2
  CIR GL7 .... 217 K1
  CIR GL7 .... 218 D6
  CIR GL7 .... 261 H4
  COTS GL54 .... 98 E5
  DSLY GL11 .... 229 K8
  EVILLE/WHL BS5 .... 336 F5
  FRCTL/WBN BS36 .... 318 A7
  FRCTL/WBN BS36 .... 318 C2
  HGRV/WHIT BS14 .... 346 D8
  HNLZ/SM/SNYPK/WT BS9 .... 324 F8
  HNLZ/SM/SNYPK/WT BS9 .... 325 J4
  HORF/LLZ BS7 .... 326 A5
  KGWD/HNM BS15 .... 337 K6
  KGWD/HNM BS15 .... 338 A3
  LED HR8 .... 20 A3
  LYD GL15 .... 223 G2
  LYD GL15 .... 224 E2
  LYD GL15 .... 225 J2
  MANG/FISH BS16 .... 327 K4
  MANG/FISH BS16 .... 337 M1
  MIM GL56 .... 103 J3
  MTCHDN GL17 .... 107 H8
  MTCHDN GL17 .... 128 C7
  OLD/WMLY/WICK BS30 .... 339 L5 [1]
  OLD/WMLY/WICK BS30 .... 340 C2
  OLD/WMLY/WICK BS30 .... 349 G3
  RSTROUD/NAIL GL6 .... 232 C5 [1]
  STNHO GL10 .... 207 G8
  STROUD GL5 .... 208 A5
  STROUD GL5 .... 232 B1
  TEWK GL20 .... 51 L4
  THNB/SVB BS35 .... 272 D7
  THNB/SVB BS35 .... 293 K1
  THNB/SVB BS35 .... 304 C5
  THNB/SVB BS35 .... 307 J1
  THNB/SVB BS35 .... 315 J2
  VGL GL2 .... 111 J4
  VGL GL2 .... 112 E7
  VGL GL2 .... 179 M2
  YATE/CS BS37 .... 310 A8
  YATE/CS BS37 .... 320 A1
Churchside MANG/FISH BS16 .. 327 K4 [1]
Church St BDWAY WR12 .... 11 H7 [1]
  BDWAY WR12 .... 32 E3
  CBATH/BATHN BA1 .... 351 H5
  CBRIS/FH BS1 .... 7 H5
  CHCAM GL55 .... 12 E8
  CHELT GL50 .... 2 D5
  CHELTS GL53 .... 116 C6
  CHNTN OX7 .... 104 C7
  CHNTN OX7 .... 125 L1
  CHNTN OX7 .... 149 K1
  CIND GL14 .... 154 E4
  CIR GL7 .... 238 D4
  CIR GL7 .... 241 K7
  CLFD GL16 .... 175 J7
  COTS GL54 .... 102 A3 [1]
  EVILLE/WHL BS5 .... 336 D2
  EVILLE/WHL BS5 .... 336 D4 [3]
  GL GL1 .... 4 D8
  LED HR8 .... 20 A3
  LYD GL15 .... 198 F5
  MIM GL56 .... 58 C6
  NWNT GL18 .... 86 C3
  RSTROUD/NAIL GL6 .... 232 E7
  SHPSTR CV36 .... 16 B5
  STNHO GL10 .... 207 J7
  STNHO GL10 .... 231 G6
  STROUD GL5 .... 208 E4
  TET GL8 .... 257 L2 [1]
  TET GL8 .... 281 M5
  TEWK GL20 .... 48 A6

  WUE GL12 .... 277 K4
Church Vw ALMDB BS32 .... 306 B7
  BRKLY GL13 .... 251 L3
  COTS GL54 .... 78 E6 [1]
  HGHW SN6 .... 266 D7
  MIM GL56 .... 36 B7
Churchview Dr GLE GL4 .... 136 F3
Church Wk HGHW SN6 .... 287 G2
  LYD GL15 .... 176 F7
  LYD GL15 .... 202 A2
Churchward Cl
  KGWD/HNM BS15 .... 337 K6 [3]
Churchward Rd
  YATE/CS BS37 .... 309 K8 [1]
Church Wy GLE GL4 .... 136 E5 [1]
  LYD GL15 .... 178 E8
  NWNT GL18 .... 86 C3
Churchways HGRV/WHIT BS14 .... 346 E7
Churchways Av HORF/LLZ BS7 .... 326 A5
Churchways Crs HORF/LLZ BS7 .. 326 A5
Churclands Rd BMSTR BS3 .... 345 K1 [3]
Churn Av CHELTE/BC GL52 .... 3 J4
Churn Cl GLE GL4 .... 263 H4
Churn Hl CIR GL7 .... 190 C6
Churston Cl
  HGRV/WHIT BS14 .... 346 C8 [3]
Cicely Wy GLE GL4 .... 137 H6
Cidermill Cl CHEP NP16 .... 270 B7 [1]
Cidermill La CHCAM GL55 .... 12 E8
Cidermill Orch CHCAM GL55 .... 11 M4
Cinderford Rd LYD GL15 .... 178 D8
Cinder Hl CLFD GL16 .... 175 K1
  LYD GL15 .... 198 F5
Cinderhill MTCHDN GL17 .... 128 F3
Cinder La CIR GL7 .... 243 C5
The Circle BMSTR BS3 .... 208 E3 [2]
Circular Rd
  HNLZ/SM/SNYPK/WT BS9 .... 335 C1
Cirencester Rd BWTH/CHD GL3 .. 138 C7
  CHELTS GL53 .... 116 C5 [3]
  CHELTS GL53 .... 116 C4 [3]
  CIR GL7 .... 239 J7
  CIR GL7 .... 242 D5
  CIR GL7 .... 263 L1
  CIR GL7 .... 264 A4 [3]
  RSTROUD/NAIL GL6 .... 234 C4
  STROUD GL5 .... 233 G4
  TET GL8 .... 282 A4
City Bank Rd CIR GL7 .... 238 D4
City Rd CBRISNE BS2 .... 336 A3
Claire's Cl STROUD GL5 .... 233 J2 [1]
The Clamp
  OLD/WMLY/WICK BS30 .... 338 E8 [3]
Clanage Rd BMSTR BS3 .... 335 G7
Clanna La LYD GL15 .... 224 B4
Clapton Rw COTS GL54 .... 123 H6
Clapton Wk
  HNLZ/SM/SNYPK/WT BS9 .... 324 D6
Clare Av HORF/LLZ BS7 .... 325 L8
Clare Ct STROUD GL5 .... 209 G4
Claremont Av HORF/LLZ BS7 .... 325 L8
Claremont Rd GL GL1 .... 5 H4
  HORF/LLZ BS7 .... 325 M8
Claremont St EVILLE/WHL BS5 .... 336 C2
Clarence Av MANG/FISH BS16.... 328 A6
Clarence Gdns
  MANG/FISH BS16 .... 328 A6 [1]
Clarence Pde CHELT GL50 .... 2 C5
Clarence Pl CBRISNE BS2 .... 6 D1
  CBRISNE BS2 .... 335 L3 [1]
Clarence Rd CBRIS/FH BS1 .... 7 G8
  CBRISNE BS2 .... 7 L2
  CHELT GL50 .... 2 E3
  CHELTE/BC GL52 .... 2 E8
  KGWD/HNM BS15 .... 337 K2
  MANG/FISH BS16 .... 327 M6
  TEWK GL20 .... 48 A7
  WUE GL12 .... 277 K4
Clarence Sq CHELT GL50 .... 2 E2
Clarence St CHELT GL50 .... 2 C4
  GL GL1 .... 4 F6
Clarendon Rd COTS GL54 .... 74 B4
  RDLND/MONT BS6 .... 335 L1
Clare Pl CHELTS GL53 .... 115 M4
Clare Rd EVILLE/WHL BS5 .... 336 D1 [2]
  KGWD/HNM BS15 .... 337 L1
  RDLND/MONT BS6 .... 335 M2
Clare St CHELTS GL53 .... 2 C9
  CHELTS GL53 .... 115 M4 [3]
  EVILLE/WHL BS5 .... 336 E3 [3]
  GL GL1 .... 4 D4
Clare Wk THNB/SVB BS35 .... 293 K1
Claridge Cl GLE GL4 .... 136 F7 [1]
Clark Cl SHPSTR CV36 .... 16 B6
Clark Dr MANG/FISH BS16 .... 327 H5
Clarken Coombe LGASH BS41 .... 334 C8
Clarke St BMSTR BS3 .... 6 F9
Clarkia Cl BWTH/CHD GL3 .... 113 H4
Clark's La CIR GL7 .... 238 D8
  LYD GL15 .... 202 D1
  SHPSTR CV36 .... 61 J6
Clark St EVILLE/WHL BS5 .... 336 C3 [2]
Clarrie Rd TET GL8 .... 282 A3
Clatworthy Dr
  HGRV/WHIT BS14 .... 346 C4
Claudians Cl GLE GL4 .... 137 G4 [1]
Claudius Wy LYD GL15 .... 201 K7
Clavell Rd HNBRY/STHM BS10 .. 325 H1
Claverham Rd
  MANG/FISH BS16 .... 327 J6 [1]
Claverton Rd West KEYN BS31.... 348 F6 [1]
Clay Bottom EVILLE/WHL BS5 .... 336 E1
Clayburn Cl VGL GL2 .... 111 G6 [1]
Clayfield YATE/CS BS37 .... 310 A6
Clayfield Rd
  BRSG/KWL/STAPK BS4 .... 337 G8 [3]
Clayfurlong Gv CIR GL7 .... 261 H3
Clay Hl EVILLE/WHL BS5 .... 337 G1
Clay La BRSTK/PCHW BS34 .... 316 E4
  OLD/WMLY/WICK BS30 .... 348 F3 [1]
  THNB/SVB BS35 .... 294 A2
Claymore Cresent
  KGWD/HNM BS15 .... 337 K2 [1]
Claypiece Rd
  BMSTRD/HC/WWD BS13 .... 345 H7
Claypit Hl YATE/CS BS37 .... 320 D4
Clay Pit Rd
  HNLZ/SM/SNYPK/WT BS9 .... 325 J8

Claypits Hl STNHO GL10 .... 205 M2
Claypits La STROUD GL5 .... 209 G7
Claypool Rd KGWD/HNM BS15 .... 337 M4
Clay Rd CLFD GL16 .... 151 L4
Clays Rd CLFD GL16 .... 175 L7
Clayton St EVILLE/WHL BS5 .... 336 D3 [3]
Clearwater Dr VGL GL2 .... 159 G2
Cleaves Av
  CHPMW/MSHF SN14 .... 343 J8
Cleave St CBRISNE BS2 .... 336 C1 [3]
Cleevale MANG/FISH BS16 .... 328 A4
Cleeve Cloud La
  CHELTE/BC GL52 .... 94 F8 [1]
Cleeve Ct CHELTE/BC GL52 .... 72 C8
Cleevecroft Av CHELTE/BC GL52 .. 72 C8
Cleeve Gdns MANG/FISH BS16 .... 327 M4
Cleeve Gv KEYN BS31 .... 347 M6
Cleeve Hl MANG/FISH BS16 .... 327 M4
Cleeve Hill Extension
  MANG/FISH BS16 .... 328 A5
Cleevelands Av CHELT GL50 .... 93 M7
Cleevelands Cl CHELT GL50 .... 94 A6
Cleeveland St CHELTW GL51 .... 2 A2
Cleeve La
  OLD/WMLY/WICK BS30 .... 339 M2
Cleeve Lawns MANG/FISH BS16 .. 327 M4
Cleeve Lodge Rd
  MANG/FISH BS16 .... 328 A4
Cleeve Mill La NWNT GL18 .... 86 D2
Cleevemount Cl
  CHELTE/BC GL52 .... 3 G1
Cleevemount Rd
  CHELTE/BC GL52 .... 94 D7
Cleeve Park Rd
  MANG/FISH BS16 .... 327 M4
Cleeve Ri NWNT GL18 .... 86 D3 [3]
Cleeve Rd
  BRSG/KWL/STAPK BS4 .... 336 D8
  CHELTE/BC GL52 .... 72 C5
  GLE GL4 .... 136 D7
  MANG/FISH BS16 .... 327 L3
  MANG/FISH BS16 .... 337 M4
  YATE/CS BS37 .... 320 A2
Cleeve View Rd CHELTE/BC GL52 .. 3 J4
Cleeve Wood Rd
  MANG/FISH BS16 .... 327 M4 [3]
Clegram Rd GL GL1 .... 135 M4
Clematis Ct CHELTE/BC GL52 .... 72 A8 [3]
Clements End Rd CLFD GL16 .... 175 L7
Clement St CBRISNE BS2 .... 7 J1
  GL GL1 .... 5 J9
Clencher's Mill La LED HR8 .... 20 E6
Clevedale MANG/FISH BS16 .... 327 M4
Clevedon Rd GL GL1 .... 136 B5
  HORF/LLZ BS7 .... 325 L8
Clevedon Sq CHELTW GL51 .... 115 J1 [3]
Clevedon Ter
  RDLND/MONT BS6 .... 335 M3 [3]
Cleveland Cl THNB/SVB BS35 .... 294 A2 [1]
Cleve Rd BRSTK/PCHW BS34 .... 316 C7
Clewson Ri HGRV/WHIT BS14 .... 346 B8 [3]
Cliff Court Dr MANG/FISH BS16 .. 327 K4
Clifford Gdns AVONM BS11 .... 324 A5
Clifford Rd MANG/FISH BS16 .... 328 A6
Cliffords HGHW SN6 .... 288 E5 [3]
Cliff Vw CHEP NP16 .... 270 C4
Clift House Rd BMSTR BS3 .... 335 H7
Clifton Down CFTN/FAIL BS8 .... 335 H3 [1]
Clifton Down Rd
  CFTN/FAIL BS8 .... 335 H4 [1]
Clifton Gv
  HNLZ/SM/SNYPK/WT BS9 .... 325 G6 [1]
Clifton Hl CFTN/FAIL BS8 .... 335 J5 [1]
Clifton Pk CFTN/FAIL BS8 .... 335 J3 [1]
Clifton Park Rd CFTN/FAIL BS8.... 335 H3 [1]
Clifton Pl EVILLE/WHL BS5 .... 7 M1
Clifton Rd CFTN/FAIL BS8 .... 335 J5 [3]
  GL GL1 .... 135 L8 [1]
Clifton St BMSTR BS3 .... 335 L8 [1]
Clifton V CFTN/FAIL BS8 .... 335 J5 [3]
Clifton Vale Cl CFTN/FAIL BS8 .... 335 J5 [3]
Cliftonwood Crs CFTN/FAIL BS8.... 6 A5
Clifton Wood Rd CFTN/FAIL BS8.... 6 A4
Cliftonwood Ter
  CFTN/FAIL BS8 .... 335 J5 [3]
Clift Pl CBRIS/FH BS1 .... 6 F6
Clift Rd BMSTR BS3 .... 335 L8 [1]
Clingre Down DSLY GL11 .... 228 E7
Clingre La DSLY GL11 .... 228 D7
Clinton Rd BMSTR BS3 .... 345 L1
Clissard Wy BUR/CRTN OX18 .... 197 L5 [1]
Clive Rd HGRV/WHIT BS14 .... 346 E4
Cloisters Rd FRCTL/WBN BS36 .... 318 A5
The Cloisters CHELTE/BC GL52 .. 72 A7 [3]
Clomoney Wy VGL GL2 .... 112 F6 [1]
Clonmel Rd
  BRSG/KWL/STAPK BS4 .... 345 M2
Close Gdns COTS GL54 .... 78 E6 [1]
  TET GL8 .... 281 M4
The Close BRSTK/PCHW BS34 .... 316 E2
  CHELTE/BC GL52 .... 94 E5
  CHELTS GL53 .... 115 M7 [1]
  CIR GL7 .... 244 E6 [1]
  CIR GL7 .... 263 J4 [1]
  CLFD GL16 .... 151 M7
  DSLY GL11 .... 229 G2
  DSLY GL11 .... 230 A4
  FRCTL/WBN BS36 .... 318 E5
  HNBRY/STHM BS10 .... 315 H6
  MANG/FISH BS16 .... 327 M8
  VGL GL2 .... 182 B6
  VGL GL2 .... 205 G8
Clothier Rd
  BRSG/KWL/STAPK BS4 .... 347 H1 [1]
Clouds Hill Av EVILLE/WHL BS5.... 337 G3
Clouds Hill Rd EVILLE/WHL BS5.... 337 G3
The Cloud WUE GL12 .... 277 K4
Clovelly Cl EVILLE/WHL BS5 .... 337 H3
Clovelly Rd EVILLE/WHL BS5 .... 337 H3
Clover Cl CLFD GL16 .... 175 L4
Cloverdale Dr
  OLD/WMLY/WICK BS30 .... 338 C8
Clover Dr VGL GL2 .... 159 G5
Clover Gnd
  HNLZ/SM/SNYPK/WT BS9 .... 325 K3
Cloverlea Rd
  OLD/WMLY/WICK BS30 .... 338 E6

Clover Leaze
  BRSTK/PCHW BS34 .... 316 F5
Clyde Av KEYN BS31 .... 348 B7
Clyde Crs CHELTE/BC GL52 .... 3 K2
Clyde Gdns EVILLE/WHL BS5 .... 337 K5
Clyde Gv BRSTK/PCHW BS34 .... 326 B1
Clyde La RDLND/MONT BS6 .... 335 K1
Clyde Rd BRSG/KWL/STAPK BS4 .. 336 C8
  BWTH/CHD GL3 .... 138 B6
  FRCTL/WBN BS36 .... 318 D3
  RDLND/MONT BS6 .... 335 K1
Clydesdale Rd COR/BOX SN13 .... 353 M6
Clyde Ter BMSTR BS3 .... 335 L8
  BRSG/KWL/STAPK BS4 .... 336 C8 [3]
Coach Cl BRKLY GL13 .... 227 G8 [3]
Coach Rd RWYE HR9 .... 106 C3
Coalpit Rd CBATH/BATHN BA1 .... 352 C7
Coalsack La FRCTL/WBN BS36 .... 318 D8
Coalville Rd FRCTL/WBN BS36 .... 318 H4
Coalway Rd CLFD GL16 .... 175 L1
Coape Rd HGRV/WHIT BS14 .... 347 H6
Coates Gdns STNHO GL10 .... 207 H3 [3]
The Cobbler's Cl
  CHELTE/BC GL52 .... 72 C4 [3]
Cobblestone Ms CFTN/FAIL BS8 .. 335 J4 [1]
Cobden St EVILLE/WHL BS5 .... 336 E4
Coberley KGWD/HNM BS15 .... 337 L5
Coberley Rd CHELTW GL51 .... 114 F3
  GLE GL4 .... 136 A8 [1]
Cobham Ct CHELTW GL51 .... 93 K8 [3]
Cobham Rd CHELTW GL51 .... 93 K8 [3]
Cobhorn Dr
  BMSTRD/HC/WWD BS13 .... 345 H7
Cobourg Rd BWTH/CHD BS6 .... 336 B2 [3]
Cochran Cl BWTH/CHD GL3 .... 113 L6 [3]
Cockatoos La RWYE HR9 .... 84 F2
Cock La CHPMW/MSHF SN14 .... 330 F6
Cock Rd KGWD/HNM BS15 .... 338 A5
Codrington Pl CFTN/FAIL BS8 .... 335 J4 [3]
Codrington Rd HORF/LLZ BS7 .... 326 A8
Cogan Rd MANG/FISH BS16 .... 328 A8
Cogsall Rd HGRV/WHIT BS14 .... 347 H5 [1]
Colchester Rd CIND GL14 .... 156 A2
  MTCHDN GL17 .... 130 C2
Colchester Crs
  BRSG/KWL/STAPK BS4 .... 345 M4
Coldharbour La
  BRSTK/PCHW BS34 .... 327 G2
  MANG/FISH BS16 .... 327 C3
  NWNT GL18 .... 64 A8
Coldharbour Rd LYD GL15 .... 198 E7
  RDLND/MONT BS6 .... 325 K8
Coldicotts Cl CHCAM GL55 .... 34 E1
Coldpark Gdns
  BMSTRD/HC/WWD BS13 .... 345 G6
Coldpark Rd
  BMSTRD/HC/WWD BS13 .... 345 G6
Cold Pool La CHELTW GL51 .... 114 E5
Coldray Cl VGL GL2 .... 5 L6
Coldrick Cl HGRV/WHIT BS14 .... 346 B8
Coldwell STNHO GL10 .... 207 K8
Coldwell Cl STNHO GL10 .... 207 K8
Coldwell La STNHO GL10 .... 207 K8
Cole Av VGL GL2 .... 135 L8
Colebridge Av VGL GL2 .... 112 E8
Colebrook Rd
  KGWD/HNM BS15 .... 337 L3
Coleford Rd CHEP NP16 .... 246 C8
  HNBRY/STHM BS10 .... 325 M3
  LYD GL15 .... 200 C3
Colemead
  BMSTRD/HC/WWD BS13 .... 345 K6
Coleridge Rd
  EVILLE/WHL BS5 .... 326 E8 [3]
Colerne Dr BWTH/CHD GL3 .... 137 K4
Cole Rd CBRISNE BS2 .... 336 D5
Colesborne Cl YATE/CS BS37 .... 320 A3 [1]
Colesbourne Rd CHELTW GL51 .... 114 F4
Coleshill Dr
  BMSTRD/HC/WWD BS13 .... 345 K6
Colin Cl THNB/SVB BS35 .... 293 K2
Colin Rd GLE GL4 .... 136 F2
College Av MANG/FISH BS16 .... 327 J6 [3]
College Baths Rd CHELTS GL53.... 2 F8
College Ct MANG/FISH BS16 .... 327 J6
College Flds CFTN/FAIL BS8 .... 335 H3
  VGL GL2 .... 112 F7
College Ga CHELTS GL53 .... 2 F8
College Gn CBRIS/FH BS1 .... 6 D4
College Lawn CHELTS GL53 .... 116 A4
College Park Dr
  HNBRY/STHM BS10 .... 325 H2
College Pl CHELT GL50 .... 2 C5 [1]
College Rd CFTN/FAIL BS8 .... 335 H3
  CHELTS GL53 .... 2 E8
  CIND GL14 .... 154 A2
  HNLZ/SM/SNYPK/WT BS9 .... 325 J4
  MANG/FISH BS16 .... 327 J6
  STROUD GL5 .... 208 C3
  TEWK GL20 .... 26 F5
College Sq CBRIS/FH BS1 .... 6 C5
College St CBRIS/FH BS1 .... 6 C5
  GL GL1 .... 4 E5
College Vw CIR GL7 .... 238 B6
Collett Cl KGWD/HNM BS15 .... 337 K6 [3]
Colletts Dr CHELTW GL51 .... 93 K8
Colletts Flds BDWAY WR12 .... 33 G3
Colletts Gdns BDWAY WR12 .... 33 G3
Collett Wy YATE/CS BS37 .... 309 L8
Colliers Break MANG/FISH BS16.. 328 D6
Colliers La CBATH/BATHN BA1.... 351 H7
Colliers Pitch LYD GL15 .... 224 B2
Colliers Wd RSTROUD/NAIL GL6 .. 232 B6
Collin Cl BDWAY WR12 .... 11 G7
Collingbourne Rd GLE GL4 .... 136 C4 [1]
Collingwood Av
  KGWD/HNM BS15 .... 338 A2 [1]
Collingwood Rd
  RDLND/MONT BS6 .... 335 K2 [3]
Collin La BDWAY WR12 .... 10 E8
Collin Rd BRSG/KWL/STAPK BS4 .. 336 F7
Collins Av BRSTK/PCHW BS34 .... 316 E5
Collins Cl RTEWK/TIB GL19 .... 66 D4
Collinson Rd
  BMSTRD/HC/WWD BS13 .... 345 K6
Colliter Crs BMSTR BS3 .... 345 J1
Collum End Ri CHELTS GL53 .... 115 M8
Colne Av CHELTE/BC GL52 .... 3 J2

Coln Sq *THNB/SVB* BS35 .... 293 L3
Colston Av *CBRIS/FH* BS1 .... 6 E4
Colston Cl *FRCTL/WBN* BS36 .. 318 A7
   MANG/FISH BS16 .... 327 M8 🛈
Colston Dl *MANG/FISH* BS16 .... 327 G7
Colston Hl *MANG/FISH* BS16 .... 326 F7
Colston Pde *CBRIS/FH* BS1 .... 7 G6
Colston Rd *EVILLE/WHL* BS5 ...... 336 E2
Colston St *CBRIS/FH* BS1 .... 6 E3
   MANG/FISH BS16 .... 327 M8
Coltham Flds *CHELTE/BC* GL52 ... 3 H7
Coltham Rd *CHELTE/BC* GL52 ...... 3 H9
Colthurst Dr *KGWD/HNM* BS15.. 337 M6
Coltman Cl *VGL* GL2 .... 5 L6
Colts Gn *YATE/CS* BS37 .... 321 C3
Columbia Cl *GL1* 5 G4
Columbia St *CHELTE/BC* GL52 .... 2 F4
Colwell Av *BWTH/CHD* GL3 ...... 137 J2
Colwyn Dr *CHELTW* GL51 .... 115 G5
Colwyn Rd *EVILLE/WHL* BS5 ..... 336 E2 🛈
Combe Cross Wk
   BMSTRD/HC/WWD BS13 .... 345 K8 🛈
Combermere La
   EVILLE/WHL BS5 .... 336 D3 🛈
Combfactory La
   EVILLE/WHL BS5 .... 336 D3 🛈
Comb Paddock
   HNLZ/SM/SNYPK/WT BS9........ 325 K4
Combrook Cl *GLE* GL4 .... 137 G7 🛈
Commercial Rd *CBRIS/FH* BS1 ...... 6 E7
   GL GL1 .... 4 C6
   RSTROUD/NAIL GL6 .... 234 A1
Commercial St *CHELT* GL50 .... 2 C9
   CIND GL14 .... 154 B3
The Common (East)
   ALMDB BS32 .... 316 E2
Commonfield Rd *AVONM* BS11 .. 324 D2
Common Hl *HGHW* SN6 .... 288 E3
Common La *CHNTN* OX7 .... 105 L1
Common Mead La
   MANG/FISH BS16 .... 327 J2
Commonmead La
   YATE/CS BS37 .... 321 H2
Common Rd
   FRCTL/WBN BS36 .... 318 B4 🛈
   KGWD/HNM BS15 .... 337 K8 🛈
   RSTROUD/NAIL GL6 .... 232 F5
The Common *BRKLY* GL13 .... 227 L8
   BRSTK/PCHW BS34 .... 316 D2
   CIR GL7 .... 238 F7
   MANG/FISH BS16 .... 327 K4
Compton Cl *BWTH/CHD* GL3 ... 113 J3 🛈
   RTEWK/TIB BS19 .... 66 D5
Compton Ct *SHPSTR* CV36 .... 61 G4
Compton Gn *KEYN* BS31 .... 348 A7
Compton Rd *CHELTW* GL51 .... 93 K7 🛈
Compton St *EVILLE/WHL* BS5 ... 336 E4
Compton's Aly *TEWK* GL20 .... 48 A5 🛈
Comyn Wk *MANG/FISH* BS16 .... 327 J6
Concorde Dr
   HNBRY/STHM BS10 .... 325 K1 🛈
Concorde Wy *GLE* GL4 .... 136 D4
Condicote La *COTS* GL54 .... 78 E6
   COTS GL54 .... 100 F4
Condover Rd
   BRSG/KWL/STAPK BS4 .... 337 H8
Conduit La *CHCAM* GL55 .... 34 D2
Conduit Pl *CBRISNE* BS2 .... 336 C2 🛈
Conduit Rd *CBRISNE* BS2 .... 336 C2
Conduit St *GL* GL1 .... 4 C4
Coneygar Rd *CIR* GL7 .... 218 C6
Coneygree La *BDWAY* WR12 .... 32 F6
Coney Hill Pde *GLE* GL4 .... 136 E4 🛈
Coney Hill Rd *GLE* GL4 .... 136 F4
Congleton Rd
   EVILLE/WHL BS5 .... 336 F3 🛈
Conham Hl *KGWD/HNM* BS15.... 337 J6
Conham Rd *KGWD/HNM* BS15... 337 H6
Conham V *KGWD/HNM* BS15 .... 337 K6
   KGWD/HNM BS15 .... 337 H6
Conifer Cl *FRCTL/WBN* BS36 ..... 318 C2
   MANG/FISH BS16 .... 327 M5 🛈
The Conifers *GL* GL1 .... 136 C4 🛈
Conigree La *TEWK* GL20 .... 48 A7
Coniston Av
   HNLZ/SM/SNYPK/WT BS9........ 325 G5
Coniston Cl
   OLD/WMLY/WICK BS30 .... 338 F5 🛈
Coniston Rd
   BRSTK/PCHW BS34 .... 316 A3
   CHELTW GL51 .... 115 G4
   VGL GL2 .... 112 C7
Connaught Rd
   BRSG/KWL/STAPK BS4 .... 346 A3
Connemara Cl *NWNT* GL18 .... 86 B4 🛈
Constable Cl *KEYN* BS31 .... 348 B5 🛈
Constable Rd *HORF/LLZ* BS7 ...... 326 C5
Constance Cl *STROUD* GL5 .... 208 B6
Constantine Av
   BRSTK/PCHW BS34 .... 317 G6
Constitution Hl *CFTN/FAIL* BS8.... 6 A4
   CFTN/FAIL BS8 .... 335 J5
Convent Cl *HNBRY/STHM* BS10.. 314 F9 🛈
Convent La *STROUD* GL5 .... 232 B4
Conway Gn *KEYN* BS31 .... 348 C3
Conway Rd
   BRSG/KWL/STAPK BS4 .... 336 E7
   BWTH/CHD GL3 .... 137 J3
Conygar Rd *TET* GL8 .... 282 A3
Conygre Gv
   BRSTK/PCHW BS34 .... 316 E8 🛈
Conygre Rd *BRSTK/PCHW* BS34.. 316 D8
Cook Cl *OLD/WMLY/WICK* BS30 . 338 F7
Cooke's Dr *THNB/SVB* BS35 ...... 315 J2
Cooks Cl *ALMDB* BS32 .... 306 E8
Cook's Folly Rd
   HNLZ/SM/SNYPK/WT BS9........ 324 F8 🛈
Cooks La *CHNTN* OX7 .... 83 H7
   FRCTL/WBN BS36 .... 318 F8 🛈
   RTEWK/TIB BS19 .... 43 M4 🛈
Cooksley Rd *EVILLE/WHL* BS5 ... 336 E3 🛈
Cooks Orch *GL* GL1 .... 5 H1
Cookspool *TET* GL8 .... 282 A3 🛈
Cookworthy Cl
   EVILLE/WHL BS5 .... 336 D5 🛈
Coomb Dr *CIND* GL14 .... 154 A6
Coombe Av *THNB/SVB* BS35 ..... 293 K1 🛈
Coombe Bridge Av
   HNLZ/SM/SNYPK/WT BS9........ 324 F5

Coombe Cl
   HNBRY/STHM BS10 .... 314 F8 🛈
Coombe Dl
   HNLZ/SM/SNYPK/WT BS9........ 324 E5
Coombe Gdns
   HNLZ/SM/SNYPK/WT BS9........ 325 G5
Coombe Glen La *CHELTW* GL51... 114 F5
Coombe La
   HNLZ/SM/SNYPK/WT BS9........ 324 F5
   STNHO GL10 .... 231 K1
   WUE GL12 .... 277 M3
Coombe Meade
   CHELTE/BC GL52 .... 72 D8 🛈
Coombe Rd *EVILLE/WHL* BS5 ..... 336 E1 🛈
   WUE GL12 .... 277 L3
Coombes Wy
   OLD/WMLY/WICK BS30 .... 338 F7
Coombe Wy
   HNBRY/STHM BS10 .... 325 H2
Coombs Rd *CLFD* GL16 .... 151 K8
Cooperage La *BMSTR* BS3 .... 6 A7
Cooperage Rd *EVILLE/WHL* BS5 . 336 E4
Co-operation Rd
   EVILLE/WHL BS5 .... 336 E2
Cooper Rd
   HNLZ/SM/SNYPK/WT BS9........ 325 H4
   THNB/SVB BS35 .... 293 K4
Coopers Cl *MALM* SN16 .... 303 J6
Coopers Dr *YATE/CS* BS37 .... 310 B6
Coopers Elm *VGL* GL2 .... 159 H1
Coopers La *MALM* SN16 .... 151 J4
Cooper's Vw *BWTH/CHD* GL3 ... 138 A6 🛈
Coopers Wy *NWNT* GL18 .... 86 D3
The Coots *HGRV/WHIT* BS14 ..... 347 G5
Copeland Dr
   HGRV/WHIT BS14 .... 346 D6 🛈
Cope Pk *ALMDB* BS32 .... 306 E6
Copford La *LGASH* BS41 .... 344 D2
Copley Ct *KGWD/HNM* BS15 ..... 338 A6 🛈
Copley Gdns *HORF/LLZ* BS7 ...... 326 D5 🛈
Copper Beech Gv *VGL* GL2 ...... 159 G2
Coppice Daw Pitch
   RTEWK/TIB BS19 .... 132 C1
Coppice Ga *CHELTW* GL51 .... 93 H6
Coppice Hl *RSTROUD/NAIL* GL6.. 234 C1
Coppice Rd *MTCHDN* GL17 .... 128 C5
The Coppice *ALMDB* BS32 .... 317 G4
   BMSTRD/HC/WWD BS13 .... 345 G7
Copsehill Rd *COTS* GL54 .... 123 C1
Copse Rd
   BRSG/KWL/STAPK BS4 .... 336 D8
   KEYN BS31 .... 348 E7
The Copse *GLE* GL4 .... 137 G4 🛈
Copt Elm Cl *CHELTS* GL53 .... 116 C5
Copt Elm Rd *CHELTS* GL53 .... 116 C5
Copthorne *HGRV/WHIT* BS14 .... 346 D6
Coral Cl *GL* GL1 .... 135 K8
Corbet Cl *AVONM* BS11 .... 324 D1
Corder's La *MIM* GL56 .... 58 C6
Cordingley Cl *BWTH/CHD* GL3 .. 113 L7
Cordwell Wk
   HNBRY/STHM BS10 .... 325 M4 🛈
Corey Cl *CBRISNE* BS2 .... 336 B2 🛈
Corfe Cl *CHELTE/BC* GL52 .... 94 E8 🛈
Corfe Crs *KEYN* BS31 .... 348 A6
Corfe Pl *OLD/WMLY/WICK* BS30 . 348 D2
Corfe Rd
   BRSG/KWL/STAPK BS4 .... 345 M4 🛈
Coriander Dr *ALMDB* BS32 .... 317 J4
   BWTH/CHD GL3 .... 113 H5
Coriander Wk
   EVILLE/WHL BS5 .... 336 E1 🛈
Corinium Ga *CIR* GL7 .... 238 D2
Cormorant Av *TEWK* GL20 .... 48 C7 🛈
Corncroft La *GLE* GL4 .... 160 E1
Corndean La *COTS* GL54 .... 96 C2
Corner Rd *GL* GL15 .... 201 H2
Cornfield Cl *ALMDB* BS32 .... 316 E2
Cornfield Dr *CHELTE/BC* GL52 ... 72 A7 🛈
   VGL GL2 .... 159 G2
The Cornfields *CHELTE/BC* GL52.. 72 A7
Cornfield Wy *EVE* WR11 .... 29 K1
Cornflower Rd *GLE* GL4 .... 137 G6
Corn Gastons *MALM* SN16 .... 303 G7 🛈
Cornhill *STROUD* GL5 .... 208 E4
Cornhill Dr *HGRV/WHIT* BS14 .... 346 C4
Cornish Gv *HGRV/WHIT* BS14 .... 347 G5 🛈
Cornish La *CHNTN* OX7 .... 105 M2
   HGRV/WHIT BS14 .... 347 G5
Cornish Wk *HGRV/WHIT* BS14... 347 G5
Cornleaze
   BMSTRD/HC/WWD BS13 .... 345 J6 🛈
Cornmeadow Dr
   CHELTW GL51 .... 92 F6 🛈
Corn St *CBRIS/FH* BS1 .... 6 F4
Cornwall Av *CHELTW* GL51 .... 115 J1
Cornwall Crs *YATE/CS* BS37 ...... 310 B8
Cornwallis Av *CFTN/FAIL* BS8 ... 335 H5 🛈
Cornwallis Crs *CFTN/FAIL* BS8 .. 335 H5
Cornwall Rd *HORF/LLZ* BS7 ...... 325 M7
Corolin Rd *VGL* GL2 .... 135 K7
Coronation Av *KEYN* BS31......... 347 M7
   MANG/FISH BS16 .... 327 J7
Coronation Cl *CHCAM* GL55 ...... 12 D8 🛈
   OLD/WMLY/WICK BS30 .... 338 C6 🛈
Coronation Gv *VGL* GL2 .... 5 M5
Coronation Pl *CBRIS/FH* BS1 .... 6 F4 🛈
Coronation Rd *BMSTR* BS3 .... 6 B7
   BMSTR BS3 .... 335 J7
   CHELTE/BC GL52 .... 94 C7
   CIND GL14 .... 154 B4
   KGWD/HNM BS15 .... 338 C4
   MANG/FISH BS16 .... 328 A6
   OLD/WMLY/WICK BS30 .... 338 D6
   STROUD GL5 .... 208 D5
   TET GL8 .... 281 M2
Coronation St *CIR* GL7 .... 242 D4
Corpus St *CHELTS* GL53 .... 2 F7
The Corriett *DSLY* GL11 .... 229 J6 🛈
Corsend Rd *RTEWK/TIB* BS19 ...... 88 E4
Corsley Wk
   BRSG/KWL/STAPK BS4 .... 346 B3 🛈
Cossham Cl *THNB/SVB* BS35 .... 293 L1 🛈
Cossham Rd *EVILLE/WHL* BS5 ... 336 F3
Cossham St *MANG/FISH* BS16 ... 328 D6
Cossham Wk *EVILLE/WHL* BS5 .. 337 J2

Cossington Rd
   BRSG/KWL/STAPK BS4.............. 346 B3
Cossins Rd *RDLND/MONT* BS6 .... 325 K8
Costard Av *SHPSTR* CV36 .... 16 A6 🛈
Costers Cl *THNB/SVB* BS35 .... 293 J5
Costiland Dr
   BMSTRD/HC/WWD BS13 .... 345 H5 🛈
Cote Dr
   HNLZ/SM/SNYPK/WT BS9........ 325 J7
Cote House La
   HNLZ/SM/SNYPK/WT BS9........ 325 J7
Cote La
   HNLZ/SM/SNYPK/WT BS9........ 325 J6
Cote Lea Pk
   HNLZ/SM/SNYPK/WT BS9........ 325 J4 🛈
Cote Paddock *HNLZ/SM/SNYPK/WT* BS9
325 J7
Cote Pk *HNLZ/SM/SNYPK/WT* BS9 325G5
Cotham Brow *RDLND/MONT* BS6 ... 335
M1 🛈
Cotham Gdns
   RDLND/MONT BS6 .... 335 K2 🛈
Cotham Gv *RDLND/MONT* BS6 ... 335 M2
Cotham Hl
   RDLND/MONT BS6 .... 335 K2 🛈
Cotham Lawn Rd
   RDLND/MONT BS6 .... 335 L2
Cotham Pk *RDLND/MONT* BS6 ... 335 L2
Cotham Pk North
   RDLND/MONT BS6 .... 335 L2
Cotham Rd *RDLND/MONT* BS6 ... 335 L3
Cotham Side
   RDLND/MONT BS6 .... 335 M2
Cotham V *RDLND/MONT* BS6 .... 335 L2
Cothar's Pitch *RWYE* HR9 .... 84 B2
Cotman Wk *HORF/LLZ* BS7 .... 326 D5
Cotrith Gv *HNBRY/STHM* BS10 .. 315 G8
Cotsmore Cl *MIM* GL56 .... 58 E6
Cotswold Av *CIR* GL7 .... 238 B4
   STNHO GL10 .... 206 B4 🛈
Cotswold Cl *CIR* GL7 .... 238 B4
   RSTROUD/NAIL GL6 .... 233 K2 🛈
   TET GL8 .... 282 A3 🛈
Cotswold Edge *CHCAM* GL55 .... 8 C7 🛈
Cotswold Gdns *MIM* GL56 .... 58 D6
   TEWK GL20 .... 48 B4
   VGL GL2 .... 112 F6 🛈
   WUE GL12 .... 277 L4
Cotswold Gv *STNHO* GL10 .... 207 J3
Cotswold La *YATE/CS* BS37 ...... 321 J3
Cotswold Md
   RSTROUD/NAIL GL6 .... 185 G4
Cotswold Rd *BMSTR* BS3 .... 335 M8
   CHELTE/BC GL52 .... 3 K1
   STROUD GL5 .... 208 A3
   YATE/CS BS37 .... 320 C5
Cotswold Vw *CHELTE/BC* GL52... 72 D8
   KGWD/HNM BS15 .... 337 M1 🛈
   RTEWK/TIB BS19 .... 68 B5 🛈
   WUE GL12 .... 276 D6 🛈
   WUE GL12 .... 296 D5 🛈
Cotswold Wy *BDWAY* WR12 .... 33 G4
   BDWAY WR12 .... 54 B3
   CBATH/BATHN BA1 .... 350 B3
   CHCAM GL55 .... 12 C7
   CHELTE/BC GL52 .... 95 J8
   CHELTW GL51 .... 139 H6
   COTS GL54 .... 75 K3
   COTS GL54 .... 96 B4
   COTS GL54 .... 117 J3
   DSLY GL11 .... 230 E6
   DSLY GL11 .... 253 C5
   RSTROUD/NAIL GL6 .... 161 H8
   STNHO GL10 .... 231 G3
   WUE GL12 .... 277 L4 🛈
   YATE/CS BS37 .... 321 J6
Cottage Fld *VGL* GL2 .... 110 F6 🛈
Cottage Pitch *NWNT* GL18 .... 86 C1
Cottage Rake Av *CHELTW* GL51 .. 93 L6
Cotteswold Ri *STROUD* GL5 ...... 208 F4
Cotteswold Rd *GLE* GL4 .... 136 C5
   TEWK GL20 .... 48 B4
Cottington Ct
   KGWD/HNM BS15 .... 338 A6 🛈
Cottisford Rd *EVILLE/WHL* BS5... 326 D7
Cottle Gdns *HGRV/WHIT* BS14 ... 347 H5
Cottle Rd *HGRV/WHIT* BS14 .... 347 H5
Cotton Cl *GLE* GL4 .... 137 H6
Cotton's La *EVE* WR11 .... 29 J2
Cottonwood Dr
   OLD/WMLY/WICK BS30 .... 338 C8
Cottrell Av *KGWD/HNM* BS15 .... 337 K1
Cottrell Rd *EVILLE/WHL* BS5 ..... 326 E8
Coulson's Cl
   HGRV/WHIT BS14 .... 346 C8 🛈
Coulson's Rd *HGRV/WHIT* BS14 . 346 B8
Coulson Wk
   KGWD/HNM BS15 .... 337 L1 🛈
Counterpool Rd
   KGWD/HNM BS15 .... 337 L4
Countership *CBRIS/FH* BS1 .... 7 G4
Counterslip Gdns
   HGRV/WHIT BS14 .... 347 H4
Countess Lilias Rd *CIR* GL7 ...... 238 C5 🛈
Countess Wk
   MANG/FISH BS16 .... 326 F5 🛈
County Court Rd *CHELT* GL50 ...... 2 D5 🛈
County St *BRSG/KWL/STAPK* BS4 .. 7 K9
Court Av *BRSTK/PCHW* BS34 ..... 317 H6 🛈
Courtbrook *CIR* GL7 .... 242 E5
Court Cl *HORF/LLZ* BS7 .... 326 A4
Court Dr *RTEWK/TIB* BS19 .... 68 F7
Courtenay St *CHELT* GL50 .... 2 D2
Courtenay Crs
   BRSG/KWL/STAPK BS4 .... 345 M4 🛈
Court Farm La *MTCHDN* GL17..... 130 C1
Court Farm Rd
   HGRV/WHIT BS14 .... 346 B8
   OLD/WMLY/WICK BS30 .... 347 M4
Courtfield Dr
   CHELTE/BC GL52 .... 116 D5 🛈
Courtfield Gv *MANG/FISH* BS16 .. 327 J7

Courtfield Rd *VGL* GL2 .... 159 G3
Court Gdn *DSLY* GL11 .... 254 D3
Court Gdns *CBATH/BATHN* BA1... 352 C8
Court La *VGL* GL2 .... 179 M1
Courthouse Gdns *DSLY* GL11 .... 229 H5
Courtiers Dr *CHELTE/BC* GL52 .... 72 C7
Courtlands *ALMDB* BS32 .... 316 E2
   KEYN BS31 .... 348 A6
Courtlands La *BMSTR* BS3 .... 335 G7
Court La *LYD* GL15 .... 224 E5
   NWNT GL18 .... 86 C3
   OLD/WMLY/WICK BS30 .... 339 K6
Court Md *BRKLY* GL13 .... 251 C8
Court Meadow *BRKLY* GL13 ...... 251 C8
   WUE GL12 .... 277 L4
Courtney Cl *TEWK* GL20 .... 48 A8
Courtney Rd *KGWD/HNM* BS15 .. 338 A4
Courtney Wy *KGWD/HNM* BS15.. 338 C4
Court Orch *WUE* GL12 .... 277 L4
Court Pl *GLE* GL4 .... 136 F5
Court Rd *BWTH/CHD* GL3 .... 138 A5
   CHELTE/BC GL52 .... 94 E7
   FRCTL/WBN BS36 .... 318 B3
   HORF/LLZ BS7 .... 326 B5
   KGWD/HNM BS15 .... 337 M4
   LYD GL15 .... 201 K5
   NWNT GL18 .... 86 D2
   OLD/WMLY/WICK BS30 .... 338 D8
   STNHO GL10 .... 206 D8
   WUE GL12 .... 275 K7
Courtside Ms
   RDLND/MONT BS6 .... 335 L2 🛈
Court View Cl *ALMDB* BS32 .... 306 C6
Court Wy *STROUD* GL5 .... 208 C6
Courville Cl *THNB/SVB* BS35 ..... 293 J7
Cousins Cl
   HNBRY/STHM BS10 .... 314 F8 🛈
Cousins Ms
   BRSG/KWL/STAPK BS4 .... 337 H5 🛈
Cousins Wy *MANG/FISH* BS16 ... 328 C3
Cousley Cl *BWTH/CHD* GL3 .... 137 J4
Couzens Cl *YATE/CS* BS37 .... 320 D1
Couzens Pl
   BRSTK/PCHW BS34 .... 317 H6 🛈
Coventry Cl *TEWK* GL20 .... 48 B7 🛈
Coventry Wk
   BRSG/KWL/STAPK BS4 .... 337 H5 🛈
Coverham Cl *CLFD* GL16 .... 151 K5 🛈
Coverham Rd *CLFD* GL16 .... 151 J6
Cowcombe Hl
   RSTROUD/NAIL GL6 .... 234 C2
Cowdray Rd
   BRSG/KWL/STAPK BS4 .... 345 M4 🛈
Cowhorn Hl
   OLD/WMLY/WICK BS30 .... 338 E7
Cow La *STROUD* GL5 .... 232 C5
Cowler Wk
   BMSTRD/HC/WWD BS13 .... 345 H7 🛈
Cowley Cl *CHELTW* GL51 .... 114 F4
Cowley Rd *GLE* GL4 .... 136 A8
Cowling Dr *HGRV/WHIT* BS14 .... 346 E6
Cowling Rd *HGRV/WHIT* BS14.... 346 E6
Cowl La *COTS* GL54 .... 74 C6
Cowlsmead *CHELTW* GL51 .... 138 F1
Cowper Rd *CHELTW* GL51 .... 115 G2 🛈
   RDLND/MONT BS6 .... 335 K2
Cowper St *EVILLE/WHL* BS5 ...... 336 E4 🛈
Cowship La *WUE* GL12 .... 295 K4
Cowslip Meadow
   CHELTE/BC GL52 .... 72 D8
Cowswell La
   RSTROUD/NAIL GL6 .... 209 L8
Coxbury & Wyegate La
   CLFD GL16 .... 174 C8
Cox Ct *OLD/WMLY/WICK* BS30 ... 338 B7
Cox La *CHNTN* OX7 .... 105 K1
Coxmoor Ct *CHNTN* OX7 .... 104 B7
Cox's Hl *HGHW* SN6 .... 287 C1
Cox's Wy *BWTH/CHD* GL3 .... 137 J5
   LYD GL15 .... 200 D2
Coxwell St *CIR* GL7 .... 238 C2
Cozens La *CHNTN* OX7 .... 104 B7
Crabbree La *CIR* GL7 .... 212 C1
   CIR GL7 .... 238 F4 🛈
Crabtree Pk *CIR* GL7 .... 242 F3
Crab Tree Pl *CHELT* GL50 .... 2 B1
Crabtree Wk
   EVILLE/WHL BS5 .... 336 F1 🛈
Craddock Cl
   OLD/WMLY/WICK BS30 .... 338 D7 🛈
Cradock Cl
   OLD/WMLY/WICK BS30 .... 338 D7 🛈
Crail Vw *COTS* GL54 .... 169 K2
Cranberry Wk
   HNLZ/SM/SNYPK/WT BS9........ 324 E3 🛈
Cranbourne Rd
   BRSTK/PCHW BS34 .... 316 B4
Cranbrook Rd
   RDLND/MONT BS6 .... 325 L8
Crandell Cl *HNBRY/STHM* BS10... 315 H7
Crane Cl *KGWD/HNM* BS15 .... 338 D3 🛈
Cranford Cl *CHELTE/BC* GL52 ..... 72 E8 🛈
Cranham *YATE/CS* BS37 .... 319 L4 🛈
Cranham Cl *GLE* GL4 .... 137 G6 🛈
   KGWD/HNM BS15 .... 338 B1 🛈
Cranham Dr *BRSTK/PCHW* BS34.. 316 E2
Cranham La *CHELTE/BC* GL52 ...... 3 H7
   HNBRY/STHM BS10 .... 325 L3
Cranham Rd *CIR* GL7 .... 238 B5
Cranleigh Court Rd
   YATE/CS BS37 .... 319 M1 🛈
Cranleigh Gdns
   HNLZ/SM/SNYPK/WT BS9........ 325 G7
Cranleigh Rd
   HGRV/WHIT BS14 .... 346 D6 🛈
Cranmoor Gn *THNB/SVB* BS35 ... 304 F3
Cranmore Av *KEYN* BS31 .... 348 A5
Cranmore Crs
   HNBRY/STHM BS10 .... 325 M2
Cranside Av *RDLND/MONT* BS6 . 325 L8
Cransley Crs
   HNLZ/SM/SNYPK/WT BS9........ 325 K7
Crantock Av
   BMSTRD/HC/WWD BS13 .... 345 K3
Crantock Dr *ALMDB* BS32 .... 306 E6
Crantock Rd *YATE/CS* BS37 .... 319 M2

Cranwell Cl *GLE* GL4 .... 136 E7
Cranwell Gv *HGRV/WHIT* BS14... 346 C6
The Crapen *DSLY* GL11 .... 229 G7
Crashmore La *TEWK* GL20 .... 28 B6
Craven Cl
   OLD/WMLY/WICK BS30 .... 338 B6
Craven Dr *BWTH/CHD* GL3 .... 113 J5
Craven Wy
   OLD/WMLY/WICK BS30 .... 338 B6
Crawley Hl *DSLY* GL11 .... 230 D8
Crawley La *DSLY* GL11 .... 230 D8
Crawshay Pl *CIND* GL14 .... 154 A3
Craydon Gv *HGRV/WHIT* BS14 ... 346 F3
Craydon Rd *HGRV/WHIT* BS14 ... 346 F3
Craydon Wk
   HGRV/WHIT BS14 .... 346 F6 🛈
The Crease *NWNT* GL18 .... 86 D3 🛈
Crediton Crs
   BRSG/KWL/STAPK BS4 .... 346 B2
Credon Rd *GLE* GL4 .... 137 G2
Crescent Cl *CLFD* GL16 .... 151 J8
   STNHO GL10 .... 207 G5
Crescentdale *VGL* GL2 .... 112 C5
Crescent Pl *CHELT* GL50 .... 2 C5
Crescent Rd *MANG/FISH* BS16 ... 327 L5
   STNHO GL10 .... 207 G5
Crescent Ter *CHELT* GL50 .... 2 D5
The Crescent *BRKLY* GL13 .... 226 F3
   BWTH/CHD GL3 .... 137 M5
   CLFD GL16 .... 151 J8
   CLFD GL16 .... 175 K1 🛈
   DSLY GL11 .... 229 H7
   HNLZ/SM/SNYPK/WT BS9........ 324 C5
   HNLZ/SM/SNYPK/WT BS9........ 325 L5
   MANG/FISH BS16 .... 327 H2
   MANG/FISH BS16 .... 327 M8
   MTCHDN GL17 .... 106 C8
   OLD/WMLY/WICK BS30 .... 339 K4
The Crest
   BRSG/KWL/STAPK BS4 .... 346 E1
Crest Wy *GLE* GL4 .... 137 H2
Creswicke Av
   KGWD/HNM BS15 .... 337 L6 🛈
Creswicke Rd
   BRSG/KWL/STAPK BS4 .... 346 A4
Crew's Hole Rd
   EVILLE/WHL BS5 .... 337 H5 🛈
Cribbs Cswy
   HNBRY/STHM BS10 .... 315 K4
Cricklade Rd *CIR* GL7 .... 238 C5
   HORF/LLZ BS7 .... 326 A7
Cricklade St *CIR* GL7 .... 238 C2
   CIR GL7 .... 240 F5
Criftycraft La *BWTH/CHD* GL3 ... 113 M7
Cripps Rd *BMSTR* BS3 .... 335 L8
   CIR GL7 .... 238 C3
   VGL GL2 .... 112 E6
Crispin Cl *THNB/SVB* BS35 .... 293 K2 🛈
Crispin Rd *COTS* GL54 .... 74 C5
Crispin Wy *KGWD/HNM* BS15 .... 338 B1
Critchford La *COTS* GL54 .... 98 D3
Crockwell St *SHPSTR* CV36 .... 61 H4
Croft Av *CHELTS* GL53 .... 116 C6
   MANG/FISH BS16 .... 326 E7 🛈
Croft Cl *BWTH/CHD* GL3 .... 113 M7
   NWNT GL18 .... 86 D2 🛈
   OLD/WMLY/WICK BS30 .... 348 F3
Crofters Wk *ALMDB* BS32 .... 316 F3
Croft Gdns *CHELTS* GL53 .... 116 D7
Croft Holm *MIM* GL56 .... 58 E6
The Croftlands *TEWK* GL20 .... 27 H5 🛈
Croft La *CIR* GL7 .... 188 C4
   HGHW SN6 .... 264 D7
Crofton Av *HORF/LLZ* BS7 .... 326 B5 🛈
Croft Rd *CHELTS* GL53 .... 116 C6
   NWNT GL18 .... 86 C2
Crofts End Rd *EVILLE/WHL* BS5 .. 337 J2
Croft St *CHELTS* GL53 .... 115 L5
The Croft *CIR* GL7 .... 242 E4
   DSLY GL11 .... 229 J7
   MANG/FISH BS16 .... 328 B6
   OLD/WMLY/WICK BS30 .... 338 E8 🛈
   RSTROUD/NAIL GL6 .... 185 G4
Croft Thorne Cl
   CHELTW GL51 .... 115 H6 🛈
Croft Vw
   HNLZ/SM/SNYPK/WT BS9 ...... 325 L5 🛈
Crokewood Wk
   AVONM BS11 .... 324 C2 🛈
Crome Rd *HORF/LLZ* BS7 .... 326 D4
Cromer Rd *EVILLE/WHL* BS5 ..... 336 E1
Cromers Cl *TEWK* GL20 .... 49 C2 🛈
Cromhall La *WUE* GL12 .... 295 G2
Cromwell Ct
   KGWD/HNM BS15 .... 338 A6 🛈
Cromwell Rd *CHELTE/BC* GL52 .... 3 J2
   CHEP NP16 .... 270 A6 🛈
   EVILLE/WHL BS5 .... 337 J3
   RDLND/MONT BS6 .... 335 M1
Cromwells Hide
   MANG/FISH BS16 .... 327 G6 🛈
Cromwell St *GL* GL1 .... 4 F7
Crooked End Pl
   MTCHDN GL17 .... 129 H3 🛈
Croomes Hl *MANG/FISH* BS16 ... 327 M5
Cropthorne Wk
   HORF/LLZ BS7 .... 326 C2 🛈
Cropthorne Rd South
   HORF/LLZ BS7 .... 326 C3 🛈
Crosby Rw *CFTN/FAIL* BS8 .... 335 J5
Crosscombe Dr
   BMSTRD/HC/WWD BS13 .... 345 K8
Cross Elms La
   HNLZ/SM/SNYPK/WT BS9........ 325 G6
Cross Farm Cl *LYD* GL15 .... 224 F3
Crossfield Rd *MANG/FISH* BS16 . 328 A8
Crossfields *COTS* GL54 .... 118 C8 🛈
Cross Hands Rd
   THNB/SVB BS35 .... 304 C8
Cross Hayes La *MALM* SN16 ..... 303 J8 🛈
Cross Keys La *GL* GL1 .... 4 E5
Crossleaze Rd
   KGWD/HNM BS15 .... 337 L8
Crossley Cl *FRCTL/WBN* BS36 .. 318 D4 🛈
Cross Leys *CHNTN* OX7 .... 105 M1
Crossman Av *FRCTL/WBN* BS36 .. 318 A4

Cross St KEYN BS31 .... 348 B4
  KGWD/HNM BS15 .... 337 L2
The Cross TEWK GL20 .... 25 J3 🔲
Cross Tree Gv ALMDB BS32 .. 316 F3 🔲
Cross Tree La CIR GL7 .... 221 K5
Crossways Rd
  BRSG/KWL/STAPK BS4 ..... 346 C2
  THNB/SVB BS35 .... 293 M2
Crow Ash CLFD GL16 .... 151 K6
Crow Ash Rd CLFD GL16 ...... 151 J6
Crowfield La NWNT GL18 ...... 63 M1
Crowgate La CLFD GL14 .... 157 C3
Crow La CBRIS/FH BS1 .... 6 F4
  HNBRY/STHM BS10 .... 325 H1
Crow Meadow WUE GL12 ..... 277 H7
Crown CI CHELTE/BC GL52 ... 72 B8
Crowndale Rd
  BRSG/KWL/STAPK BS4 ..... 336 C8
Crown Dr CHELTE/BC GL52 ... 94 B1
Crown Gdns
  OLD/WMLY/WICK BS30 ..... 338 D4
Crown HI EVILLE/WHL BS5 .... 337 H3
Crown Hill Wk EVILLE/WHL BS5 . 337 H3
Crown La LYD GL15 .... 176 E7
Crownleaze MANG/FISH BS16 . 327 K7
Crown Meadow CLFD GL16 ... 175 M2 🔲
Crown Rd KGWD/HNM BS15 .. 337 M1
  OLD/WMLY/WICK BS30 ..... 338 C5
Crows Gv ALMDB BS32 .... 306 F8
Crowther Pk HORF/LLZ BS7 .. 326 C7
Crowther Rd HORF/LLZ BS7 .. 326 C7
Crowthers Av YATE/CS BS37 . 310 E4
Crowther St BMSTR BS3 .... 335 K8 🔲
Croydon St EVILLE/WHL BS5 .. 336 D3 🔲
Crucible CI CLFD GL16 .... 175 K2
The Crunnis ALMDB BS32 ..... 317 C5
Crudwell La TET GL8 .... 282 F5
Crypt Ct GL GL1 .... 135 L8
Crythan Wk CHELTW GL51 ... 115 H6 🔲
Cuckoo La FRCTL/WBN BS36 .. 318 B8
Cuckoo Rw RSTROUD/NAIL GL6 . 233 H5
Cud La RSTROUD/NAIL GL6 ... 184 D3
Cudnall St CHELTS GL53 ...... 116 C4
Cuffington Av
  BRSG/KWL/STAPK BS4 ..... 336 F7
Culleysgate La
  OLD/WMLY/WICK BS30 ..... 340 B5
Cullimore Vw CIND GL14 ..... 154 A6
Cullingham CI RTEWK/TIB GL19 . 66 B4
Culross CI CHELT GL50 .... 94 A7
Culverhay WUE GL12 .... 277 K4
Culver HI STROUD GL5 .... 232 C3
Culverhill Rd YATE/CS BS37 .. 320 C2
Culvers Rd KEYN BS31 .... 348 A5
Culver St CBRIS/FH BS1 ...... 6 D4
  NWNT GL18 .... 86 C4
The Culvert ALMDB BS32 .... 316 F3 🔲
Culverwell Rd
  BMSTR/HC/WWD BS13 ...... 345 J7
Cumberland Basin Rd
  CFTN/FAIL BS8 .... 335 H6
Cumberland CI CBRIS/FH BS1 . 335 J6
Cumberland Crs CHELTW GL51 . 115 J2
Cumberland Gv
  RDLND/MONT BS6 .... 336 B1 🔲
Cumberland PI
  CFTN/FAIL BS8 .... 335 H5 🔲
Cumberland Rd
  CBRIS/FH BS1 .... 335 H6 🔲
Cumberland St CBRISNE BS2 .. 7 G1 🔲
Cumbria CI THNB/SVB BS35 .. 294 A2
Cunningham Gdns
  MANG/FISH BS16 .... 327 K6 🔲
Cupola CI CLFD GL16 .... 175 K2
Curland Gv HGRV/WHIT BS14 . 346 D6 🔲
Curlew CI MANG/FISH BS16 .. 327 H5 🔲
  TEWK GL20 .... 48 F2 🔲
Curlew Rd GLE GL4 .... 136 E5
  RTEWK/TIB GL19 .... 70 A6
The Cursus CIR GL7 .... 244 E6
Curtis Hayward Dr VGL GL2 .. 159 G2
Curtis La BRSTK/PCHW BS34 . 317 J8
Custom CI HGRV/WHIT BS14 .. 346 C4
Cut & Fry Rd LYD GL15 ...... 201 L1
Cutham La GLE GL4 .... 190 B8
Cuthwine PI CIR GL7 .... 244 E6
Cutler Rd
  BMSTR/HC/WWD BS13 ...... 345 H5
  STROUD GL5 .... 208 F3
Cutsdean CI CHELTE/BC GL52 . 71 M7
Cut Throat La LED HR8 ...... 20 D1
  RWYE HR9 .... 84 B6
Cuttlesheath Rd WUE GL12 .. 294 E3
Cutwell TET GL8 .... 281 M5
Cynder Wy MANG/FISH BS16 . 328 C2
Cyldre Pk RDLND/MONT BS6 .. 335 K1
Cypress Gdns CFTN/FAIL BS8 . 335 C5
Cypress Gv
  HNLZ/SM/SNYPK/WT BS9 ... 325 L5
Cypress Rd TEWK GL20 ...... 48 C7
Cypress Wk
  CHPMW/MSHF SN14 .... 343 H5
Cyrus Ct MANG/FISH BS16 ... 328 D4 🔲

D

Daffodil CI GLE GL4 .... 137 C6
Daffodil Leaze STNHO GL10 .. 207 K8
Daffodil Wy NWNT GL18 ..... 41 H8
  NWNT GL18 .... 62 C3
  NWNT GL18 .... 62 E5
  NWNT GL18 .... 63 L1
Daglingworth Pth CIR GL7 ... 212 E7
Dainty St GL GL1 .... 136 B4 🔲
Dairy Farm HGHW SN6 .... 287 C3
Dairy La EVE WR11 .... 30 B7
Daisy Bank STROUD GL5 ..... 209 C5
Daisybank Rd CHELTS GL53 .. 140 A1
Daisy Green La WUE GL12 ... 276 F1
Daisy Rd EVILLE/WHL BS5 .... 336 E1
Dakota Dr HGRV/WHIT BS14 .. 346 C7
Dalby Av BMSTR BS3 .... 335 M8
Daldry Gdns THNB/SVB BS35 . 292 C8 🔲
Dalebrook RWYE HR9 .... 84 F3 🔲
Dale CI GLE GL4 .... 136 B6

Dale St CBRISNE BS2 .... 7 J1 🔲
  COTS GL54 .... 99 J8
  EVILLE/WHL BS5 .... 337 H3
Dale Wk CHELTE/BC GL52 .... 72 C8
Dalkeith Av
  KGWD/HNM BS15 .... 337 L2 🔲
Dallaway STROUD GL5 .... 233 L3 🔲
Dalrymple Rd CBRISNE BS2 .. 336 A2 🔲
Dalston Rd BMSTR BS3 .... 6 B8 🔲
Dalton Sq CBRISNE BS2 ...... 336 A3 🔲
Damery La BRKLY GL13 ...... 251 K8 🔲
  WUE GL12 .... 251 L8 🔲
  WUE GL12 .... 275 L1 🔲
Dampier Rd BMSTR BS3 ...... 335 J8 🔲
The Damsels TET GL8 .... 282 A4 🔲
Damson CI GLE GL4 .... 137 G7
Danbury Crs
  HNBRY/STHM BS10 .... 325 L2
Danbury Wk
  HNBRY/STHM BS10 .... 325 L2 🔲
Dancey Md
  BMSTR/HC/WWD BS13 ...... 345 C5
Dancey Rd BWTH/CHD GL3 ... 113 H5 🔲
Dane CI VGL GL2 .... 112 E6 🔲
Dane La CIR GL7 .... 211 L7
Danes HI CHEP NP16 .... 270 A4
Danford La RTEWK/TIB GL19 . 88 F5
Dangerfield Av
  BMSTR/HC/WWD BS13 ...... 345 C5
Daniels Rd STROUD GL5 ...... 209 H5
Dapps HI KEYN BS31 .... 348 B6
Darell CI VGL GL2 .... 159 H4
Dark La CHELTW GL51 .... 93 J4
  CIR GL7 .... 190 C7
  MALM SN16 .... 303 H8
  RSTROUD/NAIL GL6 .... 232 C7
  RSTROUD/NAIL GL6 .... 234 A1
  STROUD GL5 .... 208 D6
Darks Rd NWNT GL18 .... 85 C5
Darley CI HNBRY/STHM BS10 . 314 F8 🔲
Darlingscote Rd SHPSTR CV36 . 15 L3
Darnell's La RWYE HR9 ...... 84 E5
Darnley Av HORF/LLZ BS7 .... 326 B5
Darren CI CLFD GL16 .... 151 K6
Dart CI THNB/SVB BS35 ...... 293 K3 🔲
  VGL GL2 .... 159 H1
Darters CI LYD GL15 .... 225 J1 🔲
Dartmoor St BMSTR BS3 ..... 6 B9
  BMSTR BS3 .... 335 K8 🔲
Dart Rd CHELTE/BC GL52 .... 3 L2 🔲
Darwin CI CHELTW GL51 ..... 114 E2
Darwin Rd GLE GL4 .... 136 B6
Daston CI STROUD GL5 ...... 209 H5
Daubeny Rd MANG/FISH BS16 . 327 K6
Davallia Dr CHELTW GL51 ... 115 H6
Daventry Rd
  BRSG/KWL/STAPK BS4 ..... 346 B2
Daventry Ter GL GL1 .... 5 G9 🔲
Davey St CBRISNE BS2 .... 336 B2
David French Ct
  CHELTW GL51 .... 115 J6 🔲
Davids CI THNB/SVB BS35 .... 293 J7
David's La THNB/SVB BS35 ... 293 J7
David's Rd HGRV/WHIT BS14 . 346 E5
David St CBRISNE BS2 .... 7 J3
Davies Dr
  BRSG/KWL/STAPK BS4 ..... 337 H6 🔲
Davies Rd MIM GL56 .... 58 E5
Davis CI
  OLD/WMLY/WICK BS30 ..... 338 B6 🔲
Davis Ct THNB/SVB BS35 .... 293 L1
Dawes CI CIR GL7 .... 220 B8
The Dawes VGL GL2 .... 159 H3
Dawley Cl FRCTL/WBN BS36 .. 318 A4 🔲
Dawlish Rd BMSTR BS3 ...... 345 M1
The Dawneys MALM SN16 .... 284 A5
Dawn Ri KGWD/HNM BS15 ... 338 C2
Daws Ct MANG/FISH BS16 .... 327 K7 🔲
Day House La WUE GL12 ..... 297 L3
Daylesford CI CHELTW GL51 .. 114 F3
Days Ct MALM SN16 .... 284 A5
Day's La MIM GL56 .... 57 C1
Day's Rd CBRISNE BS2 .... 7 M4
Deacon CI CHELTW GL51 ..... 115 H4 🔲
  FRCTL/WBN BS36 .... 318 A6
Deacons PI CHELTE/BC GL52 . 94 A1 🔲
Deadmill La CBATH/BATHN BA1 . 351 L8
Deakin Cl CHELTW GL51 ..... 93 K4 🔲
Dean Av THNB/SVB BS35 ..... 293 L1
Dean Cl KGWD/HNM BS15 .... 337 J7
Dean Ct LYD GL15 .... 201 K6
Dean Crs BMSTR BS3 .... 6 E8 🔲
  CIND GL14 .... 154 E4
Deanery Rd CBRIS/FH BS1 ... 6 C5
  KGWD/HNM BS15 .... 338 D3
Dean La BMSTR BS3 .... 6 D9
  CHELTE/BC GL52 .... 71 C6
Dean Rd CIND GL14 .... 154 E5
  YATE/CS BS37 .... 309 L8
Deans Ct CHELTW GL51 ...... 115 H4 🔲
Dean's Dr EVILLE/WHL BS5 ... 337 J1 🔲
Deansfield HGHW SN6 .... 288 F4
Deans Md AVONM BS11 ...... 324 C3
Dean's Quarry STROUD GL5 .. 233 H3
Dean's Ter GL GL1 .... 4 F2 🔲
Dean St BMSTR BS3 .... 6 D9
  CBRISNE BS2 .... 336 A3
Dean's Wk GL GL1 .... 4 E3
  MTCHDN GL17 .... 129 M4
Deans Wy CHELTE/BC GL52 ... 72 B8
  GL GL1 .... 4 F2
Deansway Rd MTCHDN GL17 .. 106 C8
Dean Vw CIND GL14 .... 154 A6
De Clifford Rd AVONM BS11 .. 324 C3
Deep Coombe Rd
  BMSTR BS3 .... 345 J1 🔲
Deep Pit Rd EVILLE/WHL BS5 . 337 H2
Deep St CHELTE/BC GL52 .... 94 D7
Deerhurst KGWD/HNM BS15 .. 338 A1
  YATE/CS BS37 .... 319 L3
Deerhurst Cl GLE GL4 .... 137 C7 🔲
  MALM SN16 .... 82 B2
Deerhurst PI VGL GL2 .... 159 G2
Deering CI AVONM BS11 ...... 324 D2
Deer Pk LYD GL15 .... 201 J1
Deer Park Rd BWTH/CHD GL3 . 137 J2 🔲

Deerswood KGWD/HNM BS15 . 338 C1
De Havilland Rd COTS GL54 .. 124 D6
Delabere Av MANG/FISH BS16 . 327 K6
Delabere Rd CHELTE/BC GL52 . 94 C1
Delavale Rd COTS GL54 ...... 74 C5
Delius Gv
  BRSG/KWL/STAPK BS4 ..... 345 M4 🔲
Delkin Rd DSLY GL11 .... 229 H7
The Dell ALMDB BS32 .... 317 C4
  GLE GL4 .... 137 C4
  HNLZ/SM/SNYPK/WT BS9 ... 325 H6
  MIM GL56 .... 35 H8 🔲
  OLD/WMLY/WICK BS30 ..... 338 E6 🔲
  TEWK GL20 .... 27 C4
Dell Vw CHEP NP16 .... 270 A3
Delmont Gv STROUD GL5 .... 208 E3
Delphinium Dr
  CHELTE/BC GL52 .... 72 A8 🔲
Delta Dr TEWK GL20 .... 48 E3
Delvin Rd HNBRY/STHM BS10 . 325 L3
Denbigh Dr CHEP NP16 ...... 270 C6
Denbigh Rd CHELTW GL51 ... 115 C5
Denbigh St CBRISNE BS2 ..... 336 A2
Dene CI KEYN BS31 .... 348 B8
Denehurst MTCHDN GL17 .... 129 H6
Dene Rd HGRV/WHIT BS14 ... 346 E7
Denham CI CHELTE/BC GL52 . 72 E8 🔲
  GL GL1 .... 159 L2
Denleigh Cl HGRV/WHIT BS14 . 346 C7
Denley CI CHELTE/BC GL52 .. 94 B1
Denmark Dr CHEP NP16 ..... 270 D4
Denmark Pl HORF/LLZ BS7 ... 326 A8 🔲
Denmark Rd GL GL1 .... 5 H2
Denmark St CBRIS/FH BS1 ... 6 D4
Dennisworth
  MANG/FISH BS16 .... 329 K6 🔲
Dennor Pk HGRV/WHIT BS14 . 346 D4
Denny Isle Dr THNB/SVB BS35 . 304 C6
Dennyview Rd CFTN/FAIL BS8 . 334 B3
Denston Wk
  BMSTR/HC/WWD BS13 ...... 345 J4
Denton Patch
  MANG/FISH BS16 .... 328 D4 🔲
Dent's La RTEWK/TIB GL19 ... 88 F8
Dentwood Gv
  HNLZ/SM/SNYPK/WT BS9 ... 324 D4
Denys Ct THNB/SVB BS35 .... 292 B8
Derby Rd GL GL1 .... 5 J8
  HORF/LLZ BS7 .... 326 A8
Derby St EVILLE/WHL BS5 .... 336 F4
Derham Rd
  BMSTR/HC/WWD BS13 ...... 345 J6
Dermot St CBRISNE BS2 ..... 336 C2 🔲
Derricke Rd HGRV/WHIT BS14 . 347 H5
Derrick Rd KGWD/HNM BS15 . 337 M3
Derry Rd BMSTR BS3 .... 345 K1 🔲
The Derry HGHW SN6 .... 287 C3
Derwent CI BRSTK/PCHW BS34 . 316 C2
  BWTH/CHD GL3 .... 138 A6
Derwent Dr TEWK GL20 ..... 48 C3
Derwent Gv KEYN BS31 ..... 348 C3
Derwent Rd EVILLE/WHL BS5 . 337 H2
Desford CI HNBRY/STHM BS10 . 325 L3
Despenser Rd TEWK GL20 ... 48 A7
Detmore CI CHELTE/BC GL52 . 116 E6
Devereaux Crs STROUD GL5 .. 207 L4
Devereaux Rd STROUD GL5 .. 207 L5
De Verose Ct KGWD/HNM BS15 . 338 A7
The Devil's Elbow
  RSTROUD/NAIL GL6 .... 233 G7
Devil's La WUE GL12 .... 296 H7
Devizes Rd COR/BOX SN13 .. 353 M7
Devon Av CHELTW GL51 ..... 115 H2
Devon Gv EVILLE/WHL BS5 ... 336 E3
Devon Rd EVILLE/WHL BS5 ... 336 E2
Devonshire Dr TEWK GL20 .. 48 B7 🔲
Devonshire Rd
  RDLND/MONT BS6 .... 325 K7
Devonshire PI CHELT GL50 .. 2 K7
Dewey CI CHELTE/BC GL52 ... 72 D8
Dewfalls Dr ALMDB BS32 .... 316 F2
Dial La MANG/FISH BS16 ..... 327 M5
Diamond CI EVILLE/WHL BS5 . 337 H4
Diamond St BMSTR BS3 ..... 335 L8 🔲
Diana Gdns ALMDB BS32 .... 317 C3
Dianas CI BWTH/CHD GL3 ... 137 H5 🔲
Dibden CI MANG/FISH BS16 .. 328 C3
Dibden La MANG/FISH BS16 .. 328 C4
  TEWK GL20 .... 51 M4
Dibden Rd MANG/FISH BS16 . 328 C3
Dickens CI GLE GL4 .... 136 B6
  HORF/LLZ BS7 .... 326 C3
Dickens Ms GLE GL4 .... 136 B6 🔲
Didsbury CI HNBRY/STHM BS10 . 325 H2
Digbeth St COTS GL54 .... 102 A3 🔲
Digby Dr TEWK GL20 .... 48 B3
Dighton Ga
  BRSTK/PCHW BS34 .... 317 C6 🔲
Dighton St CBRISNE BS2 ..... 6 F1 🔲
Dikler CI COTS GL54 .... 123 K7 🔲
Dill Av CHELTW GL51 .... 93 C7
Dimore CI VGL GL2 .... 159 G4
Dinas Rd CHELTW GL51 ..... 115 H5
Dinely St GL GL1 .... 5 C8
Dingle CI
  HNLZ/SM/SNYPK/WT BS9 ... 324 E5
Dingle Rd
  HNLZ/SM/SNYPK/WT BS9 ... 324 E4
The Dingle FRCTL/WBN BS36 . 318 A8
  HNLZ/SM/SNYPK/WT BS9 ... 324 E4
  YATE/CS BS37 .... 310 B7
Dingle Vw
  HNLZ/SM/SNYPK/WT BS9 ... 324 E4
Dinglewell GLE GL4 .... 137 H4
Dinglewood CI
  HNLZ/SM/SNYPK/WT BS9 ... 324 F4 🔲
Dings Wk CBRISNE BS2 ...... 7 L4 🔲
Discovery Rd BWTH/CHD GL3 . 137 H5 🔲
Distel CI CHELTW GL51 ...... 93 L6
Ditch La CIR GL7 .... 192 E5
Dixon Rd BRSG/KWL/STAPK BS4 . 347 H1
Dobbie Rd STRAT CV37 ...... 9 K2
Dock Gate La CFTN/FAIL BS8 . 335 H4 🔲
Dockham Rd CIND GL14 ..... 154 C3
Dockins Hill Wy MTCHDN GL17 . 130 C4
Dock La TEWK GL20 .... 27 C4
Dock Rd BRKLY GL13 .... 226 D2
Doctors HI COR/BOX SN13 ... 353 J6

Dodd Dr COTS GL54 .... 124 D7
Dodington CI GLE GL4 ...... 136 F4 🔲
Dodington La YATE/CS BS37 . 320 C5
Dodington St YATE/CS BS37 . 320 D4
Dodisham Wk MANG/FISH BS16 . 327 K5
Dog La CHELTW GL51 .... 138 F5
Dollar St CIR GL7 .... 238 C2
Dolman CI
  HNBRY/STHM BS10 .... 315 H8 🔲
Domby CI CLFD GL16 .... 175 K2
Dominion Rd MANG/FISH BS16 . 327 H8
Donald Rd
  BMSTR/HC/WWD BS13 ...... 345 H4
Doncaster Rd
  HNBRY/STHM BS10 .... 325 K2
Doncombe HI
  CHPMW/MSHF SN14 .... 343 H4
Doncombe La
  CHPMW/MSHF SN14 .... 343 H4
Donegal Rd
  BRSG/KWL/STAPK BS4 ..... 345 M1
Dongola Av HORF/LLZ BS7 ... 326 A7
Dongola Rd HORF/LLZ BS7 ... 326 A7
The Donkey Fld CIR GL7 ..... 240 A2
Donkey La MIM GL56 .... 57 C2
Donnington Ga SHPSTR CV36 . 16 B4
Donside CIR GL7 .... 214 A8
Doone Rd HORF/LLZ BS7 .... 326 B3
Dora Wk GL GL1 .... 136 B4 🔲
Dorcas Av BRSTK/PCHW BS34 . 317 H6
Dorchester Rd HORF/LLZ BS7 . 326 C4
Dorester Ct HNBRY/STHM BS10 . 315 L7
Dorian CI HORF/LLZ BS7 ..... 326 A4
Dorian Rd HORF/LLZ BS7 .... 326 A4
Dorian Wy HNBRY/STHM BS10 . 326 A3
Dorington Ct
  RSTROUD/NAIL GL6 .... 209 M7 🔲
Dormer CI FRCTL/WBN BS36 . 318 F5
Dormer Rd CHELTW GL51 ... 93 H7
  EVILLE/WHL BS5 .... 326 C6
Dorney Rd GL GL1 .... 136 A4
Dorrit CI GL GL1 .... 136 B5
Dorset Av CHELTW GL51 .... 115 J1
Dorset Gv CBRISNE BS2 ..... 336 C1 🔲
Dorset Rd
  HNLZ/SM/SNYPK/WT BS9 ... 325 K5
  KGWD/HNM BS15 .... 337 M2
Dorset St BMSTR BS3 .... 335 K8 🔲
Dorset Wy YATE/CS BS37 .... 310 C8
Doubledays HGHW SN6 ..... 288 F3
Double Vw CIND GL14 ...... 154 B4 🔲
Douglas Rd HORF/LLZ BS7 ... 326 B4
  KGWD/HNM BS15 .... 337 M4
Doulton Wy HGRV/WHIT BS14 . 346 C6
Douro CI CHELT GL52 .... 115 K2
Dovecote YATE/CS BS37 ..... 320 A4
Dovedale THNB/SVB BS35 ... 293 M4
Dove La CBRISNE BS2 .... 336 B3
Doverdale Dr VGL GL2 ...... 112 F7
Dover Hay CHELTW GL51 .... 115 H5 🔲
Dover's Vw CHCAM GL55 .... 11 M4
Dove St CBRISNE BS2 .... 6 F1
Dove St South CBRISNE BS2 . 6 F1 🔲
  CBRISNE BS2 .... 335 M3
Dovey Ct
  OLD/WMLY/WICK BS30 ..... 338 E6
Dowdeswell Ct
  HNBRY/STHM BS10 .... 315 H8 🔲
Dowding CI YATE/CS BS37 ... 320 E1 🔲
Dowding Wy BWTH/CHD GL3 . 113 L6 🔲
Dowers' La CIR GL7 .... 213 J4
Dowling Rd
  BMSTR/HC/WWD BS13 ...... 345 M8
Down Ampney Rd CIR GL7 .. 264 C5
Downend Pk HORF/LLZ BS7 . 326 B5
Downend Park Rd
  MANG/FISH BS16 .... 327 H6 🔲
Downend Rd MANG/FISH BS16 . 326 B6
  KGWD/HNM BS15 .... 337 M2
  MANG/FISH BS16 .... 327 L6
Downfield STROUD GL5 ..... 208 B3
Downfield CI THNB/SVB BS35 . 293 H6
Downfield Dr
  FRCTL/WBN BS36 .... 318 D3 🔲
Downfield La TEWK GL20 ... 26 D4
Downfield Rd CFTN/FAIL BS8 . 335 J2
  STROUD GL5 .... 208 B4
Down Hatherley La VGL GL2 . 113 C1
Downleaze
  HNLZ/SM/SNYPK/WT BS9 ... 325 H8
  MANG/FISH BS16 .... 327 M3
Down Leaze THNB/SVB BS35 . 293 J6 🔲
Downman Rd HORF/LLZ BS7 . 326 C6
Down Rd CHPMW/MSHF SN14 . 342 F1
  FRCTL/WBN BS36 .... 318 C4
  THNB/SVB BS35 .... 293 J6 🔲
Downs CI THNB/SVB BS35 ... 293 J6 🔲
Downs Cote Av
  HNLZ/SM/SNYPK/WT BS9 ... 325 H5
Downs Cote Dr
  HNLZ/SM/SNYPK/WT BS9 ... 325 H5
Downs Cote Gdns
  HNLZ/SM/SNYPK/WT BS9 ... 325 H5
Downs Cote Pk
  HNLZ/SM/SNYPK/WT BS9 ... 325 H5
Downs Cote Vw
  HNLZ/SM/SNYPK/WT BS9 ... 325 H5
Downside Close
  OLD/WMLY/WICK BS30 ..... 338 B6 🔲
Downside Rd CFTN/FAIL BS8 . 335 J2 🔲
Downs Pk East
  RDLND/MONT BS6 .... 325 J6
Downs Pk West
  RDLND/MONT BS6 .... 325 J6
Downs Rd
  HNLZ/SM/SNYPK/WT BS9 ... 325 J6
The Downs WUE GL12 ...... 296 B4
Downs Wy CIR GL7 .... 214 C5
The Down ALMDB BS32 ..... 292 F8
  THNB/SVB BS35 .... 293 H6
Downton Rd
  BRSG/KWL/STAPK BS4 ..... 345 M3
  STNHO GL10 .... 207 G5
Down Vw RSTROUD/NAIL GL6 . 210 B7
Downy Cl VGL GL2 .... 112 E6
Dowry CI CFTN/FAIL BS8 .... 335 J5 🔲
Dowry Sq CFTN/FAIL BS8 .... 335 H5 🔲

Dowty Rd CHELTW GL51 .... 115 C1
Doynton La
  CHPMW/MSHF SN14 .... 330 D8
Dozule CI STNHO GL10 ...... 207 H8
Dragon Rd FRCTL/WBN BS36 . 317 M7
Dragons Hill CI KEYN BS31 .. 348 B6
Dragons Hill Ct KEYN BS31 .. 348 B6
Dragons Hill Gdns
  KEYN BS31 .... 348 B6 🔲
Dragonswell Rd
  HNBRY/STHM BS10 .... 325 J1
Dragon Wk EVILLE/WHL BS5 . 337 H2 🔲
Drag Rd RWYE HR9 .... 126 F6
Drake CI BWTH/CHD GL3 .... 113 H4 🔲
Drake La DSLY GL11 .... 253 J2
Drake Rd BMSTR BS3 .... 335 J8
Drakes PI CHELT GL50 ...... 115 K2
Drapers Ct CHELTE/BC GL52 . 72 D8 🔲
Draper's La RTEWK/TIB GL19 . 67 K7
Draycot PI CBRIS/FH BS1 .... 6 E7
Draycott DSLY GL11 .... 229 H4
Draycott Crs DSLY GL11 ..... 229 H5
Draycott Rd HORF/LLZ BS7 .. 326 B6 🔲
Draydon Rd
  BRSG/KWL/STAPK BS4 ..... 345 L4
Drayton CI CHELTW GL51 ... 93 K6
  GLE GL4 .... 136 E7
  HGRV/WHIT BS14 .... 346 D3
Drayton Rd CHELTW GL51 ... 115 C3
  HNLZ/SM/SNYPK/WT BS9 ... 324 E3
Drayton Wy GLE GL4 .... 136 E6
Dr Brown's CI
  RSTROUD/NAIL GL6 .... 233 H5
Dr Browns Rd
  RSTROUD/NAIL GL6 .... 233 H5 🔲
Dr Crawfords Wy
  RSTROUD/NAIL GL6 .... 233 H5 🔲
Dr. Crouch's Rd
  RSTROUD/NAIL GL6 .... 209 M6
Drews CI BWTH/CHD GL3 .... 113 L7 🔲
Drews Ct BWTH/CHD GL3 .... 113 L7
Driffield Rd LYD GL15 ...... 201 L6
Drifton HI CHPMW/MSHF SN14 . 333 G4
Drift Wy CIR GL7 .... 238 A5
The Driftway SHPSTR CV36 .. 16 B5
Drinkwater CI LED HR8 ..... 19 L2 🔲
Drivemoor GLE GL4 .... 136 F8
Drivers La MIM GL56 .... 82 C2
The Drive DSLY GL11 .... 229 H7
  HGRV/WHIT BS14 .... 346 E6
  HNLZ/SM/SNYPK/WT BS9 ... 325 K6
Dr Newton's Wy STROUD GL5 . 208 D5
Druetts CI
  HNBRY/STHM BS10 .... 326 A5 🔲
Drugger's End La RGTMLV WR13 . 22 F2
Druid CI
  HNLZ/SM/SNYPK/WT BS9 ... 325 G6
Druid HI
  HNLZ/SM/SNYPK/WT BS9 ... 325 G6
Druid Rd
  HNLZ/SM/SNYPK/WT BS9 ... 324 F7
Druids CI GLE GL4 .... 136 E4 🔲
Druids Oak VGL GL2 .... 159 H3
Druid Stoke Av
  HNLZ/SM/SNYPK/WT BS9 ... 324 E6
Druid Woods
  HNLZ/SM/SNYPK/WT BS9 ... 324 E6 🔲
Drummond Ct
  OLD/WMLY/WICK BS30 ..... 338 B7 🔲
Drummond Rd CBRISNE BS2 . 336 A2 🔲
  MANG/FISH BS16 .... 327 H8 🔲
Drury La RTEWK/TIB GL19 ... 43 K7
Drybrook Rd MTCHDN GL17 . 129 L5
Dryleaze KEYN BS31 .... 348 A4
  WUE GL12 .... 277 J4
  YATE/CS BS37 .... 310 A6 🔲
Dryleaze Rd MANG/FISH BS16 . 327 H5
Dry Meadow La VGL GL2 ... 112 C4
Dubbers La EVILLE/WHL BS5 . 337 G1
Dublin Crs
  HNLZ/SM/SNYPK/WT BS9 ... 325 K5
Duchess CI CFTN/FAIL BS8 ... 335 J2
Duchess Wy EVILLE/WHL BS5 . 326 F6
Ducie Rd EVILLE/WHL BS5 ... 336 D4
  MANG/FISH BS16 .... 328 A7
Ducie St GL GL1 .... 136 B4 🔲
Duckmoor Rd BMSTR BS3 ... 335 J8
Duck St WUE GL12 .... 294 D6
Duckworth Ct CHELTS GL53 . 115 M6 🔲
Dudbridge HI STROUD GL5 .. 208 B6
Dudbridge Meadow
  STROUD GL5 .... 208 B6 🔲
Dudbridge Rd STROUD GL5 .. 208 B6
Duderstadt CI STROUD GL5 .. 208 B3 🔲
Dudley CI KEYN BS31 .... 348 A7
Dudley Ct
  OLD/WMLY/WICK BS30 ..... 338 B7 🔲
Dudley Gv HORF/LLZ BS7 ... 326 B3
Duffield's CI MONM NP25 ... 174 B1
Dugar Wk RDLND/MONT BS6 . 325 L8
Dugdale Rd GLE GL4 .... 238 C2
Duglynch La COTS GL54 .... 73 M2
Duke of York Rd CLFD GL16 . 150 A5
Duke St CHELTE/BC GL52 .... 3 C6
Dukes Wy TEWK GL20 ...... 48 B8
Dulverton PI MIM GL56 ..... 58 E5
Dulverton Rd HORF/LLZ BS7 . 325 M1 🔲
Dumaine Av BRSTK/PCHW BS34 . 317 G6
Dumbleton Gv CHELTW GL51 . 114 D5 🔲
Dunalley Pde CHELT GL50 ... 2 D3
Dunalley St CHELT GL50 .... 2 D3
Dunbar CI CHELTW GL51 .... 92 F7
Duncan Gdns
  CBATH/BATHN BA1 .... 350 C8
Duncombe La
  KGWD/HNM BS15 .... 337 J1
Duncombe Rd
  KGWD/HNM BS15 .... 337 K2 🔲
Duncroft Rd GLE GL4 .... 137 H2
Dundas CI
  HNBRY/STHM BS10 .... 325 G1 🔲
Dundonald Rd
  RDLND/MONT BS6 .... 325 K8
Dundridge Gdns
  EVILLE/WHL BS5 .... 337 J5 🔲
Dundridge La EVILLE/WHL BS5 . 337 H5
Dundry CI KGWD/HNM BS15 . 337 M5 🔲
Dundry La LGASH BS41 ..... 344 D7

Dundry Vw
BRSG/KWL/STAPK BS4 .... **346** C2
Dunford Rd *BMSTR* BS3 .... **335** M8
Dunkeld Av *BRSTK/PCHW* BS34 .. **326** B1
Dunkerry Rd *BMSTR* BS3 .... **335** M8
Dunkirk Rd *MANG/FISH* BS16 .... **327** H8
Dunlin Cl *VGL* GL2 .... **158** F1
Dunmail Rd *HNBRY/STHM* BS10.. **325** L1
Dunmore St *BMSTR* BS3 .... **7** K8 🗓
Dunns Copse *LED* HR8 .... **20** A5
Dunsdown La
CHPMW/MSHF SN14 .... **331** J6
Dunsmore Gn *RTEWK/TIB* GL19 .. **46** E6
Dunstan Gln *BWTH/CHD* GL3 ... **113** M7
Dunster Cl *CHELTW* GL51 .... **92** F8 🗓
GL GL1 .... **159** K2
Dunster Gdns *CHELTW* GL51 .... **92** F8
OLD/WMLY/WICK BS30 .. **348** D1 🗓
Dunster Gv *CHELTW* GL51 .... **92** F8
Dunster Rd *BRSG/KWL/STAPK* BS4 . **346**
B3 🗓
CHELTW GL51 .... **92** F8
KEYN BS31 .... **348** A7 🗓
Durand Cl *VGL* GL2 .... **112** E5 🗓
Durban Rd *BRSTK/PCHW* BS34 .. **316** B3
Durbin Wk *EVILLE/WHL* BS5 .... **7** M1 🗓
Durbridge Rd *RTEWK/TIB* GL19 .. **65** G2
Durdham Pk *RDLND/MONT* BS6.. **325** J8
Durham Cl *CHELTW* GL51 .... **115** J6
Durham Gv *KEYN* BS31 .... **347** M7
Durham Rd *CBRISNE* BS2 .... **336** C1 🗓
GLE GL4 .... **136** C3
WUE GL12 .... **276** B6
Durleigh Cl
BMSTRD/HC/WWD BS13 .... **345** J5
Durley Hl *KEYN* BS31 .... **347** K3
Durley La *KEYN* BS31 .... **347** M4
Durnford Av *BMSTR* BS3 .... **335** J7
Durnford St *BMSTR* BS3 .... **335** J7
Durn's Rd *WUE* GL12 .... **277** L4 🗓
Dursley Cl *YATE/CS* BS37 .... **320** A2
Dursley Rd *AVONM* BS11 .... **324** A6
DSLY GL11 .... **229** G8
VGL GL2 .... **229** H1
Durville Rd
BMSTRD/HC/WWD BS13 .... **345** K5
Durweston Wk
HGRV/WHIT BS14 .... **346** E3
Dutton Cl *HGRV/WHIT* BS14 .... **346** F5 🗓
Dutton Leys *COTS* GL54 .... **169** K2
Dutton Rd *HGRV/WHIT* BS14 .... **346** F6
Duttons La *MTCHDN* GL17 ...... **129** H5
Dutton Wk *HGRV/WHIT* BS14 .... **346** F5 🗓
Dye House Rd *WUE* GL12........... **277** H6
Dyersbrook *WUE* GL12 .... **277** K4 🗓
Dyers Cl
BMSTRD/HC/WWD BS13 .... **345** M7
Dyer's La *CHCAM* GL55 .... **12** B8
YATE/CS BS37 .... **309** J8
Dyer St *GL* GL1 .... **238** D3 🗓
Dyke House La *LED* HR8 .... **42** B4
Dylan Thomas Ct
Dynevor St *GL* GL1 .... **136** B4
Dyrham Cl
HNLZ/SM/SNYPK/WT BS9.......... **325** M1
KGWD/HNM BS15 .... **338** B3 🗓
THNB/SVB BS35 .... **273** L8
Dyrham Pde
BRSTK/PCHW BS34 .... **316** E3
Dyrham Cl *KGWD/HNM* BS15 .... **338** B3

E

Eagle Crs *MANG/FISH* BS16 .... **329** L7
Eagle Dr *BRSTK/PCHW* BS34 ...... **316** A3
Eagle Mill Cl *STROUD* GL5 .... **208** F6
Eagle Pk *CBATH/BATHN* BA1 ...... **352** B6
Eagle Rd *BRSG/KWL/STAPK* BS4 .. **346** F1
CBATH/BATHN BA1 .... **352** B6
Eagle Wy *GL* GLE GL4 .... **136** C6
Eardisland Rd *GLE* GL4 .... **160** A1 🗓
Earl Russell Wy
EVILLE/WHL BS5 .... **336** D4 🗓
Earls Cnr *MALM* SN16 .... **285** C3
Earlsmead *MANG/FISH* BS16 .... **326** F7
Earlstone Cl
OLD/WMLY/WICK BS30 .... **338** C7
Earlstone Crs
OLD/WMLY/WICK BS30 .... **338** C6 🗓
Earl St *CBRIS/FH* BS1 .... **6** F1
Early Wy *HNBRY/STHM* BS10...... **326** A3
Earthcott Rd *THNB/SVB* BS35 .... **308** A3
Easedale Cl
HNBRY/STHM BS10 .... **325** M1 🗓
East Approach Dr
CHELTE/BC GL52 .... **94** A7
Eastbourne Rd
EVILLE/WHL BS5 .... **336** D3 🗓
Eastbrook Rd *GLE* GL4 .... **136** E4
Eastbury Cl *THNB/SVB* BS35 ...... **293** L2
Eastbury Rd *MANG/FISH* BS16 .. **327** J7
Eastcote Pk *HGRV/WHIT* BS14 .. **346** D6
Eastcott Wy *BWTH/CHD* GL3 ...... **113** J5
East Cft
HNLZ/SM/SNYPK/WT BS9.......... **325** L4
East Dr *STROUD* GL5 .... **207** L4
East End *COTS* GL54 .... **169** K2
East End Rd *CHELTS* GL53 .... **116** E6 🗓
Eastern Av *GLE* GL4 .... **136** E3
MTCHDN GL17 .... **130** C2
Eastern Wy *CIND* GL14 .... **154** A7
Eastfield *HGHW* SN6 .... **287** H2
HNLZ/SM/SNYPK/WT BS9.......... **325** K4
Eastfield Dr *YATE/CS* BS37 .... **310** A2
Eastfield Rd
HNLZ/SM/SNYPK/WT BS9.......... **325** J4
RDLND/MONT BS6 .... **335** M1
RSTROUD/NAIL GL6 .... **233** K5 🗓
Eastfield Ter
HNLZ/SM/SNYPK/WT BS9.......... **325** K4
East Gable *CHELTE/BC* GL52 .... **72** D8 🗓
Eastgate St *GL* GL1 .... **4** F6
East Gv *RDLND/MONT* BS6 ...... **336** B2
East Hill Eastfield Rd
HNLZ/SM/SNYPK/WT BS9 ...... **325** J4 🗓

Eastington Rd *COTS* GL54 .... **169** K2
Eastlake Cl *HORF/LLZ* BS7 .... **326** D4
Eastland Av *THNB/SVB* BS35 .... **293** L1
Eastland Rd *THNB/SVB* BS35 .... **293** L1
Eastleigh Cl
MANG/FISH BS16 .... **328** A7 🗓
Eastleigh Rd
HNBRY/STHM BS10 .... **325** M2
MANG/FISH BS16 .... **328** A7
Eastley Cl *WUE* GL12 .... **275** G4
Eastlyn Rd
BMSTRD/HC/WWD BS13 .... **345** K3
Eastmead La
HNLZ/SM/SNYPK/WT BS9.......... **325** J5
Eastnor Rd *HGRV/WHIT* BS14 .. **346** C8
Easton Hill Rd *THNB/SVB* BS35.. **293** M1
Easton Rd *CBRISNE* BS2 .... **7** L2
EVILLE/WHL BS5 .... **336** D3
Easton Wy *EVILLE/WHL* BS5 .... **336** C2
Eastover Cl
HNLZ/SM/SNYPK/WT BS9.......... **325** J3
East Pde
HNLZ/SM/SNYPK/WT BS9.......... **324** E5
East Pk *EVILLE/WHL* BS5 .... **336** E1
East Park Dr
EVILLE/WHL BS5 .... **336** E1 🗓
East Priory Cl
HNLZ/SM/SNYPK/WT BS9.......... **325** J4
East Ridge Dr
BMSTRD/HC/WWD BS13 .... **345** H6
Eastrip La *CHPMW/MSHF* SN14 .. **343** L8
East Shrubbery
RDLND/MONT BS6 .... **335** K1 🗓
East St *BMSTR* BS3 .... **6** E9
BMSTR BS3 .... **335** L8
CBRISNE BS2 .... **7** J1
LYD GL15 .... **198** F5
MIM GL56 .... **58** D6
SHPSTR CV36 .... **61** H5
TEWK GL20 .... **48** A5 🗓
East Vw *MANG/FISH* BS16 .... **328** B5
Eastville Cl *GLE* GL4 .... **5** L8
Eastwood Crs
BRSG/KWL/STAPK BS4.......... **337** H7
Eastwood Rd
BRSG/KWL/STAPK BS4.......... **337** H7
MTCHDN GL17 .... **129** M5 🗓
Eaton Cl *HGRV/WHIT* BS14 ...... **347** G6
MANG/FISH BS16 .... **327** K7
Eaton Crs *CFTN/FAIL* BS8 .... **335** J3 🗓
Eaton Pl *CHELT* GL50 .... **2** D7
Eaton St *BMSTR* BS3 .... **335** L8 🗓
Ebenezer La
HNLZ/SM/SNYPK/WT BS9.......... **324** F5 🗓
HNLZ/SM/SNYPK/WT BS9.......... **325** G6 🗓
Ebenezer St *EVILLE/WHL* BS5 ... **336** F4 🗓
Ebley Rd *STNHO* GL10 .... **207** M5
Ebor Rd *VGL* GL2 .... **136** E2
Ebrington Cl *GLE* GL4 .... **136** F3 🗓
Eddys La *MTCHDN* GL17.......... **128** E5
Edendale Approach Rd
CHELTW GL51 .... **114** E3
Eden Gv *HORF/LLZ* BS7 .... **326** C2
Eden Park Cl
CBATH/BATHN BA1 .... **352** C7
Eden Park Dr
CBATH/BATHN BA1 .... **352** C7
Eden's Hl *NWNT* GL18 .... **65** J8
Edenwall Rd *CLFD* GL16 .... **175** L4
Edgecorner La
CHPMW/MSHF SN14 .... **323** J8
Edgecumbe Rd
RDLND/MONT BS6 .... **335** M1 🗓
Edge End Rd *CLFD* GL16 .... **151** M7
Edgefield Cl *HGRV/WHIT* BS14 .. **346** B8
Edgefield Rd *HGRV/WHIT* BS14 .. **346** B8
Edge Hills Cl *CIND* GL14 .... **154** B2
Edge Hills Rd *CIND* GL14 .... **154** B2
Edge La *RSTROUD/NAIL* GL6 .... **184** E3
Edge Rd *RSTROUD/NAIL* GL6 .... **185** G3
Edgeware Rd *BMSTR* BS3 .... **6** C8
MANG/FISH BS16 .... **327** L7 🗓
Edgewood Cl
HGRV/WHIT BS14 .... **346** D3 🗓
OLD/WMLY/WICK BS30 .... **338** C8
Edgeworth *YATE/CS* BS37 .... **319** L5
Edgeworth Cl *GLE* GL4 .... **137** G6 🗓
Edinburgh Pl *CHELTW* GL51 .... **115** G1
CLFD GL16 .... **175** M1
Edinburgh Rd *KEYN* BS31 .... **348** A7
Edington Gv
HNBRY/STHM BS10 .... **325** J1
Edmond Rd *CHEP* NP16 .... **270** D3 🗓
Edmonds Cl *STRAT* CV37 .... **9** K1
Edmund Cl *MANG/FISH* BS16 .. **327** M5 🗓
Edmund Ct *MANG/FISH* BS16 .. **329** K5
Edna Av *BRSG/KWL/STAPK* BS4 .. **337** G8
Edward Pl *TEWK* GL20 .... **48** B8
Edward Rd
BRSG/KWL/STAPK BS4 .... **336** D7 🗓
KGWD/HNM BS15 .... **338** A3 🗓
Edwards Cl *CIR* GL7 .... **240** F5
MTCHDN GL17 .... **128** C6
Edward St *CHELT* GL50........... **115** L4
EVILLE/WHL BS5 .... **336** F1 🗓
EVILLE/WHL BS5 .... **336** E3 🗓
Edwin Short Cl
OLD/WMLY/WICK BS30 .... **349** G3
Edwy Pde *GL* GL1 .... **4** F2
Effingham Rd
RDLND/MONT BS6 .... **336** A1
Egerton Brow
HORF/LLZ BS7 .... **325** M7 🗓
Egerton Rd *HORF/LLZ* BS7 ...... **325** M7
Eggshill La *YATE/CS* BS37 .... **319** M2
Eighth Av *HORF/LLZ* BS7 .... **326** D3
Elberton Rd *KGWD/HNM* BS15 .. **338** C3 🗓
Elberton Rd
HNLZ/SM/SNYPK/WT BS9.......... **324** D4
THNB/SVB BS35 .... **292** B5
Elbury Av *KGWD/HNM* BS15 .... **337** L1
Elderberry Wk
HNBRY/STHM BS10 .... **325** L1
Eldersfield Cl *COTS* GL54 .... **74** C4 🗓
VGL GL2 .... **159** G1
Elderwood Dr
OLD/WMLY/WICK BS30 .... **338** C8

Elderwood Rd
HGRV/WHIT BS14 .... **346** D4 🗓
Elderwood Wy *GL* GL1 .... **135** L8
Eldon Av *CHELTE/BC* GL52 .... **3** J5
Eldon Rd *CHELTE/BC* GL52 ...... **3** H5
Eldon Ter *BMSTR* BS3 .... **335** M8
Eldon Wy
BRSG/KWL/STAPK BS4 .... **336** E6
Eldorado Crs *CHELT* GL50 .... **115** K2
Eldorado Rd *CHELT* GL50 .... **115** J2
Eldred Cl
HNLZ/SM/SNYPK/WT BS9.......... **324** E6
Eleventh Av *HORF/LLZ* BS7 ...... **326** D2 🗓
Elfin Rd *MANG/FISH* BS16 .... **327** J6
Elf Meadow *CIR* GL7 .... **241** G4
Elgar Cl
BRSG/KWL/STAPK BS4 .... **345** M5 🗓
LED HR8 .... **19** L4
Elgin Av *HORF/LLZ* BS7 .... **326** B2
Elgin Pk *RDLND/MONT* BS6 ...... **335** K1
Elgin Rd *MANG/FISH* BS16 ...... **327** K1
Eliot Cl *HORF/LLZ* BS7 .... **326** C3
VGL GL2 .... **135** L7
Elizabeth Cl *THNB/SVB* BS35 .... **293** M3
Elizabeth Crs
BRSTK/PCHW BS34 .... **317** G2
Elizabeth Gdns *CIR* GL7 .... **241** L6
TET GL8 .... **281** M3 🗓
Elizabeths Ms
BRSG/KWL/STAPK BS4 .... **337** H5 🗓
Ellacombe Rd
OLD/WMLY/WICK BS30 .... **348** A1
Ellan Hay Rd *ALMDB* BS32 ...... **317** J5
Ellbridge Cl
HNLZ/SM/SNYPK/WT BS9.......... **324** F6 🗓
Ellenborough Rd
CHELTE/BC GL52 .... **94** C1
Ellendene Dr *TEWK* GL20 .... **49** L4
Ellenor Dr *TEWK* GL20 .... **51** L4
Ellerncroft Rd *WUE* GL12 .... **277** H3
Ellesmere *THNB/SVB* BS35 ...... **293** L3
Ellesmere Cl *GLE* GL4 .... **137** H3 🗓
Ellesmere Gv *CHELT* GL50 ...... **115** K5 🗓
Ellesmere Rd
BRSG/KWL/STAPK BS4 .... **346** F2 🗓
KGWD/HNM BS15 .... **337** M3 🗓
Ellfield Cl
BMSTRD/HC/WWD BS13 .... **345** H5
Ellicks Cl *ALMDB* BS32 .... **317** C1
Ellicott Rd *HORF/LLZ* BS7 .... **326** B5
Ellinghurst Cl
HNBRY/STHM BS10 .... **325** J1 🗓
Elliott Av *MANG/FISH* BS16 ...... **327** L2
Elliott Pl *CHELTW* GL51 .... **115** H4
Elliott Rd *CIR* GL7 .... **238** D4
Ellis Av *BMSTRD/HC/WWD* BS13.. **345** J3
Ellison Cl *BWTH/CHD* GL3 .... **137** J5
Elliston Cl *CHELTW* GL51 .... **115** G1
Elliston La *RDLND/MONT* BS6 .. **335** L1
Elliston Rd *RDLND/MONT* BS6 .. **335** L1
Ellsbridge Cl *KEYN* BS31 .... **348** D6
Ellsworth Rd
HNBRY/STHM BS10 .... **325** H1
Ellwood Rd *CLFD* GL16 .... **175** L5
Elmbridge Rd *VGL* GL2 .... **136** E1
Elmbury Dr *TEWK* GL20 .... **48** D5
Elm Cl *BRSTK/PCHW* BS34 ...... **316** F4
CHELTE/BC GL52 .... **94** C6
CHELTW GL51 .... **93** K8
CHEP NP16 .... **270** C1
STNHO GL10 .... **207** J7
STRAT CV37 .... **8** A1
YATE/CS BS37 .... **320** C2
Elm Ct *LYD* GL15 .... **224** A5
Elmcroft Crs *HORF/LLZ* BS7 ...... **326** C7
Elmdale Cl *CHEP* NP16 .... **270** A2
Elmdale Crs *THNB/SVB* BS35 .... **293** L2
Elmdale Rd *BMSTR* BS3 .... **345** K1
CFTN/FAIL BS8 .... **6** B1
Elm Dr *BWTH/CHD* GL3 .... **137** M5
Elmer St *MALM* SN16 .... **303** J6
Elmfield *KGWD/HNM* BS15 ...... **338** A5
Elmfield Av *CHELTW* GL51 .... **93** L7
Elmfield Cl *KGWD/HNM* BS15 .. **338** A5 🗓
Elmfield Rd *CHELTW* GL51 .... **2** A1
CHELTW GL51 .... **93** L7 🗓
HNLZ/SM/SNYPK/WT BS9 ...... **325** J3 🗓
Elm Garden Dr *CHELTW* GL51 .. **114** C4
Elm Gv *CHCAM* GL55 .... **13** M6
RTEWK/TIB GL19 .... **108** C7
Elmgrove Av
EVILLE/WHL BS5 .... **336** D3 🗓
Elmgrove Dr *YATE/CS* BS37 ...... **320** B1 🗓
Elmgrove Pk
RDLND/MONT BS6 .... **335** M2 🗓
Elmgrove Rd *BWTH/CHD* GL3 .... **137** H4
MANG/FISH BS16 .... **327** G8
RDLND/MONT BS6 .... **335** M2
Elmgrove Rd East *VGL* GL2 ...... **159** G4
Elmgrove Rd West *VGL* GL2 ...... **158** F4
Elm Hayes
BMSTRD/HC/WWD BS13 .... **345** H5
Elmhirst Gdns *YATE/CS* BS37 .. **320** C1 🗓
Elmhurst Av *EVILLE/WHL* BS5 .. **326** F8
Elming Down Cl *ALMDB* BS32 .. **316** F5 🗓
Elmira Rd *GLE* GL4 .... **136** B7 🗓
Elm La *RDLND/MONT* BS6 .... **335** K1
Elmlea Av
HNLZ/SM/SNYPK/WT BS9.......... **325** H6
Elmlea Rd *STNHO* GL10 .... **207** J3
Elmleaze *VGL* GL2 .... **112** F8
Elmleigh Av *MANG/FISH* BS16.. **328** C6
Elmleigh Cl *MANG/FISH* BS16 .. **328** C6 🗓
Elmleigh Rd *MANG/FISH* BS16 .. **328** C6
Elmley Rd *EVE* WR11 .... **29** K2
Elmore *KGWD/HNM* BS15 ...... **338** B1 🗓
YATE/CS BS37 .... **319** M3 🗓
Elmore La *VGL* GL2 .... **158** L1
Elmore Rd *BRSTK/PCHW* BS34 .. **316** B2
HORF/LLZ BS7 .... **326** C1
Elm Pk *BRSTK/PCHW* BS34 ...... **326** C1
Elm Rd *CHEP* NP16 .... **270** C1
CHPMW/MSHF SN14 .... **343** J6
HORF/LLZ BS7 .... **326** A6
KGWD/HNM BS15 .... **338** A5
SHPSTR CV36 .... **16** B7
STROUD GL5 .... **208** A3

Elmsdale Rd *LED* HR8 .... **19** M4
Elms Gv *BRSTK/PCHW* BS34 .... **316** D2
Elm Side *GL* GL1 .... **90** F6
Elms Rd *STNHO* GL10 .... **207** G3
The Elms *CIR* GL7 .... **245** L1
Elm St *CHELTW* GL51 .... **93** K7
Elm Tree Av *MANG/FISH* BS16 .. **328** C4
Elmtree Cl *KGWD/HNM* BS15 .. **337** M2
Elmtree Dr
BMSTRD/HC/WWD BS13 .... **345** H6
Elm Vw *CIR* GL7 .... **262** B7
Elmvil Rd *TEWK* GL20 .... **48** D4
Elm Wd *YATE/CS* BS37 .... **320** A3
Elphick Rd *GL* GL7 .... **214** B7 🗓
Elsbert Dr
BMSTRD/HC/WWD BS13 .... **345** G5
Elstree Rd *EVILLE/WHL* BS5 ...... **337** G2
Elstub La *DSLY* GL11 .... **229** G6
Elton La *HORF/LLZ* BS7 .... **335** M1
Elton Rd *CFTN/FAIL* BS8 .... **6** B2
CIND GL14 .... **154** F3
CIND GL14 .... **155** L3
HORF/LLZ BS7 .... **325** M8
KGWD/HNM BS15 .... **337** K2
Elton St *CBRISNE* BS2 .... **7** K1
Elvard Cl
BMSTRD/HC/WWD BS13 .... **345** J6
Elvard Rd
BMSTRD/HC/WWD BS13 .... **345** J6
Elvaston Rd *BMSTR* BS3 .... **336** A8
Ely Gv
HNLZ/SM/SNYPK/WT BS9.......... **324** D4
Embassy Rd *EVILLE/WHL* BS5 .. **337** G2
Embassy Wk *EVILLE/WHL* BS5 .. **337** G2
Embleton Rd
HNBRY/STHM BS10 .... **325** K1
Embrook *MIM* GL56 .... **103** G3 🗓
Emerald Cl *GL* GL1 .... **135** L8
Emersons Green La
MANG/FISH BS16 .... **328** D5
Emerson Sq *HORF/LLZ* BS7 ...... **326** C3
Emersons Wy
MANG/FISH BS16 .... **328** E4 🗓
Emery Rd
BRSG/KWL/STAPK BS4 .... **347** H2 🗓
Emet Gv *MANG/FISH* BS16 ...... **328** D5
Emet La *MANG/FISH* BS16 ...... **328** D5
Emlyn Rd *EVILLE/WHL* BS5 ...... **336** E1
Emma-chris Wy
BRSTK/PCHW BS34 .... **326** E1
Emmerson La *CIR* GL7 .... **235** H5
Emmett Wd *HGRV/WHIT* BS14 .. **346** D8
Emperor Cl *CHELTW* GL51 .... **114** F1 🗓
Empire Wy *VGL* GL2 .... **135** K6
Emra Cl *EVILLE/WHL* BS5 .... **337** H2 🗓
Enborne Cl *MANG/FISH* BS16 .. **327** J8
Enfield Rd *MANG/FISH* BS16 .... **327** J8
Engine Common La
YATE/CS BS37 .... **309** L5
England's Crs *FRCTL/WBN* BS36.. **318** A4
Englishcombe Rd
BMSTRD/HC/WWD BS13 .... **345** L8
Ennerdale Av *VGL* GL2 .... **112** C6
Ennerdale Rd
HNBRY/STHM BS10 .... **325** M1
Enterprise Wy *CHELTW* GL51 .... **93** K8
Epney Cl *BRSTK/PCHW* BS34 .... **316** B2
Epney Rd *GL* GL1 .... **135** L8
Epsom Cl *MANG/FISH* BS16 ...... **328** B2
Epworth Rd
HNBRY/STHM BS10 .... **325** J1
Erin Pk *STROUD* GL5 .... **208** C6
Erin Wk *BRSG/KWL/STAPK* BS4.. **345** M3
Ermin Pk *BWTH/CHD* GL3 .... **137** M5
Ermin Pl *GLE* GL4 .... **238** E5
Erminster Dr *BWTH/CHD* GL3 .... **137** J4
Ermin St *BWTH/CHD* GL3 .... **137** M5
Ermin Wy *BWTH/CHD* GL3 ...... **138** D7
Ermleet Rd
RDLND/MONT BS6 .... **335** L1 🗓
Ernest Barker Cl
EVILLE/WHL BS5 .... **336** D4 🗓
Ernestville Rd *MANG/FISH* BS16.. **327** H8
Eros Cl *STROUD* GL5 .... **208** C6
Errington Rd *MIM* GL56 .... **58** E6
Ervine Ter *CBRISNE* BS2 .... **336** B3
Eskdale *THNB/SVB* BS35 .... **293** M4
Esland Pl *CIR* GL7 .... **238** D5
Essery Rd *EVILLE/WHL* BS5 ...... **336** E1
Essex Av *CHELTW* GL51 .... **115** J1
Essex Cl *BWTH/CHD* GL3 .... **113** J3 🗓
Essex Pl *COTS* GL54 .... **123** G4
Esson Rd *KGWD/HNM* BS15 .... **337** K2
Estate Rd *CIND* GL14 .... **153** M1
Estcote Rd *CIR* GL7 .... **238** C2
Estcourt Cl *GL* GL1 .... **5** J1
Estcourt Rd *GL* GL1 .... **5** H1
VGL GL2 .... **5** L3
Estoril *YATE/CS* BS37 .... **320** B2
Estune Wk *LGASH* BS41 .... **344** C2
Etheldene Rd *STROUD* GL5 ...... **207** M3
Etheridge Pl *VGL* GL2 .... **5** L6 🗓
Etloe Rd *RDLND/MONT* BS6 .... **325** J7
Eton Rd *BRSG/KWL/STAPK* BS4.. **336** F8
Ettington Cl *CHELTW* GL51 .... **92** E8 🗓
Ettricke Dr *MANG/FISH* BS16 .... **327** K5
Eugene St *CBRISNE* BS2 .... **6** E1
EVILLE/WHL BS5 .... **7** K1
Evans Cl *BRSG/KWL/STAPK* BS4 .. **337** H6
Evans Rd *RDLND/MONT* BS6 .... **335** L1 🗓
Evans Wk *GLE* GL4 .... **136** D7 🗓
Evelyn Cl *CHELTS* GL53 .... **116** A6
Evelyn Rd
HNBRY/STHM BS10 .... **325** L4 🗓
Evenlode Av *CHELTE/BC* GL52 .. **3** K5 🗓
Evenlode Gdns *AVONM* BS11 .. **324** B6
MIM GL56 .... **58** E6
Evenlode Rd *GLE* GL4 .... **159** M2 🗓
Evenlode Wy *KEYN* BS31 .... **348** C8
Evercreech Rd
HGRV/WHIT BS14 .... **346** C7
Everest Av *RSTROUD/NAIL* GL6 .. **233** C5
Everest Rd *CHELTS* GL53 .... **116** A7
MANG/FISH BS16 .... **327** G7
Everlands *DSLY* GL11 .... **229** J6

Eve Rd *EVILLE/WHL* BS5 .... **336** D2
Everside Cl *DSLY* GL11 .... **229** H5 🗓
Everside La *DSLY* GL11 .... **229** H5
Evesham Rd *BDWAY* WR12 ...... **10** B7
CHELT GL50 .... **94** A4
CHELTE/BC GL52 .... **2** E3
CHELTE/BC GL52 .... **2** F2 🗓
CHELTE/BC GL52 .... **72** B7
COTS GL54 .... **74** C2
COTS GL54 .... **101** M2
Evington Rd *CHELTW* GL51 ...... **115** G1
Ewelme Cl *DSLY* GL11 .... **253** L3
Ewens Rd *CHELTE/BC* GL52 ...... **3** J8
Ewlyn Rd *CHELTS* GL53 .... **115** M5
Exeter Buildings
RDLND/MONT BS6 .... **335** K1
Exeter Rd *BMSTR* BS3 .... **6** B8
Exley Cl *OLD/WMLY/WICK* BS30.. **338** E6
Exmoor St *BMSTR* BS3 .... **335** L8
Exmouth Ct *CHELTS* GL53 ...... **115** M4 🗓
Exmouth Rd
BRSG/KWL/STAPK BS4 .... **346** B2
Exmouth St *CHELTS* GL53 ...... **115** M4
Eyer's La *CBRISNE* BS2 .... **7** J2
Eynon Cl *CHELTS* GL53 .... **115** L6

F

Faber Gv
BMSTRD/HC/WWD BS13 .... **345** L7 🗓
Fabian Dr *BRSTK/PCHW* BS34 .. **317** G6
Factory Rd *FRCTL/WBN* BS36 .... **318** B4
Failand Cresent
HNLZ/SM/SNYPK/WT BS9.......... **324** E6
Failand Wk
HNLZ/SM/SNYPK/WT BS9.......... **324** E5 🗓
Fairacre Cl *HORF/LLZ* BS7 .... **326** D4
Fairacres Cl *KEYN* BS31 .... **348** A7
Fairfax Cl *GLE* GL4 .... **238** D4
Fairfax Rd *CIR* GL7 .... **238** D4
Fairfax St *CBRIS/FH* BS1 .... **7** G3
Fairfield Av *CHELTS* GL53 .... **115** M5
Fairfield Cl
CHPMW/MSHF SN14 .... **342** B3
CLFD GL16 .... **175** K2 🗓
Fairfield Pde *CHELTS* GL53 ...... **115** M5 🗓
Fairfield Park Rd
CHELTS GL53 .... **115** M5 🗓
Fairfield Pl *BMSTR* BS3 .... **6** B9
Fairfield Rd *BMSTR* BS3 .... **6** B9
CHELTS GL53 .... **115** M5
CHEP NP16 .... **270** A5
LYD GL15 .... **201** J8
RDLND/MONT BS6 .... **336** B1
Fairfields *CIND* GL14 .... **154** A3 🗓
Fairfield St *CHELTS* GL53 .... **115** M5 🗓
Fairfield Wk *CHELTS* GL53 .... **115** M5
Fairfoot Rd
BRSG/KWL/STAPK BS4 .... **336** C8 🗓
Fairford Cl *KGWD/HNM* BS15 .. **338** B1 🗓
Fairford Crs *BRSTK/PCHW* BS34.. **316** D3
Fairford Rd *CIR* GL7 .... **218** C7
Fairford Wy *GLE* GL4 .... **136** D4 🗓
Fair Furlong
BMSTRD/HC/WWD BS13 .... **345** J7
Fairhaven *YATE/CS* BS37 .... **320** B2 🗓
Fairhaven Av *BWTH/CHD* GL3 .. **138** A5
Fairhaven Rd *CHELTS* GL53 ...... **115** M5 🗓
RDLND/MONT BS6 .... **325** L7 🗓
Fairhaven St *CHELTS* GL53 ...... **115** M5 🗓
Fair Lawn
OLD/WMLY/WICK BS30 .... **338** C7
Fairlawn
RDLND/MONT BS6 .... **336** B1 🗓
Fairlyn Dr *KGWD/HNM* BS15 .... **328** B8
Fairmile Gdns *VGL* GL2 .... **112** B6
Fairmount Rd *CHELTW* GL51 .... **115** H2
Fairoaks
OLD/WMLY/WICK BS30 .... **338** C8 🗓
Fairview *CHPMW/MSHF* SN14 .. **343** L5
Fairview *CHELTE/BC* GL52 .... **2** F5
Fair View Cl
RSTROUD/NAIL GL6 .... **232** D6 🗓
Fair View Dr *RDLND/MONT* BS6.. **335** L1
Fairview Rd *CHELTE/BC* GL52 ...... **2** E4
KGWD/HNM BS15 .... **338** B3
Fairview St *CHELTE/BC* GL52 ...... **2** F4
Fairwater Pk *GLE* GL4 .... **136** F2
Fairway *BRSG/KWL/STAPK* BS4 .. **346** F2
TEWK GL20 .... **49** G3
Fairway Cl
OLD/WMLY/WICK BS30 .... **338** D7
Fairways Av *CLFD* GL16 .... **175** K2 🗓
Falcon Cl *BRSTK/PCHW* BS34 .... **316** A3
HNLZ/SM/SNYPK/WT BS9.......... **325** H3
VGL GL2 .... **112** E5 🗓
Falcondale Rd
HNLZ/SM/SNYPK/WT BS9.......... **325** H3
Falcondale Wk
HNLZ/SM/SNYPK/WT BS9.......... **325** J3
Falcon Dr *BRSTK/PCHW* BS34 .. **316** A3
Falconer Rd *CBATH/BATHN* BA1.. **350** C8
Falcon La *LED* HR8 .... **19** H3
Falcon Wk *BRSTK/PCHW* BS34 .. **316** A3
Falcon Wy *THNB/SVB* BS35 ...... **293** M1
Faldo Cl *GLE* GL4 .... **137** H6
Falfield Rd
BRSG/KWL/STAPK BS4 .... **336** E8 🗓
GL GL1 .... **135** L8
Falfield Wk
HNBRY/STHM BS10 .... **325** L3 🗓
Falkland Pl *CHELTW* GL51 .... **92** F8
Falkland Rd
RDLND/MONT BS6 .... **336** B1 🗓
Falkner St *GL* GL1 .... **5** G9
Fallodon Ct
HNLZ/SM/SNYPK/WT BS9.......... **325** K6 🗓
Fallodon Wy
HNLZ/SM/SNYPK/WT BS9.......... **325** K6
Fallowmead
OLD/WMLY/WICK BS30 .... **338** E7
Fallows Rd *COTS* GL54 .... **169** K2
Falmouth Rd *HORF/LLZ* BS7 .... **325** M7
Fancy Rd *LYD* GL15 .... **177** C5

Fane Cl *HNBRY/STHM* BS10 ...... 315 J8 🖾
Fanshawe Rd *HGRV/WHIT* BS14.. 346 C4
Fant Hl *RBANSW* OX15 .... 17 L6
Faraday Cl *GL* GL1 .... 136 B4 🖾
Farfield La *HGHW* SN6 .... 289 G7
Far Handstones
  OLD/WMLY/WICK BS30 .... 338 C7
Farington Rd *CHELTW* GL51 .... 114 F4 🖾
Farington Rd
  HNLZ/SM/SNYPK/WT BS9...... 325 M4
Farleigh Cl *CHELTE/BC* GL52 .. 116 E5 🖾
Farleigh La *WUE* GL12 .... 295 L1
Farleigh Rd *KEYN* BS31 .... 347 M7
Farleigh Wk
  BMSTRD/HC/WWD BS13......... 345 J3
Farley Cl *BRSTK/PCHW* BS34.... 316 E4
Farman Crs *COTS* GL54 .... 124 C7
Farm Cl *MANG/FISH* BS16 .... 328 D5 🖾
  SHPSTR CV36 .... 16 A5 🖾
Farmcote *WUE* GL12 .... 297 M3
Farmcote Cl
  RSTROUD/NAIL GL6 .... 209 M7
Farmcote Gdns *COTS* GL54 .... 74 B6
Farm Ct *MANG/FISH* BS16 .... 328 A4
Farmer Rd
  BMSTRD/HC/WWD BS13......... 345 C4
Farmers La *BDWAY* WR12 .... 32 A1
Farmfield Rd *CHELTW* GL51 .... 115 H6
Farmhill La *STROUD* GL5 .... 208 B3
Farmhill La *STROUD* GL5 .... 208 B3
Farmington Ri *COTS* GL54 .... 169 K1 🖾
Farmington Rd *CHELTW* GL51 ... 115 G3
  COTS GL54 .... 169 K1
Farm La *CHELS* GL53 .... 115 K7
  CHELTW GL51 .... 138 F2
  TET GL8 .... 279 L8
  TEWK GL20 .... 27 C5
  TEWK GL20 .... 27 L3
  THNB/SVB BS35 .... 304 F8
Farm Lees *WUE* GL12 .... 276 C5
Farm Rd *MANG/FISH* BS16 .... 328 A4
  MTCHDN GL17 .... 129 H5
  RSTROUD/NAIL GL6 .... 211 L2
Farm St *GL* GL1 .... 4 F9
Farmwell Cl
  BMSTRD/HC/WWD BS13......... 345 K6 🖾
Farndale *EVILLE/WHL* BS5 .... 337 J5
Farne Cl
  HNLZ/SM/SNYPK/WT BS9...... 325 K6
Farrant Av *BWTH/CHD* BS34 .... 113 J5
Farrant Cl
  BRSG/KWL/STAPK BS4........... 345 K5
Farriers Cft
  RSTROUD/NAIL GL6 .... 209 M7 🖾
Farriers End *VGL* GL2 .... 159 H1
Farriers Reach
  CHELTE/BC GL52 .... 71 M7 🖾
The Farriers *CIR* GL7 .... 220 B7
Farr's La *CBRIS/FH* BS1 .... 6 E5
  STROUD GL5 .... 208 A4
Far Sandfield *BWTH/CHD* GL3 ... 113 L6
Farthing Cft *VGL* GL2 .... 110 F7
The Farthings *COTS* GL54 .... 142 F8
Far Wells Rd
  RSTROUD/NAIL GL6 .... 210 C3
Far Westrip *STNHO* GL10 .... 207 K3
Fauconberg Rd *CHELT* GL50 ..... 2 B6
Faulkner's Cl *CIR* GL7 .... 242 E6
Fawkes Cl *KGWD/HNM* BS15.... 338 D3
Fawkes Pl *STROUD* GL5 .... 208 E4 🖾
Fawley Dr *CHELTE/BC* GL52 .... 94 E7
Featherbed La *SHPSTR* CV36 .... 39 J5
  THNB/SVB BS35 .... 272 C5
Featherstone Rd
  MANG/FISH BS16 .... 327 H7 🖾
Feeder Rd *CBRISNE* BS2 .... 7 L6
  CBRISNE BS2 .... 336 E5
Felix Rd *EVILLE/WHL* BS5 .... 336 D3
Fell Mill La *SHPSTR* CV36 .... 16 C5
Felstead Rd
  HNBRY/STHM BS10 .... 326 A2
Feltham Rd *MANG/FISH* BS16.... 329 L6
Fenhill Cl *MIM* GL56 .... 57 K6
Fennel Cl *GLE* GL4 .... 136 E7
Fennel Dr *ALMDB* BS32 .... 317 J4
Fennell Gv
  HNBRY/STHM BS10 .... 325 J1 🖾
Fennell's Vw *STROUD* GL5 .... 209 G2
Fenshurst Gdns *LGASH* BS41 .... 344 B3
Fenswood Md *LGASH* BS41 ...... 344 A2
Fenswood Rd *LGASH* BS41 .... 344 A2
Fenton Cl *KEYN* BS31 .... 348 F8
Fenton Rd *HORF/LLZ* BS7 .... 325 M7
Fermaine Av
  BRSG/KWL/STAPK BS4........... 337 H8
Fernbank Rd
  RDLND/MONT BS6 .... 335 L1
Fernbrook Cl *MANG/FISH* BS16 .. 327 K2
Fern Cl *HNBRY/STHM* BS10 ...... 315 K8
Ferndale Av
  OLD/WMLY/WICK BS30 .... 338 B8
Ferndale Cl *CIND* GL14 .... 154 B2 🖾
  VGL GL2 .... 112 D6 🖾
Ferndale Rd *CBATH/BATHN* BA1.. 551 L8
  HORF/LLZ BS7 .... 326 C1
  RSTROUD/NAIL GL6 .... 184 C8 🖾
Ferndales Cl *CHELTW* GL51 ..... 115 H6 🖾
Ferndene *ALMDB* BS32 .... 316 F1
Ferndown *YATE/CS* BS37 .... 302 A8
Ferndown Rd *AVONM* BS11 ...... 324 C4 🖾
Ferndown Rd *LED* HR8 .... 19 M5
Ferney *DSLY* GL11 .... 253 L3
Fernhill *LA* AVONM* BS11 .... 324 D2
Fernhurst Rd
  EVILLE/WHL BS5 .... 337 H2 🖾
Fern Lawn *GLE* GL4 .... 160 F1
Fernleaze *FRCTL/WBN* BS36 .... 318 E5
Fernleigh Crs *CHELTW* GL51 .... 115 C5
Fern Rd *CLFD* GL16 .... 176 A6
  MANG/FISH BS16 .... 327 M6
Fernsteed Rd
  BMSTRD/HC/WWD BS13......... 345 H5
The Ferns *TET* GL8 .... 281 M4

Fern St *CBRISNE* BS2 .... 336 B2
Ferris Court Vw
  RSTROUD/NAIL GL6 .... 209 M7
Ferry Gdns *VGL* GL2 .... 158 F2 🖾
Ferry La *TEWK* GL20 .... 25 C3
Ferry Rd *KGWD/HNM* BS15 ...... 347 M2
Ferry St *CBRIS/FH* BS1 .... 7 C5 🖾
Ferry Wy *CHEP* NP16 .... 270 D7 🖾
Fewster Rd *STNHO* GL10 .... 207 C4
Fewster Rd *RDLND/MONT* BS6 .. 325 L7
Fewster Sq
  RSTROUD/NAIL GL6 .... 232 D7 🖾
Fiddes Rd *RDLND/MONT* BS6 .... 325 L7
Fiddler's Green La
  CHELTW GL51 .... 114 E2
The Fiddle *HGHW* SN6 .... 288 E4
Fidges La *RSTROUD/NAIL* GL6.. 210 A5
Field Badgers *CHCAM* GL55..... 34 E1
Fleld Cl *CIR* GL7 .... 263 J4
  COTS GL54 .... 73 M2
Fieldcote Dr *BWTH/CHD* GL3 ... 137 H4
Fleld Ct *TET* GL8 .... 281 M3
Field Court Dr *VGL* GL2 .... 159 G3
Field Court Gdns *VGL* GL2 ...... 159 G3
Fielden *GLE* GL4 .... 136 F8
Fleld End *BWTH/CHD* GL3 .... 113 J4
Fieldfare *GLE* GL4 .... 136 F6
Fleld Farm Cl
  BRSTK/PCHW BS34 .... 317 H7
Fieldgate Rd *CHELTE/BC* GL52 .. 72 C7
Field La *CHPMW/MSHF* SN14 ... 331 H5
  DSLY GL11 .... 228 F5
  DSLY GL11 .... 228 F7
  DSLY GL11 .... 229 M4
  OLD/WMLY/WICK BS30 .... 338 A8
  THNB/SVB BS35 .... 292 B3
  THNB/SVB BS35 .... 294 A8
Fleld Rd *CHNTN* OX7 .... 104 B8
  KGWD/HNM BS15 .... 337 L2
  RSTROUD/NAIL GL6 .... 184 C8
  STROUD GL5 .... 208 E5 🖾
Fields Rd *COTS* GL54 .... 167 K8
Fleld View Dr *MANG/FISH* BS16 .. 327 L5
Fieldways *RSTROUD/NAIL* GL6 .. 232 C7
Fiennes Cl *MANG/FISH* BS16 .... 328 A7 🖾
Fiery La *DSLY* GL11 .... 254 E1
Fifth Av *HORF/LLZ* BS7 .... 326 C2
Filbert Cl *GLE* GL4 .... 136 F8 🖾
Filby Dr *BRSTK/PCHW* BS34 .... 316 E3 🖾
Filkins Rd *CIR* GL7 .... 221 L8
Filton Av *BRSTK/PCHW* BS34 ... 316 D8
  HORF/LLZ BS7 .... 326 B5
Filton Gv *HORF/LLZ* BS7 .... 326 B5
Filton Rd *BRSTK/PCHW* BS34 ... 316 F1
  HORF/LLZ BS7 .... 326 B4
Filton Wy *GLE* GL4 .... 136 D4
Filwood Broadway
  BRSG/KWL/STAPK BS4........... 346 A3
Filwood Rd *MANG/FISH* BS16 .. 327 K8 🖾
Filwood Dr *KGWD/HNM* BS15... 338 B3
Filwood Rd *MANG/FISH* BS16 ... 327 J8
Finch Cl *THNB/SVB* BS35 .... 293 L1
Finchcroft La *CHELTE/BC* GL52.. 94 E8
Finch Rd *VGL* GL2 .... 112 F5
  YATE/CS BS37 .... 320 B3
Finlay Pl *GLE* GL4 .... 136 B6 🖾
Finlay Rd *GLE* GL4 .... 136 B6
Finstock Cl *CHELTW* GL51 .... 115 H3 🖾
Fircroft Cl *GLE* GL4 .... 137 H3
Fircroft Rd *GLE* GL4 .... 112 B6 🖾
Fire Engine La
  FRCTL/WBN BS36 .... 318 F4 🖾
Firethorne Cl *VGL* GL2 .... 112 D6 🖾
Firework Cl *KGWD/HNM* BS15 .. 338 D3
Firfield St *BRSG/KWL/STAPK* BS4.. 7 L9
Firgrove Crs *YATE/CS* BS37 ..... 320 C1
Fir Rd *CHPMW/MSHF* SN14 ..... 343 H5
Firs Cl *CHNTN* OX7 .... 125 M1
Firs Rd *RSTROUD/NAIL* GL6 ..... 232 E6
First Av *BRSG/KWL/STAPK* BS4 .. 337 C6
  DSLY GL11 .... 253 L3
The Firs *CHELTW* GL51 .... 93 K4
  STRAT CV37........................ 9 M1
Fir Tree Cl *BRSTK/PCHW* BS34.. 316 A4
  CHELTE/BC GL52 .... 94 C7
Fir Tree La *EVILLE/WHL* BS5 .... 337 J1
Fir View Rd *CIND* GL14 .... 154 A7
Firwood Dr *GLE* GL4 .... 102 A4 🖾
Fisher Av *KGWD/HNM* BS15 ..... 338 C2
Fisher Cl *COTS* GL54 .... 102 A4 🖾
Fisher Rd *KGWD/HNM* BS15 ..... 338 C2
Fishers Rd *BRKLY* GL13 .... 227 C7
Fishers Wy *STROUD* GL5 .... 208 C7
Fish Hl *BDWAY* WR12 .... 33 J4
Fisherman's Wk *CHEP* NP16 .... 270 B6 🖾
Fishpond Hl *HNBRY/STHM* BS10 .. 315 K7
Fitchett Wk
  HNBRY/STHM BS10 .... 315 H8
Fitzgerald Rd *BMSTR* BS3 .... 336 B8
Fitzhamon Pk *TEWK* GL20........ 49 H4
Fitzhardinge Wy *BRKLY* GL13 ... 227 C7
Fitzroy Rd *MANG/FISH* BS16 .... 327 K1
Fitzroy St *BRSG/KWL/STAPK* BS4 .. 7 M9
Five Acre Dr *MANG/FISH* BS16 .. 327 H4
Five Acres *DSLY* GL11 .... 253 J7
Five Mile Dr *MIM* GL56 .... 34 B8
Five Trees Cl *TET* GL8 .... 281 M3 🖾
Flaxley Rd *GLE* GL4 .... 135 M8
Flaxley St *CIND* GL14 .... 154 B3
Flaxman Cl *HORF/LLZ* BS7 ...... 326 D5
Flaxpits La *FRCTL/WBN* BS36 ... 317 M5
Flecker's Dr *CHELTW* GL51 ...... 115 H4
Fleece Rd *BDWAY* WR12 .... 32 F2
Fleet La *TEWK* GL20 .... 26 C5
Fleet Rd *TEWK* GL20 .... 26 C5
Fleming Cl *VGL* GL2 .... 112 E5
Flint Rd *CHELTW* GL51 .... 115 C5
Flisteridge Rd *MALM* GL16 ...... 285 K8
Florence Pk *ALMDB* BS32 .... 306 D6
  RDLND/MONT BS6 .... 325 K7
Florence Rd *MANG/FISH* BS16 .. 328 A4
Florida Bvd *CIR* GL7 .... 242 F6
Florida Dr *CHELTE/BC* GL52 .... 94 E7

Flowers Hl
  BRSG/KWL/STAPK BS4........... 347 G2
Flowers Hill Cl
  BRSG/KWL/STAPK BS4........... 347 G2 🖾
Flower Wy *VGL* GL2 .... 112 D7
Flowerwell Rd
  BMSTRD/HC/WWD BS13......... 345 K6 🖾
The Folders *LYD* GL15 .... 201 K8 🖾
Foley Cl *GLE* GL4 .... 135 M8 🖾
Foley Ri *RTEWK/TIB* GL19 .... 89 G5
Foley Rd *MANG/FISH* BS16 ...... 86 C3
Folland Av *BWTH/CHD* GL3 ..... 137 K5
Folland Dr *COTS* GL54 .... 124 C6
Folleigh Cl *LGASH* BS41 .... 344 D1
Folleigh Dr *LGASH* BS41 .... 344 D1
Folleigh La *LGASH* BS41 .... 344 D1
Folliot Cl *MANG/FISH* BS16 ..... 327 J3
Folly Bridge Cl
  YATE/CS BS37 .... 319 M1 🖾
Folly Brook Rd
  MANG/FISH BS16 .... 328 B1
Folly Fld *COTS* GL54 .... 123 J4 🖾
Folly La *CBRISNE* BS2 .... 7 M3
  CHELT GL50 .... 2 C1
  CLFD GL16 .... 151 J2
  MTCHDN GL17 .... 107 L5
  STROUD GL5 .... 208 E3
Folly Ri *STROUD* GL5 .... 208 F2
Folly Rd *YATE/CS* BS37 .... 308 B7
The Folly *MANG/FISH* BS16 ..... 328 B4
Fontana Cl
  OLD/WMLY/WICK BS30 .... 338 D8
Fonthill Rd *HNBRY/STHM* BS10 .. 325 M1
Fontmell Ct
  HGRV/WHIT BS14 .... 346 F4 🖾
Fontwell Dr *MANG/FISH* BS16 .. 328 B2
Footes La *FRCTL/WBN* BS36 .... 318 D4
Footshill Cl *KGWD/HNM* BS15 .. 337 L4
Footshill Dr *KGWD/HNM* BS15 .. 337 L4
Footshill Rd *KGWD/HNM* BS15 .. 337 L5
Fop St *DSLY* GL11 .... 254 C2
Forbes Cl *GLE* GL4 .... 137 H5
Forde Cl
  OLD/WMLY/WICK BS30 .... 338 B6 🖾
Fordell Pl
  BRSG/KWL/STAPK BS4........... 336 C8 🖾
Ford House Rd *NWNT* GL18...... 64 E8
Ford La *MANG/FISH* BS16 .... 328 D5
  NWNT GL18 .... 85 J4
Ford St *EVILLE/WHL* BS5 .... 336 E5 🖾
Forest Av *MANG/FISH* BS16...... 327 K8
Forest Cl *CLFD* GL16 .... 150 E5
Forest Dr *HNBRY/STHM* BS10 ... 315 L8
Forest Edge *KGWD/HNM* BS15 .. 337 L7
Foresters Rd *TEWK* GL20 .... 48 A7
Forest Hills *ALMDB* BS32 .... 306 D6
Fore St *HGHW* SN6 .... 287 H2
Forest Patch *CLFD* GL16 .... 151 J6
Forest Ri *CIND* GL14 .... 154 C2
  MTCHDN GL17 .... 128 C7
Forest Rd *CIND* GL14 .... 154 B3
  CLFD GL16 .... 151 M6
  CLFD GL16 .... 175 L4
  KGWD/HNM BS15 .... 337 M4
  LYD GL15 .... 200 D2
  LYD GL15 .... 201 J7
  MANG/FISH BS16 .... 327 K8
  MTCHDN GL17 .... 129 H5
  WUE GL12 .... 275 K7
Forest Vale Rd *CIND* GL14 ...... 129 M8
  CIND GL14 .... 153 M1
Forest Vw *CIND* GL14 .... 154 A6
Forest View Rd *BRKLY* GL13 .... 227 G7
  GLE GL4 .... 160 A2
Forest Wk *KGWD/HNM* BS15 .... 337 K1 🖾
  MANG/FISH BS16 .... 337 K1 🖾
Forge Hl *MTCHDN* GL17 .... 128 B5
Forge La *NWNT* GL18 .... 65 L8
Forrester Gn
  CHPMW/MSHF SN14 .... 343 K8
Forsdene Wk *CLFD* GL16 .... 175 M1 🖾
Forsyte Wy *GLE* GL4 .... 136 D4
Forsythia Cl *BWTH/CHD* GL3 ... 113 J5 🖾
Fortey Rd *COTS* GL54 .... 169 J1
Fortfield Rd *HGRV/WHIT* BS14 .. 346 D6
Fortfields *DSLY* GL11 .... 253 K3 🖾
Fortina Cl *CHELT* GL50 .... 93 L6 🖾
Fort La *DSLY* GL11 .... 253 K5
The Fortress *DSLY* GL11 .... 253 K5
Fort View Ter *STROUD* GL5 ...... 208 A5
Forty Acre La *STROUD* GL5 ...... 209 J4
  THNB/SVB BS35 .... 293 J8
Forty's Pitch *RWYE* HR9 .... 84 F2
The Forty *HGHW* SN6 .... 288 F4
Foscombe La *RTEWK/TIB* GL19.. 89 H2
Fosscross La *COTS* GL54 .... 192 A5
Fosse Cl *CIR* GL7 .... 238 E2
  GLE GL4 .... 137 G5
Fossedale Av *HGRV/WHIT* BS14 .. 346 D5
Fosse Folly *COTS* GL54 .... 102 A2 🖾
Fosse La *CBATH/BATHN* BA1 .... 352 C7
  COTS GL54 .... 102 A2 🖾
Fosseway Av *MIM* GL56........... 58 C7
Fosseway Cl
  CHPMW/MSHF SN14 .... 343 K8
  MIM GL56 .... 58 D7
Fosseway Dr *MIM* GL56 .... 58 D7
The Fosseway *CFTN/FAIL* BS8 ... 335 J5
Foss Fld *THNB/SVB* BS35 .... 273 C4
Foss La *THNB/SVB* BS35 .... 273 C4
Foster Cl *CHELTE/BC* GL52 ...... 72 C6
Foster St *EVILLE/WHL* BS5 .... 336 D1
Foundry La *EVILLE/WHL* BS5 .... 337 H1
Foundry Rd *CIND* GL14 .... 154 A2
  MALM SN16 .... 303 H7
Fountain Crs *WUE* GL12 .... 277 L5
Fountaine Ct
  EVILLE/WHL BS5 .... 336 E1 🖾
Fountains Dr
  OLD/WMLY/WICK BS30 .... 338 B5
Fountain St *RSTROUD/NAIL* GL6 .. 232 D8
Fountain Wy *CHEP* NP16 .... 270 B7 🖾
Four Acre Av *MANG/FISH* BS16.. 328 A3
Four Acre Cl *HGHW* SN6 .... 287 H3
Four Acre Crs *MANG/FISH* BS16 .. 328 A2
Four Acre Rd *MANG/FISH* BS16 .. 328 A2
Four Acres
  BMSTRD/HC/WWD BS13......... 345 G7

Four Acres Cl
  BMSTRD/HC/WWD BS13......... 345 H7
Fourth Av *DSLY* GL11 .... 253 L3
  HORF/LLZ BS7 .... 326 C1
Fowler's Hl *CIR* GL7 .... 218 D5
Fowler's Rd *CHNTN* OX7 .... 104 C7
Fox And Hounds La
  KEYN BS31 .... 348 B6 🖾
Fox Av *YATE/CS* BS37 .... 319 M1
Foxborough Gdns
  ALMDB BS32 .... 316 F1 🖾
Fox Cl *BWTH/CHD* CH3 .... 137 H6
  STROUD GL5 .... 207 L4
Foxcombe Rd
  HGRV/WHIT BS14 .... 346 D7 🖾
Foxcote *KGWD/HNM* BS15 .... 338 B4
  VGL GL2 .... 112 D6 🖾
Foxcote Hl *SHPSTR* CV36 .... 14 D2
Foxcote Rd *BMSTR* BS3 .... 335 J8
Foxcott *HGHW* SN6 .... 264 E7
Foxcroft Cl *ALMDB* BS32 .... 317 K5
Foxcroft Rd *EVILLE/WHL* BS5 ... 336 F3
Fox Den Rd *BRSTK/PCHW* BS34 .. 316 F8
  BRSTK/PCHW BS34 .... 326 F1
Fox Elms Rd *GLE* GL4 .... 160 A1
Foxes Bank Dr *CIR* GL7 .... 238 B5 🖾
Foxes Bridge Rd *CIND* GL14 .... 153 M2
Foxes Cl *COTS* GL54 .... 123 H5 🖾
Foxes Dell *RSTROUD/NAIL* GL6 .. 232 C6
Foxes Rw *MIM* GL56 .... 80 C7
Foxfield Av *ALMDB* BS32 .... 306 F8
Foxglove Cl *GLE* GL4 .... 137 G6
  MANG/FISH BS16 .... 327 C7 🖾
  THNB/SVB BS35 .... 293 M1 🖾
Foxglove Wy *CLFD* GL16 .... 175 L4
Foxgrove Dr *CHELTE/BC* GL52 .. 3 K5
Fox Hl *TET* GL8 .... 282 A4
Foxholes La *ALMDB* BS32 .... 292 E8
Foxleaze *HGHW* SN6 .... 288 F2
Foxleigh Crs *VGL* GL2 .... 113 G6 🖾
Foxmoor *CHELTE/BC* GL52 ...... 72 A7 🖾
Foxmoor La *STROUD* GL5 .... 207 L3
Fox's La *CLFD* GL16 .... 175 M1
Foxtail Cl *GLE* GL4 .... 136 C7
Foxwell Br *BWTH/CHD* BS34 .... 137 J3
Fraley Rd
  HNLZ/SM/SNYPK/WT BS9...... 325 K6
Frampton Ct
  OLD/WMLY/WICK BS30 .... 338 B7 🖾
Frampton Crs *MANG/FISH* BS16.. 327 L7
Frampton Dr *BDWAY* WR12 ..... 11 G7 🖾
Frampton End Rd
  FRCTL/WBN BS36 .... 318 E5
Frampton Ms *CHELTW* GL51 .... 114 D4 🖾
Frampton Rd *GL* GL1 .... 135 M4
France La *BAD* GL9 .... 312 C1
Francis Pl
  OLD/WMLY/WICK BS30 .... 338 B7
Francis Rd *BMSTR* BS3 .... 345 L1 🖾
  HNBRY/STHM BS10 .... 325 L3 🖾
Francis St *CHELTS* GL53 .... 115 M4
Francis Wy
  OLD/WMLY/WICK BS30 .... 338 F5
Francombe Gv
  HNBRY/STHM BS10 .... 326 A5
Frank Brookes Rd
  CHELTW GL51 .... 93 J7 🖾
Franklin La *CBRISNE* BS2 .... 336 D2 🖾
Franklyn St *CBRISNE* BS2 .... 336 B2
Fraser St *BMSTR* BS3 .... 335 M8
Frayne Rd *BMSTR* BS3 .... 335 J7
Frazier's Folly *CIR* GL7 .... 238 F7
Freame Rd *RSTROUD/NAIL* GL6 .. 209 M8
Frederick Pl *CFTN/FAIL* BS8...... 6 A2
Frederick Thomas Rd
  DSLY GL11 .... 229 G7
Fredrick St
  BRSG/KWL/STAPK BS4........... 7 L9 🖾
Freeland Buildings
  EVILLE/WHL BS5 .... 336 E1 🖾
Freeland Pl *CFTN/FAIL* BS8 ...... 335 H5 🖾
Freemans Cl *TEWK* GL20 .... 26 B4 🖾
Freemantle Gdns
  EVILLE/WHL BS5 .... 336 E8 🖾
Freemantle Rd
  EVILLE/WHL BS5 .... 336 E8 🖾
Freestone Rd *CBRISNE* BS2...... 7 L5
Free Tank *CBRISNE* BS2 .... 7 K5
Freezinghill La
  OLD/WMLY/WICK BS30 .... 340 C8
Fremantle La
  RDLND/MONT BS6 .... 335 M2 🖾
Fremantle Rd
  RDLND/MONT BS6 .... 335 M2 🖾
Frenchay Hl *MANG/FISH* BS16 .. 327 K4
Frenchay Park Rd
  MANG/FISH BS16 .... 327 H5
Frenchay Rd *MANG/FISH* BS16 .. 327 L4
French La *CLFD* GL16 .... 174 E4
  MONM NP25 .... 174 B3
Freshland Wy
  KGWD/HNM BS15 .... 337 K3
Fretherne Rd *GL* GL1 .... 135 M8
Frewin Cl *CHELTW* GL51 .... 114 F1
Frewins La *CIND* GL14 .... 132 D5
Friars Cl *CHELT* GL50 .... 115 K6 🖾
Friar's Wk *NWNT* GL18 .... 86 C2 🖾
Friary Grange Pk
  FRCTL/WBN BS36 .... 318 A5
Friary Rd *GLE* GL4 .... 137 C5
  HORF/LLZ BS7 .... 325 M8
Fridays Ham La *HGHW* SN6 ..... 263 K8
Friday St *RSTROUD/NAIL* GL6 .. 185 H3 🖾
  RSTROUD/NAIL GL6 .... 233 J5
  STRAT CV37........................ 8 A1
  VGL GL2 .... 156 A3
Friendship Rd
  BRSG/KWL/STAPK BS4........... 346 B1
Friezewood Rd *BMSTR* BS3 ...... 335 J8
Fripp Cl *EVILLE/WHL* BS5 .... 336 D5 🖾
Frith La *WUE* GL12 .... 296 C8
The Frith *RSTROUD/NAIL* GL6 .. 209 M8
Frithwood Cl
  RSTROUD/NAIL GL6 .... 209 M8 🖾

Frithwood Pk
  RSTROUD/NAIL GL6 .... 209 M8 🖾
Frobisher Rd *BMSTR* BS3 .... 335 J8
Frocester Hl *STNHO* GL10 .... 230 E2
Frog Furlong La *VGL* GL2 .... 112 F2
Frog La *CBRIS/FH* BS1 .... 6 C4 🖾
  DSLY GL11 .... 252 E6
  FRCTL/WBN BS36 .... 319 G3
  RTEWK/TIB GL19 .... 108 C7
  STNHO GL10 .... 230 C1
Frogmarsh La *STROUD* GL5...... 232 C2 🖾
Frogmore Rd *RTEWK/TIB* GL19 .. 108 C7
Frome Av *STROUD* GL5 .... 208 D5
Frome Brook Rd *LED* HR8 .... 19 L2
Frome Ct *THNB/SVB* BS35 .... 293 L3
  VGL GL2 .... 112 D6 🖾
Frome Gdns *STROUD* GL5 .... 208 A5
Frome Gln *FRCTL/WBN* BS36 ... 318 A7
Frome Park Rd *STROUD* GL5 .... 208 C5
Frome Pl *MANG/FISH* BS16 ...... 327 G6 🖾
Frome Rd *YATE/CS* BS37 .... 320 E2
Fromeside *STROUD* GL5 .... 208 D5
Frome St *CBRISNE* BS2 .... 7 J1 🖾
Frome Valley Rd
  MANG/FISH BS16 .... 327 H5
Frome Valley Walkway
  FRCTL/WBN BS36.................. 318 A3
  FRCTL/WBN BS36.................. 319 G1
  MANG/FISH BS16 .... 327 L4
  YATE/CS BS37 .... 309 L8
Frome Valley Wy *YATE/CS* BS37 .. 321 G3
Frome Vw *FRCTL/WBN* BS36 .... 318 D4
Frome Wy *FRCTL/WBN* BS36 .... 318 A6
Front St *STNHO* GL10 .... 231 G5
Froomshaw Rd
  MANG/FISH BS16 .... 327 J4
Frost Rd *LED* HR8 .... 19 L2
Frowens La *RWYE* HR9 .... 84 E3
Fry's Cl *MANG/FISH* BS16 .... 326 F7 🖾
Frys Hl *KGWD/HNM* BS15 .... 338 A1 🖾
  KGWD/HNM BS15 .... 338 A2 🖾
Fulbrook Cl *CHELTW* GL51 ...... 92 F6 🖾
Fulford Rd
  BMSTRD/HC/WWD BS13......... 345 K6 🖾
Fulford Wk
  BMSTRD/HC/WWD BS13......... 345 K6 🖾
Fullers Av *HGHW* SN6 .... 288 F3
Fuller's La *RTEWK/TIB* GL19 .... 88 F3
Fulmar Cl *THNB/SVB* BS35 ...... 293 M1 🖾
Fulton Rd *COTS* GL54 .... 124 D7
Furber Ct *EVILLE/WHL* BS5 ..... 337 K5
Furber Rdg *EVILLE/WHL* BS5 ... 337 K5
Furber Rd *EVILLE/WHL* BS5 ..... 337 K5
Furber V *EVILLE/WHL* BS5 ...... 337 K5
Furlong Cl *LED* HR8 .... 19 M5 🖾
Furlong La *CHELTE/BC* GL52 .... 72 B8
Furlong Meadow *SHPSTR* CV36.. 16 B7
Furlong Rd *GL* GL1 .... 136 A4
The Furlong
  HNLZ/SM/SNYPK/WT BS9...... 325 L6
Furnace Cl *CIND* GL14 .... 154 A3 🖾
Furnace La *NWNT* GL18 .... 86 B1
Furnace Va *LYD* GL15 .... 202 C1
Furnwood *EVILLE/WHL* BS5 ..... 337 J5
Furze Cft *VGL* GL2 .... 159 H4
Furze Hill Rd *SHPSTR* CV36 ..... 16 B7
Furze La *CHCAM* GL55 .... 13 H4
Furze Rd *MANG/FISH* BS16 ..... 327 L8
The Furze *GLE* GL4 .... 136 C7
Furzewood Rd
  KGWD/HNM BS15 .... 338 B3
Fylton Cft *HGRV/WHIT* BS14 .... 346 D8

G

Gabb La *RTEWK/TIB* GL19 .... 68 F5
Gable Cl *THNB/SVB* BS35 .... 315 J1
Gable Point *CHELTE/BC* GL52 ... 72 D8
Gable Rd *EVILLE/WHL* BS5........ 336 C2 🖾
Gadshill Dr *BRSTK/PCHW* BS34.. 317 G6
Gadshill Rd *CHELTS* GL53 .... 116 D8
  EVILLE/WHL BS5................... 326 E8
Gadwell Rd *TEWK* GL20 .... 48 C6
Gages Cl *KGWD/HNM* BS15 ..... 338 B4
Gages Rd *KGWD/HNM* BS15 .... 338 B4
Gainsborough Dr *GL* GL1 .... 159 L1
Gainsborough Rd *KEYN* BS31 ... 348 B6
Gallivan Cl *BRSTK/PCHW* BS34 .. 316 D4
Gallops La *CHELTE/BC* GL52..... 94 F8
Galway Rd
  BRSG/KWL/STAPK BS4........... 346 A2
Gambier Parry Gdns *VGL* GL2 .. 112 B7
Gambles La *CHELTE/BC* GL52 ... 94 E1
Gambril La *WUE* GL12 .... 275 G6
Ganborough Rd *MIM* GL56 .... 79 J3
Gander Cl
  BMSTRD/HC/WWD BS13......... 345 K6 🖾
Gander La *TEWK* GL20 .... 48 A6
  TEWK GL20 .... 50 C4
Gannaway La *TEWK* GL20 .... 48 D4
Gannet Rd *BWTH/CHD* GL3 ..... 138 A6 🖾
Gannicox Rd *STROUD* GL5 .... 208 C4
Ganzell La *DSLY* GL11 .... 253 L4
Garden City Wy *CHEP* NP16 .... 270 A3 🖾
Garden Cl *CHCAM* GL55 .... 8 F8
  CIR GL7 .... 238 C4 🖾
  EVE WR11 .... 30 B6
  HNLZ/SM/SNYPK/WT BS9...... 324 E6
Gardeners Wk *LGASH* BS41 ..... 344 D2 🖾
Gardeners Wy *NWNT* GL18 ...... 86 B3 🖾
  STNHO GL10 .... 207 J7
Gardenia Gv *CHELTW* GL51 ..... 115 H6
Garden Rd *CHELTS* GL53 .... 116 C1
The Gardens *CHELTE/BC* GL52 .. 94 A7 🖾
  MANG/FISH BS16 .... 327 H2
The Garden *STROUD* GL5 .... 232 C1 🖾
Garden Wy *VGL* GL2 .... 5 L1
Gardiner Cl *RSTROUD/NAIL* GL6 .. 210 A7
Gardiners Cl *BWTH/CHD* GL3 ... 113 J5 🖾
Gardner Av
  BMSTRD/HC/WWD BS13......... 345 H4
Gardner's La *CHELTW* GL51 ..... 93 L7
Garfield Rd *EVILLE/WHL* BS5 ... 337 J3
Garlands Rd *LYD* GL15 .... 224 C4
Garnalls Rd *GLE* GL4 .... 136 E7
Garnet St *BMSTR* BS3 .... 345 K1

Garnett Pl *MANG/FISH* BS16 ..... 328 B4
Garrett Dr *ALMDB* BS32 ..... 316 F4
Garth Rd
  BMSTRD/HC/WWD BS13 ..... 345 J3
The Garth *LED* HR8 ..... 19 M1
Garvey Cl *CHEP* NP16 ..... 270 B7
Gasferry Rd *CBRIS/FH* BS1 ..... 6 B7
The Gaskins *HORF/LLZ* BS7 ..... 326 C6
Gas La *CBRISNE* BS2 ..... 7 L5
  HGHW SN6 ..... 288 F7
Gassons Rd *CIR* GL7 ..... 244 E6
Gastons Rd *MALM* SN16 ..... 303 H8
The Gastons *AVONM* BS11 ..... 324 C3
Gasworks La *COTS* GL54 ..... 123 H6
Gatcombe Dr
  BRSTK/PCHW BS34 ..... 317 G7
Gatcombe Rd
  BMSTRD/HC/WWD BS13 ..... 345 K6
Gatehouse Av
  BMSTRD/HC/WWD BS13 ..... 345 J6
Gatehouse Cl
  BMSTRD/HC/WWD BS13 ..... 345 J6
Gatehouse Ct
  BMSTRD/HC/WWD BS13 ..... 345 K6
Gatehouse Wy
  BMSTRD/HC/WWD BS13 ..... 345 J6
Gatesby Md *BRSTK/PCHW* BS34 ..... 317 C6
Gathorne Rd *BMSTR* BS3 ..... 6 A9
Gatmeres Rd *GLE* GL4 ..... 136 E8
Gatton Rd *CBRISNE* BS2 ..... 336 C2
Gatton Wy *GLE* GL4 ..... 137 H2
Gaunt's Earthcott La
  ALMDB BS32 ..... 307 K6
Gaunt's La *CBRIS/FH* BS1 ..... 6 D4
Gaunts Rd *YATE/CS* BS37 ..... 320 D3
Gay Elms Rd
  BMSTRD/HC/WWD BS13 ..... 345 J7
Gayner Rd *HORF/LLZ* BS7 ..... 326 C2
Gays Rd *KGWD/HNM* BS15 ..... 337 K7
Gaythorne Crs *YATE/CS* BS37 ..... 319 M1
Gazelle Cl *VGL* GL2 ..... 159 H1
Gazzard Cl *FRCTL/WBN* BS36 ..... 318 H4
Gee Moors *KGWD/HNM* BS15 ..... 338 B4
Gefle Cl *CBRIS/FH* BS1 ..... 6 A7
Genista Wy *CHELTW* GL51 ..... 115 H6
Geoffrey Cl
  BMSTRD/HC/WWD BS13 ..... 345 C5
George Ct
  RSTROUD/NAIL GL6 ..... 185 H3
George Dowty Dr *TEWK* GL20 ..... 49 G2
George La *CHCAM* GL55 ..... 34 G1
  CHPMW/MSHF SN14 ..... 342 A2
  CIND GL14 ..... 154 E1
George Readings Wy
  CHELTW GL51 ..... 93 H7
George Rd *LYD* GL15 ..... 177 J3
George St *EVILLE/WHL* BS5 ..... 336 E3
  GL GL1 ..... 5 C5
  RSTROUD/NAIL GL6 ..... 210 C2
  RSTROUD/NAIL GL6 ..... 232 E7
  STROUD GL5 ..... 208 E4
George Whitefield Cl
  GLE GL4 ..... 136 E7
George Whitefield Ct
  CBRIS/FH BS1 ..... 7 H2
Georgian Cl *GLE* GL4 ..... 137 C8
Gerald Rd *BMSTR* BS3 ..... 335 J8
Geralds Wy *RSTROUD/NAIL* GL6 ..... 210 A8
Gere Cl *GLE* GL4 ..... 159 M2
Gerrard Cl
  BRSG/KWL/STAPK BS4 ..... 345 M4
Gerrard Rd *COTS* GL54 ..... 124 D8
Gerrards Rd *SHPSTR* CV36 ..... 16 C6
Gerrish Av *EVILLE/WHL* BS5 ..... 336 E3
  MANG/FISH BS16 ..... 328 B6
Gervase Rd *COTS* GL54 ..... 74 C4
Gibbsfold Rd
  BMSTRD/HC/WWD BS13 ..... 345 L8
Gibraltar Wy *CHEP* NP16 ..... 270 D7
Gibson Cl *STROUD* GL5 ..... 209 H4
Gibson Rd *BWTH/CHD* GL3 ..... 113 C4
  LED HR8 ..... 19 L2
  RDLND/MONT BS6 ..... 335 M2
Giddynap La *STROUD* GL5 ..... 232 C4
Giffard Wy *CHELTS* GL53 ..... 115 M7
Gifford Cl *VGL* GL2 ..... 112 E6
  YATE/CS BS37 ..... 309 J3
Gifford Rd *HNBRY/STHM* BS10 ..... 315 H7
Giffords Pl
  BMSTRD/HC/WWD BS13 ..... 345 J4
Gilbert HI *BRKLY* GL13 ..... 227 G7
Gilbert Rd *EVILLE/WHL* BS5 ..... 336 E3
  KGWD/HNM BS15 ..... 337 M2
  VGL GL2 ..... 112 E6
Gilberts La *GLE* GL4 ..... 160 B4
Gilda Cl *HGRV/WHIT* BS14 ..... 346 D6
Gilda Crs *HGRV/WHIT* BS14 ..... 346 D5
Gilda Sq West *HGRV/WHIT* BS14 ..... 346 D6
Gilder Rd *CHELTE/BC* GL52 ..... 94 B1
Gilders Paddock
  CHELTE/BC GL52 ..... 72 B7
Giles Av *HGHW* SN6 ..... 288 F4
Giles Cox *VGL* GL2 ..... 159 H3
Gillard Cl *KGWD/HNM* BS15 ..... 337 K3
Gillard Rd *KGWD/HNM* BS15 ..... 337 K3
Gill Av *MANG/FISH* BS16 ..... 327 K5
Gillebank Cl
  HGRV/WHIT BS14 ..... 346 F6
Gillett Cl *COTS* GL54 ..... 74 C6
Gillett's La *RBANSW* OX15 ..... 17 L7
Gillingham HI
  EVILLE/WHL BS5 ..... 337 K6
Gillingstool *THNB/SVB* BS35 ..... 293 L3
Gillray Cl *HORF/LLZ* BS7 ..... 326 C5
Gilpin Av *GLE* GL4 ..... 137 H2
Gilpin Cl *KGWD/HNM* BS15 ..... 338 B2
Gilroy Cl *OLD/WMLY/WICK* BS30 ..... 338 D3
Gilslake Av *HNBRY/STHM* BS10 ..... 315 K8
Gimson Cl *GLE* GL4 ..... 159 M1
Gipsy La *RSTROUD/NAIL* GL6 ..... 234 D2
  STNHO GL10 ..... 231 G2
Gipsy Patch La
  BRSTK/PCHW BS34 ..... 316 E5
The Glades *EVILLE/WHL* BS5 ..... 337 G1
Gladiator Cl *BWTH/CHD* GL3 ..... 138 A6

Gladstone Dr
  MANG/FISH BS16 ..... 328 A8
Gladstone La
  FRCTL/WBN BS36 ..... 318 E4
Gladstone Rd *CHELTS* GL53 ..... 116 C6
  GL GL1 ..... 135 L5
  HGRV/WHIT BS14 ..... 346 D5
  KGWD/HNM BS15 ..... 337 M2
Gladstone St *BMSTR* BS3 ..... 335 K8
  EVILLE/WHL BS5 ..... 336 F4
  MANG/FISH BS16 ..... 327 M8
Glaisdale Rd *MANG/FISH* BS16 ..... 327 J6
Glamorgan Rd *CHELTW* GL51 ..... 115 C5
Glanville Gdns
  KGWD/HNM BS15 ..... 338 A4
Glass House La *CBRISNE* BS2 ..... 336 D6
Glastonbury Cl
  OLD/WMLY/WICK BS30 ..... 338 B6
Glebe Cl *CIR* GL7 ..... 214 B7
  COTS GL54 ..... 102 A3
  LGASH BS41 ..... 344 D1
  MTCHDN GL17 ..... 106 C6
  NWNT GL18 ..... 86 B2
  VGL GL2 ..... 205 H1
Glebe Ct *NWNT* GL18 ..... 86 B2
Glebe Farm Ct *CHELTW* GL51 ..... 115 H6
Glebe Fld *ALMDB* BS32 ..... 306 C6
Glebeland Dr *TEWK* GL20 ..... 27 H5
Glebelands Rd
  BRSTK/PCHW BS34 ..... 316 C8
Glebe La *LED* HR8 ..... 261 H4
Glebe Orch *LED* HR8 ..... 40 C5
Glebe Rd *BDWAY* WR12 ..... 31 H2
  CHELTE/BC GL52 ..... 94 D7
  EVILLE/WHL BS5 ..... 337 G3
  LGASH BS41 ..... 344 E2
  NWNT GL18 ..... 86 B3
  RSTROUD/NAIL GL6 ..... 233 K5
The Glebe *CIR* GL7 ..... 211 M8
  THNB/SVB BS35 ..... 304 E4
Glebe Wy *NWNT* GL18 ..... 86 B2
Gledemoor Dr
  FRCTL/WBN BS36 ..... 318 F4
Glena Av *BRSG/KWL/STAPK* BS4 ..... 346 D1
Glenarm Rd
  BRSG/KWL/STAPK BS4 ..... 347 C1
Glenarm Wk
  BRSG/KWL/STAPK BS4 ..... 347 C1
Glen Av *CFTN/FAIL* BS8 ..... 334 B3
Glenavon Pk
  HNLZ/SM/SNYPK/WT BS9 ..... 324 E7
Glen Brook
  HNLZ/SM/SNYPK/WT BS9 ..... 324 F7
Glenburn Rd *KGWD/HNM* BS15 ..... 337 K2
Glencairn Av *GL* GL1 ..... 159 L2
Glencairn Ct *CHELTW* GL51 ..... 115 J3
Glencairn Park Rd
  CHELTW GL51 ..... 115 J3
Glen Cl *SHPSTR* CV36 ..... 16 B5
Glencoe La *MTCHDN* GL17 ..... 130 C4
Glen Ct *STNHO* GL10 ..... 207 H3
Glencoyne Sq
  HNBRY/STHM BS10 ..... 325 L1
Glendale *CFTN/FAIL* BS8 ..... 335 H5
  MANG/FISH BS16 ..... 327 L8
Glendare St *EVILLE/WHL* BS5 ..... 336 E5
Glendevon Rd
  HGRV/WHIT BS14 ..... 346 C8
Glendower Cl
  BWTH/CHD GL3 ..... 113 H1
Glen Dr
  HNLZ/SM/SNYPK/WT BS9 ..... 324 F6
Gleneagles *YATE/CS* BS37 ..... 320 A2
Gleneagles Dr
  HNBRY/STHM BS10 ..... 314 F8
Gleneagles Rd
  OLD/WMLY/WICK BS30 ..... 338 D5
Glenfall *YATE/CS* BS37 ..... 319 M4
Glenfall St *CHELTE/BC* GL52 ..... 2 F4
Glenfall Wy *CHELTE/BC* GL52 ..... 116 D5
Glenfrome Rd *CBRISNE* BS2 ..... 336 C1
  EVILLE/WHL BS5 ..... 326 D8
Glen La *BRSG/KWL/STAPK* BS4 ..... 346 F1
Glenlea Gv *CHELTW* GL51 ..... 115 H6
Glen Pk *EVILLE/WHL* BS5 ..... 336 E1
Glen Park Crs *STROUD* GL5 ..... 208 C8
Glen Park Gdns
  EVILLE/WHL BS5 ..... 337 J3
Glenroy Av *KGWD/HNM* BS15 ..... 337 K2
Glensanda Ct *CHELTW* GL51 ..... 115 J3
Glenside Cl *MANG/FISH* BS16 ..... 327 L4
Glenside Pk
  MANG/FISH BS16 ..... 327 G6
The Glen *KGWD/HNM* BS15 ..... 337 K7
  RDLND/MONT BS6 ..... 325 K8
  YATE/CS BS37 ..... 320 A1
Glenthorne Cl *STNHO* GL10 ..... 207 H2
Glentworth Rd *CFTN/FAIL* BS8 ..... 6 A4
  RDLND/MONT BS6 ..... 335 L1
Glenwood *MANG/FISH* BS16 ..... 327 L8
Glenwood Dr
  OLD/WMLY/WICK BS30 ..... 338 B7
Glenwood Rd
  HNBRY/STHM BS10 ..... 325 L4
Glevum Cl *VGL* GL2 ..... 5 L1
Glevum Wy *GLE* GL4 ..... 137 G2
Gloster Av *EVILLE/WHL* BS5 ..... 326 F8
Gloucester
  BRSTK/PCHW BS34 ..... 316 F6
Gloucester La *CBRISNE* BS2 ..... 7 K2
  CHCAM GL55 ..... 8 F8
Gloucester Pl *CHELTE/BC* GL52 ..... 2 E5
Gloucester Rd *ALMDB* BS32 ..... 306 E6
  BRKLY GL13 ..... 226 B3
  BRSTK/PCHW BS34 ..... 316 D2
  CBATH/BATHN BA1 ..... 351 J4
  CBATH/BATHN BA1 ..... 351 K6
  CHELTW GL51 ..... 114 C4
  CHEP NP16 ..... 270 C1
  CIR GL7 ..... 214 A7
  CLFD GL16 ..... 175 K1
  COTS GL54 ..... 118 B8
  HORF/LLZ BS7 ..... 335 M1
  MALM SN16 ..... 303 J7
  MANG/FISH BS16 ..... 328 A8
  MTCHDN GL17 ..... 130 D2
  NWNT GL18 ..... 87 J1
  RSTROUD/NAIL GL6 ..... 185 H1
  RTEWK/TIB GL19 ..... 66 E5
  RTEWK/TIB GL19 ..... 70 A4
  STNHO GL10 ..... 207 H3
  TEWK GL20 ..... 48 A7
  THNB/SVB BS35 ..... 293 L1
  THNB/SVB BS35 ..... 307 H1
Gloucester Rd North
  BRSTK/PCHW BS34 ..... 316 C8
  BRSTK/PCHW BS34 ..... 326 C1
  HORF/LLZ BS7 ..... 326 B2
Gloucestershire Wy
  BWTH/CHD GL3 ..... 114 B7
  CHELTE/BC GL52 ..... 73 J3
  CHEP NP16 ..... 270 A3
  CLFD GL16 ..... 176 D2
  COTS GL54 ..... 75 K6
  COTS GL54 ..... 77 H2
  COTS GL54 ..... 101 K1
  COTS GL54 ..... 121 J7
  COTS GL54 ..... 141 G6
  LYD GL15 ..... 200 C2
  LYD GL15 ..... 223 J6
  MTCHDN GL17 ..... 107 H5
  MTCHDN GL17 ..... 108 A7
Gloucester St *CBRISNE* BS2 ..... 7 H1
  CFTN/FAIL BS8 ..... 335 H4
  CIR GL7 ..... 238 B1
  COTS GL54 ..... 74 B7
  EVILLE/WHL BS5 ..... 326 F8
  NWNT GL18 ..... 86 D3
  STROUD GL5 ..... 208 E4
  WUE GL12 ..... 277 J3
Glynbridge Gdns *CHELTW* GL51 ..... 93 H6
  CHELTW GL51 ..... 115 G6
Glyndthorpe Gv
  CHELTW GL51 ..... 115 G6
Glynfield Ri *STROUD* GL5 ..... 207 L4
Glynrosa Rd *CHELTS* GL53 ..... 116 D6
Glyn V *BMSTR* BS3 ..... 345 M2
Goddard Wy *GLE* GL4 ..... 159 M1
Godfrey Cl *CHELTW* GL51 ..... 115 J4
Godfrey Ct
  OLD/WMLY/WICK BS30 ..... 338 B7
Godwin Rd *COTS* GL54 ..... 74 C4
Goffenton Dr *MANG/FISH* BS16 ..... 327 K5
Goldcrest St *STNHO* GL10 ..... 207 H3
Goldcrest Rd *YATE/CS* BS37 ..... 320 B4
Golden Cl *GL* GL1 ..... 159 L1
Golden Farm Rd *CIR* GL7 ..... 238 E3
Golden La *CHNTN* OX7 ..... 83 J6
  WUE GL12 ..... 277 H7
Golden Miller Rd *CHELT* GL50 ..... 93 L6
Golden V *BWTH/CHD* GL3 ..... 113 K5
Golden Va *STROUD* GL5 ..... 233 J2
Golden Valley La
  OLD/WMLY/WICK BS30 ..... 349 H2
Goldfinch Wy
  MANG/FISH BS16 ..... 329 L7
Golding Wy *LED* HR8 ..... 19 L1
Goldney Av *CFTN/FAIL* BS8 ..... 335 J5
  OLD/WMLY/WICK BS30 ..... 338 E4
Goldney Rd *CFTN/FAIL* BS8 ..... 335 J5
Goldsborough Cl *GLE* GL4 ..... 136 D4
Goldsbury Wk *AVONM* BS11 ..... 324 C2
Goldsmith Rd *CHELTW* GL51 ..... 115 G1
Golf Club La *BWTH/CHD* GL3 ..... 137 L7
Golf Course La
  BRSTK/PCHW BS34 ..... 316 B8
Golf Course Rd
  RSTROUD/NAIL GL6 ..... 185 H2
Gooch St
  OLD/WMLY/WICK BS30 ..... 338 E8
Goodeve Rd
  HNLZ/SM/SNYPK/WT BS9 ..... 334 F1
Goodhind St *EVILLE/WHL* BS5 ..... 336 C3
Goodier's La *TEWK* GL20 ..... 26 C5
Goodmoor Crs *BWTH/CHD* GL3 ..... 113 J5
Goodneston Rd
  MANG/FISH BS16 ..... 327 J8
Goodrich HI *RTEWK/TIB* GL19 ..... 89 J3
Goodridge Av *VGL* GL2 ..... 135 J8
Goodring HI *AVONM* BS11 ..... 324 C2
Good Shepherd Cl
  HORF/LLZ BS7 ..... 325 L7
Goodwin Ct *GL* GL1 ..... 136 A4
Goodwin Dr *HGRV/WHIT* BS14 ..... 346 B7
Goodwood Gdns
  MANG/FISH BS16 ..... 328 B2
Goodyere St *GL* GL1 ..... 4 F8
Goolden St
  BRSG/KWL/STAPK BS4 ..... 336 C8
Goose Acre *ALMDB* BS32 ..... 317 H5
  ALMDB BS32 ..... 317 J5
Goosegreen *FRCTL/WBN* BS36 ..... 318 D3
Goose Gn
  OLD/WMLY/WICK BS30 ..... 338 E2
  YATE/CS BS37 ..... 310 A8
Goose Green Wy *YATE/CS* BS37 ..... 309 L7
Gooseland Cl
  HGRV/WHIT BS14 ..... 346 B8
Gooselands *MALM* SN16 ..... 283 M6
Goose La *CIND* GL14 ..... 157 H3
  STRAT GL19 ..... 9 K1
Gopshill La *COTS* GL54 ..... 73 M2
Gordon Av *EVILLE/WHL* BS5 ..... 337 C2
Gordon Cl *EVILLE/WHL* BS5 ..... 337 C2
  VGL GL2 ..... 111 C6
Gordon Rd *CBRISNE* BS2 ..... 336 B2
  CHELTS GL53 ..... 115 L6
  EVILLE/WHL BS5 ..... 336 F1
Gore Rd *BMSTR* BS3 ..... 335 J8
Gore's Marsh Rd *BMSTR* BS3 ..... 345 J1
Gorham Cl *AVONM* BS11 ..... 324 C1
Gorlands Rd *YATE/CS* BS37 ..... 320 E2
Gorlangton Cl
  HGRV/WHIT BS14 ..... 346 C4
Gorse Cl *COTS* GL54 ..... 123 K6
  GLE GL4 ..... 137 H7
Gorse Cover Rd
  THNB/SVB BS35 ..... 304 C4
Gorse HI *EVE* WR11 ..... 29 K1
Gorse La *CFTN/FAIL* BS8 ..... 6 A4
  CHPMW/MSHF SN14 ..... 341 C3
  CLFD GL16 ..... 175 L6
Gorse Meadow *COTS* GL54 ..... 123 K7
The Gorse *COTS* GL54 ..... 123 J6

Gorsley Gdns *RWYE* HR9 ..... 84 E3
Gosditch *HGHW* SN6 ..... 264 E7
  HGHW SN6 ..... 287 C3
Gosditch St *CIR* GL7 ..... 238 C2
Gosforth Rd
  HNBRY/STHM BS10 ..... 325 K2
Goshawk Rd *VGL* GL2 ..... 135 H8
Goslet Rd *HGRV/WHIT* BS14 ..... 347 G6
Gossington Br *VGL* GL2 ..... 228 F3
Goss Wood Cnr *VGL* GL2 ..... 159 G3
Gotherington Flds
  CHELTE/BC GL52 ..... 72 A3
Gotherington La
  CHELTE/BC GL52 ..... 72 C6
Gotley Rd
  BRSG/KWL/STAPK BS4 ..... 346 F1
Gott Dr *BRSG/KWL/STAPK* BS4 ..... 336 F6
Gouda Wy *GL* GL1 ..... 4 E3
Gould Dr *TEWK* GL20 ..... 49 G2
Goulston Rd
  BMSTRD/HC/WWD BS13 ..... 345 J6
Goulston Wk
  BMSTRD/HC/WWD BS13 ..... 345 J6
Goulter St *EVILLE/WHL* BS5 ..... 336 D5
Gourney Cl *AVONM* BS11 ..... 324 D1
Gover Rd *KGWD/HNM* BS15 ..... 337 L8
Gowle Rd *STROUD* GL5 ..... 208 F5
Grace Cl *YATE/CS* BS37 ..... 320 E2
Grace Ct *MANG/FISH* BS16 ..... 327 M5
Grace Dr *COTS* GL54 ..... 169 J1
  KGWD/HNM BS15 ..... 338 C2
Grace Park Rd
  BRSG/KWL/STAPK BS4 ..... 346 F2
Grace Rd *MANG/FISH* BS16 ..... 327 L6
Graces Pitch *NWNT* GL18 ..... 86 C3
Grace Cl *MANG/FISH* BS16 ..... 327 J7
Grafton La *RTEWK/TIB* GL19 ..... 44 D5
Grafton Rd *CHELT* GL50 ..... 115 L4
  VGL GL2 ..... 5 M3
Graham Pl *CHELTW* GL51 ..... 92 F8
Graham Rd *BMSTR* BS3 ..... 335 L8
  EVILLE/WHL BS5 ..... 336 D2
  MANG/FISH BS16 ..... 328 B3
Grahamstown Gv *CHEP* NP16 ..... 270 D3
Grahamstown Rd *CHEP* NP16 ..... 270 C3
Grainger Ct *AVONM* BS11 ..... 324 A4
Grampian Cl
  OLD/WMLY/WICK BS30 ..... 338 E7
Granbrook La *CHCAM* GL55 ..... 9 G7
Granby HI *CFTN/FAIL* BS8 ..... 335 H5
Granby Rd *SHPSTR* CV36 ..... 16 D1
Grandmother's Rock La
  OLD/WMLY/WICK BS30 ..... 349 M1
Grange Av *BRSTK/PCHW* BS34 ..... 316 C5
  KGWD/HNM BS15 ..... 337 M6
Grange Cl *ALMDB* BS32 ..... 316 E1
  RSTROUD/NAIL GL6 ..... 233 H5
Grange Cl North
  HNLZ/SM/SNYPK/WT BS9 ..... 325 K5
Grange Ct *CIR* GL7 ..... 214 B7
  KGWD/HNM BS15 ..... 337 M6
  TEWK GL20 ..... 49 H2
Grange Court La
  RTEWK/TIB GL19 ..... 108 C8
Grange Court Rd *CIND* GL14 ..... 132 D7
  HNLZ/SM/SNYPK/WT BS9 ..... 325 J5
Grange Dr *CHELTE/BC* GL52 ..... 72 B8
  MANG/FISH BS16 ..... 327 L5
Grange Pk
  HNLZ/SM/SNYPK/WT BS9 ..... 325 K5
  MANG/FISH BS16 ..... 327 L3
  RWYE HR9 ..... 126 D4
Grange Rd
  BMSTRD/HC/WWD BS13 ..... 345 J6
  CFTN/FAIL BS8 ..... 335 J4
  GL GL1 ..... 159 L1
  GLE GL4 ..... 159 M2
  KEYN BS31 ..... 348 C4
  TEWK GL20 ..... 49 H2
The Grange *CHNTN* OX7 ..... 104 B7
  HNLZ/SM/SNYPK/WT BS9 ..... 324 F4
Grange Vw *STROUD* GL5 ..... 208 E3
Grangeville Cl
  OLD/WMLY/WICK BS30 ..... 338 D8
Grange Wk *CHELTS* GL53 ..... 116 D6
Grangewood Cl
  MANG/FISH BS16 ..... 327 L5
Granley Cl *CHELTW* GL51 ..... 115 H3
Granley Dr *CHELTW* GL51 ..... 115 H3
Granley Gdns *CHELTW* GL51 ..... 115 H3
Granley Rd *CHELTW* GL51 ..... 115 H3
Granna La *CHELTE/BC* GL52 ..... 72 F3
Granny's La
  KGWD/HNM BS15 ..... 338 A5
Gransmoor Gra *BWTH/CHD* GL3 ..... 137 K4
Grantham La
  KGWD/HNM BS15 ..... 337 L3
Grantham Rd *KGWD/HNM* BS15 ..... 337 L2
Grantley Crs *CIR* GL7 ..... 238 C4
Grantson Cl
  BRSG/KWL/STAPK BS4 ..... 347 C1
Granville Cl *KGWD/HNM* BS15 ..... 337 K8
Granville Rd *CBATH/BATHN* BA1 ..... 351 J4
Granville St *CHELT* GL50 ..... 2 B3
  EVILLE/WHL BS5 ..... 336 E5
  GL GL1 ..... 135 L5
Grasby Cl *GLE* GL4 ..... 137 G4
Grasington Dr *YATE/CS* BS37 ..... 320 C2
Grasmere Cl
  HNBRY/STHM BS10 ..... 325 J3
Grasmere Rd *CHELTW* GL51 ..... 115 H4
  VGL GL2 ..... 112 E7
Grass Meers Dr
  HGRV/WHIT BS14 ..... 346 C7
Grassmere Gdns
  OLD/WMLY/WICK BS30 ..... 338 F5
Gratitude Rd *EVILLE/WHL* BS5 ..... 336 C2
Gratton Rd *CHELT* GL50 ..... 115 L5
Gratton St *CHELT* GL50 ..... 2 C9
Gravel Hill Rd *YATE/CS* BS37 ..... 310 B2
Gravel Pit La *CHELTE/BC* GL52 ..... 94 E6
Gravel Pits Cl *TEWK* GL20 ..... 27 H5
Gravel Pits Rd *CHELTE/BC* GL52 ..... 94 E3
Graveney Cl
  BRSG/KWL/STAPK BS4 ..... 346 F2
Graveney Rd *COTS* GL54 ..... 169 J1
Gravney Ct *CHELTW* GL51 ..... 93 G7
Gray Cl *VGL* GL2 ..... 112 E4

Grayle Rd *HNBRY/STHM* BS10 ..... 315 H8
Grayling Cl *GLE* GL4 ..... 137 G7
Gray Rd *CIR* GL7 ..... 238 C2
Gray's Cl *HNBRY/STHM* BS10 ..... 325 G1
Gray's La *MLS6* 58 D6
Grayston Cl *TEWK* GL20 ..... 48 C3
Great Ann St *CBRISNE* BS2 ..... 7 K2
Great Brockeridge
  HNLZ/SM/SNYPK/WT BS9 ..... 325 H5
Great Dowles
  OLD/WMLY/WICK BS30 ..... 338 C7
Greatfield Dr *CHELTS* GL53 ..... 116 B6
Greatfield La *CHELTW* GL51 ..... 115 H6
Great George St *CBRIS/FH* BS1 ..... 6 B4
  CBRISNE BS2 ..... 7 J2
Great Gv *GLE* GL4 ..... 136 F4
Great Hayles Rd
  HGRV/WHIT BS14 ..... 346 C4
Great Leaze
  OLD/WMLY/WICK BS30 ..... 338 C7
Great Meadow Rd *ALMDB* BS32 ..... 317 H4
Great Norwood St *CHELT* GL50 ..... 2 B9
Great Park Rd *ALMDB* BS32 ..... 306 E8
Great Stoke Wy
  BRSTK/PCHW BS34 ..... 316 F8
  BRSTK/PCHW BS34 ..... 326 F1
Great Western Ct *GL* GL1 ..... 5 J7
Great Western La
  EVILLE/WHL BS5 ..... 336 E5
Great Western Rd
  BRKLY GL13 ..... 226 D2
  CHELT GL50 ..... 2 A4
  GL GL1 ..... 5 G5
Great Western Ter *CHELT* GL50 ..... 2 A4
Grebe Cl *GLE* GL4 ..... 136 E6
Grebe Sq *COTS* GL54 ..... 124 C7
Green Acre *BWTH/CHD* GL3 ..... 138 A6
  LYD GL15 ..... 200 D4
Greenacre Rd *HGRV/WHIT* BS14 ..... 346 C5
Greenacres *CBATH/BATHN* BA1 ..... 350 D8
  TEWK GL20 ..... 26 B4
Greenaways *NWNT* GL18 ..... 86 B2
Green Bank *BWTH/CHD* GL3 ..... 138 A7
Greenbank Av *EVILLE/WHL* BS5 ..... 336 C2
Greenbank Av West
  EVILLE/WHL BS5 ..... 336 D2
Greenbank Cl *MTCHDN* GL17 ..... 129 M5
Greenbank Rd *BMSTR* BS3 ..... 335 J7
  EVILLE/WHL BS5 ..... 336 C2
  KGWD/HNM BS15 ..... 337 M6
Greenbank Vw
  EVILLE/WHL BS5 ..... 336 E1
Green Cl *BDWAY* WR12 ..... 32 A1
  BWTH/CHD GL3 ..... 138 A7
  DSLY GL11 ..... 254 C1
Green Cft *EVILLE/WHL* BS5 ..... 337 J2
Greendale Rd *BMSTR* BS3 ..... 336 A8
  RDLND/MONT BS6 ..... 325 K7
Green Dell Cl
  HNBRY/STHM BS10 ..... 314 F8
Greenditch Av
  BMSTRD/HC/WWD BS13 ..... 345 L6
Greenditch St *THNB/SVB* BS35 ..... 305 L2
Greendown *EVILLE/WHL* BS5 ..... 337 J4
Green Dragon Rd
  FRCTL/WBN BS36 ..... 317 M6
Greenfield Av
  HNBRY/STHM BS10 ..... 325 M3
Greenfield Rd *CLFD* GL16 ..... 151 K8
  HNBRY/STHM BS10 ..... 325 M2
  MTCHDN GL17 ..... 128 C6
Greenfields Cl *SHPSTR* CV36 ..... 16 B6
Green Gdns *BWTH/CHD* GL3 ..... 138 A7
Green Hayes *YATE/CS* BS37 ..... 320 E3
Greenhill *THNB/SVB* BS35 ..... 293 K2
Greenhill Cl *CIND* GL14 ..... 154 C3
Greenhill Ct *GL* GL1 ..... 159 J1
Greenhill Down
  THNB/SVB BS35 ..... 293 J2
Greenhill Gdns *THNB/SVB* BS35 ..... 293 J2
Greenhill Gv *BMSTR* BS3 ..... 345 J1
Greenhill La *AVONM* BS11 ..... 324 E2
  THNB/SVB BS35 ..... 293 H8
Greenhill Rd *THNB/SVB* BS35 ..... 293 J2
Greenhills Cl *CHELTS* GL53 ..... 116 A6
Greenhills Rd *CHELTS* GL53 ..... 116 A6
Greenhouse La
  RSTROUD/NAIL GL6 ..... 185 J4
The Greenings
  CHELTW GL51 ..... 115 H6
Greenlands Wy
  HNBRY/STHM BS10 ..... 315 G7
Green La *BWTH/CHD* GL3 ..... 113 L8
  BWTH/CHD GL3 ..... 137 J5
  BWTH/CHD GL3 ..... 138 A5
  CHPMW/MSHF SN14 ..... 342 A3
  CHPMW/MSHF SN14 ..... 343 J8
  COTS GL54 ..... 167 L1
  FRCTL/WBN BS36 ..... 317 L4
  HNBRY/STHM BS10 ..... 314 E2
  MIM GL56 ..... 81 G4
  RWYE HR9 ..... 106 B2
  SHPSTR CV36 ..... 16 B6
  TEWK GL20 ..... 48 E4
  THNB/SVB BS35 ..... 304 D3
  VGL GL2 ..... 159 G5
  VGL GL2 ..... 182 C4
  WUE GL12 ..... 294 D2
Green Lane Cl *COTS* GL54 ..... 123 G4
  SHPSTR CV36 ..... 16 B6
Greenleaze
  BRSG/KWL/STAPK BS4 ..... 346 D1
Greenleaze Av
  MANG/FISH BS16 ..... 327 M2
Green Meadow Bank
  CHELTE/BC GL52 ..... 72 A7
Greenmore Rd
  BRSG/KWL/STAPK BS4 ..... 346 D1
Greenore *KGWD/HNM* BS15 ..... 337 L4
Greenpark Rd
  HNBRY/STHM BS10 ..... 326 A2
Greenridge Cl
  BMSTRD/HC/WWD BS13 ..... 345 G7
Green's Cl *COTS* GL54 ..... 148 B4
Green Side *MANG/FISH* BS16 ..... 328 C6
Greenside Cl
  HNBRY/STHM BS10 ..... 314 F8
Green St *BMSTR* BS3 ..... 7 J9

BWTH/CHD GL3 .... 138 A7
CHEP NP16 .... 270 A4
DSLY GL11 .... 229 L6
Greenstreet STNHO GL10 .... 207 H3 7
Green St TEWK GL20 .... 46 F3
The Green BRSTK/PCHW BS34 .... 317 G7
CHCAM GL55 .... 34 E1
CHNTN OX7 .... 83 J6
CHNTN OX7 .... 104 C6
CIND GL14 .... 155 H7
CIR GL7 .... 238 E3
CIR GL7 .... 242 D4
DSLY GL11 .... 254 E1 1
KGWD/HNM BS15 .... 338 A1
MALM SN16 .... 285 G3
MIM GL56 .... 58 D5 1
SHPSTR CV36 .... 59 M1
TET GL8 .... 282 A4
THNB/SVB BS35 .... 306 C1
WUE GL12 .... 295 K3
Greenview
OLD/WMLY/WICK BS30 .... 348 C1 1
Green Wk
BRSG/KWL/STAPK BS4 .... 346 C2 1
Green Wy BWTH/CHD GL3 .... 138 A6
Greenway CHELTE/BC GL52 .... 72 D8
Greenway Bush La BMSTR BS3 .. 335 J7
Greenway Cl CHELTW GL51 .... 138 F2 1
Greenway Dr
HNBRY/STHM BS10 .... 325 M3 2
Greenway La CHELTE/BC GL52 .... 116 D4
CHELTS GL53 .... 139 K4
CHELTW GL51 .... 138 F2
CHPMW/MSHF SN14 .... 340 F7
COTS GL54 .... 74 A2
Greenway Pk
HNBRY/STHM BS10 .... 325 M3 3
Greenway Rd CIND GL14 .... 154 A4
MIM GL56 .... 35 G8
RDLND/MONT BS6 .... 335 K1
SHPSTR CV36 .... 16 A5
Greenways COTS GL54 .... 74 D4 1
KGWD/HNM BS15 .... 338 C2 1
LYD GL15 .... 201 H8
Greenways Dr CLFD GL16 .... 175 L3
Greenways Rd YATE/CS BS37 .... 310 B7
The Greenway
MANG/FISH BS16 .... 327 L8 3
Greenwood Cl BWTH/CHD GL3 .... 137 K5
HORF/LLZ BS7 .... 326 A4 2
Greenwood Dr THNB/SVB BS35 .. 293 H7
Greenwood Rd
BRSG/KWL/STAPK BS4 .... 346 C2 2
Greet Rd COTS GL54 .... 74 D5
Gregory Ct
OLD/WMLY/WICK BS30 .... 338 C5 1
Grenadier Cl BWTH/CHD GL3 .... 137 H5
Grenadier Rd CHELTW GL51 .... 93 G7 2
Grenville Cl BWTH/CHD GL3 .... 113 H3
EVILLE/WHL BS5 .... 337 H3
Grenville Pl CBRIS/FH BS1 .... 335 H6 4
Grenville Rd RDLND/MONT BS6 .. 326 A8
Gretton Rd CHELTE/BC GL52 .... 72 E3
COTS GL54 .... 74 C4
Greve Ct
OLD/WMLY/WICK BS30 .... 338 B7 3
Grevel La CHCAM GL55 .... 12 E7
Greville Cl GL GL1 .... 112 A7
Greville Ct CHELTW GL51 .... 115 H3 3
Greville Rd BMSTR BS3 .... 6 A9
Greville St BMSTR BS3 .... 6 C9
Grevil Rd CHELTW GL51 .... 93 H7
Greyfriars Wk CIR GL7 .... 238 B5 2
Greygoose La MIM GL56 .... 82 D5
Greyhound Gdns VGL GL2 .... 112 F6
Greylag Crs TEWK GL20 .... 48 C6
Greylands Rd
BMSTRD/HC/WWD BS13 .... 345 H4
Greys Cl RSTROUD/NAIL GL6 .... 209 M7 2
Greystoke Av
HNBRY/STHM BS10 .... 325 J3
Greystoke Gdns
HNLZ/SM/SNYPK/WT BS9 .... 325 J3 2
Greystones MANG/FISH BS16 .. 328 A2 1
Greystones La COTS GL54 .... 123 J5
Grierson Cl BWTH/CHD GL3 .... 137 K5 1
Griffin Cl COTS GL54 .... 102 B3
Griffiths Av CHELTW GL51 .... 115 H3
Griffon Cl VGL GL2 .... 135 H8
Griggfield Wk
HGRV/WHIT BS14 .... 346 B4 1
Griggs Cl CHCAM GL55 .... 12 E8
Grimsbury Rd
KGWD/HNM BS15 .... 338 C3
Grimwade Cl CHELTW GL51 .... 115 H2
Grindell Rd EVILLE/WHL BS5 .... 336 F4
Grinfield Av
BMSTRD/HC/WWD BS13 .... 345 L7
Grinfield Cl
BMSTRD/HC/WWD BS13 .... 345 L7 3
Grinfield Ct
BMSTRD/HC/WWD BS13 .... 345 L7 4
Grisedale Cl VGL GL2 .... 112 E6
Grist Mill Cl CHELTW GL51 .... 92 F6
Grittleton Rd HORF/LLZ BS7 .... 326 A3
Grocyn Cl
CHPMW/MSHF SN14 .... 343 K8 1
Grosvenor Pl South
CHELTE/BC GL52 .... 2 E5
Grosvenor Rd CBRISNE BS2 .... 336 A3
STNHO GL10 .... 207 H2
VGL GL2 .... 5 M5
Grosvenor St CHELTE/BC GL52 .... 2 E6
Grosvenor Ter CHELTE/BC GL52 .... 2 E5
Ground CHNTN OX7 .... 149 L1 1
Grove Av CBRIS/FH BS1 .... 6 F6
HNLZ/SM/SNYPK/WT BS9 .... 324 E4
Grove Bank MANG/FISH BS16 .... 327 L2
Grove Crs CLFD GL16 .... 151 K8
GLE GL4 .... 136 F2
Grovefield RTEWK/TIB GL19 .... 44 D4
Grovefield Wy CHELTW GL51 .... 114 D4
Grove Gdns TET GL8 .... 281 M2
Grovelands GLE GL4 .... 137 G2
Grovelands Cl CHELTS GL53 .... 116 C5 2
Grove La CHPMW/MSHF SN14 .... 330 E4
CIR GL7 .... 238 D2
LYD GL15 .... 201 K5
VGL GL2 .... 182 B7
Grove Pk
BRSG/KWL/STAPK BS4 .... 346 F1 3
RDLND/MONT BS6 .... 335 L1
Grove Park Av
BRSG/KWL/STAPK BS4 .... 346 F1
Grove Park Rd
BRSG/KWL/STAPK BS4 .... 346 F1
STROUD GL5 .... 208 E3
Grove Rd BWTH/CHD GL3 .... 113 H5
CLFD GL16 .... 151 J5
HNLZ/SM/SNYPK/WT BS9 .... 324 F3
LYD GL15 .... 201 G2
LYD GL15 .... 201 H8
MANG/FISH BS16 .... 327 G7
RDLND/MONT BS6 .... 335 K1
Grovesend Rd THNB/SVB BS35 .. 293 K3
THNB/SVB BS35 .... 294 A4
Grove St CHELT GL50 .... 2 B4
GL GL1 .... 5 H9
The Grove CBRIS/FH BS1 .... 6 E6
CHELT GL50 .... 115 K3
CHELTE/BC GL52 .... 3 J6
MALM SN16 .... 284 E2
MIM GL56 .... 58 E6 1
OLD/WMLY/WICK BS30 .... 338 C7
STROUD GL5 .... 207 M7
TET GL8 .... 257 L3
YATE/CS BS37 .... 309 J3
Grove Vw MANG/FISH BS16 .... 327 G5 1
Guernsey Av
BRSG/KWL/STAPK BS4 .... 337 H7
Guest Av MANG/FISH BS16 .... 328 D5
Guggle La COTS GL54 .... 169 J1
Guildford Rd BRSG/KWL/STAPK BS4 337 G6
Guildings Wy STNHO GL10 .... 207 J6
Guinea La MANG/FISH BS16 .... 327 J6 3
Guinea St CBRIS/FH BS1 .... 6 F7
GL GL1 .... 5 G3
Guise Av BWTH/CHD GL3 .... 138 B7
Guise Cl VGL GL2 .... 159 H3
Gullimores Gdns
BMSTRD/HC/WWD BS13 .... 345 K7 2
Gullivers Pl YATE/CS BS37 .... 320 C3
Gullons Cl
BMSTRD/HC/WWD BS13 .... 345 J5 2
Gullon Wk
BMSTRD/HC/WWD BS13 .... 345 H6
Gully La BRKLY GL13 .... 274 A4
The Gully FRCTL/WBN BS36 .... 318 B4
Gumstool Hl TET GL8 .... 282 A4 2
Gunhouse La STROUD GL5 .... 208 F6
Gunning Cl KGWD/HNM BS15 .... 337 M5
Gunter's Hl EVILLE/WHL BS5 .... 337 J5 2
Gupshill Cl TEWK GL20 .... 48 A8 1
Gurney Av GLE GL4 .... 159 M1
Guthrie Rd CFTN/FAIL BS8 .... 335 J3
Gwentlands Cl CHEP NP16 .... 270 A4
Gwernant Rd CHELTW GL51 .... 115 H5
Gwilliam St BMSTR BS3 .... 335 M8
Gwinnette Ct CHELTW GL51 .... 139 G1
Gwy Ct CHEP NP16 .... 270 B2 1
Gwyn St CBRISNE BS2 .... 336 A2
Gyde Rd RSTROUD/NAIL GL6 .... 185 H2
Gypsy La NWNT GL18 .... 85 G5

H

Hackers La CHNTN OX7 .... 105 G7
Hacket Hl THNB/SVB BS35 .... 294 B3
Hacket La THNB/SVB BS35 .... 294 A3
Hack La SHPSTR CV36 .... 61 G2
Hadfield Cl RTEWK/TIB GL19 .... 66 D4
Hadley Ct
OLD/WMLY/WICK BS30 .... 338 D5 2
Hadley Rd DSLY GL11 .... 229 G7
Hadow Wy VGL GL2 .... 159 H3
Hadrian Cl
HNLZ/SM/SNYPK/WT BS9 .... 324 E7 2
LYD GL15 .... 201 K7
Hadrians Wy GLE GL4 .... 137 H4
Hague Av DSLY GL11 .... 229 H7 1
Hailes Rd GLE GL4 .... 136 F4
Hailes St COTS GL54 .... 74 D6
Hailey Av CHNTN OX7 .... 105 M2
Hailey Rd CHNTN OX7 .... 105 M2
Hakeburn Rd CIR GL7 .... 238 C2 3
Halbrow Crs MANG/FISH BS16 .... 327 L6
Haldon Cl BMSTR BS3 .... 345 M2
Hale Cl KGWD/HNM BS15 .... 337 M7 1
Hale La RSTROUD/NAIL GL6 .... 185 H3
Hales Cl CHELTE/BC GL52 .... 3 K5
Hales Horn Cl ALMDB BS32 .... 316 F5
Hale's Rd CHELTE/BC GL52 .... 3 H7
Halfacre Cl HGRV/WHIT BS14 .... 346 C8
Halfacre La HGRV/WHIT BS14 .... 346 D8
Halfway Br VGL GL2 .... 133 J1
Halfway Pitch
RSTROUD/NAIL GL6 .... 184 D7
Halifax Rd YATE/CS BS37 .... 309 M7
Halland Rd CHELTS GL53 .... 115 M6
Hallards Cl AVONM BS11 .... 324 B3
Hallen Cl HNBRY/STHM BS10 .... 314 F8
Hall End La YATE/CS BS37 .... 309 L1
Hallen Dr
HNLZ/SM/SNYPK/WT BS9 .... 324 E4
Hallen Rd HNBRY/STHM BS10 .... 314 E7
HNBRY/STHM BS10 .... 315 G8
Hall La CBATH/BATHN BA1 .... 350 D1
CBATH/BATHN BA1 .... 351 G1
CHPMW/MSHF SN14 .... 341 G8
YATE/CS BS37 .... 311 M6
Hallmead Cl CHELTW GL51 .... 92 F6 3
Hall Rd CHELTS GL53 .... 115 M7
Hallsfield HGHW SN6 .... 288 F3
Halls Rd KGWD/HNM BS15 .... 337 M3 3
Hall St BMSTR BS3 .... 345 K1
Halmore La BRKLY GL13 .... 227 J3
Halsbury Rd RDLND/MONT BS6 .. 325 K7
Halstock Av
MANG/FISH BS16 .... 327 H8 3
Halston Dr CBRISNE BS2 .... 336 B3
Halswell Gdns
BMSTRD/HC/WWD BS13 .... 345 K7
Halt End HGRV/WHIT BS14 .... 346 E8
Halwyn Cl
HNLZ/SM/SNYPK/WT BS9 .... 324 F6 2
Hamble Cl THNB/SVB BS35 .... 293 L3
Hambledon Cl CIR GL7 .... 239 G8 1
Hambridge La CIR GL7 .... 244 E6
Hambrook La
BRSTK/PCHW BS34 .... 317 H7
Hambrook St CHELTE/BC GL52 .... 116 D4
Hambutts Dr
RSTROUD/NAIL GL6 .... 185 G3
Hambutts Md
RSTROUD/NAIL GL6 .... 185 G3
Ham Cl CHELTE/BC GL52 .... 116 E4
Hamer St VGL GL2 .... 5 K6
Ham Farm La MANG/FISH BS16 .. 328 D5
Hamfield La BRKLY GL13 .... 226 E8
Hamilton Cft CIR GL7 .... 241 K7
Hamilton Rd BMSTR BS3 .... 6 B8
EVILLE/WHL BS5 .... 336 C3 3
Hamilton St CHELTS GL53 .... 116 C4 2
Ham La CIR GL7 .... 263 H5
CIR GL7 .... 267 G5
LGASH BS41 .... 344 F8
MANG/FISH BS16 .... 327 G5
OLD/WMLY/WICK BS30 .... 340 A2
THNB/SVB BS35 .... 272 E5
Hamlen Cl RTEWK/TIB GL19 .... 108 C7
Hamlet Cl CHELTW GL51 .... 115 G1
Hammersmith Bottom CIR GL7 .. 219 L6
Hammersmith Rd
EVILLE/WHL BS5 .... 336 F3 3
Ham Mill La STROUD GL5 .... 208 F8
Hammond Cl
BRSG/KWL/STAPK BS4 .... 346 F2 3
Hammond Dr COTS GL54 .... 169 J1 3
Hammond Gdns
HNLZ/SM/SNYPK/WT BS9 .... 325 G4 1
Hammonds HGHW SN6 .... 289 G3 1
Hammond Wy CIR GL7 .... 238 B3 1
GLE GL4 .... 136 F2 1
Hampden Cl YATE/CS BS37 .... 309 M7
Hampden Rd
BRSG/KWL/STAPK BS4 .... 336 D8 1
Hampden Wy GL GL1 .... 4 F6
Hampshire Gdns CLFD GL16 .... 175 J2
Hampshire Wy YATE/CS BS37 .. 310 B7 3
Hampstead Rd
BRSG/KWL/STAPK BS4 .... 336 E8
Hampton Cl BWTH/CHD GL3 .... 137 K4 1
CHELT GL50 .... 115 J6 3
OLD/WMLY/WICK BS30 .... 338 C6
Hampton Gv CIR GL7 .... 241 K6
Hampton Hl TET GL8 .... 257 L1
Hampton La RDLND/MONT BS6 .. 335 K2
Hampton Pk
RDLND/MONT BS6 .... 335 K2 3
Hampton Pl BWTH/CHD GL3 .... 113 J3
Hampton Rd
RDLND/MONT BS6 .... 335 K1
Hampton St
KGWD/HNM BS15 .... 337 M2 1
TET GL8 .... 281 M3
Ham Rd CHELTE/BC GL52 .... 116 E4
RTEWK/TIB GL19 .... 89 K2
Hams Rd KEYN BS31 .... 348 B4
LYD GL15 .... 201 K8
The Ham DSLY GL11 .... 230 C6
Hanbury Cl KGWD/HNM BS15 .... 337 M6
Hanbury Rd CFTN/FAIL BS8 .... 335 J3
Handel Av EVILLE/WHL BS5 .... 336 F4 3
Handel Rd KEYN BS31 .... 347 M6
Handford Wy
OLD/WMLY/WICK BS30 .... 338 D8 1
Hanford Ct HGRV/WHIT BS14 .. 346 F4 2
Hang Hill Rd LYD GL15 .... 200 C2
Hanham Rd KGWD/HNM BS15 .... 337 M5
Hanks Cl MALM SN16 .... 303 J6
Hanley La CHEP NP16 .... 246 F4
Hanman Rd GL GL1 .... 136 A4
Hannah Crs CIR GL7 .... 239 H7
Hannah Pl VGL GL2 .... 113 G4
Hannam Cl CHELTS GL53 .... 115 M7
Hannington Br HGHW SN6 .... 267 K6
Hannis Rd CHNTN OX7 .... 105 M2
Hanover Ct CBRIS/FH BS1 .... 7 H2 2
Hanover Pl CBRIS/FH BS1 .... 6 B7
Hanover St CHELT GL50 .... 2 D2
EVILLE/WHL BS5 .... 336 E4 2
Hanover Wy BWTH/CHD GL3 .... 113 H4
Hanson Av SHPSTR CV36 .... 16 A6 2
Hanstone Cl CIR GL7 .... 238 B5
Harbour Rd LYD GL15 .... 225 K3
Harbourside TEWK GL20 .... 48 B4
Harbour Vw TEWK GL20 .... 48 B4 1
Harbour Wall
HNLZ/SM/SNYPK/WT BS9 .... 324 E7 3
Harbour Wy CBRIS/FH BS1 .... 6 C6
Harbury Ms GL GL1 .... 5 K9
Harbury Rd
HNLZ/SM/SNYPK/WT BS9 .... 325 L4
Harcombe Hl FRCTL/WBN BS36 .. 318 A7
Harcombe Rd
FRCTL/WBN BS36 .... 317 M6
Harcourt Av EVILLE/WHL BS5 .. 337 J5 3
Harcourt Hl RDLND/MONT BS6 .. 325 L8
Harcourt Rd RDLND/MONT BS6 .. 325 K7
Hardenhuish Rd
BRSG/KWL/STAPK BS4 .... 336 F6
Harden Rd HGRV/WHIT BS14 .... 347 G6
Harding's Dr DSLY GL11 .... 253 J2
Hardwick Av CHEP NP16 .... 270 A3 1
Hardwick Bank Rd TEWK GL20 .... 26 E8
Hardwick Cl
BRSG/KWL/STAPK BS4 .... 337 G8
OLD/WMLY/WICK BS30 .... 338 F6 1
Hardwicke YATE/CS BS37 .... 319 L4
Hardy Av BMSTR BS3 .... 335 J8
Hardy Ct
OLD/WMLY/WICK BS30 .... 338 B6
Hardy La ALMDB BS32 .... 306 B3
Hardy Rd BMSTR BS3 .... 345 K1 3
CHELTE/BC GL52 .... 72 C7
Harebell Pl GLE GL4 .... 136 F6
Hareclive Rd
BMSTRD/HC/WWD BS13 .... 345 K6
Harefield Cl
KGWD/HNM BS15 .... 347 L1 2
Hare La GL GL1 .... 4 F5
Harescombe YATE/CS BS37 .... 320 A4
Haresdown Hl CIR GL7 .... 260 B4
Haresfield CIR GL7 .... 214 B7
Haresfield La VGL GL2 .... 159 H6
Harewood Cl GL GL1 .... 159 L2
Harewood Rd EVILLE/WHL BS5 .. 337 J2
Harford Br COTS GL54 .... 121 M1
Harford Cl
HNLZ/SM/SNYPK/WT BS9 .... 324 E4 1
Harford Dr MANG/FISH BS16 .... 327 L2
Harlech Wy
OLD/WMLY/WICK BS30 .... 348 D1
Harleston St EVILLE/WHL BS5 .... 7 K1
Harleys Fld GLE GL4 .... 136 F4
Harmer Cl HNBRY/STHM BS10 .... 315 H8
Harnham La COTS GL54 .... 142 F7
Harnhill Cl
BMSTRD/HC/WWD BS13 .... 345 K7 3
Harold Rd LYD GL15 .... 177 L8
Harolds Wy KGWD/HNM BS15 .... 337 L5
Harper Rd STROUD GL5 .... 208 A3 1
Harper's La MALM SN16 .... 303 H8
Harpfield Rd CHELTE/BC GL52 .... 94 B1
Harp Hl CHELTE/BC GL52 .... 3 L5
Harptree Ct
OLD/WMLY/WICK BS30 .... 338 C7 2
Harptree Gv BMSTR BS3 .... 345 K1 2
Harrington Av
HGRV/WHIT BS14 .... 347 G5
Harrington Cl
OLD/WMLY/WICK BS30 .... 349 G3
Harrington Dr CHELTW GL51 ... 115 G4 1
Harrington Gv
HGRV/WHIT BS14 .... 347 G5 3
Harrington Rd
HGRV/WHIT BS14 .... 347 G5
Harrington Wk
HGRV/WHIT BS14 .... 347 G5 4
Harris Barton FRCTL/WBN BS36 .. 318 C4
Harris Cl BWTH/CHD GL3 .... 113 L6
Harris Ct
OLD/WMLY/WICK BS30 .... 338 B7 3
Harris Gdns COTS GL54 .... 124 C7 2
Harris La CFTN/FAIL BS8 .... 334 B3
Harrison Cl CIND GL14 .... 155 H7 1
MANG/FISH BS16 .... 328 D5 2
Harrison Rd CHELTW GL51 .... 138 F1
Harrison Wy LYD GL15 .... 225 L1
Harris Rd HGHW SN6 .... 287 J2
Harrowdene Rd
BRSG/KWL/STAPK BS4 .... 336 D8
Harrow Rd
BRSG/KWL/STAPK BS4 .... 336 F8
Harry Stoke Rd
BRSTK/PCHW BS34 .... 317 G8
Harry Yates Wy CHELTW GL51 .... 92 F7
Hartbury Cl CHELTW GL51 .... 92 E8
Hartcliffe Rd
BRSG/KWL/STAPK BS4 .... 346 A3
Hartcliffe Wk
BRSG/KWL/STAPK BS4 .... 346 B3 1
Hartcliffe Wy BMSTR BS3 .... 345 L2
BRSG/KWL/STAPK BS4 .... 345 L4
Hartfield Av RDLND/MONT BS6 .. 335 L3
Hartgill Cl
BMSTRD/HC/WWD BS13 .... 345 K8
Hart Gn CIND GL14 .... 154 A5
Hartington Pk
RDLND/MONT BS6 .... 335 K1 3
Hartington Rd GL GL1 .... 135 L5
Hartland Rd GLE GL4 .... 136 B5
Hart La MTCHDN GL17 .... 129 G3
Hartlebury Wy
CHELTE/BC GL52 .... 116 E5
Hartley Bridge Hl
RSTROUD/NAIL GL6 .... 256 B3
Hartley Cl CHELTS GL53 .... 116 B7
YATE/CS BS37 .... 320 E2
Harts Cft YATE/CS BS37 .... 310 B7 4
Harvest Cl ALMDB BS32 .... 316 F2
Harvesters Vw
CHELTE/BC GL52 .... 71 M7 4
Harvest Gv CHELTW GL51 .... 92 F6 4
Harvest Wy VGL GL2 .... 159 H4
Harvey Cl VGL GL2 .... 135 L6
Harvey's La COTS GL54 .... 74 B6
Harwell Cl GLE GL4 .... 159 M2 3
Hasfield Cl VGL GL2 .... 159 G2
Hasfield Rd RTEWK/TIB GL19 .... 67 H7
Haskins Ct
OLD/WMLY/WICK BS30 .... 338 C7 3
Haslette Wy CHELTW GL51 .... 115 G6
Hassell Dr CBRISNE BS2 .... 7 L2
Hastings Cl BMSTR BS3 .... 345 L2 1
Hastings Hl CHNTN OX7 .... 105 G6
Hastings Pl TEWK GL20 .... 48 A7 1
Hastings Rd BMSTR BS3 .... 345 L2
CIND GL14 .... 154 A3
Hatchet La BRSTK/PCHW BS34 .... 317 G7
Hatchet Rd BRSTK/PCHW BS34 .. 317 G7
Hatchmere THNB/SVB BS35 .... 293 M3
Hatfield Rd GL GL1 .... 136 C4
Hathaway Cl VGL GL2 .... 135 K7
Hatherley YATE/CS BS37 .... 320 A4
Hatherley Brake
CHELTW GL51 .... 115 G4 2
Hatherley Court Rd
CHELTW GL51 .... 115 K4
Hatherley Ga CHELTW GL51 .... 115 K3
Hatherley La CHELTW GL51 .... 114 E3
Hatherley Rd CHELTW GL51 .... 114 F4
GL GL1 .... 136 C4
HORF/LLZ BS7 .... 326 A7
Hatherley St CHELT GL50 .... 115 K4
Hatherop Rd CIR GL7 .... 242 F4
Hathway Wk EVILLE/WHL BS5 .... 336 C3
Hatters' La YATE/CS BS37 .... 320 E2
Hatton Cl MTCHDN GL17 .... 152 C1
Havelock Rd BWTH/CHD GL3 .... 137 J3
Haven Av STNHO GL10 .... 207 G5
The Haven KGWD/HNM BS15 .... 338 A2
Haverstock Rd
BRSG/KWL/STAPK BS4 .... 336 C8
Haviland Gv CBATH/BATHN BA1 .. 350 C8
Haw Br RTEWK/TIB GL19 .... 68 D7
Hawburn Cl
BRSG/KWL/STAPK BS4 .... 346 F1
Hawcombe Ms
CHELTW GL51 .... 115 H6 12
Haweswater Cl
OLD/WMLY/WICK BS30 .... 338 F5 3
Haweswater Rd
CHELTW GL51 .... 115 G5 4
Hawk Cl GLE GL4 .... 136 F6
Hawkers Hl CIR GL7 .... 217 J1
Hawker Sq COTS GL54 .... 124 D7
Hawkesbury Rd BAD GL9 .... 297 M6
MANG/FISH BS16 .... 327 G8
Hawkesley Dr
BRSTK/PCHW BS34 .... 316 F5
Hawkfield Cl
BMSTRD/HC/WWD BS13 .... 345 M6
Hawkfield Rd
BMSTRD/HC/WWD BS13 .... 345 M6
Hawkfield Wy
BMSTRD/HC/WWD BS13 .... 345 M6 1
Hawkins Cl
OLD/WMLY/WICK BS30 .... 338 E7 2
Hawkins Crs ALMDB BS32 .... 316 F3
Hawkins St CBRISNE BS2 .... 7 J3
Hawkley Dr ALMDB BS32 .... 306 F8
Hawkridge Dr MANG/FISH BS16.. 329 L6
Hawksmoor Cl
HGRV/WHIT BS14 .... 346 C5
Hawkswood Rd CHELT GL50 .... 115 K6
Hawksworth Dr
KGWD/HNM BS15 .... 337 K7
Haw La THNB/SVB BS35 .... 306 C1
Haw Rd CLFD GL16 .... 152 A4
Haw St DSLY GL11 .... 230 B4
WUE GL12 .... 277 J4
Hawthorn Av
KGWD/HNM BS15 .... 337 K6 3
Hawthorn Cl
BRSTK/PCHW BS34 .... 316 A4
CHEP NP16 .... 270 A7 1
WUE GL12 .... 276 C7 1
Hawthorn Crs
THNB/SVB BS35 .... 293 L1 2
Hawthorn Dr BUR/CRTN OX18 .... 197 L4
BWTH/CHD GL3 .... 113 H6 1
CHELTE/BC GL52 .... 72 D8 3
CLFD GL16 .... 175 L7
Hawthorne Av GLE GL4 .... 136 E5
Hawthorne Cl MANG/FISH BS16.. 329 L6
Hawthorne Hl NWNT GL18 .... 85 K1
The Hawthornes
CHELTW GL51 .... 114 F5 2
MANG/FISH BS16 .... 328 B7
Hawthorne St
BRSG/KWL/STAPK BS4 .... 336 C8
Hawthorn Ri STROUD GL5 .... 207 M3 1
Hawthorn Rd CHELTW GL51 .... 93 G8 3
Hawthorns La KEYN BS31 .... 348 A6
Hawthorns Rd MTCHDN GL17 .... 129 L2
The Hawthorns DSLY GL11 .... 229 G6
LYD GL15 .... 201 K8
RSTROUD/NAIL GL6 .... 209 L7
Hawthorn Wy
BRSTK/PCHW BS34 .... 317 G6
SHPSTR CV36 .... 16 B7
Haycombe HGRV/WHIT BS14 ... 346 B5 1
Haycroft Cl CHELTE/BC GL52 .... 72 A7
Haycroft Dr GLE GL4 .... 136 F8
Hayden La CHELTW GL51 .... 114 C1
Hayden Rd CHELTW GL51 .... 93 G6
Haydock Cl MANG/FISH BS16 .. 328 B2 4
Haydon Gdns HORF/LLZ BS7 .... 326 D6 1
Haydons Cl CHCAM GL55 .... 12 F7 1
Hayeley Dr BRSTK/PCHW BS34... 317 G5
Hayes Cl CBRISNE BS2 .... 7 L2
Hayes Ct VGL GL2 .... 112 B5 1
Haye's La BAD GL9 .... 323 G1
CIR GL7 .... 189 L4
Hayes Rd CHELTE/BC GL52 .... 3 H4
RSTROUD/NAIL GL6 .... 232 C6
Hayfield CHPMW/MSHF SN14 .... 342 C3
Hayfield Wy CHELTE/BC GL52 .... 71 M6
Hayhedge La
RSTROUD/NAIL GL6 .... 210 F2
Hay La CIR GL7 .... 216 F1
RSTROUD/NAIL GL6 .... 256 C4
Hay Leaze YATE/CS BS37 .... 309 M7 1
The Haymarket CBRIS/FH BS1 .... 6 F2
Haymead La TET GL8 .... 279 M6
Hay Meadow SHPSTR CV36 .... 16 A5
Haymes Dr CHELTE/BC GL52 .... 94 E2
Haymes Rd CHELTE/BC GL52 .... 94 E2
Haynes La MANG/FISH BS16 .... 327 M6
Hays Cl BDWAY WR12 .... 11 G8
Hay St CHPMW/MSHF SN14 .... 342 C3
Haysum's Cl CHCAM GL55 .... 34 E1
Haythorn Ct MANG/FISH BS16 .... 328 B6
Haytor Pk
HNLZ/SM/SNYPK/WT BS9 .... 324 F5
Hayward Cl GLE GL4 .... 136 F4
Hayward Rd EVILLE/WHL BS5 .... 336 E4
MANG/FISH BS16 .... 327 M8
Haywards La CHELTE/BC GL52 .... 3 J7
Hayward's Rd CHELTE/BC GL52 .... 3 J9
Haywood Pitch RWYE HR9 .... 85 G1
Hazebrouck Cl CHELTW GL51 .... 115 G4
Hazel Av RDLND/MONT BS6 .... 335 K1
Hazelbury Dr
OLD/WMLY/WICK BS30 .... 338 E5
Hazelbury Hl COR/BOX SN13 .... 353 M5
Hazelbury Rd HGRV/WHIT BS14 .. 346 E3
Hazel Cl VGL GL2 .... 112 D6
Hazel Cote Rd
HGRV/WHIT BS14 .... 346 D7
Hazel Cresent THNB/SVB BS35.... 293 M2
Hazelcroft BWTH/CHD GL3 .... 113 K5 3
Hazeldene Rd
BRSTK/PCHW BS34 .... 316 C4
Hazel Gdns THNB/SVB BS35 .... 293 H7 1
Hazelgrove
FRCTL/WBN BS36 .... 317 M6 2
Hazel Gv HORF/LLZ BS7 .... 326 C3
Hazel La ALMDB BS32 .... 293 G8
Hazells La CIR GL7 .... 221 K6
Hazel Rd MTCHDN GL17 .... 129 M3
The Hazels GLE GL4 .... 137 G4
Hazelton Rd HORF/LLZ BS7 .... 325 M8
Hazel Wy CHPMW/MSHF SN14 .... 343 J6

Hazelwood Rd
  HNLZ/SM/SNYPK/WT BS9......... **324** F8
Hazle Cl *LED* HR8 .... **19** M5
Hazlecote La *TET* GL8......... **256** B5
Hazledean Rd *CHELTW* GL51 .. **92** F7 🔟
Hazlewood Cl *CHELT* GL50..... **115** K6
Hazlitt Cft *CHELTW* GL51 .... **92** F7
Headford Av *EVILLE/WHL* BS5 .. **337** K4
Headford Rd
  BRSG/KWL/STAPK BS4...... **345** M2
Headington Cl
  KGWD/HNM BS15 .... **337** M7 🔟
Headlam Cl *GLE* GL4 .... **159** M2 🔟
The Headlands *STROUD* GL5... **232** B1
The Headland *CHEP* NP16...... **270** C7
Headley Ct
  BMSTRD/HC/WWD BS13..... **345** K4
Headley La
  BMSTRD/HC/WWD BS13..... **345** K5
Headley Park Av
  BMSTRD/HC/WWD BS13..... **345** K4
Headley Park Rd
  BMSTRD/HC/WWD BS13..... **345** J4
Headley Rd
  BMSTRD/HC/WWD BS13..... **345** J4
Headley Wk
  BMSTRD/HC/WWD BS13..... **345** K4
Healey Dr
  CHPMW/MSHF SN14.......... **330** E5 🔟
Heapey Cl *CHELTW* GL51 .... **114** F1 🔟
Hearne Cl *CHELTS* GL53 .... **116** C5
Hearne Rd *CHELTS* GL53 .... **116** C5
Heart Meers
  HGRV/WHIT BS14 .... **346** D6 🔟
Heart of England Wy
  CHCAM GL55....................... **13** G2
Heath Cl *FRCTL/WBN* BS36...... **318** A5
Heathcote Dr *FRCTL/WBN* BS36.. **318** F4
Heathcote Rd
  MANG/FISH BS16 .... **328** A6 🔟
  MANG/FISH BS16 .... **337** K1
Heathcote Wk *KGWD/HNM* BS15 **337** L1
Heath Ct *MANG/FISH* BS16 ...... **327** M4 🔟
Heathdean Rd *BWTH/CHD* .. **113** H5 🔟
Heather Av *FRCTL/WBN* BS36.... **318** D5
  GLE GL4 .... **137** H7
Heather Cl *KGWD/HNM* BS15 ... **337** K5
  STROUD GL5 .... **208** C7
Heatherdene *HGRV/WHIT* BS14 .. **346** B4
Heathfield Cl
  CBATH/BATHN BA1 .... **350** C8
  KEYN BS31 .... **347** L6
Heathfield Crs
  HGRV/WHIT BS14 .... **346** C7
Heathfield Rd *STROUD* GL5....... **208** B2
Heathfields *MANG/FISH* BS16... **327** M3
Heath Gdns *FRCTL/WBN* BS36 .. **318** C5
  MANG/FISH BS16 .... **327** M3
Heath House La
  MANG/FISH BS16 .... **326** E6 🔟
Heath Rdg *LGASH* BS41 .... **344** C1
Heath Ri
  OLD/WMLY/WICK BS30 ...... **338** D6 🔟
Heath Rd *EVILLE/WHL* BS5 ...... **326** D8
  KGWD/HNM BS15 .... **337** K7
  MANG/FISH BS16 .... **327** M4
Heath St *EVILLE/WHL* BS5 .... **336** C1
Heathville Rd *GL* GL1 .... **5** H3
Heath Wk *MANG/FISH* BS16 ...... **327** M4
Heazle Pl *STROUD* GL5 .... **208** C7
Hebden Cl *BWTH/CHD* CL3 .... **138** B6
Heber St *EVILLE/WHL* BS5 .... **336** E4
Hebron Rd *BMSTR* BS3 .... **335** L8 🔟
Hedgeditch La *TET* GL8 .... **301** M4
Hedgemead Vw
  MANG/FISH BS16 .... **326** F6
The Hedgerow *VGL* GL2 .... **112** D7 🔟
Hedwick St *EVILLE/WHL* BS5..... **337** C4
Heggard Cl
  BMSTRD/HC/WWD BS13..... **345** J6 🔟
Helens Cl *CHELTW* GL51......... **92** F8
Hellier Wk
  BMSTRD/HC/WWD BS13..... **345** L8 🔟
Hembury Cl *VGL* GL2 .... **158** F4
Hemmingsdale Rd *VGL* GL2 .... **4** A7
Hemming Wy *CHELTE* GL52 ..... **72** E8
The Hemplelands *COTS* GL54 .... **191** M1
Hemplow Cl *HGRV/WHIT* BS14 .. **346** F4
Hempsted La *VGL* GL2 .... **135** K5
Hempton La *ALMDB* BS32 .... **316** C1
Henacre Rd *AVONM* BS11 .... **324** A3
Henbrook La *RBANSW* OX15 ...... **17** M8
Henbury Rd
  HNBRY/STHM BS10 .... **325** G1 🔟
  HNLZ/SM/SNYPK/WT BS9... **325** J3
  KGWD/HNM BS15 .... **337** K6 🔟
Henbury Road Henbury HI
  HNLZ/SM/SNYPK/WT BS9... **325** M1
Hencliffe Rd *HGRV/WHIT* BS14 .. **346** F5
Hencliffe Wy *KGWD/HNM* BS15 .. **337** K8
Henderson Rd
  KGWD/HNM BS15 .... **337** K6
Hendingham Cl *GL* GL1 .... **159** K1
Hendre Rd *BMSTR* BS3 .... **345** J1
Hendrick Dr *CHEP* NP16 .... **270** C3 🔟
Heneage La *WUE* GL12........... **275** H3
Henfield Crs
  OLD/WMLY/WICK BS30 ...... **338** D7
Henfield Rd *FRCTL/WBN* BS36 .. **318** E4
Hengaston St *BMSTR* BS3 .... **345** K1 🔟
Hengrove Av *HGRV/WHIT* BS14 .. **346** C3
Hengrove La *HGRV/WHIT* BS14 .. **346** D3
Hengrove Rd
  BRSG/KWL/STAPK BS4........ **346** C1
Hengrove Wy
  BMSTRD/HC/WWD BS13..... **345** K6
  BRSG/KWL/STAPK BS4........ **346** A5
Henleaze Av
  HNLZ/SM/SNYPK/WT BS9... **325** J6
Henleaze Gdns
  HNLZ/SM/SNYPK/WT BS9... **325** J6
Henleaze Pk
  HNLZ/SM/SNYPK/WT BS9... **325** K6
Henleaze Park Dr
  HNLZ/SM/SNYPK/WT BS9... **325** L5
Henleaze Rd
  HNLZ/SM/SNYPK/WT BS9... **325** J6

Henleaze Ter
  HNLZ/SM/SNYPK/WT BS9.... **325** K4
Henley Gv
  HNLZ/SM/SNYPK/WT BS9.... **325** K6
Henley La *COR/BOX* SN13 .... **353** K8
Henley PI *GL* GL1 .... **135** M5
Henley Rd *CHELTW* GL51 .... **92** E8
  LYD GL15 .... **200** D2
Henlow Dr *DSLY* GL11 .... **253** K3
Hennessy Cl *HGRV/WHIT* BS14 .. **346** A8
Henrietta St *CBRISNE* BS2 .... **335** M3 🔟
  CHELT GL50 .... **2** D4
  EVILLE/WHL BS5................ **336** D2 🔟
Henry Rd *GL* GL1 .... **5** H3
Henry Ryder Cl *GLE* GL4 .... **137** H5 🔟
Henry St *BMSTR* BS3 .... **7** K9
  GL GL1 .... **5** G4
Henry Williamson Ct
  OLD/WMLY/WICK BS30 .... **338** C6 🔟
Henshaw Cl
  KGWD/HNM BS15 .... **337** L1 🔟
Henshaw Rd *KGWD/HNM* BS15 .. **337** L1
Henshaw Wk *KGWD/HNM* BS15 .. **337** L1
Hensman's HI *CFTN/FAIL* BS8 ... **335** J5
Hentley Tor *WUE* GL12............. **277** L5
Hepburn Rd *CBRIS/FH* BS1 .... **336** A3
Herald Cl
  HNLZ/SM/SNYPK/WT BS9.... **324** F6
Herapath St *EVILLE/WHL* BS5 ... **336** E5
Herbert Crs *EVILLE/WHL* BS5 ... **326** F8 🔟
Herbert Howells Cl *LYD* GL15 ... **225** J7 🔟
Herbert St *BMSTR* BS3 .... **6** D9
  EVILLE/WHL BS5................ **336** E3
  GL GL1 .... **5** J8
Herberts Wy *LYD* GL15............ **201** L2
Hercules Cl *BRSTK/PCHW* BS34 .. **316** F5
Herd La *TET* GL8 .... **282** A4
Hereford PI *CHELT* GL50 .... **2** B3
Hereford Rd *CBRISNE* BS2 .... **336** C1 🔟
  LED HR8 .... **19** L1
Herkomer Cl *HORF/LLZ* BS7 ...... **326** D4
Hereward Rd *CIR* GL7 .... **238** C2
Hermitage Cl *AVONM* BS11 ...... **324** A4
Hermitage Dr *DSLY* GL11 .... **253** K3
Hermitage Rd *MANG/FISH* BS16. **327** M6
Hermitage St *CHELTS* GL53 ...... **115** M4
Hern La *NAIL* BS48 .... **344** A6
Heron Cl *CHELTW* GL51........... **115** G4
Heron Rd *EVILLE/WHL* BS5 ...... **336** D2
Heron Wy *GLE* GL4 .... **136** E6
Herridge Cl
  BMSTRD/HC/WWD BS13..... **345** K7
Herridge Rd
  BMSTRD/HC/WWD BS13..... **345** K7
Hersey Gdns
  BMSTRD/HC/WWD BS13..... **345** G8
Hersta Cl *CIR* GL7 .... **238** E3 🔟
Hertford Rd *CHELTE/BC* GL52 .... **72** B7
Hesding Cl *KGWD/HNM* BS15 ... **337** L8 🔟
Hestercombe Rd
  BMSTRD/HC/WWD BS13..... **345** K5 🔟
Hester's Way La *CHELTW* GL51... **92** F7
Hester's Way Rd *CHELTW* GL51... **92** F8
Hethersett Rd *GL* GL1 .... **5** J8
Hetton Gdns *CHELTS* GL53....... **116** C5
Hewelsfield La *LYD* GL15 .... **198** F6
Hewland Ct *AVONM* BS11 .... **324** E1 🔟
Hewlett PI *CHELTE/BC* GL52 .... **2** F6
Hewlett Rd *CHELTE/BC* GL52 .... **2** F6
Hewlett Wy *CIND* GL14 .... **154** A7
Heyford Av *EVILLE/WHL* BS5..... **326** D8
Heyron Wk
  BMSTRD/HC/WWD BS13..... **345** K7
Heywood Rd *CIND* GL14.......... **154** B2
Hiam's La *VGL* GL2 .... **89** G8
Hiatt Rd *RSTROUD/NAIL* GL6 ..... **233** C4
Hibbs Cl *CHPMW/MSHF* SN14 ... **342** B3
Hickley Gdns *BWTH/CHD* CL3 ... **138** A5
Hicks Av *DSLY* GL11................ **229** H7
  MANG/FISH BS16 .... **328** D3
Hicks Beach Rd *CHELTW* GL51 .. **92** F8
Hicks Common Rd
  FRCTL/WBN BS36............... **318** A5
Hicks Ct
  OLD/WMLY/WICK BS30 .... **338** B7 🔟
Hidcote Av *CHELTW* GL51 ...... **115** J6 🔟
Hidcote Cl
  RSTROUD/NAIL GL6 .... **209** M7 🔟
Hidcote Rd *CHCAM* GL55.......... **13** K4
Higham St
  BRSG/KWL/STAPK BS4........... **7** K8 🔟
Highbank Pk *VGL* GL2 .... **112** B6
High Bannerdown
  CBATH/BATHN BA1 .... **352** D7
High Beech Av *CLFD* GL16....... **151** M6
Highbeech Rd *LYD* GL15 .... **200** C3
  MTCHDN GL17 .... **128** C6
Highbury La *CHELTE/BC* GL52..... **2** E6
Highbury Rd *BMSTR* BS3 .... **345** L2
  HORF/LLZ BS7 .... **326** B4
  LYD GL15 .... **200** C3
  MONM NP25....................... **174** B3
Highbury Vls *CBRISNE* BS2 .... **6** C1
Highclere Rd *VGL* GL2 .... **159** G1
Highcroft
  OLD/WMLY/WICK BS30 .... **338** E5 🔟
Highdale Cl *HGRV/WHIT* BS14.... **346** D7
High Delf Wy *LYD* GL15 .... **201** G2
High Elm *KGWD/HNM* BS15 ..... **338** A5 🔟
Higher Newmarket Rd
  RSTROUD/NAIL GL6 .... **232** B7
Highett Dr *EVILLE/WHL* BS5 ... **336** C2 🔟
Highfield *LYD* GL15................ **202** D1
Highfield Av *KGWD/HNM* BS15... **337** M6
Highfield Cl *LYD* GL15 .... **200** C2
Highfield Gdns
  OLD/WMLY/WICK BS30 .... **348** E1
Highfield Gv *HORF/LLZ* BS7....... **325** M6
Highfield La *LYD* GL15 .... **201** L6
  YATE/CS BS37 .... **311** M6
Highfield PI *GLE* GL4............... **136** D4
Highfield Rd *GLE* GL4 .... **136** D4
  LYD GL15 .... **200** C2
  LYD GL15 .... **201** L6
  MTCHDN GL17 .... **129** G3
  RSTROUD/NAIL GL6 .... **184** C8

STROUD GL5 .... **209** G5
TET GL8 .... **281** M2
YATE/CS BS37 .... **320** C2
Highfields *BAD* GL9 .... **312** B1
Highfields Ap *DSLY* GL11 .... **253** L3 🔟
Highfields Cl
  BRSTK/PCHW BS34............. **317** H8
Highfield Wy
  RSTROUD/NAIL GL6 .... **210** C7
High Furlong *DSLY* GL11 .... **229** H6 🔟
High Gv
  HNLZ/SM/SNYPK/WT BS9.... **324** D4
Highgrove St
  BRSG/KWL/STAPK BS4............. **7** L9
Highgrove Wy *BWTH/CHD* CL3... **113** H4
Highland Crs *CFTN/FAIL* BS8 .... **335** J1 🔟
Highland Rd *CHELTS* GL53 ...... **116** A7
Highlands Dr *DSLY* GL11 .... **253** C7
Highland Sq *CFTN/FAIL* BS8 .... **335** J1 🔟
Highlands Rd *LGASH* BS41 ...... **344** C1
Highleaze Rd
  OLD/WMLY/WICK BS30 .... **338** E7
Highliffe Dr *VGL* GL2.............. **159** J2
Highmead Gdns
  BMSTRD/HC/WWD BS13..... **345** G7
Highmore Gdns *HORF/LLZ* BS7.. **326** E4
Highnam Cl *BRSTK/PCHW* BS34 .. **316** D2
High Nash *CLFD* GL16............. **175** K2
High Orchard St *GL* GL1 .... **4** C8
High Pk *HGRV/WHIT* BS14 ...... **346** D2
Highridge Crs
  BMSTRD/HC/WWD BS13..... **345** H6
Highridge Gn
  BMSTRD/HC/WWD BS13..... **345** G6
Highridge Pk
  BMSTRD/HC/WWD BS13..... **345** H6 🔟
Highridge Rd *BMSTR* BS3 .... **345** K1 🔟
  LGASH BS41...................... **344** C8
Highridge Wk
  BMSTRD/HC/WWD BS13..... **345** G4
High Rd *HGHW* SN6 .... **287** H2
High St *BAD* GL9.................... **298** B8
  BAD GL9 .... **323** G1
  BDWAY WR12 .... **32** F3
  BDWAY WR12 .... **33** G3 🔟
  BDWAY WR12 .... **53** M2
  BRKLY GL13 .... **251** G1
  CBATH/BATHN BA1 .... **351** M6
  CBATH/BATHN BA1 .... **352** B8
  CBRIS/FH BS1 .... **6** F5
  CFTN/FAIL BS8 .... **335** J1
  CHCAM GL55 .... **9** G7
  CHCAM GL55 .... **12** E8
  CHELT GL50 .... **2** B3
  CHELTE/BC GL52.................. **2** E5
  CHELTE/BC GL52................ **94** E7
  CHEP NP16 .... **270** A3
  CHNTN OX7 .... **149** K1
  CHPMW/MSHF SN14 .... **330** F7
  CHPMW/MSHF SN14 .... **342** A3
  CHPMW/MSHF SN14 .... **343** K8
  CIND GL14 .... **129** G8
  CIND GL14 .... **154** D3
  CIND GL14 .... **154** B2
  CIND GL14 .... **155** J7
  CIND GL14 .... **156** B2
  CIR GL7 .... **241** L6
  CIR GL7 .... **241** K7
  CIR GL7 .... **242** E4
  CIR GL7 .... **244** E8
  CIR GL7 .... **263** H5
  CIR GL7 .... **266** F5
  CLFD GL16 .... **175** J6
  CLFD GL16 .... **175** K1
  COR/BOX SN13 .... **353** M5
  COTS GL54 .... **102** A3
  COTS GL54 .... **123** H5
  COTS GL54 .... **142** D8
  COTS GL54 .... **169** J1
  DSLY GL11 .... **229** H5
  EVILLE/WHL BS5................ **336** D2
  FRCTL/WBN BS36............... **317** M5
  GL GL1 .... **136** B4
  GLE GL4 .... **161** G1
  HGHW SN6 .... **288** F4
  HNLZ/SM/SNYPK/WT BS9.... **325** J3
  KEYN BS31 .... **348** A5
  KEYN BS31 .... **349** G8
  KGWD/HNM BS15 .... **337** L6
  KGWD/HNM BS15 .... **338** D3
  KGWD/HNM BS15 .... **338** A3
  LED HR8 .... **20** A3
  LYD GL15 .... **198** F6
  LYD GL15 .... **200** C3
  LYD GL15 .... **202** D1
  LYD GL15 .... **224** F3
  LYD GL15 .... **225** J5
  MALM SN16 .... **303** J8 🔟
  MANG/FISH BS16 .... **327** L7
  MIM GL56 .... **57** G1
  MIM GL56 .... **58** C5 🔟
  MIM GL56 .... **79** K4
  MTCHDN GL17 .... **128** F6
  MTCHDN GL17 .... **128** C3
  MTCHDN GL17 .... **129** M3
  MTCHDN GL17 .... **130** C1
  NWNT GL18 .... **86** C2
  OLD/WMLY/WICK BS30 .... **338** F7
  OLD/WMLY/WICK BS30 .... **338** F4
  OLD/WMLY/WICK BS30 .... **339** K5
  OLD/WMLY/WICK BS30 .... **340** B2
  OLD/WMLY/WICK BS30 .... **349** G3
  RSTROUD/NAIL GL6 .... **210** C3
  RSTROUD/NAIL GL6 .... **233** J5 🔟
  RSTROUD/NAIL GL6 .... **234** B1
  SHPSTR CV36 .... **16** B5 🔟
  STNHO GL10 .... **207** J8
  STNHO GL10 .... **207** H4
  STROUD GL5 .... **208** B4
  STROUD GL5 .... **232** B2
  TET GL8 .... **257** K2
  TEWK GL20 .... **27** C5
  TEWK GL20 .... **48** A4
  THNB/SVB BS35 .... **293** K2
  VGL GL2 .... **155** M8
  VGL GL2 .... **181** H4
  WUE GL12 .... **277** H7
  WUE GL12 .... **277** K4 🔟

WUE GL12 .... **296** C5
WUE GL12 .... **297** M4
YATE/CS BS37 .... **308** F7
YATE/CS BS37 .... **320** D2
High Vw *CHEP* NP16 .... **270** A3 🔟
VGL GL2 .... **135** J5
Highview Rd *CIND* GL14 .... **154** C3 🔟
Highway *KGWD/HNM* BS15 ...... **338** A1
LYD GL15 .... **177** K8
MTCHDN GL17 .... **129** K5
Highview Wy *LYD* GL15 .... **200** D3
Highway *YATE/CS* BS37 .... **320** B1
Highwood Av *CHELTS* GL53 ..... **115** L5
Highwood La
  BRSTK/PCHW BS34............. **316** A4
  HNBRY/STHM BS10 .... **315** M4
Highwood Rd
  BRSTK/PCHW BS34............. **316** A4
Highworth Crs *YATE/CS* BS37 ... **319** M3
Highworth Rd
  BRSG/KWL/STAPK BS4........ **336** F5
  GL GL1 .... **136** B5
Hilirise *LYD* GL15 .... **200** D2
Hilcote Dr *COTS* GL54 .... **123** J7
Hildyard Cl *VGL* GL2 .... **159** C4
Hillands Dr *CHELTS* GL53 ...... **115** M7
Hillary Rd *CHELTS* GL53 .... **116** A7
Hill Av *BMSTR* BS3................. **336** A8
Hillborough Rd *GLE* GL4 .... **136** A8
Hill Burn
  HNLZ/SM/SNYPK/WT BS9.... **325** L5
Hillburn Rd *EVILLE/WHL* BS5.... **337** J3
Hill Cl *DSLY* GL11 .... **229** H7 🔟
  TEWK GL20 .... **27** K4
Hillcot Cl *VGL* GL2 .... **159** G2
Hill Court Rd *CHELTE/BC* GL52 ... **94** A7
Hill Crest *BRSG/KWL/STAPK* BS4.. **346** D2
  VGL GL2 .... **111** C5
Hillcrest *BRKLY* GL13 .... **227** H8
  CHPMW/MSHF SN14 .... **343** L5
  THNB/SVB BS35 .... **293** K2
Hillcrest La *CLFD* GL16 .... **151** M8
Hillcrest Rd *CLFD* GL16 .... **151** K6
  STROUD GL5 .... **208** A3
Hill End Dr *HNBRY/STHM* BS10 .. **314** F8
Hill End Rd *TEWK* GL20........... **26** B5 🔟
Hillersland La *CLFD* GL16 .... **151** J4
Hillesley Rd *WUE* GL12........... **277** L7
Hillfield *CHELTW* GL51 .... **115** H2
  STROUD GL5 .... **208** B4 🔟
Hillfield Court Rd *GL* GL1 .... **5** J4
Hillfield Dr *LED* HR8 .... **20** A2
Hillfields Av *MANG/FISH* BS16... **327** L8
Hill Gv
  HNLZ/SM/SNYPK/WT BS9.... **325** L5
Hillgrove St *CBRISNE* BS2 .... **336** A3 🔟
Hillgrove St North
  CBRISNE BS2 .... **335** M3 🔟
Hill Hay Rd *GLE* GL4 .... **136** E8
Hill House Rd *MANG/FISH* BS16 .. **328** B6
Hillier Cl *STROUD* GL5 .... **208** F2 🔟
Hillier Dr *CHELTW* GL51 .... **115** H6
Hill La *RBANSW* OX15 .... **17** L6
  STRAT CV37 .... **9** K2
  THNB/SVB BS35 .... **273** C3
  YATE/CS BS37 .... **321** K4
Hill Lawn *BRSG/KWL/STAPK* BS4. **336** F8
Hillmill La *WUE* GL12 .... **277** M7
Hill Rd *DSLY* GL11 .... **253** J2
  GLE GL4 .... **136** B7
  WUE GL12 .... **277** L5
Hillsborough Rd
  BRSG/KWL/STAPK BS4........ **336** E7
Hills Cl *KEYN* BS31 .... **348** C6
Hillsdon Rd
  HNLZ/SM/SNYPK/WT BS9.... **325** H3
Hillside *EVE* WR11 .... **29** K2
  HGHW SN6 .... **287** L6
  MANG/FISH BS16 .... **328** B6
  RSTROUD/NAIL GL6 .... **210** D7
Hillside Av *KGWD/HNM* BS15 ... **337** L3
Hillside Cl *CHELTE/BC* GL52 ..... **72** E8 🔟
  CHELTW GL51 .... **115** J4
  FRCTL/WBN BS36............... **318** E4
  LYD GL15 .... **200** D2
Hillside Gdns *CHELTE/BC* GL52 .... **72** E8
Hillside La *FRCTL/WBN* BS36 ... **318** E4 🔟
Hillside Rd *EVILLE/WHL* BS5..... **337** J4
  LGASH BS41...................... **344** D1
  MTCHDN GL17 .... **129** M2
Hillside St *BRSG/KWL/STAPK* BS4.. **7** L9
Hillside Ter *MTCHDN* GL17 ...... **128** C5 🔟
Hill St *BMSTR* BS3 .... **7** J9
  CBRIS/FH BS1 .... **6** C4
  EVILLE/WHL BS5................ **337** H3
  LYD GL15 .... **201** L3
The Hill *ALMDB* BS32 .... **306** D7
  STROUD GL5 .... **208** D4
Hilltop *LYD* GL15 .... **200** C3
Hill Top Cl *STROUD* GL5 .... **209** G4
Hilltop Gdns *EVILLE/WHL* BS5 .. **337** J4
Hill Top La *NWNT* GL18 .... **86** D1
Hill Top Rd *CHELT* GL50 .... **93** M6
Hilltop Rd *MANG/FISH* BS16..... **337** M1
Hilltop Vw *DSLY* GL11 .... **229** H7
  EVILLE/WHL BS5................ **337** J4
Hill Top Vw
  RSTROUD/NAIL GL6 .... **209** M7 🔟
Hill Vw *CFTN/FAIL* BS8 .... **6** A4
  HNLZ/SM/SNYPK/WT BS9.... **325** L5
  LYD GL15 .... **201** J8
  MANG/FISH BS16 .... **337** M1
Hill View Cl
  OLD/WMLY/WICK BS30 .... **338** E7
Hillview Dr *BWTH/CHD* CL3...... **137** H3
Hillview La *TEWK* GL20 .... **26** B4
Hillview Ri *CLFD* GL16 .... **151** J5
Hill View Rd
  BMSTRD/HC/WWD BS13..... **345** J4
  CHELTE/BC GL52 .... **3** G4
  MANG/FISH BS16 .... **329** L6
Hillview Rd *BWTH/CHD* CL3 ..... **137** H3
Hillyfield Rd
  BMSTRD/HC/WWD BS13..... **345** J1
Hilton Cl *VGL* GL2 .... **135** K5

Hinders La *RTEWK/TIB* GL19 ..... **131** M1
Hinton Cl *KEYN* BS31 .... **349** G8
Hinton Dr
  OLD/WMLY/WICK BS30 .... **338** E5
Hinton Rd *EVILLE/WHL* BS5...... **336** E2
  GL GL1 .... **136** A3
  MANG/FISH BS16 .... **327** J7 🔟
Hisnams Fld *CHELTE/BC* GL52 ... **72** B8
Hitchen Cl *CHPMW/MSHF* SN14.. **342** B3
Hitchen Hollow *CHEP* NP16 ..... **270** D7
Hitchings *LYD* GL15................ **178** D8
Hitchings Skilling
  CHPMW/MSHF SN14 .... **343** K8 🔟
The Hithe *STROUD* GL5 .... **208** D8
Hobbes Cl *MALM* SN16............ **303** H7
The Hobbins *SHPSTR* CV36 .... **16** A6
Hobb's La *CBRIS/FH* BS1 .... **6** D4 🔟
  CIR GL7 .... **189** L4
  KGWD/HNM BS15 .... **338** D2
  MTCHDN GL17 .... **107** J8
  NAIL BS48 .... **344** A7
Hobby Cl *CHELTS* GL53 .... **115** L6
Hobwell La *LGASH* BS41 .... **344** E1 🔟
Hockey's La *MANG/FISH* BS16 ... **327** J7 🔟
Hoddon La *MANG/FISH* BS16 ... **329** L6
Hodge La *MALM* SN16 .... **303** H7
Hodges Wy *CIND* GL14 .... **154** A4 🔟
Hogarth Wk *HORF/LLZ* BS7...... **326** D4
Hogues Wk
  BMSTRD/HC/WWD BS13..... **345** K7 🔟
Holbeach Wy *HGRV/WHIT* BS14.. **346** C8
Holbeck Rd *MTCHDN* GL17 ...... **128** C8
Holbrook Crs
  BMSTRD/HC/WWD BS13..... **345** M7
Holbrook La
  OLD/WMLY/WICK BS30 .... **339** J4
Holcombe Gv *KEYN* BS31 .... **347** M6
Holcot Cl *CLFD* GL16 .... **175** M1
Holcot Rd *CLFD* GL16............. **175** M2
  VGL GL2 .... **111** C5
Holdenhurst Rd
  KGWD/HNM BS15 .... **337** L2
Holder Cl *TET* GL8 .... **281** M4
Holder Rd *CHELTE/BC* GL52 ..... **94** B1 🔟
Holders La *NWNT* GL18 .... **63** M7
Holders Wk *LGASH* BS41 .... **344** B2
Holford Ct *HGRV/WHIT* BS14..... **346** D6
Holford Crs *CIR* GL7 .... **267** G5
Hollams Rd *TEWK* GL20 .... **48** B4
Holland Ct *GL* GL1 .... **5** K3
Hollies HI *RSTROUD/NAIL* GL6 ... **232** E7
Hollies La *CBATH/BATHN* BA1 ... **352** C2
Hollingham La
  RSTROUD/NAIL GL6 .... **256** A2
Hollins Cl *CHEP* NP16 .... **270** B2 🔟
Hollis Cl *LGASH* BS41............. **344** B3
Hollis Gdns *CHELTW* GL51 ...... **114** F5
Hollis Rd *CHELTW* GL51 .... **114** F5
Hollister's Dr
  BMSTRD/HC/WWD BS13..... **345** M8
Holloway *MALM* SN16 .... **303** J8
Holloway HI
  CHPMW/MSHF SN14 .... **333** G3
Holloway Rd
  RSTROUD/NAIL GL6 .... **210** C3
Hollow La *STROUD* GL5 .... **208** F4
Hollow Rd *ALMDB* BS32 .... **306** C7
  KGWD/HNM BS15 .... **338** A3
The Hollows *EVE* WR11 .... **30** D1
  FRCTL/WBN BS36............... **328** E1
The Hollow *MTCHDN* GL17 ...... **129** K4
Hollway Cl *HGRV/WHIT* BS14 .... **347** G6 🔟
Hollway Rd *HGRV/WHIT* BS14 .... **347** G6
Hollybush Cl *BAD* GL9 .... **323** J5
Hollybush La
  HNLZ/SM/SNYPK/WT BS9.... **325** G7
Holly Cl *CHEP* NP16 .... **270** A6 🔟
  EVILLE/WHL BS5................ **337** J1
  MANG/FISH BS16 .... **329** L6
  THNB/SVB BS35 .... **293** H7
Holly Crs *KGWD/HNM* BS15 ..... **338** A2 🔟
Holly Dr *CHPMW/MSHF* SN14 ... **343** H5 🔟
Holly End *VGL* GL2 .... **159** H3
Holly Gn *KGWD/HNM* BS15 ...... **338** C2
Holly Gv *MANG/FISH* BS16 ...... **327** L8
The Holly Gv *VGL* GL2 .... **159** H3
Hollyguest Rd
  KGWD/HNM BS15 .... **338** A5
Holly HI *YATE/CS* BS37 .... **309** G8
Hollyhill Rd *CIND* GL14 .... **153** M2
Holly Hill Rd *KGWD/HNM* BS15 .. **338** B3
Hollyhock La
  RSTROUD/NAIL GL6 .... **185** H3 🔟
Holly Cl *CLFD* GL16................ **176** A6
Hollyleigh Av
  BRSTK/PCHW BS34............. **326** B1
Holly Lodge Rd
  EVILLE/WHL BS5................ **337** H1
Hollymead La
  HNLZ/SM/SNYPK/WT BS9.... **325** G7
Hollyridge *HGRV/WHIT* BS14..... **346** E5
Holly Rd *SHPSTR* CV36............ **16** B7 🔟
Holly Tree Gdn *STROUD* GL5 ... **207** M5 🔟
Holly Tree PI *LYD* GL15 .... **201** M2
Holly Wk *KEYN* BS31............... **347** M8
Hollywell Rd *MTCHDN* GL17 ..... **106** C8
Hollywood La *THNB/SVB* BS35 ... **315** J4
Hollywood Rd
  BRSG/KWL/STAPK BS4........ **336** F8
Holmdale Rd
  BRSTK/PCHW BS34............. **316** D8
Holmer Crs *CHELTW* GL51 ...... **114** F5 🔟
Holme Rd *TEWK* GL20 .... **48** B8 🔟
Holmesdale Rd *BMSTR* BS3 ..... **336** A8
Holmes Gv
  HNLZ/SM/SNYPK/WT BS9.... **325** L6
Holmes Hill Rd *EVILLE/WHL* BS5.. **337** H3
Holmes St *EVILLE/WHL* BS5 ..... **336** D5 🔟
Holm La *THNB/SVB* BS35 .... **305** J1
Holmleigh Rd *GL* GL1 .... **135** L8
Holmoak Rd *KEYN* BS31 .... **347** L7
Holmwood *KGWD/HNM* BS15 ... **337** L6
Holmwood Cl
  FRCTL/WBN BS36............... **317** M5 🔟
  GL GL1 .... **159** M1 🔟
Holmwood Dr *GL* GL1 .... **159** M1
Holmwood Gdns
  HNLZ/SM/SNYPK/WT BS9.... **325** J3
Holsom Cl *HGRV/WHIT* BS14 .... **347** G5

Holsom Rd *HGRV/WHIT* BS14 .... 347 H5 🔲
Holst Gdns
  BRSG/KWL/STAPK BS4.... 345 J4
Holst Wy *GLE* GL4 .... 159 M1
Holtham Av *BWTH/CHD* GL3 .... 113 K4
Holton Rd *HORF/LLZ* BS7 .... 326 C5
Holtsdown La
  CBATH/BATHN BA1 .... 352 A3
Holts Rd *NWNT* GL18 .... 86 B3
The Holt *GLE* GL4 .... 137 G4
Holyrood Cl
  BRSTK/PCHW BS34 .... 316 F7 🔲
Holy Well Cl
  BRSG/KWL/WICK BS4 .... 337 C5 🔲
Holywell Rd *DSLY* GL11 .... 229 J7
  WUE CL12 .... 277 L3
Homeapple Hl
  OLD/WMLY/WICK BS30 .... 339 G4
Home Cl *HNBRY/STHM* BS10 .... 326 A1
  MIM GL56 .... 103 H2
Homecroft Dr *CHELTW* GL51 .... 93 G6
Home Farm Rd *CFTN/FAIL* BS8 .... 334 C4
Home Farm Wy
  THNB/SVB BS35 .... 315 J2
Homefield *RSTROUD/NAIL* GL6 .... 232 B8 🔲
  THNB/SVB BS35 .... 293 M3 🔲
  YATE/CS BS37 .... 310 A8
Homefield Cl *KEYN* BS31 .... 349 G8
Home Field Cl *MANG/FISH* BS16 .... 328 D5
Homefield Rd *KEYN* BS31 .... 349 G8
  MANG/FISH BS16 .... 329 K6
Home Gnd *HGHW* SN6 .... 288 E5
  HNLZ/SM/SNYPK/WT BS9.. 325 K4
Homeground La *CIR* GL7 .... 243 C4
Homeleaze Rd
  HNBRY/STHM BS10 .... 315 M8
Home Md
  OLD/WMLY/WICK BS30 .... 338 C7
Homemead Dr
  BRSG/KWL/STAPK BS4 .... 346 F2 🔲
Homend *LED* HR8 .... 20 A2
The Homend *LED* HR8 .... 19 M1
Home Orch *YATE/CS* BS37 .... 319 M1
Homestead *TEWK* GL20 .... 27 H5 🔲
Homestead Gdns
  MANG/FISH BS16 .... 327 K2
Homestead Rd
  BRSTK/PCHW BS34 .... 316 B8
Honeyborne Wy *WUE* CL12 .... 296 D6 🔲
Honeybourne *EVE* WR11 .... 11 L3
Honey Garston Cl
  BMSTRD/HC/WWD BS13 .... 345 K7 🔲
Honey Garston Rd
  BMSTRD/HC/WWD BS13 .... 345 K7
Honey Hill Rd *KGWD/HNM* BS15. 338 B3
Honeymead
  HGRV/WHIT BS14 .... 346 E5 🔲
Honeysuckle Cl *ALMDB* BS32 .... 317 G1 🔲
  CHELTE/BC GL52 .... 94 E8 🔲
Honeysuckle Dr *GLE* GL4 .... 137 G6
Honey Suckle La
  MANG/FISH BS16 .... 327 G7 🔲
Honeysuckle Wy
  CHELTE/BC GL52 .... 72 A6
Honiton Rd *MANG/FISH* BS16 .... 327 J8
Honyatt Rd *GL* GL1 .... 5 H5
Hookshouse La *TET* GL8 .... 280 F8
  TET GL8 .... 281 J5
Hook's La *NWNT* GL18 .... 87 H2
Hoo La *CHCAM* GL55 .... 12 D8
  RTEWK/TIB GL19 .... 69 M3
Hooper Rd *HGRV/WHIT* BS14 .... 346 F6 🔲
Hopechapel Hl
  CFTN/FAIL BS8 .... 335 H5 🔲
Hope Mill La *STROUD* GL5 .... 233 C1
Hope Orch *CHELTW* GL51 .... 92 F7
Hope Rd *BMSTR* BS3 .... 345 L1
  YATE/CS BS37 .... 319 J1
Hopes Cl *LYD* GL15 .... 225 L1
Hope Sq *CFTN/FAIL* BS8 .... 335 H5 🔲
Hope St *CHELTW* GL51 .... 93 K8
Hopetoun Rd *CBRISNE* BS2 .... 326 B8 🔲
Hopewell Gdns *AVONM* BS11 .... 324 B4
Hopewell St *GL* GL1 .... 5 H9
Hopkin Cl *THNB/SVB* BS35 .... 293 M4
Hopland Cl
  OLD/WMLY/WICK BS30 .... 338 D8
Hopp's Rd *KGWD/HNM* BS15 .... 337 M4
Hopton Rd *DSLY* GL11 .... 229 J7
Hopyard La *NWNT* GL18 .... 86 C1
The Hopyard *TEWK* GL20 .... 48 F2
Horcott Rd *GLE* GL4 .... 242 D5
Horesham Gv
  BMSTRD/HC/WWD BS13 .... 345 L6 🔲
Horfield Rd *CBRISNE* BS2 .... 6 E2
Horley Rd *CBRISNE* BS2 .... 336 C2
Hornbeam Ms *VGL* GL2 .... 112 D6 🔲
Horn La *MIM* GL56 .... 81 H5
Horns Rd *STROUD* GL5 .... 208 F5
Horsbere Rd *BWTH/CHD* GL3 .... 137 J3
Horsecroft Gdns
  OLD/WMLY/WICK BS30 .... 338 C5 🔲
Horsefair *SHPSTR* CV36 .... 16 B5 🔲
Horsefair Cl *CHELTS* GL53 .... 116 C6 🔲
Horse Fair La *HGHW* SN6 .... 289 C3
Horsefair La *NWNT* GL18 .... 86 A2
Horsefair St *CHELTS* GL53 .... 116 C5
The Horsefair *CBRIS/FH* BS1 .... 7 C2
Horse La *THNB/SVB* BS35 .... 273 M6
Horse Lane Orch *LED* HR8 .... 20 A3
Horsepool La *LYD* GL15 .... 198 E7
  OLD/WMLY/WICK BS30 .... 340 B3
Horse Pool La *RWYE* HR9 .... 126 K6 🔲
Horsepool Rd
  BMSTRD/HC/WWD BS13 .... 345 C2 🔲
The Horsepool *CLFD* GL16 .... 151 J5 🔲
Horseshoe Dr
  HNLZ/SM/SNYPK/WT BS9.. 324 E7
Horseshoe La *YATE/CS* BS37 .... 320 D2
Horse St *YATE/CS* BS37 .... 320 E3
Horsford Rd *WUE* CL12 .... 276 D6
Horslea *MTCHDN* GL17 .... 128 D6
Horsley Cl *GLE* GL4 .... 137 C6
Horsley Hl *RSTROUD/NAIL* GL6 .. 256 C1
Horsley Rd *RSTROUD/NAIL* GL6 .. 256 C1
Hortham La *ALMDB* BS32 .... 306 C5
Horton Hl *YATE/CS* BS37 .... 311 K6

Horton Rd *VGL* GL2 .... 5 K6
  YATE/CS BS37 .... 320 E1
Horton St *CBRISNE* BS2 .... 7 K4
Horwood Ct
  OLD/WMLY/WICK BS30 .... 338 C7 🔲
Horwood La *WUE* CL12 .... 296 D7
Hosey Wk
  BMSTRD/HC/WWD BS13.... 345 J6
Hospital Rd *MIM* GL56 .... 58 C5
Host St *CBRIS/FH* BS1 .... 6 E3
Hottom Gdns *HORF/LLZ* BS7.... 326 C4
Hot Water La *KGWD/HNM* BS15.. 328 B8
Hotwell Rd *CFTN/FAIL* BS8 .... 335 H5 🔲
Houlton St *CBRISNE* BS2 .... 7 J1
Hounds Rd *YATE/CS* BS37 .... 320 D3
Howard Av *EVILLE/WHL* BS5 .... 337 C3
Howard Cl *KEYN* BS31 .... 348 E8
  TEWK GL20 .... 49 C3
Howard Rd *BMSTR* BS3 .... 6 C8
  CLFD GL16 .... 151 M8
  MANG/FISH BS16 .... 327 M7
  RDLND/MONT BS6 .... 325 K7
  TEWK GL20 .... 49 C3
  THNB/SVB BS35 .... 293 L1 🔲
Howard St *EVILLE/WHL* BS5 .... 337 C1
  GL GL1 .... 136 A4
Howcroft *BWTH/CHD* GL3 .... 113 L7
Howcroft Gdns
  HNLZ/SM/SNYPK/WT BS9 .. 325 G7 🔲
Howell Rd *CHELTW* GL51 .... 93 H7
Howell's La *LYD* GL15 .... 178 E5
Howes Md
  MANG/FISH BS16 .... 328 D4 🔲
Howells Rd *TEWK* GL20 .... 48 A5
Howes Cl
  OLD/WMLY/WICK BS30 .... 338 C5
Howgate Rd *EVILLE/WHL* BS5 .... 336 E4 🔲
Howgate Cl *GLE* GL4 .... 137 H5
Howmead *BRKLY* GL13 .... 197 L8
Howsmoor La *MANG/FISH* BS16.. 328 D3
Hoylake Dr *OLD/WMLY/WICK* BS30 338 D5
Hucclecote La *BWTH/CHD* GL3 .. 137 H1
Hucclecote Rd
  BMSTRD/HC/WWD BS13 .... 345 K3
Huckford Cl *RTEWK/TIB* GL19 .... 45 J8
Huckford Rd *FRCTL/WBN* BS36 .. 318 C4
Huckley Wy *ALMDB* BS32 .... 317 H5
Huddleston Cl *COTS* GL54 .... 74 C4 🔲
Hudd's Hill Rd *EVILLE/WHL* BS5 .. 337 H3
Hudd's Vale Rd
  EVILLE/WHL BS5 .... 337 C3 🔲
Hudman's Cl *TEWK* GL20 .... 26 C5
Hudson Cl *YATE/CS* BS37 .... 320 B3
Hudson La *CIND* GL14 .... 154 A6
Hudson La *MALM* SN16 .... 303 H7
Hudson St *CHELT* GL50 .... 2 C1
Hudsons Vw *CIND* GL14 .... 154 A6
Hughenden Rd
  CFTN/FAIL BS8 .... 335 J1 🔲
  HORF/LLZ BS7 .... 326 A6
Hughes Crs *CHEP* NP16 .... 270 A4
Hughes Ter *LYD* GL15 .... 176 E6
Hulbert Cl
  BRSG/KWL/STAPK BS4 .... 347 J1 🔲
  CHELTW GL51 .... 93 J4
Hulbert Crs *CHELTW* GL51 .... 115 H6
Hulse Rd *BRSG/KWL/STAPK* BS4.. 346 F2 🔲
Humber Pl *BWTH/CHD* GL3 .... 138 B6
Humber Rd *CHELTE/BC* GL52 .... 3 K4
Humberstan Wk
  AVONM BS11 .... 324 A3 🔲
Humphreys Ct
  RSTROUD/NAIL GL6 .... 208 A2
Humphrys Barton
  BRSG/KWL/STAPK BS4 .... 337 H6
Hungerford Cl
  BRSG/KWL/STAPK BS4 .... 347 G3
Hungerford Crs
  BRSG/KWL/STAPK BS4 .... 347 G3
Hungerford Gdns
  BRSG/KWL/STAPK BS4 .... 347 G3
Hungerford Rd
  BRSG/KWL/STAPK BS4 .... 347 G3
Hungerford St *CHELT* GL50 .... 2 C2
Hungerford Wk
  BRSG/KWL/STAPK BS4 .... 347 G2
Hunger Hl *DSLY* GL11 .... 253 J3
Hung Rd *AVONM* BS11 .... 324 A5
Hunters Cl *KGWD/HNM* BS15 .... 337 L6 🔲
Hunters Dr *KGWD/HNM* BS15 .... 338 B2
Hunters Ga *GLE* GL4 .... 136 F7
Hunters Md *BAD* GL9 .... 312 C1
Hunters Rd *CHELTE/BC* GL52 .... 72 A7
  KGWD/HNM BS15 .... 337 L6
Hunters Rd East
  KGWD/HNM BS15 .... 337 L6
Hunter's Wy
  BRSTK/PCHW BS34 .... 316 D8
  COTS GL54 .... 118 C7
  STROUD GL5 .... 207 M4
Hunthill *CIND* GL14 .... 156 E1
Huntingdon Cl *STROUD* GL5 .... 207 M5 🔲
Huntingham Rd
  BMSTRD/HC/WWD BS13 .... 345 C4 🔲
Huntley Cl *GLE* GL4 .... 137 C6
Hunts Cl *BUR/CRTN* OX18 .... 173M7
Huntscote Rd *CHELTW* GL51 .... 93 J6
Huntsfield Cl *CHELT* GL50 .... 94 A7 🔲
Hunts Grove Vw *VGL* GL2 .... 159 K4
Huntsmans Cl
  CHELTE/BC GL52 .... 72 C7 🔲
Huntsmans Meet *COTS* GL54 .... 118 C7 🔲
Hurcombe Wy *BWTH/CHD* GL3... 138 A5
Hurle Crs *CFTN/FAIL* BS8 .... 335 J2
Hurle Rd *CFTN/FAIL* BS8 .... 335 K2
Hurlingham Rd
  RDLND/MONT BS6 .... 336 B1
Hurn La *KEYN* BS31 .... 348 B7
Hurst Cl *VGL* GL2 .... 112 F6
Hurston Rd
  BRSG/KWL/STAPK BS4 .... 345M3
Hurst Rd *BRSG/KWL/STAPK* BS4.. 346 B3
Hurst Wk
  BRSG/KWL/STAPK BS4 .... 346 A3
Hurstwood Rd
  MANG/FISH BS16 .... 327M6
Husbandmans Cl
  SHPSTR CV36 .... 16 B5 🔲

Hutton Cl
  HNLZ/SM/SNYPK/WT BS9 .... 324 F4
Huxley Ct *CIR* GL7 .... 263 J4
Huxley Rd *GL* GL1 .... 136 B4
Huxley Wy *CHELTE/BC* GL52 .... 71M7
Huyton Rd *EVILLE/WHL* BS5 .... 327 G8 🔲
Hyatts Wy *CHELTE/BC* GL52 .... 72 C7 🔲
Hyde Av *THNB/SVB* BS35 .... 273 K8 🔲
Hyde Cl *GL* GL1 .... 5 J4
Hyde La *CHELT* GL50 .... 93M4
  CIND GL14 .... 155 H6
  GL GL1 .... 5 J4
  VGL GL2 .... 182 A6
Hyde Park Cnr *RTEWK/TIB* GL19.. 43 J8
Jaythorpe *GLE* GL4 .... 136 F8
Jefferies Cl *GLE* GL4 .... 242 F4
Jefferies Hill Bottom
  KGWD/HNM BS15 .... 337 K6
Jeffery Ct
  OLD/WMLY/WICK BS30 .... 338 D5
Jena Rd *KEYN* BS31 .... 348 F8
Jenkin's La *RSTROUD/NAIL* GL6 .. 184 B8
Jenner Cl *GLE* GL4 .... 137 H3
  YATE/CS BS37 .... 320 F3
Jenner St *BRKLY* GL13 .... 227 C8 🔲
Jenner Wk *CHELT* GL50 .... 2 C4
Jersey Rd
  BRSG/KWL/STAPK BS4 .... 337 H7
  CHELTE/BC GL52 .... 3 H5
Jersey Rd *GL* GL1 .... 5 H8
Jersey St *CHELTE/BC* GL52 .... 2 F4
Jesson Rd *CHELTE/BC* GL52 .... 72 C8
Jessop Av *CHELT* GL50 .... 2 B5
Jessop Dr *COTS* GL54 .... 145 J3
Jessop Under/Pass *BMSTR* BS3.. 335 H7
Jewson *GLE* GL4 .... 159 M1 🔲
Jeynes Rw *TEWK* GL20 .... 48 B4
Job's La *BUR/CRTN* OX18 .... 197 L2
Jockey La *EVILLE/WHL* BS5 .... 337 J4
John Betjeman Cl
  MALM SN16 .... 303 J6 🔲
John Bevan Cl *STROUD* GL5 .... 208 F3 🔲
John Carr's Ter *CFTN/FAIL* BS8 .. 6 A4
John Daniels Wy
  BWTH/CHD GL3 .... 113 K7
John Lee Rd *LED* HR8 .... 19 L3
John of Gaunt Rd *CIR* GL7 .... 266 F5
Johnson Dr
  OLD/WMLY/WICK BS30 .... 338 B6
Johnsons La *EVILLE/WHL* BS5 .... 336 F3
Johnsons Rd *EVILLE/WHL* BS5 .... 336 F3
Johnstone Cl *RTEWK/TIB* GL19 .. 66 D5 🔲
Johnstone Rd *NWNT* GL18 .... 86 B3
John St *CBRIS/FH* BS1 .... 6 F3 🔲
  CBRISNE BS2 .... 336 C1 🔲
  KGWD/HNM BS15 .... 337 L3
  STROUD GL5 .... 208 E4 🔲
John Tame Cl *CIR* GL7 .... 242 F3
John Wesley Rd
  EVILLE/WHL BS5.... 337 K5
John Woolfe Cl *MIM* GL56 .... 35 H5
Jordans Cl *BDWAY* WR12 .... 11 G8 🔲
Jordan Wy *GL* GL2 .... 112 B6
Jordan Wk *ALMDB* BS32 .... 316 F3
Josend Crs *RTEWK/TIB* GL19 .... 66 A8
Joyford Hl *CLFD* GL16 .... 151 K5
Joy Hl *CFTN/FAIL* BS8 .... 335 H5 🔲
Joyner Rd *CHELTW* GL51 .... 93 J7
Joys Green Rd *MTCHDN* GL17 .... 128 C6
Jubilee Cl *DSLY* GL11 .... 229 C5
  LED HR8 .... 20 A5
Jubilee Crs *MANG/FISH* BS16 .... 328 C5
Jubilee Dr *TEWK* GL20 .... 26 C5
  THNB/SVB BS35 .... 293M3
Jubilee Gdns *CIR* GL7 .... 263 H5
  YATE/CS BS37 .... 320 C1 🔲
Jubilee La *WUE* CL12 .... 295 J4
Jubilee Pl *CBRIS/FH* BS1 .... 6 F6 🔲
  RTEWK/TIB GL19 .... 66 D5
Jubilee Rd
  BRSG/KWL/STAPK BS4 .... 346 E2
  CBRISNE BS2 .... 336 C2
  DSLY GL11 .... 253 J1
  EVILLE/WHL BS5 .... 337 H4
  KGWD/HNM BS15 .... 328 A8
  LYD GL15 .... 201 L1
  MTCHDN GL17 .... 130 C3
  RSTROUD/NAIL GL6 .... 232 C6
Jubilee St *CBRISNE* BS2 .... 7 K4
Jubilee Wy *BRKLY* GL13 .... 226 F3
  THNB/SVB BS35 .... 292 B3
  YATE/CS BS37 .... 309 L1
Judge's La *NWNT* GL18 .... 107 L2
Julian Cl *GLE* GL4 .... 136 F7 🔲
  HNLZ/SM/SNYPK/WT BS9.. 324 F8
Julian Rd
  HNLZ/SM/SNYPK/WT BS9.. 325 C8
Julius Rd *HORF/LLZ* BS7 .... 325M8
Julius Wy *LYD* GL15 .... 201 K7
Jumpers La *BRKLY* GL13 .... 227 C8
Junction Rd
  BRSG/KWL/STAPK BS4 .... 336 F7
  CHNTN OX7 .... 105 C7
Juniper Av *GLE* GL4 .... 136 D7
Juniper Ct *EVILLE/WHL* BS5 .... 336 E1 🔲
Juniper Wy *ALMDB* BS32 .... 317 H4
  STNHO GL10 .... 207 H3
Jupiter Rd *BRSTK/PCHW* BS34 .... 315M4
Jupiter Wy *GLE* GL4 .... 137 H5
Justice Av *KEYN* BS31 .... 349 G8
Justice Rd *MANG/FISH* BS16 .... 327 J8 🔲
Justicia Wy *CHELTW* GL51 .... 115 H6

I

Icehouse La *MIM* GL56 .... 79 J1
Icombe Cl *CHELTE/BC* GL52 .... 72 B8 🔲
Ida Rd *EVILLE/WHL* BS5 .... 336 E3 🔲
Iddesleigh Rd
  RDLND/MONT BS6 .... 325 K8 🔲
Idsall Dr *CHELTE/BC* GL52 .... 94 E7
Idstone Rd *MANG/FISH* BS16 .... 327 K7
Iford Cl *KEYN* BS31 .... 349 G8
Ilchester Crs
  BMSTRD/HC/WWD BS13 .... 345 K3
Ilchester Rd
  BMSTRD/HC/WWD BS13 .... 345 K3
Iles Cl *KGWD/HNM* BS15 .... 337M7
Ilex Cl *BMSTRD/HC/WWD* BS13 .. 345 H5
Ilminster Av
  BRSG/KWL/STAPK BS4 .... 346 B3
Ilsyn Gv *HGRV/WHIT* BS14 .... 346 F4
Imber Court Cl
  HGRV/WHIT BS14 .... 346 D3
Imjin Rd *CHELTE/BC* GL52 .... 3 M4
Imperial Circ *CHELT* GL50 .... 2 C6
Imperial La *CHELT* GL50 .... 2 C6
Imperial Rd *HGRV/WHIT* BS14.... 346 C3
  RDLND/MONT BS6 .... 335 K2 🔲
Imperial Sq *CHELT* GL50 .... 2 C7
Imperial Wk *HGRV/WHIT* BS14 .. 346 D2
Inchbrook Hl
  RSTROUD/NAIL GL6 .... 232 C5
India Rd *GL* GL1 .... 5 J8
Ingleside Rd *KGWD/HNM* BS15.. 337 L2
Inglestone Rd *WUE* CL12 .... 296 D6
Ingmire Rd *EVILLE/WHL* BS5 .... 326 D8
Ingst Rd *THNB/SVB* BS35 .... 291 L7
Inkerman Rd *HORF/LLZ* BS7 .... 326 A4
The Inner Down *WMALD* BS32 .. 292 F8
Inner Loop Rd *CHEP* NP16 .... 270 D5
Innerstone La *RTEWK/TIB* GL19 .. 65 K3
Innox Gdns
  BMSTRD/HC/WWD BS13 .... 345 J6 🔲
Innox La *CBATH/BATHN* BA1 .... 351 K6
Inns Court Av
  BRSG/KWL/STAPK BS4 .... 345M4
Inns Court Dr
  BRSG/KWL/STAPK BS4 .... 345 M5 🔲
Innsworth La *BWTH/CHD* GL3 .... 113 H4
  VGL GL2 .... 112 C6
Insley Gdns *GLE* GL4 .... 137 H3
Instow Rd
  BRSG/KWL/STAPK BS4 .... 346 A3
Instow Wk
  BRSG/KWL/STAPK BS4 .... 346 A3 🔲
Inverlea Ct *CHCAM* GL55 .... 8 F7
Ipswich Dr
  BRSG/KWL/STAPK BS4 .... 337 C5
Irby Rd *BMSTR* BS3 .... 335 J8
Irena Rd *MANG/FISH* BS16 .... 337 H1 🔲
Ireton Rd *BMSTR* BS3 .... 335 K8
Iron Acton Wy *YATE/CS* BS37 .... 309 J8
Iron Hogg La *WUE* CL12.... 274 E8
Ironmonger's La *BRKLY* GL13 .... 227 K7
Ironmould La
  BRSG/KWL/STAPK BS4 .... 347 J1
Ironstone Cl *LYD* GL15 .... 200 C3 🔲
Irving Cl *MANG/FISH* BS16 .... 328 A7 🔲
Isbourne Rd *CHELTE/BC* GL52 .... 3 L3
Isbourne Wy *COTS* GL54 .... 74 D3
Isleys Ct
  OLD/WMLY/WICK BS30 .... 338 B8 🔲
Islington Rd *BMSTR* BS3 .... 6 B8
Ismay Rd *CHELTW* GL51 .... 93 C7
Ison Hill Rd
  HNBRY/STHM BS10 .... 314 F8 🔲
Itchington Rd *THNB/SVB* BS35.... 294 C7
Ivor Rd *EVILLE/WHL* BS5 .... 336 E3
Ivory Cl *GL* GL1 .... 159 L1
Ivy Bank *CHELTE/BC* GL52 .... 94 E8 🔲
Ivy House La *RWYE* HR9 .... 84 E2
Ivy La *MANG/FISH* BS16 .... 327 J8 🔲
Ivywell Rd
  HNLZ/SM/SNYPK/WT BS9 .. 325 C8
Izod's Cl *CHCAM* GL55 .... 34 D1 🔲

J

Jackbarrow Rd *CIR* GL7 .... 188 C3
Jackson Cl *THNB/SVB* BS35 .... 304 F4 🔲
Jackson Crs *VGL* GL2 .... 113 C5
Jackson Rd *CHNTN* OX7 .... 125M1
  CIR GL7 .... 239 H8
Jacobs Cl *TET* GL8 .... 282 A2 🔲
Jacob St *CBRISNE* BS2 .... 7 K4
Jacob's Wells Rd *CFTN/FAIL* BS8.. 6 A4
Jamaica St *CBRISNE* BS2 .... 335M3
James Grieve Rd
  BWTH/CHD GL3 .... 137 H6
Jameson Cl *MIM* GL56 .... 58 C6 🔲
James Orch *BRKLY* GL13 .... 226 F3
James Rd *MANG/FISH* BS16 .... 328 A8
James St *CBRISNE* BS2 .... 336 C1
  EVILLE/WHL BS5.... 7 K1

James Wk *LYD* GL15 .... 201 H2
James Wy *BWTH/CHD* GL3 .... 137 L5
Jane St *EVILLE/WHL* BS5 .... 336 D4
Japonica Cl *CHELTW* GL51 .... 115 J6
Japonica Dr *CHELTW* GL52 .... 71M7
Jardine Dr *CHELTE/BC* GL52 .... 72 A7
Jarvis St *EVILLE/WHL* BS5 .... 336 D5
Jasmine Cl *GLE* GL4 .... 137 G6
Jasmine Gv *AVONM* BS11 .... 324 E1 🔲
Jasmine Wy *CHELTW* GL51 .... 115 H6
Jasper St *BMSTR* BS3 .... 335 K8 🔲
Javelin Wy *BWTH/CHD* GL3 .... 138 B6
Jay's Md *WUE* CL12 .... 277 L4
Jean Rd *BRSG/KWL/STAPK* BS4 .. 347 G1

K

Kansas Dr *CIR* GL7 .... 242 F6
Kathdene Gdns *HORF/LLZ* BS7 .. 326 B8
Katherine Dr *WUE* CL12 .... 276 C6 🔲
Katherine's Wk *CIR* GL7 .... 244 F7
Katifer La *MALM* SN16 .... 303 J8 🔲
Kaybourne Crs *BWTH/CHD* GL3... 113M6
Kayte Cl *CHELTE/BC* GL52 .... 94 B1
Kayte La *CHELTE/BC* GL52 .... 94 C2

Keats Av *VGL* GL2 .... 135 L7
Keats Gdns *STROUD* GL5 .... 208 C2 🔲
Keble Av
  BMSTRD/HC/WWD BS13 .... 345 H6
Keble Cl *CIR* GL7 .... 238 B6
  CIR GL7 .... 244 F6 🔲
Keble Lawns *CIR* GL7 .... 242 F4 🔲
Keble Rd *MIM* GL56 .... 58 D7
  RSTROUD/NAIL GL6 .... 210 C8
Keeds La *LGASH* BS41 .... 344 B2
Keedwell Hl *LGASH* BS41 .... 344 B2
The Keelings *CIND* GL14 .... 154 A2
Keels *HGHW* SN6 .... 288 E2
Keen's Gv *THNB/SVB* BS35 .... 304 C4
Keepers Ml *CHELTE/BC* GL52 .... 72 D8
The Keep
  OLD/WMLY/WICK BS30 .... 338 F6
Keetley Cl *SHPSTR* CV36 .... 16 B7
Keinton Wk *HNBRY/STHM* BS10.. 325 J1
Kelbra Crs *FRCTL/WBN* BS36.... 318 D5
Kellaway Av
  HNBRY/STHM BS10 .... 326 A5 🔲
  RDLND/MONT BS6 .... 325M6
Kellaway Crs *HORF/LLZ* BS7 .... 325M5
Kells Meend *CLFD* GL16 .... 151 J5
Kells Rd *CLFD* GL16 .... 151 J5
Kellys La *CHEP* NP16 .... 247 G1
Kelston La *KEYN* BS31 .... 348 F8
Kelston Gdns
  HNBRY/STHM BS10 .... 325 M3 🔲
Kelston Gv *KGWD/HNM* BS15 .... 338 A5
Kelston Rd *HNBRY/STHM* BS10 .. 325 L3
  KEYN BS31 .... 347M7
Kelston Wk *MANG/FISH* BS16 .... 327 L7
Kemble Cl *KGWD/HNM* BS15 .... 338 A5 🔲
Kemble Dr *CIR* GL7 .... 238 B5
Kemble Gv *CHELTW* GL51 .... 114 D4
Kemble Gv *GLE* GL4 .... 159M1
Kemerton Rd *CHELT* GL50 .... 115 K5
  TEWK GL20 .... 27 K4
Kemperleye Wy *ALMDB* BS32 .... 316 F4 🔲
Kempe's Cl *LGASH* BS41 .... 344 C1
Kempley Brook Dr *LED* HR8 .... 19 M2 🔲
Kempsford Acre
  CHELTE/BC GL52 .... 72 D8 🔲
Kemps La *RSTROUD/NAIL* GL6.... 185 H4
Kempton Cl *THNB/SVB* BS35 .... 273 K8 🔲
Kempton Gv *CHELTW* GL51 .... 114 F1
Kencot Wk
  BMSTRD/HC/WWD BS13 .... 345 K8
Kencourt Cl *VGL* GL2 .... 5 L4
Kendall Gdns *MANG/FISH* BS16 .. 327M7
Kendall Rd *MANG/FISH* BS16 .... 327M7
Kendal Rd *HORF/LLZ* BS7 .... 326 C4
  VGL GL2 .... 112 E8
Kendon Dr *HNBRY/STHM* BS10 .. 325M4
Kendon Wy *HNBRY/STHM* BS10.. 325M3
Kendrick St *STROUD* GL5 .... 208 E4 🔲
Kenelm Dr *CHELTS* GL53 .... 115 L5 🔲
Kenelm Gdns *CHELT* GL50 .... 115 K5 🔲
Kenelm Ri *COTS* GL54 .... 74 C4
Kenilworth *YATE/CS* BS37 .... 320 B3
Kenilworth Av *VGL* GL2 .... 5 L4
Kenilworth Cl *KEYN* BS31 .... 347M7
Kenilworth Dr
  OLD/WMLY/WICK BS30 .... 348 D2 🔲
Kenilworth Rd
  RDLND/MONT BS6 .... 335 L2 🔲
Kenmare
  BRSG/KWL/STAPK BS4 .... 346 A3
Kenmore Crs *HORF/LLZ* BS7 .... 326 A2
Kenmore Dr *HORF/LLZ* BS7 .... 326 A2
Kenmore Gv *HORF/LLZ* BS7 .... 326 A2 🔲
Kennard Ri *KGWD/HNM* BS15 .... 337 L4
Kennard Rd *KGWD/HNM* BS15 .. 337 L3
Kennedy Cl *GLE* GL4 .... 137 H2
Kennel Dr *BAD* GL9 .... 323 G1
Kennel La *BWTH/CHD* GL3 .... 138 A7
  CHNTN OX7 .... 105 K1
  MIM GL56 .... 80 C7
Kennel Lodge Rd *BMSTR* BS3 .... 335 G7
Kenneth Cl *CHELTS* GL53 .... 116 A7
Kenneth Rd
  BRSG/KWL/STAPK BS4 .... 346 F1
Kennet Rd *KEYN* BS31 .... 348 B7
Kennett Gdns *GLE* GL4 .... 137 G7
Kennet Wy *THNB/SVB* BS35 .... 293M3
Kennington Av *HORF/LLZ* BS7 .. 326 A7
  KGWD/HNM BS15 .... 337 M2 🔲
Kennion Rd *EVILLE/WHL* BS5 .... 337 J4 🔲
Kennmoor Cl
  OLD/WMLY/WICK BS30 .... 338 C5
Kenn Rd *EVILLE/WHL* BS5 .... 337 J4
Kensal Av *BMSTR* BS3 .... 336 A8
Kensal Rd *BMSTR* BS3 .... 336 A8
Kensington Av *CHELTW* GL51 .... 115 C4
Kensington Pk
  THNB/SVB BS35 .... 293 K1 🔲
Kensington Pk
  EVILLE/WHL BS5 .... 336 C2 🔲
Kensington Park Rd
  BRSG/KWL/STAPK BS4.... 346 E1
Kensington Pl *CFTN/FAIL* BS8 .... 335 J4
Kensington Rd
  EVILLE/WHL BS5 .... 337 J3 🔲
  MANG/FISH BS16 .... 327 M7 🔲
  RDLND/MONT BS6 .... 335 L2
Kent Av *YATE/CS* BS37 .... 310 B8
Kent Cl *BRSTK/PCHW* BS34 .... 316 F7
  BWTH/CHD GL3 .... 113M7
Kent End *HGHW* SN6 .... 287 J2
Kentmere Cl *CHELTW* GL51 .... 115 C4
Kenton Dr *VGL* GL2 .... 112 E6
Kenton Ms
  HNLZ/SM/SNYPK/WT BS9.. 325 L6
Kent Rd *HORF/LLZ* BS7 .... 326 A8
Kents Gn *KGWD/HNM* BS15....... 338 A8
Kent St *BMSTR* BS3 .... 335 L8 🔲
Keriston Av *BWTH/CHD* GL3 .... 113 J6
Kerrin La *LYD* GL15 .... 224 B7
Kerry Rd *BRSG/KWL/STAPK* BS4 .. 346 A2
Kersteman Rd
  RDLND/MONT BS6 .... 325 M8 🔲
Kerstin Cl *CHELT* GL50 .... 93 L6
Kestrel Cl *BRSTK/PCHW* BS34.... 316 A3 🔲
  CHELTS GL53 .... 115 L6
  THNB/SVB BS35 .... 293 M1 🔲

YATE/CS BS37 .... 320 B3
Kestrel Ct *STNHO* GL10 .... 207 H4
Kestrel Dr *MANG/FISH* BS16 .... 329 L7
Kestrel Gdns *VGL* GL2 .... 135 H8
Kestrel Wy *TEWK* GL20 .... 48 F2
Keswick Cl *GL* 5 M2
Keswick Rd *CHELTW* GL51 .... 115 G4
Keswick Wk
   HNBRY/STHM BS10 .... 325 L1
Ketch Rd *BMSTR* BS3 .... 336 B8
Kevin Cl *GLE* GL4 .... 136 F3
Kew Pl *CHELTS* GL53 .... 2 C9
Kews La *NWNT* GL18 .... 85 K3
Kewstoke Rd
   HNLZ/SM/SNYPK/WT BS9.. 325 G7
Kew Wk *BRSG/KWL/STAPK* BS4 .. 346 E3
Keynsham Bank *CHELTE/BC* GL52 .. 3 K7
Keynshambury Rd *CHELTS* GL53 .... 2 F7
Keynsham By-pass *KEYN* BS31 .. 348 A4
   OLD/WMLY/WICK BS30 .... 348 B4
Keynsham La *LYD* GL15 .... 223 L7
Keynsham St *CHELTS* GL53 .... 2 F8
   CHELTE/BC GL52 .... 3 G8
Keys Av *HORF/LLZ* BS7 .... 326 B4
Kibble's La *CIND* GL14 .... 154 A6
Kidnalls Rd *LYD* GL15 .... 201 H2
Kidnams Wk *VGL* GL2 .... 182 A6
Kidnappers La *CHELTS* GL53 .... 115 K7
   CHELTS GL53 ... 115 K6
Kilbirnie Rd *HGRV/WHIT* BS14.. 346 C8
Kildare Rd
   BRSG/KWL/STAPK BS4.. 345 M3
Kilham La *COTS* GL54 .... 142 F2
Kilkenny St *CBRISNE* BS2 .... 7 K4
Kilcott Rd *WUE* GL12 .... 297 M3
Kilmersdon Rd
   BMSTRD/HC/WWD BS13 .... 345 K5
Kilminster Ct *BWTH/CHD* GL3 .. 113 J5
Kiln Cl *KGWD/HNM* BS15 .... 337 K2
Kilnhurst Rd
   OLD/WMLY/WICK BS30 .... 348 B1
Kilvert Cl *BRSG/KWL/STAPK* BS4.. 336 F5
Kimberley Av *MANG/FISH* BS16 .. 327 L6
Kimberley Cl *LYD* GL15 .... 201 K8
   MANG/FISH BS16 .... 328 B4
   VGL GL2 .... 112 F7
Kimberley Crs *MANG/FISH* BS16.. 327 L6
Kimberley Dr *LYD* GL15 .... 201 K8
Kimberley Rd
   KGWD/HNM BS15 .... 337 M2
   MANG/FISH BS16 .... 328 B4
Kimberley Wk
   CHELTE/BC GL52 .... 116 E1
Kimbrose Wy *GL* GL1 .... 4 D6
Kimmins Rd *STNHO* GL10 .... 207 J3
Kinber Cl *CBATH/BATHN* BA1.. 350 C4
King Alfreds Rd *CHEP* NP16 .... 270 C4
King Alfred Wy *CHELTE/BC* GL52 .. 3 H7
King Arthur Cl *CHELTS* GL53 .... 116 B4
Kingcomb Cl *CHCAM* GL55 .... 12 B7
King Edward's Av *GL* GL1 .... 136 A5
Kingfisher Cl *ALMDB* BS32 .... 317 G1
   THNB/SVB BS35 .... 293 M1
Kingfisher Dr
   MANG/FISH BS16 .... 327 G5
Kingfisher Ri *VGL* GL2 .... 158 F2
Kingfisher Rd *YATE/CS* BS37 .... 320 C3
King George Cl *CHELTS* GL53.... 116 B5
King Georges Fld *COTS* GL54 .... 102 B3
King George's Rd
   BMSTRD/HC/WWD BS13 .... 345 H6
Kingham Rd *CHNTN* OX7 .... 104 F6
King Henry Cl *CHELTS* GL53 .... 116 B5
King Johns Ct *TEWK* GL20 .... 48 A4
King John's Rd
   KGWD/HNM BS15 .... 337 K1
King La *YATE/CS* BS37 .... 311 K8
Kingley Rd *STROUD* GL5 .... 208 A4
Kingrove Crs *YATE/CS* BS37 .... 320 E3
Kingrove La *YATE/CS* BS37 .... 320 E3
Kings Av *KGWD/HNM* BS15 .... 337 K7
   RDLND/MONT BS6 .... 325 L1
King's Barton St *GL* GL1 .... 4 F7
Kingsclere Dr *CHELTE/BC* GL52.. 72 A8
Kingscote *YATE/CS* BS37 .... 319 M5
Kingscote Av *CHELTW* GL51 .... 114 F4
Kingscote Cl *BWTH/CHD* GL3 .. 113 M7
   CHELTW GL51 .... 114 F4
Kingscote Dr *GLE* GL4 .... 137 G6
Kingscote Gv *CHELTW* GL51 .... 114 F4
Kingscote Pk *EVILLE/WHL* BS5 .. 337 K5
Kingscote Rd East
   CHELTW GL51 .... 114 F4
Kingscote Rd West
   CHELTW GL51 .... 114 F5
Kingscourt Cl *HGRV/WHIT* BS14.. 346 C6
Kingscourt La *STROUD* GL5 .... 208 C7
Kingscroft Rd *BWTH/CHD* GL3 .. 137 J4
Kingsdale Ct *BDWAY* WR12 .... 33 G3
Kingsditch La *CHELTW* GL51 .... 93 J7
Kingsdown *DSLY* GL11 .... 253 J1
Kingsdown Pde
   RDLND/MONT BS6 .... 6 E1
   RDLND/MONT BS6 .... 335 M3
Kings Dr *DSLY* GL11 .... 253 J1
   HORF/LLZ BS7 .... 325 L6
   KGWD/HNM BS15 .... 337 K7
Kings Elm *VGL* GL2 .... 90 F6
Kingsfield La *KGWD/HNM* BS15 .. 338 A4
   OLD/WMLY/WICK BS30 .... 338 A7
Kings Ga *TEWK* GL20 .... 48 D5
King's Head La
   BMSTRD/HC/WWD BS13.. 345 J4
   COTS GL54.... 142 F8
Kingshill *CIR* GL7 .... 238 F3
Kingshill La *CIR* GL7 .... 238 F5
   DSLY GL11 .... 253 J1
Kingshill Pk *DSLY* GL11 .... 229 J8
Kingshill Rd
   BRSG/KWL/STAPK BS4.. 346 D2
   DSLY GL11 .... 253 J1
Kingsholm Ct *GL* GL1 .... 4 F1
Kingsholm Rd
   KGWD/HNM BS15 .... 337 M2
Kingsholm Rd *GL* GL1 .... 4 F3
   HNBRY/STHM BS10 .... 325 M1

Kingsholm Sq *GL* GL1 .... 4 F1
Kingsland Cl *CBRISNE* BS2 .... 7 L4
Kingsland Rd *CBRISNE* BS2 .... 7 L4
Kingsland Road Br *CBRISNE* BS2 .. 7 L4
Kings La *GL* GL7 .... 221 M6
Kingsleigh Ct
   KGWD/HNM BS15 .... 338 B4
Kingsleigh Gdns
   KGWD/HNM BS15 .... 338 B4
Kingsley Gdns *CHELTW* GL51 .... 115 G2
Kingsley Rd *EVILLE/WHL* BS5 .... 336 E2
   GLE GL4 .... 136 C6
   RDLND/MONT BS6 .... 335 M1
Kingsmead *CIR* GL7 .... 238 E5
   CIR GL7 .... 244 E6
   GLE GL4 .... 137 G7
   RSTROUD/NAIL GL6 .... 185 G3
Kingsmead Av *CHELTW* GL51 .... 93 H7
Kingsmead Cl *CHELTW* GL51 .... 93 H7
Kings Meade *CLFD* GL16 .... 175 K1
Kings Meadow *COTS* GL54 .... 123 H3
   MALM SN16 .... 284 A6
Kingsmead Rd *CHELTW* GL51 .... 93 H7
   EVILLE/WHL BS5 .... 337 J2
Kingsmead Wk
   EVILLE/WHL BS5 .... 337 J2
Kingsmill
   HNLZ/SM/SNYPK/WT BS9.. 324 F6
King's Mill La
   KGWD/HNM BS15 .... 185 G5
King's Parade Av
   CFTN/FAIL BS8 .... 335 K2
King's Parade Ms
   CFTN/FAIL BS8 .... 335 J2
Kings Park Av *CBRISNE* BS2 .... 336 E5
King Sq *CBRISNE* BS2 .... 335 M3
King's
   BRSG/KWL/STAPK BS4.... 336 E8
   CFTN/FAIL BS8 .... 335 J4
   CHELTE/BC GL52 .... 3 H6
   STNHO GL10 .... 207 H2
   STROUD GL5 .... 208 D5
Kings Sq
   OLD/WMLY/WICK BS30 .... 348 F3
Kings St *RSTROUD/NAIL* GL6 .... 233 J5
Kingston Cl *MANG/FISH* BS16 .... 328 C4
Kingston Dr *CHELTW* GL51 .... 114 E2
   MANG/FISH BS16 .... 328 C4
Kingstone Av *GLE* GL4 .... 137 H2
Kingston Rd *BMSTR* BS3 .... 6 C8
   TEWK GL20 .... 48 F3
   VGL GL2 .... 204 E6
Kingstree St
   BRSG/KWL/STAPK BS4 .... 7 L9
King St *CBRIS/FH* BS1 .... 7 G6
   CHELT GL50 ... 2 C3
   CIR GL7 .... 238 D4
   EVILLE/WHL BS5 .... 336 E2
   KGWD/HNM BS15 .... 337 K3
   STROUD GL5 .... 208 E4
Kingsville Rd *CHELTW* GL51 .... 93 J6
Kings Wk
   BMSTRD/HC/WWD BS13.. 345 G4
King's Wall *MALM* SN16 .... 303 J8
Kingsway *BRSTK/PCHW* BS34.. 316 E5
   CIR GL7 .... 239 G5
   CLFD GL16 .... 151 M8
   DSLY GL11 .... 229 J8
   EVILLE/WHL BS5 .... 337 K4
Kingsway Av *KGWD/HNM* BS15.. 337 K3
Kingsway Crs
   KGWD/HNM BS15 .... 337 K3
Kingsway La *MTCHDN* GL17 .... 129 G4
Kingswear Rd *BMSTR* BS3 .... 345 M2
Kings Well La *COTS* GL54 .... 123 G2
Kings Weston Av *AVONM* BS11 .. 324 M3
Kings Weston Rd
   AVONM BS11 .... 324 F1
Kingswood Cl *CHELTE/BC* GL52 .. 72 B8
Kingswood Rd *WUE* GL12 .... 297 M3
Kington La *THNB/SVB* BS35 .... 293 H2
Kington Rd *THNB/SVB* BS35 .... 272 F6
King William Av *CBRIS/FH* BS1 .. 6 F5
King William Dr *CHELTS* GL53 .... 116 B5
King William St *BMSTR* BS3 .... 6 B9
Kinmoor *GLE* GL4 .... 136 F8
Kinsale Rd *HGRV/WHIT* BS14.. 346 E4
Kinsale Wk
   BRSG/KWL/STAPK BS4 .... 346 A2
Kinsham La *TEWK* GL20 .... 27 K7
Kinvara Rd
   BRSG/KWL/STAPK BS4.. 346 A3
Kipling Cl *VGL* GL2 .... 135 L7
Kipling Rd *CHELTW* GL51 .... 115 G2
   DSLY GL11 .... 253 L4
   HORF/LLZ BS7 .... 326 D2
Kirby Rd *COTS* GL54 .... 124 D8
Kirkby Rd *AVONM* BS11 .... 324 C2
Kirtlington Rd
   EVILLE/WHL BS5 .... 326 D8
Kitchener Av *GL* GL1 .... 136 A6
Kitefield *HGHW* SN6 .... 288 F3
Kite Hay Cl *MANG/FISH* BS16 .. 327 G6
Kites Cl *ALMDB* BS32 .... 316 E1
Kitesnest La *STROUD* GL5 .... 208 C7
Klondyke Av *LYD* GL15 .... 201 K8
Knap La *RSTROUD/NAIL* GL6 .... 185 H4
   WUE GL12 .... 275 K8
Knapp Cl *LED* HR8 .... 19 M2
Knapp La *CHELT* GL50 .... 2 B4
   DSLY GL11 .... 229 H6
   DSLY GL11 .... 230 C6
   LED HR8 .... 20 A2
   LYD GL15 .... 224 C5
   RSTROUD/NAIL GL6 .... 209 K1
   RSTROUD/NAIL GL6 .... 233 K3
Knapp Rdg *LED* HR8 .... 20 A1
Knapp Rd *CHELT* GL50 .... 2 B4
   THNB/SVB BS35 .... 293 M2
   WUE GL12 .... 277 L4
Knapps La *EVILLE/WHL* BS5 .... 337 J3
The Knapp *DSLY* GL11 .... 253 J1
   YATE/CS BS37 .... 310 B6
Knightcott Rd *CFTN/FAIL* BS8.. 334 B3
Knighton Rd
   HNBRY/STHM BS10 .... 326 A2

Knightsbridge Crs
   CHELTS GL53 .... 3 H9
Knights Crs *NWNT* GL18 .... 86 A3
Knights Wy *NWNT* GL18 .... 86 A3
   TEWK GL20 .... 48 C5
Knightwood Rd
   BRSTK/PCHW BS34 .... 317 H6
Knockley Patch *LYD* GL15 .... 200 D1
Knole Cl *ALMDB* BS32 .... 306 B7
Knole La *HNBRY/STHM* BS10 .. 315 J8
Knole Pk *ALMDB* BS32 .... 306 B8
Knoll Hl
   HNLZ/SM/SNYPK/WT BS9.. 324 F8
The Knoll *CIR* GL7 .... 266 F4
   STROUD GL5 .... 208 F4
Knollys End *VGL* GL2 .... 159 H3
Knovill Cl *AVONM* BS11 .... 324 D2
Knowle Rd
   BRSG/KWL/STAPK BS4 .. 336 C8
Knowles Rd *GL* GL1 .... 136 B4
Knowsley Rd
   MANG/FISH BS16 .... 327 G8
Knox Rd *LYD* GL15 .... 200 F4
Kyderminster Rd *COTS* GL54 .... 74 C4
Kyght Cl *KGWD/HNM* BS15 .... 338 C3
Kylross Av *HGRV/WHIT* BS14.. 346 D6
Kynges Mill Cl *MANG/FISH* BS16.. 327 J4

L

The Labbott *KEYN* BS31 .... 348 A6
Laburnum Ct *CHELTW* GL51 .... 114 E1
Laburnum Gdns *VGL* GL2 .... 159 H2
Laburnum Gv *MANG/FISH* BS16.. 327 K7
Laburnum Rd *GL* GL1 .... 135 M6
   KGWD/HNM BS15 .... 337 L6
   STNHO GL10 .... 207 G4
Laburnum Wk *STNHO* GL10 .... 207 H4
Lacca Cl *VGL* GL2 .... 112 F6
Lacemakers La *MALM* SN16 .... 303 J6
Lacey Rd *HGRV/WHIT* BS14.. 347 G5
Lacock Dr
   OLD/WMLY/WICK BS30 .... 338 B6
Lacy Cl *VGL* GL2 .... 112 E5
Ladd Cl *KGWD/HNM* BS15 .... 338 B4
Ladden Ct *THNB/SVB* BS35 .... 293 L3
The Ladder *RSTROUD/NAIL* GL6 .. 232 E7
Ladies Mile
   HNLZ/SM/SNYPK/WT BS9.. 335 H2
Ladman Gv *HGRV/WHIT* BS14.. 347 G5
Ladman Rd *HGRV/WHIT* BS14.. 347 G6
Ladybellegate St *GL* GL1 .... 4 D6
Lady Chapel Rd *GLE* GL4 .... 137 G5
Lady Margaret Ct
   CHEP NP16 .... 270 B7
Lady Md *HGHW* SN6 .... 288 F3
Ladysmith Rd *CHELTE/BC* GL52 .. 3 M3
   GL GL1 .... 136 A5
   RDLND/MONT BS6 .... 325 K7
Ladywell Cl *VGL* GL2 .... 135 K4
Laggar La *STROUD* GL5 .... 232 B2
Lake La *VGL* GL2 .... 109 K8
   VGL GL2 .... 181 J5
Lakemead Gv
   BMSTRD/HC/WWD BS13.. 345 H5
Lake Rd *HNBRY/STHM* BS10 .. 325 L4
Lakers Cl *CLFD* GL16 .... 151 K5
Lakeside *CIR* GL7 .... 242 D5
   CIR GL7 .... 263 K4
   MANG/FISH BS16 .... 327 G8
Lake Side *NWNT* GL18 .... 86 C2
Lakeside Av *LYD* GL15 .... 225 L1
Lakeside Dr *LYD* GL15 .... 225 L1
Lake St *CHELTE/BC* GL52 .... 94 D6
   VGL GL2 .... 133 M6
Lake View Rd *EVILLE/WHL* BS5.. 336 F3
Lakewood Crs
   HNBRY/STHM BS10 .... 325 K5
Lakewood Rd
   HNBRY/STHM BS10 .... 325 K5
Lambert Av *CHELTW* GL51 .... 138 F2
Lambert Cl
   BRSG/KWL/STAPK BS4.. 345 M5
   CHELTW GL51 .... 138 F2
Lambert Dr *CHELTW* GL51 .... 138 F2
Lambert Gdns *CHELTW* GL51 .... 138 F2
Lamberts Fld *COTS* GL54 .... 123 J6
Lamb La *CIND* GL14 .... 154 B3
Lambley Rd *EVILLE/WHL* BS5 .... 337 G3
Lambourn La *VGL* GL2 .... 113 G8
Lambourne Av
   RTEWK/TIB GL19 .... 108 D8
Lambourne Cl *LED* HR8 .... 20 A5
Lambourn Rd *KEYN* BS31 .... 348 C7
Lambrook Rd *MANG/FISH* BS16.. 327 J7
Lambs Barn Pitch *NWNT* GL18 .... 64 B8
Lambsdowne *DSLY* GL11 .... 229 H8
Lambsquay Rd *CLFD* GL16 .... 175 L5
Lamb St *CBRISNE* BS2 .... 7 K2
Lamord Ga *BRSTK/PCHW* BS34.. 317 G6
Lampern Vw *DSLY* GL11 .... 254 D2
Lampeter Rd
   HNLZ/SM/SNYPK/WT BS9.. 325 H4
The Lampreys *GLE* GL4 .... 136 D5
Lampton Av
   BMSTRD/HC/WWD BS13.. 346 A3
Lampton Gv
   BMSTRD/HC/WWD BS13.. 346 A3
Lampton Rd *LGASH* BS41 .... 344 B2
Lanaway Rd
   MANG/FISH BS16 .... 327 K5
Lancashire Rd *HORF/LLZ* BS7 .... 326 A8
Lancaster Cl
   BRSTK/PCHW BS34 .... 316 F7
Lancaster La *LYD* GL15 .... 201 K6
Lancaster Dr *LYD* GL15 .... 201 K6
Lancaster Rd *CBRISNE* BS2 .... 336 C1
   CIR GL7 .... 267 G5
   TEWK GL20 .... 48 B7
   YATE/CS BS37 .... 310 A8
Lancaster St
   EVILLE/WHL BS5 .... 336 E4
Lancaut La *CHEP* NP16 .... 246 B5
Lancelot Ct *VGL* GL2 .... 204 F7
Landseer Av *HORF/LLZ* BS7 .... 326 D4
The Land *FRCTL/WBN* BS36 .... 318 E4

Lane End *COTS* GL54 .... 148 B3
Lanercost Rd
   HNBRY/STHM BS10 .... 325 L1
Lanesborough Ri
   HGRV/WHIT BS14 .... 346 F4
Lanescourt *TEWK* GL20 .... 48 A5
The Lanes *CHELTS* GL53 .... 115 J7
The Lane *BDWAY* WR12 .... 32 B6
   MIM GL56 .... 81 M4
   RSTROUD/NAIL GL6 .... 207 M1
   SHPSTR CV36 .... 38 C3
   SHPSTR CV36 .... 38 C8
   THNB/SVB BS35 .... 315 H1
Langdale Gdns *VGL* GL2 .... 112 E6
Langdale Rd *CHELTW* GL51 .... 115 H4
   MANG/FISH BS16 .... 327 H7
Langdon Rd *CHELTS* GL53 .... 115 M5
Langet *CIR* GL7 .... 263 G4
Langetts Rd *CLFD* GL16 .... 175 K1
Langfield Cl
   HNBRY/STHM BS10 .... 315 H8
Langford Rd
   BMSTRD/HC/WWD BS13.. 345 H3
Langford Wy *KGWD/HNM* BS15.. 338 A4
Langham Rd
   BRSG/KWL/STAPK BS4 .. 346 D1
Langhill Av
   BRSG/KWL/STAPK BS4 .. 345 M4
The Langland *LED* HR8 .... 19 M1
Langley Crs *BMSTR* BS3 .... 345 G2
Langley Mow
   MANG/FISH BS16 .... 328 D4
Langley Rd *COTS* GL54 .... 73 K6
   GLE GL4 .... 136 D6
Langridge La
   CBATH/BATHN BA1 .... 350 D4
Langston Cl *CHNTN* OX7 .... 105 C6
Langthorn Cl *FRCTL/WBN* BS36 .. 318 D4
Langtoft Rd *STROUD* GL5 .... 209 G4
Langton Cl *GLE* GL4 .... 137 G2
Langton Court Rd
   BRSG/KWL/STAPK BS4.. 336 F6
Langton Grove Rd
   CHELTS GL53 .... 116 C4
Langton Pk *BMSTR* BS3 .... 6 C9
Langton Pl *CHELTS* GL53 .... 116 C4
Langton Rd
   BRSG/KWL/STAPK BS4.. 336 F6
Langton Wy
   BRSG/KWL/STAPK BS4 .. 337 G5
Lanham Gdns *VGL* GL2 .... 159 H4
Lannett Rd *GL* GL1 .... 136 A5
Lansdown *STROUD* GL5 .... 208 E4
   YATE/CS BS37 .... 320 A3
Lansdown Castle Dr
   CHELTW GL51 .... 115 H3
Lansdown Cl *CHELTW* GL51 .... 115 J3
   KGWD/HNM BS15 .... 337 M1
Lansdown Crs *CHELT* GL50 .... 115 K3
Lansdown Crescent La
   CHELT GL50 .... 2 A7
Lansdown La
   CBATH/BATHN BA1 .... 350 D8
   OLD/WMLY/WICK BS30 .... 349 K3
Lansdown Lodge Dr
   CHELTW GL51 .... 115 J3
Lansdown Pde *CHELT* GL50 .... 115 K3
Lansdown Pk
   CBATH/BATHN BA1 .... 351 G8
Lansdown Place La *CHELT* GL50.. 2 A7
Lansdown Rd
   CBATH/BATHN BA1 .... 350 C4
   CFTN/FAIL BS8 .... 335 J4
   CHELT GL50 ... 2 A8
   CHELTW GL51 .... 115 J3
   GL GL1 .... 5 J2
   KEYN BS31 .... 349 G8
   KGWD/HNM BS15 .... 337 M1
   MANG/FISH BS16 .... 329 L5
   RDLND/MONT BS6 .... 335 L2
Lansdown Ter
   RDLND/MONT BS6 .... 325 M6
Lansdown Terrace La *CHELT* GL50.. 2 A6
Lansdown Vw
   KGWD/HNM BS15 .... 338 A3
Lansdown Wk *CHELT* GL50 .... 2 A7
   LYD GL15 .... 200 D3
Lantern Cl *BRKLY* GL13 .... 227 G8
   CIND GL14 .... 154 A3
Lapdown La *BAD* GL9 .... 331 M2
Laphams Ct
   OLD/WMLY/WICK BS30 .... 338 B7
Lapwing Cl *ALMDB* BS32 .... 316 F1
   TEWK GL20 .... 48 F2
Lapwing Gdns
   MANG/FISH BS16 .... 327 H5
Larch Cl *CHELTS* GL53 .... 116 D6
The Larches *GLE* GL4 .... 137 G4
Larchmere Gv *CHELTW* GL51 .... 115 G6
Larch Ri *CHELTS* GL53 .... 115 K7
Larch Rd *CHPMW/MSHF* SN14 .. 343 H5
   KGWD/HNM BS15 .... 328 A8
Larch Wy *BRSTK/PCHW* BS34.. 316 A4
Larchwood Dr *GLE* GL4 .... 136 A8
Larkfield *FRCTL/WBN* BS36 .... 318 F4
Larkham Cl *GLE* GL4 .... 136 D8
Larkhay Rd *BWTH/CHD* GL3 .... 137 J2
Larkhill Cl *CHEP* NP16 .... 270 A1
Lark Ri *CLFD* GL16 .... 151 J7
Larkrise *DSLY* GL11 .... 229 H6
Lark's Fld *MANG/FISH* BS16 .... 327 G6
Larksfield Rd *MTCHDN* GL17 .... 129 M5
   STROUD GL5 .... 208 C7
Lark's La *YATE/CS* BS37 .... 308 D4
Larksleaze Rd
   OLD/WMLY/WICK BS30 .... 348 A1
Larkspear Cl *GLE* GL4 .... 136 A8
Larkspur Cl *THNB/SVB* BS35 .... 293 M1
Larput Pl *CHELT* GL50 .... 2 C1
Lasbury Gv
   BMSTRD/HC/WWD BS13.. 345 L6
Lasne Crs *BWTH/CHD* GL3 .... 138 B7
Lassington Gv *VGL* GL2 .... 110 E6
Lassington La *VGL* GL2 .... 110 E6
Latchen *MTCHDN* GL17 .... 131 H1
Latchen Orch *MTCHDN* GL17 .. 131 H1

Latimer Cl
   BRSG/KWL/STAPK BS4.. 337 G7
Latimer Rd *CIND* GL14 .... 154 C2
Latteridge La *THNB/SVB* BS35 .. 308 C3
Latteridge Rd *YATE/CS* BS37 .... 308 C3
Latton Rd *HORF/LLZ* BS7 .... 326 B3
Launceston Av
   KGWD/HNM BS15 .... 337 K6
Launceston Rd
   KGWD/HNM BS15 .... 337 K2
Laundry Rd *CLFD* GL16 .... 174 E4
Laura Cl *VGL* GL2 .... 5 L1
Laurel Av *TEWK* GL20 .... 48 C7
Laureldene *CLFD* GL16 .... 175 L6
Laurel Dr *CHELTE/BC* GL52 .... 94 D7
   CHPMW/MSHF SN14 .... 343 H5
Laurel Ga *GLE* GL4 .... 137 H7
The Laurels *GL* GL1 .... 136 B4
   HNBRY/STHM BS10 .... 315 J5
   MANG/FISH BS16 .... 328 C5
Laurel St *KGWD/HNM* BS15 .... 337 M3
Laurence Cl *CHELTW* GL51 .... 138 F1
Laurie Crs
   HNLZ/SM/SNYPK/WT BS9.. 325 M5
Laurie Lee Ct
   OLD/WMLY/WICK BS30 .... 338 C6
Lavender Cl *THNB/SVB* BS35.... 293 M2
Lavender La *CIR* GL7 .... 238 C4
Lavender Ms *CHELTE/BC* GL52 .. 72 A8
Lavender Rd *CHELTW* GL51 .... 115 H6
Lavender Vw *GLE* GL4 .... 137 H7
Lavender Wy *ALMDB* BS32 .... 317 H4
Lavenham Rd *YATE/CS* BS37 .... 319 K1
Lavers Cl *KGWD/HNM* BS15 .... 338 A5
Lavington Dr *VGL* GL2 .... 135 L7
Lavington Rd *EVILLE/WHL* BS5.. 337 K5
Lawford Av *BRSTK/PCHW* BS34.. 316 E5
Lawfords Ga *CBRISNE* BS2 .... 7 K2
Lawn Av *MANG/FISH* BS16 .... 327 K6
Lawn Crs *CHELTW* GL51 .... 139 G1
Lawn Rd *MANG/FISH* BS16 .... 327 K6
   RTEWK/TIB GL19 .... 89 J3
Lawnside *RSTROUD/NAIL* GL6 .. 232 B7
Lawnside Rd *LED* HR8 .... 19 M3
Lawns Pk *STROUD* GL5 .... 232 B1
Lawns Rd *CHELTE/BC* GL52 .... 72 D4
The Lawns *CHELTE/BC* GL52 .... 72 D4
   GLE GL4 .... 136 F8
   STNHO GL10 .... 207 G3
Lawrence Av
   EVILLE/WHL BS5 .... 336 D2
Lawrence Cl
   CHELTE/BC GL52 .... 116 D5
   KGWD/HNM BS15 .... 338 C1
Lawrence Dr *YATE/CS* BS37 .... 319 K1
Lawrence Gv *DSLY* GL11 .... 253 H1
   HNLZ/SM/SNYPK/WT BS9.. 325 K6
Lawrence Hl *CBRISNE* BS2 .... 7 L2
   EVILLE/WHL BS5 .... 336 D4
Lawrence Rd *CIR* GL7 .... 238 B4
   TET GL8 .... 257 M2
Lawrence's Meadow
   CHELTE/BC GL52 .... 72 C3
Lawrence Wy *GL* GL1 .... 4 E2
Lawrence Wy North *GL* GL1 .... 111 M7
Lawrence Weston Rd
   AVONM BS11 .... 324 E2
Lawson Gld *CHELTS* GL53 .... 116 C7
Laxey Rd *HORF/LLZ* BS7 .... 326 B4
Laxton Cl *THNB/SVB* BS35 .... 292 C3
Laxton Dr *WUE* GL12 .... 277 H7
Laxton Rd *BWTH/CHD* GL3 .... 137 J5
   CHELTW GL51 .... 115 G1
Laymore Rd *CIND* GL14 .... 153 M2
Laynes Rd *BWTH/CHD* GL3 .... 137 J3
Lays Dr *KEYN* BS31 .... 347 L7
Leacey Ct *BWTH/CHD* GL3 .... 113 J4
Lea Crs *VGL* GL2 .... 112 E6
Leacy Ms *BWTH/CHD* GL3 .... 113 J4
Leadon Cl *BWTH/CHD* GL3 .... 138 A6
Leadon Wy *LED* HR8 .... 19 L2
Leafield Rd *CIR* GL7 .... 242 F4
Leaholme Gdns
   HGRV/WHIT BS14 .... 346 C8
Leaman Cl *YATE/CS* BS37 .... 320 D2
Leamington Av *BDWAY* WR12 .. 32 F1
Leaping Stocks Rd
   RWYE HR9 .... 126 E5
Leap V *MANG/FISH* BS16 .... 328 C3
Leap Valley Crs
   MANG/FISH BS16 .... 328 B3
Lea Rd *BWTH/CHD* GL3 .... 138 B6
Lears Dr *CHELTE/BC* GL52 .... 72 C8
Leaside Cl *DSLY* GL11 .... 229 J7
Leasow La *COTS* GL54 .... 123 L7
The Leasows *CHCAM* GL55 .... 34 D1
Leaze Cl *BRKLY* GL13 .... 227 G8
The Leazes *STROUD* GL5 .... 208 F4
The Leaze *CIR* GL7 .... 263 H5
   HGHW SN6 .... 287 H2
   YATE/CS BS37 .... 319 M1
Lechlade Rd *CIR* GL7 .... 220 D8
   CIR GL7 .... 245 L1
   FGDN SN7 .... 269 G2
   HGHW SN6 .... 268 C5
Lechmere Rd *CHELTW* GL51 .... 93 G8
Leckhampton Farm Ct
   CHELTS GL53 .... 115 K8
Leckhampton Ga
   CHELTW GL51 .... 115 J7
Leckhampton Hl *CHELTS* GL53 .. 139 L4
Leckhampton La *CHELTW* GL51 .. 139 J1
Leckhampton Rd *CHELTS* GL53 .. 115 M7
Leda Av *HGRV/WHIT* BS14.. 346 C4
Ledbury Rd *MANG/FISH* BS16 .. 327 L7
Ledbury Road Crs
   RTEWK/TIB GL19 .... 66 C4
Ledmore Rd *CHELTS* GL53 .... 116 D5
Lee Cl *BRSTK/PCHW* BS34 .... 316 B3
   CHELTW GL51 .... 93 H8
Lee Rd *TEWK* GL20 .... 49 G3
Lees Hl *KGWD/HNM* BS15 .... 338 A1
Lees La *OLD/WMLY/WICK* BS30.. 338 C6
Leicester Sq
   MANG/FISH BS16 .... 327 M8
Leicester St *BMSTR* BS3 .... 6 E9

Leicester Wk
  BRSG/KWL/STAPK BS4............337 H6
Leigh La *CBATH/BATHN* BA1......341 J4
  YATE/CS BS37............329 K2
Leigh Rd *CFTN/FAIL* BS8............335 K3
Leigh St *BMSTR* BS3............335 J7 [3]
Leighton Rd *BMSTR* BS3............6 B8
  BRSG/KWL/STAPK BS4............346 C1
  CBATH/BATHN BA1............350 C8
  CHELTE/BC GL52............3 C5
Leinster Av
  BRSG/KWL/STAPK BS4............345 M3
  BRSG/KWL/STAPK BS4............346 A3
Leinster Cl *CHELTW* GL51............92 E7
Leland Cl *MALM* SN16............303 J5
Lemon La *CBRISNE* BS2............336 A3
Lena Av *EVILLE/WHL* BS5............336 E2
Lena St *EVILLE/WHL* BS5............336 D2
The Lennards *CIR* GL7............263 J4
Lenover Gdns
  BMSTRD/HC/WWD BS13............345 K7
Lensbrook *LYD* GL15............202 C4
Leonard La *CBRIS/FH* BS1............6 E3
Leonard Rd *EVILLE/WHL* BS5............336 E4
  GL GL1............136 B5
Leonards Av *EVILLE/WHL* BS5..336 E5
Leopold Rd *RDLND/MONT* BS6......336 A1
Letch Hill Rd *COTS* GL54............123 J4
Letch La *COTS* GL54............123 H6
Leven Cl *VGL* GL2............112 F7
Lever's HI *DSLY* GL11............230 E5
Lewington Rd
  MANG/FISH BS16............327 L7
Lewins Md *CBRIS/FH* BS1............6 E3
Lewin St *EVILLE/WHL* BS5............336 F4 [3]
Lewis Av *VGL* GL2............112 B5
Lewis Cl *OLD/WMLY/WICK* BS30..338 F6
Lewisham Rd *GL* GL1............136 A6
Lewis La *CIR* GL7............238 D3
Lewis Rd
  BMSTRD/HC/WWD BS13............345 J3
  CHELTE GL51............114 F1
  CHNTN OX7............105 M1
Lewis St *CBRISNE* BS2............7 M6
  CBRISNE BS2............336 D6
Lewiston Rd *STROUD* GL5............233 J2 [1]
Lewis Wy *CHEP* NP16............270 B7 [3]
Lewton La *FRCTL/WBN* BS36............318 A4
Leyland Wk
  BMSTRD/HC/WWD BS13............345 H7
Ley La *THNB/SVB* BS35............292 B8
Ley Orch *BDWAY* WR12............11 H7
Ley Rd *CIND* GL14............133 H5
Leysbourne *CHCAM* GL55............12 E8 [3]
Leyson Rd *CHELTW* GL51............114 E5
The Leys *BRKLY* GL13............227 G7
  CHNTN OX7............105 M1
The Ley *COR/BOX* SN13............353 M6
Leyton Vis *RDLND/MONT* BS6......335 K1
Libby's Dr *STROUD* GL5............208 C8
Libertus Ct *CHELTW* GL51............115 J2 [3]
Libertus Rd *CHELTW* GL51............115 H2
Lichfield Dr *CHELT* GL50............115 J6
Lichfield Rd
  BRSG/KWL/STAPK BS4............337 G5
  GLE GL4............136 B5
Lidderdale Rd *COTS* GL54............124 D8
Liddington Cl *CHELTS* GL53............115 M1 [2]
Liddington Rd *VGL* GL2............113 G8
Lifford Gdns *BDWAY* WR12............32 E3
Lightenbrook La *VGL* GL2............204 E8
Lightwood La
  RSTROUD/NAIL GL6............184 A8
Lilac Cl *CHELT* GL51............115 J6
  HNBRY/STHM BS10............325 L2
Lilac Wy *GL* GL1............135 L8
  VGL GL2............159 C2
Lillian St *EVILLE/WHL* BS5............336 E3 [3]
Lilliesfield Av *GLE* GL4............137 G3
Lilliput Av *YATE/CS* BS37............320 C3
Lilliput Ct *YATE/CS* BS37............320 C3
Lilly Hall La *LED* HR8............19 H6
Lilstock Av *HORF/LLZ* BS7............326 B7
Lilton Wk
  BMSTRD/HC/WWD BS13............345 J2 [3]
Lilymead Av
  BRSG/KWL/STAPK BS4............336 C8
Limber HI *CHELTW* GL51............93 L6
Lime Av *BAD* GL9............322 E2
Lime Cl *CHELTE/BC* GL52............94 C6
  CHPMW/MSHF SN14............343 H6
  HNBRY/STHM BS10............315 K8
Lime Cft *YATE/CS* BS37............310 C7
Lime Gv *STROUD* GL5............208 E4 [3]
  THNB/SVB BS35............293 H6
Lime Kiln Cl *BRSTK/PCHW* BS34..347 J3
Lime Kiln Gdns *ALMDB* BS32............306 F8 [2]
Limekiln Gv *VGL* GL2............110 F6
Limekiln La *RSTROUD/NAIL* GL6..210 E4
Limekiln Rd *WUE* GL12............309 L1
Limerick Rd *RDLND/MONT* BS6......335 L1
Lime Rd *BMSTR* BS3............6 A9
  KGWD/HNM BS15............337 J6
  TEWK GL20............48 C8
Limes Cl *CIR* GL7............238 C3
Limes Pl *HGHW* SN6............264 E7
Limes Rd *CIR* GL7............261 H4
The Limes *BAD* GL9............323 C1
  VGL GL2............112 A6 [3]
Limestone Link
  CBATH/BATHN BA1............352 C5
  CHPMW/MSHF SN14............341 J6
Lime St *RTEWK/TIB* GL19............67 J3
Lime Tree Av *BDWAY* WR12............32 F2
Lime Wy *LYD* GL15............201 K7
Linacre Crs *CIR* GL7............238 B5 [1]
Lincoln Av *CHELTW* GL51............115 J6
Lincoln Cl *KEYN* BS31............347 L7
  TEWK GL20............47 M7
Lincoln Green La *TEWK* GL20............47 M8
Lincoln St *EVILLE/WHL* BS5............336 D4
Lincombe Av *MANG/FISH* BS16..327 M6 [1]
Lincombe Rd *MANG/FISH* BS16..327 L6
Linden Av *CHELTE/BC* GL52............94 C6
Linden Cl
  CHEP NP16............270 A6 [3]
  CHPMW/MSHF SN14............343 H5 [2]
  FRCTL/WBN BS36............318 A5

  KGWD/HNM BS15............337 K1
Linden Dr *ALMDB* BS32............316 F3
Linden Rd *GL* GL1............135 M4
  RDLND/MONT BS6............325 K7
Lindrea St *BMSTR* BS3............335 K8 [3]
Lindsay Rd *HORF/LLZ* BS7............326 C7
Linegar Wood Rd *CIND* GL14......154 A6
The Line *RWYE* HR9............84 C5
Linfoot Rd *TET* GL8............281 M4
Lingfield Pk *FRCTL/WBN* BS36..46 A8
Linkend Rd *RTEWK/TIB* GL19............46 A8
Link Rd *BRSTK/PCHW* BS34............316 B8
  LYD GL15............201 H1
  TEWK GL20............48 B5 [3]
  YATE/CS BS37............320 B2
The Links *CLFD* GL16............175 J2 [3]
Links Vw *CIR* GL7............214 B6
Linnell Cl *HORF/LLZ* BS7............326 D5 [3]
Linnet Cl *BRSTK/PCHW* BS34............316 A3
  GLE GL4............136 E6
Linsley Wy *BRSTK/PCHW* BS34............316 A3
Lintern Crs
  OLD/WMLY/WICK BS30............338 C5
Lintham Dr *KGWD/HNM* BS15......338 B5
Linton Rd *RWYE* HR9............84 E3
Linwell Cl *CHELTW* GL51............93 K6
Linworth Rd *CHELTE/BC* GL52............72 C5
Lion Cl *VGL* GL2............159 H1 [3]
Lipson Rd *CHELTW* GL51............93 G7
Lisburn Rd
  BRSG/KWL/STAPK BS4............346 A3
Lisle Pl *WUE* GL12............277 J4
Litfield Rd *CFTN/FAIL* BS8............335 H3
Lithgow Rd *COTS* GL54............124 D8
Little Acorns *CHELTE/BC* GL52............72 A6
Little Ann St *CBRISNE* BS2............7 K2
Little Birch Cft
  HGRV/WHIT BS14............346 C8
Little Bishop St *CBRISNE* BS2....336 A3 [3]
Little Bristol La *WUE* GL12............276 C6
Little Caroline Pl
  CFTN/FAIL BS8............335 H6 [3]
Little Cleevemount
  CHELTE/BC GL52............3 G1
Littlecote Cl *CHELTE/BC* GL52....72 A8 [3]
Littledean *YATE/CS* BS37............320 A5
Littledean Hill Rd *CIND* GL14......154 C3
Little Dowles
  OLD/WMLY/WICK BS30............338 C7 [2]
Littledown Rd *CHELTS* GL53............116 A1 [3]
Little Elmbridge *VGL* GL2............112 F7
Little Fld *GLE* GL4............136 F4 [3]
Littlefield *VGL* GL2............159 G1
Little George St *CBRISNE* BS2............7 K1
Little Green La *THNB/SVB* BS35...304 C4
Little Hayes
  MANG/FISH BS16............327 K5 [2]
Little Headley Cl
  BMSTRD/HC/WWD BS13............345 K4
Little Herbert's Cl *CHELTS* GL53...116 D6
Little Herbert's Rd *CHELTS* GL53...116 D6
Little Holbury *VGL* GL2............182 A6
Little Horcott La *CIR* GL7............242 E5 [3]
Little King St *CBRIS/FH* BS1............6 F5 [3]
Little Marcle Rd *LED* HR8............19 L4
Littlemead *COR/BOX* SN13............353 M6
Little Meadow *ALMDB* BS32............317 H5
Little Normans *VGL* GL2............112 E6
Little Orch *CHELTE/BC* GL52............72 A7 [3]
Little Paradise *BMSTR* BS3............6 A9
Little Parr Cl
  MANG/FISH BS16............326 E6 [3]
Little Paul St *CBRISNE* BS2............335 L3
Little Stoke La
  BRSTK/PCHW BS34............316 E4
Little Stoke Rd
  HNLZ/SM/SNYPK/WT BS9............325 G7
Littleton Rd *BMSTR* BS3............345 M1
Little Trewen La *RWYE* HR9............126 B2
Little Withey Md
  HNLZ/SM/SNYPK/WT BS9............325 H5
Littlewood Cl *HGRV/WHIT* BS14...346 D8
Littleworth *CHCAM* GL55............12 D8
Livia Wy *LYD* GL15............201 K7
Llandilo St *GL* GL1............136 B4 [3]
Llanthony Rd *VGL* GL2............4 A8
Lime Tree Ct *GL* GL1............136 A6 [3]
Lobleys Dr *GLE* GL4............137 H6
Lockemor Rd
  BMSTRD/HC/WWD BS13............346 B7
Lockeridge La *UUSV* WR8............23 K1
Lock Gdns
  BMSTRD/HC/WWD BS13............345 G4
Locking HI *STROUD* GL5............208 E4 [3]
Lockingwell Rd *KEYN* BS31............347 M6
Lockleaze Rd *HORF/LLZ* BS7............326 C5
Locombe HI *CIR* GL7............220 D3
Locombe Pl *WUE* GL12............277 L5
Loden Brook Cl *LED* HR8............19 M2
Lodersfield *CIR* GL7............244 E7
Lodge Cswy *MANG/FISH* BS16....327 H8
Lodge Dr *LGASH* BS41............344 D1
  OLD/WMLY/WICK BS30............348 L1 [1]
Lodge Gdns *LYD* GL15............198 F5 [1]
Lodge HI *KGWD/HNM* BS15............337 L1
Lodge La *LYD* GL15............200 C8
Lodgemore Cl *STROUD* GL5............208 C4
Lodgemore La *STROUD* GL5............208 C4
Lodge Rd *KGWD/HNM* BS15............337 L1
  OLD/WMLY/WICK BS30............339 J3 [1]
  YATE/CS BS37............319 J1
Lodgeside Av
  KGWD/HNM BS15............337 L2 [2]
Lodgeside Gdns
  KGWD/HNM BS15............337 L2
Lodge St *CBRIS/FH* BS1............6 D3
Lodge Wk *MANG/FISH* BS16............327 M5
Lodore Rd *MANG/FISH* BS16......327 H8 [3]
Lodway Rd
  BRSG/KWL/STAPK BS4............346 L1
Logan Rd *HORF/LLZ* BS7............325 M8
Logus Ct
  OLD/WMLY/WICK BS30............338 B7 [1] [3]

Loiterpin *LYD* GL15............178 D7
Lombard St *BMSTR* BS3............6 E9 [3]
Lomond Rd *HORF/LLZ* BS7............326 B2 [3]
London Rd *CBRISNE* BS2............336 B2 [1]
  CHELTE/BC GL52............2 F7
  CHELTE/BC GL52............117 G7
  CHELTS GL53............3 H9
  CIR GL7............238 D3
  COR/BOX SN13............353 M5
  GL GL1............5 H4
  MIM GL56............58 D5
  OLD/WMLY/WICK BS30............338 E4
  OLD/WMLY/WICK BS30............340 A5
  SHPSTR CV36............16 B7
  STROUD GL5............208 E5
  TET GL8............281 M3 [1]
  TET GL8............282 A3
London Rd East
  CBATH/BATHN BA1............352 C5
London St *KGWD/HNM* BS15......337 M3
Lone La *MONM* NP25............174 A4
Longacre Rd *HGRV/WHIT* BS14...346 C8
Long Acres *LED* HR8............19 M3
Long Acres Cl
  HNLZ/SM/SNYPK/WT BS9............324 F4
Long Ashton Rd *LGASH* BS41......344 C2
Longaston Cl *VGL* GL2............204 F7
Longaston La *VGL* GL2............204 F6
Long Beach Rd
  OLD/WMLY/WICK BS30............348 C1
Longborough Dr *GLE* GL4............137 G6
Long Cl *ALMDB* BS32............317 C5
  MANG/FISH BS16............327 L5
Long Cft *CHELTW* GL51............309 M6
Long Cross *AVONM* BS11............324 A3
Longden Rd *MANG/FISH* BS16....328 B5
Long Eaton Dr
  HGRV/WHIT BS14............346 D3
Long Eights *TEWK* GL20............48 F3 [2]
Long Fld *VGL* GL2............110 F5
Longfield *VGL* GL2............159 C3 [3]
Longfield Rd *HORF/LLZ* BS7............326 A8
Longford *YATE/CS* BS37............319 L3
Longford Av
  HNBRY/STHM BS10............325 M3
Longford La *VGL* GL2............112 C5
Longford Ms *VGL* GL2............112 B5 [3]
Long Furlong *CHELTE/BC* GL52....72 B4 [3]
Long Furlong La *TET* GL8............281 L6
Long Handstones
  OLD/WMLY/WICK BS30............338 C7
Longhill Rd *GL* GL1............212 D2
Longhope Cl *GLE* GL4............137 G6 [3]
Longhope Rd *RTEWK/TIB* GL19...108 B8
Longland Ct *VGL* GL2............112 D7 [3]
  VGL GL2............112 D6 [2]
Longland Gdns *VGL* GL2............112 D7
Longlands Cl *CHELTE/BC* GL52....72 D7 [3]
Longlands Rd *CHELTE/BC* GL52...72 D8 [3]
Longleat Av *GL* GL1............159 L2
Longleat Cl
  HNLZ/SM/SNYPK/WT BS9............325 L6 [1]
Longlength La
  RSTROUD/NAIL GL6............256 E3
Long Marston Rd *STRAT* CV37......8 E3
Long Md *YATE/CS* BS37............310 A6
Longmead Av *HORF/LLZ* BS7......325 M6
Long Meadow
  MANG/FISH BS16............326 F6
Longmeadow Rd *KEYN* BS31......347 L7
Longmoor Rd *BMSTR* BS3............345 J1
Longmore Av *COTS* GL54............124 D7
Long Mynd Av *CHELTW* GL51......115 C5
Longney Pl *BRSTK/PCHW* BS34...316 B2 [3]
Longney Rd *GL* GL1............135 L8
Longreach Gv
  HGRV/WHIT BS14............346 F4
Longridge La *RTEWK/TIB* GL19...89 H5
Long Rd *MANG/FISH* BS16............328 C6
Long Rw *CBRIS/FH* BS1............7 G5 [3]
  HGHW SN6............266 D7 [3]
Longs Dr *YATE/CS* BS37............309 L8 [1]
  YATE/CS BS37............319 M1 [3]
Longsmith St *GL* GL1............4 E5 [3]
Longsplatt *COR/BOX* SN13............353 L8
Long St *DSLY* GL11............253 K2
  TET GL8............282 A4 [3]
  WUE GL12............277 K4
Longs Vw *WUE* GL12............276 C5
Longtree Cl *TET* GL8............281 M2
Longville Cl *GLE* GL4............137 H6
Longway Av *CHELTS* GL53............116 B7
  HGRV/WHIT BS14............346 B7
Longwood
  BRSG/KWL/STAPK BS4............347 J1
Longwood La *CFTN/FAIL* BS8......334 A7
The Lonk *CLFD* GL16............151 K5
Lonsdale Rd *VGL* GL2............136 E1
Loop Rd *CHEP* NP16............270 D5
Lorain Wk *HNBRY/STHM* BS10...325 H1
Lord Eldon Dr *CHEP* NP16............270 B7 [3]
Lords Gn *CHELTE/BC* GL52............72 E8
Lord's HI *CLFD* GL16............175 K1
Lords Piece Rd *CHNTN* OX7............105 M2
Loriners Cl *VGL* GL2............159 H1
Lorton Rd *HNBRY/STHM* BS10...325 J2
The Lotts *STNHO* GL10............287 H3
Louisa St *CBRISNE* BS2............7 K4
Louise Av *MANG/FISH* BS16......328 C6 [3]
Lovedays Md *STROUD* GL5............208 E3
Love La *CIR* GL7............238 D5
  YATE/CS BS37............310 C7
  YATE/CS BS37............320 C5
Lovelinch Gdns *LGASH* BS41......344 B2 [3]
Lovell Av
  OLD/WMLY/WICK BS30............338 F7 [2]
Lovell's HI *KGWD/HNM* BS15......337 K6 [1]
Loveringe Cl
  HNBRY/STHM BS10............315 H7
Lover's La *MALM* SN16............303 J4
Lovers Wk *RWYE* HR9............84 F3
Lovett Rd *RTEWK/TIB* GL19............66 D4
Lowbourne *HNRY/WHIT* BS14......346 B5
Lowdilow La *CHELTW* GL51............92 F2 [3]
Lower Ashley Rd
  EVILLE/WHL BS5............336 C2 [3]
  RDLND/MONT BS6............336 B2
Lower Berrycroft *BRKLY* GL13...227 C8 [3]

Lower Castle St *CBRISNE* BS1............7 H2
Lower Chapel La
  FRCTL/WBN BS36............318 E4
Lower Chapel Rd
  KGWD/HNM BS15............337 L6 [3]
Lower Cheltenham Pl
  RDLND/MONT BS6............336 B2
Lower Churchfield Rd
  STROUD GL5............208 F5 [3]
Lower Church La *CBRISNE* BS2............6 D3
Lower Church St *CHEP* NP16......270 B2
Lower Clifton HI *CFTN/FAIL* BS8......6 A4
  CFTN/FAIL BS8............335 J3
Lower Cock Rd
  KGWD/HNM BS15............338 B4
Lower College St *CBRIS/FH* BS1...6 C5 [3]
Lower Common *LYD* GL15............224 C2
Lower Court Rd *ALMDB* BS32......306 C6
Lower Cft *CIR* GL7............242 F4
Lower End *CHNTN* OX7............83 H7
Lower Fallow Cl
  HGRV/WHIT BS14............346 B8 [3]
Lower Gay St *CBRISNE* BS2......335 M3 [3] [3]
Lower Grove Rd
  MANG/FISH BS16............327 G7 [3]
Lower Guinea St *CBRIS/FH* BS1......6 F7
Lower Hanham Rd
  KGWD/HNM BS15............337 L6
Lower High St *CHCAM* GL55............12 D8
Lower House Crs
  BRSTK/PCHW BS34............316 D7
Lower Kingsdown Rd
  CBATH/BATHN BA1............353 H8
  COR/BOX SN13............353 J7
Lower Kitesnest La
  RSTROUD/NAIL GL6............184 B8
Lower Knole La
  HNBRY/STHM BS10............315 J8
Lower Lamb St *CBRIS/FH* BS1......6 C5
Lower Lode La *TEWK* GL20............47 L7
Lower Maudlin St
  CBRIS/FH BS1............6 F2 [3]
Lower Meadow *VGL* GL2............159 H4
Lower Mill St *CHELTW* GL51......115 L1
Lower Moor Rd *YATE/CS* BS37...310 A7
Lower Newmarket Rd
  RSTROUD/NAIL GL6............232 D7
Lower Northend
  CBATH/BATHN BA1............352 B6
Lower Park Rw *CBRIS/FH* BS1............6 E3 [3]
Lower Park St *COTS* GL54............102 A3
Lower Poole Rd *DSLY* GL11............253 K3
Lower Quay St *GL* GL1............4 D4
Lower Redland Rd
  RDLND/MONT BS6............335 K1
Lower Rd *CIND* GL14............178 D2
  CLFD GL16............151 K6
  LED HR8............19 L4
  LYD GL15............177 J8
  LYD GL15............198 F6
Lower Sidney St *BMSTR* BS3............335 J7
Lower Station Approach Rd
  CBRIS/FH BS1............7 J6 [3]
Lower Station Rd
  MANG/FISH BS16............327 H7
Lower Stone Cl
  FRCTL/WBN BS36............318 E3
Lower St *MIM* GL56............57 H1
  RSTROUD/NAIL GL6............184 B8
  STROUD GL5............208 C5
Lower Tockington Rd
  ALMDB BS32............306 D3
Lower Tuffley La *VGL* GL2............135 K7
Lower Washwell La
  RSTROUD/NAIL GL6............185 H3
Loweswater Cl *CHELTW* GL51......115 H4
Loweswater Rd *CHELTW* GL51...115 H4
Lowfield Rd *TET* GL8............281 M3
Lowlis Cl *HNBRY/STHM* BS10......315 H8 [3]
Lowther Rd
  HNBRY/STHM BS10............325 L1 [3]
Loxton Sq *HGRV/WHIT* BS14......346 C8
Lucas Cl *BRSG/KWL/STAPK* BS4...346 F1
Luccombe HI
  RDLND/MONT BS6............335 K1 [3]
Luckington Rd *HORF/LLZ* BS7......326 A3
Luckley Av
  BMSTRD/HC/WWD BS13............345 L6 [3]
Luckwell Rd *BMSTR* BS3............335 K8
Lucky La *BMSTR* BS3............6 E8 [3]
Ludgate HI *WUE* GL12............277 L4 [3]
Ludlow Cl *CBRISNE* BS2............336 B2
  KEYN BS31............347 M6
  OLD/WMLY/WICK BS30............348 D1
Ludlow Rd *HORF/LLZ* BS7............326 C4
Ludwell Cl *FRCTL/WBN* BS36............317 M6 [3]
The Luggs *STNHO* GL10............207 J8 [3]
Luke La *BWTH/CHD* GL3............113 C5
Lullington Rd
  BRSG/KWL/STAPK BS4............346 D1
Lulsgate Rd
  BMSTRD/HC/WWD BS13............345 J3
Lulworth Crs *MANG/FISH* BS16...328 B3 [3]
Lulworth Rd *KEYN* BS31............348 A7
Lurgan Wk
  BRSG/KWL/STAPK BS4............345 M2
Lurks La *RSTROUD/NAIL* GL6......184 D7
Lux Furlong
  HNLZ/SM/SNYPK/WT BS9............324 D4
Luxton St *EVILLE/WHL* BS5............336 D3 [3]
Lych Gate Ms *LYD* GL15............225 J1
Lydbrook Cl *YATE/CS* BS37......319 M3 [3]
Lyddington Rd *HORF/LLZ* BS7......326 A2
Lydfield Rd *LYD* GL15............201 J8
Lydford Wk *BMSTR* BS3............345 L1
Lydiard Cft *KGWD/HNM* BS15......337 L7
Lydney Rd *HNBRY/STHM* BS10...325 M3
  LYD GL15............200 C4
  MANG/FISH BS16............328 A7
Lydstep Ter *BMSTR* BS3............6 C9
Lyefield Rd East *CHELTS* GL53...116 C5
Lyefield Rd West *CHELTS* GL53...116 C5
Lye La *CHELTE/BC* GL52............72 F5
Lygon Ct *CIR* GL7............242 F5 [3]
Lynbrook *LGASH* BS41............344 B2
Lynch Ct
  OLD/WMLY/WICK BS30............338 D7 [1] [3]
Lynch Rd *BRKLY* GL13............226 F8

  RSTROUD/NAIL GL6............210 C8
Lyncombe Wk
  MANG/FISH BS16............337 K1 [3]
Lyncroft *VGL* GL2............134 B4
Lyndale Av
  HNLZ/SM/SNYPK/WT BS9............324 E6
Lyndale Rd *EVILLE/WHL* BS5............336 F3
  YATE/CS BS37............319 M2
Lynde Cl
  BMSTRD/HC/WWD BS13............345 K7
Lyndhurst Cl *CHELTE/BC* GL52....72 D8 [3]
Lyndhurst Rd
  HNLZ/SM/SNYPK/WT BS9............325 H4
  KEYN BS31............348 B8
Lyndley Cha *CHELTE/BC* GL52......71 M7
Lyng Cl *GLE* GL4............137 G3
Lynmouth Rd *BWTH/CHD* GL3......137 H5
  CBRISNE BS2............336 C1 [3]
Lynn Rd *MANG/FISH* BS16............326 F6 [3]
Lynton Pl *EVILLE/WHL* BS5............336 E3
Lynton Rd *BMSTR* BS3............345 M2
  GLE GL4............137 H4
Lynton Wy *MANG/FISH* BS16......327 K2
Lynwood Rd *LYD* GL15............201 J6
Lynworth La *TEWK* GL20............26 B5
Lynworth Pl *CHELTE/BC* GL52......3 K1
Lyons Court Rd
  HGRV/WHIT BS14............346 F4
Lypiatt Dr *CHELT* GL50............2 A8
Lypiatt La *CHELT* GL50............2 A8
Lypiatt Rd *CHELT* GL50............2 A9
Lypiatt Vw *RSTROUD/NAIL* GL6...209 L2 [1]
Lyppiatt Rd *EVILLE/WHL* BS5............336 F3
Lyppincourt Rd
  HNBRY/STHM BS10............315 J8
Lysander Ct *BWTH/CHD* GL3......113 L6 [3]
Lysander Rd
  BRSTK/PCHW BS34............315 L5
  BRSTK/PCHW BS34............315 K5
Lysander Wk
  BRSTK/PCHW BS34............317 C6 [3]
Lysons Av *GL* GL1............135 M4
Lytchet Dr *MANG/FISH* BS16......328 B3 [3]
Lytton Gv *HORF/LLZ* BS7............326 C3
  KEYN BS31............348 C6
Lyveden Gdns
  BMSTRD/HC/WWD BS13............345 K6 [3]
Lyvedon Wy *LGASH* BS41............344 D2

M

Mabel's Furlong *LED* HR8............20 A5
Macarthur Rd *COTS* GL54............169 J1
Macauley Rd *HORF/LLZ* BS7......326 C3
Macey's
  BMSTRD/HC/WWD BS13............345 M8 [3]
Machen Rd *CLFD* GL16............151 M8
Machin Cl *HNBRY/STHM* BS10...315 H8
Machin Gdns
  HNBRY/STHM BS10............315 J8 [3]
Machin Rd *HNBRY/STHM* BS10...315 H8
The Macies *CBATH/BATHN* BA1...350 D8
Mackenzie Wy *CHELTW* GL51......93 J6
Mackie Av *BRSTK/PCHW* BS34...326 D1
Mackie Gv *BRSTK/PCHW* BS34...326 D1
Mackie Rd *BRSTK/PCHW* BS34...326 D1
Macmillan Wy *CIR* GL7............189 M4
  CIR GL7............213 H2
  CIR GL7............235 L6
  COTS GL54............121 M8
  COTS GL54............122 F2
  COTS GL54............168 D1
  MIM GL56............103 K1
  SHPSTR CV36............61 H7
  TET GL8............258 F2
  TET GL8............281 G5
  TET GL8............300 C3
Macmillian Wy *TET* GL8............281 H3
Macrae Ct *KGWD/HNM* BS15......338 A3 [3]
Madeline Cl
  MANG/FISH BS16............337 H1 [3]
Madison Cl *YATE/CS* BS37............319 M1
Madleaze Rd *GL* GL1............4 B9
Madocke Rd *CHEP* NP16............270 C4 [3]
Maesbury *KGWD/HNM* BS15......338 A5
Maesknoll Rd
  BRSG/KWL/STAPK BS4............336 C8
Magdala Rd *GL* GL1............5 H7
Magdalene Pl *CBRISNE* BS2............336 B2
Magdalen Rd *TET* GL8............281 M3
Maggs Cl *HNBRY/STHM* BS10......315 L8
Maggs La *EVILLE/WHL* BS5............337 G1
  HGRV/WHIT BS14............346 D7
Magnolia Cl *CHEP* NP16............270 B6 [3]
Magnolia Wk *VGL* GL2............159 G2 [3]
Magpie Bottom La
  KGWD/HNM BS15............337 L5 [1]
Magpie Ct *STNHO* GL10............207 H3 [3]
Maida Vale *CHELTS* GL53............115 M5 [1]
Maidenhall *VGL* GL2............110 F6
Maidenhead Rd
  BMSTRD/HC/WWD BS13............345 M8
Maidstone St *BMSTR* BS3............336 B8
Main Rd *CLFD* GL16............151 M7
  LYD GL15............201 H1
  LYD GL15............224 C5
  LYD GL15............224 B7
  MANG/FISH BS16............328 E7
  RSTROUD/NAIL GL6............184 B7
Main St *BDWAY* WR12............11 G7
  CHNTN OX7............125 M1
  EVE WR11............30 C2
  MIM GL56............81 L8
  SHPSTR CV36............38 C3
  TEWK GL20............28 F7
Main Vw *FRCTL/WBN* BS36............318 F4
Maisemore *YATE/CS* BS37............319 M4
Maisemore Av
  BRSTK/PCHW BS34............316 D2
Maitlands *GLE* GL4............160 B6
Makin Cl
  OLD/WMLY/WICK BS30............338 E6 [2]
Malago Rd *BMSTR* BS3............335 L8

Malago Wk
BMSTRD/HC/WWD BS13 .... 345 G7 8

Malden Rd *CHELTE/BC* GL52 ...... 2 F3
The Maldens *SHPSTR* CV36 ...... 16 A6
Maldon Gdns *GL* GL1 .... 136 B4
Maldowers La *EVILLE/WHL* BS5 .. 337 J2
Malet Cl *VGL* GL2 .... 112 E6 8
Mallard Cl *ALMDB* BS32 .... 316 F1
  EVILLE/WHL BS5 .... 337 H2
  VGL GL2 .... 158 F2
  YATE/CS BS37 .... 320 C3
Malleson Rd *CHELTE/BC* GL52 .. 72 B3
Mallow Cl *THNB/SVB* BS35 ...... 293 M1
The Mall *CFTN/FAIL* BS8 .... 335 H4
Malmains Dr *MANG/FISH* BS16 .. 327 K2
Malmesbury Cl
  OLD/WMLY/WICK BS30 .... 338 B6 8
  RDLND/MONT BS6 .... 325 L7 8
Malmesbury Rd *CHELTW* GL51 .. 93 J6
  GLE GL4 .... 136 B4
  SWDNW SN5 .... 287 H8
Malmsey Cl *TEWK* GL20 .... 48 B3
Malthouse La *CHELT* GL50 ...... 2 D2
  COTS GL54 .... 74 C6
  COTS GL54 .... 123 G1 8
  SHPSTR CV36 .... 61 H5
Malthouse Wk *TET* GL8 .... 281 M3 8
The Maltings *MALM* SN16 ...... 303 J8
Malvern Cl *EVILLE/WHL* BS5 .... 337 H4
Malvern Dr
  OLD/WMLY/WICK BS30 .... 338 E6
  THNB/SVB BS35 .... 293 M3
Malvern Pl *CHELT* GL50 .... 115 K3
Malvern Rd
  BRSG/KWL/STAPK BS4 .... 336 F8
  CHELT GL50 .... 115 K2
  EVILLE/WHL BS5 .... 337 H4
  GL GL1 .... 5 H1
  RTEWK/TIB GL19 .... 66 E4
The Malverns *GLE* GL4 .... 136 F5
Malvern St *CHELTW* GL51 ...... 93 K7
Malvern Wy *CLFD* GL16 .... 152 A4
Mancroft Av *AVONM* BS11 ...... 324 B4
Mandalay Dr *VGL* GL2 .... 90 F6
Mandara Gv *GLE* GL4 .... 136 F7
Mandarin Wy *CHELTW* GL51 .... 93 K6
Mangotsfield Rd
  MANG/FISH BS16 .... 328 B7
Manilla Rd *CFTN/FAIL* BS8 ...... 335 J4
Mankley Rd *STNHO* GL10 ...... 207 H7
Manley Gdns *VGL* GL2 .... 112 E6 8
Mannings Rd *MTCHDN* GL17 .. 129 M2
Manor Av *DSLY* GL11 .... 229 H6
Manor Cl *ALMDB* BS32 .... 306 D2
  CIR GL7 .... 214 B6
  CIR GL7 .... 242 F4 8
  DSLY GL11 .... 229 C5
  FRCTL/WBN BS36 .... 318 E5
  RSTROUD/NAIL GL6 .... 233 H5
  TEWK GL20 .... 50 C5
The Manor Cl *CFTN/FAIL* BS8 .. 334 C3
Manor Ct *CHELTW* GL51 .... 93 J5
Manor Court Dr *HORF/LLZ* BS7 .. 326 A4
Manor Farm *COTS* GL54 ...... 124 A7 8
Manor Farm Cl *CHNTN* OX7 .. 104 B6
Manor Farm Crs *ALMDB* BS32 .. 316 F2
Manor Gdns *STROUD* GL5 ...... 232 C1
Manor Gv *ALMDB* BS32 .... 316 D1 8
  MANG/FISH BS16 .... 328 C2
Manor La *CFTN/FAIL* BS8 ...... 334 B3
  CHELTE/BC GL52 .... 72 D3
  FRCTL/WBN BS36 .... 318 B4
  SHPSTR CV36 .... 16 B5
  WUE GL12 .... 276 C7
  WUE GL12 .... 277 L4 8
Manor Orch *HGHW* SN6 .... 289 G3
Manor Pk *ALMDB* BS32 .... 306 E1
  CHELTW GL51 .... 114 F6
  RDLND/MONT BS6 .... 325 K8
  TEWK GL20 .... 48 C3
  VGL GL2 .... 113 G7
Manor Pl *MANG/FISH* BS16 .... 327 G2
  TEWK GL20 .... 48 B8 8
Manor Rd
  BMSTRD/HC/WWD BS13 ...... 345 H5
  CFTN/FAIL BS8 .... 334 B5
  CHELTW GL51 .... 93 J5
  HORF/LLZ BS7 .... 326 A7
  KEYN BS31 .... 348 C8
  LYD GL15 .... 201 L8
  MANG/FISH BS16 .... 327 H6
  MANG/FISH BS16 .... 328 C1
  OLD/WMLY/WICK BS30 .... 339 L6
  YATE/CS BS37 .... 309 J4
Manor St *RSTROUD/NAIL* GL6 .. 210 C2
Manor Wk *THNB/SVB* BS35 .... 273 L8
Manor Wy *YATE/CS* BS37 ...... 320 E1
Manse Gdns *CHELTW* GL51 .... 115 H4 8
The Manse La *RWYE* HR9 ...... 84 E2
Mansel Cl *KEYN* BS31 .... 348 E8
Mansell Av *SHPSTR* CV36 ...... 16 A6
Mansell's La *CIND* GL54 ...... 154 B2 8
Mansfield Ms *VGL* GL2 .... 159 H4 8
Mansfield St *BMSTR* BS3 ...... 345 K1
Manston Cl *HGRV/WHIT* BS14 .. 346 E4
Manworthy Rd
  BRSG/KWL/STAPK BS4 .... 336 F8
Manx Rd *HORF/LLZ* BS7 ...... 326 A4
Maple Av *CHEP* NP16 .... 270 A4
  MANG/FISH BS16 .... 327 L8
  THNB/SVB BS35 .... 293 L2
Maple Cl *BRSTK/PCHW* BS34 .. 316 E4
  DSLY GL11 .... 229 J8
  HGRV/WHIT BS14 .... 346 F6
  OLD/WMLY/WICK BS30 .... 338 D7
  VGL GL2 .... 159 G3
Maple Ct *VGL* GL2 .... 113 G7 8
Maple Dr *BWTH/CHD* GL3 ...... 137 M4
  CHELTS GL53 .... 116 D6
  STROUD GL5 .... 208 C2
Mapleleaze
  BRSG/KWL/STAPK BS4 .... 336 F8
Maplemeade *HORF/LLZ* BS7 .. 325 L7 8
Mapleridge La *YATE/CS* BS37 .. 310 C4
Maple Rd
  BRSG/KWL/STAPK BS4 .... 336 F6
  HORF/LLZ BS7 .... 325 M6

The Maples *CIR* GL7 .... 238 B6
  GLE GL4 .... 137 G5 8
Maplestone Rd
  HGRV/WHIT BS14 .... 346 C8
Maple Wk *KEYN* BS31 .... 347 M7
  MANG/FISH BS16 .... 329 L6
Marbeck Rd
  HNBRY/STHM BS10 .... 325 K2
Marchant Cl *CHELTW* GL51 .... 93 H8
Mardale Cl
  HNBRY/STHM BS10 .... 325 L1 8
Marden Rd *KEYN* BS31 .... 348 C7
Mardon Rd
  BRSG/KWL/STAPK BS4 .... 336 F5
Mardyke Ferry Rd
  CBRIS/FH BS1 .... 6 A6
Marefield Cl *GLE* GL4 .... 137 G4 8
Margaret Rd *LED* HR8 .... 19 M3
  TEWK GL20 .... 48 B7
Margate St *BMSTR* BS3 .... 336 A8
Margery La *CLFD* GL16 .... 175 G7
Margrett Rd *CHELT* GL50 ...... 2 C2
Marguerite Rd
  BMSTRD/HC/WWD BS13 ...... 345 H3
Marians Wk *CLFD* GL16 .... 151 J5
Marigold Wk *BMSTR* BS3 ...... 345 J1
Marina Gdns *MANG/FISH* BS16 .. 327 G8
Mariners Dr
  HNLZ/SM/SNYPK/WT BS9 .... 324 F7
Mariners' Pth
  HNLZ/SM/SNYPK/WT BS9 .... 324 F7
Marion Rd *KGWD/HNM* BS15 .. 337 K8
Marion Wk *EVILLE/WHL* BS5 .. 337 J4
Marissal Cl *HNBRY/STHM* BS10 .. 315 G8
Marissal Rd *HNBRY/STHM* BS10 .. 315 G8
Mariston Wy
  OLD/WMLY/WICK BS30 .... 338 E5
Marjoram Cl *GLE* GL4 .... 137 H6 8
Marjoram Pl *ALMDB* BS32 ...... 317 H4
Market La *COTS* GL54 .... 74 D2
Market Pde *GL* GL1 .... 4 F5
Market Pl *CHPMW/MSHF* SN14 .. 342 C3
  CHPMW/MSHF SN14 .... 343 K6
  CIR GL7 .... 238 C2
  CIR GL7 .... 242 E4 8
  CLFD GL16 .... 175 K1 8
  COR/BOX SN13 .... 353 M5
  SHPSTR CV36 .... 16 B5 8
  TET GL8 .... 282 A4 8
Market Sq *COTS* GL54 .... 102 A3 8
  MANG/FISH BS16 .... 327 L8 8
Market St *CHELTW* GL51 ...... 2 A3
  CIND GL14 .... 154 B2 8
  LED HR8 .... 19 M3
  RSTROUD/NAIL GL6 .... 232 D8 8
  WUE GL12 .... 277 K4
Mark La *CBRIS/FH* BS1 .... 6 D4
Marksbury Rd *BMSTR* BS3 .... 345 L1
Marlborough Av
  EVILLE/WHL BS5 .... 327 G8 8
Marlborough Cl
  CHELTE/BC GL52 .... 72 A8 8
  CHELTS GL53 .... 116 B5 8
Marlborough Crs *GLE* GL4 .... 136 C5
Marlborough Dr
  MANG/FISH BS16 .... 327 K2
Marlborough Hl
  RDLND/MONT BS6 .... 6 E1
Marlborough Hill Pl
  CBRISNE BS2 .... 6 E1 8
Marlborough Rd *GLE* GL4 ...... 136 C4
Marlborough St *CBRIS/FH* BS1 .. 6 F1
  CBRISNE BS2 .... 6 E2
  EVILLE/WHL BS5 .... 327 G8 8
Marle Hl *RSTROUD/NAIL* GL6 .. 234 B1
Marle Hill Pde *CHELT* GL50 .. 2 D2
Marle Hill Rd *CHELT* GL50 .... 2 D1
Marlepit Gv
  BMSTRD/HC/WWD BS13 ...... 345 H5 8
Marleyfield Cl
  BWTH/CHD GL3 .... 113 J4 8
Marleyfield Wy *BWTH/CHD* GL3 .. 113 J4
Marley La *RSTROUD/NAIL* GL6 .. 234 D2
Marlfield Wk
  BMSTRD/HC/WWD BS13 ...... 345 G4
Marling Cl *STROUD* GL5 .... 232 D3
Marling Crs *STROUD* GL5 ...... 208 A4
Marling Rd *EVILLE/WHL* BS5 .. 337 J4 8
Marlowe Rd *DSLY* GL11 .... 229 H7
Marlwood Dr
  HNBRY/STHM BS10 .... 315 J8
Marmaduke St *BMSTR* BS3 .... 336 B8
Marment Rd *DSLY* GL11 .... 229 G7
Marmion Crs
  HNBRY/STHM BS10 .... 315 H8
Marne Cl *HGRV/WHIT* BS14 .... 346 F6
Marram Cl *GLE* GL4 .... 137 H6
Marshacre La *THNB/SVB* BS35 .. 292 B5
Marshall Av *SHPSTR* CV36 .... 16 A6
Marsham Wy
  OLD/WMLY/WICK BS30 .... 338 A6
Marsh Cl *CHELTW* GL51 .... 2 A1
  FRCTL/WBN BS36 .... 318 A7
Marsh Common
  THNB/SVB BS35 .... 304 F5
Marsh Dr *CHELTW* GL51 .... 2 B1
Marshfield La
  OLD/WMLY/WICK BS30 .... 349 J2
Marshfield Rd *BAD* GL9 .... 332 A2
  MANG/FISH BS16 .... 327 K7
Marsh Gdns *CHELTW* GL51 .... 2 B1
Marsh La *CHELTW* GL51 .... 2 B1
  CHPMW/MSHF SN14 .... 323 K7
  EVILLE/WHL BS5 .... 336 E4
  STNHO GL10 .... 207 H8
Marshmouth La *COTS* GL54 .. 123 J6 8
Marsh Rd *BMSTR* BS3 .... 335 H8
  CHEP NP16 .... 270 B6
  STNHO GL10 .... 207 G7
Marsh St *CBRIS/FH* BS1 ...... 6 E4
Marsh Ter *CHELTW* GL51 ...... 2 B1
Marshwall La *ALMDB* BS32 .. 306 B5
Marsh Wy *CLFD* GL16 .... 175 L7
Marsland Rd *CHELTW* GL51 .. 114 F1
Marston Rd
  BRSG/KWL/STAPK BS4 .... 346 D1 8
  CHELTE/BC GL52 .... 94 B7

Marten Cl *BWTH/CHD* GL3 .... 137 J6
Marten Rd *CHEP* NP16 .... 270 A5
Martin Cl *BRSTK/PCHW* BS34 .. 316 A3
  CIR GL7 .... 238 C4 8
Martindale Rd *BWTH/CHD* GL3 .. 113 K5
Martingale Rd
  BRSG/KWL/STAPK BS4 .... 336 F7
Martins Cl *KGWD/HNM* BS15 .. 337 L6 8
Martins Cft
  CHPMW/MSHF SN14 .... 343 L8
Martin's Rd *KGWD/HNM* BS15 .. 337 L6
The Martins *CHEP* NP16 ...... 270 C2 8
  STROUD GL5 .... 207 M3
Martin St *BMSTR* BS3 .... 335 K8 8
Martins Wy *LED* HR8 .... 19 M5
Martlock Crs *BMSTR* BS3 ...... 345 L2
Martock Rd *BMSTR* BS3 ...... 345 L2
  KEYN BS31 .... 348 C8
Marwood Rd
  BRSG/KWL/STAPK BS4 .... 346 A3 8
Marybush La *CBRISNE* BS2 .... 7 H3 8
Marygold Leaze
  OLD/WMLY/WICK BS30 .... 338 C7 8
Mary Gv *VGL* GL2 .... 110 F6
Mary Rose Av *BWTH/CHD* GL3 .. 113 H4
Mary St *EVILLE/WHL* BS5 ...... 336 F3 8
Mascot Rd *BMSTR* BS3 .... 335 M8
Masefield Av *VGL* GL2 .... 135 L7
Masefield Rd *CIR* GL7 .... 238 E5 8
Masefield Wy *HORF/LLZ* BS7 .. 326 C4 8
Maskelyne Av
  HNBRY/STHM BS10 .... 325 M4
Mason Rd *STROUD* GL5 .... 209 H4
Masons Vw *FRCTL/WBN* BS36 .. 318 A4
Massey Pde *GL* GL1 .... 136 B4 8
Massey Rd *GLE* GL4 .... 136 C4
  LED HR8 .... 19 L3 8
Materman Rd *HGRV/WHIT* BS14 .. 347 G6
Matford Cl *FRCTL/WBN* BS36 .. 318 A6
  HNBRY/STHM BS10 .... 315 M7
Matford La *BRKLY* GL13 .... 251 H7
Mathern Wy *CHEP* NP16 ...... 270 A6 8
Mathews Wy *STROUD* GL5 .... 208 B3
Matson Av *GLE* GL4 .... 136 E8 8
Matson La *GLE* GL4 .... 160 D1
Matson Pl *GL* GL1 .... 136 C4
Matthews Cl *HGRV/WHIT* BS14 .. 347 H5
Matthew's Rd
  EVILLE/WHL BS5 .... 336 E4 10
Maugersbury Pk *COTS* GL54 .. 102 A4
Maules La *MANG/FISH* BS16 .. 327 H1
Maunsell Rd *AVONM* BS11 .... 324 D1
Maurice Rd *RDLND/MONT* BS6 .. 336 A1
Mautravers Cl *ALMDB* BS32 .. 316 F4
Mawley Rd *CIR* GL7 .... 218 D6
Maxse Rd
  BRSG/KWL/STAPK BS4 .... 336 D8
Mayalls Cl *RTEWK/TIB* GL19 .. 68 E5
The Mayalls *TEWK* GL20 ...... 26 C5
Maybec Gdns
  EVILLE/WHL BS5 .... 337 J5 8
Maybourne
  BRSG/KWL/STAPK BS4 .... 347 J1 8
Maybrook St *BRKLY* GL13 ...... 227 G8
May Bush La *RWYE* HR9 .... 126 E6
Maycliffe Pk *RDLND/MONT* BS6 .. 336 B1
Maycroft La *BRKLY* GL13 ...... 251 K5
  DSLY GL11 .... 251 M6
May Evans Cl *DSLY* GL11 ...... 229 H6 8
Mayfair Cl *VGL* GL2 .... 135 K3
Mayfield Av *MANG/FISH* BS16 .. 337 J1
Mayfield Cl *CHELTE/BC* GL52 .. 94 B1 8
Mayfield Dr *BWTH/CHD* GL3 .. 137 H2
  GLE GL4 .... 137 H3
Mayfield Pk *MANG/FISH* BS16 .. 337 J1
Mayfield Pk North
  MANG/FISH BS16 .... 337 J1
Mayfield Pk South
  MANG/FISH BS16 .... 337 J1
Mayfields *KEYN* BS31 .... 348 A6
May La *CHCAM* GL55 .... 13 L7
  DSLY GL11 .... 253 J2
May Meadow La *MTCHDN* GL17 .. 130 C2
Maynard Cl
  BMSTRD/HC/WWD BS13 ...... 345 L6
Maynard Rd
  BMSTRD/HC/WWD BS13 ...... 345 L6
Mayo Rd *SHPSTR* CV36 .... 16 B4
Maypole Gn *LYD* GL15 .... 200 C3
Maypole Rd *LYD* GL15 .... 200 C3
May's Crs *COTS* GL54 .... 169 J1
Mays La *TET* GL8 .... 257 M3
May St *KGWD/HNM* BS15 ...... 337 L2
Maythorn Dr *CHELTW* GL51 .. 92 F7 8
Maytree Av
  BMSTRD/HC/WWD BS13 ...... 345 K4
Maytree Cl
  BMSTRD/HC/WWD BS13 ...... 345 K4
May Tree Cl *CIR* GL7 .... 236 F5
May Tree Sq *GLE* GL4 .... 136 E4
Mayville Av *BRSTK/PCHW* BS34 .. 316 C8
Maywood Crs *MANG/FISH* BS16 .. 327 K7
Maywood Rd *MANG/FISH* BS16 .. 327 L7
Maze St *EVILLE/WHL* BS5 ...... 336 D5 8
Maze Wk *CLFD* GL16 .... 151 J5
Mead Cl *AVONM* BS11 .... 324 A5 8
  CHELTS GL53 .... 116 A6
Meade-king Gv *CHELTE/BC* GL52 .. 72 D8
Meadgate *MANG/FISH* BS16 .. 328 D3
Mead La *KEYN* BS31 .... 349 H7
  LYD GL15 .... 225 H2
  THNB/SVB BS35 .... 305 M1
Meadoway *CHELTE/BC* GL52 .. 94 A1
Meadowbank *LYD* GL15 .... 201 L8
Meadow Cl *CHELTW* GL51 ...... 114 E2 8
  CIR GL7 .... 238 C4
  LYD GL15 .... 202 B2
  MANG/FISH BS16 .... 328 B4
  TEWK GL20 .... 48 D3
Meadow Court Dr
  OLD/WMLY/WICK BS30 .... 338 E8
Meadowcroft *GLE* GL4 .... 137 G6
  MANG/FISH BS16 .... 328 C3 8
Meadowland Rd
  HNBRY/STHM BS10 .... 315 G7
Meadow La *CHELTW* GL51 ...... 115 G6 8
Meadow La (West) *STROUD* GL5 .. 208 A5
Meadowleaze *VGL* GL2 .... 112 F8

Meadow Md *FRCTL/WBN* BS36 .. 318 D3
  YATE/CS BS37 .... 310 A6
Meadow Pk *CBATH/BATHN* BA1 .. 352 D7
Meadow Rd *CIND* GL14 .... 154 C3
  CIR GL7 .... 238 C4
  STNHO GL10 .... 207 H3
  WUE GL12 .... 275 K7
  YATE/CS BS37 .... 320 C2 8
Meadows Dean *MTCHDN* GL17 .. 130 D2
Meadowside
  THNB/SVB BS35 .... 293 M3 8
Meadowside Dr
  HGRV/WHIT BS14 .... 346 C8
The Meadows
  KGWD/HNM BS15 .... 337 M7
Meadow St *CBRISNE* BS2 ...... 7 H2 8
Meadowsweet Av
  BRSTK/PCHW BS34 .... 316 D8
Meadow V *DSLY* GL11 .... 229 H7 8
  STROUD GL5 .... 207 J2
Meadow Vw *FRCTL/WBN* BS36 .. 318 E4
Meadow Wy *ALMDB* BS32 ...... 317 G4
  BWTH/CHD GL3 .... 113 K4 8
  CHNTN OX7 .... 104 B7
  CIR GL7 .... 263 C4
  STROUD GL5 .... 208 A5 8
Meadvale Cl *VGL* GL2 .... 112 B5 8
Meadway
  HNLZ/SM/SNYPK/WT BS9 .... 324 E5
  THNB/SVB BS35 .... 293 K4
Mead Wy *RSTNHO* GL10 ...... 207 G5 8
Meardon Rd
  HGRV/WHIT BS14 .... 347 G5 8
Mede Cl *CBRIS/FH* BS1 .... 7 G7 8
Medical Av *CFTN/FAIL* BS8 .... 6 C2 8
Medina Cl *THNB/SVB* BS35 .... 293 L4 8
Medoc Cl *CHELTW* GL51 ...... 93 K6
Medway Cl *KEYN* BS31 .... 348 B8 8
Medway Ct *THNB/SVB* BS35 .. 293 M3
Medway Crs *BWTH/CHD* GL3 .. 138 B6
Medway Dr *FRCTL/WBN* BS36 .. 318 D4
  KEYN BS31 .... 348 C8
Meeks Well La *RWYE* HR9 .... 126 E5
Meenhurst Rd *CIND* GL14 .... 154 A4
Meend La *MTCHDN* GL17 ...... 129 G4
Meerbrook Wy *VGL* GL2 ...... 159 H4 8
Meere Bank *AVONM* BS11 .... 324 D2
Meerstone Wy *GLE* GL4 ...... 136 F8
Meg Thatchers Cl
  EVILLE/WHL BS5 .... 337 K4 8
Melbourne Cl *CHELTS* GL53 .. 115 L5
  STNHO GL10 .... 207 G2
Melbourne Dr *STNHO* GL10 .. 207 G3
  YATE/CS BS37 .... 320 D2
Melbourne Rd *HORF/LLZ* BS7 .. 325 M7
Melbourne St East *GL* GL1 .... 136 C4
Melbourne St West *GL* GL1 .. 136 B4 8
Melbury Rd
  BRSG/KWL/STAPK BS4 .... 346 C1
Melick Cl *GLE* GL4 .... 136 C6 8
Melita Rd *RDLND/MONT* BS6 .. 326 A8
Mellent Av
  BMSTRD/HC/WWD BS13 ...... 345 L8
Melmore Gdns *CIR* GL7 .... 238 E5
Melody Wy *VGL* GL2 .... 113 G6 8
Melrose Av *CFTN/FAIL* BS8 .... 335 K3 8
  YATE/CS BS37 .... 320 B1
Melrose Cl *YATE/CS* BS37 ...... 320 C1
Melrose Pl *CFTN/FAIL* BS8 .... 335 K3
Melton Crs *HORF/LLZ* BS7 .... 326 C4
Melville Cl *COTS* GL54 .... 123 H3
Melville Rd *BWTH/CHD* GL3 .. 113 K6
  RDLND/MONT BS6 .... 335 K2
Melville Ter *BMSTR* BS3 ...... 335 L8
Melvin Sq
  BRSG/KWL/STAPK BS4 .... 346 A2
Memorial Cl *KGWD/HNM* BS15 .. 337 K7
Memorial Rd *KGWD/HNM* BS15 .. 337 K6
Mendip Cl *CHELTE/BC* GL52 .. 3 J1
  KEYN BS31 .... 347 M6
  VGL GL2 .... 159 G3 8
Mendip Crs *MANG/FISH* BS16 .. 328 C4
Mendip Rd *BMSTR* BS3 .... 335 M8
  CHELTE/BC GL52 .... 3 J2
Mendip Vw
  OLD/WMLY/WICK BS30 .... 339 L4
Mendip View Av
  MANG/FISH BS16 .... 327 J8
Meon Cl *STRAT* CV37 .... 9 K2
Meon Rd *CHCAM* GL55 .... 13 L7
Merchants Md *VGL* GL2 .... 158 F2 8
Merchants Rd *CFTN/FAIL* BS8 .. 335 J4
  GL GL1 .... 4 C8
Merchant St *CBRIS/FH* BS1 .... 7 G2
Mercia Dr *CBRISNE* BS2 ...... 336 C1
Mercian Cl *CIR* GL7 .... 238 D4 8
Mercian Wy *CHEP* NP16 ...... 270 C4
Mercia Rd *COTS* GL54 .... 74 C5 8
  GL GL1 .... 4 E3
Mercier Cl *YATE/CS* BS37 ...... 320 D1
Mercury Wy *GLE* GL4 .... 137 H5
Merestones Cl *CHELT* GL50 .. 115 K5
Merestones Dr *CHELT* GL50 .. 115 K5 8
Merestones Rd *CHELT* GL50 .. 115 K5
Merevale Rd *VGL* GL2 .... 5 M3
Merfield Rd
  BRSG/KWL/STAPK BS4 .... 346 D1 8
Meridian Pl *CFTN/FAIL* BS8 .... 6 A3
Meridian Rd *RDLND/MONT* BS6 .. 335 L2 8
Meridian V *CFTN/FAIL* BS8 .... 6 A3

Meriet Av
  BMSTRD/HC/WWD BS13 ...... 345 K7
Merioneth St *BMSTR* BS3 ...... 336 B8
Meriton St *CBRISNE* BS2 ...... 336 D6
Merlin Cl *CHELTS* GL53 .... 115 L6
  HNLZ/SM/SNYPK/WT BS9 .... 325 H3
Merlin Dr *VGL* GL2 .... 159 G1
Merlin Hvn *WUE* GL12 .... 277 J4
Merlin Rdg *MANG/FISH* BS16 .. 329 L7 8
Merlin Rd *BRSTK/PCHW* BS34 .. 315 L5
Merlin Wy *CHELTS* GL53 ...... 115 L6
  YATE/CS BS37 .... 320 B4
Merrett's Orch *VGL* GL2 ...... 204 F8
Merriville Gdns *CHELTW* GL51 .. 93 J8 8
Merriville Rd *CHELTW* GL51 .. 93 J8
Merrymouth Rd *CHNTN* OX7 .. 149 J1
Merrywalks *STROUD* GL5 ...... 208 D4
Merryweather Rd *ALMDB* BS32 .. 316 E3
Merrywood Rd *BMSTR* BS3 .... 335 L8
Mersey Rd *CHELTE/BC* GL52 .. 3 K4
Merstham Rd *CBRISNE* BS2 .. 336 C1 10
Merton Rd *HORF/LLZ* BS7 .... 326 A6
The Mertons *CIND* GL14 ...... 155 H7 8
Mervyn Rd *HORF/LLZ* BS7 .... 326 A7
Meteor Wy *BWTH/CHD* GL3 .. 138 A6 8
Metford Gv *RDLND/MONT* BS6 .. 325 K8
Metford Pl
  RDLND/MONT BS6 .... 325 L8 8
Metford Rd *RDLND/MONT* BS6 .. 325 K8
Metz Wy *GL* GL1 .... 5 H6
  GLE GL4 .... 136 E3
  VGL GL2 .... 5 K7
The Mews *LED* HR8 .... 19 M2
Meysey Cl *CIR* GL7 .... 241 L6
Michaelmas Ct *GL* GL1 .... 5 J3
Michael Pym's Rd
  MALM SN16 .... 303 J6 8
Michaels Md *CIR* GL7 .... 238 B5
Michaels Wy *CLFD* GL16 ...... 175 L7 8
Mickle Md *VGL* GL2 .... 110 F6 8
Middle Av *CBRIS/FH* BS1 ...... 6 E5 8
Middle Cft *GLE* GL4 .... 136 F4
Middlecroft *STNHO* GL10 ...... 206 B4
Middledorn Rd
  CHPMW/MSHF SN14 .... 341 J2
Middle Gnd *HGHW* SN6 .... 288 E3
Middlehay Ct *CHELTE/BC* GL52 .. 72 A8 8
Middle Hl *RSTROUD/NAIL* GL6 .. 210 A7
  STROUD GL5 .... 208 F4
Middle Hill Crs
  RSTROUD/NAIL GL6 .... 210 B8
Middle Leazes *STROUD* GL5 .. 208 F4
Middle Rd *BUR/CRTN* OX18 .. 172 D5
  KGWD/HNM BS15 .... 328 A8
  STROUD GL5 .... 209 G8
Middle Spillman's *STROUD* GL5 .. 208 C5
Middle St *CHEP* NP16 .... 270 A3 8
  STROUD GL5 .... 208 E4
Middleton Lawn *VGL* GL2 ...... 113 G4 8
Middleton Rd *AVONM* BS11 .... 324 B3
Middle Tynings
  RSTROUD/NAIL GL6 .... 232 C7 8
Middle Wy *CHEP* NP16 .... 270 B6
Midland Rd *CBRISNE* BS2 ...... 7 K3
  CIR GL7 .... 238 D5
  GL GL1 .... 4 F9
  MANG/FISH BS16 .... 327 M7
  STNHO GL10 .... 207 G3
Midland St *CBRISNE* BS2 ...... 7 K4
Midland Ter
  MANG/FISH BS16 .... 327 H8 8
Midland Wy *THNB/SVB* BS35 .. 293 K3
Midway *RSTROUD/NAIL* GL6 .. 210 B8
Midwinter Av *CHELTW* GL51 .. 2 A1
Midwinter Gdns *CHELTW* GL51 .. 93 L7
Midwinter Rd *COTS* GL54 ...... 169 J1
Milbourne La *MALM* SN16 .... 303 L7
Milbourne Rd *MALM* SN16 .... 303 L7
Mildred St *EVILLE/WHL* BS5 .. 336 E4
Mile End Rd *CLFD* GL16 ...... 151 L8
Miles Ct
  OLD/WMLY/WICK BS30 .... 338 B7 11
Miles Rd *CFTN/FAIL* BS8 ...... 335 J2
Milestone Wk *CLFD* GL16 .... 175 L7
Milford Av
  OLD/WMLY/WICK BS30 .... 339 K4
Milford Cl *VGL* GL2 .... 112 D6
Milford St *BMSTR* BS3 .... 6 C9
Millard Cl *HNBRY/STHM* BS10 .. 325 L1 8
Mill Av *BDWAY* WR12 .... 32 D4
  CBRIS/FH BS1 .... 6 F5
Millbank *DSLY* GL11 .... 229 J6
Millbank Cl
  BRSG/KWL/STAPK BS4 .... 337 G8
Millbridge Rd *BWTH/CHD* GL3 .. 137 J4
Millbrook Av
  BRSG/KWL/STAPK BS4 .... 337 H8 8
Millbrook Cl *GL* GL1 .... 5 J7
  OLD/WMLY/WICK BS30 .... 338 E5
Millbrook Gdns *CHELTW* GL51 .. 115 K1 8
  RWYE HR9 .... 106 C3 8
Millbrook Gn *LYD* GL15 .... 224 F2
Millbrook Ley *MIM* GL56 ...... 80 C7
Millbrook Rd *YATE/CS* BS37 .. 319 K1
Millbrook St *CHELTW* GL51 .. 115 K1
  GL GL1 .... 5 H7
Mill Cl *CIR* GL7 .... 263 J4
  FRCTL/WBN BS36 .... 318 E4
  WUE GL12 .... 277 L5
Mill Crs *YATE/CS* BS37 .... 319 K7
Millend *LYD* GL15 .... 202 E1
Millend La *STNHO* GL10 ...... 206 B4
Miller Cl *RTEWK/TIB* GL19 .... 89 J3
  VGL GL2 .... 112 F6 8
Miller Craddock Wy *LED* HR8 .. 19 M5 8
Miller's Court Rd *RGTMLV* WR13 .. 22 E5
  RGTMLV WR13 .... 23 G6
Millers Dr
  OLD/WMLY/WICK BS30 .... 338 E6
Millers Dyke *VGL* GL2 .... 158 F2 8
Millers Gn *MTCHDN* GL17 .... 129 K4
Mill Farm Dr *STROUD* GL5 .... 208 A3
Millfield *EVE* WR11 .... 30 D1 8
  THNB/SVB BS35 .... 293 L1
Millfield Dr
  OLD/WMLY/WICK BS30 .... 338 E5
Millfields *BWTH/CHD* GL3 .... 137 J3

Millground Rd
BMSTRD/HC/WWD BS13 345 G7
Mill Gv VGL GL2 158 F2
Millham Rd CHELTE/BC GL52 72 C7
Mill Hl CHEP NP16 222 B4
LYD GL15 222 D3
Millhill La CLFD GL16 175 H5
Millhouse Dr CHELT GL50 93 L6
Milliman Cl
BMSTRD/HC/WWD BS13 345 L6
Millin Av GLE GL4 135 M8
Milling Cl HGHW SN6 287 H2 1
Milling Crs LYD GL15 224 F3
Mill La ALMDB BS32 306 C2
BMSTR BS3 6 E9
BWTH/CHD GL3 138 B5
CHCAM GL55 8 F7
CHELTE/BC GL52 71 G7
CHELTE/BC GL52 94 E7
CIR GL7 242 D4
CIR GL7 245 G8
COR/BOX SN13 353 L4
COTS GL54 74 C6 3
COTS GL54 101 J4
COTS GL54 123 G1
FRCTL/WBN BS36 318 D3
MALM SN16 303 J8
MTCHDN GL17 131 J2
NWNT GL18 85 H5
OLD/WMLY/WICK BS30 338 E6
OLD/WMLY/WICK BS30 340 B2
OLD/WMLY/WICK BS30 349 H2
RSTROUD/NAIL GL6 161 L5
RTEWK/TIB GL19 44 A7
RTEWK/TIB GL19 66 A3
TET GL8 257 L2
WUE GL12 275 G4
YATE/CS BS37 321 H5
Mill Pitt Gdns BWTH/CHD GL3 137 J3
Millpond End STROUD GL5 232 C1 2
Mill Rd FRCTL/WBN BS36 317 M7
Mills Cl BDWAY WR12 32 F3
Mill St CHELTE/BC GL52 94 D6
TEWK GL20 47 M5 1
Mill Vw COTS GL54 169 J1
Millview MIM GL56 57 H1
Millward Gv MANG/FISH BS16 327 L7
Mill Wy DSLY GL11 229 H7
Milne Pastures TEWK GL20 48 E4 1
Milner Gn
OLD/WMLY/WICK BS30 338 C6
Milner Rd HORF/LLZ BS7 326 B6
Milo Pl GL GL1 136 A5
Milsom St CHELT GL50 2 C3
EVILLE/WHL BS5 7 L1
Milton Av CHELTW GL51 115 G2 2
VGL GL2 135 L6
Milton Cl YATE/CS BS37 319 M1
Milton Gv STROUD GL5 209 G4
Milton Pk EVILLE/WHL BS5 336 E4 11
Milton Pl CIR GL7 242 D5
Milton Rd CHELTW GL51 115 H2
HORF/LLZ BS7 326 A5
YATE/CS BS37 319 M1
Miltons Cl
BMSTRD/HC/WWD BS13 345 M7
Milton St CIR GL7 242 D5
Milverton Gdns
RDLND/MONT BS6 336 B1 7
Milward Rd KEYN BS31 348 A5
Mimosa Av CHELTW GL51 115 J7
Mina Rd CBRISNE BS2 326 B8
Minehead Rd
BRSG/KWL/STAPK BS4 346 B2
Mine Pitts La RWYE HR9 126 E7
Minerva Cl GLE GL4 137 H5
Minerva Wk LYD GL15 201 K6
Minetts Av CHELTE/BC GL52 72 C8
Minety La MALM SN16 285 K5
Minnow La BUR/CRTN OX18 172 D5
Minor's La HNBRY/STHM BS10 314 C3
Minsmere Rd KEYN BS31 348 C8
Minster Cl CHELTE/BC GL52 72 A7
Minster Gdns GLE GL4 137 H5 4
Minstrel Wy BWTH/CHD GL3 113 H3
Minton Cl HGRV/WHIT BS14 346 D6
Minto Rd CBRISNE BS2 336 C1
Miserden Rd CHELTW GL51 114 F3
Miss Grace's La CHEP NP16 222 E8
Mission Rd YATE/CS BS37 309 J7
Mitchell La CBRIS/FH BS1 7 G5
Mitchell Wk
OLD/WMLY/WICK BS30 338 F5 4
Mitford Br SHPSTR CV36 38 C4
Mitre Pitch WUE GL12 277 L4 3
Mitre St CHELTS GL53 2 E7
Mitton Wy TEWK GL20 48 C3
Mivart St EVILLE/WHL BS5 336 D1
Moat Bank TEWK GL20 24 B6
Moat La CHELTW GL51 92 E5
RTEWK/TIB GL19 66 D3
RTEWK/TIB GL19 108 E3
The Moat CHNTN OX7 104 B6
VGL GL2 159 H2 2
Modecombe Gv
HNBRY/STHM BS10 315 H8 3
Moffat Rd RSTROUD/NAIL GL6 232 C6
Mogg St CBRISNE BS2 336 C1
Mogridge Cl BWTH/CHD GL3 137 J4 1
Molesworth Cl
BMSTRD/HC/WWD BS13 345 J7
Molesworth Dr
BMSTRD/HC/WWD BS13 345 J7
Monarch Cl GLE GL4 137 G7 3
Monarch's Wy BAD GL9 298 A8
CHCAM GL55 12 F6
CHCAM GL55 34 D4
CIR GL7 236 D6
COTS GL54 101 J7
COTS GL54 123 H6
COTS GL54 145 H8
COTS GL54 168 B5
COTS GL54 191 H1
EVILLE/WHL BS5 336 F5
KGWD/HNM BS15 347 K1
LGASH BS41 344 A1
MIM GL56 79 M5
MIM GL56 102 B2
OLD/WMLY/WICK BS30 339 L5
OLD/WMLY/WICK BS30 348 B4
TET GL8 279 J5
TET GL8 281 M4 1
WUE GL12 298 B3
YATE/CS BS37 320 E4
Monica Dr CHELT GL50 94 A7
Monkey Meadow TEWK GL20 49 G2 5
Monkey Puzzle Cl
STROUD GL5 208 A5 2
Monk Rd HORF/LLZ BS7 325 M7
Monks Av KGWD/HNM BS15 337 K3 1
Monks Cft CHELTW GL51 115 G2
Monks La TEWK GL20 49 G8
Monks Meadow LED HR8 40 B5 1
Monks Pk MALM SN16 303 M7
Monk's Park Av HORF/LLZ BS7 326 A2
Monks Park Wy
HNBRY/STHM BS10 326 A3
Monkton Rd KGWD/HNM BS15 337 K7
Monmouth Hl ALMDB BS32 305 M7
Monmouth Rd CLFD GL16 151 M5
HORF/LLZ BS7 325 M7
KEYN BS31 347 M6
Monmouth St BMSTR BS3 336 B8 2
Monsdale Cl
HNBRY/STHM BS10 325 J1
Monsdale Dr
HNBRY/STHM BS10 315 J8
Monson Av CHELT GL50 2 D3
Montague Cl
BRSTK/PCHW BS34 317 G6 5
Montague Hl CBRISNE BS2 335 M3 12
Montague Hl South
CBRISNE BS2 6 F1 2
Monterey Cl TEWK GL20 48 C8
Montfort Rd VGL GL2 112 D6
Montgomery Cl
BWTH/CHD GL3 137 K5 2
Montgomery Rd
CHELTW GL51 114 F5 4
Montgomery St BMSTR BS3 7 J9
BMSTR BS3 336 B8 3
Montpellier GL GL1 4 E7
Montpellier Dr CHELT GL50 2 D7
Montpellier Gv CHELT GL50 2 C9
Montpellier Pde CHELT GL50 2 C8
Montpellier Retreat CHELT GL50 2 C9
Montpellier Rd LYD GL15 200 E2
Montpellier Spa Rd CHELT GL50 2 C7
Montpellier St CHELT GL50 2 B7
Montpellier Ter CHELT GL50 2 B8
Montpellier Vls CHELT GL50 2 C9
Montpellier Wk CHELT GL50 2 B7
Montreal Av HORF/LLZ BS7 326 B3
Montrose Av
RDLND/MONT BS6 335 L2
Montrose Dr
OLD/WMLY/WICK BS30 338 D5
Montrose Pk
BRSG/KWL/STAPK BS4 346 F1
Montroy Cl
HNLZ/SM/SNYPK/WT BS9 325 L5
Montserrat STROUD GL5 208 F8
Moon Cl CHPMW/MSHF SN14 353 K1 1
Moon's La RSTROUD/NAIL GL6 210 D6
Moon St CBRISNE BS2 7 G1
Moor Court Dr CHELTE/BC GL52 3 H3
Moor Croft Dr
OLD/WMLY/WICK BS30 338 B7
Moordell Cl YATE/CS BS37 319 M2
Moorend Crs CHELTS GL53 115 L5
Moorend Gdns AVONM BS11 324 B4
Moorend Gld CHELTS GL53 116 B5
Moorend Gv CHELTS GL53 115 L6
Moorend La VGL GL2 204 F8
Moorend Park Rd CHELTS GL53 115 L5
Moorend Rd CHELTS GL53 115 M6
MANG/FISH BS16 317 M8
RTEWK/TIB GL19 67 H2
Moorend St CHELTS GL53 115 L5
Moore Rd COTS GL54 123 H5
Moorfield Rd BWTH/CHD GL3 138 B6
Moorgate CIR GL7 244 D7
Moor Gv AVONM BS11 324 B3
Moor Hall Pl STROUD GL5 208 A3 2
Moorhen Ct VGL GL2 158 F1
Moorhill St EVILLE/WHL BS5 336 D2 7
Moorhouse La AVONM BS11 314 B6
HNBRY/STHM BS10 314 D7
Moorland Cl CIND GL14 154 B2 5
Moorland Rd YATE/CS BS37 319 M2
Moorlands Rd MANG/FISH BS16 337 J1
Moor La ALMDB BS32 306 B4
CIR GL7 242 F5
COTS GL54 123 J4
Moorpark Av YATE/CS BS37 319 L2
Moors Av CHELTW GL51 93 J7
Moorslade La WUE GL12 275 G3
Moor St CHEP NP16 270 A3
GL GL1 136 B4
VGL GL2 181 J2
Mop Hale MIM GL56 35 H8
Mopla Rd CHEP NP16 270 B1
Moravian Rd KGWD/HNM BS15 337 M3
Morcroft Pl LYD GL15 201 G2 1
Morden Wk
HGRV/WHIT BS14 346 F4 3
Morestall Dr CIR GL7 238 B5 3
Moreton Cl CHELTE/BC GL52 94 C1
HGRV/WHIT BS14 346 C7
Moreton La TEWK GL20 27 H4
Morgans La MTCHDN GL17 129 K5
Morgan St CBRISNE BS2 336 B2
Mork La LYD GL15 198 F4
Mork Rd LYD GL15 198 E4
Morlands Dr CHELTS GL53 116 D7
Morley Av BWTH/CHD GL3 113 J5
MANG/FISH BS16 328 C7
Morley Cl BRSTK/PCHW BS34 316 D4
MANG/FISH BS16 327 M8
Morley Rd BMSTR BS3 6 C8
MANG/FISH BS16 327 M8
Morley Sq HORF/LLZ BS7 326 A7 1
Morley St CBRISNE BS2 336 C2
EVILLE/WHL BS5 336 D4
Morley Ter KGWD/HNM BS15 337 M2 7
Morman Cl MTCHDN GL17 129 M3
Morningside Cl
CHELTE/BC GL52 94 E7 2
Mornington Dr CHELTS GL53 115 M5 7
Mornington Rd
CFTN/FAIL BS8 335 J1 6
Morpeth Rd
BRSG/KWL/STAPK BS4 345 M3
Morpeth St GL GL1 136 B4 10
Morris Cl LYD GL15 177 L8
Morris Hill Cl CHELTW GL51 93 K5
Morris La CBATH/BATHN BA1 352 D8
Morris Orch DSLY GL11 229 H5
Morris Rd BDWAY WR12 32 F3
HORF/LLZ BS7 326 C6
Morse La MTCHDN GL17 129 J3
Morse Rd EVILLE/WHL BS5 336 E4 12
MTCHDN GL17 129 J4
Mortimer Rd
BRSTK/PCHW BS34 326 D2
CFTN/FAIL BS8 335 J4
VGL GL2 112 E6 3
Morton St EVILLE/WHL BS5 336 D4 3
GL GL1 136 B4
THNB/SVB BS35 273 L7
Morton Wy THNB/SVB BS35 294 A3
Morwent Cl GLE GL4 137 G5
Mosedale MIM GL56 58 E6
Moselle Dr BWTH/CHD GL3 113 J5
Mosley Crs STROUD GL5 208 A4 1
Mosley Rd STROUD GL5 208 A3
Mottershead Dr VGL GL2 113 G4
Mottershead Rd CIR GL7 239 H8
Moulder Rd TEWK GL20 48 C5
Mountbatten Cl YATE/CS BS37 309 M8
Mount Cl FRCTL/WBN BS36 318 B3
MTCHDN GL17 129 M5
Mount Crs FRCTL/WBN BS36 318 A6
Mounteney's La WUE GL12 296 F5
Mount Gdns KGWD/HNM BS15 337 M5
Mount Hill Rd
KGWD/HNM BS15 337 L5
Mountjoy's La CIND GL14 154 B2 6
Mountjoy's Lane End
CIND GL14 154 B2 7
Mount Pleasant CHEP NP16 270 A3
CIR GL7 244 E7
LYD GL15 225 L1
WUE GL12 277 L4
Mount Pleasant Cl
COTS GL54 102 B3 1
Mount Pleasant Rd CIND GL14 154 B4
Mount Pleasant Ter BMSTR BS3 6 B9
Mount St CIR GL7 238 C4
GL GL1 4 D4 2
Mousell La CIND GL14 154 B3
Mousetrap La COTS GL54 123 G5
Mow Barton
BMSTRD/HC/WWD BS13 345 G5
YATE/CS BS37 319 M1 4
Mowberry Cl VGL GL2 112 E6 5
Mowbray Av TEWK GL20 48 B8
Mowbray Rd HGRV/WHIT BS14 346 E4
Mowcroft Rd
BMSTRD/HC/WWD BS13 345 L7
Moxham Dr
BMSTRD/HC/WWD BS13 345 L7
Moyle Old School La
CHEP NP16 246 C7 1
Muirfield
OLD/WMLY/WICK BS30 338 C5
Mulberry Cl KGWD/HNM BS15 338 A3
VGL GL2 159 G3
Mulberry Dr KGWD/HNM BS15 338 B2
Mulberry Wk
HNLZ/SM/SNYPK/WT BS9 324 E3 4
Muller Av HORF/LLZ BS7 326 B7
Muller Rd EVILLE/WHL BS5 326 E8 5
HORF/LLZ BS7 326 B5
Mulling Cl
CHPMW/MSHF SN14 343 K8 3
Mulready Cl HORF/LLZ BS7 326 E5
Mumbleys La THNB/SVB BS35 293 G4
Munday Cl
RSTROUD/NAIL GL6 209 M7 7
Munsley Gv GLE GL4 136 E8
Murford Av
BMSTRD/HC/WWD BS13 345 K7
Murford Wk
BMSTRD/HC/WWD BS13 345 K7
Murray Cl CHELTE/BC GL52 72 B6 1
Murray St BMSTR BS3 6 D9
Murrells Rd CLFD GL16 127 K8
Murvagh Cl CHELTS GL53 2 F9 1
Muscroft Rd CHELTE/BC GL52 94 F7
Musgrove Cl AVONM BS11 324 E1
Mushet Pl CLFD GL16 175 J2
Mutsilver Ms VGL GL2 113 G6 5
Muzzle Patch VGL GL2 109 M3
Myers Rd VGL GL2 5 L6
Myrtle Cl GLE GL4 136 C6
Myrtle Dr AVONM BS11 324 A6
Myrtle Pl CHEP NP16 270 B2 3
Myrtle Rd CBRISNE BS2 6 D1
The Myrtles CHEP NP16 270 C1
Myrtle St BMSTR BS3 6 B9
Mythe Rd TEWK GL20 48 A3

N

Naas La LYD GL15 225 M4
VGL GL2 159 J4
Nags Head Hl EVILLE/WHL BS5 337 J5
Nailsea Cl
BMSTRD/HC/WWD BS13 345 J4
Nailsworth Av YATE/CS BS37 320 A2
Naishcombe Hl
OLD/WMLY/WICK BS30 339 L4
The Naite THNB/SVB BS35 272 F5
Napier Miles Rd AVONM BS11 324 C3
Napier Rd CBATH/BATHN BA1 350 C8
EVILLE/WHL BS5 336 D1
RDLND/MONT BS6 335 K1
Napier St EVILLE/WHL BS5 336 D5 3
GL GL1 5 H7 1
Napping La MTCHDN GL17 131 H1
The Napping MTCHDN GL17 107 H8
Narles Rd VGL GL2 205 J8
Narroways Rd CBRISNE BS2 326 C8
Narrowcut La
RSTROUD/NAIL GL6 256 B2
Narrow La MANG/FISH BS16 328 A7
Narrow Pln CBRISNE BS2 7 H4
Narrow Quay CBRIS/FH BS1 6 E5
The Narrows CHCAM GL55 34 A1
Naseby Wk EVILLE/WHL BS5 337 H2
Nash Cl KEYN BS31 348 C6 2
Nash Dr HORF/LLZ BS7 326 E4
Nash's La CHCAM GL55 13 M5
Nash Wy CLFD GL16 175 K2 3
Nasse Ct DSLY GL11 229 H6
Nastend La STNHO GL10 206 D3
Nature Cl BWTH/CHD GL3 137 M6
Naunton Crs CHELTS GL53 115 M5
Naunton La CHELTS GL53 115 M5
Naunton Pde CHELTS GL53 115 M4
Naunton Park Cl CHELTS GL53 116 A5
Naunton Park Rd CHELTS GL53 116 A5
Naunton Rd GLE GL4 136 E4
Naunton Ter CHELTS GL53 115 M4
Naunton Wy CHELTS GL53 115 M5
Neads Dr
OLD/WMLY/WICK BS30 338 E6 3
Neath Rd EVILLE/WHL BS5 336 F3 7
Nebsworth La SHPSTR CV36 13 M2
Needham Av VGL GL2 159 K5
Nelson Rd MANG/FISH BS16 327 M6 4
MANG/FISH BS16 327 M7 5
Nelson St BMSTR BS3 345 J1 2
CBRIS/FH BS1 6 F3
CHEP NP16 270 B3 1
GL GL1 136 B5
STROUD GL5 208 E4
TEWK GL20 48 A5 3
Nene Cl VGL GL2 159 G1
Neptune Cl GLE GL4 137 H5 5
Neston Wk
BRSG/KWL/STAPK BS4 346 B3 5
Netham Rd EVILLE/WHL BS5 336 F5
Nethercote Dr COTS GL54 123 J6 2
Nethercote Farm Dr COTS GL54 123 J7
Netherend Crs LYD GL15 224 B6
Netherhope La CHEP NP16 246 D6
Netheridge Cl VGL GL2 135 J7
Netherley La RTEWK/TIB GL19 44 D3
Netherwood Gdns CHELTW GL51 93 J8
Nettlestone Cl
HNBRY/STHM BS10 315 G7 1
Nettleton Rd CHELTW GL51 115 G4
CHPMW/MSHF SN14 323 K8
GL GL1 5 G6
Nevalan Dr EVILLE/WHL BS5 337 J5
Neville Rd KGWD/HNM BS15 338 A1
TEWK GL20 48 B6
Nevil Rd HORF/LLZ BS7 326 A7
Newark Rd GL GL1 135 L5
New Barn Av CHELTE/BC GL52 94 C7
New Barn Cl CHELTE/BC GL52 94 C7
New Barn La CHELTE/BC GL52 94 A6
Newbrick Rd
BRSTK/PCHW BS34 317 J6
Newbridge Cl
BRSG/KWL/STAPK BS4 336 F5
Newbridge Rd
BRSG/KWL/STAPK BS4 336 F5
New Brunswick Av
EVILLE/WHL BS5 337 K4
New Buildings
MANG/FISH BS16 327 H7
Newbury Pk LED HR8 19 M2
Newbury Rd HORF/LLZ BS7 326 C4
New Charlotte St BMSTR BS3 6 F8
New Cheltenham Rd
KGWD/HNM BS15 337 M2
New Church St TET GL8 281 M4
Newcombe Dr
HNLZ/SM/SNYPK/WT BS9 324 E7 4
Newcombe Rd
HNLZ/SM/SNYPK/WT BS9 325 H4
Newcourt Pk CHELTS GL53 116 C5
Newcourt Rd CHELTS GL53 116 C6
New Cut DSLY GL11 254 D2
Newent Av KGWD/HNM BS15 337 K4
Newent La RTEWK/TIB GL19 108 B8
Newerne St LYD GL15 201 J8
New Fosseway Rd
HGRV/WHIT BS14 346 D5
Newfoundland Rd CBRISNE BS2 7 J1
CBRISNE BS2 336 C2 13
Newfoundland St CBRISNE BS2 7 H1
Newfoundland Wy CBRISNE BS2 7 K1
Newgate CBRIS/FH BS1 7 G3
Newgrounds La VGL GL2 204 C5
New Inn La GL GL1 4 F5
TET GL8 257 L3
New John St BMSTR BS3 335 L8 7
New Kingsley Rd CBRISNE BS2 7 J4 1
Newland Dr
BMSTRD/HC/WWD BS13 345 J7 1
Newland Rd
BMSTRD/HC/WWD BS13 345 J7
Newlands Av FRCTL/WBN BS36 318 E4
Newlands Rd KEYN BS31 347 M7
The Newlands
MANG/FISH BS16 327 K4
Newland St CLFD GL16 175 H2
GL GL1 5 H4 1
Newland Wk
BMSTRD/HC/WWD BS13 345 J8
New La THNB/SVB BS35 293 L6
New Leaze ALMDB BS32 306 E8
Newleaze Gdns TET GL8 281 L3 1
Newlyn Av
HNLZ/SM/SNYPK/WT BS9 324 F6
Newlyn Wk
BRSG/KWL/STAPK BS4 346 D2 1
Newlyn Wy YATE/CS BS37 320 B1
Newman Cl YATE/CS BS37 319 K7
Newmarket Rd
RSTROUD/NAIL GL6 232 C7
Newmills Hl RWYE HR9 127 G1
New Mills La WUE GL12 298 A2
New Mills Wy LED HR8 19 L2
Newnham Cl HGRV/WHIT BS14 346 F4
Newnham Pl
BRSTK/PCHW BS34 316 B2 1
Newnton Hl TET GL8 282 D1
Newnton Rd TET GL8 282 B5
Newpit La
OLD/WMLY/WICK BS30 339 H8
Newport St BMSTR BS3 336 A8 2
Newquay Rd
BRSG/KWL/STAPK BS4 346 B3
New Queen St BMSTR BS3 7 G9
KGWD/HNM BS15 337 K2
New Rd BRSTK/PCHW BS34 316 B8
BRSTK/PCHW BS34 316 F7
BRSTK/PCHW BS34 326 E1
CHCAM GL55 13 M6
CHELTE/BC GL52 94 E2
CHNTN OX7 125 M1
CIND GL14 152 E2
CLFD GL16 152 E3
CLFD GL16 175 M2
CLFD GL16 176 D1
DSLY GL11 229 G7
DSLY GL11 253 G7
LYD GL15 176 F8
LYD GL15 200 B3
LYD GL15 201 H5
LYD GL15 202 C1
LYD GL15 224 C1
MIM GL56 58 D5
MTCHDN GL17 130 C2
MTCHDN GL17 152 C1
RGTMLV WR13 22 B2
RSTROUD/NAIL GL6 233 H6
STRAT CV37 8 A1
STROUD GL5 208 A7
THNB/SVB BS35 306 C1
WUE GL12 277 H5
WUE GL12 294 E5
YATE/CS BS37 309 J3
New Rutland Ct CHELT GL50 2 C3
Newry Wk
BRSG/KWL/STAPK BS4 346 A2
New Stadium Rd
EVILLE/WHL BS5 336 D1
New Station Rd
MANG/FISH BS16 327 J7
Newstead Rd GLE GL4 137 G3
New St BDWAY WR12 32 A1
BRKLY GL13 226 E3
CBRISNE BS2 7 J2
CHELT GL50 2 B4
CHELTS GL53 116 D6 5
CHNTN OX7 83 M8
GL GL1 4 E9
LED HR8 19 M4
MTCHDN GL17 130 C2
RSTROUD/NAIL GL6 185 H3
SHPSTR CV36 16 B5
STNHO GL10 207 J8
WUE GL12 276 C5
New Thomas St CBRISNE BS2 7 J3
Newton Av GLE GL4 136 E4
Newton Cl CHELTW GL51 115 G1
KGWD/HNM BS15 338 C2
LED HR8 20 A5 1
RTEWK/TIB GL19 108 C8
Newton Rd CHELTW GL51 115 G1
OLD/WMLY/WICK BS30 338 C6
Newton St EVILLE/WHL BS5 7 L1
Newtown WUE GL12 276 C6
Newtown Rd CIND GL14 129 M8
New Tyning La YATE/CS BS37 311 L8
New Wk KGWD/HNM BS15 337 K6
New Walls BRSG/KWL/STAPK BS4 7 K8
Niblett Cl KGWD/HNM BS15 338 B5 1
Niblett's Hl EVILLE/WHL BS5 337 J5
Nibley La YATE/CS BS37 309 H8
Nibley Rd AVONM BS11 324 A6
Nicholas La EVILLE/WHL BS5 337 J5
Nicholas Rd EVILLE/WHL BS5 336 D2
Nicholas St BMSTR BS3 7 H8 1
Nicholettes
OLD/WMLY/WICK BS30 338 F6
Nicholls La FRCTL/WBN BS36 318 A4
Nicolson Cl BWTH/CHD GL3 113 G5
Niebull Cl MALM SN16 303 J6
Nigel Pk AVONM BS11 324 A4
Nightingale Cl
FRCTL/WBN BS36 318 C5
THNB/SVB BS35 293 M1 6
Nightingale La
FRCTL/WBN BS36 318 C4 1
Nind La WUE GL12 277 K7
Nine Elms Rd VGL GL2 113 G7
Nine Tree Hl CBRISNE BS2 335 M2
Nine Wells Rd CLFD GL16 151 K5
Ninth Av HORF/LLZ BS7 326 D2
Noake Rd BWTH/CHD GL3 137 J3
Noble Av
OLD/WMLY/WICK BS30 338 E7
Nodens Wy LYD GL15 201 L7
Norbury Av GLE GL4 136 D7
Norden Dr RWYE HR9 106 B4 2
Nordown Cl DSLY GL11 229 H7
Nordown Rd DSLY GL11 229 H7
Norfolk Av CBRISNE BS2 7 H1
CHELTW GL51 115 H2
RDLND/MONT BS6 336 A1 3
Norfolk Gv KEYN BS31 347 L7
Norfolk Pl BMSTR BS3 335 L8
Norfolk St GL GL1 4 D7
Norland Rd CFTN/FAIL BS8 335 H3 1
Norley Rd HORF/LLZ BS7 326 B4
Norluck Ct SHPSTR CV36 16 B5 3
Normal Ter CHELT GL50 2 C3
Norman Ball Wy VGL GL2 5 L6
Normanby Rd
EVILLE/WHL BS5 336 D2 3
Norman Gv
KGWD/HNM BS15 337 M1 1
Norman Hl DSLY GL11 229 H7 3
Norman Rd CBRISNE BS2 336 C1 11
KEYN BS31 348 F8
OLD/WMLY/WICK BS30 338 D3
Normanton Rd
CFTN/FAIL BS8 335 J1 2
Norman Wy MTCHDN GL17 129 G3

Norrisville Rd RDLND/MONT BS6 .... 336 A2 6
Norse Wy CHEP NP16 270 D4
Nortenham Cl
CHELTE/BC GL52 71 M7 5
North Av MTCHDN GL17 129 M3
TEWK GL20 49 J3
Northbank Cl CHELTW GL51 .... 114 D4 3
Northbrook Rd GLE GL4 136 E2
Northcote Rd CFTN/FAIL BS8 335 H2
EVILLE/WHL BS5 337 G3
MANG/FISH BS16 328 B5
Northcote St
EVILLE/WHL BS5 336 D2 9
Northcot La MIM GL56 35 K7
North Cft
OLD/WMLY/WICK BS30 338 F7 3
North Devon Rd
MANG/FISH BS16 327 J6
Northdown Cl LED HR8 19 L2 3
North East Rd
THNB/SVB BS35 293 L1 4
Northen Cl CIR GL7 267 G5
Northend Av KGWD/HNM BS15 .. 337 M1
Northend Rd KGWD/HNM BS15 .. 338 A1
Northfield YATE/CS BS37 319 M3
Northfield Av KGWD/HNM BS15.. 337 M6
Northfield Rd EVILLE/WHL BS5 .. 337 K4
GLE GL4 136 B6
TET GL8 282 A3
Northfield Sq GLE GL4 136 B6 3
Northfields Rd
RSTROUD/NAIL GL6 232 D7
Northfield Ter CHELT GL50 2 D3
Northgate St GL GL1 4 E5
North Green St
CFTN/FAIL BS8 335 H5 11
North Hall Ms CHELTE/BC GL52 3 H4
North Hill Rd CIR GL7 238 E5 2
North Home Rd CIR GL7 238 E4
Northington La CIND GL14 179 L5
Northlands Wy TET GL8 282 A3
Northleach Wk AVONM BS11 .. 324 B6 1
North Leaze LGASH BS41 344 D1
Northleaze TET GL8 282 A3
Northmead LED HR8 19 M2
Northmead La YATE/CS BS37 308 F5
North Meadow Rd HGHW SN6 288 E3
Northmoor La CIR GL7 263 J2
Northover Rd
HNLZ/SM/SNYPK/WT BS9 325 H2
North Pk KGWD/HNM BS15 338 A2
North Pl CHELT GL50 2 E4
CHELTE/BC GL52 2 E4
North Rd BMSTR BS3 335 J7 4
BRSTK/PCHW BS34 317 G7
CFTN/FAIL BS8 334 F5
CLFD GL16 151 M8
FRCTL/WBN BS36 318 B4
GL GL1 5 H1
RDLND/MONT BS6 335 M1
RTEWK/TIB GL19 108 C8
THNB/SVB BS35 293 L1
YATE/CS BS37 309 K5
YATE/CS BS37 319 L1
North Rd East CHELTW GL51 114 D4
North Rd West CHELTW GL51 114 D4
North Stoke La
OLD/WMLY/WICK BS30 349 J3
North St BMSTR BS3 6 A9
BMSTR BS3 335 J7
CBRIS/FH BS1 7 G1
CHELT GL50 2 D4
COTS GL54 74 C5
MANG/FISH BS16 327 M6
OLD/WMLY/WICK BS30 338 E7
WUE GL12 296 C5
Northumberland Rd RDLND/MONT BS6 335 L1
Northumbria Dr
HNLZ/SM/SNYPK/WT BS9 325 K6
North Upton La GLE GL4 137 G4
North Vw MANG/FISH BS16 .... 327 M7 4
RDLND/MONT BS6 325 J7
Northville Rd HORF/LLZ BS7 326 C2
North Wall HGHW SN6 288 F3
Northway BRSTK/PCHW BS34 .... 316 D7
North Wy CIR GL7 238 C3 2
Northway La TEWK GL20 48 C4
Northwaylane TEWK GL20 48 F3
Northway La TEWK GL20 49 G2
Northwick Rd HORF/LLZ BS7 326 B3
THNB/SVB BS35 304 F3
Northwood Cl CIND GL14 154 B2
Northwoods Wk
HNBRY/STHM BS10 315 M8 1
Norton Cl COTS GL54 74 C4
KGWD/HNM BS15 338 B4 7
RWYE HR9 126 D4 1
Norton Rdg
RSTROUD/NAIL GL6 232 B6 2
Norton Rd
BRSG/KWL/STAPK BS4 346 C1
Norton Vw CHCAM GL55 8 F8
Nortonwood
RSTROUD/NAIL GL6 232 B6
Norwich Dr
BRSG/KWL/STAPK BS4 337 G5
CHELTW GL51 115 J5
Norwood Rd CHELT GL50 115 L4
Nostle Rd COTS GL54 169 K2
Notch Rd CIR GL7 188 C3
Notgrove Cl CHELTW GL51 115 G3 2
GL GL1 159 L1
Notley Pl BWTH/CHD GL3 137 J4
Nottingham Rd CHELTE/BC GL52.. 72 B6
HORF/LLZ BS7 326 A8
Nottingham St BMSTR BS3 336 B8 4
Nourse Cl CHELTS GL53 115 K7
Nova Scotia Pl CBRIS/FH BS1 ... 335 J6 3
Novers Crs
BRSG/KWL/STAPK BS4 345 L3
Novers Hl
BRSG/KWL/STAPK BS4 345 L3
Novers La
BRSG/KWL/STAPK BS4 345 L4
Novers Park Dr
BRSG/KWL/STAPK BS4 345 L3
Novers Park Rd
BRSG/KWL/STAPK BS4 345 M3
Novers Rd
BRSG/KWL/STAPK BS4 345 L3
Noverton Av CHELTE/BC GL52 94 F7
Noverton La CHELTE/BC GL52 94 E7
Nugent Hl RDLND/MONT BS6 335 M2
Nunnery La DSLY GL11 253 J4
Nunny Cl CHELTW GL51 114 E2
Nupdown Rd THNB/SVB BS35 .... 249 G6
Nup End RTEWK/TIB GL19 89 J3
Nupend Gdns MTCHDN GL17 ... 131 H1 3
Nupend La MTCHDN GL17 131 G1
Nup End La RTEWK/TIB GL19 89 J3
The Nurseries
CHELTE/BC GL52 94 A1 3
WUE GL12 294 D6
Nursery Cl CHCAM GL55 9 H6
CIR GL7 238 D5
MIM GL56 58 D4
STROUD GL5 208 F5 3
Nursery Gdns
HNBRY/STHM BS10 315 J8
Nursery Rd
CHPMW/MSHF SN14 343 J8 2
CIR GL7 238 E5 3
The Nursery BMSTR BS3 335 K8 7
STNHO GL10 207 J7
Nursery Vw CIR GL7 238 E8
Nut Cft GLE GL4 136 D4
Nutfield Gv BRSTK/PCHW BS34 .. 326 D1
Nutgrove Av BMSTR BS3 336 A8
Nuthatch Dr MANG/FISH BS16 .... 327 H5
Nuthatch Gdns
MANG/FISH BS16 327 J5
Nuthill GLE GL4 137 H8
Nutley Av GL GL1 159 L1
Nutmeg Cl GLE GL4 136 F7 2
Nut Orchard La TEWK GL20 26 B5 2
Nympsfield KGWD/HNM BS15 .... 338 A1
Nympsfield Rd GL GL1 135 L8
RSTROUD/NAIL GL6 231 M6
RSTROUD/NAIL GL6 232 C7

O

Oak Av CHELTE/BC GL52 3 J9
Oakbank GLE GL4 136 A7
Oakbrook Dr CHELTW GL51 114 E4
Oak Cl BRSTK/PCHW BS34 316 F4
CHEP NP16 270 A6
YATE/CS BS37 309 M8
Oak Crs LYD GL15 224 A5
Oakcroft Cl GLE GL4 136 F8 2
Oakdale Av MANG/FISH BS16 327 M3
Oakdale Cl MANG/FISH BS16 328 A3
Oakdale Ct MANG/FISH BS16 ... 328 A4 1
Oakdale Rd HGRV/WHIT BS14 346 C3
MANG/FISH BS16 328 A3
Oakdene Av EVILLE/WHL BS5 326 F8
Oak Dr BWTH/CHD GL3 137 M5
DSLY GL11 229 J8
STROUD GL5 208 D5
TEWK GL20 48 F3
Oakenhill Rd
BRSG/KWL/STAPK BS4 347 G1
Oakenhill Wk
BRSG/KWL/STAPK BS4 347 G1
Oakes La BAD GL9 322 D5
Oakfield Gv CFTN/FAIL BS8 6 A1
Oakfield Pl CFTN/FAIL BS8 6 A1
Oakfield Rd CFTN/FAIL BS8 335 J3
CHELTE/BC GL52 72 C8
KEYN BS31 348 B8
KGWD/HNM BS15 337 M4
Oakfields CLFD GL16 175 J1
Oakfield St CHELT GL50 115 K4
The Oak Fld CIND GL14 154 C3
Oakfield Wy BRKLY GL13 226 F2
Oakford La CBATH/BATHN BA1 352 C3
CHPMW/MSHF SN14 352 D1
Oakham Rd MIM GL56 82 D2
Oakhanger Dr AVONM BS11 324 D2
Oakhill HNBRY/STHM BS10 314 E7
Oakhill Av
OLD/WMLY/WICK BS30 348 E1
Oakhill Pitch LYD GL15 223 G5
Oakhill Rd MTCHDN GL17 130 C1 1
Oakhunger La BRKLY GL13 226 E7
Oakhurst Cl BWTH/CHD GL3 113 H6
Oakhurst Ri CHELTE/BC GL52 3 K8
Oakhurst Rd
HNLZ/SM/SNYPK/WT BS9 325 H6
Oakland Av CHELTE/BC GL52 3 H1
Oakland Dr LED HR8 19 M4
Oakland Rd EVILLE/WHL BS5 ... 337 G3 2
MTCHDN GL17 129 M5 2
RDLND/MONT BS6 335 K2 3
Oaklands CIR GL7 238 C5
CLFD GL16 175 L7
Oaklands Cl
MANG/FISH BS16 328 D6 1
Oaklands Dr ALMDB BS32 306 C7
MANG/FISH BS16 327 J3
OLD/WMLY/WICK BS30 348 E1 2
Oaklands Pk LYD GL15 200 F2
Oaklands Rd
MANG/FISH BS16 328 C6 4
Oakland St CHELTS GL53 116 C4 5
Oak La EVILLE/WHL BS5 337 H1
TEWK GL20 27 G5
Oaklea Rd LYD GL15 177 L8
Oakleaze FRCTL/WBN BS36 318 F4 3
Oakleaze Rd THNB/SVB BS35 293 L2
Oakleigh Av EVILLE/WHL BS5 .. 336 F3 3
Oakleigh Gdns
OLD/WMLY/WICK BS30 348 E1
Oakley Flats CIR GL7 266 F5
Oakley Rd CHELTE/BC GL52 3 K6
CIR GL7 238 B5
HORF/LLZ BS7 326 B4
Oakley Wy LYD GL15 200 C4
Oak Manor Dr CHELTE/BC GL52 3 J5
Oakmeade Pk
BRSG/KWL/STAPK BS4 346 D1 4
Oak Meadow LYD GL15 201 K5
Oakridge VGL GL2 110 F5
Oakridge Cl GLE GL4 137 G6 7
KGWD/HNM BS15 338 C4
Oak Rd CHPMW/MSHF SN14 343 H6
CIR GL7 265 G4
HGHW SN6 265 J7
HORF/LLZ BS7 326 A6
Oaksey Rd MALM SN16 285 L7
Oaks La RWYE HR9 85 J8
The Oaks CHELTW GL51 114 F5
CIR GL7 261 H4 1
GLE GL4 137 G5
Oak St CIR GL7 244 E7
Oak Tree Av MANG/FISH BS16 329 K7
Oak Tree Cl KGWD/HNM BS15 .. 337 L8 2
VGL GL2 159 G4
Oaktree Ct AVONM BS11 324 A4
Oaktree Crs ALMDB BS32 316 D1
Oaktree Gdn GLE GL4 136 E8 3
Oaktree Gdns
BMSTRD/HC/WWD BS13 345 G6
Oak Tree Wk KEYN BS31 347 M8
Oak Wy CIND GL14 154 E3
CIR GL7 263 H5
RTEWK/TIB GL19 108 C8
STNHO GL10 207 H4
Oakwood Av
HNLZ/SM/SNYPK/WT BS9 325 K5
Oakwood Cl CIND GL14 154 B2 3
LYD GL15 200 C2
Oakwood Dr BWTH/CHD GL3 137 H5
Oakwood Rd CLFD GL16 175 L6
HNLZ/SM/SNYPK/WT BS9 325 K5
LYD GL15 200 C2
Oatfield VGL GL2 159 G1
Oatfield Rd VGL GL2 181 J5
Oathill La CIR GL7 259 J3
Oatlands Av HGRV/WHIT BS14 .... 346 C5
Oatleys Crs LED HR8 19 L3
Oatleys Rd LED HR8 19 M4
Oatleys Ter LED HR8 19 M4
Oberon Av EVILLE/WHL BS5 337 G1
O'brien Rd CHELTW GL51 93 J7 2
Ocker Hl RSTROUD/NAIL GL6 208 A1
Octavia Pl LYD GL15 201 K7
Oddington Rd COTS GL54 102 B3
Offas Cl CHEP NP16 270 C4
Offa's Dyke Pth CHEP NP16 222 C8
LYD GL15 222 A1
Office Rd CIND GL14 154 A4
Ogbourne CHPMW/MSHF SN14 .. 343 K8
Ogbourne Cl VGL GL2 113 G8
Okebourne Cl
HNBRY/STHM BS10 315 K7
Okebourne Rd
HNBRY/STHM BS10 315 K8
Okus Rd CHELTS GL53 116 C6
Oldacre Dr CHELTE/BC GL52 72 C6
Old Alexander Rd MALM SN16 .... 303 G7
Old Ashley Hl
RDLND/MONT BS6 336 B1 3
Old Aust Rd ALMDB BS32 306 E5
Old Bath Rd CHELTS GL53 2 F9
CHELTS GL53 116 A6
Old Bread St CBRISNE BS2 7 J4
Old Brewery La TET GL8 281 M4 2
Oldbridge Rd HGRV/WHIT BS14 .. 346 E8
Old Bristol Rd
RSTROUD/NAIL GL6 232 D8
Old Bulwark Rd CHEP NP16 270 A4
Old Burford Rd CHNTN OX7 125 M1
Oldbury Cha
OLD/WMLY/WICK BS30 348 C1
Oldbury Cl CHELTW GL51 92 F8 3
Oldbury Court Dr
MANG/FISH BS16 327 K5 3
Oldbury Court Rd
MANG/FISH BS16 327 J6
Oldbury La
OLD/WMLY/WICK BS30 339 M6
THNB/SVB BS35 273 K7
Oldbury Orch BWTH/CHD GL3 .... 113 M7
Oldbury Rd CHELTW GL51 92 F8
TEWK GL20 48 A5
Oldbutt Rd SHPSTR CV36 16 A6
Old Cheltenham Rd VGL GL2 112 F7
Old Coach Rd CHEP NP16 270 E8
CHPMW/MSHF SN14 343 L1
Old Common
RSTROUD/NAIL GL6 233 K4
The Old Common
RSTROUD/NAIL GL6 209 M7
Old Court Dr RTEWK/TIB GL19 .... 109 K2
Old Dam Rd LYD GL15 201 L4
Old Dean Rd MTCHDN GL17 106 C8
Old Down Hl ALMDB BS32 306 E1
Old Down Rd BAD GL9 322 E3
Oldends La STNHO GL10 206 F3
Old Farm La EVILLE/WHL BS5 .. 337 K5 3
Oldfield TEWK GL20 48 B5
Oldfield Crs CHELTW GL51 115 H3
Oldfield Pl CFTN/FAIL BS8 335 H6
Oldfield Rd CFTN/FAIL BS8 335 J6 4
Oldfields La THNB/SVB BS35 307 L4
Old Forge Cl CHNTN OX7 125 M1
Old Gloucester Rd
CHELTW GL51 114 A1
COTS GL54 122 E5
FRCTL/WBN BS36 317 K4
MANG/FISH BS16 327 K3
THNB/SVB BS35 293 K6
WUE GL12 294 D1
Old Hall Cl BDWAY WR12 31 G2 1
Old Hl MTCHDN GL17 131 J1
TET GL8 257 M2
Old Horsley Rd
RSTROUD/NAIL GL6 232 D8
Old Hospital La TEWK GL20 48 B4 2
Old King Street Ct
CBRIS/FH BS1 7 G2 1
Oldlands Av FRCTL/WBN BS36 .... 318 E5
Old La (Simmonds La)
RWYE HR9 85 G3
Old London Rd WUE GL12 277 J3
Old Manor Cl WUE GL12 276 C6
Old Manor Gdns CHCAM GL55 9 G7
Old Manor La TEWK GL20 48 C3
Old Market RSTROUD/NAIL GL6 .. 232 D7
Old Market St CBRISNE BS2 7 J3
Oldmead Wk
BMSTRD/HC/WWD BS13 345 G4
Old Millbrook Ter
CHELTW GL51 115 K1 2
Old Mill Cl YATE/CS BS37 319 K7
The Old Ml BDWAY WR12 32 E3 1
Oldminster Rd BRKLY GL13 226 E2
Old Moat VGL GL2 112 A1
Old Monmouth Rd
MTCHDN GL17 131 H1
Old Neighbourhood
RSTROUD/NAIL GL6 234 A1
Old Orchard Ct CIR GL7 218 C6
The Old Orch MALM SN16 303 J6
Old Painswick Rd GLE GL4 136 D5 1
Old Pk CBRISNE BS2 6 D2 1
Old Park Hl CBRISNE BS2 6 D3
Old Quarry Ri AVONM BS11 324 A4
Old Railway Cl MALM SN16 303 J7 2
Old Rectory Cl STROUD GL5 208 C6
Old Rectory Gdns MIM GL56 79 K4 1
Old Rectory Rd WUE GL12 277 H7
Old Reddings Cl
CHELTW GL51 114 E4 2
Old Reddings Rd CHELTW GL51 .. 114 E4
Old Rd CHELTE/BC GL52 94 E3
CLFD GL16 175 M2
SHPSTR CV36 16 B6
VGL GL2 111 J3
Old Rw GL GL1 5 H8
Old Sneed Av
HNLZ/SM/SNYPK/WT BS9 324 F7
Old Sneed Pk
HNLZ/SM/SNYPK/WT BS9 324 F7
Old Sneed Rd
HNLZ/SM/SNYPK/WT BS9 324 F7
Old Station Dr CHELTS GL53 115 M5
Old Station Rd NWNT GL18 86 B2
Old Station Wy CLFD GL16 175 K2
Old Town WUE GL12 277 K4
Old Town Ms LYD GL15 225 H1
Old Tram Rd GL GL1 4 D7
Old Vicarage La CIR GL7 261 H4
Oldwood La YATE/CS BS37 309 K3
Olio La CHELTS GL53 2 E8
Olive Gdns THNB/SVB BS35 293 H7 2
Olive Gv DSLY GL11 253 J1
Oliver's La MALM SN16 303 J8 4
Ollney Rd RSTROUD/NAIL GL6 233 H5
Olveston Rd HORF/LLZ BS7 326 A6
Olympus Cl
BRSTK/PCHW BS34 316 F5 2
Olympus Pk VGL GL2 159 J1
Olympus Rd BRSTK/PCHW BS34.. 315 M4
Onslow Rd NWNT GL18 86 D3
Oram Ct OLD/WMLY/WICK BS30.. 338 B7
The Orangery GLE GL4 137 G4 5
Orange St CBRISNE BS2 7 J1
Orchard Av BDWAY WR12 33 G3
CBRIS/FH BS1 6 D4 4
CHELTW GL51 115 H1
CHEP NP16 270 A6
THNB/SVB BS35 293 L2
Orchard Bank COTS GL54 148 B4 1
Orchard Bvd
OLD/WMLY/WICK BS30 338 D7
Orchard Cl CHCAM GL55 9 G6 1
CHNTN OX7 83 J6
CIR GL7 244 D7 1
CLFD GL16 127 K7
CLFD GL16 175 H6
DSLY GL11 229 H6
FRCTL/WBN BS36 318 A5
HNLZ/SM/SNYPK/WT BS9 325 H6
KEYN BS31 347 M5 1
KGWD/HNM BS15 338 A3
LYD GL15 224 F3
MTCHDN GL17 130 C1
RWYE HR9 106 B4
SHPSTR CV36 16 B6 3
STNHO GL10 207 K8 1
TEWK GL20 27 H5
VGL GL2 112 A6
VGL GL2 158 F4
WUE GL12 276 C6
YATE/CS BS37 320 B1
Orchard Ct COTS GL54 73 M1
RSTROUD/NAIL GL6 185 H3
STNHO GL10 207 G4 1
TEWK GL20 48 B5 5
Orchard Dr BWTH/CHD GL3 113 M7
TEWK GL20 26 B4
THNB/SVB BS35 291 J4 1
Orchard End RTEWK/TIB GL19 .. 69 G6 2
Orchard Farm Cl CHEP NP16 .. 270 D4 1
Orchard Fld TET GL8 257 L3 1
Orchard Gdns
KGWD/HNM BS15 338 B3
Orchard Ga LYD GL15 202 D1 1
Orchard Gra THNB/SVB BS35 ... 293 K1 3
The Orchard Gv
CHELTW GL51 138 F2 2
Orchard La CBRIS/FH BS1 6 D4
LED HR8 19 M3
Orchard Lea THNB/SVB BS35 ... 293 J6 5
Orchard Leaze DSLY GL11 228 F7
Orchard Md RSTROUD/NAIL GL6.. 185 H4
RSTROUD/NAIL GL6 232 D7 3
Orchard Pl LED HR8 20 A5
Orchard Rdg TEWK GL20 24 B6
Orchard Ri CIND GL14 155 H7
DSLY GL11 229 H8 1
MIM GL56 79 K3 1
RTEWK/TIB GL19 109 L2
THNB/SVB BS35 306 C1
Orchard Rd CHELTE/BC GL52 72 B8
CLFD GL16 175 K1
COTS GL54 74 B6
EVILLE/WHL BS5 337 H3 3
FRCTL/WBN BS36 318 F4 4
HORF/LLZ BS7 326 A7
KGWD/HNM BS15 338 A3
LGASH BS41 344 B1
LYD GL15 225 K1
MANG/FISH BS16 329 K6
MTCHDN GL17 128 C6
NWNT GL18 64 B6
STROUD GL5 207 L5
TEWK GL20 51 L4
VGL GL2 113 G7
Orchard Sq EVILLE/WHL BS5 .... 336 F4 7
The Orchards KGWD/HNM BS15.. 338 B3
LYD GL15 201 J8
Orchard St CBRIS/FH BS1 6 D4
WUE GL12 277 K4
The Orchard
BRSTK/PCHW BS34 317 H6
CIR GL7 242 E4 2
DSLY GL11 254 D2
LYD GL15 224 B6
WUE GL12 294 D6
Orchard V KGWD/HNM BS15 338 B4
Orchard Vw STROUD GL5 208 C7
Orchard Wk WUE GL12 277 H7 1
Orchard Wy BWTH/CHD GL3 113 K4
CHELTW GL51 93 H8
CHNTN OX7 104 B7
CLFD GL16 151 K5
RTEWK/TIB GL19 108 D7
Oridge St RTEWK/TIB GL19 66 C8
Oriel Gv MIM GL56 58 D7
Oriel Rd CHELT GL50 2 D6
Oriole Wy GLE GL4 136 E5
Orion Dr BRSTK/PCHW BS34 316 F5
Orland Wy
OLD/WMLY/WICK BS30 338 C8
Orlebar Gdns AVONM BS11 324 D1
Orlham La LED HR8 19 K6
Ormerod Rd CHEP NP16 270 D4
HNLZ/SM/SNYPK/WT BS9 325 G7
Ormond Pl CHELT GL50 2 D5 3
Ormonds Cl ALMDB BS32 317 G1
Ormsley Cl BRSTK/PCHW BS34 .... 316 E3
Orpen Gdns HORF/LLZ BS7 326 D6
Orpheus Av BRSTK/PCHW BS34 .. 316 F5
Orrisdale Ter CHELTS GL53 2 E7
Orwell Cl MALM SN16 303 J6 3
Orwell Dr KEYN BS31 348 B7
Orwell St BMSTR BS3 336 A8 3
Osborne Av HORF/LLZ BS7 326 B8 2
Osborne Cl
BRSTK/PCHW BS34 316 F7 5
Osborne Rd BMSTR BS3 6 C8
CFTN/FAIL BS8 335 J2
THNB/SVB BS35 304 B4
Osborne Ter BMSTR BS3 345 K1 9
Osborne Vls CBRISNE BS2 6 D1 1
Osbourne Av GL GL1 159 L2
Osier Cl GLE GL4 136 C7
Osprey Cl GLE GL4 136 F6
Osprey Dr STNHO GL10 207 H3
Osprey Pk THNB/SVB BS35 273 M8
Osprey Rd CHELTS GL53 115 L6
EVILLE/WHL BS5 336 E4 13
Osric Rd GL GL1 136 B5
Othello Cl CHELTW GL51 115 G1
Otterford Cl
HGRV/WHIT BS14 346 D6 6
Otter Rd BWTH/CHD GL3 137 H6
Otters Fld COTS GL54 74 D3
Ottery Cl AVONM BS11 324 C2
Ottrells Md ALMDB BS32 306 E8
Oval Ap VGL GL2 181 H6
The Oval GL GL1 135 M5
VGL GL2 181 H6
Overbrook Cl GLE GL4 136 E2
Overbrook Dr CHELTE/BC GL52 3 H1
Overbrook Rd VGL GL2 159 G3
Overbury Rd GL GL1 5 K9
Overbury St CHELTS GL53 116 C4 6
Over Cswy GL GL1 111 K8
Overhill Rd CIR GL7 214 B7
Over La ALMDB BS32 306 C7
ALMDB BS32 315 L2
Overley Rd CIR GL7 212 D6
Overndale Rd MANG/FISH BS16 .. 327 L6
Overnhill Ct MANG/FISH BS16 327 L6
Overnhill Rd MANG/FISH BS16 .... 327 L6
Over Old Rd VGL GL2 89 G6
Overton La VGL GL2 180 E1
Overton Park Rd CHELT GL50 2 A5
Overton Rd HORF/LLZ BS7 335 M1
Owen Gv
HNLZ/SM/SNYPK/WT BS9 325 K6
Owen St EVILLE/WHL BS5 336 D3 11
Owl Cl GLE GL4 136 F6
Owls End Rd CHELTE/BC GL52 ... 72 C7 5
Owls Eye Cl CLFD GL16 151 M7 1
Owls Head Rd
KGWD/HNM BS15 338 A5
Oxbarton BRSTK/PCHW BS34 317 H6
The Oxebode GL GL1 4 E5
Oxen Leaze ALMDB BS32 317 G1 3
Oxford Cl CHELTE/BC GL52 3 G7
Oxford Pas CHELT GL50 2 D4
Oxford Pl CFTN/FAIL BS8 335 H5 12
EVILLE/WHL BS5 336 C2 14
Oxford Rd GL GL1 5 H3
Oxfordshire Wy COTS GL54 123 J4
Oxford St BMSTR BS3 7 K9 1
CBRISNE BS2 7 L5
CHELTE/BC GL52 2 F7
CHEP NP16 270 A3 7
EVILLE/WHL BS5 336 E4 14
GL GL1 5 G4
LYD GL15 225 J1
MALM SN16 303 J8
MIM GL56 58 D6 1
RDLND/MONT BS6 335 L3
Oxford Wy CHELTW GL51 115 J6
Oxleaze
BMSTRD/HC/WWD BS13 345 M7
Oxleaze Cl TET GL8 281 M3
Oxleaze Rd TET GL8 259 G6
Oxmead Cl CHELTE/BC GL52 72 D7
Oxmoor GLE GL4 136 F8
Oxstalls Dr VGL GL2 112 D7 3
Oxstalls La VGL GL2 5 M2
Oxstalls Wy VGL GL2 5 M1
VGL GL2 112 D6 3
Oxway Cl SHPSTR CV36 16 B5
Ozleworth KGWD/HNM BS15 .. 338 C3 4

P

Packer's Rd *CIND* GL14 .... 154 B3
Packhorse La *CIR* GL7 .... 217 K1
Paddock Cl *ALMDB* BS32 .... 316 F1
MANG/FISH BS16 .... 328 E5 🔢
Paddock Gdns
HGRV/WHIT BS14 .... 346 C7
THNB/SVB BS35 .... 293 J6
VGL GL2 .... 112 F6
Paddock Ri *STNHO* GL10 .... 207 H4
The Paddocks *CIR* GL7 .... 214 C6
THNB/SVB 293M2
Padin Cl *RSTROUD/NAIL* GL6 .... 210 A7
Padstow Rd
BRSG/KWL/STAPK BS4 .... 346 A3
Paganhill Est *STROUD* GL5 .... 208 B3
Paganhill La *STROUD* GL5 .... 208 B4
Page Rd *MANG/FISH* BS16 .... 327M7
Page's La *TEWK* GL20 .... 25 M6
Pagets Rd *CHELTE/BC* GL52 .... 94 C1
Painswick Av
BRSTK/PCHW BS34 .... 316 D1
Painswick Dr *YATE/CS* BS37 .... 320 A3 🔢
Painswick Old Rd *STROUD* GL5 .... 208 E1
Painswick Rd *BWTH/CHD* GL3 .... 137 M8
CHELT GL50 .... 115 L4
GLE GL4 .... 136 F7
GLE GL4 .... 161 L4
RSTROUD/NAIL GL6 .... 208 D1
STROUD GL5 .... 208 D3
Palmdale Cl
OLD/WMLY/WICK BS30 .... 348 C1 🔢
Palmer Av *GLE* GL4 .... 137 H6
Palmers Cl
OLD/WMLY/WICK BS30 .... 338 C5
Palmers Leaze *ALMDB* BS32 .... 317 J4
Palmerston Rd
RDLND/MONT BS6 .... 325 K7 🔢
Palmerston St *BMSTR* BS3 .... 335 K8
Palm Rd *CHPMW/MSHF* SN14.. .. 343 J6
TEWK GL20 .... 48 C7
Palmyra Rd *BMSTR* BS3 .... 345 K1
Pancake La *RTEWK/TIB* GL19 .... 91 L2
Parabola Cl *CHELT* GL50 .... 2 B6
Parabola La *CHELT* GL50 .... 2 A6
Parabola Rd *CHELT* GL50 .... 2 A6
The Parade *AVONM* BS11 .... 324 A5 🔢
YATE/CS BS37 .... 320 C2 🔢
Paragon Ter *CHELT* GL50 .... 2 D8
The Paragon
CFTN/FAIL BS8 .... 335 H5 🔢
Parawell La *LYD* GL15 .... 200 A4
Park Av *ALMDB* BS32 .... 316 C1
BMSTR BS3 .... 336 A8
EVILLE/WHL BS5.. .... 337 G3
FRCTL/WBN BS36 .... 318 A5
FRCTL/WBN BS36 .... 318 D4
VGL GL2 .... 112 E6
Park Brake *VGL* GL2 .... 110 F7
Parkbury Cl *CHELTW* GL51 .... 115 J1
Park Cl *CIR* GL7 .... 242 F4
KEYN BS31 .... 347 M6
KGWD/HNM BS15 .... 338 A4
LYD GL15 .... 199 C6
OLD/WMLY/WICK BS30 .... 338 D6 🔢
TET GL8 .... 282 A4
Park Crs *EVILLE/WHL* BS5 .... 336 F3
MANG/FISH BS16 .... 327 L2
OLD/WMLY/WICK BS30 .... 338 D6
Park Dr *VGL* GL2 .... 159 H2
Parkend Br *VGL* GL2 .... 182 B1
Parkend Rd *CLFD* GL16 .... 175M3
Park End Rd *GL* GL1 .... 136 A4
Parkend Rd *LYD* GL15 .... 177 K8
LYD GL15 .... 200 D2
Parkend Wk *CLFD* GL16 .... 175 L7
CLFD GL16 .... 175M2
Parker Pl *BDWAY* WR12 .... 32 F3
Parkers Av
OLD/WMLY/WICK BS30 .... 339 L4
Parkers Barton
EVILLE/WHL BS5 .... 336 D5 🔢
Parkers Cl *HNBRY/STHM* BS10 .... 316 A7
Parkers La *MIM* GL56 .... 58 C6
Parker St *BMSTR* BS3 .... 335 K8 🔢
Park Farm *COTS* GL54 .... 123 H4
Park Farm Ct
OLD/WMLY/WICK BS30 .... 338 B7 🔢
Parkfield Av *EVILLE/WHL* BS5.. .. 336 F4 🔢
Parkfield Rd *MANG/FISH* BS16 .... 329 J4
RDLND/MONT BS6 .... 325 L6
Park Gv *LYD* GL15 .... 200 F2
Park HI *AVONM* BS11 .... 324 A5
LYD GL15 .... 200 F2
Park Hill Common *LYD* GL15 .... 223 J7
Park Hill La *LYD* GL15 .... 222 F7
Park Hill Rd *LYD* GL15 .... 223 J7
Parkhurst Av
MANG/FISH BS16 .... 327 K7 🔢
Parkland Rd *CHELTS* GL53 .... 116 B7
DSLY GL11 .... 229 H7
Parklands *KGWD/HNM* BS15 .... 337 M3 🔢
MALM SN16 .... 303 G2
VGL GL2 .... 159 G2
WUE GL12 .... 277 K3
Parklands Cl *MALM* SN16 .... 303 G2
Parkland Sq *CIR* GL7 .... 238 D5
Parklands Rd *BMSTR* BS3 .... 335 C4
Parkland Wy *THNB/SVB* BS35.. .. 273 K8
Park La *CHELTE/BC* GL52 .... 94 D5
CIR GL7 .... 238 C3
COTS GL54 .... 118 D2
DSLY GL11 .... 252 F4
FRCTL/WBN BS36 .... 318 C4
MALM SN16 .... 302 F7
STROUD GL5 .... 232 B5
VGL GL2 .... 278 C3
Park Md *MALM* SN16 .... 303 H7
Park Ms *CHELT* GL50 .... 115 L5
Park Pl *CBRISNE* BS2 .... 6 D2
CFTN/FAIL BS8 .... 6 B2
CHELT GL50 .... 115 L4
EVILLE/WHL BS5.. .... 327 G8

HGHW SN6 .... 287 H3
Park Rd *AVONM* BS11 .... 324 A5
BMSTR BS3 .... 6 B7
CHCAM GL55 .... 34 D1
CLFD GL16 .... 151 K8
GL GL1 .... 4 F7
HORF/LLZ BS7 .... 326 B2
KEYN BS31 .... 348 A6
KGWD/HNM BS15 .... 337M2
MALM SN16 .... 303 G6
MANG/FISH BS16 .... 326 F6
MANG/FISH BS16 .... 328 A6
MIM GL56 .... 35 G8
NWNT GL18 .... 88 A7
OLD/WMLY/WICK BS30 .... 338 D6
RSTROUD/NAIL GL6 .... 232 E8
STNHO GL10 .... 207 G5
STROUD GL5 .... 208 F5
THNB/SVB BS35 .... 293 K1
WUE GL12 .... 275 K7
Park Road Crs
RSTROUD/NAIL GL6 .... 232 E8 🔢
Park Rw *CBRIS/FH* BS1 .... 6 C3
FRCTL/WBN BS36 .... 318 C3
Parkside *CLFD* GL16 .... 175 K1
Parkside Av *FRCTL/WBN* BS36 .. .. 318 A5
Parkside Dr *BWTH/CHD* GL3 .... 113 H5
Parkside Gdns *EVILLE/WHL* BS5.. .. 326 D7
Park Rd *MTCHDN* GL17 .... 130 D2
Parkstone Av *HORF/LLZ* BS7.. .. 326 B5
Park St *BAD* GL9 .... 312 C1
BRSG/KWL/STAPK BS4 .... 7 M9
CBRIS/FH BS1 .... 6 C3
CHELT GL50 .... 2 B4
CIR GL7 .... 238 C2 🔢
CIR GL7 .... 242 F4
COTS GL54 .... 102 A3
EVILLE/WHL BS5.. .... 337 H3 🔢
GL GL1 .... 4 F4
YATE/CS BS37 .... 308 F7
Park Street Av *CBRIS/FH* BS1 .... 6 C3 🔢
The Park *ALMDB* BS32 .... 306 E8
CHELT GL50 .... 115 A4
COTS GL54 .... 102 A4
KEYN BS31 .... 338 A3
KGWD/HNM BS15 .... 338 A3
MANG/FISH BS16 .... 327 K2
OLD/WMLY/WICK BS30 .... 348 D2
TEWK GL20 .... 48 F2
Park Vw *CHEP* NP16 .... 270 D3
CIR GL7 .... 214 B7
KGWD/HNM BS15 .... 338 A4
MTCHDN GL17 .... 129 C3
VGL GL2 .... 181 H4
Park View Av *THNB/SVB* BS35 .. .. 293 L1
Park View Dr *STROUD* GL5 .... 208 A3 🔢
Park View Rd *BRKLY* GL13 .... 226 F8
Parkwall Crs
OLD/WMLY/WICK BS30 .... 338 B7
Parkwall Rd
OLD/WMLY/WICK BS30 .... 338 C7
Parkway *BRSTK/PCHW* BS34 .... 317 J7
Park Wy *CIR* GL7 .... 238 D7
OLD/WMLY/WICK BS30 .... 338 D6
Park Wood Cl *HGRV/WHIT* BS14.. .. 346 B7
Parkwood Crs *BWTH/CHD* GL3.. .. 137 H5
Parkwood Gv *CHELTS* GL53 .... 116 C7
Parliament St
BRSG/KWL/STAPK BS4 .... 7 L9 🔢
GL GL1 .... 4 E7
STROUD GL5 .... 208 E4
Parliment Cl *STROUD* GL5 .... 208 E4 🔢
Parnall Crs *YATE/CS* BS37 .... 319 L1
Parnall Rd *MANG/FISH* BS16 .... 327M5
Parragate Rd *CIND* GL14 .... 154 A2
Parr Cl *BWTH/CHD* GL3 .... 113 H4
Parry Rd *GL* GL1 .... 136 B5
Parry's Cl
HNLZ/SM/SNYPK/WT BS9.. .. 325 G6
Parrys Gv
HNLZ/SM/SNYPK/WT BS9.. .. 325 G6
Parry's La
HNLZ/SM/SNYPK/WT BS9.. .. 325 H6
Parslow Barton
EVILLE/WHL BS5 .... 337 J4 🔢
Parsonage Farm *HGHW* SN6.. .. 288 F4 🔢
Parsonage Rd *LGASH* BS41 .... 344 F1
Parsonage St *DSLY* GL11 .... 253 J2 🔢
Parsons Av *BRSTK/PCHW* BS34 .. .. 317 H6
Parsons Cl *SHPSTR* CV36 .... 16 B6
Parsons Ct
RSTROUD/NAIL GL6 .... 233 J5 🔢
Parsons La *CHCAM* GL55 .... 11 M5
RTEWK/TIB GL19 .... 44 A8
Parsons Paddock
HGRV/WHIT BS14 .... 346 C4 🔢
Parson St *BMSTR* BS3 .... 345 L2
Parsons Wk
HNBRY/STHM BS10 .... 338 C4
Partition St *CBRIS/FH* BS1 .... 6 C5 🔢
Parton Dr *BWTH/CHD* GL3 .... 113 L6
Parton Rd *BWTH/CHD* GL3 .... 113 K5
Partridge Cl *STNHO* GL10 .... 207 H3 🔢
VGL GL2 .... 135 L6
Partridge Rd *MANG/FISH* BS16.. .. 329 L7
Partridge Wy *CIR* GL7 .... 238 E2
Passage Rd *HNBRY/STHM* BS10.. .. 315 H7
HNBRY/STHM BS10 .... 315 J8 🔢
HNLZ/SM/SNYPK/WT BS9.. .. 325 J3
VGL GL2 .... 159 H2
VGL GL2 .... 181 G3
Passage Road Brentry HI
HNBRY/STHM BS10 .... 315 J8
Passage St *CBRIS/FH* BS1 .... 7 H4
Pastor's HI *LYD* GL15 .... 200 D3
Pasture La *MIM* GL56 .... 57 H1
Patch Elm La *YATE/CS* BS37 .... 309 G4
The Patches *MTCHDN* GL17 .... 129 H5
Patch La *YATE/CS* BS37 .... 309 J3
Paterson Rd *CIR* GL7 .... 238 E3
Pates Av *CHELT* GL51 .... 115 K1
Patseamur Ms *VGL* GL2 .... 113 G6 🔢
Patterdale Cl *CHELT* GL51 .... 93 H6 🔢
Paulman Gdns *LGASH* BS41 .... 344 B3 🔢
Paul Md *RSTROUD/NAIL* GL6 .... 184 D2
Pauls Cft *HGHW* SN6 .... 289 G4
Paul's Ri *STROUD* GL5 .... 232 C1
Paul St *CBRISNE* BS2 .... 6 D1

GL GL1 .... 136 B4 🔢
Paulton Dr *HORF/LLZ* BS7 .... 325 L7
Paultow Av *BMSTR* BS3 .... 336 A8
Paultow Rd *BMSTR* BS3 .... 336 A8
Pauntley Court Dr
RTEWK/TIB GL19 .... 65 G4
Pavey Cl
BMSTRD/HC/WWD BS13 .... 345 L7
Pavey Rd
BMSTRD/HC/WWD BS13 .... 345 L7
Pavilion Rd *CHEP* NP16 .... 290 D1
Pawlett Rd
BMSTRD/HC/WWD BS13 .... 345 L8
Pawlett Wk
BMSTRD/HC/WWD BS13 .... 345 L8 🔢
Paxhill La *TEWK* GL20 .... 26 B4
Paybridge Rd
BMSTRD/HC/WWD BS13 .... 345 H7
Payford Br *RTEWK/TIB* GL19.. .. 65 H3
Paygrove La *VGL* GL2 .... 112 F7
Payne Dr *EVILLE/WHL* BS5 .... 336 D4
Paynes Meadow *VGL* GL2 .... 182 B6
Paynes Pitch *BWTH/CHD* GL3.. .. 113M8
Peach La *TEWK* GL20 .... 48 C7
Peache Rd *MANG/FISH* BS16.. .. 328 A5
Peacock Cl *CHELTW* GL51 .... 114 F1 🔢
GLE GL4 .... 137 G6
NWNT GL18 .... 86 C3 🔢
Peacock Gdns *NWNT* GL18 .... 86 C3 🔢
Peacock La *CIND* GL14 .... 154 A6
Peacocks La *KGWD/HNM* BS15.. .. 337 L3
Peak La *DSLY* GL11 .... 230 C4
Peakstile Piece
CHELTE/BC GL52 .... 72 D8 🔢
Pearces HI *MANG/FISH* BS16.. .. 327 K4
Pearce Wy *VGL* GL2 .... 135 K7
Pearcroft Rd *STNHO* GL10 .... 207 H5
Pearl St *BMSTR* BS3 .... 335 K8
The Pear Orch *TEWK* GL20 .... 49 G2 🔢
Pearsall Rd
OLD/WMLY/WICK BS30 .... 348 A1
Peart Cl
BMSTRD/HC/WWD BS13 .... 345 G6
VGL GL2 .... 5 L6
Peart Dr
BMSTRD/HC/WWD BS13 .... 345 G7
Pear Tree Cl *CHCAM* GL55 .... 34 E1 🔢
CHELTE/BC GL52 .... 72 E8 🔢
VGL GL2 .... 159 C4
Pear Tree Hey *YATE/CS* BS37 .. .. 310 A6 🔢
Peartree La *EVILLE/WHL* BS5.. .. 337 K5
KGWD/HNM BS15 .... 338 B1 🔢
Pear Tree Rd *ALMDB* BS32 .... 316 E1
Pearwood Wy *GL* GL1 .... 159 L1 🔢
Pecked La *CHELTE/BC* GL52 .... 72 C7
Peel Cl *CHELTS* GL53 .... 116 E6 🔢
Peel St *CBRISNE* BS2 .... 336 B3
Pegasus Gdns *VGL* GL2 .... 159 H1
Pegasus Rd *BRSTK/PCHW* BS34.. .. 315M4
Peghouse Cl *STROUD* GL5 .... 208 F3
Peghouse Ri *STROUD* GL5 .... 208 F3
Pelham Crs *BWTH/CHD* GL3 .... 113 J5
Pemberton Ct
MANG/FISH BS16 .... 327 L6 🔢
Pembery Rd *BMSTR* BS3 .... 6 C8
Pembridge Cl *CHELTE/BC* GL52 .. .. 116 F5
Pembroke Av *AVONM* BS11 .... 324 A5
Pembroke Gv *CFTN/FAIL* BS8.. .. 335 J4
Pembroke Pl *CFTN/FAIL* BS8.. .. 335 J6 🔢
Pembroke Rd *AVONM* BS11 .... 324 A5 🔢
BMSTR BS3 .... 6 C8
CFTN/FAIL BS8 .... 335 J2
CHELTW GL51 .... 115 C5
CHEP NP16 .... 270 A6
KGWD/HNM BS15 .... 338 A1 🔢
Pembroke St *CBRISNE* BS2 .... 7 H1
CIND GL14 .... 154 B3
GL GL1 .... 5 C8
Pembroke V *CFTN/FAIL* BS8 .... 335 J3
Pembury Rd *GLE* GL4 .... 136 A7
Penard Wy *KGWD/HNM* BS15 .. .. 338 B4 🔢
Penda Pl *CHEP* NP16 .... 270 C3
Pendennis Av
MANG/FISH BS16 .... 327 M7 🔢
Pendennis Pk
BRSG/KWL/STAPK BS4 .... 346 F1
Pendennis Rd *MANG/FISH* BS16.. .. 327M6
Pendil Cl *CHELTW* GL51 .... 93 K5
Pendock Cl
OLD/WMLY/WICK BS30 .... 348 E2 🔢
VGL GL2 .... 159 G2 🔢
Pendock Ct
MANG/FISH BS16 .... 328 D4 🔢
Pendock Rd *FRCTL/WBN* BS36.. .. 318 A6
MANG/FISH BS16 .... 327 K5
Penfield Rd *CBRISNE* BS2 .... 336 C1
Penharva Cl *CHELTW* GL51 .... 93 J8 🔢
Penhill Rd *GLE* GL4 .... 136 D6
Penmoel La *CHEP* NP16 .... 246 C8
Penmoyle Gdns *CHEP* NP16 .... 246 C7 🔢
Pennard Ct *HGRV/WHIT* BS14.. .. 346 D6
Penn Dr *MANG/FISH* BS16 .... 327 L2
Penngrove
OLD/WMLY/WICK BS30 .... 338 C8 🔢
Pennine Cl *VGL* GL2 .... 159 G3
Pennine Rd *CHELTE/BC* GL52.. .. 94 D7
OLD/WMLY/WICK BS30 .... 338 E7
Penn La *STNHO* GL10 .... 207 K8
Pennlea
BMSTRD/HC/WWD BS13 .... 345 K4
Penn St *CBRIS/FH* BS1 .... 7 H2
Pennsylvania Av *CHELTW* GL51.. .. 93 H8
Penny Cl *VGL* GL2 .... 112 F7
Pennylands Bank *BDWAY* WR12 .. .. 32 C1
Penny La *STNHO* GL10 .... 207 K8
Pennyroyal Gv
MANG/FISH BS16 .... 327 G6 🔢
Pennywell Rd *EVILLE/WHL* BS5.. .. 7 K1
EVILLE/WHL BS5 .... 336 C1 🔢
Pen Park Rd
HNBRY/STHM BS10 .... 315 L8
Penpole Av *AVONM* BS11 .... 324 A5
Penpole La *AVONM* BS11 .... 324 A4
Penpole Pk *AVONM* BS11 .... 324 A4 🔢
Penpole Pl *AVONM* BS11 .... 324 A5
Penrith Rd *CHELT* GL51 .... 115 H5
Penrose Cl *HGRV/WHIT* BS14.. .. 346 B5
Penrose Cl *RSTROUD/NAIL* GL6.. .. 184 A8

Penrose Dr
BRSTK/PCHW BS34 .... 316 F4 🔢
Penrose Rd *VGL* GL2 .... 112 F5
Pensfield Pk
HNBRY/STHM BS10 .... 315M7
Pensford Ct *HGRV/WHIT* BS14 .... 346 F6 🔢
Pensile Rd *RSTROUD/NAIL* GL6.. .. 232 F7
Pentathlon Wy *CHELT* GL50 .... 93 M6 🔢
Pentire Av
BMSTRD/HC/WWD BS13 .... 345 J4
Pentland Av *THNB/SVB* BS35.. .. 294 A3
Perch Cl *CLFD* GL16 .... 152 A7
Perch Cl *CLFD* GL16 .... 152 A7
Percival Rd *CFTN/FAIL* BS8 .... 335 H4
Percy St *GL* GL1 .... 136 B4 🔢
Peregrine Cl *VGL* GL2 .... 135 H8
Peregrine Rd *CHELTS* GL53 .... 115 L6
Perricks Cl *CIND* GL14 .... 132 C6
Perrinpit Rd *FRCTL/WBN* BS36.. .. 307M8
Perrinsfield *CIR* GL7 .... 244 F5
Perrott Rd *KGWD/HNM* BS15 .. .. 338 C2 🔢
Perry Cl *FRCTL/WBN* BS36 .... 317M7
NWNT GL18 .... 86 D3
Perrycroft Av
BMSTRD/HC/WWD BS13 .... 345 J5
Perrycroft Rd
BMSTRD/HC/WWD BS13 .... 345 J5
Perrygrove Rd *CLFD* GL16 .... 175 K3
Perrymans Cl *MANG/FISH* BS16.. .. 327 J5
Perry Orch *STROUD* GL5 .... 207 M3 🔢
Perry Rd *CBRIS/FH* BS1 .... 6 C4
Perrys Lea *ALMDB* BS32 .... 316 F1 🔢
Perry St *EVILLE/WHL* BS5 .... 336 C3 🔢
Perry Wy *VGL* GL2 .... 181 K7
Persh La *VGL* GL2 .... 111 H4
Perth *STNHO* GL10 .... 207 G2
Perwell Cl *TEWK* GL20 .... 27 G4
Pesley Cl
BMSTRD/HC/WWD BS13 .... 345 H7
Petercole Dr
BMSTRD/HC/WWD BS13 .... 345 J5
VGL GL2 .... 5 L6
Peter Pennell Cl *CHELTW* GL51.. .. 93 G7
Peters Fld *VGL* GL2 .... 111 G6 🔢
Peterson Sq
BMSTRD/HC/WWD BS13 .... 345 L8 🔢
Peter's St *STNHO* GL10 .... 206 B8
Peter's Ter *EVILLE/WHL* BS5.. .. 336 D4
Petersway Gdns
EVILLE/WHL BS5 .... 337 J5 🔢
Petherton Cl *KGWD/HNM* BS15.. .. 338 A4
Petherton Gdns
HGRV/WHIT BS14 .... 346 D4
Petherton Rd
HGRV/WHIT BS14 .... 346 D5
Pettigrove Gdns
KGWD/HNM BS15 .... 338 A4
Pettigrove Rd
KGWD/HNM BS15 .... 338 A5
Pettycroft *MTCHDN* GL17 .... 129 G4
Petty La *CHELTE/BC* GL52 .... 73 H8
Petty Marsh *LYD* GL15 .... 198 F7
Peverell Cl *VGL* GL2 .... 159 L3
Pevelands *DSLY* GL11 .... 229 H6
Pevensey Wk
BRSG/KWL/STAPK BS4 .... 345 M4 🔢
Peverell Cl *HNBRY/STHM* BS10.. .. 315 H8
Peverell Dr *HNBRY/STHM* BS10.. .. 315 H8
Pheasant La *CHELTW* GL51 .... 114 C2
Pheasant Md *STNHO* GL10 .... 207 H3 🔢
The Pheasantry *CIR* GL7 .... 265 G4
Pheasant Wy *CIR* GL7 .... 238 F2
Phelps Wy *RTEWK/TIB* GL19 .... 109 L3
Philadelphia Ct *CBRIS/FH* BS1.. .. 7 H2 🔢
Philippa Cl *HGRV/WHIT* BS14.. .. 346 C4
Philip's Cl *LYD* GL15 .... 201 M2
Philip St *BMSTR* BS3 .... 6 F9
CBRISNE BS2 .... 336 D6
GL GL1 .... 135 M4 🔢
Phillimore Gdns *VGL* GL2 .... 181 J6
Phillimore Rd *DSLY* GL11 .... 229 G7
Phillips Rd *BDWAY* WR12 .... 32 F2
Phippen St *CBRIS/FH* BS1 .... 7 C6 🔢
Phipps St *BMSTR* BS3 .... 6 A8
Phoenix Dr *CHEP* NP16 .... 270 C7 🔢
Phoenix Gv *RDLND/MONT* BS6.. .. 325 L6
Phoenix Wy *CIR* GL7 .... 238 C3 🔢
Piccadilly *COTS* GL54 .... 98 E5
STROUD GL5 .... 208 D8
Piccadilly Wy *CHELTE/BC* GL52 .. .. 94 F7 🔢
Pickedmoor La *THNB/SVB* BS35.. .. 272 F6
Pickering Cl *CHELTS* GL53 .... 115 L5 🔢
Pickering Rd *CHELTS* GL53 .... 115 L5 🔢
Picton La *RDLND/MONT* BS6.. .. 336 A2
Picton St *RDLND/MONT* BS6.. .. 336 A2
The Piece *BWTH/CHD* GL3 .... 113 L7
Pigeon House Dr
BMSTRD/HC/WWD BS13 .... 345 M7 🔢
Pigeon La *TEWK* GL20 .... 28 C3
Pigott Av
BMSTRD/HC/WWD BS13 .... 345 J7
Pike Cnr *BDWAY* WR12 .... 11 G7
Pike House Cl *HGHW* SN6 .... 288 E3
Pike La *RSTROUD/NAIL* GL6 .... 232 D8
Pike Rd *CIR* GL7 .... 188 C3
CLFD GL16 .... 151 K8
Pile Marsh *EVILLE/WHL* BS5 .... 336 F4
Pilford Av *CHELTS* GL53 .... 116 A7
Pilford Cl *CHELTS* GL53 .... 116 A6
Pilford Ct *CHELTS* GL53 .... 116 A6
Pilford Rd *CHELTS* GL53 .... 116 A8
Pilgrim Cl *GLE* GL4 .... 137 G5 🔢
Pilgrims Wy
MANG/FISH BS16 .... 327 M3 🔢
Pilgrims Whf
BRSG/KWL/STAPK BS4 .... 337 C3 🔢
Pilgrove Cl *CHELTW* GL51 .... 92 F6
Pilgrove Wy *CHELTW* GL51 .... 92 F6
Pilkington Cl
BRSTK/PCHW BS34 .... 326 E1
Pillcroft Cl *CHELTW* GL51 .... 138 C7
Pillcroft Rd *CHELTW* GL51 .... 138 C6
Pilley Crs *CHELTS* GL53 .... 115M1
Pilley La *CHELTS* GL53 .... 115M1
Pillingers Rd *KGWD/HNM* BS15.. .. 337 L4
Pill La *MIM* GL56 .... 82 B2

Pillowell Rd *LYD* GL15 .... 201 G2
Pillows Green Rd
RTEWK/TIB GL19 .... 66 E3
Pill Rd *CFTN/FAIL* BS8 .... 334 B2
Pilning St *THNB/SVB* BS35.. .. 305 L3
Pimpernel Md *ALMDB* BS32 .... 317 G4 🔢
Pincoate *VGL* GL2 .... 110 F5
Pincot La *RSTROUD/NAIL* GL6.. .. 184 F4
Pincots La *WUE* GL12 .... 296 D8
Pine Bank *CHELTE/BC* GL52 .... 72 D8
Pine Cl *CHELTE/BC* GL52 .... 3 J8
THNB/SVB BS35 .... 293 L2
Pine Crest Wy *LYD* GL15 .... 200 C3 🔢
Pinecroft *HGRV/WHIT* BS14 .... 346 B4 🔢
Pinedale *LYD* GL15 .... 223M5
Pine Gv *HORF/LLZ* BS7 .... 325 M8 🔢
Pinemount Rd *BWTH/CHD* GL3.. .. 137 J4
Pine Ridge Cl
HNLZ/SM/SNYPK/WT BS9.. .. 324 E7 🔢
Pine Rd *HNBRY/STHM* BS10.. .. 315 K8
Pinery Rd *GLE* GL4 .... 137 G4 🔢
Pines Rd
OLD/WMLY/WICK BS30 .... 348 E2
The Pines *COTS* GL54 .... 74 D3 🔢
Pinetrees *CHELTS* GL53 .... 116 B6
Pine Tree Dr *GLE* GL4 .... 137 G3
Pine Tree Wy *LYD* GL15 .... 202 B1
Pinetum Dr *VGL* GL2 .... 110 B7
Pineway *GLE* GL4 .... 136 D5
Pinewood *KGWD/HNM* BS15 .. .. 338 B2 🔢
Pinewood Cl *CIND* GL14 .... 154 C2
HNLZ/SM/SNYPK/WT BS9.. .. 325 K4
Pinewood Rd *VGL* GL2 .... 159 G3
Pinewood Wy
CHPMW/MSHF SN14 .... 343 G4
Pinford La *RWYE* HR9 .... 84 A6
Pingry La *CLFD* GL16 .... 175 H5
Pinhay Rd
BMSTRD/HC/WWD BS13 .... 345 K5 🔢
Pinkers Md *MANG/FISH* BS16.. .. 328 E5
Pinlocks *GLE* GL4 .... 137 G8
Pinnells End La *DSLY* GL11 .... 229M3
Pintail Cl *VGL* GL2 .... 158 F2
Pioneer Pk
BRSG/KWL/STAPK BS4 .... 336 E6
Pipe La *CBRIS/FH* BS1 .... 6 D4
Piper Rd *YATE/CS* BS37 .... 310 A8 🔢
Pipers Gv *VGL* GL2 .... 110 F6 🔢
Pippin Cl *BWTH/CHD* GL3 .... 137 J5 🔢
NWNT GL18 .... 86 D3 🔢
Pippin Ct
OLD/WMLY/WICK BS30 .... 338 B7 🔢
Pippins Rd *TEWK* GL20 .... 27 H5
Pirton Crs *BWTH/CHD* GL3 .... 113 K6
Pirton La *BWTH/CHD* GL3 .... 113 J5
Pitch And Pay La
HNLZ/SM/SNYPK/WT BS9.. .. 325 C8
Pitchcombe *YATE/CS* BS37 .... 319 L4 🔢
Pitchcombe Gdns
HNLZ/SM/SNYPK/WT BS9.. .. 324 F4
Pitch La *RDLND/MONT* BS6 .... 335M2
The Pitch *RSTROUD/NAIL* GL6.. .. 233 L1
Pithay Ct *CBRIS/FH* BS1 .... 6 F3 🔢
Pitman Pl *WUE* GL12 .... 277 L5
Pitman Rd *CHELTW* GL51 .... 115 G2
Pitt Rd *HORF/LLZ* BS7 .... 326 A6
Pittsfield *HGHW* SN6 .... 288 F4
Pitt St *GL* GL1 .... 4 E4 🔢
Pittville Circ *CHELTE/BC* GL52.. .. 3 G1
Pittville Circus Rd
CHELTE/BC GL52 .... 3 G3
Pittville Cir *THNB/SVB* BS35.. .. 273 L8 🔢
Pittville Crs *CHELTE/BC* GL52.. .. 3 G2
Pittville Crescent La
CHELTE/BC GL52 .... 3 G2
Pittville Lawn *CHELTE/BC* GL52 .. .. 2 F2
Pittville Ms *CHELTE/BC* GL52 .... 2 F3
Pittville St *CHELTE/BC* GL52 .... 2 D5
Pittway Av *SHPSTR* CV36 .... 16 A5
Pixash La *KEYN* BS31 .... 348 D6
Place HI *NWNT* GL18 .... 85 H3
The Plain *RSTROUD/NAIL* GL6.. .. 208 C1
Plaister's End *LED* HR8 .... 19 M1 🔢
Plantation Crs *TEWK* GL20 .... 27 H5 🔢
Players Cl *MANG/FISH* BS16 .... 317 K7
Playford Gdns *AVONM* BS11 .... 324 A3
Pleasant Rd *MANG/FISH* BS16.. .. 327M6
Pleasant Stile *CIND* GL14 .... 154 E5
Pleydells *HGHW* SN6 .... 288 F3 🔢
The Pleydells *CIR* GL7 .... 239 M2 🔢
The Plies *CIR* GL7 .... 242 E5
Plock Ct *VGL* GL2 .... 112 B6
Ploughmans Wy *VGL* GL2 .... 159 G5 🔢
Plover Cl *YATE/CS* BS37 .... 319 L1
Plummer's HI *EVILLE/WHL* BS5.. .. 337 C3
Plumpton Ct
MANG/FISH BS16 .... 328 B2 🔢
Plum Tree Cl *GLE* GL4 .... 137 G7 🔢
Pochard Cl *VGL* GL2 .... 158 F1
Pockhill La *COTS* GL54 .... 123 G5
Podsmead Pl *GL* GL1 .... 135M6
Podsmead Rd *GL* GL1 .... 135M7
Poets Cl *EVILLE/WHL* BS5 .... 336 F3 🔢
Poets Pth *LED* HR8 .... 41 G1
NWNT GL18 .... 41 K7
Poets' Path No 1 *NWNT* GL18.. .. 41 L7
NWNT GL18 .... 64 L1
Poets' Path No 2 *NWNT* GL18.. .. 42 A6
Point Rd *TET* GL8 .... 257 L3
Polefield Gdns *CHELTW* GL51 .... 115 K3
Pollards La *LYD* GL15 .... 202 C2
Polly Barnes Cl
KGWD/HNM BS15 .... 337 K6 🔢
Polly Barnes HI
KGWD/HNM BS15 .... 337 K6
Polygon Rd *CFTN/FAIL* BS8 .... 335 J5 🔢
Pomfrett Gdns
HGRV/WHIT BS14 .... 347 G6 🔢
Pomphrey HI *MANG/FISH* BS16.. .. 328 C3 🔢
Ponsford Rd
BRSG/KWL/STAPK BS4 .... 346 D2
Ponting Cl *EVILLE/WHL* BS5 .... 337 J2 🔢
Pool Cl *MIM* GL56 .... 82 B2
Pool Cnr *ALMDB* BS32 .... 306 D1
Poole Court Dr *YATE/CS* BS37.. .. 320 A1
Poole Gnd *VGL* GL2 .... 110 F6 🔢
Pooles La *STROUD* GL5 .... 208 A7 🔢

Pooles Whf *CFTN/FAIL* BS8 .... **335** J6
Pooles Wharf Ct
  CFTN/FAIL BS8 .... **335** J6 🔢
Poole Wy *CHELT* GL50 .... **2** B3
Pool Gastons Rd *MALM* SN16 ...... **303** H7
Poolhay Cl *RTEWK/TIB* GL19 .... **67** M1 🔢
Pool Rd *KGWD/HNM* BS15 .... **328** A8
Poolway Cl *CLFD* GL16 .... **175** K1 🔢
Poolway Pl *CLFD* GL16 .... **175** L1
Poolway Ri *CLFD* GL16 .... **151** K8
Poolway Rd *CLFD* GL16 .... **151** L8
Popes Cl *CHELT* GL50 .... **2** C2
Pope's Ct *CIR* GL7 .... **214** A7
Popes Meade *VGL* GL2 .... **111** G6 🔢
Poplar Av
  HNLZ/SM/SNYPK/WT BS9 ...... **324** F5 🔢
Poplar Cl *GL* GL1 .... **135** M7
  OLD/WMLY/WICK BS30 .... **338** E5 🔢
Poplar Dr *MANG/FISH* BS16 .... **329** K6
Poplar La *WUE* GL12 .... **296** D7
Poplar Pl *MANG/FISH* BS16 .... **327** J8 🔢
Poplar Rd
  BMSTRD/HC/WWD BS13 .... **345** H4
  EVILLE/WHL BS5 .... **337** H2
  KGWD/HNM BS15 .... **337** J6
  OLD/WMLY/WICK BS30 .... **338** F5 🔢
Poplars Cl *CHCAM* GL55 .... **34** D1
The Poplars *CHELTW* GL51 .... **115** G6
Poplar Ter *KGWD/HNM* BS15 .... **338** B3 🔢
  VGL GL2 .... **159** G4
Poppy Fld *VGL* GL2 .... **111** G5 🔢
Poppy Md *ALMDB* BS32 .... **317** G4
Porchester Rd *BWTH/CHD* GL3 ... **137** H4
Porlock Rd *BMSTR* BS3 .... **335** M8 🔢
Portland Pl *CHELTE/BC* GL52 .... **2** F3 🔢
  MANG/FISH BS16 .... **327** M8 🔢
  CHELTE/BC GL52 .... **2** F3
Portland Sq *CBRISNE* BS2 .... **7** H1
  CHELTE/BC GL52 .... **2** E4
Portland St *CBRISNE* BS2 .... **335** L3 🔢
  CFTN/FAIL BS8 .... **335** H4
  CHELTE/BC GL52 .... **2** E4
  MANG/FISH BS16 .... **327** M8 🔢
Port La *STROUD* GL5 .... **233** H2
Portmeirion Cl
  HGRV/WHIT BS14 .... **346** C6 🔢
Porturet Wy *CHELTS* GL53 .... **116** D5 🔢
Portwall La *CBRIS/FH* BS1 .... **7** G6
Portwall La East *CBRIS/FH* BS1 .. **7** H6 🔢
Portwall Rd *CHEP* NP16 .... **270** A3
Portway *GLE* GL4 .... **161** N2 🔢
  HNLZ/SM/SNYPK/WT BS9 ...... **324** E8 🔢
  HNLZ/SM/SNYPK/WT BS9 ...... **335** G2 🔢
Portway La *YATE/CS* BS37 .... **320** E1
Portwell *HGHW* SN6 .... **288** F4 🔢
Postlip Wy *CHELTW* GL51 .... **114** F3 🔢
Post Office La *CHELT* GL50 .... **2** D5
  CHELTE/BC GL52 .... **73** G8
  MIM GL56 .... **35** K7
  TEWK GL20 .... **48** A5 🔢
Post Office Sq *CIR* GL7 .... **238** C7
The Post Paddocks *LYD* GL15 .... **224** A6
Potlicker's La *CIR* GL7 .... **193** C7
Potters Croft *CHEP* NP16 .... **270** D7
Potters Field Rd
  CHELTE/BC GL52 .... **72** E8
Potters La *SHPSTR* CV36 .... **15** J2
Potters Pond *WUE* GL12 .... **277** K4
Pound Cl *BWTH/CHD* GL3 .... **138** A7
  CIR GL7 .... **238** E7
  LED HR8 .... **19** M4
  SHPSTR CV36 .... **16** B5 🔢
  TEWK GL20 .... **26** B5
Pound Dr *MANG/FISH* BS16 .... **327** H6
Pound Farm La *RWYE* HR9 .... **84** E2
Pound Hl *TET* GL8 .... **257** L3 🔢
Pound La *CHCAM* GL55 .... **8** F3
  COTS GL54 .... **124** A7
  MANG/FISH BS16 .... **327** H7
  VGL GL2 .... **158** E6
  VGL GL2 .... **179** M1
Pound Meadow *LED* HR8 .... **19** M4
Pound Rd *KGWD/HNM* BS15 ..... **338** B1
The Pound *ALMDB* BS32 .... **306** C6
  COTS GL54 .... **124** A7
Pountney Dr
  EVILLE/WHL BS5 .... **336** D3 🔢
Powells Wy *TET* GL8 .... **282** V7
Powis La *TET* GL8 .... **257** M2
Pow's Rd *KGWD/HNM* BS15 ...... **337** M4
Poyntz Ct
  OLD/WMLY/WICK BS30 .... **338** B8 🔢
Poyntz Rd
  BRSG/KWL/STAPK BS4........... **346** B3
Preddy's La *EVILLE/WHL* BS5 ...... **337** J3
Prescott *YATE/CS* BS37 .... **319** M3 🔢
Prescott Av *GLE* GL4 .... **136** D7
Prescott Wk *CHELTE/BC* GL52 .... **94** D7
Press Moor Dr
  OLD/WMLY/WICK BS30 .... **338** B7 🔢
Prestbury *YATE/CS* BS37 .... **319** M3 🔢
Prestbury Rd *CHELTE/BC* GL52 .... **2** F3
Preston Brook Cl *LED* HR8 .... **19** M2
Preston Cl *CHEP* NP16 .... **270** B7 🔢
Preston Wk
  BRSG/KWL/STAPK BS4 .... **346** C2
Prestwick Cl
  BRSG/KWL/STAPK BS4 .... **346** F2 🔢
Pretoria Rd
  BRSTK/PCHW BS34 .... **316** M4
Prewett St *CBRIS/FH* BS1 .... **7** G7
Price St *GL* GL1 .... **135** M4
Priddy Ct *HGRV/WHIT* BS14....... **346** D6
Priddy Dr *HGRV/WHIT* BS14 ...... **346** D6
Priestwood Cl I
  HNBRY/STHM BS10 .... **315** J8 🔢
Primrose Cl *ALMDB* BS32 .... **316** F1 🔢
  GLE GL4 .... **136** C7 🔢
  KGWD/HNM BS15 .... **337** K2
Primrose Cl *MIM* GL56 .... **58** D6
Primrose Dr *CLFD* GL16 .... **175** L4
  THNB/SVB BS35 .... **293** M1
Primrose Hill Rd *LYD* GL15....... **201** J7
Primrose La *KGWD/HNM* BS15 ... **337** L3
Primrose Wy *LYD* GL15 .... **201** L8
Prince Albert Ct
  BWTH/CHD GL3 .... **137** L5
Prince Charles Rd *CIR* GL7.......... **242** F4

Prince Crs *RTEWK/TIB* GL19 .... **66** D5
Prince Rupert Rd *LED* HR8 .... **19** L2
Princes Ct
  OLD/WMLY/WICK BS30 .... **338** B7
Princes' La *CFTN/FAIL* BS8 .... **335** H5
Prince's Pl *HORF/LLZ* BS7 .... **326** A8 🔢
Prince's St *CHELT* GL50 .... **115** K4
  STROUD GL5 .... **208** A3 🔢
Princess Cl *KEYN* BS31 .... **348** A6
Princess Elizabeth Wy
  CHELTW GL51 .... **114** F2
Princess Gdns
  MANG/FISH BS16 .... **326** F5 🔢
Princess Rw *CBRISNE* BS2 .... **6** F1
Princess Royal Rd *LYD* GL15 ..... **200** D2
Princess St *BMSTR* BS3 .... **7** G8
  CBRISNE BS2 .... **7** L4
Prince's St *CBRISNE* BS2 .... **336** B3
  CHELTE/BC GL52 .... **3** G6
Princess Victoria St
  CFTN/FAIL BS8 .... **335** H5
Prince St *CBRIS/FH* BS1 .... **6** E6
  GL GL1 .... **5** G6 🔢
Prinknash Cl *GLE* GL4 .... **136** E7 🔢
Prinknash Rd *GLE* GL4 .... **136** E7 🔢
Priors Lea *YATE/CS* BS37 .... **320** A2
Priory Av
  HNLZ/SM/SNYPK/WT BS9 ...... **325** J4
Priory Court Rd
  HNLZ/SM/SNYPK/WT BS9 ...... **325** J4
Priory Dene
  HNLZ/SM/SNYPK/WT BS9 ...... **325** J4 🔢
Priory Flds *RSTROUD/NAIL* GL6 .. **256** B3
Priory Gdns *HORF/LLZ* BS7 ...... **326** B3
Priory La *CHELTE/BC* GL52 .... **72** C7
Priory Pl *CHELTS* GL53 .... **2** F7
Priory Rd
  BRSG/KWL/STAPK BS4 .... **346** D1
  CFTN/FAIL BS8 .... **6** B1
  GL GL1 .... **4** E3 🔢
  KEYN BS31 .... **348** A4
Priory St *CHELTE/BC* GL52 .... **2** F7
Priory Ter *CHELTE/BC* GL52 .... **3** G6
Priory Wk *CHELTE/BC* GL52 .... **3** G6
Priory Wy *TET* GL8 .... **282** A3 🔢
Pritchard St *CBRISNE* BS2 .... **7** H1
Private Rd *STROUD* GL5 .... **208** D8
Probertsbarn La *CLFD* GL16 ..... **128** A5
Probyn Cl *MANG/FISH* BS16 ... **327** J4 🔢
Progress Cl *LED* HR8 .... **19** L1
Promenade *CHELT* GL50 .... **2** C6
Prospect *COR/BOX* SN13 .... **353** K7
Prospect Av
  KGWD/HNM BS15 .... **337** K2 🔢
Prospect Cl
  FRCTL/WBN BS36 .... **318** A7 🔢
  THNB/SVB BS35 .... **315** H1
Prospect Crs *KGWD/HNM* BS15 .. **338** B1
Prospect Gdns
  CBATH/BATHN BA1 .... **352** B6
Prospect La
  FRCTL/WBN BS36 .... **318** B3 🔢
Prospect Pl *CIR* GL7 .... **238** D4
  CLFD GL16 .... **175** K1 🔢
  EVILLE/WHL BS5 .... **336** E3
Prospect Rd *CIND* GL14 .... **154** A3
  THNB/SVB BS35 .... **304** C5
Prospect Rw *RWYE* HR9 .... **84** F3
Prosper La *CLFD* GL16 .... **175** M2
Providence La *LGASH* BS41 .... **344** B1
Providence Pl *CBRISNE* BS2 ...... **7** J4 🔢
Providence Vw *LGASH* BS41 ..... **344** C2 🔢
Prudham St *EVILLE/WHL* BS5 ... **336** E2 🔢
Pry La *BDWAY* WR12 .... **32** C3
Puck Pit La *COTS* GL54 .... **74** D5
Puckrup La *TEWK* GL20 .... **25** L6
Pudicott La *CHCAM* GL55 .... **35** L1
Pullar Cl *CHELTE/BC* GL52 .... **72** B7 🔢
Pullen Ct *CHELTE/BC* GL52 .... **72** C3
Pullens Rd *RSTROUD/NAIL* GL6 .. **185** M2
Pullin Cl *OLD/WMLY/WICK* BS30.. **338** F7
Pullnoggin Pool La *RWYE* HR9.... **126** D5
Pumphreys Rd *CHELTS* GL53...... **116** C6
Pump La *ALMDB* BS32 .... **292** F7
  CBRIS/FH BS1 .... **7** G7
  TET GL8 .... **282** E7
Purbeck Wy *CHELTE/BC* GL52 ..... **94** E8
Purcell Rd *BWTH/CHD* GL3 .... **113** H3
Purcell Wk
  BRSG/KWL/STAPK BS4 .... **345** M4 🔢
Purdown Rd *HORF/LLZ* BS7 ...... **326** B6
Purley Av *CIR* GL7 .... **238** D3 🔢
Purley Rd *CIR* GL7 .... **238** D3
Pursey Dr *ALMDB* BS32 .... **317** G5
Purslane Cl *GLE* GL4 .... **136** D7
Purton Cl *KGWD/HNM* BS15 ..... **338** A5
Purton Pl *LYD* GL15 .... **225** L1
Purton Rd *HORF/LLZ* BS7 .... **337** M1 🔢
Puxley Cl *HGRV/WHIT* BS14 .... **347** G5 🔢
Puzzle Cl *LYD* GL15 .... **200** C3 🔢
Pye Cft *ALMDB* BS32 .... **307** G8
Pyecroft Av
  HNLZ/SM/SNYPK/WT BS9 ...... **325** K4
Pyke Rd *TEWK* GL20 .... **48** D5
Pylers Wy *LYD* GL15 .... **225** K1
Pylle Hill Crs *BMSTR* BS3 .... **7** J9
Pynne Cl *HGRV/WHIT* BS14 ...... **347** G5 🔢
Pynne Rd *HGRV/WHIT* BS14 .... **347** H6 🔢
Pyrton Ms *CHELTW* GL51 .... **115** G6 🔢
Pystol La *LYD* GL15 .... **198** F6

Q section:

Quabbs La *MTCHDN* GL17 .... **129** L4
The Quadrangle *YATE/CS* BS37.... **319** L7
Quadrant East
  MANG/FISH BS16 .... **327** L8 🔢
The Quadrant
  RDLND/MONT BS6 .... **325** K8 🔢
Quadrant West
  MANG/FISH BS16 .... **327** L8
Quail Cl *GLE* GL4 .... **137** G4
Quail Mdw *TET* GL8 .... **281** M3 🔢
Quaker La *THNB/SVB* BS35 ...... **293** K2 🔢
Quaker's Cl
  MANG/FISH BS16 .... **327** M3 🔢

Quakers' Friars *CBRIS/FH* BS1 ...... **7** G2 🔢
Quaker's Rd *MANG/FISH* BS16 .... **327** M3
Quantock Cl
  OLD/WMLY/WICK BS30 .... **338** E6
Quantock Rd *BMSTR* BS3 .... **335** M8
  VGL GL2 .... **159** C3
Quarhouse La *STROUD* GL5 .... **233** J1
The Quarries *ALMDB* BS32 .... **306** D6
Quarrington Rd *HORF/LLZ* BS7 .. **326** A4
Quarry Barton
  MANG/FISH BS16 .... **317** L7
Quarry Cl *CIR* GL7 .... **214** B7
Quarry Gdns *DSLY* GL11 .... **228** F7
Quarry Hl *COR/BOX* SN13 .... **353** M5
Quarry La *AVONM* BS11 .... **324** E2
  CHPMW/MSHF SN14 .... **343** K8
  FRCTL/WBN BS36 .... **318** A7
  RWYE HR9 .... **84** F3
Quarry Md *THNB/SVB* BS35 ...... **293** H6
Quarry Rd *KGWD/HNM* BS15 ... **337** M5
  MANG/FISH BS16 .... **327** L4 🔢
  THNB/SVB BS35 .... **293** H6
  YATE/CS BS37 .... **320** C2
Quarry Steps *CFTN/FAIL* BS8 ... **335** J1 🔢
The Quarry *CIR* GL7 .... **217** H1
  CIR GL7 .... **242** F4
  DSLY GL11 .... **228** F7
Quarry Vw *CIR* GL7 .... **220** B8
Quarry Wy *MANG/FISH* BS16.... **327** C6
  MANG/FISH BS16 .... **328** C2
Quat Goose La *CHELT* GL51 ...... **93** J4
Quayside *CHEP* NP16 .... **222** B4
Quayside La *EVILLE/WHL* BS5 .. **337** H5 🔢
Quay St *CBRIS/FH* BS1 .... **6** F3 🔢
  GL GL1 .... **4** F9 🔢
  TEWK GL20 .... **48** A5 🔢
The Quay *GL* GL1 .... **4** C5
Quedgeley *YATE/CS* BS37 .... **319** L3
Queen Anne's Rd *CIR* GL7 .... **238** C5 🔢
Queen Charlotte St
  CBRIS/FH BS1 .... **6** F4 🔢
Queen Charlton La
  HGRV/WHIT BS14 .... **346** F6
Queen Elizabeth Rd *CIR* GL7 ... **238** E3 🔢
Queens Acre *CIND* GL14 .... **155** H7
Queen's Av *CFTN/FAIL* BS8 .... **6** B2
  SHPSTR CV36 .... **16** A5
Queen's Circ *CHELT* GL50 .... **2** C6 🔢
Queens Cl *BWTH/CHD* GL3........ **137** J2
Queen's Ct *LED* HR8 .... **19** M3
Queensdale Crs
  BRSG/KWL/STAPK BS4 .... **346** C2
Queens Down Gdns
  BRSG/KWL/STAPK BS4 .... **336** D8
Queen's Dr *HORF/LLZ* BS7 ...... **325** L7
  KGWD/HNM BS15 .... **337** K7
  STROUD GL5 .... **208** A4
Queens Fld *CIR* GL7 .... **242** F4
Queens Ga
  HNLZ/SM/SNYPK/WT BS9 ...... **324** F4
Queenshill Rd
  BRSG/KWL/STAPK BS4 .... **346** C6
Queensholm Av
  MANG/FISH BS16 .... **328** A2 🔢
Queensholm Cl
  MANG/FISH BS16 .... **328** A2 🔢
Queensholm Crs
  MANG/FISH BS16 .... **327** M2
Queensholm Dr
  MANG/FISH BS16 .... **328** A3 🔢
Queens La *CHELT* GL50 .... **2** B7
Queensmead
  RSTROUD/NAIL GL6 .... **185** G4
  TEWK GL20 .... **27** J5
Queens Pde *CBRIS/FH* BS1 .... **6** B8
Queen Sq *CBRIS/FH* BS1 .... **6** E5
  KEYN BS31 .... **349** H8 🔢
Queen Square Av
  CBRIS/FH BS1 .... **6** F5 🔢
Queen's Retreat
  CHELTW GL51 .... **115** K1 🔢
Queen's Rd
  BMSTRD/HC/WWD BS13 .... **345** H7
  BRSG/KWL/STAPK BS4 .... **346** E2
  CFTN/FAIL BS8 .... **6** A2
  CFTN/FAIL BS8 .... **335** J4
  CFTN/FAIL BS8 .... **335** J4
  CHELTW GL51 .... **115** J3
  CHEP NP16 .... **270** A5
  EVILLE/WHL BS5 .... **337** H4
  HORF/LLZ BS7 .... **326** B7
  KEYN BS31 .... **347** M7
  LGASH BS41 .... **345** H8
  MANG/FISH BS16 .... **329** K6
  OLD/WMLY/WICK BS30 .... **338** C7
  STNHO GL10 .... **207** H4
  STROUD GL5 .... **208** D5
  TEWK GL20 .... **48** B7
Queens Sq *COTS* GL54 .... **74** C6
Queen St *CBRISNE* BS2 .... **7** H3
  CHELTW GL51 .... **2** A1
  CIR GL7 .... **238** D4
  COTS GL54 .... **167** J6
  EVILLE/WHL BS5 .... **337** K4
  KGWD/HNM BS15 .... **337** K4
  LYD GL15 .... **201** K7
Queens Wk *THNB/SVB* BS35 .... **273** M8
Queensway *BRSTK/PCHW* BS34... **316** E5
  CLFD GL16 .... **175** M1
Queen's Wy *LED* HR8 .... **19** M3
  WUE GL12 .... **277** K5
Queen Victoria Rd
  RDLND/MONT BS6 .... **325** J7
Queen Victoria St *CBRISNE* BS2 ... **7** M4
Queenwood Gv *CHELTE/BC* GL52.. **94** F6
Quenneys Cl *GLE* GL4 .... **136** E8
Querns La *CIR* GL7 .... **238** C3 🔢
Querns Rd *CIR* GL7 .... **238** C3
Quickthorn Cl *HGRV/WHIT* BS14.. **346** C5
Quietways *STNHO* GL10 .... **207** G3
Quinton Cl *BWTH/CHD* GL3 ...... **113** K5 🔢

R section:

Rackham Cl *HORF/LLZ* BS7 .... **326** D5

Rackhay *CBRIS/FH* BS1 .... **6** F4 🔢
Radburn Cl *MIM* GL56 .... **58** E6 🔢
Radley Rd *MANG/FISH* BS16 ..... **327** K7
Radnor Pl *CLFD* GL16 .... **115** C5 🔢
  HNLZ/SM/SNYPK/WT BS9 ...... **325** K6
  HORF/LLZ BS7 .... **325** M6
Raeburn Rd *EVILLE/WHL* BS5 .... **337** K4
Rag La *WUE* GL12 .... **295** M6
Raglan Pl *HORF/LLZ* BS7 .... **325** M8 🔢
  THNB/SVB BS35 .... **293** K3
Raglan Rd *HORF/LLZ* BS7 .... **325** M8
Raglan St *GL* GL1 .... **5** H7
Raglan Wy *CHEP* NP16 .... **270** B6
  DSLY GL11 .... **254** D2
Raikes Rd *GL* GL1 .... **135** M5
Railton Jones Cl
  BRSTK/PCHW BS34 .... **317** C8
Railway Dr *CLFD* GL16 .... **175** K1
Railway Rd *CIND* GL14 .... **154** A6
Railway Ter *MANG/FISH* BS16 ... **327** L7
Raleigh Rd *BMSTR* BS3 .... **6** A9
  BMSTR BS3 .... **335** J7
Ralph Rd *HORF/LLZ* BS7 .... **326** B7
Ram Hl *FRCTL/WBN* BS36 .... **318** F7
Ramscombe La
  CBATH/BATHN BA1 .... **352** B5
Ramsdale Rd *VGL* GL2 .... **135** K8
Ramsey Rd *HORF/LLZ* BS7 .... **326** B4
Rance Pitch *GLE* GL4 .... **161** C1
Randall Cl *KGWD/HNM* BS15 .... **338** B1
Randall Rd *CFTN/FAIL* BS8 .... **335** J5
  COTS GL54 .... **124** D8
Randalls Fld
  RSTROUD/NAIL GL6 .... **185** H4 🔢
Randalls Gn *RSTROUD/NAIL* GL6.. **210** B8
Randolph Av
  BMSTRD/HC/WWD BS13 .... **345** K6
  YATE/CS BS37 .... **309** M7
Randolph Cl
  BMSTRD/HC/WWD BS13 .... **345** K6
  CHELTS GL53 .... **116** B5 🔢
Randwick Rd *GL* GL1 .... **159** M1
Rangers Av *DSLY* GL11 .... **253** K4
Rangers Wk *KGWD/HNM* BS15 .. **337** L6
The Range *GLE* GL4 .... **110** F6
Ranmoor *GLE* GL4 .... **136** F8
Rannoch Rd
  BRSTK/PCHW BS34 .... **326** B1
Ratcliffe Dr *BRSTK/PCHW* BS34 .. **317** C6
Ratcliff Lawns *CHELTE/BC* GL52.. **94** D3
Rathbone Cl *FRCTL/WBN* BS36 .. **318** E6
Rathmore Ct *COTS* GL54 .... **74** C5
Ravendale Dr
  OLD/WMLY/WICK BS30 .... **338** D8
Ravenglass Crs
  HNBRY/STHM BS10 .... **325** L1
Ravenhead Dr
  HGRV/WHIT BS14 .... **346** D3
Ravenhill Av *BMSTR* BS3 .... **346** B1
Ravenhill Rd *BMSTR* BS3 .... **336** B8
Ravensgate Rd *CHELTS* GL53 .... **116** D7
Ravenswood Rd
  RDLND/MONT BS6 .... **335** L2
Rawens Wd
  OLD/WMLY/WICK BS30 .... **338** D8 🔢
Rayens Cross Rd *LGASH* BS41 .. **344** B2
Rayleigh Rd
  HNLZ/SM/SNYPK/WT BS9 ...... **324** F4
Raymend Rd *BMSTR* BS3 .... **336** A4
Raymend Wk *BMSTR* BS3 .... **336** A4
Raymill
  BRSG/KWL/STAPK BS4 .... **347** J1 🔢
Raymore Ri *LGASH* BS41 .... **344** D3
Raynes Rd *BMSTR* BS3 .... **335** J8
Reaburn Cl *CHELTE/BC* GL52 ... **116** D5 🔢
Read Wy *CHELTE/BC* GL52 .... **94** B1
Rea La *VGL* GL2 .... **135** H6
Rectory Ct *COTS* GL54 .... **101** J4
  GLE GL4 .... **161** C1
  YATE/CS BS37 .... **310** B8 🔢
Rectory La *BRSTK/PCHW* BS34 .. **316** C5
  HGHW SN6 .... **289** C3
  TET GL8 .... **257** L2
  VGL GL2 .... **135** J5
  WUE GL12 .... **295** J2
Rectory Meadow
  MTCHDN GL17 .... **107** G7
Rectory Rd *FRCTL/WBN* BS36 ... **318** D3
  GLE GL4 .... **136** E7
Red Admiral Dr *GLE* GL4 .... **137** C7
Redbrook Rd *MONM* NP25 .... **174** B3
Redcar Ct *FRCTL/WBN* BS36 ... **328** B2 🔢
Redcatch Rd *BMSTR* BS3 .... **346** B1
  BRSG/KWL/STAPK BS4 .... **346** C1
Redcliffe Backs *CBRIS/FH* BS1 ..... **7** G4
Redcliffe Pde East *CBRIS/FH* BS1.. **6** F6
Redcliffe Pde West *CBRIS/FH* BS1.. **6** F6
Redcliffe Wy *CBRIS/FH* BS1 .... **6** F6
Redcliff Hl *CBRIS/FH* BS1 .... **7** G7
Redcliff Mead La *CBRIS/FH* BS1 .. **7** H6
Redcliff St *CBRIS/FH* BS1 .... **7** G5
Redcross St *CBRISNE* BS2 .... **7** J3
Redding Cl *VGL* GL2 .... **159** C2
Reddings Cl *LYD* GL15 .... **224** A5
Reddings La *CIND* GL14 .... **154** C3
Reddings Pk *CHELTW* GL51 ..... **114** F4 🔢
Reddings Rd *CHELTW* GL51 ..... **114** E4
The Reddings *CHELTW* GL51 .... **114** D4
  CHEP NP16 .... **270** B6 🔢
  KGWD/HNM BS15 .... **338** B1
Red Ditch La *RTEWK/TIB* GL19 ... **65** J1
Redesdale Pl *MIM* GL56 .... **58** C7
Redfield Hl
  OLD/WMLY/WICK BS30 .... **338** F7
Redfield Rd *BRSTK/PCHW* BS34.. **316** D4
Redford Crs
  BMSTRD/HC/WWD BS13 .... **345** G8
Redford La *MANG/FISH* BS16 ... **329** M7
Redford Wk
  BMSTRD/HC/WWD BS13 .... **345** H8 🔢
Redgrove Pk *CHELTW* GL51 ..... **114** F4
Redgrove Rd *CHELTW* GL51 ...... **93** H7
Redham La *THNB/SVB* BS35 ..... **305** K2
Redhill Cl *MANG/FISH* BS16 ..... **327** C8
Redhill Dr *MANG/FISH* BS16 .... **327** C8
Red House La *THNB/SVB* BS35 .. **292** A5
Red House La *ALMDB* BS32 ...... **306** C4
Redhouse La *CLFD* GL16 .... **127** K8 🔢

Red House La
  HNLZ/SM/SNYPK/WT BS9 ...... **325** C5
Redhouse La *STROUD* GL5 .... **207** M3
Redland Cl *VGL* GL2 .... **112** D7
Redland Court Rd
  RDLND/MONT BS6 .... **325** L8
Redland Green Rd
  RDLND/MONT BS6 .... **335** L1
Redland Gv *RDLND/MONT* BS6 .. **335** L1
Redland Hl *RDLND/MONT* BS6 .. **335** J1
Redland Pk *RDLND/MONT* BS6 .. **335** K2
Redland Rd
  RDLND/MONT BS6 .... **325** K8 🔢
  RDLND/MONT BS6 .... **335** M1
Redland Ter
  RDLND/MONT BS6 .... **335** J1 🔢
Red La *TEWK* GL20 .... **48** A4
Red Lion La *HGHW* SN6 .... **289** C3
Rednock Dr *DSLY* GL11 .... **253** J1
Redpoll Wy *GLE* GL4 .... **136** E5
Red Rover Cl *CHELT* GL50 .... **93** L6
Redshelf Wk
  HNBRY/STHM BS10 .... **315** L8
Redstart Wy *GLE* GL4 .... **136** E5
Redthorne Wy *CHELTW* GL51 ... **115** C6
Red Well Rd *GLE* GL4 .... **160** E1
Redwick Cl *AVONM* BS11 .... **324** E1
Redwick Gdns *THNB/SVB* BS35 . **304** E4
Redwick Rd *THNB/SVB* BS35 .... **304** D2
Redwing Wy *VGL* GL2 .... **112** F6
Redwing Gdns
  MANG/FISH BS16 .... **327** C5 🔢
Redwood Cl *GL* GL1 .... **135** M7
  OLD/WMLY/WICK BS30 .... **338** C8 🔢
Redwood Ct *TEWK* GL20 .... **49** C2 🔢
Redwood Wy
  CHPMW/MSHF SN14 .... **343** J6
Reed Cl *HNBRY/STHM* BS10 .... **325** M4 🔢
Reed Ct
  OLD/WMLY/WICK BS30 .... **338** B8 🔢
Reedley Rd
  HNLZ/SM/SNYPK/WT BS9 ...... **325** C6
Reedling Cl *MANG/FISH* BS16 .. **327** C5 🔢
Reeds *HGHW* SN6 .... **288** E3
Reeds Farm Rd *MALM* SN16 .... **303** J7
Reevers Rd *NWNT* GL18 .... **86** D3
Reeves Ct *CIR* GL7 .... **238** A5 🔢
Regency Dr
  BRSG/KWL/STAPK BS4 .... **347** J1 🔢
Regent Rd *BMSTR* BS3 .... **6** F8 🔢
Regents Cl *THNB/SVB* BS35 ..... **273** K8
Regent St *CFTN/FAIL* BS8 .... **335** J5
  CHELT GL50 .... **4** F9
  KGWD/HNM BS15 .... **337** L3
  LYD GL15 .... **201** J8
  STNHO GL10 .... **207** H5
Regent Wy *CHEP* NP16 .... **270** A3 🔢
Regis Cl *CHELTS* GL53 .... **116** C6
Reine Barnes Cl *DSLY* GL11 ..... **253** K3
Remenham Dr
  HNLZ/SM/SNYPK/WT BS9 ...... **325** K6 🔢
Remenham Pk
  HNLZ/SM/SNYPK/WT BS9 ...... **325** K6
Remus Cl *GLE* GL4 .... **137** H5 🔢
Rendcomb Cl *CIR* GL7 .... **137** C7 🔟
Rendcomb Dr *CIR* GL7 .... **238** A4
Repton Rd
  BRSG/KWL/STAPK BS4 .... **336** E8
Reservoir Rd *GLE* GL4 .... **136** B7
  STROUD GL5 .... **209** G4
Reynolds Cl *KEYN* BS31 .... **348** C6
Reynold's Wk *HORF/LLZ* BS7 .. **326** C4
Ribble Cl *BWTH/CHD* GL3 .... **138** B6
Ribblesdale *THNB/SVB* BS35 .... **293** L3
Ricardo Rd *RSTROUD/NAIL* GL6 .. **233** H5
Richard Pl *TEWK* GL20 .... **48** B8
Richards Cl *CHELTW* GL51 .... **93** K7 🔢
Richeson Cl *HNBRY/STHM* BS10.. **325** H1
Richeson Wk
  HNBRY/STHM BS10 .... **325** H1
Richmond Av
  BRSTK/PCHW BS34 .... **317** C6
  GLE GL4 .... **136** E5
  RDLND/MONT BS6 .... **336** B1 🔢
Richmond Cl *KEYN* BS31 .... **347** M7
Richmond Cl *HGHW* SN6 .... **287** H2
Richmond Dl *CFTN/FAIL* BS8 .. **335** J1 🔢
Richmond Dr *CHELTE/BC* GL52 ... **3** K5
Richmond Gdns *VGL* GL2 .... **112** E6
Richmond Hl *CFTN/FAIL* BS8 ...... **6** A2
Richmond Hill Av *CFTN/FAIL* BS8.. **6** A3
Richmond La *CFTN/FAIL* BS8 .... **335** H4
Richmond Park Rd *CFTN/FAIL* BS8 **335** J4
Richmond Rd *EVILLE/WHL* BS5.. **337** C3
  MANG/FISH BS16 .... **329** J5
  RDLND/MONT BS6 .... **336** B1 🔟
The Richmonds *GLE* GL4 .... **136** F7
Richmond St *BMSTR* BS3 .... **7** J9
Richmond Ter *CFTN/FAIL* BS8 .. **335** J4
Rickyard Wy *VGL* GL2 .... **182** A6
The Ride *KGWD/HNM* BS15 ...... **338** C1
Ridgehill
  HNLZ/SM/SNYPK/WT BS9 ...... **325** L6
Ridgemont Rd *STROUD* GL5 ..... **209** G4
Ridgemount Cl *BWTH/CHD* GL3.. **137** M5
Ridge Pl *MTCHDN* GL17 .... **152** C1
The Ridge *AVONM* BS11 .... **324** A4
  FRCTL/WBN BS36 .... **318** E4
  RSTROUD/NAIL GL6 .... **209** L7
Ridgeview *LGASH* BS41 .... **344** D1 🔢
Ridgeway *FRCTL/WBN* BS36 ..... **318** E4
  LED HR8 .... **20** E4
  LYD GL15 .... **177** L8
  YATE/CS BS37 .... **320** C1
Ridgeway Ct
  HNBRY/STHM BS10 .... **325** H2
Ridgeway Crs *RWYE* HR9 .... **126** D3
Ridgeway Gdns
  HGRV/WHIT BS14 .... **346** E6
Ridgeway La *HGRV/WHIT* BS14 .. **346** F7
Ridgeway Pde
  EVILLE/WHL BS5 .... **337** C8 🔢
Ridgeway Rd *LGASH* BS41 .... **344** C2
  MANG/FISH BS16 .... **327** C6
The Ridgeway
  HNBRY/STHM BS10 .... **325** J2

MALM SN16 .... **284** A5
RSTROUD/NAIL GL6 .... **209** M7
Riding Barn HI
  OLD/WMLY/WICK BS30 .... **339** H5
Ridingleaze *AVONM* BS11 ...... **324** C2
Ridings CI *YATE/CS* BS37 ...... **320** E2
Ridings Rd *FRCTL/WBN* BS36 ... **318** E5
The Ridings
  BMSTRD/HC/WWD BS13 .... **345** K4
  FRCTL/WBN BS36 .... **318** E5
  RSTROUD/NAIL GL6 .... **232** E8
  VGL GL2 .... **111** J4
Ridler Rd *LYD* GL15 .... **225** L1
Rigsby's La *MALM* SN16 .... **286** B6
Ringer's CI *RTEWK/TIB* GL19 ... **69** G6
Ring Fence *LYD* GL15 .... **223** M5
Ringfield CI
  RSTROUD/NAIL GL6 .... **232** E8
Ringwood Crs
  HNBRY/STHM BS10 .... **325** M2
Ripley Rd *EVILLE/WHL* BS5 ..... **337** G2
Ripon Ct *MANG/FISH* BS16 ..... **328** B2
Ripon Rd *BRSG/KWL/STAPK* BS4 . **337** G5
Rippledale CI *CHELTW* GL51 .... **115** G4
Risdale Rd *BMSTR* BS3 .... **345** G2
Rising Sun La *CHELTE/BC* GL52 .. **95** G1
Rissington CI *CHELTW* GL51 ... **115** G3 🖻
Rissington Rd *COTS* GL54 ..... **123** J6 🖻
  GLE GL4 .... **160** A1
Rivelands Rd *CHELTW* GL51 .... **93** K4 🖻
Riverland Dr
  BMSTRD/HC/WWD BS13 .... **345** H7
Riverleaze
  HNLZ/SM/SNYPK/WT BS9 ...... **324** D6
River Leys *CHELTW* GL51 .... **93** H6
Rivermead CI *VGL* GL2 .... **112** A6
River Rd *YATE/CS* BS37 .... **320** C2 🖻
River St *CBRISNE* BS2 .... **7** J2
Riverside *COTS* GL54 .... **74** D5
Riverside CI *AVONM* BS11 ...... **324** B6
  CHELTE/BC GL52 .... **116** D5 🖻
Riverside Ct
  BRSG/KWL/STAPK BS4 .... **337** H5
Riverside Pk *THNB/SVB* BS35 .... **304** B5
Riverside Wk
  EVILLE/WHL BS5 .... **337** H5 🔟
Riverside Wy *KGWD/HNM* BS15 ... **337** L8
Riversley Rd *VGL* GL2 .... **136** E1
River St *CBRISNE* BS2 .... **7** J2
River Vw *CHEP* NP16 .... **270** A3 🖻
  MANG/FISH BS16 .... **327** G6
Riverview Wy *CHELTW* GL51 ..... **93** J7
River Wy *CIR* GL7 .... **263** K4
  SHPSTR CV36 .... **16** C4
Riverwood Rd
  MANG/FISH BS16 .... **327** L2
Riviera Crs *MANG/FISH* BS16 ... **328** A7
Roach's La *BAD* GL9 .... **322** E2
Road HI *CHPMW/MSHF* SN14 ..... **352** F2
  COR/BOX SN13 .... **353** C3
Robbers Rd *STNHO* GL10 .... **207** L1
Robbins CI *ALMDB* BS32 .... **317** H5
  CHPMW/MSHF SN14 .... **342** B3
  STROUD GL5 .... **207** L5
Robbins Ct *MANG/FISH* BS16 ... **328** D5
Robel Av *FRCTL/WBN* BS36 ..... **318** C3
Robert Burns Av *CHELTW* GL51 .. **114** F4
Robert Ct *MANG/FISH* BS16 .... **328** A4
Robert Franklin Wy *CIR* GL7 ... **263** K4
Robert Raikes Av *GLE* GL4 ..... **159** M1 🖻
Roberts CI *CHELTE/BC* GL52 .... **72** B7 🖻
  CIR GL7 .... **214** B8
Robertson Dr
  BRSG/KWL/STAPK BS4 .... **337** H5
Robertson Rd *CHELTW* GL51 .... **138** F1 🖻
  EVILLE/WHL BS5 .... **336** E1
Roberts Rd *BWTH/CHD* GL3 ..... **113** H4
  CHELTE/BC GL52 .... **94** F7 🖻
Robert St *EVILLE/WHL* BS5 ..... **336** D1 🖻
  EVILLE/WHL BS5 .... **336** D4 🔟
Robin CI *HNBRY/STHM* BS10 .... **325** K1
  RSTROUD/NAIL GL6 .... **210** A8 🖻
  TEWK GL20 .... **48** F2 🖻
Robin Ct *STNHO* GL10 .... **207** H3
Robinhood St *GL* GL1 .... **135** M4
Robins CI *CHELTE/BC* GL52 ..... **3** J3
Robins End *VGL* GL2 .... **112** F4 🖻
Robinson CI *NWNT* GL18 .... **86** C2
Robinson Dr
  EVILLE/WHL BS5 .... **336** C3 🔟
Robinson La *CIR* GL7 .... **189** L4
Robinson Rd *GL* GL1 .... **135** M4
Robinson's Meadow *LED* HR8 .... **19** M2
Robinswood Gdns *GLE* GL4 ..... **136** B6
Robin Wy *YATE/CS* BS37 .... **320** B4
Rochester Rd
  BRSG/KWL/STAPK BS4 .... **337** G6
  CHELT GL50 .... **115** J6 🖻
Rock And Fountain La
  CIND GL14 .... **156** F2
Rock CI
  BRSG/KWL/STAPK BS4 .... **347** L6 🔟
Rockfield *CHPMW/MSHF* SN14.... **343** K8
Rockingham Gdns
  AVONM BS11 .... **324** C3 🖻
Rockland Gv
  MANG/FISH BS16 .... **326** F6 🖻
Rockland Rd *MANG/FISH* BS16 .. **327** L4
Rock La *BRSTK/PCHW* BS34 ..... **317** H7
  CIND GL14 .... **156** E2
  CLFD GL16 .... **175** K3
Rockleaze
  HNLZ/SM/SNYPK/WT BS9 ...... **335** G1
Rockleaze Av
  HNLZ/SM/SNYPK/WT BS9 ...... **325** G8
Rockleaze Rd
  HNLZ/SM/SNYPK/WT BS9 ...... **335** G1
Rockness HI
  RSTROUD/NAIL GL6 .... **256** D1
Rock Rd *DSLY* GL11 .... **228** F7
  KEYN BS31 .... **348** A6
  OLD/WMLY/WICK BS30 .... **339** M3
Rockside Av *MANG/FISH* BS16 .. **328** B3
Rockside Dr
  HNLZ/SM/SNYPK/WT BS9 ...... **325** K5
Rockside Gdns
  FRCTL/WBN BS36 .... **318** E3
  MANG/FISH BS16 .... **328** B3 🖻
Rocks Rd *MTCHDN* GL17 .... **128** C5

The Rocks *CLFD* GL16 .... **175** K6
Rockstowes Wy
  HNBRY/STHM BS10 .... **315** M8
  THNB/SVB BS35 .... **293** K3
The Rock
  BRSG/KWL/STAPK BS4 .... **337** G8
Rock Villa La *CHEP* NP16 ..... **270** B2
Rockwell Av *AVONM* BS11 ...... **324** D2
Rockwood Rd *CHEP* NP16 .... **270** A4
Rodborough *YATE/CS* BS37 ..... **319** L4
Rodborough Av *STROUD* GL5 .... **208** D5
Rodborough HI *STROUD* GL5 .... **208** D5
Rodborough La *STROUD* GL5 .... **208** E6
Rodbourne Rd
  HNBRY/STHM BS10 .... **325** M4
Rodfords Md *HGRV/WHIT* BS14 .. **346** C4
Rodford Wy *YATE/CS* BS37 ..... **319** L4
Rodley Rd *LYD* GL15 .... **201** L8
Rodley Sq *LYD* GL15 .... **201** L8
Rodmead Wk
  BMSTRD/HC/WWD BS13 .... **345** J7 🖻
Rodney Av *KGWD/HNM* BS15 ..... **337** J3
Rodney CI *VGL* GL2 .... **112** D7
Rodney Crs *BRSTK/PCHW* BS34 .. **316** C7
  RDLND/MONT BS6 .... **2** D6
Rodney Rd *CHELT* GL50 .... **2** D6
  KGWD/HNM BS15 .... **337** J2
Rodney Wk *KGWD/HNM* BS15 ..... **337** J2
Rodway HI *MANG/FISH* BS16 .... **328** C7
Rodway Rd *BRSTK/PCHW* BS34 ... **316** C6
  MANG/FISH BS16 .... **328** C6
Rodway Vw *KGWD/HNM* BS15 .... **328** B8
Roebuck Mdw
  MTCHDN GL17 .... **129** H5 🖻
Roegate Dr
  BRSG/KWL/STAPK BS4 .... **337** G3 🖻
Rogers CI
  OLD/WMLY/WICK BS30 .... **338** D6
Rokeby Av *RDLND/MONT* BS6 .... **335** L2
The Rollers *RSTROUD/NAIL* GL6 . **232** D7
Rolleston Wy *CHELTW* GL51 .... **115** H4 🖻
Rolling Stones *CHCAM* GL55 .... **12** E8
Roman Farm Ct
  AVONM BS11 .... **324** E1 🖻
Roman Hackle Av *CHELT* GL50 .. **93** L6
Roman Rd *CHELTW* GL51 .... **115** J2
  GLE GL4 .... **137** G5
Roman Wk
  BRSG/KWL/STAPK BS4 .... **336** E8
  BRSTK/PCHW BS34 .... **317** G6 🖻
Roman Wy *CIND* GL14 .... **154** D3
  CIR GL7 .... **244** F6
  CLFD GL16 .... **175** K2
  COTS GL54 .... **123** J4
  HNLZ/SM/SNYPK/WT BS9 ...... **324** E7
Romney Av *HORF/LLZ* BS7 ...... **326** D6
Romney CI *GL* GL1 .... **136** A6
Romney Rd *TET* GL8 .... **281** L3 🖻
Ronald Rd *MANG/FISH* BS16 .... **327** H5 🖻
Ronayne Wk *MANG/FISH* BS16... **327** L5
Ron Golding CI *MALM* SN16 .... **303** J6
Rookery La *BRKLY* GL13 .... **227** G4
  CLFD GL16 .... **175** G7
  OLD/WMLY/WICK BS30 .... **330** B8
  THNB/SVB BS35 .... **305** J5
Rookery Wk
  BRSG/KWL/STAPK BS4 .... **336** C8
  VGL GL2 .... **112** F5
Rookery Wy *HGRV/WHIT* BS14 ... **346** B7
Rooksmoor HI *STROUD* GL5 ..... **208** C8
Roosevelt Av *CHELTE/BC* GL52 .. **3** J9
Ropewalk *TEWK* GL20 .... **48** B5
The Rope Wk *STROUD* GL5 ...... **209** G8
Rose Acre *HNBRY/STHM* BS10 ... **315** J8
Rose & Crown Pas *CHELT* GL50.. **2** D4
Rosebay Md
  MANG/FISH BS16 .... **327** G7 🖻
Roseberry Pk *EVILLE/WHL* BS5 .. **336** F3
Roseberry Rd *EVILLE/WHL* BS5 .. **336** E4
Rosebery Av *CBRISNE* BS2 ...... **336** C2 🔟
  GL GL1 .... **136** A6
Rosebery Mt *DSLY* GL11 .... **253** L3 🖻
Rosebery Pk *DSLY* GL11 .... **253** L3
Rosebery Rd *DSLY* GL11 .... **253** L3
Rose CI *FRCTL/WBN* BS36 ...... **318** A7
Rosedale Av *STNHO* GL10 ...... **207** H4
Rosedale Rd *MANG/FISH* BS16 .. **327** K8
Rosefield Crs *TEWK* GL20 ..... **48** C5
Rose Green Rd *EVILLE/WHL* BS5.. **336** F1
Rosehill Ct *GR* GL7 .... **214** C8
Rosehill St *CHELTE/BC* GL52 ... **3** H8
Rose Hip Wy *CHELTE/BC* GL52 .. **72** A7 🖻
Rose La *FRCTL/WBN* BS36 ...... **318** A7
Roselarge Gdns *HNBRY/STHM* BS10 ....
325 J1 🖻
Rosemary CI *ALMDB* BS32 ...... **317** H4
  GLE GL4 .... **136** E7
Rosemary La *CHEP* NP16 .... **246** F1
  EVILLE/WHL BS5 .... **336** E1
Rosemary Ter *WUE* GL12 .... **277** K5
Rose Md *HORF/LLZ* BS7 .... **326** C4 🖻
Rose Oak Dr
  FRCTL/WBN BS36 .... **318** F4 🖻
Rose Oak Gdns
  FRCTL/WBN BS36 .... **318** F4 🖻
Rose Oak La *FRCTL/WBN* BS36 .. **318** F4
Rose Rd *EVILLE/WHL* BS5 ...... **337** G4
Rosery CI
  HNLZ/SM/SNYPK/WT BS9 ...... **325** J3
The Rosery *MANG/FISH* BS16 ... **327** L8 🖻
Roses La *CHNTN* OX7 .... **83** H7
Rose St *CBRIS/FH* BS1 .... **7** H6
Roseville Av
  OLD/WMLY/WICK BS30 .... **348** C1
Rose Wk *MANG/FISH* BS16 ..... **327** L8 🖻
Rose Wy *CIR* GL7 .... **238** E5
Rosewood Av *THNB/SVB* BS35 ... **293** H6
Rosling Rd *HORF/LLZ* BS7 ..... **326** A5
Roslyn Rd *RDLND/MONT* BS6 .... **335** L1
Rossall Av *BRSTK/PCHW* BS34 .. **316** E5
Rossall Rd
  BRSG/KWL/STAPK BS4 .... **336** F8
Ross CI *YATE/CS* BS37 .... **320** D1
Rossiter's La *EVILLE/WHL* BS5 . **337** J5
Rosslyn Wy *THNB/SVB* BS35 .... **273** L8 🖻
Ross Rd *CLFD* GL16 .... **151** J4
  MTCHDN GL17 .... **106** C8

NWNT GL18 .... **86** B2
Rothermere CI
  CHELTW GL51 .... **115** H6 🔞
Rothleigh *CHELTW* GL51 .... **115** G6
Rougemont Gv *CHEP* NP16 ..... **270** B7 🖻
The Roundabouts
  STROUD GL5 .... **233** H2 🔟
Round Barrow CI
  CHPMW/MSHF SN14 .... **343** J8
Roundmoor CI *KEYN* BS31 ...... **348** F8
Roundmoor Gdns
  HGRV/WHIT BS14 .... **346** F4 🖻
Roundways *FRCTL/WBN* BS36 .... **318** E5
Rouses La *CIR* GL7 .... **221** K6
Rousham Rd *EVILLE/WHL* BS5 ... **326** C8
Rowacres *HGRV/WHIT* BS14 ..... **346** B5
Rowan CI
  CHPMW/MSHF SN14 .... **343** J6 🖻
  MANG/FISH BS16 .... **337** J1
Rowanfield Rd *CHELTW* GL51 ... **115** J2
Rowan Gdns *BWTH/CHD* GL3 .... **137** M4
Rowan Gv *DSLY* GL11 .... **229** J8
The Rowans *CHELTE/BC* GL52.... **72** D8
  MALM SN16 .... **303** H7 🖻
Rowan Wy *CHELTW* GL51 .... **115** G6 🔞
  KGWD/HNM BS15 .... **337** K8 🖻
Rowberrow *HGRV/WHIT* BS14 .... **346** B4
Rowcroft *STROUD* GL5 .... **208** D4
Rowcroft Retreat
  STROUD GL5 .... **208** D4 🖻
Rowland Av
  MANG/FISH BS16 .... **326** E7 🖻
Rowlandson Gdns
  HORF/LLZ BS7 .... **326** D5 🖻
Rowley *DSLY* GL11 .... **229** J8
Rowley St *BMSTR* BS3 .... **335** L8 🖻
Rownham CI *BMSTR* BS3 .... **335** G7 🖻
Rownham HI *CFTN/FAIL* BS8 .... **335** G5 🖻
Rownham Md *CFTN/FAIL* BS8 .. **335** J6 🖻
The Row *THNB/SVB* BS35 .... **291** J4
Roxton Dr *CHELTW* GL51 .... **114** E4
Royal Albert Rd
  RDLND/MONT BS6 .... **325** J7
Royal CI *HNBRY/STHM* BS10 .... **314** F8
Royal Crs *CHELT* GL50 .... **2** C5
Royal Fort Rd *CFTN/FAIL* BS8 .. **6** D2
Royal Oak Ms *CHELT* GL50 ..... **2** C5
Royal Oak Rd *GL* GL1 .... **4** C4
  MTCHDN GL17 .... **128** F6
Royal Parade Ms *CHELT* GL50... **2** B7
Royal Pk *CFTN/FAIL* BS8 ...... **335** J4
Royal Rd *MANG/FISH* BS16 ..... **328** C5
Royal Spring *MTCHDN* GL17 .... **131** K2
Royal Well La *CHELT* GL50 ..... **2** C5
Royal Well PI *CHELT* GL50 ..... **2** C5
Royal Well Rd *CHELT* GL50 ..... **2** C5
Royal York Crs
  CFTN/FAIL BS8 .... **335** H5 🖻
Royal York Vls
  CFTN/FAIL BS8 .... **335** J5 🔟
Royate HI *EVILLE/WHL* BS5 .... **336** F1
Roycroft Rd
  BRSTK/PCHW BS34 .... **326** D1
Roy King Gdns
  OLD/WMLY/WICK BS30 .... **338** E6
Royston Wk
  HNBRY/STHM BS10 .... **325** M1
Rozel Rd *HORF/LLZ* BS7 .... **326** A5
Ruardean Rd *MTCHDN* GL17 .... **129** G5
Rubens CI *KEYN* BS31 .... **348** C6 🖻
Ruby St *BMSTR* BS3 .... **335** K8
Rudford CI *BRSTK/PCHW* BS34 .. **316** D2
Rudge CI *KGWD/HNM* BS15 ..... **338** B1
The Rudge *VGL* GL2 .... **111** K3
Rudgeway Pk *THNB/SVB* BS35.... **307** C2
Rudgewood CI
  BMSTRD/HC/WWD BS13 .... **345** M7 🖻
Rudhall Gv *HNBRY/STHM* BS10 .. **326** A4
Rudhall Vw *RWYE* HR9 .... **106** D3 🖻
Rudthorpe Rd *HORF/LLZ* BS7 ... **326** A6
Ruffet CI *CLFD* GL16 .... **175** K3
Ruffet Rd *FRCTL/WBN* BS36 .... **318** D7
The Ruffitt *CIND* GL14 .... **154** D2
Rugby Rd
  BRSG/KWL/STAPK BS4 .... **336** F8
Rumsey CI *GLE* GL4 .... **137** G7
Runnings Rd *CHELTW* GL51 ..... **93** J6
The Runnings *CHELTW* GL51 .... **93** J5
Runnymead Av
  BRSG/KWL/STAPK BS4 .... **346** F2
Runnymede *CHELTW* GL51 ...... **115** G6 🖻
  KGWD/HNM BS15 .... **338** A2 🔟
Runswick Rd
  BRSG/KWL/STAPK BS4 .... **336** E8
Rupert St *CBRIS/FH* BS1 ...... **6** F5
  EVILLE/WHL BS5 .... **336** E4
Ruscombe Rd
  RSTROUD/NAIL GL6 .... **208** A2
Rush CI *ALMDB* BS32 .... **316** F1
Rushley La *COTS* GL54 .... **74** D6
Rushmead La
  CHPMW/MSHF SN14 .... **342** A1
Rushton Dr *FRCTL/WBN* BS36.... **318** F4
Rushworth CI *CHELTW* GL51 .... **114** F1
Rushy *OLD/WMLY/WICK* BS30..... **338** C3
Rushyleaze *LYD* GL15 .... **225** K1
Rushy Wy *MANG/FISH* BS16 .... **328** C2
Ruskin Gv *HORF/LLZ* BS7 ...... **326** C3
Ruspidge CI *GLE* GL4 .... **137** G6 🖻
Ruspidge Rd *CIND* GL14 .... **154** A7
Russell Av *KGWD/HNM* BS15.... **337** M4
Russell Gv *RDLND/MONT* BS6 ... **325** L6
Russell PI *CHELTW* GL51 ...... **2** A2
Russell Rd *MANG/FISH* BS16 ... **337** K1
  RDLND/MONT BS6 .... **325** K7
Russell St *CHELTW* GL51 ...... **2** A2
  GL GL1 .... **4** F6
  STROUD GL5 .... **208** E4 🔟
Russell Town Av
  EVILLE/WHL BS5............ **336** D3
Russet CI *GL* GL1 .... **135** K8
  LED HR8 .... **19** L3
  TEWK GL20 .... **27** H5 🖻
  THNB/SVB BS35 .... **292** C8
Russet Gv *WUE* GL12 .... **277** H7 🖻
Russet Rd *CHELTW* GL51 .... **93** H8
Russett Wy *NWNT* GL18 .... **86** D3
Russ St *CBRISNE* BS2 .... **7** J4

Rustic CI *GLE* GL4 .... **136** E7
Rutherford CI
  OLD/WMLY/WICK BS30 .... **338** C8 🖻
Rutherford Wy *CHELTW* GL51 ... **93** J6
Ruthven Rd
  BRSG/KWL/STAPK BS4 .... **346** A3
Rutland Av
  OLD/WMLY/WICK BS30 .... **348** C1
Rutland Rd *HORF/LLZ* BS7 ..... **326** A8 🖻
Ryalls La *VGL* GL2 .... **205** G6
Rydal Rd *VGL* GL2 .... **5** M1
Ryder CI *DSLY* GL11 .... **229** J7
Ryde Rd
  BRSG/KWL/STAPK BS4 .... **346** D1 🖻
Rye Av *CHELTW* GL51 .... **92** F6 🖻
Rye CI *BMSTRD/HC/WWD* BS13 ... **345** C5
Ryeclose *COTS* GL54 .... **123** J6
Rye Crs *COTS* GL54 .... **123** K6 🖻
Ryecroft Ri *LGASH* BS41 ...... **344** D2
Ryecroft Rd *FRCTL/WBN* BS36 .. **318** C3
Ryecroft St *GL* GL1 .... **5** G9
Ryedown La
  OLD/WMLY/WICK BS30 .... **348** E2
Ryelands *GL* GL1 .... **135** G8
Ryelands CI *STNHO* GL10 ...... **207** C3 🖻
Ryelands Rd *LYD* GL15 .... **200** D3
  STNHO GL10 .... **207** G3
The Ryelands
  RSTROUD/NAIL GL6 .... **207** M2
Ryeleaze CI *STROUD* GL5 ...... **208** E4 🖻
Ryeleaze Rd *STROUD* GL5 ...... **208** E4 🔟
Ryeworth Dr *CHELTE/BC* GL52 .. **116** D4
Ryeworth Rd *CHELTE/BC* GL52... **116** D4
Ryland CI *TET* GL8 .... **282** A2
Ryland PI *CBRISNE* BS2 .... **336** C1 🖻
Rylestone CI *FRCTL/WBN* BS36.. **318** B3
Rylestone Gv
  HNLZ/SM/SNYPK/WT BS9 ...... **325** H6
Rysdale Rd
  HNLZ/SM/SNYPK/WT BS9 ...... **325** H5

S

Sabre CI *VGL* GL2 .... **135** J8
Sabrina Wy
  HNLZ/SM/SNYPK/WT BS9 ...... **324** E7
  LYD GL15 .... **201** K7
Saddlers CI *CHELT* GL50 ...... **2** C5
Saddlers Rd *VGL* GL2 .... **159** H1
Sadlers Av *SHPSTR* CV36 ...... **16** A5
Sadlier CI *AVONM* BS11 .... **324** B3
Saffron CI *GLE* GL4 .... **136** C6
Saffron Rd *TEWK* GL20 .... **48** A5 🖻
Sages Md *ALMDB* BS32 .... **317** G3 🖻
St Agnes Av
  BRSG/KWL/STAPK BS4 .... **346** B1
St Agnes CI
  BRSG/KWL/STAPK BS4 .... **346** B1 🖻
St Agnes Wk
  BRSG/KWL/STAPK BS4 .... **346** B1 🖻
St Aidans CI *CHELTW* GL51 .... **115** G1 🖻
  EVILLE/WHL BS5 .... **337** K5 🖻
St Aidan's Rd *EVILLE/WHL* BS5 . **337** J6
St Albans CI *CHELT* GL50 ..... **115** J6 🖻
St Alban's Rd
  RDLND/MONT BS6 .... **325** K7
  VGL GL2 .... **135** L6
St Aldams Dr *MANG/FISH* BS16.. **329** K6
St Aldate St *GL* GL1 .... **4** F5
St Aldhelms Rd *MALM* SN16 .... **303** H7
St Aldwyn Rd *GL* GL1 .... **136** B5
St Aldwyn's CI *HORF/LLZ* BS7 . **326** B3 🖻
St Andrews
  OLD/WMLY/WICK BS30 .... **338** D5
  RTEWK/TIB GL19 .... **89** J3
  YATE/CS BS37 .... **320** B2
St Andrew's Av *CHEP* NP16 .... **270** A4 🖻
St Andrews CI *TEWK* GL20 ..... **49** H4
St Andrew's Rd
  RDLND/MONT BS6 .... **336** B1 🔟
  RDLND/MONT BS6 .... **336** A1 🖻
St Annal's Rd *CIND* GL14 ..... **154** B3
St Anne's Av *KEYN* BS31 ...... **347** M5
  CHELTE/BC GL52 .... **2** F5
  OLD/WMLY/WICK BS30 .... **338** D7
St Anne's Dr *FRCTL/WBN* BS36 . **318** E6
  OLD/WMLY/WICK BS30 .... **339** K4
St Anne's Park Rd
  BRSG/KWL/STAPK BS4 .... **337** G6
St Anne's Rd
  BRSG/KWL/STAPK BS4 .... **336** F5
  CHELTE/BC GL52 .... **2** F5
  EVILLE/WHL BS5 .... **337** K5
St Anne's Ter
  BRSG/KWL/STAPK BS4 .... **337** G6
  CHELTE/BC GL52 .... **2** F5
St Annes Wy *GL* GL15 .... **198** F6
St Ann Ct *CHEP* NP16 .... **270** B2
St Ann Wy *GL* GL1 .... **4** C8
St Arild's Rd *BAD* GL9 .... **299** K7
St Aubin's Av
  BRSG/KWL/STAPK BS4 .... **337** H8
St Augustine's Pde *CBRIS/FH* BS1 . **6** E4
St Augustine's PI *CBRIS/FH* BS1 .. **6** E4 🖻
St Barbara's CI *TEWK* GL20 ... **49** J4 🖻
St Barnabas CI *GLE* GL4 ...... **136** A7
  OLD/WMLY/WICK BS30 .... **338** E4 🖻
St Bartholomews *NWNT* GL18 .. **86** C3 🖻
St Bartholomews CI
  DSLY GL11 .... **229** H6 🖻
St Bartholomew's Rd
  HORF/LLZ BS7 .... **326** B8 🖻
St Bede's Rd *KGWD/HNM* BS15 .. **337** L1 🖻
St Bernard's Rd *AVONM* BS11... **324** A5
St Brelades Gv
  BRSG/KWL/STAPK BS4 .... **337** G6
St Brendan's Rd *STROUD* GL5 .. **209** G4 🖻
St Briavels Dr *YATE/CS* BS37 .. **319** M3 🖻
St Briavels Rd *LYD* GL15 ..... **223** K8
Saintbridge CI *GLE* GL4 ...... **136** D6 🖻
Saintbridge PI *GLE* GL4 ...... **136** D6 🖻
St Bruel's CI *LYD* GL15 ...... **199** G6 🖻
St Catherine St *GL* GL1 ...... **4** E3
St Clements Ct *KEYN* BS31 .... **348** A7

St Clements Rd *KEYN* BS31 .... **348** A6
St Cloes Pitch *STROUD* GL5 .... **232** C3
St Cyril's Rd *STNHO* GL10 ..... **207** H4 🖻
St David's Av
  OLD/WMLY/WICK BS30 .... **338** D6
St Davids CI *CHELTW* GL51 .... **115** J5
  CHEP NP16 .... **270** A4 🖻
  GL GL1 .... **135** L8
St David's Crs
  BRSG/KWL/STAPK BS4 .... **337** G6
  DSLY GL11 .... **253** H1 🖻
St Davids Rd *TEWK* GL20 ...... **49** H4
  THNB/SVB BS35 .... **293** C2
St Dennis La *MALM* SN16 ...... **303** J8 🖻
St Dunstan's Rd *BMSTR* BS3 ... **345** L1
St Edwards Ct *MIM* GL56 ...... **58** C7 🖻
St Edwards Dr *COTS* GL54 ..... **58** C7 🖻
St Edward's Rd *CFTN/FAIL* BS8 . **6** A5 🖻
St Edwards Wk *CHELTS* GL53 ... **116** C5 🖻
St Edyth's Rd
  HNLZ/SM/SNYPK/WT BS9 ...... **324** D5
St Ewens Rd *CHEP* NP16 ...... **270** A5
St Fagans Ct
  OLD/WMLY/WICK BS30 .... **348** D1 🖻
St Francis Dr *FRCTL/WBN* BS36 . **318** B5
  OLD/WMLY/WICK BS30 .... **339** K4
St Francis Rd *BMSTR* BS3 ..... **335** J7 🖻
  KEYN BS31 .... **347** L5
St Gabriel's Rd
  EVILLE/WHL BS5 .... **336** C3 🔞
St George Rd *CHEP* NP16 ...... **270** A4
St Georges Av
  EVILLE/WHL BS5 .... **337** H5 🔞
  STNHO GL10 .... **207** J7
St George's CI *CHELTW* GL51 .. **115** K1 🖻
  DSLY GL11 .... **229** K8
  GL GL1 .... **135** L8
  MIM GL56 .... **58** D6
  STNHO GL10 .... **207** J7 🖻
St George's Dr *CHELTW* GL51 .. **115** K1
St Georges Rd *BWTH/CHD* GL3... **137** M6
  CBRIS/FH BS1 .... **6** C5
  CHELT GL50 .... **2** A4
  CHELTW GL51 .... **115** K1
  DSLY GL11 .... **229** J8
  KEYN BS31 .... **347** M6
  TEWK GL20 .... **49** H3
St George's St *CHELT* GL50 ... **2** C4
St Georges Wy *CHEP* NP16 .... **270** D7 🖻
St Giles Barton *WUE* GL12 .... **297** M3 🖻
St Gregory's Rd *HORF/LLZ* BS7 . **326** B3
St Gregory's Wk
  HORF/LLZ BS7 .... **326** C3 🖻
St Helena Rd
  RDLND/MONT BS6 .... **325** K7
St Helens Dr
  OLD/WMLY/WICK BS30 .... **339** L4
  OLD/WMLY/WICK BS30 .... **348** E1
St Helen's Wk *EVILLE/WHL* BS5 . **337** J2
St Helier Av
  BRSG/KWL/STAPK BS4 .... **337** H8 🖻
St Hilary CI
  HNLZ/SM/SNYPK/WT BS9 ...... **324** F6
St Ivel Wy
  OLD/WMLY/WICK BS30 .... **338** E5
St James' CI *VGL* GL2 .... **159** H2
St James Ct *MIM* GL56 .... **58** C7 🖻
St James Pk *CLFD* GL16 .... **175** G4
St James' PI *CHELT* GL50 ..... **2** B9
St James' Sq *CHELT* GL50 ..... **2** C5
St James's St *MANG/FISH* BS16 . **328** C2
St James St *CHELTE/BC* GL52 .. **2** E6
  GL GL1 .... **5** H9
St James Av *BWTH/CHD* GL3 .... **113** J4
  CHELTE/BC GL52 .... **2** F5
St John's Br *CBRIS/FH* BS1 ... **6** E2 🖻
St John's CI *CHELTE/BC* GL52 .. **72** B7 🖻
  CIR GL7 .... **214** B8
  SHPSTR CV36 .... **39** J5
St Johns Ct *KEYN* BS31........ **348** A5
St John's Crs *BMSTR* BS3 ..... **346** A1
St John's La *BMSTR* BS3 ...... **335** L8
  BMSTR BS3 .... **345** M1
  GL GL1 .... **4** E5
St John's Rd *BMSTR* BS3 ...... **6** E8
  BMSTR BS3 .... **335** L8 🖻
  CFTN/FAIL BS8 .... **335** J2
  CIR GL7 .... **238** C1
  MTCHDN GL17 .... **129** G3
  SHPSTR CV36 .... **39** J5
  VGL GL2 .... **205** G8
St Johns Sq *CIND* GL14 .... **154** A5
St John's St *BMSTR* BS3 ...... **335** L8 🔟
  CIR GL7 .... **244** F7
  CLFD GL16 .... **175** J1 🖻
  MALM SN16 .... **303** K8
St John St *BAD* GL9 .... **298** C8
  THNB/SVB BS35 .... **293** K2
St Johns Wy *YATE/CS* BS37 .... **320** E1
St Joseph's Rd
  HNBRY/STHM BS10 .... **315** K9
St Judes Wk *CHELTS* GL53 ..... **116** B4
St Keyna Rd *KEYN* BS31 .... **348** A6
St Kilda Pde *GL* GL1 .... **5** G6
St Ladoc Rd *KEYN* BS31 .... **347** M5
St Laud CI
  HNLZ/SM/SNYPK/WT BS9 ...... **324** E6
St Lawrence CI *CIR* GL7 ...... **238** E1
  VGL GL2 .... **90** A8
St Lawrence Rd *CIR* GL7 ...... **244** E7
  GLE GL4 .... **136** F4
St Leonard's *MALM* SN16 ...... **285** M8
St Leonards CI *GLE* GL4 ...... **161** G1
St Leonard's
  EVILLE/WHL BS5 .... **336** E1 🔞
  HORF/LLZ BS7 .... **326** A5
St Lucia CI *HORF/LLZ* BS7 .... **326** A3
St Lucia Crs *HORF/LLZ* BS7 ... **326** A4
St Luke's Crs *BMSTR* BS3 ..... **7** J8
St Luke's Gdns
  BRSG/KWL/STAPK BS4 .... **347** C1
St Luke's PI *CHELTS* GL53 ..... **2** E7
St Luke's Rd *BMSTR* BS3 ...... **7** H8
  CHELT GL50 .... **2** D7
St Lukes St *GL* GL1 .... **4** D8
St Margaret's CI *KEYN* BS31 ... **347** M5 🖻

St Margaret's Dr
 HNLZ/SM/SNYPK/WT BS9 ...... **325** L6 🔲
 TEWK GL20 .... **51** K4
St Margaret's Rd *CHELT* GL50 .... **2** D3
 GLE GL4 .... **137** H3 🔲
 MTCHDN GL17 .... **129** C3
 TEWK GL20 .... **51** L4
St Marks Cl *KEYN* BS31 .... **348** A5 🔲
St Mark's Rd *EVILLE/WHL* BS5.... **336** D2
St Mark's Ter
 EVILLE/WHL BS5 .... **336** D2 🔲
St Mark St *GL* GL1 .... **4** F2
St Martin's Gdns
 BRSG/KWL/STAPK BS4 ...... **346** D2 🔲
St Martin's La
 CHPMW/MSHF SN14 .... **342** B3
St Martin's Pk
 CHPMW/MSHF SN14 .... **342** B3 🔲
St Martin's Rd
 BRSG/KWL/STAPK BS4 .... **346** D1
St Martin's Wk
 BRSG/KWL/STAPK BS4 ...... **346** D2 🔲
St Mary's Cl *CIR* GL7 .... **267** C5
 COTS GL54............................. **101** J3
St Marys Dr *CIR* GL7 .... **242** F4
St Marys Fld *CIR* GL7 .... **241** K6
St Mary's HI *STROUD* GL5....... **232** C5
 MALM SN16 .... **303** J7 🔲
 TEWK GL20 .... **48** A5
St Mary's Rd *CFTN/FAIL* BS8 .... **334** F5 🔲
 CIR GL7 .... **238** E3 🔲
 TET GL8 .... **281** M3
 TEWK GL20 .... **47** M5
St Mary's Sq *GL* GL1 .... **4** D4
 LYD GL15 .... **201** L8
St Mary's St *GL* GL1 .... **4** E4
 MALM SN16 .... **303** J8 🔲
 RSTROUD/NAIL GL6 .... **185** H3 🔲
St Mary St *CHEP* NP16 .... **270** A4
 THNB/SVB BS35 .... **293** K3 🔲
St Mary's Wy *YATE/CS* BS37 .... **320** B1
St Matthew's Av
 RDLND/MONT BS6 .... **335** M2 🔲
St Matthew's Rd
 RDLND/MONT BS6 .... **335** M3
St Matthias Pk *CBRISNE* BS2 ...... **7** J2
St Michaels Av *CHELTE/BC* GL52 .... **72** C8
St Michael's Cl
 FRCTL/WBN BS36.................... **318** A4
 MTCHDN GL17 .... **130** C1
St Michaels Ct
 KGWD/HNM BS15 .... **337** K3 🔲
St Michael's HI *CBRISNE* BS2 ...... **335** L3
St Michael's Pk *CFTN/FAIL* BS8 ...... **6** C1
St Michaels Pl *STROUD* GL5.... **207** M3 🔲
St Michaels Rd *CHELT* GL50 .... **115** K6
 CIR GL7 .... **238** C4 🔲
St Michael's Sq *GL* GL1 .... **4** E7
St Nicholas Cl *TEWK* GL20 ...... **50** C5
St Nicholas Dr *CHELT* GL50 .... **93** M6
St Nicholas Pk
 EVILLE/WHL BS5 .... **336** D1 🔲
St Nicholas' Rd *CBRISNE* BS2 .... **336** B2
 HGRV/WHIT BS14 .... **346** E7
St Nicholas St *CBRIS/FH* BS1 .... **6** F4 🔲
St Oswald's Rd *GL* GL1 .... **4** E1
 RDLND/MONT BS6 .... **325** K8
St Patricks Rd *TEWK* GL20...... **49** H4
St Pauls Ct *MIM* GL56 .... **58** C7 🔲
St Paul's La *CHELT* GL50 .... **2** C3
St Paul's Pde *CHELT* GL50 .... **2** D3
St Paul's Rd *BMSTR* BS3 .... **6** E8
 CFTN/FAIL BS8 .... **6** A2
 CHELT GL50 .... **2** C2
 GL GL1 .... **4** E9
St Paul's St North *CHELT* GL50 .... **2** C3
St Paul's St South *CHELT* GL50 .... **2** C3
St Paul St *CBRISNE* BS2 .... **7** H1
St Peters Cl *CHELTW* GL51 .... **93** J8
 CIND GL14 .... **155** J7 🔲
 CIR GL7 .... **259** L2
St Peters Ct *MIM* GL56 .... **58** C7 🔲
St Peter's Crs *FRCTL/WBN* BS36 .. **318** D4
St Peters Rd *BMSTRD/HC/WWD* BS13....... **345** J4
 CIR GL7 .... **238** C3
 GLE GL4 .... **136** E8
St Peter's Sq *CHELTW* GL51 .... **93** J7 🔲
St Peter's Wk
 HNLZ/SM/SNYPK/WT BS9 ...... **325** K6
St Peters Wy *COTS* GL54 .... **74** C5
St Philips Cswy
 BRSG/KWL/STAPK BS4 .... **336** E7
 CBRISNE BS2............................ **336** D5
St Philip's Cl *BWTH/CHD* GL3 .... **137** J3 🔲
St Philips Rd *CBRISNE* BS2 .... **7** K3
St Phillips Rd *CBRISNE* BS2 .... **7** L3
St Phillip's St *CHELT* GL50 ...... **115** L4
St Pierre Dr
 OLD/WMLY/WICK BS30 .... **338** D5 🔲
St Ronan's Av
 RDLND/MONT BS6 .... **335** L2
St Saviours Ri *FRCTL/WBN* BS36.. **318** D5
St Silas St *CBRISNE* BS2 .... **7** M6
St Stephen's Av *CBRIS/FH* BS1 .... **6** E4 🔲
St Stephens Cl *CHELT* GL50 .... **115** K4
 KGWD/HNM BS15 .... **328** A8 🔲
St Stephen's Rd *CHELT* GL50.... **115** K4
 MANG/FISH BS16 .... **328** M8
St Stephen's St *CBRIS/FH* BS1 .... **6** E3
St Swithins *LYD* GL15 .... **201** L1
St Swithuns Rd *GL* GL1 .... **135** J5
St Tecla Rd *CHEP* NP16 .... **270** A5
St Tewdric Rd *CHEP* NP16 .... **270** A4
St Thomas St *CBRIS/FH* BS1 .... **7** G5
St Vincent's HI
 RDLND/MONT BS6 .... **335** J1 🔲
St Vincent's Rd
 CFTN/FAIL BS8 .... **335** J5 🔲
St Vincent Wy
 BWTH/CHD GL3 .... **113** J3 🔲
St Werburgh's Pk
 CBRISNE BS2.......................... **336** C1
St Werburgh's Rd
 CBRISNE BS2.......................... **336** B1 🔲
St Whites Rd *CIND* GL14........... **154** A5
St Whytes Rd
 BRSG/KWL/STAPK BS4........... **345** M3

Salamanca Rd *CHELTE/BC* GL52 ...... **3** M3
Salcombe Rd
 BRSG/KWL/STAPK BS4........... **346** C3
Salem Rd *FRCTL/WBN* BS36 ...... **318** B4
Salisbury Av *CHELTW* GL51 ...... **115** J6
 KGWD/HNM BS15 .... **337** K3
Salisbury Gdns
 MANG/FISH BS16 .... **328** A6
Salisbury Rd
 BRSG/KWL/STAPK BS4........... **336** F6
 MANG/FISH BS16 .... **328** A5
 RDLND/MONT BS6 .... **335** M1
Salisbury St *EVILLE/WHL* BS5 ... **336** D5
Salix Ct *CHELTW* GL51 .... **115** H7
Sallis Cl *TEWK* GL20 .... **48** F1
Sallybarn Cl
 OLD/WMLY/WICK BS30 .... **348** A1
Sallysmead Cl
 BMSTRD/HC/WWD BS13......... **345** K7 🔲
Sallys Wy *FRCTL/WBN* BS36 .... **318** B4
Salmons Wy *MANG/FISH* BS16 .... **328** C3
Salter's La *COTS* GL54 .... **75** H5
Salter St *BRKLY* GL13 .... **227** G8
Salthrop Rd *HORF/LLZ* BS7 ...... **326** A8
Saltmarsh Dr *AVONM* BS11 ...... **324** C2
Salt Wy *COTS* GL54................ **218** B2
Saltwell Av *HGRV/WHIT* BS14 .... **346** E6
Samian Wy *BRSTK/PCHW* BS34 .. **317** C6
Sampsons Rd
 BMSTRD/HC/WWD BS13......... **345** L7
Samuel St *EVILLE/WHL* BS5 ...... **336** E3 🔲
Samuel White Rd
 KGWD/HNM BS15 .... **337** L8
Samuel Wright Cl
 OLD/WMLY/WICK BS30 .... **338** F6 🔲
Sanatorium Rd *GLE* GL4 .... **161** L4 🔲
Sandalwood Dr *VGL* GL2 .... **135** K4
Sandbach Rd
 BRSG/KWL/STAPK BS4........... **336** F7
Sandbed Rd *CBRISNE* BS2 .... **336** C1
Sandburrows Rd
 BMSTRD/HC/WWD BS13......... **345** G5
Sandburrows Wk
 BMSTRD/HC/WWD BS13 .... **345** H5 🔲
Sandcroft *HGRV/WHIT* BS14 .... **346** B5
Sandfield *LED* HR8 .... **42** F5
Sandfield La *EVE* WR11 .... **30** A1
Sandfield Rd *BWTH/CHD* GL3 .... **113** M6
The Sandfield *TEWK* GL20 .... **49** G2
Sandford Leaze *TET* GL8 .... **257** L2
Sandford Mill Cl *CHELTS* GL53 .... **3** C9 🔲
Sandford Mill Rd *CHELTS* GL53 .... **3** C9
Sandford Rd *CFTN/FAIL* BS8 .... **335** J6 🔲
 CHELTS GL53............................. **2** E9
 LYD GL15 .... **224** D3
Sandford St *CHELT* GL50 .... **2** D7
Sandford Wy *GL* GL1 .... **159** K1
Sandgate Rd
 BRSG/KWL/STAPK BS4........... **336** F8
Sand HI *BRSG/KWL/STAPK* BS4 .... **336** E7
Sandholme Cl
 MANG/FISH BS16 .... **328** A3 🔲
Sandholme Rd
 BRSG/KWL/STAPK BS4........... **336** F8
Sandhurst Cl
 BRSTK/PCHW BS34 .... **316** D2
Sandhurst La *VGL* GL2 .... **90** B8
 VGL GL2 .... **111** M5
Sandhurst Rd
 BRSG/KWL/STAPK BS4........... **336** F7 🔲
 CHELTE/BC GL52 .... **116** D5
 GL GL1 .... **4** F1
Sandling Av *HORF/LLZ* BS7 ...... **326** C4
Sandown Cl *MANG/FISH* BS16 .... **328** B2
Sandown Rd
 BRSG/KWL/STAPK BS4........... **336** F7
 BRSTK/PCHW BS34 .... **316** B8 🔲
 CHELTE/BC GL52 .... **72** B7
Sandpiper Cl *VGL* GL2 .... **158** F2 🔲
Sandpits La *BAD* GL9 .... **312** B2
 RSTROUD/NAIL GL6 .... **207** L3
Sandpool La *CIR* GL7 .... **236** A8
Sandringham Av *GL* GL1 .... **159** L2
 MANG/FISH BS16 .... **328** A3
Sandringham Pk
 MANG/FISH BS16 .... **328** A3 🔲
Sandringham Rd
 BRSG/KWL/STAPK BS4........... **336** F8
 BRSTK/PCHW BS34 .... **316** F7
Sands Cl *BDWAY* WR12 .... **32** F2
Sands Croft Av *BDWAY* WR12 .... **33** G2
Sands HI *CHPMW/MSHF* SN14 .... **331** G8
Sands La *EVE* WR11 .... **10** A1
Sandstar Cl *VGL* GL2 .... **112** F6 🔲
The Sands *BDWAY* WR12 .... **32** F2
Sandstone Ri *FRCTL/WBN* BS36 .... **317** M7
Sandtumps *LYD* GL15 .... **223** L5
Sandwich Rd
 BRSG/KWL/STAPK BS4........... **336** F7 🔲
Sandy Cl *ALMDB* BS32 .... **317** C5
Sandycroft Rd *BWTH/CHD* GL3 .... **113** J4
Sandy La *CHELTS* GL53 .... **116** B7
 COTS GL54............................. **124** B7
 EVILLE/WHL BS5...................... **326** E8
 LYD GL15 .... **198** E8
 THNB/SVB BS35 .... **291** J4
Sandy Lane Rd *CHELTS* GL53 .... **116** B6 🔲
Sandyleaze
 HNLZ/SM/SNYPK/WT BS9....... **325** G4
 VGL GL2 .... **112** F9
Sandy Ldg *YATE/CS* BS37........ **320** A3
Sandy Park Rd
 BRSG/KWL/STAPK BS4........... **336** E7
Sandy Pluck La *CHELTW* GL51.... **138** D3
Sandyway La *RWYE* HR9 .... **126** C5
Saniger La *BRKLY* GL13 .... **226** E4
Sankey Gv *MIM* GL56 .... **58** D7
Sappercombe La *CHELTS* GL53 .... **116** D6
Sapperton Rd *GLE* GL4 .... **136** B6
Sapphire Cl *GL* GL1 .... **159** K1
Sarah St *EVILLE/WHL* BS5 .... **336** D4
Sargent's La *RWYE* HR9 .... **84** F4
Sargent St *BMSTR* BS3 .... **7** G8
Sarnedy Rd *CLFD* GL16........... **175** K1
Sarum Crs *HNBRY/STHM* BS10 .... **325** L2
Sassoon Ct
 OLD/WMLY/WICK BS30 .... **338** B6 🔲

Satchfield Cl
 HNBRY/STHM BS10 .... **325** H1
Satchfield Crs
 HNBRY/STHM BS10 .... **325** H1
Sates Wy
 HNLZ/SM/SNYPK/WT BS9....... **325** L5
Saturn Cl *GLE* GL4 .... **137** H5
Saunders Cl *MTCHDN* GL17 .... **107** K6
 RWYE HR9 .... **106** C3
Saunders Rd *MANG/FISH* BS16 .. **328** A7 🔲
Saunton Wk
 BRSG/KWL/STAPK BS4........... **346** A3 🔲
Savage HI *CLFD* GL16 .... **174** E4
Savages Wood Rd *ALMDB* BS32.. **316** F3
Saville Cl *CHELT* GL50 .... **94** A7
Saville Gate Cl
 HNLZ/SM/SNYPK/WT BS9....... **325** H7 🔲
Saville Pl *CFTN/FAIL* BS8 .... **335** J5 🔲
Saville Rd
 HNLZ/SM/SNYPK/WT BS9....... **325** H8
Savoy Rd
 BRSG/KWL/STAPK BS4........... **336** F7
Saw Mill La *THNB/SVB* BS35 .... **293** K2 🔲
Sawpit La *RTEWK/TIB* GL19 ...... **69** G6
Sawpits La *MIM* GL56 .... **103** J2
Sawpitts La *RWYE* HR9 .... **126** D5
Sawyers Ri *RTEWK/TIB* GL19 .... **89** J5
Saxon Cl *HGHW* SN6 .... **288** F4
 VGL GL2 .... **112** E6 🔲
Saxon Pl *CHEP* NP16 .... **270** C4
Saxon Rd *CBRISNE* BS2 .... **336** C1
 VGL GL2 .... **238** E2
Saxon Wy *ALMDB* BS32 .... **316** E2
 CHELTE/BC GL52 .... **3** J7
 LED HR8 .... **19** L1
Sayers Crs *BWTH/CHD* GL3 ...... **138** A6 🔲
Saylittle Ms *VGL* GL2 .... **113** A6 🔲
Say Wk *OLD/WMLY/WICK* BS30.. **338** F4
Scandrett Cl
 HNBRY/STHM BS10 .... **315** G8 🔲
Scantleberry Cl
 MANG/FISH BS16 .... **327** M3 🔲
Scar HI *RSTROUD/NAIL* GL6 ...... **232** F6
Scarr Rd *NWNT* GL18 .... **64** C6
School Cl *BRSTK/PCHW* BS34 .... **316** E3
 CLFD GL16.............................. **175** M1
 DSLY GL11.............................. **229** G7
 EVILLE/WHL BS5...................... **336** F1
 HGRV/WHIT BS14 .... **346** B7
 SHPSTR CV36 .... **61** H5
School Crs *LYD* GL15 .... **201** K6
 RTEWK/TIB GL19 .... **66** E5
Schooler's La *MIM* GL56 .... **81** L8
School HI *CHEP* NP16 .... **270** A3
 CIR GL7 .... **188** C3
 CIR GL7 .... **214** A7
School La *BAD* GL9 .... **323** G1
 CBATH/BATHN BA1 .... **352** B7
 CHELTE/BC GL52 .... **94** E3
 CHELTW GL51 .... **139** G1
 CIR GL7 .... **238** D4
 CIR GL7 .... **240** A3
 CIR GL7 .... **241** K7
 CIR GL7 .... **263** H4
 COTS GL54............................. **142** F1
 HGHW SN6 .... **266** D7
 MIM GL56 .... **57** G1
 MTCHDN GL17 .... **107** G7
 MTCHDN GL17 .... **128** F4
 MTCHDN GL17 .... **128** C3
 RSTROUD/NAIL GL6 .... **211** M2
 TEWK GL20 .... **28** B4
 VGL GL2 .... **158** F3
 VGL GL2 .... **159** G3
 VGL GL2 .... **182** A6
School Md *CHELTW* GL51 ...... **115** J1
School Ms *GLE* GL4 .... **136** D7 🔲
School Rd *BDWAY* WR12 .... **31** G7
 BRSG/KWL/STAPK BS4........... **336** C8
 BRSG/KWL/STAPK BS4........... **347** G1
 CHELTE/BC GL52 .... **72** C7
 CHELTS GL53.......................... **116** D5
 CIR GL7 .... **261** H4
 DSLY GL11.............................. **253** L3
 FRCTL/WBN BS36.................... **318** B3
 KGWD/HNM BS15 .... **337** L3
 LYD GL15 .... **201** H2
 MTCHDN GL17 .... **128** C5 🔲
 MTCHDN GL17 .... **129** G3
 OLD/WMLY/WICK BS30 .... **338** C7
 RSTROUD/NAIL GL6 .... **233** J5
 RTEWK/TIB GL19 .... **68** F7
 STRAT CV37.............................. **8** A1
 TEWK GL20 .... **51** L4
 WUE GL12.............................. **277** K4
School Wk *YATE/CS* BS37......... **320** A1
School Wy *THNB/SVB* BS35 ..... **304** C5 🔲
The Scop *ALMDB* BS32 .... **306** C6
Scott Av *VGL* GL2 .... **135** L7
Scott Ct
 OLD/WMLY/WICK BS30 .... **338** B6 🔲
Scott Lawrence Cl
 MANG/FISH BS16 .... **327** J4 🔲
Scott Wk
 OLD/WMLY/WICK BS30 .... **338** F4
Scott Wy *YATE/CS* BS37 .... **320** B3
Scowles Rd *CLFD* GL16 .... **175** G1
Scrubbett's La *TET* GL8 .... **279** H2
Seabright Cl *CHELTW* GL51 ...... **93** G6 🔲
Seabroke Rd *GL* GL1 .... **5** H7
Seabrook Rd *BWTH/CHD* GL3 .... **137** M6
Seacome Rd *CHELTW* GL51 ...... **115** G1 🔲
Seagry Cl *HNBRY/STHM* BS10.... **326** A2
Sea Mills La
 HNLZ/SM/SNYPK/WT BS9....... **324** C7
Searle Court Av
 BRSG/KWL/STAPK BS4........... **337** G6
Seaton Rd *EVILLE/WHL* BS5 ...... **336** E2 🔲
Seawalls Rd
 HNLZ/SM/SNYPK/WT BS9....... **334** F1
Sebert St *GL* GL1 .... **5** G2
Second Av *DSLY* GL11 .... **253** L3
Secret La *GL* GL1 .... **4** F3 🔲
Sedbury La *CHEP* NP16 .... **270** C2
Seddon Rd *CBRISNE* BS2 .... **336** C1 🔲
Sedgefield Gdns
 MANG/FISH BS16 .... **328** B2 🔲

Sedgewick Gdns *CHELTW* GL51 .. **114** F5
Sedgley Cl *GL* GL1 .... **159** L1
Sedgley Rd *CHELTE/BC* GL52.... **72** B7
Sefton Park Rd *HORF/LLZ* BS7 .. **326** B8
Sefton Wk *CHELTW* GL51 .... **114** F5
Selborne Rd *CHELTE/BC* GL52 .... **72** B7
 HORF/LLZ BS7 .... **326** B6
Selbrooke Crs *MANG/FISH* BS16.. **327** L5
Selby Rd *EVILLE/WHL* BS5 .... **337** H2
Selden Rd *HGRV/WHIT* BS14 .... **347** G6
Selkirk Cl *CHELTE/BC* GL52 .... **3** G3
Selkirk Gdns *CHELTE/BC* GL52 ...... **3** G3
Selkirk Rd *KGWD/HNM* BS15 .... **337** L1
Selkirk St *CHELTE/BC* GL52 .... **2** F3
Sellars Rd *VGL* GL2 .... **158** F4
Selley Wk
 BMSTRD/HC/WWD BS13......... **345** J6
Selsey Rd *STROUD* GL5........... **232** A1
Selsley HI *STROUD* GL5............ **232** A1
Selworthy *CHELTE/BC* GL51 ..... **115** C6 🔲
 KGWD/HNM BS15 .... **338** A4
Selworthy Cl *KEYN* BS31 .... **347** M6
Selworthy Rd
 BRSG/KWL/STAPK BS4........... **346** D1
Selwyn Cl *STNHO* GL10 .... **207** J6
Selwyn Rd *GLE* GL4 .... **136** B6
Seneca Pl *EVILLE/WHL* BS5 ...... **336** F4 🔲
Seneca St *EVILLE/WHL* BS5 ...... **336** F4
Seneca Wy *CHELTW* GL51 .... **93** K6
Serio Rd *GL* GL1 .... **4** E3
Sevelm *CHELTW* GL51 .... **115** G6 🔲
Seven Acres *GLE* GL4 .... **136** F4
Seven Acres La
 CBATH/BATHN BA1 .... **352** B6
Sevenacres Rd
 RSTROUD/NAIL GL6 .... **232** C7
Sevenleaze La
 RSTROUD/NAIL GL6 .... **160** F5
 RSTROUD/NAIL GL6 .... **184** D1
Seven Stars Rd *CIND* GL14 ...... **154** A1
Seventh Av *GLE* GL4 .... **159** M1
 HORF/LLZ BS7 .... **326** D2 🔲
Seven View Rd *THNB/SVB* BS35.. **293** L1
Severn Av *CHEP* NP16 .... **270** C4
Severnbank Av *LYD* GL15 .... **201** L8
Severn Br *THNB/SVB* BS35 .... **291** C3
Severn Cl *WUE* GL12 .... **276** C7 🔲
Severn Crs *CHEP* NP16 .... **270** A4
Severn Dr *BRKLY* GL13 .... **227** G7
 THNB/SVB BS35 .... **293** K1
Severn La *BRKLY* GL13 .... **250** A2
Severn Oaks *VGL* GL2 .... **159** H4
Severn Rd *AVONM* BS11 .... **314** B3
 BRKLY GL13 .... **226** D3
 CHELTE/BC GL52 .... **3** J3
 DSLY GL11.............................. **229** G7
 GL GL1 .... **4** B7
 HNBRY/STHM BS10 .... **314** B1
 LYD GL15 .... **225** K1
 STNHO GL10 .... **207** G3
 THNB/SVB BS35 .... **304** F2
Severn St *CIND* GL14 .... **155** J7
Severnvale Dr *VGL* GL2 .... **159** C2
Severn Vw *CIND* GL14 .... **154** C2
Severn View Rd *LYD* GL15 ...... **177** L8
 LYD GL15 .... **223** M5
Severn Wy *BRKLY* GL13 .... **203** L6
 BRKLY GL13 .... **226** C6
 BRSTK/PCHW BS34 .... **316** B2
 GL GL1 .... **4** B3
 KEYN BS31 .... **348** B7
 RTEWK/TIB GL19 .... **69** C4
 THNB/SVB BS35 .... **291** G4
 THNB/SVB BS35 .... **304** B5
 VGL GL2 .... **135** H4
 VGL GL2 .... **179** K2
Severnwood Gdns
 THNB/SVB BS35 .... **304** C6
Sevier St *CBRISNE* BS2 .... **336** C1
Seymour Av *HORF/LLZ* BS7 ..... **326** A7 🔲
Seymour Ga *CHCAM* GL55 .... **12** E8 🔲
Seymour Pl *COTS* GL54 .... **74** C6
 TEWK GL20 .... **48** A6
Seymour Rd *EVILLE/WHL* BS5 .... **336** C2
 GL GL1 .... **135** M5
 HORF/LLZ BS7 .... **326** A7
 KGWD/HNM BS15 .... **337** L2 🔲
 MANG/FISH BS16 .... **327** M7
Seyton Wk *BRSTK/PCHW* BS34... **317** G6
Sezincote Cl
 RSTROUD/NAIL GL6 .... **209** M6 🔲
Shackel Hendy Ms
 MANG/FISH BS16 .... **328** D6 🔲
Shackleton Av *YATE/CS* BS37 .... **320** B3
Shackleton Cl *BWTH/CHD* GL3 .... **113** K6
Shadwell Rd *HORF/LLZ* BS7 ..... **325** M8
Shaftesbury Av
 RDLND/MONT BS6 .... **336** A2
Shaft Rd *THNB/SVB* BS35 .... **304** C3
Shakespeare Av *HORF/LLZ* BS7 .. **326** C3
 VGL GL2 .... **135** L7
Shakespeare Ct *TEWK* GL20 .... **48** A5 🔲
Shakespeare Rd *CHELTW* GL51.... **115** G2
 DSLY GL11.............................. **253** L4
Shaldon Rd *HORF/LLZ* BS7 ...... **326** C7
Shalford Cl *CIR* GL7 .... **238** B4 🔲
The Shallows *KEYN* BS31 .... **349** H8
The Shambles *STROUD* GL5 .... **208** E4 🔲
Shamrock Cl *BWTH/CHD* GL3 .... **113** H5
Shamrock Rd
 EVILLE/WHL BS5...................... **326** F8 🔲
Shanklin Dr
 BRSTK/PCHW BS34 .... **316** D8 🔲
Shannon Ct *THNB/SVB* BS35 .... **293** M3 🔲
Shannon Wy *TEWK* GL20 .... **48** E4
Shapcott Cl
 BRSG/KWL/STAPK BS4........... **346** D2 🔲
Shaplands
 HNLZ/SM/SNYPK/WT BS9....... **325** H7
Sharps Wy *CHEP* NP16 .... **270** B6 🔲
Sharry La *STRAT* CV37................ **9** G1
Shaw Green La *CHELTE/BC* GL52.. **94** D5
Shaymoor La *THNB/SVB* BS35 .. **305** H7
Shearmore Cl *HORF/LLZ* BS7 ... **326** C3
Shearwater Gv *VGL* GL2 .... **112** F5
Sheene La *BMSTR* BS3 .... **335** L8
Sheep Fair La
 CHPMW/MSHF SN14 .... **342** B4

Sheepscombe Cl
 CHELTW GL51 .... **115** G3 🔲
Sheeps Cft
 BMSTRD/HC/WWD BS13......... **345** J7
Sheep St *BUR/CRTN* OX18 .... **173** M6
 CHCAM GL55 .... **34** D1
 CIR GL7 .... **238** C3
 COTS GL54............................. **102** A3
 SHPSTR CV36 .... **16** B5
Sheepwood Cl
 HNBRY/STHM BS10 .... **325** J2
Sheepwood Rd
 HNBRY/STHM BS10 .... **325** J1
Sheevaun Ct *VGL* GL2 .... **112** F6 🔲
Sheldare Barton
 EVILLE/WHL BS5...................... **337** K4 🔲
Sheldrake Dr *MANG/FISH* BS16 .. **327** H5
Shelduck Rd *GL* GL2 .... **158** E2
Shellard Rd *BRSTK/PCHW* BS34 .. **316** C8
Shellards La *THNB/SVB* BS35 ... **293** L1
 THNB/SVB BS35 .... **308** B1
Shellards Rd
 OLD/WMLY/WICK BS30 .... **338** B8
Shelley Av *CHELTW* GL51 .... **115** G2
 VGL GL2 .... **135** L7
Shelley Cl *EVILLE/WHL* BS5 ...... **337** H3
Shelley Rd *CHELT* GL51 .... **115** G2
Shelley Wy *HORF/LLZ* BS7 ...... **326** C3
Shellmor Av *BRSTK/PCHW* BS34.. **316** D2
Shellmor Cl *ALMDB* BS32 .... **316** F2 🔲
 BRSTK/PCHW BS34 .... **316** E2
Shelly Rd *DSLY* GL11 .... **253** L4
Shephard Md *TEWK* GL20 .... **47** M6
Shepherdine Cl *GL* GL15 .... **201** L8
Shepherd Rd *GL* GL1 .... **135** K8
Shepherd's Cl *CHCAM* GL55 ...... **34** D1
 LED HR8 .... **19** M5
 MANG/FISH BS16 .... **328** A6
 STROUD GL5 .... **208** F3 🔲
Shepherds Cft *STROUD* GL5 .... **208** F3
Shepherd's Leaze *WUE* GL12 ... **277** L5 🔲
Shepherds Md *TET* GL8 .... **282** A2
Shepherds Wk *WUE* GL12 .... **277** L5 🔲
Shepherds Wy *BWTH/CHD* GL3 .. **113** H4
 CIR GL7 .... **238** C5
 COTS GL54............................. **102** B3
 COTS GL54............................. **169** H1
Shepherds Well *STROUD* GL5 ... **232** F2 🔲
Sheppard Rd *MANG/FISH* BS16 .. **327** L5
Sheppard Wy
 RSTROUD/NAIL GL6 .... **233** C4
Shepperdine Rd
 THNB/SVB BS35 .... **248** F7
Shepton Wk *BMSTR* BS3 .... **345** L1
Sherborne Cl *STNHO* GL10....... **207** H3 🔲
Sherborne La *COTS* GL54 .... **148** B5
Sherborne Pl *CHELTE/BC* GL52 .... **2** F5
Sherborne St *CHELTE/BC* GL52 .... **2** F4
 CIR GL7 .... **244** E7
 COTS GL54............................. **123** H5
 GL GL1 .... **5** C4
Sherbourne Av *ALMDB* BS32 ... **317** C5
Sherbourne Cl
 KGWD/HNM BS15 .... **338** B1
Sherbourne Ct *STNHO* GL10 ... **207** H3 🔲
Sherbourne Rd *EVILLE/WHL* BS5.. **337** C3
Shergar Cl *GLE* GL4 .... **136** F7
Sheridan Rd *HORF/LLZ* BS7 ..... **326** C2
Sheridan Wy
 OLD/WMLY/WICK BS30 .... **348** C5
Sherrin Wy
 BMSTRD/HC/WWD BS13......... **345** C8
The Sherry *COTS* GL54 .... **76** E6
Sherston Cl *MANG/FISH* BS16 ... **327** K6
Sherston Rd *HORF/LLZ* BS7 ..... **326** A3 🔲
 MALM SN16 .... **303** G7
Sherwell Rd
 BRSG/KWL/STAPK BS4........... **337** C8
Sherwood Cl *KEYN* BS31 .... **348** A6
Sherwood Gn *VGL* GL2 .... **112** B5
Sherwood Rd *KEYN* BS31 .... **348** A6
 KGWD/HNM BS15 .... **337** J2
 TET GL8 .... **281** M7
Shetland Dr
 HNBRY/STHM BS10 .... **325** M2
Shields Av *HORF/LLZ* BS7 .... **326** C3
Shiels Dr *ALMDB* BS32 .... **316** F4 🔲
Shilton Cl *KGWD/HNM* BS15 .... **338** B4 🔲
Shimsey Cl *MANG/FISH* BS16 ... **327** L5 🔲
Shipham Cl *HGRV/WHIT* BS14 .. **346** D6
Ship La *CBRIS/FH* BS1................ **7** G7
Shipley Mow *MANG/FISH* BS16.. **328** D5
Shipley Rd
 HNLZ/SM/SNYPK/WT BS9....... **325** J3
Shipnran Ct
 MANG/FISH BS16 .... **328** A7 🔲
Shipston Rd *SHPSTR* CV36 .... **61** H4
Shipton HI *MALM* SN16 .... **303** J7 🔲
Shipton's Grave La
 RSTROUD/NAIL GL6 .... **256** C2
Shipway Ct *CHELTE/BC* GL52 .... **72** B7 🔲
Shirehampton Rd *AVONM* BS11.. **324** C4
 HNLZ/SM/SNYPK/WT BS9....... **324** E5 🔲
Shire HI *CHPMW/MSHF* SN14 .... **332** B4
Shire Wy *YATE/CS* BS37 .... **319** L5
Shockerwick La
 CBATH/BATHN BA1 .... **352** D7
Shophouse Rd *LYD* GL15 .... **175** K8
Shop La *BAD* GL9 .... **323** G1
Short Hedges Cl *COTS* GL54 ..... **169** K2 🔲
Shorthill Rd *YATE/CS* BS37 ...... **319** L7
Shortlands Rd *AVONM* BS11 .... **324** C2 🔲
Short La *LGASH* BA41 .... **344** B1
Short St *CBRISNE* BS2 .... **7** M6
 CHELTS GL53.......................... **115** L5
Short Wy *THNB/SVB* BS35 .... **293** K4
Shortwood HI *MANG/FISH* BS16.. **328** F6
Shortwood Rd
 BMSTRD/HC/WWD BS13......... **346** A8
 MANG/FISH BS16 .... **329** A7
 RSTROUD/NAIL GL6 .... **232** B2
Shortwood Vw
 KGWD/HNM BS15 .... **338** B3 🔲
Shortwood Wk
 BMSTRD/HC/WWD BS13......... **346** A8 🔲
Shotts La *NWNT* GL18............... **85** C5
Shoulderway La *SHPSTR* CV36 ... **38** B2

Showering Cl
  HGRV/WHIT BS14 ...... **346** F6 🔟
Showering Rd
  HGRV/WHIT BS14 ...... **346** F6
Shrubbery Cottages
  RDLND/MONT BS6 ...... **335** K1 🔟
Shrubbery Rd *MANG/FISH* BS16.. **327** M6
Shrublands *CHELTS* GL53 ...... **116** B6
Shurdington Rd
  BWTH/CHD GL3 ...... **138** B6
  CHELTS GL53 ...... **115** K6
  CHELTW GL51 ...... **138** E3
Shutehay Dr *DSLY* GL11 ...... **229** H6
Shuter Rd
  BMSTRD/HC/WWD BS13 ...... **345** H6 🔟
Shute St *STNHO* GL10 ...... **207** J8
Shutter La *CHELTE/BC* GL52 ...... **72** B3
Sibland *THNB/SVB* BS35.. ...... **293** M3
Sibland Cl *THNB/SVB* BS35 ...... **293** M3 🔟
Sibland Rd *THNB/SVB* BS35 ...... **293** M2
Sibland Wy *THNB/SVB* BS35 ...... **293** L3
Sibree Cl *RSTROUD/NAIL* GL6 ...... **209** L8
Sidcot *BRSG/KWL/STAPK* BS4 ...... **347** J1
Siddington Rd *CIR* GL7 ...... **238** E5
Sideland Cl *HGRV/WHIT* BS14 ...... **347** C5
Sidelands Rd *MANG/FISH* BS16.. **327** C5
Sidings Rd *CHNTN* OX7 ...... **104** F6
The Sidings *WUE* GL12 ...... **276** D6 🔟
Sidmouth Gdns *BMSTR* BS3 ...... **345** M1 🔟
Sidmouth Rd *BMSTR* BS3 ...... **345** M1
Sidney Dr *CHELTE/BC* GL52 ...... **2** F7
  GL GL1 ...... **5** J7
Signal Rd *MANG/FISH* BS16 ...... **328** A7
Silbury Rd *BMSTR* BS3 ...... **345** G1
Silcock Cl *BWTH/CHD* GL3 ...... **113** H4
Silcox Rd
  BMSTRD/HC/WWD BS13 ...... **345** L7 🔟
Silklands Gv
  HNLZ/SM/SNYPK/WT BS9 ...... **324** E5 🔟
Silk Mill La *COTS* GL54 ...... **74** D6
Silley's Cl *CHEP* NP16 ...... **270** E1 🔟
Silverbirch Cl
  BRSTK/PCHW BS34 ...... **316** F4
Silver Birch Cl *VGL* GL2 ...... **159** G2 🔟
Silver Cl *GL* GL1 ...... **135** L8
Silverhill Rd *HNBRY/STHM* BS10.. **315** C8
Silver St *CBRIS/FH* BS1 ...... **6** F2 🔟
  CHPMW/MSHF SN14 ...... **343** K8
  CIND GL14 ...... **154** E4
  CIR GL7 ...... **238** C2 🔟
  CIR GL7 ...... **263** H3
  DSLY GL11 ...... **253** K2 🔟
  DSLY GL11 ...... **253** K2 🔟
  MALM SN16 ...... **303** J8 🔟
  MTCHDN GL17 ...... **130** C2
  TET GL8 ...... **282** A4 🔟
  VGL GL2 ...... **156** A8
Silverthorn Cl *CHELT* GL50 ...... **115** K6 🔟
Silverthorne La *CBRISNE* BS2 ...... **7** L6
Silverton Ct
  BRSG/KWL/STAPK BS4 ...... **346** B2 🔟
Silvertree Gdns *STROUD* GL5 ...... **209** G8 🔟
Silverwood Wy
  CHELTW GL51 ...... **115** G6 🔟
Simmonds Rd *GLE* GL4 ...... **137** H4
Simmonds Vw
  BRSTK/PCHW BS34 ...... **317** H7
Simon Rd *VGL* GL2 ...... **112** E6
Simpson Rd *SHPSTR* CV36 ...... **16** B6
Sims La *VGL* GL2 ...... **135** H7
Sinclair Rd *CHELTW* GL51 ...... **138** F2
Sinderberry Dr *TEWK* GL20 ...... **49** C2
Sinope St *GL* GL1 ...... **5** H7
Sion Hl *CFTN/FAIL* BS8 ...... **335** H5
Sion La *CFTN/FAIL* BS8 ...... **335** H4
Sion Pl *CFTN/FAIL* BS8 ...... **335** H4
Sion Rd *BMSTR* BS3 ...... **335** L8 🔟
Sir John's La *EVILLE/WHL* BS5.. **326** D7
  HORF/LLZ BS7 ...... **326** D7
Siskin Rd *COTS* GL54 ...... **124** C6
Sissinghurst Gv *CHELTW* GL51 . **115** J6 🔟
Sisson End *VGL* GL2 ...... **136** F1
Sisson Rd *VGL* GL2 ...... **136** E1
Siston Cl *KGWD/HNM* BS15 ...... **338** C1
Siston La
  OLD/WMLY/WICK BS30 ...... **339** G2
Siston Pk *KGWD/HNM* BS15 ...... **338** C1
Sivell Cl *VGL* GL2 ...... **112** C5
Six Acres *GLE* GL4 ...... **137** H8
Sixth Av *HORF/LLZ* BS7 ...... **326** C2
Skillicorne Ms *CHELTW* GL51 ...... **115** J3 🔟
Skinner St *GL* GL1 ...... **4** F3
Skippon Ct *KGWD/HNM* BS15 ...... **338** A6 🔟
Skylark Wy *GLE* GL4 ...... **136** D6
Slade Brook *STROUD* GL5 ...... **209** G3
Slade Rd *LYD* GL15 ...... **177** K8
The Slade *DSLY* GL11 ...... **253** K3 🔟
Slad La *RSTROUD/NAIL* GL6 ...... **209** J1
  STROUD GL5 ...... **209** H3
Slad Rd *RSTROUD/NAIL* GL6 ...... **185** K5
  STROUD GL5 ...... **208** F3
The Slad *CIND* GL14 ...... **154** F3
Slaney St *GL* GL1 ...... **136** B4
Sleep La *HGRV/WHIT* BS14.. ...... **346** E6
Slimbridge Cl *YATE/CS* BS37 ...... **320** B4
Slimbridge La *BRKLY* GL13 ...... **227** K2
Slimbridge Rd *GL* GL1 ...... **135** M8
Sloan St *EVILLE/WHL* BS5 ...... **336** F3
Slough La *CHPMW/MSHF* SN14 . **341** H7
Slymbridge Av
  HNBRY/STHM BS10 ...... **315** J7
Smallbrook Rd *BDWAY* WR12 ...... **32** F1
Small La *MANG/FISH* BS16 ...... **327** C6
Small St *CBRIS/FH* BS1 ...... **6** F3 🔟
  CBRISNE BS2.. ...... **7** M6
Smarts Gn *YATE/CS* BS37 ...... **320** E3
Smeaton Rd *CBRIS/FH* BS1 ...... **335** H4
Smith Barry Crs *COTS* GL54 ...... **124** D7
Smith Barry Rd *COTS* GL54 ...... **124** D7
Smithmead
  BMSTRD/HC/WWD BS13 ...... **345** K6
Smiths Ct *TEWK* GL20 ...... **48** A3 🔟
Smiths Hl *CLFD* GL16 ...... **176** A5
Smith's La *TEWK* GL20 ...... **48** A5 🔟
Smith St *CHPMW/MSHF* SN14 ... **333** J4
Smithville Cl *LYD* GL15 ...... **199** G5
Smithville Pl *LYD* GL15 ...... **199** G6

Smithy Cl *CLFD* GL16 ...... **127** K8
Smithy La *COTS* GL54 ...... **74** C2
Smithyman Ct *CIND* GL14 ...... **155** J7 🔟
The Smithy *CIR* GL7 ...... **238** E4 🔟
  LYD GL15 ...... **178** E8 🔟
Smythe Cft *HGRV/WHIT* BS14.. ... **346** C8
Smythe Rd *CHELTW* GL51 ...... **93** K5
Smyth Rd *BMSTR* BS3 ...... **335** J2
Snake Dr *CIR* GL7 ...... **218** C6
Snead Pk *GLE* GL4 ...... **137** H6 🔟
Sneedhams Rd *GLE* GL4 ...... **160** D1
Snipehill Br *CHEP* NP16 ...... **270** E1
Snipe Rd *COTS* GL54 ...... **124** C7 🔟
Snowberry Wk
  EVILLE/WHL BS5 ...... **337** C3 🔟
Snowdon Cl *MANG/FISH* BS16 ... **327** H7
Snowdon Gdns *BWTH/CHD* GL3.. **113** J4
Snowdonia Rd *TEWK* GL20 ...... **48** C7
Snowdon Rd *MANG/FISH* BS16... **327** H6
Snowdrop Cl *GLE* GL4 ...... **137** C6 🔟
Snowshill Cl *GLE* GL4 ...... **136** F4 🔟
Snowshill Dr *CHELTE/BC* GL52 ... **72** A4 🔟
Snowshill Rd *BDWAY* WR12.. ...... **32** F4
  GLE GL4 ...... **137** C4
Snowswick La *FGDN* SN7 ...... **269** C4
Sodbury Rd *WUE* GL12 ...... **296** C8
Solent Wy *THNB/SVB* BS35 ...... **293** M4 🔟
Solsbury La *CBATH/BATHN* BA1 .. **352** A7
Solway Rd *CHELTW* GL51 ...... **92** F8
Somerby Cl *ALMDB* BS32 ...... **316** F4 🔟
Somerdale Av
  BRSG/KWL/STAPK BS4.. ...... **346** C8
Somerdale Rd *KEYN* BS31 ...... **348** B4
Somerdale Rd North
  KEYN BS31 ...... **348** B4
Somerford Rd *CIR* GL7 ...... **238** C4
Somergate Rd *CHELTW* GL51 ...... **92** F7
Somermead *BMSTR* BS3 ...... **345** L2
Somerset Av *CHELTW* GL51 ...... **115** J1
  DSLY GL11 ...... **253** K3
  YATE/CS BS37 ...... **310** B8
Somerset Cl *WUE* GL12 ...... **277** G7
Somerset Crs
  BRSTK/PCHW BS34 ...... **317** H6 🔟
Somerset Pl *GL* GL1 ...... **4** D8 🔟
  TEWK GL20 ...... **48** B8 🔟
Somerset Rd
  BRSG/KWL/STAPK BS4.. ...... **336** C8
  CIND GL14 ...... **154** A4
Somerset Sq *CBRIS/FH* BS1.. ...... **7** G7
Somerset St *CBRIS/FH* BS1 ...... **7** H7
  CBRISNE BS2.. ...... **335** M3
Somerset Ter *BMSTR* BS3 ...... **336** A8
Somerset Wy *CHEP* NP16 ...... **270** B6
Somerton Cl *KGWD/HNM* BS15 .. **338** C4
Somerton Rd *HORF/LLZ* BS7 ...... **326** A5 🔟
Somerville Ct *CIR* GL7 ...... **238** B5 🔟
Somme Rd *CHELTE/BC* GL52 ...... **3** M3
Sommerville Rd
  RDLND/MONT BS6 ...... **326** A8
Sommerville Rd South
  RDLND/MONT BS6 ...... **336** B1 🔟
Sopwith Rd *COTS* GL54 ...... **124** C6
Sorrel Cl *GLE* GL4.. ...... **136** C7
  THNB/SVB BS35 ...... **293** M1
Soundwell Rd
  KGWD/HNM BS15 ...... **337** L2 🔟
Southall Ter *NWNT* GL18 ...... **107** L1
Southam La *CHELTE/BC* GL52 ...... **94** B3
South Av *TEWK* GL20 ...... **49** J4
  YATE/CS BS37 ...... **319** K2
Southbank *STROUD* GL5 ...... **232** B1
Southbrook Rd *GLE* GL4 ...... **136** E2
South Cerney Rd *CIR* GL7 ...... **238** F7
South Cl *VGL* GL2.. ...... **5** M1
Southcourt Cl *CHELTS* GL53 ...... **115** M6
Southcourt Dr *CHELTS* GL53 ...... **115** M6
South Cft
  HNLZ/SM/SNYPK/WT BS9 ...... **325** L4
South Dene
  HNLZ/SM/SNYPK/WT BS9 ...... **325** C5
Southdown Rd
  HNLZ/SM/SNYPK/WT BS9 ...... **325** H3
The Southend *LED* HR8 ...... **20** A4
Southend La *NWNT* GL18 ...... **86** C4
Southern Av *CFTN/FAIL* BS8 ...... **6** A5 🔟
Southernhay *CFTN/FAIL* BS8.. ...... **6** A5
  MANG/FISH BS16 ...... **327** L7
Southernhay Av *CFTN/FAIL* BS8 .. **6** A5
Southern Rd *CHELTS* GL53.. ...... **116** A7
Southey Av *KGWD/HNM* BS15 ... **337** M2
Southey St *CBRISNE* BS2 ...... **336** B2
Southfield
  RSTROUD/NAIL GL6 ...... **233** H5 🔟
  TET GL8 ...... **281** M5
Southfield Ap *CHELTS* GL53.. ...... **116** A7
Southfield Av
  KGWD/HNM BS15 ...... **338** A2
Southfield Cl *CHELTS* GL53 ...... **116** A7
Southfield Ct
  HNLZ/SM/SNYPK/WT BS9 ...... **325** J4 🔟
Southfield Ri *CHELTS* GL53 ...... **116** A7
Southfield Rd *CLFD* GL16 ...... **151** K8
  GLE GL4 ...... **136** B7
  HNLZ/SM/SNYPK/WT BS9 ...... **325** J4
  RDLND/MONT BS6 ...... **335** M2 🔟
  STROUD GL5 ...... **232** C1
Southgate Crs *STROUD* GL5 ...... **208** C6 🔟
Southgate Dr *CHELTS* GL53 ...... **3** G7
Southgate Gdns
  STROUD GL5 ...... **208** C6 🔟
South Gn *GL* GL1 ...... **4** E6
South Green St
  CFTN/FAIL BS8 ...... **335** H5 🔟
South Gv *RDLND/MONT* BS6.. ...... **325** L6
South Hayes *EVILLE/WHL* BS5.. ... **326** D7
Southleigh Rd *CFTN/FAIL* BS8.. ...... **6** A1
South Liberty La *BMSTR* BS3 ...... **345** G2
  BMSTRD/HC/WWD BS13 ...... **345** K1 🔟
South Lynn Gdns
  SHPSTR CV36 ...... **16** B6 🔟
Southmead Cir *CIR* GL7 ...... **238** E5
Southmead La
  RSTROUD/NAIL GL6 ...... **186** C5
Southmead Rd
  BRSTK/PCHW BS34 ...... **326** A2

HNBRY/STHM BS10 ...... **325** L3
HNLZ/SM/SNYPK/WT BS9.. ...... **325** K4
Southmead Wy
  HNBRY/STHM BS10 ...... **325** M3
Southover Cl
  HNBRY/STHM BS9.. ...... **325** J3
South Pde *LED* HR8 ...... **20** A4
South Rd *ALMDB* BS32 ...... **306** F5
  BMSTR BS3 ...... **335** L8 🔟
  CLFD GL16 ...... **151** J8
  CLFD GL16 ...... **175** M1
  KGWD/HNM BS15 ...... **337** M3
  LYD GL15 ...... **201** J7
  RDLND/MONT BS6 ...... **335** L1
Southsea Rd
  BRSTK/PCHW BS34 ...... **316** C4
Southside *TET* GL8 ...... **302** A3
Southside Cl *AVONM* BS11.. ...... **324** D4
South St *BMSTR* BS3 ...... **335** K8
  DSLY GL11 ...... **254** E2
South Vw *FRCTL/WBN* BS36 ...... **318** D4
  MANG/FISH BS16 ...... **328** A6
South View Crs
  FRCTL/WBN BS36 ...... **318** F5
South View Ri
  FRCTL/WBN BS36 ...... **318** F5
South View Wy *CHELTE/BC* GL52 .. **94** E7
Southview Pl *BMSTR* BS3 ...... **6** E8
Southville Rd *BMSTR* BS3 ...... **6** D8
South Wy *CIR* GL7 ...... **238** C3
Southway Dr
  OLD/WMLY/WICK BS30 ...... **338** F6
Southwell St *CBRISE* BS2 ...... **6** D1
Southwood Av
  HNLZ/SM/SNYPK/WT BS9.. ...... **324** E3
Southwood Cl *CIND* GL14 ...... **154** B2
Southwood Dr
  HNLZ/SM/SNYPK/WT BS9.. ...... **324** D3
Southwood Dr East
  HNLZ/SM/SNYPK/WT BS9.. ...... **324** E3
Southwood La *CHELT* GL50 ...... **2** B8
Sovereign Cha *RTEWK/TIB* GL19 .. **66** E4
Spa Gdns *TEWK* GL20 ...... **48** D4
Spalding Cl *CBRISNE* BS2.. ...... **336** C6
Spaniorum Vw *THNB/SVB* BS35.. **315** H1
Spark Hl *DSLY* GL11 ...... **229** H5 🔟
Spa Rd *GL* GL1 ...... **4** D8
Spar Rd *YATE/CS* BS37 ...... **319** M1
Sparrow Hl *CLFD* GL16 ...... **151** J8
Sparrows La *RWYE* HR9 ...... **84** F4
Spartan Cl *GLE* GL4 ...... **137** C5 🔟
Spartley Dr
  BMSTRD/HC/WWD BS13 ...... **345** H5
Spartley Wk
  BMSTRD/HC/WWD BS13 ...... **345** H5 🔟
Speculation Rd *CIND* GL14 ...... **129** M8
Speech House Rd *CIND* GL14 ...... **153** L5
  CLFD GL16 ...... **152** A8
  CLFD GL16 ...... **152** E7
Speedwell *CLFD* GL16 ...... **151** M7
Speedwell Av
  EVILLE/WHL BS5 ...... **336** F4 🔟
Speedwell Cl *GLE* GL4 ...... **137** C6
  THNB/SVB BS35 ...... **293** M1
Speedwell Rd *EVILLE/WHL* BS5.. **337** H2
  KGWD/HNM BS15 ...... **337** K2
Spencer Cl *BWTH/CHD* GL3 ...... **137** H4
Spencer's Tft *THNB/SVB* BS35 ... **293** K5
Spenser Av *CHELTW* GL51 ...... **115** C2
Spenser Rd *CHELTW* GL51 ...... **115** C2
Sperringate *CIR* GL7 ...... **238** D4 🔟
Spey Cl *THNB/SVB* BS35 ...... **293** L3
  VGL GL2 ...... **159** H1
Spider La *STROUD* GL5 ...... **208** F5
Spillman's Pitch *STROUD* GL5 ... **208** C5 🔟
Spillman's Rd *STROUD* GL5 ...... **208** C5
The Spindles *CHELTS* GL53 ...... **115** J7
Spine Rd East *HGHW* SN6 ...... **263** J8
Spine Rd West *GLE* GL4 ...... **286** C1
Spinnaker Rd *VGL* GL2 ...... **135** K3
Spinney Ct *STROUD* GL5 ...... **233** H2 🔟
Spinney Rd *GLE* GL4 ...... **136** F4
The Spinney *ALMDB* BS32 ...... **317** C4
  CHELTE/BC GL52 ...... **94** A7
  CIR GL7 ...... **244** E7
  FRCTL/WBN BS36 ...... **318** D4 🔟
Spires Vw *MANG/FISH* BS16 ...... **327** C6 🔟
Spire Wy *GLE* GL4 ...... **136** F3
Spitalgate La *CIR* GL7 ...... **238** C2
Spital La *HGHW* SN6 ...... **289** C4
Spittle Leys *COTS* GL54 ...... **74** C5
Splatt Br *VGL* GL2 ...... **205** C1
Spout Hl *LYD* GL15 ...... **224** A4
Spouthouse La *DSLY* GL11 ...... **229** H6
Spout La *MTCHDN* GL17 ...... **129** K4
Spratsgate La *CIR* GL7 ...... **238** C7
  CIR GL7 ...... **262** C6
Spread Eagle Rd *GL* GL1 ...... **4** F5
Springbank Cl *CHELTW* GL51 ...... **92** F7
Springbank Dr *CHELTW* GL51 ...... **92** E8
Springbank Gv *CHELTW* GL51 ...... **92** E8
Springbank Rd *CHELTW* GL51 ...... **92** E8
Springbank Wy *CHELTW* GL51 ...... **92** F7
Spring Di *RTEWK/TIB* GL19 ...... **133** C1
Springdale *RWYE* HR9 ...... **84** F3 🔟
Springdale Cl *VGL* GL2 ...... **158** F3
Springfield *COTS* GL54 ...... **123** C6
  DSLY GL11 ...... **229** C7
  MIM GL56 ...... **35** H8
  TEWK GL20 ...... **48** D4
  THNB/SVB BS35 ...... **293** L3 🔟
  VGL GL2 ...... **159** G4
Springfield Av *HORF/LLZ* BS7 ...... **326** B6
  MANG/FISH BS16 ...... **328** C5
Springfield Cl *CHELTW* GL51 ...... **114** D4
  CLFD GL16 ...... **175** K1
  MANG/FISH BS16 ...... **328** C4 🔟
  SHPSTR CV36 ...... **16** B7
Springfield Dr *CIND* GL14 ...... **154** A1
Springfield Gv
  HNLZ/SM/SNYPK/WT BS9.. ...... **325** K6
Springfield La *BDWAY* WR12.. ...... **32** E2
Springfield Rd *CIR* GL7 ...... **218** C6
  CIR GL7 ...... **238** B5
  LYD GL15 ...... **201** J7
  MANG/FISH BS16 ...... **328** C5 🔟
  RDLND/MONT BS6 ...... **335** M2
  SHPSTR CV36 ...... **16** B7

STROUD GL5 ...... **207** M3 🔟
STROUD GL5 ...... **208** E3
Springfields *BRSTK/PCHW* BS34.. **326** C1
  TET GL8 ...... **282** B3
Springfields Ct *DSLY* GL11 ...... **229** C7
Spring Gdns
  BRSG/KWL/STAPK BS4.. ...... **346** C2
  CIR GL7 ...... **218** C6
  CIR GL7 ...... **244** E7
Spring Gv *LED* HR8 ...... **20** A5
Spring Hl *CBRISNE* BS2 ...... **335** M5 🔟
Spring Meadow Rd *LYD* GL15 ...... **201** J7
Springhill *DSLY* GL11 ...... **229** M7
Spring Hl *KGWD/HNM* BS15 ...... **338** A1
  RSTROUD/NAIL GL6 ...... **232** D7
  STNHO GL10 ...... **206** C3
Springhill Cl *RSTROUD/NAIL* GL6.. **232** D7
Springhill Crs
  RSTROUD/NAIL GL6 ...... **232** D7
Springhill (Old Court)
  DSLY GL11 ...... **229** K8 🔟
Spring La *CHELTE/BC* GL52 ...... **94** D6
  CHELTE/BC GL52 ...... **95** G1
  CHNTN OX7 ...... **125** K7
  STROUD GL5 ...... **208** E5
  STROUD GL5 ...... **209** G8
Springleaze
  BRSG/KWL/STAPK BS4.. ...... **346** C2
  MANG/FISH BS16 ...... **328** C4
Spring Meadow Rd *LYD* GL15.. ... **201** J7
The Springs *LYD* GL15 ...... **201** J8 🔟
Spring St *BMSTR* BS3 ...... **7** H8
Spring Street Pl *BMSTR* BS3 ...... **7** H8
Springvale *COTS* GL54 ...... **123** H3
Springville Cl
  OLD/WMLY/WICK BS30 ...... **338** C8 🔟
Springwell Gdns
  HNBRY/STHM BS10 ...... **314** F9
Springwood Dr
  HNBRY/STHM BS10 ...... **314** F9
Spruce Ride *CLFD* GL16 ...... **153** G7
Spruce Rd *CLFD* GL16 ...... **151** M7
Spruce Wy
  BRSTK/PCHW BS34 ...... **316** A4 🔟
Squires Cl *RSTROUD/NAIL* GL6 ... **209** L8
Squires Ct
  OLD/WMLY/WICK BS30 ...... **338** B8 🔟
Squires Leaze *THNB/SVB* BS35.. **293** M1
The Squires *BDWAY* WR12 ...... **32** B1 🔟
Squirrel Cl *VGL* GL2 ...... **159** G4
Stackpool Rd *BMSTR* BS3 ...... **6** E8
Stadium Rd *RDLND/MONT* BS6 .. **325** L6
Stafford Cl *CLFD* GL16 ...... **151** M8 🔟
Stafford Crs *THNB/SVB* BS35 ...... **293** K2
Stafford Rd *CBRISNE* BS2 ...... **336** C1 🔟
Staffords Ct
  OLD/WMLY/WICK BS30 ...... **338** C5 🔟
Stafford St *BMSTR* BS3 ...... **6** E9
  BMSTR BS3 ...... **335** M8
Stag Hl *LYD* GL15 ...... **177** J8
Stainer Cl
  BRSG/KWL/STAPK BS4.. ...... **345** M5 🔟
Staites Orch *GLE* GL4 ...... **137** G8
Stamage's La
  RSTROUD/NAIL GL6 ...... **185** G4
Stambourne La *BRKLY* GL13 ...... **227** G3
Stamp's Meadow *VGL* GL2 ...... **112** B6 🔟
Stanborough La *COTS* GL54 ...... **120** F4
Stanbridge Cl
  MANG/FISH BS16 ...... **328** B5 🔟
Stanbridge Rd
  MANG/FISH BS16 ...... **328** B5
Stanbury Av *MANG/FISH* BS16 .. **327** K6
Stanbury Ms *BWTH/CHD* GL3 ...... **137** K5
Stanbury Rd *BMSTR* BS3 ...... **336** A8
Stancombe La *COTS* GL54 ...... **74** D5
Stancombe Vw *COTS* GL54 ...... **74** D5
Standfast Rd
  HNBRY/STHM BS10 ...... **315** H9
Standish Av *BRSTK/PCHW* BS34.. **316** D2
Standish Cl
  HNBRY/STHM BS10 ...... **325** H2 🔟
Standish La *VGL* GL2 ...... **182** E5
Standle La *DSLY* GL11 ...... **252** C1
Standon Wy
  HNBRY/STHM BS10 ...... **325** L1 🔟
Stanfield Cl *HORF/LLZ* BS7 ...... **326** D5 🔟
Stanford Cl *FRCTL/WBN* BS36.. ... **318** B3
Stanford Rd *LYD* GL15 ...... **201** H8
  TEWK GL20 ...... **49** C3
Stanhope Rd
  OLD/WMLY/WICK BS30 ...... **348** B1
Stanhope St *CBRISNE* BS2.. ...... **7** L7
Stank La *VGL* GL2 ...... **158** E5
Stanks La *UUSV* WR8 ...... **24** B1
Stanleigh Ter *VGL* GL2 ...... **111** J4
Stanley Av *BRSTK/PCHW* BS34 .. **326** D1
  HORF/LLZ BS7 ...... **326** A8
Stanley Cha *EVILLE/WHL* BS5 ...... **336** F1
Stanley Crs *BRSTK/PCHW* BS34 .. **326** D1
Stanley Gdns
  OLD/WMLY/WICK BS30 ...... **338** D7
Stanley Hl *BRSG/KWL/STAPK* BS4.. **7** L9
Stanley Md *ALMDB* BS32 ...... **317** G1 🔟
Stanley Pk *EVILLE/WHL* BS5 ...... **336** D2
Stanley Park Rd
  MANG/FISH BS16 ...... **328** A8
Stanley Pl *CHELTW* GL51 ...... **92** F8 🔟
Stanley Rd *CHELTE/BC* GL52 ...... **3** L7
  GL GL1 ...... **136** A5
  KGWD/HNM BS15 ...... **338** D2
  RDLND/MONT BS6 ...... **335** L1
Stanley St *BMSTR* BS3 ...... **335** L8 🔟
Stanley St North
  BMSTR BS3 ...... **335** L9 🔟
Stanley St South *BMSTR* BS3 ...... **335** L8
Stanley Ter *BMSTR* BS3 ...... **345** J1 🔟
  GL GL1 ...... **136** A4 🔟
The Stanley *GLE* GL4 ...... **161** H1
Stanley Vw *STROUD* GL5 ...... **208** B6
Stanley Wk *GLE* GL4 ...... **161** H2
Stanmoor *GLE* GL4 ...... **136** F8
Stansby Crs *BWTH/CHD* GL3 ...... **113** J5

Stanshawe Crs *YATE/CS* BS37 ... **320** A2
Stanshawes Dr *YATE/CS* BS37 ... **319** M2
Stanshaw Rd *MANG/FISH* BS16 .. **327** J4
Stanshaws Cl
  BRSTK/PCHW BS34 ...... **316** D1
Stanthill Dr *DSLY* GL11 ...... **253** K3
Stanton Cl *KGWD/HNM* BS15 ...... **338** B2
Stanton Dr *CHELTW* GL51 ...... **93** J4
Stanton Rd *HNBRY/STHM* BS10 .. **326** A2
  STROUD GL5 ...... **208** A3
  TEWK GL20 ...... **48** B4
Stanton Wy *CHELTW* GL51 ...... **115** C3 🔟
Stantway La *CIND* GL14 ...... **156** E3
Stanway
  OLD/WMLY/WICK BS30 ...... **348** D2
Stanway Rd *BDWAY* WR12 ...... **53** L2
  CHELTW GL51 ...... **114** F3
  GLE GL4 ...... **136** E4
Stanway Wood Dr
  CHELTE/BC GL52 ...... **72** A7 🔟
Stanwick Crs *CHELTW* GL51 ...... **93** K6 🔟
Stanwick Dr *CHELTW* GL51 ...... **93** K6
Stanwick Gdns *CHELTW* GL51 ...... **93** K7
Staple Gv *KEYN* BS31 ...... **347** M6
Staple Grove Crs
  EVILLE/WHL BS5 ...... **337** J4 🔟
Staplehill Rd *MANG/FISH* BS16 ... **327** J7
Staples Rd *YATE/CS* BS37 ...... **319** M1 🔟
Stapleton Cl
  MANG/FISH BS16 ...... **326** F6 🔟
Stapleton Rd *EVILLE/WHL* BS5 ...... **7** L1
  EVILLE/WHL BS5 ...... **326** E8
  EVILLE/WHL BS5 ...... **336** D1
Star Barn Rd *FRCTL/WBN* BS36.. **318** A4
Star Hl *RSTROUD/NAIL* GL6 ...... **232** C6
Star La *MANG/FISH* BS16 ...... **327** H6
  TET GL8 ...... **257** M4
Starling Cl *STNHO* GL10 ...... **207** H3 🔟
Station Av *MANG/FISH* BS16 ...... **327** J4
Station Cl *BWTH/CHD* GL3 ...... **113** M6
  OLD/WMLY/WICK BS30 ...... **338** E3
  YATE/CS BS37 ...... **320** F3
Station Dr *TEWK* GL20 ...... **27** H5
Station La *HORF/LLZ* BS7 ...... **326** C7
  MTCHDN GL17 ...... **131** H1
  TEWK GL20 ...... **48** B4
Station Rd *AVONM* BS11 ...... **324** A5
  BAD GL9 ...... **323** H3
  BDWAY WR12 ...... **32** D2
  BRKLY GL13 ...... **227** C5
  BRSG/KWL/STAPK BS4.. ...... **346** F1
  BRSTK/PCHW BS34 ...... **316** C8
  BRSTK/PCHW BS34 ...... **316** E5
  BWTH/CHD GL3 ...... **113** L7
  CHCAM GL55 ...... **12** F8
  CHELTE/BC GL52 ...... **72** C7
  CHEP NP16 ...... **270** A3
  CHNTN OX7 ...... **104** B8
  CHNTN OX7 ...... **105** M1
  CIND GL14 ...... **155** H6
  CIR GL7 ...... **244** F6
  CIR GL7 ...... **261** H4
  CIR GL7 ...... **263** J4
  CLFD GL16 ...... **175** L4
  COTS GL54 ...... **118** C7
  COTS GL54 ...... **123** H4
  DSLY GL11 ...... **229** J6
  EVE WR11 ...... **29** L3
  FRCTL/WBN BS36 ...... **318** A7
  FRCTL/WBN BS36 ...... **318** E6
  GL GL1 ...... **5** G6
  HNBRY/STHM BS10 ...... **315** C8
  HORF/LLZ BS7 ...... **326** D7
  KEYN BS31 ...... **348** A5
  KGWD/HNM BS15 ...... **338** B8
  LYD GL15 ...... **224** B8
  LYD GL15 ...... **225** J2
  MANG/FISH BS16 ...... **327** J7
  MIM GL56 ...... **35** H8
  MIM GL56 ...... **58** D5
  OLD/WMLY/WICK BS30 ...... **338** E4
  RDLND/MONT BS6 ...... **335** M1
  RSTROUD/NAIL GL6 ...... **232** C2
  SHPSTR CV36 ...... **16** B4
  STROUD GL5 ...... **232** C2
  TEWK GL20 ...... **25** J3
  TEWK GL20 ...... **28** F7
  TEWK GL20 ...... **48** B4
  THNB/SVB BS35 ...... **304** D5
  THNB/SVB BS35 ...... **305** H7
  WUE GL12 ...... **276** C6
  WUE GL12 ...... **296** C5
  YATE/CS BS37 ...... **308** F8
  YATE/CS BS37 ...... **319** L1
Station Ter *CHELT* GL50 ...... **2** B4
  CIND GL14 ...... **154** A2
  TEWK GL20 ...... **48** A5
Station Ter *CIND* GL14 ...... **154** A2
Station Wy *MANG/FISH* BS16 ...... **327** J7
Staunton Cl *GLE* GL4 ...... **137** G7 🔟
Staunton Flds
  HGRV/WHIT BS14 ...... **346** E8
Staunton La *HGRV/WHIT* BS14 ... **346** E7
Staunton Rd *CLFD* GL16 ...... **150** E6
  CLFD GL16 ...... **151** G7
Staunton Wy
  HGRV/WHIT BS14 ...... **346** F7 🔟
Staveley Crs
  HNBRY/STHM BS10 ...... **325** L1
Staverton Connection
  CHELTW GL51 ...... **114** B2
Stavordale Gv
  HGRV/WHIT BS14 ...... **346** D5
Staynes Crs
  KGWD/HNM BS15 ...... **338** A3 🔟
Steam Mills Rd *CIND* GL14 ...... **129** M7
Stean Bridge Rd *ALMDB* BS32 ... **317** C5
Steel Av *LYD* GL15 ...... **201** K8
Steel Ct *OLD/WMLY/WICK* BS30 .. **338** B8
Steel Mills *KEYN* BS31 ...... **348** B7
Steels La *SHPSTR* CV36 ...... **39** J6
Steeple Cl *GLE* GL4 ...... **136** F3 🔟
Steeple Vw *LYD* GL15 ...... **225** J1 🔟
Steep St *CHEP* NP16 ...... **270** A3
Stella Gv *BMSTR* BS3 ...... **345** J1
Stella Wy *CHELTE/BC* GL52 ...... **71** M7
Stenders Rd *MTCHDN* GL17 ...... **130** C2
The Stenders *MTCHDN* GL17 ...... **130** B2

Stephens Dr OLD/WMLY/WICK BS30 ...... 338 B6
Stephens Pl CLFD GL16 ...... 175 M1
Stephen St EVILLE/WHL BS5 ...... 336 E3
Stepney Rd EVILLE/WHL BS5 ...... 336 E2
Stepney Wk EVILLE/WHL BS5 ...... 336 E2
Stepping Stone La RSTROUD/NAIL GL6 ...... 185 G5
Steps Cl DSLY GL11 ...... 229 H5
Step's La TET GL8 ...... 233 L8
Stepstairs La CIR GL7 ...... 238 D4
Sterling Cl COTS GL54 ...... 102 B5
Sterling Cl CHELTW GL51 ...... 115 K1
Sterncourt Rd MANG/FISH BS16 ...... 327 J4
Sterrys Rd RWYE HR9 ...... 85 G3
Stevans Cl VGL GL2 ...... 112 C6
Stevens Crs BMSTR BS3... ...... 7 J9
Stevens Wk ALMDB BS32 ...... 316 F3
Stevens Wy RSTROUD/NAIL GL6. 256 D2
Steward Rd TEWK GL20 ...... 49 G3
Stewarts Mill La GLE GL4 ...... 137 G7
Steway La CBATH/BATHN BA1 .. 352 C6
Stgiles'sroad TEWK GL20 ...... 27 G5
Stibbs Ct OLD/WMLY/WICK BS30 ... 338 B7
Stibbs Hl EVILLE/WHL BS5 ...... 337 J4
Sticky La VGL GL2 ...... 159 G5
Stidcote La WUE GL12 ...... 295 H6
Stidcot La WUE GL12 ...... 294 E6
Stile Acres AVONM BS11 ...... 324 C2
Stillhouse La BMSTR BS3... ...... 6 F8
Stillingfleet Rd BMSTRD/HC/WWD BS13... 345 L6
Stilman Cl BMSTRD/HC/WWD BS13... 345 H2
Stinchcombe YATE/CS BS37 ... 320 A2
Stirling Cl YATE/CS BS37 ...... 309 M7
Stirling Rd BRSG/KWL/STAPK BS4 ...... 336 E8
KEYN BS31 ...... 348 A7
Stirling Wy GL GL1 ...... 159 K1
The Stirrup STROUD GL5 ...... 207 M4
Stocken Cl BWTH/CHD GL3 ... 137 K5
Stock Hl THNB/SVB BS35 ...... 292 D2
Stock La BRKLY GL13 ...... 227 G8
Stockley Wy GLE GL4 ...... 160 F5
The Stocks RSTROUD/NAIL GL6 . 207 M1
Stockton Cl HGRV/WHIT BS14 ...... 346 B7
OLD/WMLY/WICK BS30 ... 338 D8
Stockwell Av MANG/FISH BS16.. 328 C5
Stockwell Cl MANG/FISH BS16 .. 328 C5
Stockwell Dr MANG/FISH BS16.. 328 C5
Stockwell Gn CIND GL14 ...... 154 B5
Stockwell La CHELTE/BC GL52 ... 72 FB
LYD GL15 ...... 224 F3
Stockwells MIM GL56 ...... 58 D6
Stockwood Crs BRSG/KWL/STAPK BS4 ...... 346 B1
Stockwood Hl KEYN BS31 ...... 347 L4
Stockwood La HGRV/WHIT BS14 ...... 347 G6
Stockwood Ms BRSG/KWL/STAPK BS4 ...... 337 H6
Stockwood Rd BRSG/KWL/STAPK BS4 ...... 347 H2
HGRV/WHIT BS14 ...... 347 G6
Stoke Bridge Av BRSTK/PCHW BS34 ...... 316 F5
Stokefield Cl THNB/SVB BS35 ... 293 K2
Stoke Gv HNLZ/SM/SNYPK/WT BS9.. 325 G5
Stoke Hamlet HNLZ/SM/SNYPK/WT BS9 . 325 H5
Stoke Hl HNLZ/SM/SNYPK/WT BS9 . 325 G7
Stoke La BRSTK/PCHW BS34... 316 C5
HNLZ/SM/SNYPK/WT BS9 . 325 H5
MANG/FISH BS16 ...... 327 G4
Stokeleigh Wk HNLZ/SM/SNYPK/WT BS9 . 324 E6
Stokemead BRSTK/PCHW BS34 ...... 316 E3
Stoke Mdw ALMDB BS32 ...... 316 F2
Stoke Paddock Rd HNLZ/SM/SNYPK/WT BS9 . 324 F5
Stoke Park Cl CHELTE/BC GL52 ...... 72 B7
Stoke Park Ct CHELTE/BC GL52 .. 72 A7
Stoke Park Rd HNLZ/SM/SNYPK/WT BS9 . 325 G8
Stoke Park Rd South HNLZ/SM/SNYPK/WT BS9 . 325 G8
Stoke Rd CHELTE/BC GL52... 71 H6
HNLZ/SM/SNYPK/WT BS9 . 325 H8
Stokes Ct OLD/WMLY/WICK BS30 ... 338 C7
Stokes Cft CBRIS/FH BS1... 336 A3
Stokes Rd TEWK GL20 ...... 47 J3
Stoke View Rd MANG/FISH BS16 ...... 327 H8
Stoneberry Rd HGRV/WHIT BS14 ...... 346 C8
Stone Br MIM GL56 ...... 37 K6
Stonebridge Pk EVILLE/WHL BS5... ...... 336 F1
Stonechat Av GLE GL4 ...... 136 E6
Stonechat Gdns MANG/FISH BS16 ...... 327 G5
Stone Cl GLE GL4 ...... 137 G4
Stonecote Rdg RSTROUD/NAIL GL6 ...... 209 M7
Stonecroft Cl CHELTE/BC GL52 ...... 72 A7
Stoneford La EVE WR11 ...... 10 F1
Stonehenge Rd GLE GL4 ...... 136 D2
Stonehill OLD/WMLY/WICK BS30 ... 338 A7
Stonehouse Ct COTS GL54 ... 101 J4
Stonelea DSLY GL11 ...... 228 F7
Stoneleigh Cl CHELTS GL53 ... 115 M8
Stoneleigh Crs BRSG/KWL/STAPK BS4 ...... 346 C1
Stoneleigh Dr OLD/WMLY/WICK BS30 ... 338 B6

Stoneleigh Rd BRSG/KWL/STAPK BS4 ...... 346 C1
Stoneleigh Wk BRSG/KWL/STAPK BS4 ...... 346 C1
The Stone Rd RTEWK/TIB GL19... 66 D5
Stones La HGHW SN6 ...... 288 D2
Stoneville St CHELTW GL51 ...... 2 A3
Stoney Fld VGL GL2 ...... 111 G6
Stoney Pool CIR GL7 ...... 240 F5
Stoney Rd RWYE HR9 ...... 85 G4
Stoney Stile Rd THNB/SVB BS35 ...... 293 J6
Stony Riding RSTROUD/NAIL GL6 ...... 234 B1
Storrington Rd STNHO GL10 ... 207 H4
Stothard Rd HORF/LLZ BS7 ... 326 D4
Stottbury Rd HORF/LLZ BS7 ... 326 C8
Stoulgrove La CHEP NP16 ...... 246 C7
Stourden Dr OLD/WMLY/WICK BS30 ... 338 B7
Stover Rd YATE/CS BS37 ...... 319 J1
Stow Br COTS GL54 ...... 101 K8
Stow Cl CHELTW GL51 ...... 115 J2
Stowe La LYD GL15 ...... 198 E1
Stowell Hill Rd WUE GL12 ...... 294 D5
Stowell Ms GLE GL4 ...... 136 F4
Stowe Rd LYD GL15 ...... 198 D4
Stow Hill Rd WUE GL12 ...... 294 C5
Stowick Crs AVONM BS11 ...... 324 E2
Stow Rd CHNTN OX7 ...... 103 L8
CHNTN OX7 ...... 125 L1
CIR GL7 ...... 214 F7
MIM GL56 ...... 58 C7
Strachans Cl STROUD GL5 ...... 208 C2
Stradbrook Av EVILLE/WHL BS5.. 337 K4
Stradling Rd AVONM BS11 ...... 324 E1
Straight La RTEWK/TIB GL19... 66 E4
Straight St CBRISNE BS2 ...... 7 J4
Strand La CIND GL14 ...... 156 B4
Stratford Cl HGRV/WHIT BS14 ...... 346 B8
VGL GL2 ...... 135 L7
Stratford Rd SHPSTR CV36 ... 16 B5
STRAT CV37 ...... 8 F5
STROUD GL5 ...... 208 B3
Strathmore Rd HORF/LLZ BS7 .. 326 A5
Stratton Hts CIR GL7 ...... 214 B6
Stratton Rd GL GL1 ...... 5 H9
KEYN BS31 ...... 349 G8
Stratton St CBRISNE BS2 ...... 7 H1
Strawberry La CIR GL7 ...... 241 L7
Strawbridge Rd EVILLE/WHL BS5 ...... 336 D4
Stream Cl HNBRY/STHM BS10 .. 315 H8
Stream La NWNT GL18 ...... 86 F1
Streamleaze THNB/SVB BS35 ... 293 L3
Streamside CHELTE/BC GL52 ... 72 B7
Stream Side MANG/FISH BS16 .. 328 B5
Streamside STROUD GL5 ...... 208 E4
Streamside Rd YATE/CS BS37 .. 320 C2
The Stream MANG/FISH BS16... 327 K1
The Street BAD GL9 ...... 299 L8
DSLY GL11 ...... 230 A3
DSLY GL11 ...... 252 F7
DSLY GL11 ...... 254 D2
HGHW SN6 ...... 264 D7
HGHW SN6 ...... 265 M5
HGHW SN6 ...... 266 C7
MALM SN16 ...... 284 A6
MALM SN16 ...... 285 H3
RSTROUD/NAIL GL6 ...... 256 B2
STNHO GL10 ...... 207 G8
STROUD GL5 ...... 208 C8
TET GL8 ...... 299 L1
TET GL8 ...... 301 M3
THNB/SVB BS35 ...... 292 C8
THNB/SVB BS35 ...... 293 K6
VGL GL2 ...... 181 H8
Stretford Av EVILLE/WHL BS5 ...... 336 F3
Stretford Rd EVILLE/WHL BS5 .. 336 F3
Strickland Rd CHELTE/BC GL52... 3 H8
Stride Cl THNB/SVB BS35 ...... 304 C5
Striguil Rd CHEP NP16 ...... 270 D5
Stringer's Cl STROUD GL5 ...... 208 C7
Stringer's Dr STROUD GL5 ...... 208 C6
Strode Common THNB/SVB BS35 ...... 293 H6
Strode Gdns THNB/SVB BS35 ... 293 H6
Strongbow Rd CHEP NP16 ...... 270 A5
Stroud Rd AVONM BS11 ...... 324 A6
BRSTK/PCHW BS34 ...... 316 A3
CIR GL7 ...... 237 J3
GL GL1 ...... 136 A4
GLE GL4 ...... 160 A1
RSTROUD/NAIL GL6 ...... 184 F5
RSTROUD/NAIL GL6 ...... 210 C2
RSTROUD/NAIL GL6 ...... 232 D7
Stuart St EVILLE/WHL BS5 ...... 336 E4
Studland Dr CHELTE/BC GL52 ... 94 E7
Stump La BWTH/CHD GL3 ...... 137 K3
Stumpwell La WUE GL12 ...... 276 F1
Sturden La MANG/FISH BS16 ... 317 L8
Sturdon Rd BMSTR BS3... ...... 335 J8
Sturmer Rd YATE/CS BS37 ...... 310 A7
Sturminster Cl HGRV/WHIT BS14 ...... 346 F5
Sturminster Rd HGRV/WHIT BS14 ...... 346 E6
Sturmyes Rd RSTROUD/NAIL GL6 ...... 210 C8
Sudbrook Wy GLE GL4 ...... 136 D6
Sudeley Dr CIR GL7 ...... 263 H5
Sudgrove Pk GLE GL4 ...... 137 G6
Sudmeadow Rd VGL GL2 ...... 135 K2
Suffolk Cl TET GL8 ...... 282 A2
Suffolk Pde CHELT GL50 ...... 2 C9
Suffolk Pl CIR GL7 ...... 264 F4
Suffolk Rd CHELT GL50 ...... 2 B8
Suffolk Sq CHELT GL50 ...... 2 B8
Sugar Tump RWYE HR9 ...... 84 F3
Sugley La RSTROUD/NAIL GL6... 256 A1
Sulgrave Cl GL GL1 ...... 159 L2
Summer Cl STROUD GL5 ...... 209 G4

Summer Crs STROUD GL5 ...... 209 G4
Summerfield Cl CHELTW GL51... 93 H6
MIM GL56 ...... 35 H8
Summerhayes OLD/WMLY/WICK BS30 ... 338 F6
Summer Hl BRSG/KWL/STAPK BS4... 7 L9
Summerhill Rd EVILLE/WHL BS5... ...... 337 H3
Summerhill Ter EVILLE/WHL BS5 ...... 337 H4
Summerhouse La CHEP NP16 ...... 270 B7
Summerland Dr BWTH/CHD GL3 ...... 113 J8
Summerleaze KEYN BS31 ...... 348 A4
LYD GL15 ...... 225 K1
MANG/FISH BS16 ...... 327 L8
Summerleaze Rd LYD GL15 ...... 225 K1
Summers Dr OLD/WMLY/WICK BS30 ... 340 C2
Summersfield Cl RSTROUD/NAIL GL6 ...... 233 K5
Summersfield Rd RSTROUD/NAIL GL6 ...... 233 K4
Summers Md YATE/CS BS37 ... 310 A6
Summers Rd CBRISNE BS2 ... 336 C2
COTS GL54 ...... 74 C5
Summer St BMSTR BS3... ...... 6 C9
STROUD GL5 ...... 209 G4
Sundale RWYE HR9 ...... 84 E3
Sundays Hl ALMDB BS32 ...... 306 C7
Sundayshill La BRKLY GL13 ...... 274 B3
Sunderland Ct BWTH/CHD GL3 ...... 113 L6
Sunderland Pl CFTN/FAIL BS8... 6 A1
Sundridge Pk YATE/CS BS37 ... 320 A3
Sun Green Cl LYD GL15 ...... 200 C2
Sun Green Rd LYD GL15 ...... 200 C2
The Sunground TET GL8 ...... 257 L2
Sunningdale YATE/CS BS37 ... 320 A3
Sunningdale Dr OLD/WMLY/WICK BS30 ... 338 D5
Sunny Bank CLFD GL16 ...... 151 J8
KGWD/HNM BS15 ...... 337 K2
Sunnybank Rd CLFD GL16 ...... 151 J8
Sunnycroft Cl CHELTE/BC GL52 ... 94 C4
Sunnycroft Ms GL GL1 ...... 136 A6
Sunnydene BRSG/KWL/STAPK BS4... 336 F6
Sunnyfield La CHELTW GL51 ... 114 C6
Sunnyfield Rd VGL GL2 ...... 158 F3
Sunny Hl HNLZ/SM/SNYPK/WT BS9... 324 E4
Sunnyhill Dr AVONM BS11 ...... 324 A5
Sunnymead KEYN BS31 ...... 348 B8
Sunnymead Cl MTCHDN GL17 129 M3
Sunnyside FRCTL/WBN BS36 ... 318 D4
HNLZ/SM/SNYPK/WT BS9 ... 325 G6
Sunnyside La MANG/FISH BS16 . 327 K1
YATE/CS BS37 ...... 319 L2
Sunnyvale Dr OLD/WMLY/WICK BS30 ... 338 D8
Sunny Wk KGWD/HNM BS15... 337 K2
Sunridge MANG/FISH BS16 ... 327 M5
Sunrise Gv BRSG/KWL/STAPK BS4... 336 F7
Sun Rise Rd LYD GL15 ...... 200 C2
Sunset Cl CHELTE/BC GL52 ...... 94 C3
Sunset Pl RTEWK/TIB GL19 ...... 108 C8
Sunshine Cl LED HR8 ...... 19 L2
Sun St CHELTW GL51 ...... 2 A1
TEWK GL20 ...... 48 A4
Sun Tump LYD GL15 ...... 200 C3
Surrey Av CHELTW GL51 ...... 115 J1
Surrey Rd HORF/LLZ BS7 ...... 326 A8
Surrey St CBRISNE BS2 ...... 7 H1
Suspension Br CFTN/FAIL BS8... 335 G4
Sussex Av CHELTW GL51 ...... 115 J1
Sussex Gdns BWTH/CHD GL3 ... 137 K4
Sussex St CBRISNE BS2 ...... 7 L4
Sutherland Av MANG/FISH BS16 ...... 328 A4
YATE/CS BS37 ...... 309 M7
Sutherland Pl CFTN/FAIL BS8... 335 J1
Sutton Av BRSG/KWL/STAPK BS4... 336 F7
Sutton Cl DSLY GL11 ...... 253 K3
Sutton La RBANSW OX15 ...... 39 L3
Sutton Rd CIND GL14 ...... 154 D5
CIND GL14 ...... 178 B1
Swagwater La HGRV/WHIT BS14 . 346 B5
Swainswick La CBATH/BATHN BA1 ...... 351 M8
Swaish Dr OLD/WMLY/WICK BS30 ... 338 B7
Swallow Crs VGL GL2 ...... 112 F5
Swallow Cft STNHO GL10 ...... 206 B4
Swallow Dr BRSTK/PCHW BS34... 316 A3
Swallow Pk THNB/SVB BS35... 273 L8
Swallows Ct BRSTK/PCHW BS34 ...... 317 G7
Swallowtail Cl CHELTW GL51 ... 114 F1
Swan Cl CIR GL7 ...... 244 E7
MIM GL56 ...... 58 C6
Swane Rd HGRV/WHIT BS14 ... 347 H5
Swan La FRCTL/WBN BS36 ... 317 L3
HGHW SN6 ...... 287 K6
LYD GL15 ...... 178 E3
Swanley La BRKLY GL13 ...... 251 L6
Swanmoor Crs HNBRY/STHM BS10 ...... 315 J7
Swan Rd GL GL1 ...... 5 G3
LYD GL15 ...... 201 J8
Swanscombe Pl CHELTW GL51 ...... 115 G6
Swansfield CIR GL7 ...... 244 F5
Swan St STROUD GL5 ...... 208 E4
Swanswell Dr CHELTW GL51 ... 115 G3
Sweden La TEWK GL20... ...... 50 F1
Sweetbriar Cl CHELTE/BC GL52 ... 72 A7
Sweetbriar St GL GL1 ...... 4 F3
Sweets Cl KGWD/HNM BS15 ... 338 A1
Sweets Rd KGWD/HNM BS15 ... 337 M1
Swells Hl STROUD GL5 ...... 233 G2
Swift Rd GLE GL4 ...... 136 F6
Swifts Hill Vw STROUD GL5 ...... 209 G2
Swilgate Rd TEWK GL20 ...... 48 A6

Swindon Cl CHELTW GL51 ...... 2 A1
Swindon La CHELTW GL51 ...... 93 K5
Swindon Rd CHELT GL50 ...... 2 B3
CHELTW GL51 ...... 93 K6
CIR GL7 ...... 238 F5
HGHW SN6 ...... 289 G4
Swindon St CHELTW GL51 ...... 2 B3
Swinhay Rd WUE GL12 ...... 276 C4
Swish La MTCHDN GL17 ...... 129 K4
Swiss Rd BMSTR BS3... ...... 345 H1
Swordfish Cl BWTH/CHD GL3 ... 113 L6
Swynford Cl CIR GL7 ...... 266 F5
Sybil Rd GLE GL4 ...... 136 E5
Sycamore Av CHEP NP16 ...... 270 A6
Sycamore Cl EVILLE/WHL BS5... 337 C2
GL GL1 ...... 135 M7
KGWD/HNM BS15 ...... 337 K8
Sycamore Dr BRSTK/PCHW BS34 ...... 316 A4
STROUD GL5 ...... 208 F3
THNB/SVB BS35 ...... 293 L2
Sycamore Rd MTCHDN GL17 .. 129 M5
TEWK GL20 ...... 49 G3
Sydenham Hl RDLND/MONT BS6 ...... 335 M2
Sydenham La RDLND/MONT BS6 ...... 335 M2
Sydenham Rd BRSG/KWL/STAPK BS4... 336 C8
CHELTE/BC GL52 ...... 3 G6
RDLND/MONT BS6 ...... 335 M2
Sydenham Rd South CHELTE/BC GL52 ...... 3 C7
Sydenham Ter GL GL1 ...... 136 A4
Sydenham Villas Rd CHELTE/BC GL52 ...... 3 C7
Sydenham Wy KGWD/HNM BS15 ...... 337 L8
Sydney St STNHO GL10 ...... 207 G2
Sydney Rw CBRIS/FH BS1... ...... 6 A7
Sylvan Cl CLFD GL16 ...... 175 K2
Sylvan Wy HNLZ/SM/SNYPK/WT BS9.. 324 D5
Sylvia Av BMSTR BS3... ...... 336 B8
Symes Av BMSTRD/HC/WWD BS13... 345 L8
Symington Rd MANG/FISH BS16 ...... 327 K6
Symn La WUE GL12 ...... 277 K4
Synwell La WUE GL12 ...... 277 L4
Syon Rd RSTROUD/NAIL GL6 ... 233 K5
Syston Wy KGWD/HNM BS15 ... 337 M2

Tabernacle Pitch WUE GL12 ... 277 K4
Tabernacle Rd KGWD/HNM BS15 ...... 337 L5
WUE GL12 ...... 277 J3
Tabernacle Wk STROUD GL5 ... 208 D6
Tabrams Pitch RSTROUD/NAIL GL6 ...... 232 E7
Tackley Rd EVILLE/WHL BS5 ... 326 D8
Tadwick La CBATH/BATHN BA1... 351 K6
CBATH/BATHN BA1 ...... 351 G2
Tailor's La STRAT CV37 ...... 9 J2
Tainmor Cl VGL GL2 ...... 113 G6
Tait's Hl DSLY GL11 ...... 228 E7
Tait's Hill Rd DSLY GL11 ...... 228 F8
Talbot Av KGWD/HNM BS15 ... 337 K2
Talbot Ms GL GL1 ...... 135 M5
Talbot Rd BRSG/KWL/STAPK BS4... 346 D1
CHELTW GL51 ...... 115 J3
Talbot Sq COTS GL54 ...... 101 M3
Talboys Wk TET GL8 ...... 282 A3
Talgarth Rd HORF/LLZ BS7 ... 326 B7
Tallard's Pl CHEP NP16 ...... 270 C7
Tall Elms Cl BWTH/CHD GL3 ... 113 K6
Tallis Gv BRSG/KWL/STAPK BS4... 345 M5
Tallis Rd BWTH/CHD GL3 ...... 113 H3
Tally Ho La COTS GL54 ...... 98 E6
Tamar Cl THNB/SVB BS35 ...... 293 M4
Tamar Dr KEYN BS31 ...... 348 C7
Tamarisk Cl CHELTW GL51 ...... 115 J7
Tamar Rd BWTH/CHD GL3 ... 138 B5
CBRISNE BS2 ...... 336 E5
CHELTE/BC GL52 ...... 3 K3
Tamesis Dr CIR GL7 ...... 261 H4
Tamorth Rd KEYN BS31 ...... 348 A7
Tanglewood Wy RSTROUD/NAIL GL6 ...... 209 M7
Tanhouse La YATE/CS BS37 ... 309 L4
Tankard's Cl CFTN/FAIL BS8... 6 D2
Tankards Hl MIM GL56 ...... 36 E1
Tanner Cl OLD/WMLY/WICK BS30 ... 338 B6
Tanners Cl BWTH/CHD GL3 ... 138 A5
CHPMW/MSHF SN14 ...... 342 A3
Tanner's Rd CHELTW GL51 ...... 93 H8
Tanner's Ct CHELTW GL51 ...... 93 H8
Tanorth Cl HGRV/WHIT BS14 ... 346 C8
Tanorth Rd HGRV/WHIT BS14 .. 346 B8
The Tanyard OLD/WMLY/WICK BS30 ... 348 D1
Tapscott Ct WUE GL12 ...... 277 J4
Tapsters OLD/WMLY/WICK BS30 ... 338 C7
Target Cl LED HR8 ...... 19 L2
STROUD GL5 ...... 209 H4
Tarlton Cl GLE GL4 ...... 137 G7
Tarnock Av HGRV/WHIT BS14 .. 346 C4
Tarragon Pl ALMDB BS32 ...... 317 H4
Tarrington Rd GL GL1 ...... 136 B8
Tatchley La CHELTE/BC GL52... 94 D7
Taunton Wk HORF/LLZ BS7 ... 326 C4
Taurus Cl VGL GL2 ...... 112 B6
Taverner Cl BRSG/KWL/STAPK BS4... 345 M4
Tavistock Rd BRSG/KWL/STAPK BS4 ...... 346 B2
Tavistock Wk BRSG/KWL/STAPK BS4 ...... 346 B2
Tayberry Gv CHELTW GL51 ...... 115 H7
Tayler Rd COTS GL54 ...... 169 J1

Taylor Cl KGWD/HNM BS15 ..... 338 B3
Taylor Gdns BMSTRD/HC/WWD BS13... 345 H7
Taylors Gnd VGL GL2 ...... 159 H1
Tayman Cl HNBRY/STHM BS10 ...... 326 A5
Tayman Rdg OLD/WMLY/WICK BS30 ... 348 F3
Taynton Cl OLD/WMLY/WICK BS30 ... 348 D1
Teal Cl ALMDB BS32 ...... 316 F1
VGL GL2 ...... 158 F2
Teasel Cl VGL GL2 ...... 112 B6
Teasel Md ALMDB BS32 ...... 317 G4
Teddington Gdns GLE GL4 ...... 136 C5
Ted Preston Cl TEWK GL20 ...... 48 B7
Teewell Av MANG/FISH BS16 ... 328 A7
Teewell Cl MANG/FISH BS16 ... 328 A7
Teewell Hl MANG/FISH BS16 ... 328 A7
Teignmouth Cl BRSG/KWL/STAPK BS4... 346 C2
Telegraph St SHPSTR CV36 ... 16 B5
Telephone Av CBRIS/FH BS1... 6 E4
Telford's Br VGL GL2 ...... 111 K7
Telford Wk EVILLE/WHL BS5 ... 337 J2
Teme Cl CHELTE/BC GL52 ...... 3 J5
Templar Rd YATE/CS BS37 ... 310 A8
Temple Back CBRIS/FH BS1... 7 H4
Temple Cl GLE GL4 ...... 137 G5
LYD GL15 ...... 201 H8
Templefields COTS GL54 ...... 118 B8
Temple Ga CBRIS/FH BS1... 7 H4
Templeland Rd BMSTRD/HC/WWD BS13... 345 H6
Temple Rose St CBRIS/FH BS1... 7 H5
Temple St BMSTR BS3... ...... 345 K1
CBRIS/FH BS1... ...... 7 G4
KEYN BS31 ...... 348 A6
Temple Wy CBRIS/FH BS1... 7 H5
Templeway U/P CBRISNE BS2... 7 J3
Templeway West LYD GL15 ...... 201 H8
Tenby Rd KEYN BS31 ...... 347 M7
Tenby St EVILLE/WHL BS5 ...... 336 D4
Tennessee Gv RDLND/MONT BS6 ...... 325 L6
Tenniscourt Rd KGWD/HNM BS15 ...... 338 C2
Tennis Rd BRSG/KWL/STAPK BS4... 346 B1
Tennyson Av VGL GL2 ...... 135 L7
Tennyson Cl KEYN BS31 ...... 348 B5
Tennyson Rd CHELTW GL51 ...... 115 H2
DSLY GL11 ...... 253 L4
HORF/LLZ BS7 ...... 326 A6
Tensing Rd CHELTS GL53 ...... 116 A7
Tenth Av HORF/LLZ BS7 ...... 326 D2
Tereslake Gn HNBRY/STHM BS10 ...... 315 M7
Tern Cl GLE GL4 ...... 136 E2
Terrell Gdns EVILLE/WHL BS5 ...... 336 F4
Terrell St CBRISNE BS2 ...... 6 E2
Terry Ruck Cl CHELTW GL51 ... 114 F1
Tetbury Cl BRSTK/PCHW BS34 ... 316 E3
Tetbury Hl MALM SN16 ...... 303 J6
TET GL8 ...... 257 L5
Tetbury La MALM SN16 ...... 283 M5
RSTROUD/NAIL GL6 ...... 233 G7
RSTROUD/NAIL GL6 ...... 256 F1
TET GL8 ...... 279 L8
Tetbury Rd CIR GL7 ...... 237 M5
GLE GL4 ...... 160 A2
KGWD/HNM BS15 ...... 337 K3
Tetbury St RSTROUD/NAIL GL6... 233 G7
Teviot Rd KEYN BS31 ...... 348 C7
Tewkesbury Rd CBRISNE BS2 ...... 336 C1
CHELTW GL51 ...... 92 F5
COTS GL54 ...... 101 J2
NWNT GL18 ...... 86 C2
TEWK GL20 ...... 48 B2
VGL GL2 ...... 112 B6
Tewther Rd BMSTRD/HC/WWD BS13... 345 G4
Teyfant Rd BMSTRD/HC/WWD BS13... 346 A1
Teyfant Wk BMSTRD/HC/WWD BS13... 346 A1
Thackeray Cl STRAT CV37 ...... 9 J1
Thackeray Wk HORF/LLZ BS7 .. 326 C3
Thames Cl WUE GL12 ...... 276 C3
Thames La HGHW SN6 ...... 289 G3
Thames Pth CIR GL7 ...... 237 G8
CIR GL7 ...... 244 D8
HGHW SN6 ...... 289 H3
Thames Rd CHELTE/BC GL52... 3 J3
Thames St CIR GL7 ...... 244 E8
Thames Vw HGHW SN6 ...... 287 H3
Thanet Rd BMSTR BS3... ...... 345 K1
Thatchers EVILLE/WHL BS5 ...... 337 K4
Thatchers End CHELTE/BC GL52 ...... 72 D8
Theescombe Hl STROUD GL5 ... 232 D5
The High Gv CHELTE/BC GL52 ... 72 A8
Theocs Cl TEWK GL20 ...... 47 M7
There-and-back-again La CFTN/FAIL BS8 ...... 6 C3
Theresa Av HORF/LLZ BS7 ... 326 A7
Theresa St GL GL1 ...... 135 M4
Thessaly Rd CIR GL7 ...... 214 A7
Theyer Cl BWTH/CHD GL3 ... 138 A6
Theynes Cft LGASH BS41 ...... 344 D2
Thicket Av MANG/FISH BS16 ... 327 L8
Thicket Rd MANG/FISH BS16 ... 327 L7
Thicket Wk THNB/SVB BS35 ... 293 L2
Thickwood La CHPMW/MSHF SN14 ...... 343 L5
Thiery Rd BRSG/KWL/STAPK BS4... 346 C1
Thingwall Pk MANG/FISH BS16 . 327 G8
Third Av DSLY GL11 ...... 253 L3
HORF/LLZ BS7 ...... 326 C2
Thirlestaine Rd CHELTS GL53 ... 2 D9
Thirlmere Ct OLD/WMLY/WICK BS30 ... 338 F5

Thirlmere Rd
BRSTK/PCHW BS34......... **316** C3 [1]
CHELTW GL51........... **115** G4
Thistledown Cl *CHELTW* GL51.. **92** F7 [7]
Thistle Downs *TEWK* GL20........ **48** F2
Thistle St *BMSTR* BS3........ **335** K8 [1]
Thomas Cl *MANG/FISH* BS16..... **328** D3
Thomas Cl *LED* HR8........... **19** L2
Thomas Moore Cl
BWTH/CHD GL3............ **113** J5 [3]
Thomas Pring Wk
EVILLE/WHL BS5.......... **337** J2 [8]
Thomas Stock Gdns *GLE* GL4 .. **137** G5 [3]
Thomas St *CBRISNE* BS2..... **336** A3 [15]
CHEP NP16.............. **270** A3 [17]
CIR GL7................. **238** C2
GL GL1.................... **5** G8
Thomas St North
RDLND/MONT BS6.......... **335** M2
Thomond Cl *CHELTW* GL51..... **93** L7 [3]
Thompson Dr *CHELTS* GL53...... **115** M7
Thompson Rd *CIR* GL7........ **239** H7
HGRV/WHIT BS14........ **347** C5 [7]
STROUD GL5............ **208** F3
Thompson Wy *VGL* GL2........ **112** F5
Thomson Rd
EVILLE/WHL BS5......... **336** D3 [15]
Thoresby *CHELT* GL50........ **94** A6 [1]
Thoresby Av *GL* GL1.......... **159** L2
Thornbury Cl *CHELTW* GL51..... **115** K1
Thornbury Rd *THNB/SVB* BS35 .. **293** J6
Thorncliffe Dr *CHELTW* GL51 .. **115** K3 [1]
Thorndale *CFTN/FAIL* BS8...... **335** J3
Thornhaugh Ms
CHELTW GL51............ **115** G6 [16]
Thornhayes Cl
FRCTL/WBN BS36......... **318** C3 [1]
Thornhill Cl *GL* GL1.......... **135** M6 [1]
The Thornhills
MANG/FISH BS16......... **327** K6
Thornleigh Rd *HORF/LLZ* BS7 .. **326** A6
Thornmead Gv
HNBRY/STHM BS10........ **325** J1 [1]
Thorns Farm *YATE/CS* BS37 .... **320** A2 [3]
Thorn Tree Dr *CHEP* NP16..... **270** B7 [10]
Thornwell Rd *CHEP* NP16...... **270** B6
Thornycroft Cl *HORF/LLZ* BS7 .. **326** D4
Threadneedle St
STROUD GL5............. **208** E4 [16]
Three Ashes La *NWNT* GL18..... **64** C8
Three Queens' La *CBRIS/FH* BS1 .. **7** G5
Three Sisters La
CHELTE/BC GL52......... **94** F8
Three Wells Rd
BMSTRD/HC/WWD BS13.... **345** H7
Thrissell St *EVILLE/WHL* BS5..... **7** L1
Throgmorton Rd
BRSG/KWL/STAPK BS4..... **346** B4
Thrupp La *STROUD* GL5....... **233** H1
Thrush Cl *GLE* GL4.......... **136** E5
Thurlestone *HGRV/WHIT* BS14.. **346** B6
Thurlow Rd *EVILLE/WHL* BS5.... **336** E1
Thurstons Barton
EVILLE/WHL BS5.......... **337** G2 [4]
Tibberton *KGWD/HNM* BS15..... **338** C3
Tibberton Gv *CHELTW* GL51.... **114** D4
Tibberton La *RTEWK/TIB* GL19 .. **108** D7
Tibbiwell La *RSTROUD/NAIL* GL6.. **185** H3
Tibbott Rd *HGRV/WHIT* BS14.... **346** E6
Tibbott Wk *HGRV/WHIT* BS14.. **346** E6
Tiberius Av *LYD* GL15........ **201** K7 [3]
Tichborne Rd *EVILLE/WHL* BS5.. **336** E4
Tide Gv *AVONM* BS11......... **324** C4
Tidenham Wy
BRSTK/PCHW BS34........ **316** B2
Tidswell Cl *GL* GL1.......... **159** H3
Tilemans La *SHPSTR* CV36...... **16** A4
Tilling Rd *HNBRY/STHM* BS10.. **326** A4
Tilling Wk *HNBRY/STHM* BS10.. **326** A4
Tillis Vw *CLFD* GL16......... **150** D6
Tilney Rd *CHELT* GL50....... **93** M7
Tilnor Crs *DSLY* GL11......... **229** H7
Tilsdown *DSLY* GL11.......... **229** H7
Tilsdown Cl *DSLY* GL11...... **229** G7
Tilsley Rd *CHNTN* OX7....... **105** M2
Tilting Rd *THNB/SVB* BS35..... **293** K1
Timbercombe La *CHELTS* GL53.. **116** D8
Timber Dene *MANG/FISH* BS16.. **326** F7
Timbercombe Wk
HGRV/WHIT BS14........ **346** E6 [1]
Timbrells Cl *CIR* GL7......... **263** H4
Timmis Cl *GLE* GL4.......... **136** E7 [3]
Timms Gn *BDWAY* WR12...... **11** G7
Timperley Wy *CHELTW* GL51.... **114** F6
Timsbury Rd *BMSTR* BS3...... **346** A1
Tindell Ct
OLD/WMLY/WICK BS30..... **338** B7 [10]
Tinglesfield *CIR* GL7......... **214** B7
Tinker's Cl *MIM* GL56......... **58** D6
Tinkley La *STNHO* GL10...... **231** G5
Tinmans Gn *MONM* NP25...... **174** B3 [1]
Tintern Av *EVILLE/WHL* BS5.... **336** F3 [11]
Tintern Cl
OLD/WMLY/WICK BS30..... **338** B5 [2]
Tintern Rd *GLE* GL4.......... **135** M8
Tippetts Rd *KGWD/HNM* BS15.. **337** M5
Tirle Bank Wy *TEWK* GL20..... **48** D5
Tirlebrookgra *TEWK* GL20...... **49** J4
Tirley Cl *GL* GL1............ **159** G2
Tirley St *RTEWK/TIB* GL19..... **68** B5
Tiverton Cl *CHELTW* GL51..... **92** F8 [3]
Tiverton Wk *MANG/FISH* BS16.. **337** J1
Tivoli La *CHELT* GL50......... **2** A9
Tivoli Ms *CHELT* GL50......... **2** A8
Tivoli Rd *CHELT* GL50......... **2** A9
Tivoli St *CHELT* GL50......... **2** A9
Tivoli Wk *CHELT* GL50....... **115** K3 [7]
Toadsmoor Rd
RSTROUD/NAIL GL6....... **233** K2
Tobacco Cl *COTS* GL54....... **74** B7 [1]
Tobacconist Rd
RSTROUD/NAIL GL6....... **233** J5
Tobyfield Cl *CHELTE/BC* GL52... **72** C8
Tobyfield La *CHELTE/BC* GL52.. **72** B8 [1]
Tobyfield Rd *CHELTE/BC* GL52.. **72** C8
Tockington La *ALMDB* BS32..... **306** C5

Tockington Park La
THNB/SVB BS35.......... **307** G3
Toghill La
OLD/WMLY/WICK BS30..... **340** C2
Toll *CFTN/FAIL* BS8......... **335** H4
Toll Bridge Rd
CBATH/BATHN BA1........ **352** A8
Toll Down Wy
CHPMW/MSHF SN14....... **343** K8
Tolsey La *TEWK* GL20........ **48** A5
Tommy's Turn La *RBANSW* OX15 .. **39** M1
Tommy Taylor's La *CHELT* GL50 .. **93** M7
Tom Price Cl *CHELTE/BC* GL52.... **2** F5
Tone Dr *BWTH/CHD* GL3...... **138** B6
Tooke Rd *RSTROUD/NAIL* GL6 .. **233** C4
Top Rd *CIND* GL14.......... **178** B2
CIR GL7................ **266** E4
Torchacre Ri *DSLY* GL11....... **253** J2
Tormarton Crs
HNBRY/STHM BS10........ **315** H7
Tormarton Rd *BAD* GL9....... **322** C6
CHPMW/MSHF SN14....... **343** M8
Toronto Rd *HORF/LLZ* BS7..... **326** C3
Torpoint Rd *BMSTR* BS3...... **345** M2
Torrance Cl
OLD/WMLY/WICK BS30..... **338** F5
Torridge Rd *KEYN* BS31...... **348** C7
Torrington Av
BRSG/KWL/STAPK BS4..... **346** B3
Tortworth Rd *HORF/LLZ* BS7.... **326** A6
Totshill Dr
BMSTRD/HC/WWD BS13..... **346** A7
Totshill Gv
BMSTRD/HC/WWD BS13 .. **346** A7 [1]
Totterdown La *CIR* GL7....... **242** E6
Totts La *CHPMW/MSHF* SN14.. **343** K8
Touching End La
CHPMW/MSHF SN14....... **342** B3 [1]
Touchstone Av
BRSTK/PCHW BS34........ **317** G6
Tower Cl *GLE* GL4........... **136** F5
Tower Hi *CBRISNE* BS2........ **7** H4
Tower House Dr
RTEWK/TIB GL19......... **44** A8
Tower La *CBRIS/FH* BS1........ **6** F5
OLD/WMLY/WICK BS30..... **338** C5
Tower Rd *KGWD/HNM* BS15... **337** L2
LYD GL15.............. **177** K8
Tower Rd North
KGWD/HNM BS15......... **338** D3
Tower Rd South
KGWD/HNM BS15......... **338** D5
Tower St *CBRIS/FH* BS1........ **7** H5
CIR GL7................ **238** D3
Townsend *ALMDB* BS32....... **306** B7
MTCHDN GL17............ **128** F4
MTCHDN GL17............ **130** C1
Townsend Cl *HGRV/WHIT* BS14.. **347** H6
LYD GL15.............. **199** G6
Townsend Rd *HGRV/WHIT* BS14.. **347** H6
Townsend St *CHELTW* GL51...... **2** B2
Toy La *CHNTN* OX7.......... **105** L1
Tozers Hl
BRSG/KWL/STAPK BS4 ... **346** E1 [1]
T Parkside Cl *BWTH/CHD* GL3.. **113** H5
Trafalgar Dr *BWTH/CHD* GL3.... **113** H3
Trafalgar Rd *CIR* GL7........ **238** C1 [7]
Trafalgar St *CHELT* GL50....... **2** C1
Trafalgar Ter *BMSTR* BS3...... **345** K1 [2]
Traherne Cl *LED* HR8......... **20** A5
Trajan Cl *GLE* GL4.......... **137** H5 [7]
Tralee Wk
BRSG/KWL/STAPK BS4..... **345** M2
The Tram Rd *CLFD* GL16...... **175** J1
Tramway Rd
BRSG/KWL/STAPK BS4..... **336** E8
CIND GL14............. **154** A7
Tranmere Av
HNBRY/STHM BS10........ **315** J7
Tranmere Gv
HNBRY/STHM BS10........ **315** J7
Tranton La *THNB/SVB* BS35.... **249** L7
Tratman Wk
HNBRY/STHM BS10....... **315** H8 [7]
Travers Cl
BRSG/KWL/STAPK BS4 ... **345** M5 [4]
Travers Wk *BRSTK/PCHW* BS34 .. **317** C6
Tredegar Rd *MANG/FISH* BS16 .. **327** K8
Tredworth Rd *GL* GL1........ **136** B4
Treefield Pl *CBRISNE* BS2..... **336** C1 [8]
Treelands Cl *CHELTS* GL53...... **115** M6
Treelands Dr *CHELTS* GL53...... **115** M6
Tree Leaze *YATE/CS* BS37...... **320** B1
Tregannon Rd *BMSTR* BS3...... **345** H2
Trelawney Av
EVILLE/WHL BS5......... **336** F3 [12]
Trelawney Pk
BRSG/KWL/STAPK BS4..... **336** F8
Trelawney Rd
RDLND/MONT BS6......... **335** L2
Trenchard Gdns *CIR* GL7...... **239** H8
Trenchard St *CBRIS/FH* BS1..... **6** D4
Trench La *ALMDB* BS32....... **306** F8
FRCTL/WBN BS36......... **317** H1
Trendlewood Pk
MANG/FISH BS16......... **327** G7
Trenley Rd *DSLY* GL11....... **230** B4
Trent Dr *THNB/SVB* BS35...... **293** M4
Trent Gv *KEYN* BS31........ **348** C7
Trentham Cl *CBRISNE* BS2.... **336** C1 [17]
Trent Rd *BWTH/CHD* GL3..... **138** B6
Tresham Cl *ALMDB* BS32...... **316** F1
Tretawn Gdns *TEWK* GL20..... **48** D5
Trevelyan Wk
HNBRY/STHM BS10....... **315** H8 [3]
Treverdowe Wk
HNBRY/STHM BS10....... **314** F8
Trevethin Cl
KGWD/HNM BS15........ **337** L4 [1]
Trevisa Cl *BWTH/CHD* GL13.... **227** G8
Trevisa Gv *HNBRY/STHM* BS10 .. **315** L7
Trevor Rd *BWTH/CHD* GL3..... **137** H5
Trewsbury Rd *CIR* GL7....... **236** F5
Triangle South *CFTN/FAIL* BS8.... **6** B3
The Triangle *VGL* GL2....... **112** E8
Triangle West *CFTN/FAIL* BS8.... **6** B3
Tribune Pl *GLE* GL4......... **137** G5

Trident Cl *MANG/FISH* BS16.... **328** C2
Trier Wy *GL1................ **4** E9
Trimnells *CHPMW/MSHF* SN14 .. **343** K8
Trinity Dr *RSTROUD/NAIL* GL6 .. **233** L5 [1]
Trinity La *CHELTE/BC* GL52...... **2** L2
Trinity Rd *CBRISNE* BS2........ **7** L2
CIR GL7................ **238** C4
GLE GL4................ **137** H5
MTCHDN GL17............ **129** M5
STROUD GL5............ **208** F5 [3]
Trinity St *CBRISNE* BS2........ **7** L2
TEWK GL20............. **48** A5
Trinity Wk *CBRISNE* BS2........ **7** K2
Trinity Wy *CIND* GL14....... **154** B2
Troon *YATE/CS* BS37........ **320** A3
Troon Dr
OLD/WMLY/WICK BS30..... **338** D5 [4]
Troopers' Hill Rd
EVILLE/WHL BS5......... **337** H5
Trotman Av *DSLY* GL11....... **229** H6
Troughton Pl *TEWK* GL20...... **48** C5
Trowbridge Rd
HNBRY/STHM BS10........ **325** J7
Trowbridge Wk
HNBRY/STHM BS10...... **325** L2 [3]
Trubshaw Ct *BWTH/CHD* GL3 .. **113** L6
Truro Rd *BMSTR* BS3....... **335** K8
Tryes Rd *CHELT* GL50........ **115** L5
Trygrove *GLE* GL4......... **136** F5 [3]
Trym Cross Rd
HNLZ/SM/SNYPK/WT BS9.... **324** E6
Trymleaze
HNLZ/SM/SNYPK/WT BS9 .. **324** E6 [3]
Trym Rd
HNLZ/SM/SNYPK/WT BS9.... **325** J4
Trym Side
HNLZ/SM/SNYPK/WT BS9.... **324** E6
Trymwood Cl
HNBRY/STHM BS10........ **325** H1
Tucker St *CBRISNE* BS2........ **7** J1
Tuckett La *MANG/FISH* BS16 .. **327** L4 [2]
Tuckwell Rd *CIR* GL7......... **267** C5
Tudor Cl *OLD/WMLY/WICK* BS30.. **338** E8
Tudor Lodge Dr *CHELT* GL50 ... **115** L4
Tudor Pl *TEWK* GL20........ **48** B7
Tudor Rd *CBRISNE* BS2....... **336** B2 [2]
CIR GL7................ **238** E2 [3]
EVILLE/WHL BS5.......... **336** E2
KGWD/HNM BS15......... **337** L6
Tudor St *GL* GL1........... **135** L5
Tudor Wk *CLFD* GL16....... **151** J5 [3]
Tuffley Av *GL* GL1.......... **135** L5
Tuffley Crs *GL* GL1.......... **135** M6
Tuffley La *GL* GL1........... **135** L3
Tuffley Rd *HNBRY/STHM* BS10 .. **325** L3
Tufthorn Av *CLFD* GL16..... **175** K2 [7]
Tufthorn Cl *CLFD* GL16....... **175** L3
Tufthorn Rd *CLFD* GL16....... **175** L4
Tufton Av *AVONM* BS11....... **324** C3
Tugela Rd
BMSTRD/HC/WWD BS13.... **345** H4
Tug Wilson Closel *TEWK* GL20 .. **49** G1 [4]
The Tulworths *VGL* GL2....... **112** D6 [1]
Tunacre *VGL* GL2.......... **110** F5
Tuners La *MALM* SN16....... **284** A5
Tunstall Cl
HNLZ/SM/SNYPK/WT BS9.... **325** G7
Turkdean Rd *CHELTW* GL51.... **115** G5
Turley Rd *EVILLE/WHL* BS5..... **336** F2 [3]
Turnberry
OLD/WMLY/WICK BS30..... **338** D5 [3]
Turnbridge Rd
HNBRY/STHM BS10........ **315** L7
Turnbury *YATE/CS* BS37....... **320** A3
Turner Cl *KEYN* BS31........ **348** C6
Turner Gdns *HORF/LLZ* BS7.... **326** D5 [3]
Turner Rd *DSLY* GL11....... **229** C7
Turners Cl *VGL* GL2......... **110** F7
Turners Ct
OLD/WMLY/WICK BS30..... **338** B7 [20]
Turnpike Av *WUE* GL12....... **277** L5 [3]
Turnpike Cl *YATE/CS* BS37..... **320** A1 [7]
Turnpike End *CHEP* NP16..... **270** D7
Turnpike Ga *WUE* GL12...... **296** C5
Turnstone Dr *VGL* GL2........ **158** F2
Turtlegate Av
BMSTRD/HC/WWD BS13.... **345** G7
Turtlegate Wk
BMSTRD/HC/WWD BS13.... **345** G7
Turville Dr *HORF/LLZ* BS7..... **326** C5
Tusculum Wy *MTCHDN* GL17... **130** C1
Tutnalls St *LYD* GL15........ **201** K8
Tutton Hi *CHPMW/MSHF* SN14.. **343** K8
Tweed Cl *THNB/SVB* BS35..... **293** L3
Tweenbrook Av *GL* GL1..... **136** A5
Tweeny La
OLD/WMLY/WICK BS30..... **338** F5
The Twenties *CIR* GL7........ **238** E7
Twenty Acres Rd
HNBRY/STHM BS10....... **325** L1 [7]
Twickenham Rd
RDLND/MONT BS6........ **325** L6 [4]
Twinberrow La *DSLY* GL11..... **253** K4
Twixtbears *TEWK* GL20....... **48** A4 [2]
Two Acres Rd *HGRV/WHIT* BS14.. **346** C4
Two Hedges Rd *CHELTE/BC* GL52.. **72** C8
Two Mile Ct
KGWD/HNM BS15......... **337** K3 [3]
Twomile Hill Rd
KGWD/HNM BS15......... **337** K3
Two Mile La *VGL* GL2........ **110** D7
The Twynings
KGWD/HNM BS15......... **338** A1
Twyver Bank *GLE* GL4....... **137** H8
Twyver Cl *GLE* GL4......... **137** H7
Tybalt Wy *BRSTK/PCHW* BS34.. **317** G6
Tylea Cl *CHELTW* GL51...... **114** E4
Tyler Cl *KGWD/HNM* BS15..... **338** A5
Tyler's La *MANG/FISH* BS16 .. **327** M6 [3]
Tyler St *CBRISNE* BS2......... **7** L5
Tylers Wy *CHEP* NP16....... **270** D3
LYD GL15.............. **177** L8
RSTROUD/NAIL GL6....... **185** L8
YATE/CS BS37........... **310** B6 [3]
Tyndale Av *MANG/FISH* BS16 .. **327** J7 [3]
YATE/CS BS37........... **309** M8
Tyndale Cl *DSLY* GL11....... **253** G7 [1]
Tyndale Rd *BWTH/CHD* GL3.... **137** J3

DSLY GL11............. **228** F7
KGWD/HNM BS15....... **338** A1 [3]
Tyndale Vw *THNB/SVB* BS35 .. **293** K3 [3]
Tyndall Av *CFTN/FAIL* BS8...... **6** D2
Tyndall Rd *EVILLE/WHL* BS5.... **336** D3 [1]
Tyndalls Park Ms *CFTN/FAIL* BS8.. **6** C1
Tyndall's Park Rd *CFTN/FAIL* BS8.. **6** B1
Tyndalls Wy
HNBRY/STHM BS10....... **326** A3
Tyne Rd *HORF/LLZ* BS7....... **325** M8
Tyne St *CBRISNE* BS2........ **336** C1
Tyning Cl *HGRV/WHIT* BS14..... **346** C4
YATE/CS BS37........... **320** A1
Tyning Rd *BMSTR* BS3....... **336** B8
Tynings Ct *BWTH/CHD* GL3 .. **113** M6 [3]
Tynings Rd *RSTROUD/NAIL* GL6 .. **232** C7
The Tynings
RSTROUD/NAIL GL6....... **233** K4 [3]
Tynte Av
BMSTRD/HC/WWD BS13.... **345** M8
Tyntesfield Rd
BMSTRD/HC/WWD BS13.... **345** J4
Tyrone Wk
BRSG/KWL/STAPK BS4..... **346** A3 [3]
Tyrrel Wy *BRSTK/PCHW* BS34.. **317** C5
Tythe Ct *DSLY* GL11........ **229** H6
Tytherington Rd
THNB/SVB BS35......... **294** B5
Tythe Rd *BDWAY* WR12...... **32** F2
Tythings Crs *NWNT* GL18...... **86** B3
The Tythings *NWNT* GL18..... **86** B3

U

Uley Rd *DSLY* GL11.......... **253** L3
Ullenwood Rd *GLE* GL4...... **136** F4 [3]
Ullswater Cl
OLD/WMLY/WICK BS30..... **338** F5 [3]
YATE/CS BS37........... **310** A8
Ullswater Rd *CHELTW* GL51.... **115** G4 [3]
HNBRY/STHM BS10........ **325** K2
Undercliff Av *CHELTS* GL53...... **115** M8
Undercliff Ter *CHELTS* GL53...... **115** M8
Underhill *CHEP* NP16........ **222** B4
Underhill Rd *GLE* GL4........ **136** E7
WUE GL12.............. **276** C6
Underwood Cl *THNB/SVB* BS35 .. **293** J7
Union Rd *CBRISNE* BS2........ **7** L4
CLFD GL16.............. **151** L8
Union St *CBRIS/FH* BS1......... **6** F2
CHELTE/BC GL52......... **2** F4
COTS GL54.............. **102** A3
DSLY GL11............. **253** K3
GL GL1.................. **5** G3
STROUD GL5............ **208** E4
Unity Rd *KEYN* BS31........ **348** C6
Unity St *CBRIS/FH* BS1......... **6** D4 [3]
CBRISNE BS2............. **7** J3
KGWD/HNM BS15......... **338** A5
University Farm *MIM* GL56...... **58** C6 [3]
University Rd *CFTN/FAIL* BS8..... **6** B3
University Wk *CFTN/FAIL* BS8.... **6** C1
Unlawater La *CIND* GL14...... **155** J6
Unwin Cl *CHELTW* GL51...... **114** E4
Unwin Rd *CHELTW* GL51..... **114** E4
Upcott *HGHW* SN6.......... **264** C7
Up Hatherley Wy *CHELTW* GL51 .. **114** F6
Uphill Rd *HORF/LLZ* BS7...... **326** B6 [3]
MTCHDN GL17............ **128** C7
Upjohn Crs
BMSTRD/HC/WWD BS13.... **345** M8
Uplands Cl *CIND* GL14....... **154** C2 [3]
Uplands Rd *MANG/FISH* BS16 .. **327** L8
STROUD GL5............ **208** E3
Upper Bath Rd
THNB/SVB BS35.......... **293** K3 [3]
Upper Bath St *CHELT* GL50..... **2** B9
Upper Belgrave Rd
CFTN/FAIL BS8.......... **335** J1
Upper Belmont Rd
HORF/LLZ BS7........... **326** A8
Upper Bilson Rd *CIND* GL14.... **154** A2
Upper Byron Pl *CFTN/FAIL* BS8.... **6** B3
Upper Chapel La
FRCTL/WBN BS36......... **318** E4
Upper Cheltenham Pl
RDLND/MONT BS6........ **336** A2
Upper Church La *STROUD* GL5.. **207** M4
Upper Church St *CHEP* NP16.... **270** A2
Upper Churnside *CIR* GL7...... **238** E3
Upper Cranbrook Rd
RDLND/MONT BS6........ **325** K7
Upperfield Rd *CHELTW* GL51... **93** J6 [3]
Upperfields *LED* HR8........ **20** A2
Upper Hall Cl *LED* HR8....... **20** A3
Upper Hayes Rd
RSTROUD/NAIL GL6....... **232** C6
Upper Kitesnest La
RSTROUD/NAIL GL6....... **184** B8
Upper Leazes *STROUD* GL5..... **208** F4
Upper Ley *COR/BOX* SN13..... **353** M6
Upper Lynch Rd
RSTROUD/NAIL GL6....... **210** C8
Upper Maudlin St *CBRISNE* BS2 .. **6** E2
Upper Mill La *CHELTE/BC* GL52 .. **94** F6
Upper Nelson St
CHEP NP16............. **270** A3 [3]
Upper Norwood St
CHELTS GL53............ **115** L5 [3]
Upper Park Rd *CHELTE/BC* GL52 .. **3** G8
Upper Perry Hl *BMSTR* BS3...... **6** A6
Upper Poole Rd *DSLY* GL11..... **253** K3
Upper Quay St *GL* GL1......... **5** G3
Upper Queen's Rd
STNHO GL10............ **207** H4 [3]
Upper Rd *LED* HR8.......... **20** A1
LYD GL15.............. **201** H2
Upper Rodley Rd *CIND* GL14.... **156** F5
Upper Sandhurst Rd
BRSG/KWL/STAPK BS4..... **336** F7
Upper Springfield Rd
STROUD GL5............ **208** E3 [3]
Upper Station Rd
MANG/FISH BS16......... **327** L7

Upper Stone Cl
FRCTL/WBN BS36......... **318** E4
Upper Stowfield Rd
MTCHDN GL17............ **128** A4
Upper St *BRSG/KWL/STAPK* BS4 .. **7** M9
Upper St *CHPMW/MSHF* SN14 .. **330** F7
Upper Sydney St
BMSTR BS3............. **335** K8 [12]
Upper Tockington Rd
THNB/SVB BS35.......... **306** C1
Upper Tynings
RSTROUD/NAIL GL6....... **232** C7 [7]
The Upper Tynings
RSTROUD/NAIL GL6....... **207** M3
Upper Washwell
RSTROUD/NAIL GL6....... **185** H2
Upper Wells St *CBRIS/FH* BS1 .. **6** D4 [3]
Upthorpe La *DSLY* GL11...... **229** K6
Upthorpe La *DSLY* GL11...... **229** K5
Upton Cl *GLE* GL4.......... **137** G4
Upton Gdns *TET* GL8........ **281** M2
Upton HI *GLE* GL4.......... **160** F2
Upton La *GLE* GL4.......... **137** H6
GLE GL4............... **160** B6
Upton Rd *BMSTR* BS3........ **6** A8
Upton St *GL* GL1........... **5** H9
Urfords Dr *MANG/FISH* BS16 .... **327** L5 [3]
Usk Wy *BWTH/CHD* GL3...... **138** B6

V

Vaisey Fld *VGL* GL2......... **182** B6
Vaisey Rd *CIR* GL7......... **214** B7
Vale Bank *GL* GL2.......... **155** M8
Valens Ter *COR/BOX* SN13..... **353** L5
Valentine Cl *CHEP* NP16...... **270** B7
HGRV/WHIT BS14........ **346** D6
Valerian Cl *AVONM* BS11...... **324** B5
Vale Rd *CIR* GL7........... **214** B7
Vale St
BRSG/KWL/STAPK BS4..... **336** C8 [7]
The Vale *MANG/FISH* BS16..... **329** H4
Vale View Ter
CBATH/BATHN BA1........ **352** B8
Vale View Ter
CBATH/BATHN BA1........ **351** L8
STROUD GL5............ **209** G5
Valley Rd *DSLY* GL11........ **229** H7
Valley Vw *DSLY* GL11........ **229** H7
Valley We *DSLY* GL11........ **229** H7
The Valls *ALMDB* BS32....... **317** H5
Valma Rocks
EVILLE/WHL BS5......... **337** J5 [3]
Van Der Breen St
RSTROUD/NAIL GL6....... **210** C2
Vandyck Av *KEYN* BS31....... **348** B5
Varley Av *BWTH/CHD* GL3..... **137** K5 [3]
Varnister Cl *MTCHDN* GL17.... **129** H3
Varnister Rd *MTCHDN* GL17.... **129** G3
Vassall Ct *MANG/FISH* BS16.... **327** K6
Vassall Rd *MANG/FISH* BS16 .... **327** K6
Vatch La *RSTROUD/NAIL* GL6.... **209** L7
Vatch Vw *STROUD* GL5....... **209** G2
Vattingstone La
THNB/SVB BS35.......... **293** M5
Vaughan Cl *HNBRY/STHM* BS10 .. **315** H8
Vauxhall *NWNT* GL18....... **86** A3
Vauxhall Rd *GL* GL1......... **5** H8
Vauxhall Ter *GL* GL1......... **5** H7
Vayre Cl *YATE/CS* BS37....... **320** C2
Velhurst Dr *RSTROUD/NAIL* GL6 .. **209** M8
Velthouse La *MTCHDN* GL17.... **131** J1
The Vennings *DSLY* GL11...... **229** H5
Venns Acre *WUE* GL12....... **277** K5
Vensfield Rd *VGL* GL2......... **159** G1
Vention La *MTCHDN* GL17..... **128** C5
Ventnor Rd *BRSTK/PCHW* BS34 .. **316** D8
EVILLE/WHL BS5.......... **337** H2
Vera Rd *MANG/FISH* BS16..... **337** H1
Verbena Cl *GLE* GL4........ **137** G6 [3]
Vernal Cl *GLE* GL4......... **137** H6
Vernals La *WUE* GL12....... **276** C5
Verney Cl *CHELTS* GL53...... **116** A5 [1]
Verney Rd *STNHO* GL10..... **207** H4
The Verneys *CHELTS* GL53..... **116** A5 [7]
Vernon Cl *KEYN* BS31....... **348** F8
Vernon St
BRSG/KWL/STAPK BS4..... **7** K8 [3]
Verrier Rd *EVILLE/WHL* BS5 .. **336** E4 [13]
Vertican Rd *VGL* GL2......... **112** F5
Vervain Cl *BWTH/CHD* GL3..... **113** J4
Verwood Dr
OLD/WMLY/WICK BS30..... **348** E2
Vetch Cl *GLE* GL4.......... **136** C7
Viburnum Vw *GLE* GL4...... **137** H6 [3]
Vicarage Cl *BWTH/CHD* GL3.... **113** L7
CHELTW GL51............ **139** G1
LYD GL15.............. **225** J2 [2]
Vicarage Ct *CLFD* GL16...... **175** K1 [3]
KGWD/HNM BS15......... **337** K6 [3]
Vicarage La *BDWAY* WR12...... **32** A1
BWTH/CHD GL3.......... **138** A6
CHPMW/MSHF SN14....... **343** L8
SHPSTR CV36............ **61** H5
THNB/SVB BS35......... **292** C8
VGL GL2................ **179** M1
WUE GL12.............. **181** H8
Vicarage Rd *BMSTR* BS3...... **6** B9
BMSTRD/HC/WWD BS13.... **345** H5
CFTN/FAIL BS8.......... **334** F5
EVILLE/WHL BS5.......... **336** E5

FRCTL/WBN BS36.................. 318 E6
GL GL1 .... 136 C4
KGWD/HNM BS15............. 337 K6
THNB/SVB BS35 .... 304 E4
Vicarage St RSTROUD/NAIL GL6.. 185 H3
Vicars Cl MANG/FISH BS16 ...... 327 K7
Vickers Rd COTS GL54 .... 124 D6
Victoria Av EVILLE/WHL BS5 ..... 336 E4
Victoria Cl THNB/SVB BS35 ...... 273 K8
Victoria Ct THNB/SVB BS35 ...... 304 C5
Victoria Dr STNHO GL10............ 206 B4
Victoria Gdns
  CBATH/BATHN BA1............... 352 B8
  RDLND/MONT BS6 .... 335 M2
Victoria Gv BMSTR BS3 .... 7 G8
Victoria Pde EVILLE/WHL BS5 .... 336 E3
Victoria Pk KGWD/HNM BS15.. 337 M3
  MANG/FISH BS16 .... 327 J6
Victoria Pl BMSTR BS3 .... 335 L8
  CHELTE/BC GL52 .... 3 G5
Victoria Retreat CHELT GL50 .... 2 C9
Victoria Rd CBRISNE BS2........... 7 L7
  CHEP NP16 .... 270 B6
  CIR GL7 .... 218 D6
  CIR GL7 .... 238 D3
  CLFD GL16 .... 175 J1
  KEYN BS31 .... 348 F8
  KGWD/HNM BS15 .... 337 L6
  LED HR8 .... 19 L4
  LYD GL15 .... 201 J8
  OLD/WMLY/WICK BS30 .... 338 F6
  STROUD GL5 .... 233 H2
  VGL GL2 .... 112 B5
Victoria Sq CFTN/FAIL BS8........ 335 J4
Victoria Ter CBRIS/FH BS1 .... 7 G4
  CHELT GL50 .... 2 C2
  CIND GL14 .... 154 A3
  COTS GL54 .... 123 H6
  GL GL1 .... 5 G8
  MANG/FISH BS16 .... 327 M7
  RSTROUD/NAIL GL6 .... 185 H3
Victoria Ter CBRISNE BS2 .... 7 M6
  CFTN/FAIL BS8 .... 335 H5
  CHELTE/BC GL52 .... 3 H6
Victoria V CIND GL14................ 154 A3
Victoria Wk RDLND/MONT BS6 .. 335 M2
Victor Rd BMSTR BS3 .... 335 L8
Victor St CBRISNE BS2 .... 7 M4
  EVILLE/WHL BS5 .... 336 D5
Victory Cl BWTH/CHD CL3 .... 113 J3
Victory Rd GL GL1 .... 136 B4
  RSTROUD/NAIL GL6 .... 185 H4
View Ct OLD/WMLY/WICK BS30 .. 339 L5
Vigor Rd
  BMSTRD/HC/WWD BS13...... 345 K6
Viking Wy LED HR8.................. 19 L2
Village Av COTS GL54 .... 99 K7
Village Cl YATE/CS BS37 .... 319 M2
Village Rd CHELTW GL51 .... 93 H7
Villa Wy LED HR8 .... 19 M5
Villiers Rd EVILLE/WHL BS5 .... 336 D2
Vilner La THNB/SVB BS35 .... 293 K4
Vilverie Md CHELTE/BC GL52 .... 71 M7
Vimpany Cl HNBRY/STHM BS10 .. 315 H8
Vimpennys La THNB/SVB BS35 .. 314 F2
Vincent Av GL GL1 .... 159 L2
Vincent Cl AVONM BS11............ 324 E1
Vine Ct CHELT GL51 .... 2 B2
Vineries Cl CHELTS GL53.......... 115 L7
Viner's La BAD GL9.................. 323 K5
Vine Ter GL GL1 .... 5 G2
Vine Wy TEWK GL20 .... 48 B8
Vineyard La WUE GL12 .... 277 H6
Vineyards Cl CHELTS GL53 .... 116 D7
Vineyard St COTS GL54 .... 74 C6
Vining Wk EVILLE/WHL BS5 ..... 336 D3
Vinney La STNHO GL10 .... 311 C3
Vinny Av MANG/FISH BS16 ...... 328 C4
Vintery Leys
  HNLZ/SM/SNYPK/WT BS9...... 325 K4
Virginia Cl YATE/CS BS37 .... 320 C2
Virginia Rd TEWK GL20 .... 49 G3
Vittoria Wk CHELT GL50............ 2 A5
Vivian St BMSTR BS3 .... 335 M8
Vizard Cl DSLY GL11 .... 253 K3
Vowell Cl
  BMSTRD/HC/WWD BS13....... 345 K7
Voxwell La CHELTE/BC GL52 .... 72 A8
Voyce Cl GLE GL4 .... 159 M1
Vulcan Wy GLE GL4.................. 137 H5
Vyners Cl CIR GL7 .... 238 C5
Vyvyan Rd CFTN/FAIL BS8........ 335 J4
Vyvyan Ter CFTN/FAIL BS8 .... 335 J4

W

Wade Rd YATE/CS BS37 .... 309 J8
Wades La RSTROUD/NAIL GL6.. 184 E8
Wades Rd BRSTK/PCHW BS34.. 316 D8
Wade St CBRISNE BS2 .... 7 J1
Wadham Cl CIR GL7 .... 220 B8
Wadham Dr MANG/FISH BS16 .. 327 K2
Wadham Gv MANG/FISH BS16 .. 328 D6
Wagtail Dr TEWK GL20 .... 48 F2
Wainbridge Crs
  THNB/SVB BS35 .... 304 C4
Wainbrook Dr EVILLE/WHL BS5 .. 336 F1
Wainlode La RTEWK/TIB GL19.... 90 D1
Wakefield Cl CIR GL7 .... 266 F5
Wakeford Rd
  MANG/FISH BS16 .... 328 C4
Walden Rd KEYN BS31 .... 348 C7
Waldrist Cl CHELTW GL51 .... 93 H6
Walham La VGL GL2 .... 112 A7
Walker Cl EVILLE/WHL BS5 .... 336 D4
  MANG/FISH BS16 .... 328 C4
Walkers Gdn COTS GL54........... 169 K2
Walker's La MTCHDN GL17 .... 129 H4
Walker St CBRISNE BS2 .... 6 D1
Walker Wy THNB/SVB BS35 ...... 293 K4
Walkley Hl STROUD GL5 .... 208 C6
Walkley Rd TEWK GL20 .... 48 B4
Walk Mill La WUE GL12............. 277 H7
The Walk WUE GL12 .... 277 H7
Wallbridge STROUD GL5 .... 208 D4

Wallingford Rd
  BRSG/KWL/STAPK BS4.......... 345 M4
Walliscote Av
  HNLZ/SM/SNYPK/WT BS9...... 325 L5
Walliscote Rd
  HNLZ/SM/SNYPK/WT BS9...... 325 L5
Wallscourt Rd
  BRSTK/PCHW BS34 .... 326 D1
Wallscourt Rd South
  BRSTK/PCHW BS34 .... 326 D2
Wallsend La
  CHPMW/MSHF SN14............ 331 K6
Walnut Av YATE/CS BS37 .... 320 C1
Walnut Bank Dr TEWK GL20 ..... 50 D4
Walnut Cl BDWAY WR12........... 32 E3
  CHELTE/BC GL52 .... 94 A7
  CLFD GL16 .... 175 M2
  GLE GL4 .... 136 F8
  KEYN BS31 .... 347 L7
  THNB/SVB BS35 .... 293 M2
Walnut Crs KGWD/HNM BS15 ... 338 B3
Walnut Dr CHPMW/MSHF SN14 .. 343 H5
Walnut La KGWD/HNM BS15 .... 338 C3
Walnut Tree Cl ALMDB BS32 .... 306 C6
Walnut Wk
  BMSTRD/HC/WWD BS13....... 345 J5
Walsh Av HGRV/WHIT BS14....... 346 C4
Walshe Av YATE/CS BS37 .... 320 E2
Walsingham Rd
  RDLND/MONT BS6 .... 336 A1
Walterbush Rd CHNTN OX7 ...... 105 M2
Walter St BMSTR BS3 .... 335 J7
Walton Av
  BRSG/KWL/STAPK BS4.......... 336 F6
Walton Cl GLE GL4 .... 137 G8
  KEYN BS31 .... 347 M7
  OLD/WMLY/WICK BS30......... 348 E2
Walton Heath YATE/CS BS37 .... 320 B2
Walton Ri
  HNLZ/SM/SNYPK/WT BS9...... 325 J3
Walton St EVILLE/WHL BS5 ...... 336 D2
Walwyn Cl MTCHDN GL17 .... 130 C2
Wansbeck Rd KEYN BS31 .... 348 C7
Wanscow Wk
  HNLZ/SM/SNYPK/WT BS9...... 325 K5
Wapley Hl YATE/CS BS37 .... 320 A7
Wapley Rd YATE/CS BS37 .... 320 C8
Wapping Rd CBRIS/FH BS1 ...... 6 E6
Ward Av VGL GL2 .... 113 G5
Ward Cl CHELTE/BC GL52 .... 72 C7
Warden Hill Cl CHELTW GL51 ... 115 H5
Warden Hill Rd CHELTW GL51 .. 115 H5
Warden Rd BMSTR BS3 .... 6 D9
Wardens' Wy COTS GL54.......... 97 J2
  COTS GL54 .... 99 H8
Wardour Rd
  BRSG/KWL/STAPK BS4.......... 345 M3
Ward Rd COTS GL54.................. 169 J1
Wards Rd CHELTW GL51 .... 114 F5
Warend Hl DSLY GL11 .... 253 J5
Warleigh Dr CBATH/BATHN BA1 .. 352 C8
Warman Cl HGRV/WHIT BS14..... 347 H5
Warman Rd HGRV/WHIT BS14 .. 347 H5
Warmer's Inn La MALM SN16 ... 302 F3
Warmington Rd
  HGRV/WHIT BS14 .... 346 E3
Warminster Rd
  CBRISNE BS2 .... 336 C1
Warneford Pl MIM GL56 .... 58 D6
Warner Cl KGWD/HNM BS15 .... 338 B5
The Warns
  OLD/WMLY/WICK BS30......... 338 C7
Warren Cl ALMDB BS32 .... 306 F8
  BWTH/CHD CL3 .... 113 J4
  CHELTW GL51 .... 115 H5
Warren Ct DSLY GL11 .... 252 F7
Warren Dr LED HR8 .... 20 A4
Warren Gdns
  HGRV/WHIT BS14 .... 347 H6
Warren La LGASH BS41 .... 344 A3
  RWYE HR9 .... 106 C1
Warren Rd BRSTK/PCHW BS34 .. 316 D8
  TEWK GL20 .... 48 F3
Warren Slade CHEP NP16 .... 270 B6
Warren Wy YATE/CS BS37 .... 310 A8
Warrington Rd
  BRSG/KWL/STAPK BS4.......... 346 F1
Warth La THNB/SVB BS35 .... 290 E8
  VGL GL2 .... 156 A7
Warwick Av
  EVILLE/WHL BS5 .... 336 D2
  GL GL1 .... 159 L2
Warwick Cl
  OLD/WMLY/WICK BS30......... 348 D1
  STROUD GL5 .... 208 C7
  THNB/SVB BS35 .... 293 J2
Warwick Crs CHELTE/BC GL52 .. 116 D5
Warwick Pl CHELTE/BC GL52 .... 2 E4
  SHPSTR CV36 .... 16 A5
  TEWK GL20 .... 48 B7
Warwick Rd
  EVILLE/WHL BS5 .... 336 D2
  KEYN BS31 .... 347 M7
  RDLND/MONT BS6 .... 335 K2
Washingpool Hill Rd
  ALMDB BS32 .... 306 E1
Washing Pound La
  HGRV/WHIT BS14 .... 346 D7
Washington Av
  EVILLE/WHL BS5 .... 336 E2
Washmeres
  CHPMW/MSHF SN14............ 353 K1
Wasley Rd CHELTW GL51 .... 115 H3
Watch Elm Cl ALMDB BS32 ...... 317 G5
Watchhill Av
  BMSTRD/HC/WWD BS13....... 345 H5
Watchhill Cl
  BMSTRD/HC/WWD BS13....... 345 H5
Waterbridge Rd
  BMSTRD/HC/WWD BS13....... 345 H6
Watercress Rd CBRISNE BS2..... 326 B8
Waterdale Cl
  HNBRY/STHM BS10 .... 325 L4
  VGL GL2 .... 158 F3
Waterdale Gdns
  HNLZ/SM/SNYPK/WT BS9...... 325 L4
Waterford Cl THNB/SVB BS35... 293 M3

Waterford Rd
  HNLZ/SM/SNYPK/WT BS9 ... 325 K5
Watergates
  CHPMW/MSHF SN14............ 343 L8
Watergripla TEWK GL20............. 28 C4
Water La BMSTR BS3 .... 336 B8
  BRSG/KWL/STAPK BS4.......... 346 F2
  CBRIS/FH BS1 .... 7 H4
  CHELTE/BC GL52 .... 116 D5
  KGWD/HNM BS15 .... 347 K1
  STROUD GL5 .... 208 A7
  STROUD GL5 .... 233 G3
  WUE GL12 .... 277 K5
Waterloo La CIR GL7................. 242 D5
Waterloo Pl CBRISNE BS2 .... 7 K3
Waterloo Rd CBRISNE BS2........ 7 K3
Waterloo St CBRISNE BS2 .... 7 K2
  CFTN/FAIL BS8 .... 335 H4
  CHELT GL50 .... 2 E3
  CLFD GL16 .... 175 J1
The Waterloo CIR GL7 .... 238 D2
Waterloo Wy TEWK GL20 .... 27 H5
Watermans Ct VGL GL2............. 158 F2
Water Meadow VGL GL2 .... 159 G4
Watermill Cl CHELTW GL51 .... 92 F7
Watermoor Ct
  BWTH/CHD CL3 .... 113 K6
Watermoor Rd CIR GL7 .... 238 D5
Watermoor Wy CIR GL7 .... 238 D4
Watermore Cl
  FRCTL/WBN BS36................. 318 C4
Watershoot Cl
  CHELTE/BC GL52 .... 94 C6
Waterside Ct COTS GL54........... 118 C7
  VGL GL2 .... 158 F2
Waterside Dr ALMDB BS32 .... 316 C2
Water's La
  HNLZ/SM/SNYPK/WT BS9...... 325 J4
Waters Reach VGL GL2 .... 135 K5
Waters Rd KGWD/HNM BS15 .... 337 L3
Water St DSLY GL11 .... 253 K2
Waters Wy CHEP NP16 .... 270 A4
Waterton Cl BWTH/CHD CL3 .... 137 K5
Waterwheel Cl VGL GL2 .... 158 F2
Watery La GLE GL4 .... 161 H3
  LED HR8 .... 40 A4
  LYD GL15 .... 201 G8
  NWNT GL18 .... 86 A4
  OLD/WMLY/WICK BS30 .... 340 C3
  RWYE HR9 .... 106 B5
  SHPSTR CV36 .... 16 B5
  VGL GL2 .... 134 D4
  VGL GL2 .... 181 H8
Wathen Rd RDLND/MONT BS6 .. 326 B8
Watkins Yd
  HNLZ/SM/SNYPK/WT BS9 ... 325 J3
Watledge Bank
  RSTROUD/NAIL GL6 .... 232 D6
Watledge Cl TEWK GL20 .... 48 B5
Watledge Rd STROUD GL5......... 232 D5
Watley's End Rd
  FRCTL/WBN BS36................. 318 A4
Watson Av
  BRSG/KWL/STAPK BS4.......... 346 C2
Watson Gv GLE GL4 .... 137 H6
Watson's Rd
  OLD/WMLY/WICK BS30 .... 338 C6
Watters Cl FRCTL/WBN BS36 .... 318 F5
Watts Cl BWTH/CHD CL3 .... 137 J4
Wavell Cl YATE/CS BS37 .... 309 M7
Waveney Rd KEYN BS31............ 348 C8
Waverley Rd RDLND/MONT BS6 .. 335 L2
  VGL GL2 .... 136 E1
  YATE/CS BS37 .... 319 K1
Waverley St
  EVILLE/WHL BS5 .... 336 C2
Wayfield Gdns
  CBATH/BATHN BA1............... 352 B7
Wayford Cl KEYN BS31............. 348 C8
Waylands Rd HGHW SN6.......... 289 G4
Wayleaze FRCTL/WBN BS36 ...... 318 F4
Wayside Rd FRCTL/WBN BS36 .. 318 D4
Weald Cl GLE GL4 .... 136 E6
Weavers Cl DSLY GL11 .... 253 K3
  WUE GL12 .... 277 H8
Weavers Rd CIR GL7 .... 238 E3
  VGL GL2 .... 159 H1
Webb Crs CHNTN OX7 .... 105 M1
Webb Rd TET GL8 .... 281 L2
Webbs Heath
  OLD/WMLY/WICK BS30 .... 338 F4
Webbs Wy MALM SN16 .... 303 J6
Webbs Wood Rd ALMDB BS32 ... 317 H5
Webley Rd MTCHDN GL17 .... 129 H5
Wedgewood Rd
  MANG/FISH BS16 .... 327 M4
Wedgwood Cl
  HGRV/WHIT BS14 .... 346 D6
Wedgwood Dr VGL GL2 .... 112 E6
Wedmore Cl KGWD/HNM BS15.. 338 B4
Wedmore Rd KEYN BS31........... 348 F7
Wedmore V BMSTR BS3 .... 346 A1
Weedon Cl CBRISNE BS2 .... 336 C1
Weigh Bridge Ct CHCAM GL55 .. 12 E7
Weight Rd EVILLE/WHL BS5 ...... 336 E4
Weir Bridge Cl GLE GL4 .... 137 G3
Weir La CFTN/FAIL BS8 .... 334 A6
  CHPMW/MSHF SN14............ 342 B3
Welch Rd CHELTW GL51 .... 93 G7
Welland Ct CHELTE/BC GL52 .... 94 C7
Welland Dr CHELTE/BC GL52 .... 94 C7
Welland Lodge Rd
  CHELTE/BC GL52 .... 94 B7
Welland Rd KEYN BS31 .... 348 B7
  VGL GL2 .... 159 H1
Wellborook Rd CHELTE/BC GL52 .. 72 B6
Well Cl CHEP NP16 .... 270 B7
  LGASH BS41 .... 344 D2
  TEWK GL20 .... 49 G2
Well Cross Rd GLE GL4 .... 136 B7
Well End STROUD GL5 .... 209 G3
Wellesley Rd CHELT GL50......... 2 E2
Wellesley St GL GL1 .... 136 B5
Wellfield TEWK GL20 .... 48 D4
Wellgarth Rd BRSG/KWL/STAPK BS4.. 346 C1
Wellgarth Wk
  BRSG/KWL/STAPK BS4.......... 346 C2

Well Hl RSTROUD/NAIL GL6 ...... 233 J5
Well House Cl
  HNLZ/SM/SNYPK/WT BS9...... 335 G1
Welling Cl DSLY GL11 .... 253 K4
Wellington Av
  RDLND/MONT BS6 .... 336 A2
Wellington Crs HORF/LLZ BS7 .. 326 A5
Wellington Dr
  HNLZ/SM/SNYPK/WT BS9...... 325 M5
  YATE/CS BS37 .... 319 K1
Wellington Hl HORF/LLZ BS7 .... 326 A5
Wellington Hl West
  HNLZ/SM/SNYPK/WT BS9...... 325 L4
Wellington La CHELT GL50........ 2 E2
  CHELTE/BC GL52 .... 2 E3
  RDLND/MONT BS6 .... 336 A2
Wellington Pk CFTN/FAIL BS8... 335 J2
Wellington Rd CBRISNE BS2 .... 7 H2
  CHELTE/BC GL52 .... 2 F2
  COTS GL54 .... 124 C8
  KGWD/HNM BS15 .... 337 M1
  MIM GL56 .... 58 E6
  YATE/CS BS37 .... 310 A7
Wellington Sq CHELT GL50 ...... 2 E2
Wellington St CHELT GL50......... 2 D7
  GL GL1 .... 4 F7
Wellington Wk
  HNBRY/STHM BS10 .... 325 L4
Well La BAD GL9....................... 313 C6
  COTS GL54 .... 98 E5
  COTS GL54 .... 102 A3
  MTCHDN GL17 .... 129 K4
Wellmeadow CLFD GL16 .... 150 D5
Wellmeadow La CLFD GL16 ...... 151 K4
Well Pl CHELT GL50 .... 115 K2
Wells Cl CHELTW GL51 .... 115 H6
  HGRV/WHIT BS14 .... 346 E6
Wells Gdns BDWAY WR12 .... 33 G3
Wells Rd BRSG/KWL/STAPK BS4 .. 7 K8
  BRSG/KWL/STAPK BS4.......... 346 D1
  GLE GL4 .... 136 E2
  HGRV/WHIT BS14 .... 346 D3
  RSTROUD/NAIL GL6 .... 210 C3
Wells St BMSTR BS3 .... 335 J7
Wellstead Av YATE/CS BS37 .... 319 M2
Wellsway KEYN BS31 .... 348 B5
Welsford Av MANG/FISH BS16 .. 326 E7
Welsford Rd MANG/FISH BS16 .. 326 E7
Welsh Back CBRIS/FH BS1 .... 6 F6
Welsh House La NWNT GL18 .... 64 D3
Welsh Wy CIR GL7 .... 213 G1
  CIR GL7 .... 217 H5
Welton Wk KGWD/HNM BS15 ... 337 L1
Welveland La GLE GL4 .... 137 G2
Welwyn Ms CHELTW GL51 .... 115 G6
Wendover Gdns CHELT GL50 .... 115 K2
The Wend MTCHDN GL17 .... 131 H1
Wenlock Rd TEWK GL20 .... 48 B6
Wenmore Cl MANG/FISH BS16 .. 327 M2
Wentforth Dr
  KGWD/HNM BS15 .... 337 L1
Wentworth
  OLD/WMLY/WICK BS30 .... 338 C5
  YATE/CS BS37 .... 320 A2
Wentworth Cl CHELTW GL51 .... 92 F8
  VGL GL2 .... 112 D6
Wentworth Rd HORF/LLZ BS7 .. 325 M8
Werth La RTEWK/TIB GL19 .... 46 F8
Wesley Av KGWD/HNM BS15.... 337 M6
Wesley Cl LYD GL15 .... 224 F3
  MANG/FISH BS16 .... 327 M8
Wesley Hl KGWD/HNM BS15 .... 337 M2
Wesley La
  OLD/WMLY/WICK BS30 .... 338 D6
Wesley Pl CFTN/FAIL BS8 .... 335 J1
  HORF/LLZ BS7 .... 326 A7
  LYD GL15 .... 201 G2
  STNHO GL10 .... 207 G8
Wesley St BMSTR BS3 .... 335 L8
Wessex Av HORF/LLZ BS7 .... 326 B4
Wessex Dr CHELTE/BC GL52 .... 3 H4
Westacre Cl HNBRY/STHM BS10.. 325 J1
Westal Pk CHELTW GL51 .... 115 K4
West Approach Dr
  CHELTE/BC GL52 .... 94 A7
West Av MTCHDN GL17 .... 129 M3
Westbourne Av KEYN BS31 ...... 348 A6
Westbourne Cl
  HNLZ/SM/SNYPK/WT BS9...... 325 H4
Westbourne Dr CHELTE/BC GL52 .. 3 H4
  VGL GL2 .... 159 G4
Westbourne Pl CFTN/FAIL BS8 .. 6 A1
Westbourne Rd
  EVILLE/WHL BS5 .... 336 D3
  MANG/FISH BS16 .... 328 B3
West Broadway
  HNLZ/SM/SNYPK/WT BS9...... 325 M5
Westbrook Rd
  BRSG/KWL/STAPK BS4.......... 346 F3
Westbury Court Rd
  HNLZ/SM/SNYPK/WT BS9...... 325 H4
Westbury Hl
  HNLZ/SM/SNYPK/WT BS9...... 325 J4
Westbury La
  HNLZ/SM/SNYPK/WT BS9...... 324 E4
Westbury Pk
  RDLND/MONT BS6 .... 325 J7
Westbury Rd CFTN/FAIL BS8 ... 335 J1
  CHELTS GL53 .... 116 A7
  GL GL1 .... 135 M8
  HNLZ/SM/SNYPK/WT BS9...... 325 J5
West Coombe
  HNLZ/SM/SNYPK/WT BS9...... 324 F5
Westcote Rd GLE GL4 .... 159 M2
Westcourt Dr
  OLD/WMLY/WICK BS30 .... 338 D7
West Cft
  HNLZ/SM/SNYPK/WT BS9...... 325 L4
West Dene
  HNLZ/SM/SNYPK/WT BS9...... 324 F4
Westdown Gdns CHELTE/BC GL52.. 3 G5
West Dr CHELT GL50 .... 115 K2
Westend DSLY GL11 .... 228 F7
West End BMSTR BS3 .... 6 D8
  CBRISNE BS2 .... 6 E1
  CBRISNE BS2 .... 335 M3

CHNTN OX7 .... 104 B7
COTS GL54 .... 169 J1
RSTROUD/NAIL GL6 .... 233 H5
THNB/SVB BS35 .... 272 E5
West End La BDWAY WR12 .... 32 C4
  BWTH/CHD CL3 .... 137 K5
Westend La THNB/SVB BS35 .... 272 D5
Westend Pde GL GL1 .... 4 A3
Westend Rd WUE GL12 .... 296 A4
Westend Ter GL GL1 .... 4 B3
Westering Cl
  MANG/FISH BS16 .... 328 C6
Westerleigh Cl
  MANG/FISH BS16 .... 328 B4
Westerleigh Rd
  MANG/FISH BS16 .... 328 C4
  MANG/FISH BS16 .... 328 A5
  MANG/FISH BS16 .... 329 K5
  YATE/CS BS37 .... 319 K7
Westerley Cl CIND GL14 .... 154 B4
Western Av CHEP NP16 .... 270 A6
  FRCTL/WBN BS36................. 318 C3
Western Dr HGRV/WHIT BS14 .. 346 A4
Western Hlrd TEWK GL20 .... 50 F1
Western Rd CHELT GL50 .... 115 K2
  HORF/LLZ BS7 .... 326 A5
Western Wy NWNT GL18 .... 41 K8
Westfield DSLY GL11 .... 253 J1
West Fld VGL GL2 .... 110 F6
Westfield Av BWTH/CHD CL3 ... 137 M5
  TEWK GL20 .... 49 G3
Westfield Cl KEYN BS31 .... 347 L6
  KGWD/HNM BS15 .... 337 M6
Westfield Ct CIND GL14............ 154 B2
Westfield La
  BRSTK/PCHW BS34 .... 317 G8
Westfield Pk RDLND/MONT BS6 .. 335 K2
Westfield Pl CFTN/FAIL BS8 ..... 335 H4
Westfield Rd BWTH/CHD CL3 ... 137 M5
  CIND GL14 .... 154 B2
  HNLZ/SM/SNYPK/WT BS9...... 325 J3
Westfields WUE GL12 .... 277 J4
Westfield Ter VGL GL2 .... 112 A6
Westfield Wy ALMDB BS32 ...... 316 F1
Westgate St GL GL1 .... 4 B3
West Gv RDLND/MONT BS6 ..... 336 B2
West Hay Gv CIR GL7 .... 261 H4
Westland Av
  OLD/WMLY/WICK BS30 .... 338 E7
Westland Rd VGL GL2 .... 158 F4
West La CIR GL7 .... 261 H4
West Leaze Pl ALMDB BS32...... 317 G5
Westleigh Cl
  HNBRY/STHM BS10 .... 325 M2
  YATE/CS BS37 .... 319 L2
Westleigh Pk HGRV/WHIT BS14 .. 346 C3
Westleigh Rd
  HNBRY/STHM BS10 .... 325 L2
West Littleton Rd
  CHPMW/MSHF SN14............ 341 M1
West MI CFTN/FAIL BS8 .... 335 M4
West Market Pl CIR GL7 .... 238 C2
Westmarsh La THNB/SVB BS35 .. 272 E5
Westmead Rd EVILLE/WHL BS5 .. 337 K4
  VGL GL2 .... 112 F6
West Mill La HGHW SN6 .... 288 E3
Westminster Cl
  HNLZ/SM/SNYPK/WT BS9...... 325 J4
Westminster Rd
  EVILLE/WHL BS5 .... 336 F3
Westmoreland Rd
  RDLND/MONT BS6 .... 325 K8
Weston Av EVILLE/WHL BS5 .... 336 F4
Weston Cl
  HNLZ/SM/SNYPK/WT BS9...... 324 E4
Weston Ct SHPSTR CV36 .... 61 J5
Weston Crs HORF/LLZ BS7 ...... 326 A5
Weston Rd GL GL1 .... 4 E9
  LGASH BS41 .... 344 B2
Westons Brake
  MANG/FISH BS16 .... 328 C2
Westons Hill Dr
  MANG/FISH BS16 .... 328 C3
Westons Wy KGWD/HNM BS15 .. 338 B4
Westover Cl
  HNLZ/SM/SNYPK/WT BS9...... 325 H2
Westover Ct BWTH/CHD CL3 ... 113 K4
Westover Dr
  HNLZ/SM/SNYPK/WT BS9...... 325 J3
Westover Gdns
  HNLZ/SM/SNYPK/WT BS9 ... 325 H3
Westover Ri
  HNLZ/SM/SNYPK/WT BS9...... 325 J2
Westover Rd
  HNLZ/SM/SNYPK/WT BS9...... 325 J3
West Pde
  HNLZ/SM/SNYPK/WT BS9...... 324 E4
West Pk CFTN/FAIL BS8 .... 335 K3
West Park Rd MANG/FISH BS16 .. 328 A6
West Priory Cl
  HNLZ/SM/SNYPK/WT BS9 ... 325 J4
West Rdg FRCTL/WBN BS36 ..... 318 D4
Westridge Rd WUE GL12 .... 277 J3
Westrip Pl RSTROUD/NAIL GL6 .. 207 M3
West Rocke Av
  HNLZ/SM/SNYPK/WT BS9...... 324 F4
West Shrubbery
  RDLND/MONT BS6 .... 335 K1
West St BMSTR BS3 .... 345 K1
  CBRISNE BS2 .... 7 K3
  CHNTN OX7 .... 104 B6
  KGWD/HNM BS15 .... 337 M3
  MALM SN16 .... 303 H8
  OLD/WMLY/WICK BS30......... 338 E7
  SHPSTR CV36 .... 16 B6
  TET GL8 .... 281 M4
  WUE GL12 .... 294 C6
West Town Dr
  BRSG/KWL/STAPK BS4.......... 346 F2
West Town Gv
  BRSG/KWL/STAPK BS4.......... 346 F3
West Town La
  BRSG/KWL/STAPK BS4.......... 346 F2
  HGRV/WHIT BS14 .... 346 D3
West Town Pk
  BRSG/KWL/STAPK BS4.......... 346 F3
West Tynings
  RSTROUD/NAIL GL6 .... 232 C7

West Vw CIND GL14 .... 154 B4 [2]
 NWNT GL18 .... 86 B3
 THNB/SVB BS35 .... 293 H7
Westview RTEWK/TIB GL19 .. 69 G6
West View Rd BMSTR BS3 .... 335 K8
 CBATH/BATHN BA1 .... 352 C8
 KEYN BS31 .... 348 A6
Westward Gdns LGASH BS41 .. 344 D1 [2]
Westward Rd
 BMSTRD/HC/WWD BS13 .... 345 H4
 STROUD GL5 .... 207 M5
West Wy CIR GL7 .... 238 C3
 CIR GL7 .... 244 E6
Westwick Rd RTEWK/TIB GL19 .. 108 C7
Westwood Crs
 BRSG/KWL/STAPK BS4 .... 336 F6 [2]
Westwood La
 CHELTE/BC GL52 .... 94 F8 [3]
Westwood Rd
 BRSG/KWL/STAPK BS4 .... 346 F3
Westwoods CBATH/BATHN BA1 .. 352 D8
Wetherby Ct
 FRCTL/WBN BS36 .... 328 B2 [2]
Wetherell Pl CFTN/FAIL BS8 .... 6 A3
Wetherleigh Dr VGL GL2 .... 110 F6
Wexford Rd
 BRSG/KWL/STAPK BS4 .... 345 M3
Weyhouse Cl STROUD GL5 .... 208 F6 [1]
Weymouth Rd BMSTR BS3 .... 345 M1
Whaddon Av CHELTE/BC 3 J4
Whaddon Dr CHELTE/BC GL52 ... 3 H3
Whaddon Rd CHELTE/BC GL52 .. 3 L3
Whaddon Wy GLE GL4 .... 159 M2
Wharfdale Wy STNHO GL10 .... 207 C5
 VGL GL2 .... 158 F3
Wharfedale THNB/SVB BS35 ... 293 M3
The Wharfings HGHW SN6 .... 266 F5
The Wharf La CIR GL7 .... 244 F7
 CIR GL7 .... 266 F5
Wharf Rd MANG/FISH BS16 .... 327 H7 [1]
The Wharf COR/BOX SN13 .... 353 M5
Wharncliffe Cl
 HGRV/WHIT BS14 .... 346 D6 [3]
Wharncliffe Gdns
 HGRV/WHIT BS14 .... 346 D6
Whatley Rd CFTN/FAIL BS8 .... 335 J2
Wheatfield Ct CHCAM GL55 .... 8 F7
Wheatfield Dr ALMDB BS32 .... 316 F2
Wheat Hl TET GL8 .... 281 L3
Wheathill Cl KEYN BS31 .... 347 L6
Wheatland Dr CHELTW GL51 ... 92 F7 [3]
The Wheatridge (East) GLE GL4 .. 136 F7
The Wheatridge GLE GL4 .... 136 F7
Wheatsheaf Dr CHELTE/BC GL52 .. 71 M7
Wheatstone Cl TEWK GL20 .... 49 G2 [3]
Wheatstone Rd GL GL1 .... 136 A4
Wheatway GLE GL4 .... 136 F5
Wheelers Wk STROUD GL5 .... 208 B2
Whelford Rd CIR GL7 .... 266 F4
Whimbrel Rd VGL GL2 .... 158 E2
Whimsey Rd CIND GL14 .... 129 M8
 CIND GL14 .... 153 M1
Whinchat Gdns
 MANG/FISH BS16 .... 327 H5 [2]
Whip La RSTROUD/NAIL GL6 .... 232 D6
Whippington Ct CBRIS/FH BS1 ... 7 G2 [3]
Whitby Rd
 BRSG/KWL/STAPK BS4 .... 336 E7 [1]
Whitchurch La
 BMSTRD/HC/WWD BS13 .... 345 J4
 HGRV/WHIT BS14 .... 346 A6
Whitebeam Cl VGL GL2 .... 112 D6 [1]
Whitechapel Rd LYD GL15 .... 200 D2 [3]
Whitecourt DSLY GL11 .... 254 C2
Whitecroft RSTROUD/NAIL GL6 .. 232 D7
Whitecroft Rd LYD GL15 .... 200 E2
Whitecross Av
 HGRV/WHIT BS14 .... 346 E5 [2]
White Cross Rd LYD GL15 .... 225 J1
Whitecross Sq CHELTS GL53 ... 116 A4
Whitefield Av EVILLE/WHL BS5 .. 337 J1
 KGWD/HNM BS15 .... 337 M6 [3]
Whitefield Cl
 CBATH/BATHN BA1 .... 352 D7 [1]
 STNHO GL10 .... 207 G5
Whitefield Rd EVILLE/WHL BS5 .. 337 J1
Whitefields CHELTE/BC GL52 .. 71 M7
 YATE/CS BS37 .... 320 E2 [1]
Whitefriars La HGHW SN6 .... 263 G8
Whitehall Av EVILLE/WHL BS5 .. 337 G2
Whitehall Gdns
 EVILLE/WHL BS5 .... 336 F3 [14]
Whitehall La VGL GL2 .... 109 M4
Whitehall Rd EVILLE/WHL BS5 .. 336 E3
White Hart La COTS GL54 .... 102 A3
White Hart St CHELTW GL51 .... 2 B1
Whitehill La MTCHDN GL17 .... 129 L3
White Horse La
 RSTROUD/NAIL GL6 .... 185 H3 [2]
White Horse Rd HGHW SN6 .... 288 F3
Whitehouse La BMSTR BS3 .... 6 F9
 NWNT GL18 .... 85 H2
 TET GL8 .... 301 L3
Whitehouse Pk STROUD GL5 .. 208 A4
Whitehouse Pl BMSTR BS3 .... 7 G8
Whitehouse Rd
 THNB/SVB BS35 .... 304 C8
Whitehouse St BMSTR BS3 .... 7 G9
Whitehouse Wy
 CHELTE/BC GL52 .... 72 D8
Whiteladies Rd CFTN/FAIL BS8 .. 6 C1
 CFTN/FAIL BS8 .... 335 J1
Whitelands Rd CIR GL7 .... 238 E2
Whiteleaze
 HNBRY/STHM BS10 .... 325 L4 [3]
White Lion Pk MALM SN16 .... 303 H3 [4]
White Lodge Rd
 MANG/FISH BS16 .... 328 B7
Whitemarsh Cl CHELTW GL51 .. 92 F7 [3]
Whites Hl EVILLE/WHL BS5 .... 337 J5
Whiteshill MANG/FISH BS16 .. 317 M8
White St EVILLE/WHL BS5 .... 7 K1
White Tree Rd
 HNLZ/SM/SNYPK/WT BS9 .... 325 K7
Whitewall La THNB/SVB BS35 .. 294 B1
Whitewater Rd TET GL8 .... 279 L7
White Wy CIR GL7 .... 190 E2
 CIR GL7 .... 214 D5

Whiteway DSLY GL11 .... 253 L4
Whiteway Cl
 BRSG/KWL/STAPK BS4 .... 337 G5 [3]
 DSLY GL11 .... 253 L4 [2]
 EVILLE/WHL BS5 .... 337 J3
Whiteway Ms EVILLE/WHL BS5 .. 337 J3
Whiteway Rd EVILLE/WHL BS5 .. 337 J2
 GLE GL4 .... 136 D6
The Whiteway CIR GL7 .... 214 D6
Whiteway Md EVILLE/WHL BS5 .. 337 J3
Whiteway Vw CIR GL7 .... 214 B8
Whitewell Cl GLE GL4 .... 137 G4 [7]
Whitewood Rd
 EVILLE/WHL BS5 .... 337 H2 [1]
Whitfield Cl
 KGWD/HNM BS15 .... 337 M1 [3]
Whitfield Rd THNB/SVB BS35 .. 293 L1 [3]
Whitfield St GL GL1 .... 4 F6 [3]
Whiting Rd
 BMSTRD/HC/WWD BS13 .... 345 J7
Whitland Av
 BMSTRD/HC/WWD BS13 .... 345 K6 [3]
Whitland Rd
 BMSTRD/HC/WWD BS13 .... 345 K6
Whitley Cl YATE/CS BS37 .... 309 L8
Whitley Md BRSTK/PCHW BS34 .. 317 G8
Whitlow La CIND GL14 .... 132 E2
Whitmead Gdns
 BMSTRD/HC/WWD BS13 .... 345 L7 [3]
Whitminster La VGL GL2 .... 181 J6
Whitmore Av
 BRSG/KWL/STAPK BS4 .... 337 J8
Whitmore Rd COTS GL54 .... 74 B4
The Whitmores COTS GL54 .... 123 H1 [1]
Whitson St CBRIS/FH BS1 .... 6 F1
Whittington Rd CHELTW GL51 .. 114 F3
 MANG/FISH BS16 .... 327 L5
Whittington Wy LYD GL15 .... 200 D4
Whittle Av GLE GL4 .... 159 M2
Whittle Cl CHELTW GL51 .... 114 E2 [2]
Whittles La VGL GL2 .... 181 G7
Whittlestone Rd COTS GL54 .... 101 J3 [1]
Whittlestone Hollow
 COTS GL54 .... 101 J3
Whittock Rd HGRV/WHIT BS14 .. 346 F6
Whittock Sq HGRV/WHIT BS14 .. 346 F4 [3]
Whittucks Cl KGWD/HNM BS15 .. 337 M7
Whittucks Rd
 KGWD/HNM BS15 .... 337 M6 [1]
Whitwell Rd HGRV/WHIT BS14 .. 346 E5
Whitworth Ms
 BWTH/CHD GL3 .... 137 L5 [1]
Whitworth Rd CIR GL7 .... 238 C4 [2]
Whornes Orch GLE GL4 .... 137 H8
Whytes Cl
 HNLZ/SM/SNYPK/WT BS9 .... 325 J3
Wick Crs BRSG/KWL/STAPK BS4 .. 336 F8
The Wickets HORF/LLZ BS7 .... 326 B2
 KGWD/HNM BS15 .... 337 M1 [3]
Wickfield La CHELTE/BC GL52 .. 73 H7
Wickham Cl YATE/CS BS37 .... 320 F3
Wickham Gln MANG/FISH BS16 .. 326 F6
Wickham Hl MANG/FISH BS16 .. 326 F6
Wickham Vw
 MANG/FISH BS16 .... 326 F7 [3]
Wick House Cl KEYN BS31 .... 348 F4
Wick La OLD/WMLY/WICK BS30 .. 349 J2 [3]
 RTEWK/TIB GL19 .... 69 H7
Wicklow Rd
 BRSG/KWL/STAPK BS4 .... 346 A3
Wickridge Cl STROUD GL5 .... 208 E3
Wick Rd BRSG/KWL/STAPK BS4 .. 336 F8
 MALM SN16 .... 285 J3
 THNB/SVB BS35 .... 304 E4
Wick St RSTROUD/NAIL GL6 .... 185 G7
Wickwar Rd WUE GL12 .... 277 G7
 YATE/CS BS37 .... 309 J3
Wickwater La CIR GL7 .... 263 L7
Widcombe HGRV/WHIT BS14 .. 346 C6
Widcombe Cl
 EVILLE/WHL BS5 .... 337 J4 [3]
Widden St GL GL1 .... 5 H7
Wigmore Cl GLE GL4 .... 137 G5 [9]
Wigton Crs HNBRY/STHM BS10 .. 325 L1
Wilbye Gv
 BRSG/KWL/STAPK BS4 .... 345 M5 [3]
Wilcox Cl KGWD/HNM BS15 .... 337 M3
Wildcountry La LGASH BS41 .... 344 A4
 NAIL BS48 .... 344 A6
Wildcroft Rd
 HNLZ/SM/SNYPK/WT BS9 .... 325 K6
Wildlife Wk BWTH/CHD GL3 .... 138 A7 [3]
Wildmoorway La CIR GL7 .... 263 K4
Wilkes Av BWTH/CHD GL3 .... 137 J3
Wilkes Meadow CLFD GL16 .... 151 M8
Wilkinson Rd CIR GL7 .... 238 C6
Willada Cl BMSTR BS3 .... 345 L1
Willcox Dr CHELTE/BC GL52 .... 72 D8
Willersey Rd CHELTW GL51 .... 115 C3
 EVE WR11 .... 10 A1
William Gough Cl
 CHELTW GL51 .... 92 F6 [3]
William Mason Cl
 EVILLE/WHL BS5 .... 336 D4 [13]
Williams Cl
 OLD/WMLY/WICK BS30 .... 348 B1
William Smith Cl CHNTN OX7 .. 105 C7
Williamson Rd HORF/LLZ BS7 .. 326 B8
Williams Orch VGL GL2 .... 110 F6
William St BMSTR BS3 .... 7 G8
 BMSTR BS3 .... 7 J9
 CBRISNE BS2 .... 7 L4
 CBRISNE BS2 .... 336 B2
 EVILLE/WHL BS5 .... 336 E3 [10]
 MANG/FISH BS16 .... 327 K8 [2]
Willinton Rd
 BRSG/KWL/STAPK BS4 .... 346 B4
Willis Rd KGWD/HNM BS15 .... 338 B1
Willis Wk TEWK GL20 .... 49 G2
Willmott Cl HGRV/WHIT BS14 .. 346 B8 [3]
Willoughby Cl BMSTRD/HC/WWD BS13
 345 J4
Willoughby Rd
 HORF/LLZ BS7 .... 326 A6 [3]
Willow Av GLE GL4 .... 136 D4
Willow Bank Rd TEWK GL20 .... 51 K5
Willow Bed Cl MANG/FISH BS16 .. 327 K5
Willowbrook Dr CHELTW GL51 .. 92 F7

Willow Cl BRSTK/PCHW BS34 .. 316 A4
 CHELTE/BC GL52 .... 72 D8
 DSLY GL11 .... 229 J8 [1]
 EVE WR11 .... 29 K4
 LGASH BS41 .... 344 B2
 OLD/WMLY/WICK BS30 .... 338 F5
 OLD/WMLY/WICK BS30 .... 339 K5
 WUE GL12 .... 276 C7
Willowcroft Cl GLE GL4 .... 136 F8 [3]
Willow End MIM GL56 .... 82 C2
The Willowfalls
 CBATH/BATHN BA1 .... 352 A8 [3]
Willow Gv CIR GL7 .... 263 J5
 MANG/FISH BS16 .... 337 L1 [3]
Willow Hts LYD GL15 .... 201 K6
Willowherb Cl CHELTE/BC GL52 .. 3 M2
 CHELTE/BC GL52 .... 94 E8 [3]
Willowleaze VGL GL2 .... 112 F8
Willow Park Dr
 CHELTE/BC GL52 .... 72 B7 [3]
Willow Rd BDWAY WR12 .... 11 G8
 CHELTS GL53 .... 116 E7 [3]
 CHELTS GL53 .... 116 D6
 KGWD/HNM BS15 .... 337 L8 [3]
 STNHO GL10 .... 207 G4
 STNHO GL10 .... 207 J7
The Willows ALMDB BS32 .... 316 F3
 MTCHDN GL17 .... 131 H1
 VGL GL2 .... 159 G2
 YATE/CS BS37 .... 319 M1 [3]
Willow View Cl MALM SN16 .... 303 H7 [3]
Willow Wk HNBRY/STHM BS10 .. 315 K8
 KEYN BS31 .... 347 M7
Willow Wy FRCTL/WBN BS36 .. 318 E5 [2]
 GLE GL4 .... 136 D4
Willsbridge Hl
 OLD/WMLY/WICK BS30 .... 348 C1
Wills Dr EVILLE/WHL BS5 .... 336 C3
Willway St BMSTR BS3 .... 7 G9
 CBRISNE BS2 .... 7 K3
Wilmot Ct
 OLD/WMLY/WICK BS30 .... 338 C5 [3]
Wilshire Av KGWD/HNM BS15 .. 337 M6
Wilson Pl CBRISNE BS2 .... 336 B3 [3]
Wilson Rd CHELTW GL51 .... 138 F2
Wilson St CBRISNE BS2 .... 7 H1
Wilton Cl HNBRY/STHM BS10 .. 325 L3
Wilton Rd GL GL1 .... 135 M5
Wiltshire Av YATE/CS BS37 .... 310 C8
Wiltshire Pl
 KGWD/HNM BS15 .... 328 A8 [3]
Wimbledon Rd
 RDLND/MONT BS6 .... 325 L6
Wimborne Cl CHELTW GL51 .... 115 C5
Wimborne Rd BMSTR BS3 .... 345 L2 [3]
Winash Cl HGRV/WHIT BS14 .. 346 F4
Wincanton Cl
 FRCTL/WBN BS36 .... 328 B2 [3]
Wincel Rd COTS GL54 .... 74 D5
Winchcombe Rd EVE WR11 .... 30 D2
 FRCTL/WBN BS36 .... 318 D3 [3]
 GLE GL4 .... 160 A1 [3]
Winchcombe St CHELTE/BC GL52 .. 2 E5
Winchester Av
 BRSG/KWL/STAPK BS4 .... 336 F8 [3]
Winchester Dr GLE GL4 .... 136 A4
Winchester Rd
 BRSG/KWL/STAPK BS4 .... 336 F8
Winchester Wy CHELTW GL51 .. 115 H5
Wincroft
 OLD/WMLY/WICK BS30 .... 338 E7
Windcliff Crs AVONM BS11 .... 324 A3
Windermere Cl CHELTW GL51 .. 115 G4 [3]
Windermere Rd
 BRSTK/PCHW BS34 .... 316 C3
 CHELTW GL51 .... 115 C4
 VGL GL2 .... 112 E7
Windermere Wy
 OLD/WMLY/WICK BS30 .... 338 F5
Windmill Cl BMSTR BS3 .... 7 G9
Windmill Fld GLE GL4 .... 136 F4
Windmill Hl BMSTR BS3 .... 335 M8
Windmill La HNBRY/STHM BS10 .. 314 F8
Windmill Rd CIR GL7 .... 261 H3
 STROUD GL5 .... 232 F4
Windrush Ct THNB/SVB BS35 .. 293 L3
Windrush Rd CHELTE/BC GL52 .. 3 K3
 GLE GL4 .... 160 A1
 KEYN BS31 .... 348 C7
Windrush Wy COTS GL54 .... 120 D2
Windsor Av OLD/WMLY/WICK BS30 .. 337 K5
Windsor Cl
 BRSTK/PCHW BS34 .... 317 G7 [3]
Windsor Ct MANG/FISH BS16 .. 328 A4
Windsor Crs
 HNBRY/STHM BS10 .... 314 E7
Windsor Dr GL GL1 .... 159 L1 [3]
 LYD GL15 .... 201 K5
 YATE/CS BS37 .... 309 M8
 YATE/CS BS37 .... 319 M1
Windsor Gv
 EVILLE/WHL BS5 .... 336 D3 [17]
Windsor La DSLY GL11 .... 254 C3
Windsor Pl CFTN/FAIL BS8 .... 335 H5
 MANG/FISH BS16 .... 328 C6
Windsor Rd DSLY GL11 .... 253 L2 [3]
 OLD/WMLY/WICK BS30 .... 348 B1 [3]
 RDLND/MONT BS6 .... 336 A1
 TET GL8 .... 281 M3
Windsor St CHELTE/BC GL52 .... 3 G2
Windsor Ter BMSTR BS3 .... 7 J9
 CFTN/FAIL BS8 .... 335 H5 [17]
Windyridge Gdns CHELTW GL51 .. 93 L6
Windyridge Rd CHELTW GL51 .. 93 K6
Wineberry Cl EVILLE/WHL BS5 .. 336 F2
Wine St CBRIS/FH BS1 .... 6 F3
Winfield NWNT GL18 .... 86 B3
Winfield Rd
 OLD/WMLY/WICK BS30 .... 338 E4
Winford Gv
 BMSTRD/HC/WWD BS13 .... 345 J3
Wingfield Rd BMSTR BS3 .... 346 A1
Wing La TEWK GL20 .... 27 M3
Winkworth Pl CBRISNE BS2 .... 336 B2 [3]
Winnycroft La GLE GL4 .... 160 E2

Winsbury Wy ALMDB BS32 .... 316 E3
Winscombe Cl KEYN BS31 .... 347 M5
Winsford St EVILLE/WHL BS5 .. 7 L1 [3]
Winsham Cl
 HGRV/WHIT BS14 .... 346 D6 [3]
Winsley Rd GLE GL4 .... 136 E7
 RDLND/MONT BS6 .... 335 M2 [3]
Winston Cl LED HR8 .... 20 A5 [3]
Winstonian Rd CHELTE/BC GL52 .. 3 G4
Winston Rd BWTH/CHD GL3 .... 113 K6
Winterbotham Rd CHELTW GL51 .. 92 F8
 DSLY GL11 .... 229 H6
Winterbourne Hl
 FRCTL/WBN BS36 .... 317 M6
Winterbourne Rd
 BRSTK/PCHW BS34 .... 317 G5
Winterspring La WUE GL12 .... 278 B8
Winterstoke Cl BMSTR BS3 .... 345 K1 [13]
Winterstoke Rd BMSTR BS3 .... 335 H8
Winterway MIM GL56 .... 35 H8
Wintles Cl MTCHDN GL17 .... 130 C2
Wintle's Hl CIND GL14 .... 156 C3
Wintles La CIND GL14 .... 132 A5
Winton Cl CHELTW GL51 .... 115 H4
Winton Rd CHELTW GL51 .... 115 H4
Winton St BRSG/KWL/STAPK BS4 .. 7 K9
Wirewood Cl CHELTW GL51 .... 270 B1
Wirewood Crs CHEP NP16 .... 270 C1
Wishford Cl VGL GL2 .... 113 C7
Wisloe Rd VGL GL2 .... 229 C1
Wistaria Av YATE/CS BS37 .... 320 C2 [3]
Wistaria Rd TET GL8 .... 281 M3
Wisteria Wy BWTH/CHD GL3 .. 113 H5
Wistley Rd CHELTS GL53 .... 116 D7
Witchell Rd
 EVILLE/WHL BS5 .... 336 E4 [17]
Witch Hazel Rd
 BMSTRD/HC/WWD BS13 .... 346 A8
Witcombe YATE/CS BS37 .... 319 L4
Witcombe Cl KGWD/HNM BS15 .. 338 A2
Witcombe Pl CHELTE/BC GL52 .. 2 F6
Witham Rd KEYN BS31 .... 348 C8
Witherlies Rd
 MANG/FISH BS16 .... 327 H5 [3]
The Withers CHELTE/BC GL52 .. 72 B7
Withey Cl West
 HNLZ/SM/SNYPK/WT BS9 .... 325 G6
The Witheys HGRV/WHIT BS14 .. 346 E7
Withington Cl
 OLD/WMLY/WICK BS30 .... 348 E1 [3]
Withleigh Rd
 BRSG/KWL/STAPK BS4 .... 346 D1 [3]
Withy Br CHELTW GL51 .... 92 D5
Withybridge Gdns CHELTW GL51 .. 92 C3
Withybridge La CHELTW GL51 .. 92 C3
Withy Cl East
 HNLZ/SM/SNYPK/WT BS9 .... 325 H6
Withyfield Rd CHELTE/BC GL52 .. 72 C7
Withyholt Pk CHELTS GL53 .... 116 B6 [3]
Withymead Rd
 CHPMW/MSHF SN14 .... 342 D3
Withy Ms GLE GL4 .... 136 D6
Withypool CHELTW GL51 .... 115 G6 [13]
Withypool Gdns
 HGRV/WHIT BS14 .... 346 D6 [10]
Withy Wy DSLY GL11 .... 229 H6
Withywood Rd
 BMSTRD/HC/WWD BS13 .... 345 H7
Witley Lodge Cl
 CHELTW GL51 .... 114 F5 [3]
Witney Cl KEYN BS31 .... 348 F8
Witpit La CIR GL7 .... 239 H4
Woburn Av GLE GL4 .... 159 L2
Woburn Cl
 OLD/WMLY/WICK BS30 .... 338 B6 [3]
Woburn Rd EVILLE/WHL BS5 .. 326 D8
Woefuldane Bottom
 RSTROUD/NAIL GL6 .... 233 K6
Wolds End Cl CHCAM GL55 .... 12 E7
Wolferton Rd
 RDLND/MONT BS6 .... 336 B1
Wolford Rd MIM GL56 .... 37 L8
Wolfridge Gdns
 HNBRY/STHM BS10 .... 315 J7
Wolfridge La THNB/SVB BS35 .. 293 H7
Wolfridge Ride THNB/SVB BS35 .. 293 H7
Wolseley Rd HORF/LLZ BS7 .... 325 M8
 VGL GL2 .... 136 E1
Woodbine Cl GLE GL4 .... 137 G6 [3]
Woodbine Rd
 EVILLE/WHL BS5 .... 336 F3 [15]
Woodborough Cl
 RSTROUD/NAIL GL6 .... 185 H4 [3]
Woodborough St
 EVILLE/WHL BS5 .... 336 D2 [14]
Woodbridge La COTS GL54 .... 166 F1 [3]
Woodbridge Rd
 BRSG/KWL/STAPK BS4 .... 346 C1
Woodchester
 KGWD/HNM BS15 .... 328 A8 [3]
 YATE/CS BS37 .... 320 A5
Woodchester Rd
 HNBRY/STHM BS10 .... 325 L4 [3]
Woodcock Cl GLE GL4 .... 136 E6
 STNHO GL10 .... 207 H2
Woodcock La STNHO GL10 .... 207 H3
Woodcote KGWD/HNM BS15 .. 337 M5 [3]
 VGL GL2 .... 112 D6 [3]
Woodcote Rd MANG/FISH BS16 .. 337 K1
Woodcote Wk
 MANG/FISH BS16 .... 337 K1
Woodcroft Av
 EVILLE/WHL BS5 .... 336 F2 [3]
Woodcroft Cl
 BRSG/KWL/STAPK BS4 .... 337 G7
 CHEP NP16 .... 246 C7
Woodcroft La CHEP NP16 .... 246 C7
Woodcroft Rd
 BRSG/KWL/STAPK BS4 .... 337 G7
Wood Edge Rd CLFD GL16 .... 175 L5
Woodend KGWD/HNM BS15 .. 337 M5 [3]
Woodend Cl GLE GL4 .... 137 G3
Woodend La BRKLY GL13 .... 273 M1
 CIND GL14 .... 179 M7
 DSLY GL11 .... 228 E4
 DSLY GL11 .... 229 H5
 RWYE HR9 .... 84 C4
Woodend Rd FRCTL/WBN BS36 .. 318 D4

MTCHDN GL17 .... 129 M5
Wood End St LED HR8 .... 42 F4
Wood End Wk
 HNLZ/SM/SNYPK/WT BS9 .... 324 E5
Woodfield Rd DSLY GL11 .... 229 M5
 LED HR8 .... 19 M5
 RDLND/MONT BS6 .... 335 K2
Woodgate Cl CHELTS GL53 .... 116 E6 [3]
 GLE GL4 .... 137 G3 [3]
Woodgate Rd CIND GL14 .... 154 B2
 CLFD GL16 .... 151 L6
Woodgrove Rd
 HNBRY/STHM BS10 .... 324 F1
Woodhall Rd
 MANG/FISH BS16 .... 328 B5 [3]
Woodhouse Av ALMDB BS32 .... 306 F4
Woodhouse Cl ALMDB BS32 .... 306 F4
 CIR GL7 .... 238 B5
Woodhouse Dr STROUD GL5 .... 208 D5
Woodhouse Gv HORF/LLZ BS7 .. 326 A5
Woodington Ct
 OLD/WMLY/WICK BS30 .... 338 B7 [21]
Woodland Av DSLY GL11 .... 253 J1 [3]
 KGWD/HNM BS15 .... 337 M1 [3]
Woodland Cl BDWAY WR12 .... 31 H2 [3]
Woodland Dr DSLY GL11 .... 253 J1 [3]
Woodland Gn GLE GL4 .... 137 G3
Woodland Gv
 HNLZ/SM/SNYPK/WT BS9 .... 324 F5
Woodland Pl LYD GL15 .... 177 L8
Woodland Ri LYD GL15 .... 176 F5
 LYD GL15 .... 201 K7
Woodland Rd CFTN/FAIL BS8 .... 6 C2
 CFTN/FAIL BS8 .... 335 L3
 CLFD GL16 .... 151 H4
 LYD GL15 .... 176 F5
 LYD GL15 .... 200 C2
 MTCHDN GL17 .... 129 M3
 WUE GL12 .... 275 K7
Woodlands ALMDB BS32 .... 306 F8
 MANG/FISH BS16 .... 328 A5 [3]
 STNHO GL10 .... 207 G8
Woodlands Cl LYD GL15 .... 200 F2
Woodlands Dr STROUD GL5 .... 209 G3 [3]
Woodlands La ALMDB BS32 .... 316 E1
 BRKLY GL13 .... 250 C2
Woodlands MI STROUD GL5 .... 209 G3 [3]
Woodlands Reach CIND GL14 .. 154 B3
Woodlands Ri MANG/FISH BS16 .. 327 M5
Woodlands Rd CHELT GL50 .... 115 J6
 CIR GL7 .... 238 B5
 WUE GL12 .... 276 C7
The Woodlands STROUD GL5 .. 208 F3 [3]
Woodland Ter
 KGWD/HNM BS15 .... 337 M4
 RDLND/MONT BS6 .... 335 K1 [3]
Woodland Vw CIR GL7 .... 189 L4 [3]
Woodland Wy
 HNLZ/SM/SNYPK/WT BS9 .... 337 L1
Wood La CHPMW/MSHF SN14 .. 333 K3
 EVE WR11 .... 29 K1
 NWNT GL18 .... 85 J4
 RSTROUD/NAIL GL6 .... 232 E7
 SHPSTR CV36 .... 39 J5
 VGL GL2 .... 113 J1
 YATE/CS BS37 .... 311 J2
Woodlea CHPMW/MSHF SN14 .. 343 L5
Woodleaze
 HNLZ/SM/SNYPK/WT BS9 .... 324 D5
Woodleigh THNB/SVB BS35 .... 293 L2
Woodleigh Cl LED HR8 .... 19 L3
Woodleigh Fld VGL GL2 .... 111 G5 [3]
Woodleigh Gdns
 HGRV/WHIT BS14 .... 346 E5
Woodleigh Rd LED HR8 .... 19 M3
Woodmancote DSLY GL11 .... 253 K3
 YATE/CS BS37 .... 319 M3
Woodmancote Rd
 RDLND/MONT BS6 .... 336 A2 [3]
Woodmancote V
 CHELTE/BC GL52 .... 72 D8 [10]
Woodmans Cl YATE/CS BS37 .... 320 D3
Woodmans Rd YATE/CS BS37 .... 320 D3
Woodmans V YATE/CS BS37 .... 320 E3 [3]
Woodmans Wy CHELTE/BC GL52 .. 72 B8
Woodmarsh Cl
 HGRV/WHIT BS14 .... 346 C7
Woodmead Gdns
 BMSTRD/HC/WWD BS13 .... 345 L7
Woodmead La
 OLD/WMLY/WICK BS30 .... 340 C2
Woodpecker Crs
 MANG/FISH BS16 .... 329 L7 [3]
Woodpecker Av VGL GL2 .... 135 L6
Woodpeckers Cl
 RTEWK/TIB GL19 .... 89 J2 [3]
Wood Rd CLFD GL16 .... 151 M7
 KGWD/HNM BS15 .... 337 M3
Woodrow Wy VGL GL2 .... 135 J8
Woodruff Cl GLE GL4 .... 136 D6
Woodside LYD GL15 .... 223 L5
Woodside Av CIND GL14 .... 154 B3
Woodside Dr BUR/CRTN OX18 .. 197 L4
Woodside Gv
 HNBRY/STHM BS10 .... 314 F8
Woodside La STNHO GL10 .... 231 H1
Woodside Rd
 BRSG/KWL/STAPK BS4 .... 337 G5
 FRCTL/WBN BS36 .... 318 F4
 KGWD/HNM BS15 .... 337 L3
 LYD GL15 .... 223 L7
 MANG/FISH BS16 .... 327 L4
Woods Orch GLE GL4 .... 160 A1
Woods Orchard Rd GLE GL4 .. 160 A1
Woodstock Av
 RDLND/MONT BS6 .... 335 L2 [3]
Woodstock Cl
 KGWD/HNM BS15 .... 338 B3 [3]
 TET GL8 .... 257 K2 [3]
Woodstock La TET GL8 .... 257 K2
Woodstock Rd
 KGWD/HNM BS15 .... 338 B4 [10]
 RDLND/MONT BS6 .... 335 K1
Woodstock Ter DSLY GL11 .... 254 E2
Wood St EVILLE/WHL BS5 .... 336 D1 [3]
 STROUD GL5 .... 208 F3

TEWK GL20 .... 47 G2
Woodview Cl *AVONM* BS11 ..... 324 A4
Woodview Rd *DSLY* GL11 ... 229 J7
Woodville Cl *CLFD* GL16 ..... 151 M7
Woodville Rd *CIND* GL14 ..... 154 C3
TEWK GL20 ..... 48 B8
Woodville Rd West *CIND* GL14 ... 154 B3
Woodward Cl *TET* CL8 ... 281 M2
Woodward Dr
OLD/WMLY/WICK BS30 ..... 338 B7
Woodwell Rd *AVONM* BS11 ..... 324 A5
Woodyleaze Dr
KGWD/HNM BS15 ..... 337 L5
Woolaston Common *LYD* GL15 ... 223 M4
Woolcot St *RDLND/MONT* BS6 ... 335 K1
Woolley La *CBATH/BATHN* BA1 .... 351 J6
Woolley Rd *HGRV/WHIT* BS14 .. 347 G6
Woolstone La *CHELTE/BC* GL52 ... 72 B2
Woolstrop Wy *VGL* GL2 ..... 135 J8
Woolthorpe La *VGL* GL2 ..... 156 A8
Wootton Crs
BRSG/KWL/STAPK BS4.. 337 G5
Wootton Pk *HGRV/WHIT* BS14 .. 346 D2
Wootton Rd
BRSG/KWL/STAPK BS4.. 337 G5
Worcester Cl *MANG/FISH* BS16... 337 K1
Worcester Pde *GL* GL1 ..... 4 F3
Worcester Rd *CFTN/FAIL* BS8 ... 335 J3
CHNTN OX7 ..... 83 M8
CHNTN OX7 ..... 105 K1
CIND GL14 ..... 154 C2
KGWD/HNM BS15 ..... 337 M2
LED HR8 ..... 20 A3
RTEWK/TIB GL19 ..... 66 F8
Worcestershire Wy
RGTMLV WR13 ..... 21 K3
Worcester St *GL* GL1 ..... 4 F4
Worcester Ter *CFTN/FAIL* BS8... 335 J3
Worcester Wk *CLFD* GL16 ..... 151 M8
Worchester Road
RTEWK/TIB GL19 ..... 67 H5

Worcestershire Way Link
TEWK GL20 ..... 24 F8
The Wordens *STROUD* GL5 ... 207 M3
Wordsworth Av *CHELTW* GL51 115 G2
Wordsworth Rd *DSLY* GL11 ... 253 L4
HORF/LLZ BS7 ..... 326 C4
Working La *COTS* GL54 ..... 73 M2
Worldsend La *BRKLY* GL13 ..... 250 A3
World's End La *KEYN* BS31 ..... 348 E6
Worley Rdg *RDLND/MONT* GL6... 232 C7
Wormcliff La *COR/BOX* SN13 ... 353 J7
Wormwood HI
RSTROUD/NAIL GL6 ..... 256 B2
Worrall Rd *CFTN/FAIL* BS8 ..... 335 J1
Worrel's La *MANG/FISH* BS16 ... 317 M8
Worsley St *EVILLE/WHL* BS5 ... 336 F4
Worth Cl *KGWD/HNM* BS15 ... 338 B5
Wortheys Cl *MALM* SN16 ..... 303 J6
Worthing Rd
BRSTK/PCHW BS34 ..... 316 B3
The Worthys *ALMDB* BS32 ... 317 J5
Wortley Rd *WUE* GL12 ..... 277 L5
Wotton Cl *GLE* GL4 ..... 136 F2
Wotton Crs *WUE* GL12 ..... 277 L5
Wotton Rd *WUE* GL12 ..... 276 C6
YATE/CS BS37 ..... 309 G7
Wragg Castle La
RSTROUD/NAIL GL6 ..... 184 E5
Wraxall Gv
BMSTRD/HC/WWD BS13 .. 345 H3
Wraxall Rd *KGWD/HNM* BS15 .. 338 C5
OLD/WMLY/WICK BS30 ..... 338 C5
Wrenbert Rd *MANG/FISH* BS16... 327 M6
Wren Cl *GLE* GL4 ..... 136 D5
Wren Dr *MANG/FISH* BS16 ..... 327 H5
Wren Ter *VGL* GL2 ..... 112 F5
Wright Cl *COTS* GL54 ..... 124 C6
Wright Rd *COTS* GL54 ..... 124 C6
Wrington Cl *BRSTK/PCHW* BS34.. 316 E4
Wrington Crs
BMSTRD/HC/WWD BS13 ... 345 J4
Wroughton Dr
BMSTRD/HC/WWD BS13 ... 345 M7

Wroughton Gdns
BMSTRD/HC/WWD BS13 ...... 345 M7
Wroxham Dr
BRSTK/PCHW BS34 ...... 316 E3
Wyatt Av
BMSTRD/HC/WWD BS13 ...... 345 H6
Wyatt Cl
BMSTRD/HC/WWD BS13 ...... 345 H6
Wychavon Wy *TEWK* GL20 ...... 52 A2
Wychbury Cl *CHELTS* GL53 ... 115 M6
Wychovon Wy *EVE* WR11 ..... 29 L6
Wychwood *KGWD/HNM* BS15 .... 337 M5
Wyck Beck Rd
HNBRY/STHM BS10 ...... 315 J7
Wycliffe Rd
HNLZ/SM/SNYPK/WT BS9... 325 K4
Wycombe Gv
BRSG/KWL/STAPK BS4 ...... 346 F1
Wydelands *MIM* GL56 ..... 35 K7
Wyebank Av *CHEP* NP16 ..... 270 C3
Wyebank Cl *CHEP* NP16 ..... 270 C3
Wyebank Crs *CHEP* NP16 ..... 270 C3
Wyebank Pl *CHEP* NP16 ..... 270 C3
Wyebank Ri *CHEP* NP16 ..... 270 C3
Wyebank Rd *CHEP* NP16 ..... 270 C3
Wyebank Vw *CHEP* NP16 ..... 270 C3
Wyebank Wy *CHEP* NP16 ..... 270 C3
Wye Ct *THNB/SVB* BS35 ..... 293 L3
Wye Crs *CHEP* NP16 ..... 270 A4
Wye Croft Cl
HNBRY/STHM BS10 ...... 315 M8
Wyedale Av
HNLZ/SM/SNYPK/WT BS9... 324 D4
Wye Rd *BWTH/CHD* GL3 ..... 138 B6
Wye Valley Wk *CHEP* NP16 ..... 222 A3
CHEP NP16 ..... 246 A8
RWYE HR9 ..... 128 C4
Wye View La *RWYE* HR9 ..... 126 E5
Wykis Cl *KGWD/HNM* BS15 ..... 338 A6
Wyman's La *CHELTW* GL51 ..... 93 K5
Wyman's Rd *CHELTE/BC* GL52 ...... 3 J2

Wymbush Crs
BMSTRD/HC/WWD BS13 ...... 345 L6
Wymbush Gdns
BMSTRD/HC/WWD BS13 ...... 345 L6
Wyndbrook La *RTEWK/TIB* GL19 .. 44 B4
Wyndham Crs
BRSG/KWL/STAPK BS4.. 337 H8
Wynols Cl *CLFD* GL16 ..... 175 M1
Wynols Hill La *CLFD* GL16 ..... 151 K8
Wynols Rd *CLFD* GL16 ..... 175 M1
The Wynstones
KGWD/HNM BS15 ..... 337 L4
Wynyards Cl *TEWK* GL20 ..... 48 B5
Wyvern Rd *CHEP* NP16 ..... 290 D1

Y

Yanleigh Cl
BMSTRD/HC/WWD BS13...... 344 E5
Yanley La *LGASH* BS41 ...... 344 D3
The Yard *EVE* WR11 ..... 30 D1
Yarlington Cl *CHELTE/BC* GL52 .. 72 A7
Yarnolds *CHELTW* GL51 ..... 138 F2
Yarrow Cl *GLE* GL4 ..... 136 C7
Yartleton La *MTCHDN* GL17 ... 107 H4
Yate Rd *YATE/CS* BS37 ..... 308 F7
Yate Rocks *YATE/CS* BS37 ..... 310 B4
Yellow Hundred Cl *DSLY* GL11 ... 253 K2
Yeoman Cl *LED* HR8 ..... 19 L1
Yeomans Cl
HNLZ/SM/SNYPK/WT BS9 ..... 324 F6
Yeomanside Cl
HGRV/WHIT BS14 ..... 346 E6
Yeomeads *LGASH* BS41 ..... 344 B2
The Yetts *CHEP* NP16 ..... 270 D4
Yewcroft Cl *HGRV/WHIT* BS14 .. 346 C7
Yew Tree Cl *CHELTW* GL51 ..... 93 L6
Yewtree Cl *DSLY* GL11 ..... 228 F8
Yew Tree Dr *CHELTE/BC* GL52 .. 72 C3

KGWD/HNM BS15 ..... 328 B8
Yew Tree Wy *BWTH/CHD* GL3 .... 113 J6
STROUD GL5 ..... 209 G8
Yokehouse La
RSTROUD/NAIL GL6 ..... 185 H6
York Av *HORF/LLZ* BS7 ..... 326 B7
York Cl *BRSTK/PCHW* BS34 ... 316 F7
FRCTL/WBN BS36 ..... 328 B2
YATE/CS BS37 ..... 310 A7
York Gdns *CFTN/FAIL* BS8 ..... 335 H5
FRCTL/WBN BS36 ..... 318 B3
Yorkley La *LYD* GL15 ..... 201 K2
Yorkley Wood Rd *LYD* GL15 ... 201 J2
York Pl *CBRIS/FH* BS1 ..... 6 C5
CFTN/FAIL BS8 ..... 6 A3
York Rd *BMSTR* BS3 ..... 7 G8
CIND GL14 ..... 154 C2
EVILLE/WHL BS5 ..... 336 E2
GLE GL4 ..... 136 E3
MANG/FISH BS16 ..... 328 A7
RDLND/MONT BS6 ..... 336 A2
TEWK GL20 ..... 48 A7
York Rw *CHELTE/BC* GL52 ..... 94 C7
York St *CBRISNE* BS2 ..... 7 G1
CBRISNE BS2 ..... 336 B1
CBRISNE BS2 ..... 336 C1
CFTN/FAIL BS8 ..... 335 J1
CHELTE/BC GL52 ..... 2 F4
EVILLE/WHL BS5 ..... 336 E4
Youngs Ct *MANG/FISH* BS16 ... 328 D3
Youngs Orch *STROUD* GL5 ..... 233 J2

Z

Zetland Rd *RDLND/MONT* BS6 .... 335 M1
Zinnia Cl *BWTH/CHD* GL3 ..... 113 H4
Zion HI *RSTROUD/NAIL* GL6 ..... 184 B8
Zoons Rd *BWTH/CHD* GL3 ..... 137 J5

Index - featured places

3-D Gallery
CBRISNE BS2 ..... 6 E2
Abbey House Studio & Gallery
CHEP NP16 ..... 222 A6
Abbeymead Primary School
GLE GL4 ..... 137 H6
Abbotswood Infant School
YATE/CS BS37 ..... 319 M5
Abbotswood Surgery
YATE/CS BS37 ..... 319 M4
ABC Cinema
CFTN/FAIL BS8 ..... 335 K3
Air Balloon Hill Junior &
Infant School
EVILLE/WHL BS5 ..... 337 J4
Airthrie School
CHELT GL50 ..... 115 K2
Alderman Knight School
TEWK GL20 ..... 48 E4
Allen School House
OLD/WMLY/WICK BS30 ..... 338 C6
All Saints Exhibition Centre
CBRIS/FH BS1 ..... 6 F3
Almondsbury Business Centre
ALMDB BS32 ..... 306 F8
Almondsbury
C of E VC Primary School
ALMDB BS32 ..... 306 C7
Almondsbury Surgery
ALMDB BS32 ..... 306 C6
Almondsbury Town
Football Club
ALMDB BS32 ..... 306 C7
Alstone Trading Estate
CHELTW GL51 ..... 115 J2
Amberley House School
CFTN/FAIL BS8 ..... 335 J2
Amberley Parochial School
STROUD GL5 ..... 232 E4
Amberley Ridge
Special School
STROUD GL5 ..... 232 E2
Amelia Nutt Clinic
BMSTRD/HC/WWD BS13 .. 345 H7
Amphitheatre
CBRIS/FH BS1 ..... 6 D6
Anchor Business Centre
RDLND/MONT BS6 ..... 335 K2
Anderson Gallery
BDWAY WR12 ..... 33 G3
Andoversford
Industrial Estate
COTS GL54 ..... 118 D8
Andoversford Primary School
COTS GL54 ..... 118 C8
Andoversford Sports Club
COTS GL54 ..... 118 C8
Ann Edwards School
CIR GL7 ..... 263 H5
The Archway School
STROUD GL5 ..... 208 B3
Aretians RFC Clubhouse
BRSTK/PCHW BS34 ..... 316 D4
Army Apprentices College
CHEP NP16 ..... 270 D8
Arnolsfield Trading Estate
WUE GL12 ..... 296 C6
Arnolfini Gallery
CBRIS/FH BS1 ..... 6 E6
Art Gallery
CHELT GL50 ..... 2 C8
Arthur Dye CP School
CHELTW GL51 ..... 92 F7

Ashchurch Business Centre
TEWK GL20 ..... 48 F3
Ashchurch County
Primary School
TEWK GL20 ..... 49 H4
Ashleworth C of E
Primary School
RTEWK/TIB GL19 ..... 89 J3
Ashley Down Junior School
HORF/LLZ BS7 ..... 326 A6
Ashley Down OB Rugby Club
HORF/LLZ BS7 ..... 326 D3
Ashley Trading Estate
RDLND/MONT BS6 ..... 336 B1
Ashmead Business Park
KEYN BS31 ..... 348 D6
Ashton Gate Primary School
BMSTR BS3 ..... 335 J7
Ashton Keynes C of E School
HCHW SN6 ..... 287 G2
Ashton Park School
BMSTR BS3 ..... 335 G8
Ashton under Hill
Primary School
EVE WR11 ..... 29 K3
Ashton Vale Primary School
BMSTR BS3 ..... 345 H1
Ashville Industrial Estate
VGL GL2 ..... 135 L6
Ashville Trading Estate
CHELTW GL51 ..... 93 K5
Ashville Trading Estate
VGL GL2 ..... 135 L6
Ashwicke Hall (School)
CHPMW/MSHF SN14 ..... 342 E7
Avening School
TET GL8 ..... 257 K2
Avlon Works
HNBRY/STHM BS10 ..... 304 D8
Avon Business Park
MANG/FISH BS16 ..... 327 J8
Avon County Council
BMSTR BS3 ..... 346 A1
Avondale Business Centre
MANG/FISH BS16 ..... 337 L1
Avon & Somerset
Constabulary
CBRIS/FH BS1 ..... 6 F2
Avon Trading Estate
CBRISNE BS2 ..... 7 L6
Axiom Arts Centre
CHELTE/BC GL52 ..... 2 E4
Aylburton C of E School
LYD GL15 ..... 224 F2
Azure Gallery
HNLZ/SM/SNYPK/WT BS9 .. 325 H4
Badminton Road Trading Estate
YATE/CS BS37 ..... 319 L2
Badminton School
HNLZ/SM/SNYPK/WT BS9 .. 325 J6
Badocks Wood Primary School
HNBRY/STHM BS10 ..... 325 L3
Badsey First School
EVE WR11 ..... 10 A1
Baileys Court Primary School
ALMDB BS32 ..... 317 H5
Balaclava Industrial Estate
MANG/FISH BS16 ..... 327 H8
Balcarras School
CHELTS GL53 ..... 116 E6
Bank Leaze Primary School
AVONM BS11 ..... 324 D1

Bankside Industrial Estate
LED HR8 ..... 19 L4
Bank Yard Industrial Estate
WUE GL12 ..... 277 J4
Bannerman Road
Primary School
EVILLE/WHL BS5 ..... 336 D2
Barley Close Primary School
MANG/FISH BS16 ..... 328 C5
Barnack Trading Centre
BMSTR BS3 ..... 345 L2
The Barn Business Centre
COTS GL54 ..... 148 C3
Barn Close Surgery
BDWAY WR12 ..... 32 F3
Barnwood Business Centre
GLE GL4 ..... 136 F2
Barnwood Business Centre
GLE GL4 ..... 137 H2
Barnwood C of E
Primary School
GLE GL4 ..... 136 F2
Barrett Industrial Estate
GL GL1 ..... 4 D1
Barrow Hospital
NAIL BS48 ..... 344 C5
Barrs Court Primary School
OLD/WMLY/WICK BS30 ..... 338 B6
Bartongate Surgery
GL GL1 ..... 5 G7
Barton Hill Primary School
EVILLE/WHL BS5 ..... 336 D5
Barton Hill Trading Estate
EVILLE/WHL BS5 ..... 336 D5
Batheaston Medical Centre
CBATH/BATHN BA1 ..... 352 B7
Batheaston Primary School
CBATH/BATHN BA1 ..... 352 B7
Battledown Industrial Estate
CHELTE/BC GL52 ..... 3 J7
Beachley Road
Doctors Surgery
CHEP NP16 ..... 270 C3
The Beacon Medical Practice
RSTROUD/NAIL GL6 ..... 185 G4
Beacon Rise Junior School
KGWD/HNM BS15 ..... 337 M5
Beaufort Community School
GL GL1 ..... 159 K1
Bedminster Down School
BMSTRD/HC/WWD BS13 ... 345 H4
Beeches Trading Estate
YATE/CS BS37 ..... 319 J1
Beech Green CP School
VGL GL2 ..... 159 H2
Beechwood Shopping Centre
CHELTE/BC GL52 ..... 2 E5
Beehive Trading Estate
EVILLE/WHL BS5 ..... 337 G4
Begbrook Primary School
MANG/FISH BS16 ..... 327 H4
Bells Hotel & the Royal
Forest of Dean Golf Club
CLFD GL16 ..... 175 K1
Benhall Infant School
CHELTW GL51 ..... 114 F4
Berkeley Association
Football Club
BRKLY GL13 ..... 227 H7
Berkeley Castle
BRKLY GL13 ..... 251 H1
Berkeley Hospital
BRKLY GL13 ..... 227 G8

Berkeley Leisure Centre
BRKLY GL13 ..... 227 G4
Berkeley Primary School
BRKLY GL13 ..... 227 G8
Berkeley Vale
Community School
BRKLY GL13 ..... 227 G4
Berkhampstead School
CHELTE/BC GL52 ..... 3 H4
Berry Hill R F C
CLFD GL16 ..... 151 K5
Bettridge School
CHELTW GL51 ..... 115 J5
Bibury C of E Primary School
CIR GL7 ..... 217 K1
Birdlip School
BWTH/CHD GL3 ..... 163 H2
Birdwell Primary School
LGASH BS41 ..... 344 C3
Bishop Road Primary School
HORF/LLZ BS7 ..... 325 M7
Bishops Cleeve Primary School
CHELTE/BC GL52 ..... 72 B8
Bishops Cleeve Sports Centre
CHELTE/BC GL52 ..... 94 C1
Bishopston House Clinic
HORF/LLZ BS7 ..... 326 A7
Bishopsworth C of E School
BMSTRD/HC/WWD BS13 ... 345 H5
Bishopsworth Swimming Pool
BMSTRD/HC/WWD BS13 ... 345 J5
Bisley Blue Coat School
RSTROUD/NAIL GL6 ..... 210 C3
Blackberry Hill Hospital
MANG/FISH BS16 ..... 327 H6
Blackhorse CP School
MANG/FISH BS16 ..... 328 C3
Blaise Hamlet (NT)
HNBRY/STHM BS10 ..... 324 F1
Blakeney CP School
LYD GL15 ..... 202 D1
Bledington County
Primary School
CHNTN OX7 ..... 125 M1
Blockley C of E School
MIM GL56 ..... 35 G8
Blue Coat Church of
England Primary School
WUE GL12 ..... 277 K4
Bond Industrial Estate
EVE WR11 ..... 10 A5
Bonds Mill Trading Estate
STNHO GL10 ..... 206 E4
Bonville Business Centre
BRSG/KWL/STAPK BS4 ... 347 H1
Bourton Industrial Estate
COTS GL54 ..... 123 H4
Bourton on the Water County
Primary School
COTS GL54 ..... 123 H4
Bowden Hall (Hotel)
GLE GL4 ..... 137 J8
Bowling Club
CHELT GL50 ..... 2 B8
Bowling Hill Business Park
YATE/CS BS37 ..... 320 C2
Bownham Park School
STROUD GL5 ..... 232 F1
Box C of E School
COR/BOX SN13 ..... 353 M5
Box Surgery
COR/BOX SN13 ..... 353 M5

Bradgate Surgery
HNBRY/STHM BS10 ..... 315 J8
Brailes C of E Primary School
RBANSW OX15 ..... 17 M8
Brailes Golf Club
RBANSW OX15 ..... 39 M2
Bream Sports Club
LYD GL15 ..... 200 C3
Bredon Hancocks
Endowed First School
TEWK GL20 ..... 27 G4
Bredon School
TEWK GL20 ..... 47 G2
Brentry Hospital
HNBRY/STHM BS10 ..... 325 K1
Brentry Primary School
HNBRY/STHM BS10 ..... 315 K1
Briarwood School
MANG/FISH BS16 ..... 327 K8
Brickhampton Court Golf Club
BWTH/CHD GL3 ..... 113 K3
Brickwell Swimming Pools
RSTROUD/NAIL GL6 ..... 233 M4
Bridge Farm Junior &
Infant School
HGRV/WHIT BS14.. 346 D2
Bridge House Gallery
CIR GL7 ..... 244 D7
Brimscombe C of E
Primary School
STROUD GL5 ..... 233 H2
Brimscombe Mills Estate
STROUD GL5 ..... 233 H2
Brimscombe Port
Business Park
STROUD GL5 ..... 233 H2
Brimsham Green School
YATE/CS BS37 ..... 309 M7
Brislington Retail Park
BRSG/KWL/STAPK BS4 ... 347 G2
Brislington School
BRSG/KWL/STAPK BS4 ... 347 H3
Brislington Trading Estate
BRSG/KWL/STAPK BS4 ... 347 H1
Bristol Baptist College
CFTN/FAIL BS8 ..... 335 H3
Bristol Business Park
MANG/FISH BS16 ..... 327 H2
Bristol Cathedral
CBRIS/FH BS1 ..... 6 D5
Bristol Cathedral School
CBRIS/FH BS1 ..... 6 D5
Bristol City Council
AVONM BS11 ..... 324 C4
Bristol City Council
BMSTR BS3 ..... 7 G8
Bristol City Council
BMSTRD/HC/WWD BS13 .. 345 K7
Bristol City Council
BRSG/KWL/STAPK BS4 ... 336 E7
Bristol City Council
BRSG/KWL/STAPK BS4 ... 337 H8
Bristol City Council
BRSG/KWL/STAPK BS4 ... 345 M4
Bristol City Council
BRSG/KWL/STAPK BS4 ... 346 C1
Bristol City Council
CBRIS/FH BS1 ..... 6 C4
Bristol City Council
CBRIS/FH BS1 ..... 7 G3
Bristol City Council
CBRIS/FH BS1 ..... 7 K6

Bristol City Council
CBRIS/FH BS1 .... **7** G1
Bristol City Council
CBRISNE BS2 .... **336** B2
Bristol City Council
CFTN/FAIL BS8 .... **6** A3
Bristol City Council
CFTN/FAIL BS8 .... **6** C2
Bristol City Council
CFTN/FAIL BS8 .... **335** J6
Bristol City Council
EVILLE/WHL BS5 .... **336** F4
Bristol City Council
EVILLE/WHL BS5 .... **336** D1
Bristol City Council
HGRV/WHIT BS14 .... **346** B6
Bristol City Council
HGRV/WHIT BS14 .... **346** E3
Bristol City Council
HNBRY/STHM BS10 .... **315** K8
Bristol City Council
HNBRY/STHM BS10 .... **325** M1
Bristol City Council
HNBRY/STHM BS10 .... **325** K3
Bristol City Council
HNBRY/STHM BS10 .... **326** A5
Bristol City Council
HNLZ/SM/SNYPK/WT BS9 ..... **335** J1
Bristol City Council
HORF/LLZ BS7 .... **326** B2
Bristol City Football Club
BMSTR BS3 .... **335** H8
Bristol Civil Service
Sports Club
HORF/LLZ BS7 .... **326** B5
Bristol Clifton &
West of England
Zoological Society
CFTN/FAIL BS8 .... **335** H3
Bristol County Court
CBRISNE BS2 .... **6** E2
Bristol County Sports Club
CBRIS/FH BS1 .... **6** D3
Bristol Crown Court
CBRIS/FH BS1 .... **6** E3
Bristol Dental Hospital
CBRIS/FH BS1 .... **6** E2
Bristol General Hospital
CBRIS/FH BS1 .... **6** F7
Bristol Grammar School
CFTN/FAIL BS8 .... **6** B2
Bristol Grammar School
CFTN/FAIL BS8 .... **334** A8
Bristol Harlequins RFC
BRSG/KWL/STAPK BS4 ..... **347** J1
Bristol Ice Rink
CBRIS/FH BS1 .... **6** D3
Bristol Industrial Museum
CBRIS/FH BS1 .... **6** D7
Bristol North Baths
HORF/LLZ BS7 .... **325** M8
Bristol Old Vic
(New Vic Theatre &
Theatre Royal)
CBRIS/FH BS1 .... **6** E4
Bristol Old Vic Theatre School
CFTN/FAIL BS8 .... **335** J2
Bristol Old Vic Theatre School
HNLZ/SM/SNYPK/WT BS9 ..... **335** H2
Bristol Rovers Football Club
BRSG/KWL/STAPK BS4 ..... **347** H2
Bristol Royal Hospital for Sick
Children
CFTN/FAIL BS8 .... **6** D2
Bristol Royal Infirmary
CBRISNE BS2 .... **6** E1
Bristol South Swimming Pool
BMSTR BS3 .... **6** D9
Bristol Steiner Waldorf School
CFTN/FAIL BS8 .... **6** A3
Bristol University
CFTN/FAIL BS8 .... **6** D3
Bristol Vale Trading Estate
BMSTR BS3 .... **345** A3
British Empire &
Commonwealth Museum
CBRIS/FH BS1 .... **7** J6
The British School
WUE GL12 .... **277** L5
Broadfield House
Glass Museum
CIR GL7 .... **238** C2
Broadlands School
KEYN BS31 .... **347** M5
Broadmead Lane
Industrial Estate
KEYN BS31 .... **348** C4
Broadwalk Shopping Centre
BRSG/KWL/STAPK BS4 ..... **346** D1
Broadway County
Infant School
YATE/CS BS37 .... **320** B1
Broadway Dental Health Centre
BDWAY WR12 .... **32** F3
Broadway Primary School
BDWAY WR12 .... **33** G2
Broadway Trading Estate
CIR GL7 .... **263** J6
Broadway United
Football Club
BDWAY WR12 .... **32** D3
Brockeridge Infant School
FRCTL/WBN BS36 .... **318** E4
Brockworth
Comprehensive School
BWTH/CHD GL3 .... **138** B5
Brockworth County
Primary Infant School
BWTH/CHD GL3 .... **138** A5
Bromesberrow C of E School
LED HR8 .... **43** H2
Bromley Heath Infant School
MANG/FISH BS16 .... **328** A3
Bromley Heath Junior School
MANG/FISH BS16 .... **328** A3
Bromsberrow Heath
Business Park
LED HR8 .... **42** E5

Brookfield School
CHELTW GL51 .... **115** J4
Brooklea Clinic
BRSG/KWL/STAPK BS4 ..... **337** G6
Brookside Business Centre
TEWK GL20 .... **48** D4
Broomhill Infant School
BRSG/KWL/STAPK BS4 ..... **337** H8
Broomhill Jm School
BRSG/KWL/STAPK BS4 ..... **337** H8
Brunston Surgery
CLFD GL16 .... **175** J2
B Tech Business Park
CIR GL7 .... **238** D5
Burford Cottage Hospital
BUR/CRTN OX18 .... **173** M6
Burford Golf Club
BUR/CRTN OX18 .... **173** M8
Burford School
BUR/CRTN OX18 .... **173** M7
Burford Surgery
BUR/CRTN OX18 .... **173** M6
Burnbush Primary School
HGRV/WHIT BS14 .... **346** F6
Burnbush School
HGRV/WHIT BS14 .... **346** F5
Bush Industrial Estate
EVILLE/WHL BS5 .... **336** F3
Business Park
VGL GL2 .... **4** B7
The Business Park
BMSTRD/HC/WWD BS13 ..... **346** A8
Bussage C of E
Primary School
RSTROUD/NAIL GL6 .... **209** M7
Butcher Row Folk Museum
LED HR8 .... **20** A3
Cab & Guildhall
CBRIS/FH BS1 .... **6** F3
Cabot Primary School
CBRISNE BS2 .... **336** B3
Cabot Tower
CFTN/FAIL BS8 .... **6** B4
Cadbury Heath CP School
OLD/WMLY/WICK BS30 .... **338** D5
Cadbury Heath Health Centre
OLD/WMLY/WICK BS30 .... **338** C6
Cainscross Parish Council
STROUD GL5 .... **207** M5
Callicroft Infant School
BRSTK/PCHW BS34 .... **316** B3
Callicroft Junior School
BRSTK/PCHW BS34 .... **316** A3
Callowell CP School
STROUD GL5 .... **208** C2
Calton Junior School
GL GL1 .... **136** A5
Cam Everlands CP School
DSLY GL11 .... **229** J7
Cam Hopton School
DSLY GL11 .... **229** J7
Cam House School
DSLY GL11 .... **253** J1
Cam Sports Club
DSLY GL11 .... **229** J7
Canons House
CBRIS/FH BS1 .... **6** D6
The Card Gallery
YATE BS37 .... **320** D2
Carla Trading Estate
BMSTR BS3 .... **335** H8
Carlyle Business Centre
CBRISNE BS2 .... **7** M4
Carrant Brook Junior School
TEWK GL20 .... **49** G2
Carrick Business Park
BRSG/KWL/STAPK BS4 ..... **347** H1
Cascade Swimming Pool
TEWK GL20 .... **48** A5
Cashes Green CP School
RSTROUD/NAIL GL6 .... **207** M3
Castle Business Centre
THNB/SVB BS35 .... **293** K2
Castle CP School
KEYN BS31 .... **347** M8
Castle Hill CP School
BWTH/CHD GL3 .... **138** A7
Castlemorton School
RGTMLV WR13 .... **22** E4
The Castle School
THNB/SVB BS35 .... **293** K1
Cattle Market Industrial Estate
GL GL1 .... **4** E1
Cedars Health Clinic
GL GL1 .... **4** F6
Central Technology College
GLE GL4 .... **136** D6
Central Trading Estate
BRSG/KWL/STAPK BS4 ..... **336** D7
Central Trading Estate
VGL GL2 .... **135** J8
Centurion Industrial Estate
VGL GL2 .... **135** K6
Chalford Hill County
Primary School
RSTROUD/NAIL GL6 .... **234** B1
Chandag County &
Infant School
KEYN BS31 .... **348** C6
Charborough Road CP School
BRSTK/PCHW BS34 .... **326** B1
Charfield CP School
WUE GL12 .... **276** B6
Charles Street Industrial
Estate
GL GL1 .... **5** G7
Charlotte Keel Health Clinic
EVILLE/WHL BS5 .... **336** C2
The Charlton Kings Clinic
CHELTE/BC GL52 .... **116** C4
Charlton Kings County
Infants School
CHELTS GL53 .... **116** D5
Charlton Kings Junior School
CHELTS GL53 .... **116** D6
Chatterton House
CBRIS/FH BS1 .... **7** G6

Cheddar Grove Primary School
BMSTRD/HC/WWD BS13 ..... **345** J3
Cheltenham Borough Council
CHELTW GL51 .... **93** J7
Cheltenham Bournside
School & Sixth Form Centre
CHELTW GL51 .... **115** J5
Cheltenham College
CHELTS GL53 .... **2** D9
Cheltenham College
CHELTS GL53 .... **2** F9
Cheltenham College
Junior School
CHELTS GL53 .... **2** D9
Cheltenham Cricket Club
CHELTE/BC GL52 .... **3** H5
Cheltenham General Hospital
CHELTS GL53 .... **2** E8
Cheltenham & Gloucester
College of Higher Education
CHELT GL50 .... **115** L5
Cheltenham & Gloucester
College of Higher Education
CHELTE/BC GL52 .... **94** B7
Cheltenham & Gloucester
College of Higher Education
CHELTW GL51 .... **2** B1
Cheltenham Kingsmead School
CHELTW GL51 .... **93** H7
Cheltenham Ladies College
CHELT GL50 .... **2** A6
Cheltenham Ladies College
CHELT GL50 .... **2** C6
Cheltenham Ladies College
CHELT GL50 .... **115** K3
Cheltenham North Rugby Club
CHELTE/BC GL52 .... **71** L7
Cheltenham Race Course
CHELTE/BC GL52 .... **94** C5
Cheltenham Retail Park
CHELTW GL51 .... **93** H6
Cheltenham Road Surgery
VGL GL2 .... **5** L3
Cheltenham Saracens
Sports Club
CHELT GL50 .... **2** D3
Cheltenham Saracens
Sports Club
CHELTW GL51 .... **93** J8
Cheltenham Synagogue
CHELT GL50 .... **2** B5
Cheltenham Theatre & Arts Club
CHELT GL50 .... **2** E6
Cheltenham Town Association
Football Club
CHELTE/BC GL52 .... **3** H2
Cheltenham Tutorial College
CHELT GL50 .... **2** C4
Chelworth Industrial Estate
HGHW SN6 .... **288** C6
Chepstow Castle
CHEP NP16 .... **270** A2
Chepstow County Court
CHEP NP16 .... **270** B3
Chepstow Museum
CHEP NP16 .... **270** A2
Cherry Garden Primary School
OLD/WMLY/WICK BS30 .... **348** D1
Chesterfield Hospital
CFTN/FAIL BS8 .... **335** J5
Chester Park Primary School
MANG/FISH BS16 .... **327** J8
Chesterton County
Primary School
CIR GL7 .... **238** C5
Childswickham School
BDWAY WR12 .... **32** B1
Chipping Campden School
CHCAM GL55 .... **12** E7
Chipping Edge Estate
YATE/CS BS37 .... **320** D2
Chipping Sodbury Library
YATE/CS BS37 .... **320** D2
Chipping Sodbury School
YATE/CS BS37 .... **320** D3
The Chipping Surgery
WUE GL12 .... **277** J4
Chosen Hill Former
Pupils Rugby Football Club
BWTH/CHD GL3 .... **113** M6
Chosen Hill School
BWTH/CHD GL3 .... **114** A6
Christchurch C of E
Primary School
CFTN/FAIL BS8 .... **335** J4
Christ Church C of E School
RSTROUD/NAIL GL6 .... **234** A1
Christ Church C of E Vc
Infant School
MANG/FISH BS16 .... **327** M6
Christchurch Junior School
MANG/FISH BS16 .... **327** M6
Christchurch School
CHELTW GL51 .... **115** K2
Christ the King RC School
THNB/SVB BS35 .... **293** L2
Churcham School
VGL GL2 .... **133** K1
Churchdown School
BWTH/CHD GL3 .... **113** K6
Churchdown Village
County Junior School
BWTH/CHD GL3 .... **113** L7
Churchdown Village
Infant School
BWTH/CHD GL3 .... **113** L6
Churchill Industrial Estate
CHELTS GL53 .... **115** M5
Church of England School
CLFD GL16 .... **175** J7
Church Street Gallery
COTS GL54 .... **101** M3
Cirencester Business Estate
CIR GL7 .... **238** E5
Cirencester College
CIR GL7 .... **238** A3

Cirencester
Comprehensive School
CIR GL7 .... **237** M3
Cirencester County
Junior School
CIR GL7 .... **238** D3
Cirencester Golf Club
CIR GL7 .... **214** B5
Cirencester Hospital
CIR GL7 .... **238** B4
Cirencester Kingshill School
CIR GL7 .... **238** F2
Cirencester Polo Club
CIR GL7 .... **238** A3
Cirencester Rugby Union Club
CIR GL7 .... **238** C1
Cirencester Town Council
CIR GL7 .... **238** C2
Cirencester Town
Football Club
CIR GL7 .... **238** A4
City Business Park
CBRIS/FH BS1 .... **6** F3
City Business Park
EVILLE/WHL BS5 .... **7** L2
City Council Offices
CIR GL7 .... **4** C6
City of Bristol College
BMSTR BS3 .... **346** A1
City of Bristol College
CBRIS/FH BS1 .... **6** B5
City of Bristol College
HORF/LLZ BS7 .... **326** B7
City & Port of Bristol
Social & Sports Club
AVONM BS11 .... **324** A6
Civil Service Sports Club
CHELTW GL51 .... **93** H6
Civil Sports Club
GL GL1 .... **5** G1
Claremont Special School
RDLND/MONT BS6 .... **325** L6
Cleeve School
CHELTE/BC GL52 .... **94** C1
Cleeve View Infant School
CHELTW GL51 .... **93** L7
Clifton Cathedral Church
CFTN/FAIL BS8 .... **335** J3
Clifton Clinic
CFTN/FAIL BS8 .... **335** J4
Clifton College
CFTN/FAIL BS8 .... **335** H3
Clifton College
Preparatory School
CFTN/FAIL BS8 .... **335** H2
Clifton College Sports Club
CFTN/FAIL BS8 .... **334** D4
Clifton Down Shopping Centre
CFTN/FAIL BS8 .... **335** K2
The Clifton Gallery
CFTN/FAIL BS8 .... **335** H4
Clifton High Junior School
CFTN/FAIL BS8 .... **335** J4
Clifton High School
CFTN/FAIL BS8 .... **335** H3
Clifton Rugby Club
HNBRY/STHM BS10 .... **315** H6
Close Farm Surgery
OLD/WMLY/WICK BS30 .... **338** D6
Club House
LED HR8 .... **18** A3
Club House
TEWK GL20 .... **47** L8
Clyde House Surgery
RDLND/MONT BS6 .... **335** K1
Coalway County Junior &
Infant School
CLFD GL16 .... **175** M2
Coberley School
CHELTS GL53 .... **140** C6
Cold Aston C of E
Primary School
COTS GL54 .... **121** M7
Coleford County
Primary School
CLFD GL16 .... **151** K5
Coleford Health Centre
CLFD GL16 .... **175** K2
Coleford Road Surgery
CHEP NP16 .... **270** B1
Colerne C of E Primary School
CHPMW/MSHF SN14 .... **343** K8
Colerne Rugby Football Club
CHPMW/MSHF SN14 .... **343** H8
College House
MANG/FISH BS16 .... **327** J6
College of Art & Technology
GL GL1 .... **4** E6
College of St Mathias
C of E (A) Infant School
MANG/FISH BS16 .... **327** J6
College Pharmacy
CHELT GL50 .... **2** C9
The College Yard Surgery
GL GL1 .... **4** D4
Coln Gallery
CIR GL7 .... **238** C2
Coln Gallery
CIR GL7 .... **242** C6
Coln House Special School
CIR GL7 .... **242** D5
Colston Hall
CBRIS/FH BS1 .... **6** E3
Colston House Tennis Club
CIR GL7 .... **221** M8
Colstons Collegiate
Lower School
MANG/FISH BS16 .... **326** F6
Colstons Giris School
RDLND/MONT BS6 .... **336** A1
Colstons Primary School
RDLND/MONT BS6 .... **335** L3
Colstons School
MANG/FISH BS16 .... **326** F6
Commercial House
Station Road Business Parkt
TEWK GL20 .... **48** B5

Community Health Authority
KEYN BS31 .... **348** A5
Community Services Clinic
TEWK GL20 .... **48** B5
The Compton Clinic
RDLND/MONT BS6 .... **325** J7
Coney Hill Infant School
GLE GL4 .... **136** E4
Coniston Primary School
BRSTK/PCHW BS34 .... **316** B2
Connaught Infant &
Primary School
BRSG/KWL/STAPK BS4 ..... **346** A2
Connoisseur Gallery
TET GL8 .... **282** A4
Conygre Medical Centre
BRSTK/PCHW BS34 .... **316** C8
Copse Surgery
RTEWK/TIB GL19 .... **66** E4
Corbett House Clinic
EVILLE/WHL BS5 .... **336** D4
Corinium Business Park
CIND GL14 .... **129** M8
Corinium Museum
CIR GL7 .... **238** C2
Coroners Court
CBRISNE BS2 .... **336** A3
Cossham Memorial Hospital
KGWD/HNM BS15 .... **337** L1
Cotham Galleries
RDLND/MONT BS6 .... **335** K2
Cotham Grammar School
RDLND/MONT BS6 .... **335** L2
Cotham Park Rugby Club
CFTN/FAIL BS8 .... **334** C5
Cotham Road Surgery
RDLND/MONT BS6 .... **335** L3
Cotswold Bowl (Cheltenham)
CHELTW GL51 .... **93** K6
Cotswold Chine Home School
RSTROUD/NAIL GL6 .... **232** F6
Cotswold District Council
CIR GL7 .... **238** C3
Cotswold Edge Golf Club
WUE GL12 .... **254** B8
Cotswold Motor Museum &
Toy Collection
COTS GL54 .... **123** G5
Cotswold Nuffield Hospital
CHELTW GL51 .... **115** J3
Cotswold School
COTS GL54 .... **123** H4
Cotswold Sports Centre
CIR GL7 .... **238** B3
The Cotswold Teddy
Bear Museum
BDWAY WR12 .... **33** G3
Council Offices
GLE GL4 .... **136** E4
Council Offices
MIM GL56 .... **58** D5
Council Offices
TEWK GL20 .... **47** M6
County Library
GL GL1 .... **4** D4
County Police Court
CHCAM GL55 .... **12** E7
Courtney Primary School
KGWD/HNM BS15 .... **338** B4
Courtside Surgery
YATE/CS BS37 .... **320** A2
Courtyard Shopping Centre
CHELT GL50 .... **2** B6
Cowdy Gallery
NWNT GL18 .... **86** C3
The Craft Gallery
HORF/LLZ BS7 .... **326** B2
Cribbs Causeway
Shopping Centre
BRSTK/PCHW BS34 .... **315** L5
Cricklade Hotel & Country Club
HGHW SN6 .... **288** D4
Cricklade Leisure Centre
HGHW SN6 .... **288** E3
Cricklade Town Council
HGHW SN6 .... **288** F3
Croft Primary School
RSTROUD/NAIL GL6 .... **185** G3
Crofts End Industrial Estate
EVILLE/WHL BS5 .... **337** G2
Crofts End Trading Estate
EVILLE/WHL BS5 .... **337** G2
Crooks Industrial Estate
CHELTS GL53 .... **115** M5
Crossways Junior &
Infant School
THNB/SVB BS35 .... **293** M2
Crown Court
CBRIS/FH BS1 .... **6** F2
Crudwell C of E Primary School
MALM SN16 .... **284** B5
The Crypt School
GL GL1 .... **135** M7
Culverhay Surgery
WUE GL12 .... **277** K4
Culverhill School
YATE/CS BS37 .... **319** M4
Custom House
CBRIS/FH BS1 .... **6** F5
Cutlers Brook Junior School
CBRISNE BS2 .... **336** C1
Daniels Industrial Estate
STROUD GL5 .... **208** B6
Darcy Galleries
CHELT GL50 .... **2** B9
David Hamiltons Practice
RDLND/MONT BS6 .... **335** K2
Dean Close Junior School
CHELTW GL51 .... **115** J3
Dean Close School
CHELTW GL51 .... **115** H3
Dean Heritage Museum
CIND GL14 .... **178** C1
Dean Lane Family Practice
BMSTR BS3 .... **6** D1
Deerhurst C of E
Primary School
RTEWK/TIB GL19 .... **69** G6

Deers Wood Primary School
  KGWD/HNM BS15 .... 338 C1
The Dell Primary School
  CHEP NP16 .... 270 A2
Dene Magna
  Community School
  MTCHDN GL17 .... 130 D3
Denmark Road High
  School for Girls
  GL GL1 .... 5 H2
The Diane Breen Gallery
  CIR GL7 .... 217 K1
Didbrook CP School
  COTS GL54 .... 53 K8
Dilke Memorial Hospital
  CIND GL14 .... 153 L5
Dinglewell Primary School
  GLE GL4 .... 137 H4
Dixon Business Centre
  BRSG/KWL/STAPK BS4 .... 347 H1
Docks Industrial Estate
  AVONM BS11 .... 314 A3
The Doctors Surgery
  EVILLE/WHL BS5 .... 336 D2
Dodington Parish Council
  YATE/CS BS37 .... 320 C3
Dodington Park
  YATE/CS BS37 .... 321 J7
Dormer House PNEU School
  MIM GL56 .... 58 D5
Down Ampney C of E
  Primary School
  CIR GL7 .... 265 C4
Downend Cricket Club
  MANG/FISH BS16 .... 327 M5
Downend School
  MANG/FISH BS16 .... 328 A6
Downend Surgery
  MANG/FISH BS16 .... 327 M6
Downs Fitness &
  Health Centre
  RDLND/MONT BS6 .... 335 J1
Dr Bells C of E School
  MANG/FISH BS16 .... 327 J7
Drybrook Primary School
  MTCHDN GL17 .... 129 L4
Drybrook Rugby Football Club
  MTCHDN GL17 .... 129 M3
Drybrook Surgery
  MTCHDN GL17 .... 129 L4
Duckmoor Road Industrial
  Estate
  BMSTR BS3 .... 335 H8
Dunalley County Primary
  School
  CHELT GL50 .... 2 E1
Dunalley Street School
  CHELT GL50 .... 2 D3
Dunmail Primary School
  HNBRY/STHM BS10 .... 325 L1
Dursley C of E Primary School
  DSLY GL11 .... 253 L3
Dursley Day Hospital
  DSLY GL11 .... 252 F2
Dursley Magistrates Court
  DSLY GL11 .... 229 H8
Dursley Town Council
  DSLY GL11 .... 253 K2
Eagles Wood Business Park
  ALMDB BS32 .... 306 E8
Eastbrook Road
  Trading Estate
  GLE GL4 .... 136 E3
Eastcombe CP School
  RSTROUD/NAIL GL6 .... 209 M6
Eastern Avenue Retail Park
  GLE GL4 .... 5 M9
East Gloucestershire NHS Trust
  CHELTW GL51 .... 115 G1
Eastington CP School
  STNHO GL10 .... 206 C3
Eastington Trading Estate
  STNHO GL10 .... 206 B2
Eastnor Castle
  LED HR8 .... 20 F5
Eastnor C of E Primary School
  LED HR8 .... 20 E4
Easton Business Centre
  EVILLE/WHL BS5 .... 336 D3
Easton CEVA Primary School
  EVILLE/WHL BS5 .... 7 M1
Easton Leisure Centre
  EVILLE/WHL BS5 .... 7 M1
Eastpark Trading Estate
  EVILLE/WHL BS5 .... 336 F2
Eastville Health Centre
  EVILLE/WHL BS5 .... 336 D1
Ebley Industrial Estate
  STROUD GL5 .... 207 M5
Eight Bells Gallery
  TET GL8 .... 282 A4
Eldersfield Lawn School
  RTEWK/TIB GL19 .... 68 A1
The Ellen Badger Hospital
  SHPSTR CV36 .... 16 C5
Ellwood County Primary
  School
  CLFD GL16 .... 175 M6
Ellwood Football Club
  CLFD GL16 .... 176 A6
Elmbridge Junior School
  VGL GL2 .... 136 E1
Elmbridge Rugby Club
  VGL GL2 .... 112 F8
Elmfield Junior School
  CHELTW GL51 .... 93 L7
Elmlea Infant School
  HNLZ/SM/SNYPK/WT BS9 .... 325 H6
Elmlea Junior School
  HNLZ/SM/SNYPK/WT BS9 .... 325 H6
Elm Park School
  FRCTL/WBN BS36 .... 318 A5
The Elms Day Hospital
  THNB/SVB BS35 .... 293 K2
Embleton Junior School
  HNBRY/STHM BS10 .... 325 K2
English Bicknor C of E Primary
  CLFD GL16 .... 127 L7

English Estates Workshops
  CIND GL14 .... 153 M2
Evergreen Industrial Estate
  CIR GL7 .... 263 H6
Everyman Theatre
  CHELT GL50 .... 2 D5
Exhibition Centre
  CBRIS/FH BS1 .... 6 D5
Explore @ Bristol
  CBRIS/FH BS1 .... 6 D5
The Eye Clinic
  CBRIS/FH BS1 .... 7 G2
Fairfield Grammar School
  RDLND/MONT BS6 .... 336 B1
Fairford C of E Primary School
  CIR GL7 .... 242 E3
Fairford Football Club
  CIR GL7 .... 243 G4
Fairford Hospital
  CIR GL7 .... 242 E4
Fair Furlong Primary School
  BMSTRD/HC/WWD BS13 ...... 345 J7
Fairway Industrial Centre
  BRSTK/PCHW BS34 .... 316 B8
Falconride Primary School
  KGWD/HNM BS15 .... 338 A2
The Family Practice
  RDLND/MONT BS6 .... 335 L3
Family & Youth Court
  CBRIS/FH BS1 .... 6 F3
Farmors School
  CIR GL7 .... 242 E3
Feathers Gallery
  BDWAY WR12 .... 32 F4
Federated Primary Schools of
  Ebrington & St James
  CHCAM GL55 .... 34 E1
Ferry Steps Trading Estate
  CBRISNE BS2 .... 7 L8
Field Court C of E
  Junior & Infant School
  VGL GL2 .... 159 H3
Filand School
  MALM SN16 .... 303 H5
Filton Avenue Junior School
  HORF/LLZ BS7 .... 326 C4
Filton Clinic
  HORF/LLZ BS7 .... 326 C1
Filton College
  BRSTK/PCHW BS34 .... 316 C7
Filton High School
  BRSTK/PCHW BS34 .... 316 F8
Filton Hill CP School
  BRSTK/PCHW BS34 .... 316 D7
Filton Park School
  BRSTK/PCHW BS34 .... 326 B1
Filton Recreation Centre
  BRSTK/PCHW BS34 .... 326 C1
Filton Shield Road School
  HORF/LLZ BS7 .... 326 C2
Filton Town Council
  BRSTK/PCHW BS34 .... 326 C1
Filwood Swimming Baths
  BRSG/KWL/STAPK BS4 .... 346 A3
Finlay Primary School
  GLE GL4 .... 136 C5
Fire Service Technical College
  MIM GL56 .... 59 G5
Fire Station
  CBRIS/FH BS1 .... 7 H4
The Firs Surgery
  CHPMW/MSHF SN14 .... 343 J8
Fishponds Health Centre
  MANG/FISH BS16 .... 327 K7
The Florence Brown School
  BRSG/KWL/STAPK BS4 .... 345 M3
The Florence Brown School
  CBRISNE BS2 .... 7 J2
Flower Gallery
  FRCTL/WBN BS36 .... 317 M5
Folk House
  CBRIS/FH BS1 .... 6 D3
Fonthill Junior School
  HNBRY/STHM BS10 .... 326 A1
Forest Health Care
  CIND GL14 .... 154 B3
Forest Hills Golf Club
  CLFD GL16 .... 151 L7
Forest of Dean District Council
  CIND GL14 .... 154 B2
Forest of Dean District Council
  CLFD GL16 .... 175 J1
Forest View Primary School
  CIND GL14 .... 154 C2
Forest View Upper School
  CIND GL14 .... 154 C2
Fosse Cross Industrial Estate
  CIR GL7 .... 191 K4
Fosse Way Business Centre
  MIM GL56 .... 58 D5
Foster Almshouses
  CBRIS/FH BS1 .... 6 E3
Fouracres Primary School
  BMSTRD/HC/WWD BS13 ...... 345 G7
Foxmoor CP School
  STROUD GL5 .... 207 M4
Frampton Cotterell
  C of E School
  FRCTL/WBN BS36 .... 318 C3
Frampton on Severn
  C of E School
  VGL GL2 .... 181 H5
Francis Woodcock
  Trading Estate
  GL GL1 .... 5 J9
Frenchay C of E School
  MANG/FISH BS16 .... 327 K4
Frenchay Health Authority
  MANG/FISH BS16 .... 327 L6
Frenchay Hospital
  MANG/FISH BS16 .... 327 K3
Frenchay Village Museum
  MANG/FISH BS16 .... 327 H4
The Friends of
  Gloucester Cathedral
  GL GL1 .... 4 E4
Frithwood Surgery
  RSTROUD/NAIL GL6 .... 209 M7

Frome Bank Junior School
  YATE/CS BS37 .... 309 M8
Fromeside Clinic
  MANG/FISH BS16 .... 327 L1
Fulford Special School
  BMSTRD/HC/WWD BS13 ...... 345 L7
Gable House Surgery
  MALM SN16 .... 303 J8
The Galleries Shopping Centre
  CBRIS/FH BS1 .... 7 G2
The Gallery
  CIR GL7 .... 238 C3
Gastrells CP School
  STROUD GL5 .... 208 C7
Gas Works
  HNBRY/STHM BS10 .... 314 D3
Gay Elms Junior & Infant School
  BMSTRD/HC/WWD BS13 ...... 345 J7
Georgian House
  CBRIS/FH BS1 .... 6 C4
Glebe Infant School
  NWNT GL18 .... 86 B2
Glenfall CP School
  CHELTE/BC GL52 .... 116 E5
Glenfrome Primary School
  EVILLE/WHL BS5 .... 326 E7
Glevum Industrial Estate
  GLE GL4 .... 136 C2
Glevum Shopping Centre
  GLE GL4 .... 136 F7
Gloucester City
  Association Football Club
  VGL GL2 .... 135 K3
Gloucester City Council
  GL GL1 .... 4 C5
Gloucester City Council
  GL GL1 .... 4 F8
Gloucester City Council
  GL GL1 .... 4 E1
Gloucester
  County Constabulary
  GL GL1 .... 5 D4
Gloucester
  County Constabulary
  STNHO GL10 .... 207 H4
Gloucester County Council
  CHELT GL50 .... 2 A8
Gloucester County Council
  CHELT GL50 .... 115 K3
Gloucester County Council
  GLE GL4 .... 136 C4
Gloucester County Council
  VGL GL2 .... 206 B1
Gloucester Crown &
  County Court
  GL GL1 .... 4 D6
Gloucester Folk Museum
  GL GL1 .... 4 C5
Gloucester Retail Park
  GLE GL4 .... 136 E2
Gloucester Road
  Industrial Estate
  MALM SN16 .... 303 J7
Gloucester Road
  Primary School
  CHELTW GL51 .... 115 K1
Gloucester Royal Hospital
  GL GL1 .... 5 K5
Gloucester Rugby Football Club
  GL GL1 .... 4 F2
Gloucestershire
  Aviation Museum
  BWTH/CHD BS14 .... 113 L3
Gloucestershire
  College of Arts & Technology
  GL GL1 .... 4 F7
Gloucestershire
  Community Health Centre
  GL GL1 .... 5 H5
Gloucestershire County Council
  CHELTS GL53 .... 2 F7
Gloucestershire County Council
  CHELTW GL51 .... 114 B4
Gloucestershire County Council
  CIR GL7 .... 238 D5
Gloucestershire County Council
  CLFD GL16 .... 175 J1
Gloucestershire County Council
  COTS GL54 .... 123 J4
Gloucestershire County Council
  GL GL1 .... 4 F6
Gloucestershire County Council
  GL GL1 .... 4 D4
Gloucestershire County Council
  GL GL1 .... 5 K3
Gloucestershire County Council
  GL GL1 .... 5 K8
Gloucestershire County Council
  KGWD/HNM BS15 .... 338 A3
Gloucestershire County Council
  STROUD GL5 .... 208 D4
Gloucestershire County
  Cricket Club
  HORF/LLZ BS7 .... 326 A8
Gloucestershire County
  Library Arts &
  Museums Service
  CHELT GL50 .... 2 A4
Gloucestershire Health
  Authority
  GL GL1 .... 4 D6
Gloucestershire Islamic
  Secondary School for Girls
  GL GL1 .... 5 H7
Gloucestershire Royal Hospital
  GL GL1 .... 5 J4
Gloucester Sports Club
  GL GL1 .... 4 D8
Glynne Wickham
  Studio Theatre
  CFTN/FAIL BS8 .... 6 C3
Golf Course
  HGHW SN6 .... 288 D3
Goodridge Industrial Estate
  VGL GL2 .... 135 J7
Goodridge Trading Estate
  VGL GL2 .... 135 J8

Gordon League Rugby
  Football Club
  VGL GL2 .... 135 K4
Gorsley Goffs C of E
  Primary School
  RWYE HR9 .... 84 E2
Granby House Clinic
  BMSTR BS3 .... 335 L8
Grange Infant School
  GL GL1 .... 159 L1
Grange Junior School
  GL GL1 .... 135 L8
Grange Road Surgery
  BMSTRD/HC/WWD BS13 ...... 345 H6
Greatfield Park Primary School
  CHELT GL51 .... 115 H6
Great Rissington CP School
  COTS GL54 .... 148 C4
Great Western Business Park
  YATE/CS BS37 .... 309 K8
The Great Western
  Railway Museum
  CLFD GL16 .... 175 K1
Gretton School
  COTS GL54 .... 73 M2
Greyholme Surgery
  CHELTE/BC GL52 .... 72 B7
Greystones Gallery
  CIR GL7 .... 244 E7
Grimsbury Park School
  OLD/WMLY/WICK BS30 .... 338 D4
Grove Industrial Estate
  BRSTK/PCHW BS34 .... 316 D4
Grove Road Day Hospital
  RDLND/MONT BS6 .... 335 J1
Hadwen Practice
  GLE GL4 .... 137 G7
Hambrook CP School
  MANG/FISH BS16 .... 317 M8
Hambrook Sports Club
  MANG/FISH BS16 .... 317 M8
Hampton Street
  Industrial Estate
  TET GL8 .... 281 L2
Hanham Abbots Junior School
  KGWD/HNM BS15 .... 337 L7
Hanham Business Park
  KCWD/HNM BS15 .... 337 K6
Hanham C of E Primary School
  KGWD/HNM BS15 .... 337 K7
Hanham High School
  KGWD/HNM BS15 .... 337 L7
Hanham Surgery
  KGWD/HNM BS15 .... 337 M7
Hannah More Primary School
  CBRISNE BS2 .... 7 K4
The Happening Art Gallery
  RDLND/MONT BS6 .... 335 K2
Hardwicke Parochial
  Primary School
  VGL GL2 .... 159 G5
Hareclive Primary School
  BMSTRD/HC/WWD BS13 ...... 345 L7
Haresfield C of E Primary
  School
  STNHO GL10 .... 183 K2
Harewood Junior &
  Infant School
  GL GL1 .... 159 L2
Harlequin Gallery
  CHELTE/BC GL52 .... 2 E5
Hartcliffe Health Centre
  BMSTRD/HC/WWD BS13 ...... 345 L7
Hartcliffe School
  BMSTRD/HC/WWD BS13 ...... 346 A7
Hartpury College
  RTEWK/TIB GL19 .... 110 D1
Harveys Wine Museum
  CBRIS/FH BS1 .... 6 D4
Hatherley Infant School
  GL GL1 .... 136 C4
Hatherop Castle School
  CIR GL7 .... 218 E4
Hatherop C of E School
  CIR GL7 .... 218 E4
Hawkesbury Upton
  Primary School
  BAD GL9 .... 298 B8
Hayward Road
  Industrial Estate
  MANG/FISH BS16 .... 327 M8
Headley Park Primary School
  BMSTRD/HC/WWD BS13 ...... 345 K4
Heath House Priory Hospital
  HORF/LLZ BS7 .... 326 D7
Heathville Road Surgery
  GL GL1 .... 5 H4
Hempsted School
  VGL GL2 .... 135 J4
Henbury Court Junior &
  Primary School
  HNBRY/STHM BS10 .... 315 H8
Henbury Manor School
  HNBRY/STHM BS10 .... 325 G1
Henbury Old Boys A F C
  HNBRY/STHM BS10 .... 325 H1
Henbury School
  HNBRY/STHM BS10 .... 315 G8
The Henbury Surgery
  HNBRY/STHM BS10 .... 315 H8
Henbury Swimming Pool
  HNBRY/STHM BS10 .... 325 H1
Henfield Business Park
  FRCTL/WBN BS36 .... 328 F1
Hengrove School
  HGRV/WHIT BS14 .... 346 D4
Henleaze Infant School
  RDLND/MONT BS6 .... 325 L6
The Herd AFC Club House
  CIR GL7 .... 238 B4
The Heron Primary School
  GLE GL4 .... 136 F6
The Heywood School
  CIND GL14 .... 154 C1
Heywood Sports Centre
  CIND GL14 .... 154 C1
Highbridge Infant School
  BMSTRD/HC/WWD BS13 ...... 345 H5

Highcroft Junior School
  FRCTL/WBN BS36 .... 318 E3
Highnam Business Centre
  VGL GL2 .... 110 E6
Highnam School
  VGL GL2 .... 110 F6
The High Street Medical Centre
  STNHO GL10 .... 207 G3
Hillesley C of E Va
  Primary School
  WUE GL12 .... 298 A3
Hillfields Park Primary School
  MANG/FISH BS16 .... 327 L8
Hillview County
  Primary School
  BWTH/CHD GL3 .... 137 H3
The Hindu Temple
  EVILLE/WHL BS5 .... 336 E3
Hippodrome Theatre
  CBRIS/FH BS1 .... 6 E4
H & L Estate
  STROUD GL5 .... 208 A5
H & L Trading Estate
  STROUD GL5 .... 208 A5
HM Young Offender Institute
  WUE GL12 .... 274 F4
Holloway Dental
  Health Centre
  HGRV/WHIT BS14 .... 347 G6
Hollywood Bowl
  CBRISNE BS2 .... 336 E6
Holst Birthplace Museum
  CHELTE/BC GL52 .... 2 E3
Holts Health Centre
  NWNT GL18 .... 86 C3
Holy Apostles C of E School
  CHELTE/BC GL52 .... 3 K6
Holy Family RC Primary School
  BRSTK/PCHW BS34 .... 316 D3
Holymead Infant School
  BRSG/KWL/STAPK BS4 .... 346 F1
Holymead School
  BRSG/KWL/STAPK BS4 .... 336 F8
Holy Trinity Primary School
  ALMDB BS32 .... 316 E1
Holy Trinity School
  CHELTE/BC GL52 .... 2 F4
Homedowns Business Park
  TEWK GL20 .... 49 G6
Homeopathic Hospital
  CFTN/FAIL BS8 .... 335 L3
Honeybourne
  Airfield Industrial Estate
  EVE WR11 .... 11 K2
Hopelands School
  STNHO GL10 .... 207 H4
Hopes Hill Primary School
  MTCHDN GL17 .... 131 K2
Horcott Industrial Estate
  CIR GL7 .... 242 D6
Horcott Road Industrial Estate
  CIR GL7 .... 242 E5
Horfield C of E School
  HNBRY/STHM BS10 .... 325 M4
Horfield Health Centre
  HORF/LLZ BS7 .... 326 C5
Horfield Sports Centre
  HORF/LLZ BS7 .... 326 B4
Horsley School
  RSTROUD/NAIL GL6 .... 256 B2
Horton Primary School
  YATE/CS BS37 .... 311 L6
Hospital
  PTSHD/EG BS20 .... 324 A7
Hotspots Indoor Sports Centre
  BRSG/KWL/STAPK BS4 .... 347 H1
Hotwells Primary School
  CFTN/FAIL BS8 .... 335 H5
Ilminster Avenue
  Junior School
  BRSG/KWL/STAPK BS4 .... 346 C3
Inchbrook Trading Estate
  STROUD GL5 .... 232 C4
Innsworth County
  Primary School
  VGL GL2 .... 112 F5
Innsworth Technology Park
  VGL GL2 .... 112 E4
The Institute of
  Cosmetic Surgery
  CFTN/FAIL BS8 .... 335 J2
Iron Acton C of E School
  YATE/CS BS37 .... 309 G7
Jama Al-Karim Mosque
  GL GL1 .... 5 G7
JHP Business Centre
  CIR GL7 .... 238 D3
John Blockley Gallery
  COTS GL54 .... 102 E7
John Cabot City
  Technology College
  KGWD/HNM BS15 .... 337 L4
John Masefield High School
  LED HR8 .... 19 M4
The John Milton Health Clinic
  HNBRY/STHM BS10 .... 315 J8
The John M Museum
  TEWK GL20 .... 48 A6
Jorrocks Estate
  YATE/CS BS37 .... 319 L7
Joys Green CP School
  MTCHDN GL17 .... 128 C6
Jubilee Public Baths
  BRSG/KWL/STAPK BS4 .... 346 D1
Katerine Lady Berkeley School
  WUE GL12 .... 277 H5
Kemble County
  Primary School
  CIR GL7 .... 261 H4
Kennedy Way Surgery
  YATE/CS BS37 .... 320 A2
Kensington Business Centre
  CHELT GL50 .... 2 C7
Keynsham County
  Primary School
  KEYN BS31 .... 347 M6
Keynsham Hospital
  KEYN BS31 .... 348 B7

Keynsham Leisure Centre
 KEYN BS31 .... 348 B6
Keynsham Rugby Club
 KEYN BS31 .... 347 M4
Keynsham Town Football Club
 KEYN BS31 .... 347 M4
King Edmund Community
 School
 YATE/CS BS37 .... 320 A2
Kingfisher Business Park
 STROUD GL5 .... 233 G1
Kingham County
 Primary School
 CHNTN OX7 .... 104 C6
Kingham Hill School
 CHNTN OX7 .... 104 D2
Kings Business Park
 CBRISNE BS2 .... 336 E5
Kings Chase Shopping Centre
 KGWD/HNM BS15 .... 337 M3
Kings Court Primary School
 YATE/CS BS37 .... 320 A3
Kingsditch Retail Park
 CHELTW GL51 .... 93 J3
Kingsdown Golf Club
 COR/BOX SN13 .... 353 K8
Kingsdown Sports Centre
 RDLND/MONT BS6 .... 335 L3
Kingsfield School
 KGWD/HNM BS15 .... 338 C3
Kingsholm C of E
 Primary School
 GL GL1 .... 5 G3
Kings School
 GL GL1 .... 4 E4
Kings Stanley C of E
 Primary School
 STNHO GL10 .... 207 J7
Kings Stanley County
 Infant School
 STNHO GL10 .... 207 J8
Kings Theatre
 GL GL1 .... 5 G7
Kingsweston School
 AVONM BS11 .... 324 C3
Kingswood Borough Council
 MANG/FISH BS16 .... 327 M7
Kingswood County
 Primary School
 WUE GL12 .... 277 G6
Kingswood District Council
 KGWD/HNM BS15 .... 337 M4
Kingswood Health Centre
 KGWD/HNM BS15 .... 338 A3
Kingswood Leisure Centre
 MANG/FISH BS16 .... 327 M8
Kirtlands Preparatory School
 BDWAY WR12 .... 33 G3
Knightsbridge Business Centre
 CHELTW GL51 .... 92 A1
Knowle Junior Mixed School
 BRSG/KWL/STAPK BS4 .... 336 C8
Knowle Park Junior School
 BRSG/KWL/STAPK BS4 .... 346 C2
Ladygrove Business Park
 MTCHDN GL17 .... 130 E2
Lakers School
 CLFD GL16 .... 151 L6
Lakeside Primary School
 CHELTW GL51 .... 115 G4
The Lake Surgery
 HNBRY/STHM BS10 .... 325 K4
Lansdown Industrial Estate
 CHELTW GL51 .... 115 J2
Larkfield Infant School
 VGL GL2 .... 113 G5
Larkhall Football Club
 CBATH/BATHN BA1 .... 351 K8
Lawnwood Road
 Industrial Estate
 EVILLE/WHL BS5 .... 336 D3
Lawrence Hill Health Centre
 CBRISNE BS2 .... 7 M2
Lawrence Hill Industrial Estate
 EVILLE/WHL BS5 .... 336 E3
Lawrence Hill Industrial Park
 EVILLE/WHL BS5 .... 336 D3
Lawrence Weston School
 AVONM BS11 .... 324 D2
Lea C of E County
 Primary School
 RWYE HR9 .... 106 B3
Leckhampton Industrial Estate
 CHELTS GL53 .... 115 M8
Leckhampton Primary School
 CHELTS GL53 .... 115 L7
Leckhampton Surgery
 CHELTS GL53 .... 115 L5
Leconfield Cheltenham College
 CHELTS GL53 .... 2 D8
Ledbury Market Surgery
 LED HR8 .... 19 M3
Ledbury Primary School
 LED HR8 .... 19 M3
Ledbury Town Football Club
 LED HR8 .... 19 L5
Leigh C of E School
 HGHW SN6 .... 287 L6
Leigh Court Business Centre
 CFTN/FAIL BS8 .... 334 C1
Leighterton County
 Primary School
 TET GL8 .... 279 L8
Leisure Centre
 CLFD GL16 .... 151 L5
Leisure Centre
 GL GL1 .... 5 G6
Leonard Stanley C of E
 Primary School
 STNHO GL10 .... 207 H7
Lewis Road Surgery
 BMSTRD/HC/WWD BS13 .... 345 J3
Liberty Industrial Park
 BMSTR BS3 .... 345 J2
Library, Museum & Art Gallery
 CHELT GL50 .... 2 D4
Liddington Industrial Estate
 CHELTS GL53 .... 115 M6

Linden Primary School
 GL GL1 .... 135 M5
Linear Business Park
 CIND GL14 .... 154 A4
Little Dean Hall
 CIND GL14 .... 154 E4
Littledean Primary School
 CIND GL14 .... 154 E3
Little Stoke Junior School
 BRSTK/PCHW BS34 .... 316 F5
Llanthony Industrial Estate
 VGL GL2 .... 4 A7
Llanthony Secunda Priory
 VGL GL2 .... 4 B8
Lockleaze School
 HORF/LLZ BS7 .... 326 E3
Lodge Causeway
 Trading Estate
 MANG/FISH BS16 .... 327 H8
London Road Medical Practice
 GL GL1 .... 5 J4
Long Ashton Surgery
 LGASH BS41 .... 344 B2
Longborough C of E
 Primary School
 MIM GL56 .... 79 K3
Longbrook Trading Estate
 BMSTR BS3 .... 335 G8
Long Compton Junior &
 Infant School
 SHPSTR CV36 .... 61 H5
Longford Special School
 VGL GL2 .... 112 D6
Longhope C of E
 Primary School
 MTCHDN GL17 .... 107 G7
Longhope Industrial Estate
 MTCHDN GL17 .... 107 H8
Longlevens Primary School
 VGL GL2 .... 112 E7
Longlevens R F C
 VGL GL2 .... 112 D6
Longlevens Surgery
 VGL GL2 .... 112 E7
Longney C of E
 Primary School
 VGL GL2 .... 157 L6
Longwell Green CP School
 OLD/WMLY/WICK BS30 .... 338 B8
Lonsdale Business Centre
 KGWD/HNM BS15 .... 337 L1
Lord Chancellors Department
 CBRIS BS1 .... 6 F3
Lord Chancellors Department
 CFTN/FAIL BS8 .... 335 H4
Love Lane Industrial Estate
 CIR GL7 .... 238 D5
Love Lane Trading Estate
 CIR GL7 .... 238 D5
Luckwell Road School
 BMSTR BS3 .... 335 J8
Lydbrook County
 Primary School
 MTCHDN GL17 .... 128 C8
Lydbrook Health Centre
 MTCHDN GL17 .... 128 C7
Lydney C of E School
 LYD GL15 .... 201 J8
Lydney Cricket Club
 LYD GL15 .... 201 J8
Lydney & District Hospital
 LYD GL15 .... 201 H8
Lydney Golf Club
 LYD GL15 .... 225 L1
Lydney Health Centre
 LYD GL15 .... 201 K8
Lydney Industrial Estate
 LYD GL15 .... 225 M3
Lydney Rugby Football Club
 LYD GL15 .... 201 K8
Lydney Yacht Club
 LYD GL15 .... 226 A3
Lyntony House
 Reading School
 HORF/LLZ BS7 .... 325 M8
Lynworth Primary School
 CHELTE/BC GL52 .... 3 L1
Madleaze Trading Estate
 GL GL1 .... 4 C9
Maidenhill School
 STNHO GL10 .... 207 H2
Malago Surgery
 BMSTR BS3 .... 335 L8
Malago Vale Trading Estate
 BMSTR BS3 .... 335 M8
The Mall Gallery
 CFTN/FAIL BS8 .... 335 H4
The Mall
 BRSTK/PCHW BS34 .... 315 M5
Malmesbury Business Park
 MALM SN16 .... 303 H6
Malmesbury C of E
 Primary School
 MALM SN16 .... 303 H7
Malmesbury Cricket Club
 MALM SN16 .... 303 J7
Malmesbury School
 MALM SN16 .... 303 G8
Malmesbury Swimming Pool
 MALM SN16 .... 303 G7
Malvern View Business Park
 CHELTE/BC GL52 .... 71 M7
Mangotsfield School
 MANG/FISH BS16 .... 328 D7
Mangotsfield United
 Football Club
 MANG/FISH BS16 .... 328 D6
Manor Brook School
 THNB/SVB BS35 .... 273 L8
Manor C of E School
 FRCTL/WBN BS36 .... 318 E5
Manor Farm Associated
 Football Club
 HNLZ/SM/SNYPK/WT BS9 .... 324 D6
Manor Park Business Centre
 CHELTW GL51 .... 93 J6
Maritime Heritage Centre
 CBRIS/FH BS1 .... 6 B6

Market
 GL GL1 .... 4 E6
Market Theatre
 LED HR8 .... 19 M3
Marling School
 STROUD GL5 .... 208 B4
Marlwood School
 THNB/SVB BS35 .... 293 H6
Marshfield Primary School
 CHPMW/MSHF SN14 .... 342 C3
Martor Industrial Estate
 CHPMW/MSHF SN14 .... 342 C1
Marybrook Medical Centre
 BRKLY GL13 .... 227 G7
Matson Rugby Club House
 GLE GL4 .... 136 E8
May Park Primary School
 EVILLE/WHL BS5 .... 336 E1
Mead Lane Industrial Estate
 LYD GL15 .... 225 H3
The Meadows Primary School
 OLD/WMLY/WICK BS30 .... 348 F3
Mead Park Industrial Estate
 CHELTS GL53 .... 115 M5
Medical Surgery
 CIND GL14 .... 156 B3
Merchants Quay Shopping Centre
 GL GL1 .... 4 C6
Merrywood School
 BRSG/KWL/STAPK BS4 .... 346 B2
Meteor Business Park
 BWTH/CHD GL3 .... 113 L2
Meysey Hampton
 C of E School
 CIR GL7 .... 241 K7
Midland Way Business Park
 THNB/SVB BS35 .... 293 K3
The Milestone School
 VGL GL2 .... 112 D6
Millcot Gallery
 TEWK GL20 .... 47 M5
Millpond Primary School
 EVILLE/WHL BS5 .... 336 C2
Minchinhampton Golf Club
 TET GL8 .... 257 M1
Minsterworth School
 VGL GL2 .... 134 B4
Minto Road Industrial Centre
 RDLND/MONT BS6 .... 336 B1
Miserden C of E Primary School
 RSTROUD/NAIL GL6 .... 187 J5
Mitcheldean Endowed
 Primary School
 MTCHDN GL17 .... 130 C2
Mitcheldean Surgery
 MTCHDN GL17 .... 130 C1
Mitton Manor Primary School
 TEWK GL20 .... 48 C3
The Moat Infant School
 GLE GL4 .... 136 D7
Monk Meadow Dock
 VGL GL2 .... 135 L4
Monkscroft Junior &
 Infant School
 CHELTW GL51 .... 115 G2
Monks Park School
 HORF/LLZ BS7 .... 326 B2
Monks Park Surgery
 HORF/LLZ BS7 .... 326 B3
Monmouthshire
 County Council
 CHEP NP16 .... 270 A3
Montpelier Health Centre
 RDLND/MONT BS6 .... 336 A2
Montpellier Gallery
 CHELT GL50 .... 2 A6
Moore Cottage Hospital
 COTS GL54 .... 123 H5
Moore Health Centre
 COTS GL54 .... 123 H4
Moreton-in-Marsh Hospital
 MIM GL56 .... 58 C5
Moreton Wanderers
 Football Club
 MIM GL56 .... 58 E6
Mosque Centre
 COTS GL54 .... 123 G1
The Mount
 CBATH/BATHN BA1 .... 352 E6
Mount Zion School
 RDLND/MONT BS6 .... 335 M2
Much Marcle C of E
 Primary School
 LED HR8 .... 40 B4
Museum
 CBATH/BATHN BA1 .... 350 F7
Museum, Library & Art Gallery
 GL GL1 .... 4 F6
Museum of Advertising &
 Packaging
 GL GL1 .... 4 D6
Naas House
 LYD GL15 .... 225 M3
Nailsworth Mills Estate
 RSTROUD/NAIL GL6 .... 232 E7
National Star Centre College
 CHELTS GL53 .... 139 L5
National Waterways Museum
 GL GL1 .... 4 C7
Natural Health Clinic
 RDLND/MONT BS6 .... 335 K3
Naunton Downs Golf Club
 COTS GL54 .... 99 J8
Naunton Park Primary School
 CHELTS GL53 .... 116 A5
Newbridge Industrial Estate
 BRSG/KWL/STAPK BS4 .... 336 F5
Newent Community School
 NWNT GL18 .... 86 B4
Newent Sports Centre
 NWNT GL18 .... 86 B3
Newent Town
 Associated Football Club
 NWNT GL18 .... 86 F3
Newent Town Council
 NWNT GL18 .... 86 B3
New Fosseway School
 HGRV/WHIT BS14 .... 346 D4

Newnham C of E School
 CIND GL14 .... 155 J6
Newnham Surgery
 CIND GL14 .... 155 H7
The New Olympus Theatre
 GL GL1 .... 5 G8
New Siblands School
 THNB/SVB BS35 .... 293 M2
Newtown Trading Estate
 TEWK GL20 .... 48 E4
Northavon Business Centre
 YATE/CS BS37 .... 309 L8
North Avon Magistrates Court
 YATE/CS BS37 .... 320 A2
North Bristol Rugby
 Football Club
 ALMDB BS32 .... 306 C8
North Cerney Primary School
 CIR GL7 .... 190 C6
Northleaze Primary School
 LGASH BS41 .... 344 D1
North Nibley C of E
 Primary School
 DSLY GL11 .... 252 F6
Northridge Business Centre
 YATE/CS BS37 .... 319 L1
North Road CP School
 YATE/CS BS37 .... 309 K7
North Star Business Park
 VGL GL2 .... 135 K8
Northville Family Practice
 HORF/LLZ BS7 .... 326 D2
Northway County
 Infant School
 TEWK GL20 .... 49 G2
Northway Trading Estate
 TEWK GL20 .... 49 G4
Northwick Business Centre
 MIM GL56 .... 35 J5
North Wilts District Council
 MALM SN16 .... 303 H7
Norton C of E School
 VGL GL2 .... 90 E7
Novers Hill Trading Estate
 BMSTR BS3 .... 345 L2
Novers Lane Jmi School
 BRSG/KWL/STAPK BS4 .... 345 L4
Oakdene School
 CIND GL14 .... 154 B3
Oakfield Business Park
 KGWD/HNM BS15 .... 337 M4
Oak Hill Primary School
 TEWK GL20 .... 51 L4
Oakridge Parochial School
 RSTROUD/NAIL GL6 .... 210 E8
Oatley Trading Estate
 KGWD/HNM BS15 .... 337 M2
Odeon Cinema
 CBRIS/FH BS1 .... 6 F3
Odeon Cinema
 CHELTE/BC GL52 .... 2 E5
Offas Mead CP School
 CHEP NP16 .... 270 C2
Off Centre Gallery
 BMSTR BS3 .... 335 M8
Old Bristolians Sports Club
 CFTN/FAIL BS8 .... 334 B7
Oldbury Court Infant School
 MANG/FISH BS16 .... 327 L4
Oldbury Court Jm School
 MANG/FISH BS16 .... 327 L4
Oldbury-on-Severn
 C of E School
 THNB/SVB BS35 .... 272 D6
Old Coalyard Farm Estate
 COTS GL54 .... 169 H1
Old Cryptians RFC
 GLE GL4 .... 136 A7
The Old Estate Sawmill
 Workshops
 CIR GL7 .... 218 F4
Old Inchbrook School
 RSTROUD/NAIL GL6 .... 232 C5
Oldland Surgery
 OLD/WMLY/WICK BS30 .... 338 E8
The Old Mill Museum
 COTS GL54 .... 123 G1
Old Print Gallery
 BDWAY WR12 .... 32 F4
Old Quarries Industrial Estate
 TET GL8 .... 282 A5
Old Sodbury County
 Primary School
 YATE/CS BS37 .... 321 K3
Old Sucians R F C
 CBATH/BATHN BA1 .... 350 F7
Old Wharf Industrial Estate
 LED HR8 .... 19 L5
Olveston & Elberton
 Primary School
 THNB/SVB BS35 .... 292 C8
The Open University
 CBRIS/FH BS1 .... 7 G5
Optimax Laser Eye Clinic
 CBRIS/FH BS1 .... 6 E4
The Orchard Medical Centre
 DSLY GL11 .... 229 H6
The Orchard Medical Centre
 KGWD/HNM BS15 .... 337 M3
The Other Surgery
 CFTN/FAIL BS8 .... 335 K2
Our Lady of Lourdes RC School
 KGWD/HNM BS15 .... 338 A4
Our Lady of the Rosary
 RC Primary School
 AVONM BS11 .... 324 C3
Overbury First School
 TEWK GL20 .... 28 B4
Overndale School
 YATE/CS BS37 .... 321 J4
Overton Park Surgery
 CHELT GL50 .... 2 B5
Oxstalls Community School
 VGL GL2 .... 112 C7
The Palace Theatre
 CIND GL14 .... 154 B3
Parkend School
 LYD GL15 .... 177 G7

The Park Primary School
 STNHO GL10 .... 207 G4
The Park School
 KGWD/HNM BS15 .... 338 A3
Park Surgery
 CIR GL7 .... 238 B3
Parkwall CP School
 OLD/WMLY/WICK BS30 .... 338 C7
Parkway Trading Estate
 CBRISNE BS2 .... 336 C1
Parliament School
 STROUD GL5 .... 209 H4
Parnall Road Industrial Estate
 MANG/FISH BS16 .... 327 J8
Parson Street Primary School
 BMSTR BS3 .... 345 L1
Parton Manor Infant School
 BWTH/CHD GL3 .... 113 K5
Parton Manor Junior School
 BWTH/CHD GL3 .... 113 K5
Patchway C of E
 Primary School
 BRSTK/PCHW BS34 .... 316 E2
Patchway Health Clinic
 BRSTK/PCHW BS34 .... 316 C3
Patchway High School
 ALMDB BS32 .... 316 D2
Patchway Town Council
 BRSTK/PCHW BS34 .... 316 B3
Patchway Trading Estate
 BRSTK/PCHW BS34 .... 315 M3
Pates Grammar School
 CHELTW GL51 .... 93 G8
Pauntley C of E Primary School
 NWNT GL18 .... 64 E4
Pavilion Business Park
 CIND GL14 .... 129 M8
Pebworth CP School
 STRAT CV37 .... 8 A1
Pembroke Junior &
 Infant School
 CHEP NP16 .... 270 A5
Pembroke Road Surgery
 CFTN/FAIL BS8 .... 335 J2
Pendock C of E School
 RTEWK/TIB GL19 .... 44 D4
Pen Park School
 HNBRY/STHM BS10 .... 325 M1
Perry Court Junior &
 Infant School
 HGRV/WHIT BS14 .... 346 C5
Petherton Road Infant School
 HGRV/WHIT BS14 .... 346 D4
Philblack Works
 HNBRY/STHM BS10 .... 314 B3
Phoenix Business Park
 BMSTR BS3 .... 345 J1
Phoenix NHS Trust
 KGWD/HNM BS15 .... 337 L7
Phoenix Surgery
 CIR GL7 .... 238 B4
Phoenix Surgery
 CIR GL7 .... 263 H4
Phoenix Trading Estate
 STROUD GL5 .... 209 G8
The Picture House
 CBRIS/FH BS1 .... 7 G1
Pillowell CP School
 LYD GL15 .... 201 H2
Pilning CP School
 THNB/SVB BS35 .... 305 G5
Pittville Comprehensive School
 CHELTE/BC GL52 .... 94 B7
Pittville Sports Centre
 CHELTW GL51 .... 93 L7
Pixash Business Centre
 KEYN BS31 .... 348 D6
Playhouse Theatre
 CHELT GL50 .... 2 B6
Plump Hill County
 Primary School
 MTCHDN GL17 .... 130 A7
Portrait Gallery
 HORF/LLZ BS7 .... 326 B2
Portway School
 AVONM BS11 .... 324 A4
Powells C of E School
 CIR GL7 .... 238 B2
The Practice
 CFTN/FAIL BS8 .... 6 B3
Prices Mill Surgery
 RSTROUD/NAIL GL6 .... 232 D8
Prim School
 THNB/SVB BS35 .... 293 K3
Primsdown Industrial Estate
 CHNTN OX7 .... 83 L8
Prinknash Abbey
 GLE GL4 .... 161 K3
Prior Park Preparatory School
 HGHW SN6 .... 289 G4
Priory Doctors Surgery
 BRSG/KWL/STAPK BS4 .... 346 D1
Priory Industrial Estate
 TET GL8 .... 282 A3
Priory Ruins
 GL GL1 .... 4 E6
The Priory Surgery
 BRSG/KWL/STAPK BS4 .... 346 D1
Pucklechurch C of E
 Primary School
 MANG/FISH BS16 .... 329 L5
QEH Theatre
 CFTN/FAIL BS8 .... 6 A3
Quakers Friars
 CBRIS/FH BS1 .... 7 H2
Quedgeley Trading Estate East
 STNHO GL10 .... 183 G6
Quedgeley Trading Estate West
 VGL GL2 .... 158 F6
Queen Elizabeth Hospital
 CFTN/FAIL BS8 .... 6 B3
Queen Margaret County School
 TEWK GL20 .... 48 A7
Querns Business Centre
 CIR GL7 .... 238 C4
Querns School
 CIR GL7 .... 238 C3

Temple House Doctors Surgery
 KEYN BS31 .... **348** A6
Temple Industrial Estate
 CHELTE/BC GL52 .... **3** H2
The Temple
 MTCHDN GL17 .... **131** H1
Temple Trading Estate
 CBRISNE BS2 .... **336** D6
Ten Pin Alley
 GL GL1 .... **4** E7
Tetbury Gallery
 TET GL8 .... **282** A4
Tetbury Industrial Estate
 TET GL8 .... **282** B3
Tewkesbury Abbey School
 TEWK GL20 .... **48** A5
Tewkesbury Business Centre
 TEWK GL20 .... **48** E3
Tewkesbury C of E School
 TEWK GL20 .... **48** B5
Tewkesbury Cottage Hospital
 TEWK GL20 .... **48** A5
Tewkesbury Grant Maintained
 Comprehensive School
 TEWK GL20 .... **48** E4
Tewkesbury Museum
 TEWK GL20 .... **48** A5
Tewkesbury Rugby
 Football Club Ltd
 TEWK GL20 .... **48** A6
Tewkesbury Squash Club
 TEWK GL20 .... **48** D4
Teyfant Primary School
 BMSTRD/HC/WWD BS13 .... **346** A7
Thomas Keble School
 RSTROUD/NAIL GL6 .... **210** A6
Thornbury Health Centre
 THNB/SVB BS35 .... **293** L2
Thornbury Hospital
 THNB/SVB BS35 .... **293** L2
Thornbury Leisure Centre
 THNB/SVB BS35 .... **293** K4
Thornwell Junior School
 CHEP NP16 .... **270** B6
Thrupp Primary School
 STROUD GL5 .... **209** G8
Tibberton Primary School
 VGL GL2 .... **109** L2
Tirlebrook CP School
 TEWK GL20 .... **48** D5
Tockington Manor School
 ALMDB BS32 .... **306** E1
Toddington Primary School
 COTS GL54 .... **52** F6
Toll House Clinic
 YATE/CS BS37 .... **320** E2
Tortworth VC Primary School
 WUE GL12 .... **275** L4
Totterdown Bridge Estate
 CBRISNE BS2 .... **7** M8
Town Council
 MALM SN16 .... **303** J7
Towncrest Sports Club
 TEWK GL20 .... **48** B5
Transport Museum
 GL GL1 .... **4** D5
Tredworth Infant School
 GL GL1 .... **136** B4

Tredworth Junior School
 GL GL1 .... **136** B4
Trinity C of E School
 BAD GL9 .... **323** J5
Trinity College
 HNLZ/SM/SNYPK/WT BS9 .... **325** G7
TT Trading Estate
 YATE/CS BS37 .... **320** E2
Tuffley Primary School
 GLE GL4 .... **160** A2
Tuffley Trading Estate
 VGL GL2 .... **135** K7
Tutthorn Industrial Estate
 CLFD GL16 .... **175** L3
Tutshill Church of
 England School
 CHEP NP16 .... **246** B8
Twigworth C of E School
 VGL GL2 .... **112** B4
Two Mile Hill Junior &
 Infant School
 KGWD/HNM BS15 .... **337** K3
Twyford House Cricket Club
 AVONM BS11 .... **324** B4
Twyning CP School
 TEWK GL20 .... **26** C5
Tyning Junior & Mixed School
 HGRV/WHIT BS14 .... **346** C4
The Tynings CP School
 MANG/FISH BS16 .... **328** B4
Uley C of E Primary School
 DSLY GL11 .... **254** E2
United Bristol
 Healthcare NHS Trust
 CBRIS/FH BS1 .... **6** F2
University of Bristol
 CBRIS/FH BS1 .... **6** D3
University of Bristol
 CFTN/FAIL BS8 .... **6** C2
University of Bristol
 CFTN/FAIL BS8 .... **335** J5
University of Bristol
 HNLZ/SM/SNYPK/WT BS9 .... **325** H7
University of Bristol Childrens
 Hospital
 CFTN/FAIL BS8 .... **6** D1
University of the
 West of England
 CBRIS/FH BS1 .... **6** F4
University of the
 West of England
 MANG/FISH BS16 .... **327** G6
University of the
 West of England Bristol
 BMSTR BS3 .... **335** G6
University of the
 West of England Bristol
 MANG/FISH BS16 .... **326** F2
University of the
 West of England Bristol
 MANG/FISH BS16 .... **327** J6
University of the West of
 England Bristol
 RDLND/MONT BS6 .... **325** J8
Uplands CP School
 STROUD GL5 .... **208** E3
Upper Horfield Primary School
 HORF/LLZ BS7 .... **326** C3

Upton St Leonards
 C of E (C) School
 GLE GL4 .... **137** H8
Upton St Leonards
 Primary School
 GLE GL4 .... **161** G1
Venture Business Centre
 .... **4** B9
Victoria Park County
 Infant School
 BMSTR BS3 .... **336** A8
Victoria Rooms
 CFTN/FAIL BS8 .... **6** A2
Wadehurst Industrial Park
 CBRISNE BS2 .... **7** M3
Walcot Rugby Club
 CBATH/BATHN BA1 .... **350** E6
Wallis Estate
 CBRISNE BS2 .... **326** B8
Wallsworth Hall
 VGL GL2 .... **112** C1
Walmore Hill Primary School
 CIND GL14 .... **157** H1
Walton House Gallery
 CIND GL14 .... **101** M3
Wansdyke School
 HGRV/WHIT BS14 .... **346** B4
Warden Hill Primary School
 CHELTW GL51 .... **115** J6
Ward Industrial Estate
 LYD GL15 .... **225** J3
Warmley C of E School
 OLD/WMLY/WICK BS30 .... **338** E5
Watermoor C of E
 Controlled Primary School
 CIR GL7 .... **238** D4
Watershed Arts Complex
 CBRIS/FH BS1 .... **6** E5
Watledge Surgery
 TEWK GL20 .... **48** B5
Waycroft Primary School
 HGRV/WHIT BS14 .... **347** G6
Wellesley CP School
 YATE/CS BS37 .... **319** M5
Wellsway School
 KEYN BS31 .... **348** C6
Westbury Bazaar & Gallery
 HNLZ/SM/SNYPK/WT BS9 .... **325** J4
Westbury on Severn C of E Primary
 School
 CIND GL14 .... **156** B2
Westbury-on-Trym C of E
 Primary School
 HNLZ/SM/SNYPK/WT BS9 .... **325** J4
Westbury-on-Trym Practice
 HNLZ/SM/SNYPK/WT BS9 .... **325** H5
Westbury Park School
 RDLND/MONT BS6 .... **325** J8
Westbury Surgery
 CIND GL14 .... **156** A2
Westlands School
 CHELTW GL51 .... **115** J4
Westonbirt School
 TET GL8 .... **301** G3
Weston House Group Practice
 CHELT GL50 .... **2** C2
Weston Park Primary School
 AVONM BS11 .... **324** B3

Westpoint Trading Estate
 KGWD/HNM BS15 .... **337** M4
West Town Lane Infant School
 BRSG/KWL/STAPK BS4 .... **346** E2
West Town Lane Junior School
 BRSG/KWL/STAPK BS4 .... **346** E2
West Walk Surgery
 YATE/CS BS37 .... **320** A2
Westwing School
 THNB/SVB BS35 .... **293** G3
Whaddon Primary School
 CHELTE/BC GL52 .... **3** L3
Whimsey Industrial Estate
 CIND GL14 .... **153** M1
Whitchuch Health Centre
 HGRV/WHIT BS14 .... **346** C6
Whitchurch Parish Council
 HGRV/WHIT BS14 .... **346** E7
Whitchurch Primary School
 HGRV/WHIT BS14 .... **346** E7
Whitchurch VA School
 RWYE HR9 .... **126** E3
Whitecross Business Park
 LYD GL15 .... **225** J1
Whitecross School
 LYD GL15 .... **225** H1
Whitefield Fishponds School
 MANG/FISH BS16 .... **327** H7
Whitehall Primary &
 Infant School
 EVILLE/WHL BS5 .... **336** F2
Whitehall Trading Estate
 EVILLE/WHL BS5 .... **336** E3
White Knight Gallery
 .... **2** B9
Whiteladies Medical Group
 CFTN/FAIL BS8 .... **335** J2
Whiteshill Primary School
 RSTROUD/NAIL GL6 .... **184** B8
Whitminster Endowed
 Primary School
 VGL GL2 .... **182** A6
Whitminster Sports Club
 VGL GL2 .... **182** A6
Wick School
 OLD/WMLY/WICK BS30 .... **339** K5
Wick Surgery
 OLD/WMLY/WICK BS30 .... **339** M5
Wickwar Primary School
 WUE GL12 .... **296** D6
Wickwar Trading Estate
 WUE GL12 .... **296** D4
Wicliffe Industrial Centre
 STROUD GL5 .... **208** C5
Widden Infant School
 GL GL1 .... **5** H6
Widden Junior School
 GL GL1 .... **5** H7
Wildscreen @ Bristol
 CBRIS/FH BS1 .... **6** D5
Willersey Industrial Estate
 BDWAY WR12 .... **11** G6
Willersey School
 BDWAY WR12 .... **11** H7
William Budd Health Centre
 BRSG/KWL/STAPK BS4 .... **345** M3
Willow Green Infant School
 CBRISNE BS2 .... **336** C1

Willow Tree Surgery
 CLFD GL16 .... **175** K1
Wilverley Trading Estate
 BRSG/KWL/STAPK BS4 .... **347** G2
Winchcombe Business Centre
 COTS GL54 .... **74** D3
Winchcombe C of E Infant School
 COTS GL54 .... **74** C6
Winchcombe Junior School
 COTS GL54 .... **74** C6
Winchcombe School
 COTS GL54 .... **74** D4
Wincombe Trading Estate
 BRSG/KWL/STAPK BS4 .... **7** K8
Windmill Farm Business Centre
 BMSTR BS3 .... **6** E9
Windmill Hill City Farm
 BMSTR BS3 .... **6** F9
Winfield Hospital
 VGL GL2 .... **112** B4
Withington C of E School
 COTS GL54 .... **142** D7
Withington Primary School
 COTS GL54 .... **142** E7
Withywood School
 BMSTRD/HC/WWD BS13 .... **345** J6
Woodchester Endowed Primary
 School
 STROUD GL5 .... **232** C1
Woodfield Infants School
 DSLY GL11 .... **229** G6
Woodmancote CP School
 CHELTE/BC GL52 .... **72** D7
Wood Road Industrial Centre
 KGWD/HNM BS15 .... **337** M3
Woodside County Primary School
 MTCHDN GL17 .... **129** H6
Woodstock Special School
 KGWD/HNM BS15 .... **338** A4
Wotton Sports Centre
 WUE GL12 .... **277** H5
Wotton Under Edge Town Council
 WUE GL12 .... **277** J4
Wycliffe College
 STNHO GL10 .... **207** H4
Wyedean School
 CHEP NP16 .... **270** C3
Wynstones School
 GLE GL4 .... **160** A3
Yate Leisure Centre
 YATE/CS BS37 .... **320** A1
Yate Town Council
 YATE/CS BS37 .... **320** A1
Yate Town Football Club
 YATE/CS BS37 .... **309** K8
YHA
 CBRIS/FH BS1 .... **6** E6
YMCA
 BRSG/KWL/STAPK BS4 .... **7** H7
Yorkley County School
 LYD GL15 .... **177** K5
Yorkley Health Centre
 LYD GL15 .... **177** K8
Zhong Yi Clinic
 CFTN/FAIL BS8 .... **335** K2

Page 48
B8
1 Abbey Meadow
2 Holme Rd
3 Manor Cl
4 Somerset Pl
5 Woodville Rd

Page 72
A7
1 Bishops Meadow
2 The Cloisters
3 Cornfield Dr
4 Foxmoor
5 Little Orch
6 Rosehip Wy
7 Stanway Wood Gv
8 Stonecroft Cl
9 Yarlington Cl

B7
1 Buckland Cl
2 Gilders Paddock
3 Pullar Cl
4 Roberts Cl
5 St John's Cl
6 Shipway Ct
7 Stoke Park Cl
8 Streamside
9 Willow Park Dr

C7
1 Hisnams Fld
2 Icombe Cl
3 Tobyfield La

C7
1 Birchfield Rd
2 Bootenhay Rd
3 Cares Cl
4 Huntsmans Cl
5 Owls End Rd
6 Ward Cl

D8
1 Anderson Cl
2 Coombe Meade
3 Drapers Cl
4 East Gable
5 Hawthorn Dr
6 Kempsford Acre
7 Lyndhurst Cl
8 Peakstile Piece
9 Thatchers End
10 Woodmancote V

Page 93
G8
1 Blenheim Sq
2 Brown Cl
3 Hawthorn Rd
4 Lechmere Rd

H6
1 Attwood Cl
2 Patterdale Cl
3 Summerfield Cl

I5
1 Aldridge Cl
2 Bullingham Ct
3 Carlton Pl
4 Marsh Cl
5 Midwinter Av
6 Russell Pl
7 Russell St
8 Vine Ct
9 White Hart St

J6
1 Pentathlon Wy

Page 94
E8
1 Corfe Cl
2 Honeysuckle Cl
3 Ivy Bank
4 Willowherb Cl

Page 112
B6
1 Fircroft Rd
2 Stamp's Meadow
3 Taurus Cl
4 Teasel Cl
5 Tewkesbury Rd

D6
1 Alders Grn
2 Ashmead
3 Ferndale Cl
4 Firethorne Cl
5 Foxcote
6 Hornbeam Ms
7 Longland Cl
8 Oxstalls Wy
9 The Tulworths
10 Wentworth Cl
11 Whitebeam Cl
12 Woodcote

E6
1 Dane Cl
2 Gifford Cl
3 Gilbert Rd
4 Langdale Gdns
5 Lea Crs
6 Malet Cl
7 Manley Gdns
8 Mortimer Rd
9 Mowbrey Cl
10 Saxon Cl
11 Wedgwood Dr

Page 113
G7
1 Maple Ct

H5
1 Heathdean Rd

J3
1 Compton Cl
2 Essex Cl
3 St Vincent Wy
4 Thomas Moore Cl
5 Victory Cl

J5
1 Berryfield Gld
2 Forsythia Cl
3 Gardiners Cl
4 Kilminster Ct

K5
1 Andorra Wy
2 Chadbournes
3 Hazelcroft
4 Quinton Cl

L7
1 Barnhay
2 Chapel Hay Cl
3 Drews Cl

Page 115
G1
1 Amberley Rd
2 St Aidans Cl
3 Seacome Rd

G2
1 Cowper Rd
2 Milton Av
3 Wordsworth Av

G3
1 Chedworth Wy
2 Notgrove Cl
3 Rissington Cl
4 Sheepscombe Cl
5 Stanton Wy

G4
1 Harrington Dr
2 Hatherley Brake
3 Ullswater Rd
4 Windermere Rd

G5
1 Caernarvon Cl
2 Colwyn Dr
3 Glamorgan Rd
4 Haweswater Rd

G6
1 Arlingham
2 Ashcott Ms
3 Aysgarth Av
4 Beechmore Dr
5 Calverley Ms
6 Chasely Crs
7 Clynderwe Gv
8 Larchmere Gv
9 Meadow La
10 Pyrton Ms
11 Rowan Wy
12 Selworthy
13 Severn
14 Silverwood Wy
15 Swainscombe Dr
16 Thornhaugh Ms
17 Welwyn Ms
18 Withypool

H3
1 Church Rd
2 Finstock Cl
3 Granley Cl
4 Granley Dr
5 Greville Ct
6 Lansdown Castle Dr

H4
1 Bronte Cl
2 Browning Ms
3 Chapman Wy
4 Deacon Cl
5 Deans Ct
6 Grainere Rd
7 Manse Gdns
8 Rolleston Wy

H5
1 Dover Hay
2 Warden Hill Cl

H6
1 Amaranth Cl
2 Barwick Rd
3 Charlton Cl
4 Croft Thorne Cl
5 Crythan Wk
6 Ferndales Cl
7 Genista Wy
8 Globe Farm Ct
9 Gleniea Gv
10 Griasfield La
11 The Greenings
12 Hawcombe Ms
13 Rothermere Cl

H7
1 Tayberry Gv

J1
1 Clavedon Sq

J2
1 Libertus Ct
2 Stow Cl

J3
1 Sincairn Cl
2 Lansdown Cl
3 Lansdown Lodge Dr
4 Sicilicome Ms

K1
1 Camelia Cl
2 David French Ct
3 Hampton Cl
4 Hidcote Av
5 Rochester Rd
6 St Albans Cl
7 Sissinghurst Gv

Page 116
L3
1 Leckhampton Ga

K1
1 Millbrook Gdns
2 Old Millbrook Ter
3 Queen's Retreat
4 St George's Cl
5 Sterling Ct

K2
1 Wendover Gdns

K3
1 Thorncliffe Dr
2 Tivoli Wk

K4
1 Bakehouse La

K5
1 Ellesmere Cl
2 Kenelm Gdns
3 Merestones Dr

K7
1 Friars Cl
2 Kidnappers' La
3 Silverthorn Cl

K7
1 The Alders
2 Bryony Bank
3 Chestnut Rd

L1
1 Leckhampton Farm Ct

L2
1 Devonshire St
2 Hereford Pl
3 Knapp La

L3
1 Lansdown Wk
2 Parabola Rd
3 Queens La

L4
1 Andover Wk
2 Brandon Pl
3 Saddlers La
4 St James' Pl
5 Tivoli Ms

L5
1 Brooksdale La
2 Kenelm Dr
3 Pickering Cl
4 Pickering Rd
5 Upper Norwood St

M1
1 Ambrose Pl
2 Baynham Wy
3 Chester Wk
4 Church St
5 Jenner Wk
6 Oxford Pas
7 Rose & Crown Pas
8 Royal Oak Ms
9 St George's Pl

M2
1 Clarence Pde
2 Clarence St
3 College Pl
4 County Court Rd
5 High St
6 Imperial Circ
7 Imperial Sq
8 Oriel Rd
9 Ormond Pl
10 Post Office La
11 Promenade
12 Queen's Circ
13 Regent St
14 Royal Well Pl
15 Royal Well Rd
16 Royal Well Rd

M3
1 Bath Ville Ms
2 Belmore Pl
3 Calderwood Ct
4 Cedar Court Rd
5 Eaton Pl
6 Glensanda Ct
7 Montpellier Dr
8 Montpellier Retreat
9 Paragon Ter
10 Trafalgar St
11 Vittoria Wk

M4
1 Bath Ter
2 Bethesda St
3 Chapel La
4 Clare St
5 Exmouth Ct
6 St Luke's Pl
7 Victoria Retreat

M5
1 Badminton Cl
2 Fairfield Park Rd
3 Fairfield St
4 Fairhaven Rd
5 Fairhaven St
6 Maida Vale Rd
7 Mornington Dr

M6
1 Charnwood Cl
2 Charnwood Wk
3 Duckworth St
4 Wychbury Cl

M8
1 Stoneleigh Cl

Page 116
A1
1 Albert Pl
2 Albion Pl
3 Back Albert Pl
4 Berkeley Av
5 Clarence St
6 Columbia St
7 Gloucester Pl
8 Jersey St
9 North Pl
10 Portland Rd
11 Portland Sq
12 Trinity La
13 Warwick Pl
14 Winchcombe St

A2
1 Albion St
2 Barratt's Mill La
3 Berkeley Ct
4 Berkeley Pl
5 Crosvenor Pl South
6 Crosvenor St
7 Crosvenor Ter
8 Hewlett Pl
9 Highbury La
10 St Anne's Rd
11 Sherborne St
12 Tom Price Ct
13 Vernon Pl
14 Winchcombe St
15 Witcombe Pl

A5
1 Verney Cl
2 The Verneys

B1
1 All Saints' Villas Rd
2 Fairview Cl
3 Glenfall St
4 Pittville Circ
5 Pittville Circus Rd
6 St Anne's Cl
7 Whaddon Dr

B2
1 Brighton Rd
2 Fairview Rd
3 Victoria Pl
4 Westdown Gdns

B3
1 Oxford Cl

B5
1 Marlborough Cl
2 Randolph Cl

C4
1 Cirencester Rd
2 Hamilton St
3 Langton Grove Rd
4 Langton Pl
5 Oakland St
6 Oxford St

D1
1 Hill View Rd
2 Ilsbourne Rd
3 Ladysmith Rd
4 Salamanca Rd
5 Whaddon Rd

D5
1 Acomb Crs
2 Courtfield Dr
3 Lawrence Cl
4 Porturet Wy
5 Redburn Cl
6 Riverside Cl
7 Water La

D6
1 Cedar La
2 Church Piece
3 Chyrosa Rd
4 Little Herbert's Cl
5 New St

D7
1 Chatcombe Cl

E1
1 Kimberley Wk

E5
1 Carisbrooke Dr

E6
1 Farleigh Cl

E6
1 Balcarras Retreat
2 East End Rd
3 Peel Cl
4 Woodgate Cl

E7
1 Birch Cl
2 Willow Rd

Page 135
M1
1 Archdeacon Ct
2 Barbican Rd
3 Barbican Wy
4 Barrack Sq
5 Bearland
6 Berkeley St
7 Longsmith St
8 Lower Quay St
9 Mount St
10 Priory Rd
11 Quay St
12 Upper Quay St

Page 136
A1
1 Bull La
2 Cross Keys La
3 Hare La
4 Market Pde
5 New Inn La
6 St Mary's St
7 Spread Eagle Rd
8 Station Rd

A2
1 Bell La
2 Brunswick Sq
3 Hampden Wy
4 Parliament St
5 Southgate St
6 Whitfield St

M3
1 Beechwood Gv
2 Cherrywood Gdns
3 Coberley Rd

M4
1 Claremont Rd
2 George St
3 Newland St
4 Wellington Pde

A3
1 Albert St
2 Bedford St
3 Cambridge St
4 Charles St
5 Eastgate St
6 King's Barton St
7 Napier St
8 Nettleton Rd
9 Park St
10 Raglan St
11 St Kilda Pde
12 Sinope St
13 Widden St

B4
1 Carmarthen St
2 Dainty St
3 Dora Wk
4 Ducie St
5 Faraday Cl
6 The Laurels
7 Llandilo St
8 Massey Pde
9 Melbourne St West
10 Morpeth St
11 Paul St
12 Percy St

C2
1 Alington Cl
2 Great Western Ct
3 Magdala Rd
4 Millbrook Cl

D2
1 Armscroft Gdns
2 Etheridge Pl

D4
1 Fairford Wy
2 Stonehenge Rd

D4
1 Old Painswick Rd

E4
1 Amberley Rd
2 Chatcombe Rd
3 Saintbridge Cl

D7
1 Evans Wk
2 School Ms

A5
1 Armscroft Ms

E4
1 Coney Hill Pde
2 Druids Cl

E5
1 Ashgrove Wy
2 Church Wy

E7
1 Brindle Cl
2 Drayton Cl
3 George Whitefield Cl
4 Prinknash Cl
5 Prinknash Rd
6 Timmis Cl

E8
1 Gatmeres Rd
2 Matson Av
3 Oaktree Gdn

F2
1 Hammond Wy
2 Wotton Ct

F3
1 Ebrington Cl
2 Julian Cl
3 Steeple Cl

F4
1 Blake Hill Wy
2 Dodington Cl
3 Little Fld
4 Snowshill Cl
5 Ullenwood Rd

F5
1 Trygrove

F7
1 Claridge Cl
2 Nutmeg Cl

F8
1 Filbert Cl
2 Oakcroft Cl
3 Walnut Cl
4 Willowcroft Cl

Page 137
G4
1 Claudians Cl
2 The Copse
3 Grasby Cl
4 Marefield Cl
5 The Orangery
6 Pinery Rd
7 Whitewell Cl

G5
1 Brierley Cl
2 Broadwell Cl
3 Chaceley Cl
4 Cranham Cl
5 Edgeworth Cl
6 Longhope Cl
7 Oakridge Cl
8 Peacock Cl
9 Ruspidge Cl
10 Snowdrop Cl
11 Sudgrove Pk
12 Verbena Cl
13 Woodbine Cl

H3
1 Alderton Cl
2 Apple Tree Cl
3 Birdwood Cl
4 Blackberry Cl
5 Combrook Cl
6 Deerhurst Cl
7 Grayling Cl
8 Monarch Cl
9 Plum Tree Cl
10 Rendcomb Cl
11 Staunton Cl
12 Tarlton Cl

H5
1 Augustine Wy
2 Dianas Cl
3 Henry Ryder Cl
4 Minster Gdns
5 Neptune Cl
6 Remus Cl
7 Trajan Cl

H7
1 Bilberry Cl
2 Buddleia Cl

L5
1 Whitworth Ms

Page 154
B2
1 Edge Hills Cl
2 Ferndale Cl
3 Market St
4 Marshall's La
5 Moreland Cl
6 Mountjoy's La
7 Mountjoy's Lane End
8 Oakwood Cl

Page 159
G3
1 Ashleworth Gdns
2 Cheviot Cl
3 Coss Wood Cnr
4 Mendip Cl

Page 207
H3
1 Blackbird Cl
2 Cedar Gdns
3 Chaffinch Ct
4 Coates Gdns
5 Glen Ct
6 Goldcrest Cl
7 Greenstreet
8 Magpie Ct
9 Partridge Cl
10 Pheasant Mead
11 Sherbourne Ct
12 Starling Cl

M3
1 Hawthorn Ri
2 Perry Orch
3 St Michael's Pl
4 Springfield Rd
5 The Wordens

Page 208
H3
1 Harper Rd
2 Moor Hall Pl
3 Park View Dr
4 Princes Rd

A4
1 Mosley Crs

C2
1 Birches Cl
2 The Circle
3 The Square
4 Upper Springfield Rd

D2
1 Bedford St
2 Fawkes Pl
3 Gloucester St
4 John St
5 Kendrick St
6 King St
7 Lime Gv
8 Locking Hl
9 Parliment Ct
10 Russell St
11 Ryeleaze Cl
12 Ryeleaze Rd
13 The Shambles
14 Streamside
15 Swan St
16 Threadneedle St

F3
1 John Bevan Cl
2 Shepherds Cl
3 Sycamore Dr
4 The Woodlands

F4
1 The Knoll
2 Wood St

F6
1 Churchfield Rd
2 Lower Churchfield Rd
3 Nursery Cl
4 Trinity Rd

F6
1 Weyhouse Cl

Page 233
H4
1 Burleigh Tor

H5
1 Dr Crawfords Wy
2 Southfield

K4
1 The Tynings

Page 238
B5
1 Foxes Bank Dr
2 Greyfriars Wk
3 Linacre Crs
4 Masefield Rd
5 Michaels Mead
6 Morestall Dr
7 Somerville St

C2
1 Black Jack St
2 Cosditch St
3 Hakeburn Rd
4 Park St
5 Silver St
6 West Market Pl

C4
1 Beaufort Ct
2 Garden Cl
3 Grantley Crs
4 Limes Cl
5 Martin Cl
6 St Michaels Rd
7 Whitworth Rd

D4
1 Bridge End
2 Mercian Cl
3 Sperringate
4 Watermoor Wy

D5
1 Bridge Cl

E4
1 The Smithy

Page 270
A3
1 Bank Sq
2 Beaufort Cl
3 Carden City Wy
4 Hardwick Av
5 High Vw
6 Middle St
7 Oxford St
8 Regent Wy
9 River Vw
10 Thomas St
11 Upper Nelson St

A8
1 Ash Cl
2 Holly Cl
3 Linden Cl
4 Mathern Wy

B4
1 Fisherman's Wk
2 Magnolia Cl
3 The Reddings
4 Sharps Wy
5 Warren Slade

H5
1 Stoke Hamlet
2 Stoke La

H7
1 Saville Gate Cl

B7
1 Bishops Cl
2 Cidermill Rd
3 Fountain Wy
4 Lady Margaret Ct
5 Lewis Wy
6 Lord Eldon Dr
7 Preston Cl
8 Rougemont Gv
9 Thorn Tree Dr
10 Well Cl

C4
1 Madocke Rd

Page 293
K1
1 Coombe Av
2 Kensington Cl
3 Orchard Gra

Page 316
F1
1 Boursland Cl
2 Campion Dr
3 Foxborough Gdns
4 Perrys Lea
5 Primrose Cl
6 Teal Cl

G7
1 Blackthorn Dr
2 Garrett Dr
3 Kemperleye Wy
4 Shiels Dr
5 Somerby Cl

F5
1 Elming Down Cl
2 Olympus Cl

G1
1 Balmoral Rd
2 Chevening Cl
3 Holyrood Cl
4 Lancaster Cl
5 Osborne Cl

Page 317
G6
1 Cerimon Ga
2 Charbon Ga
3 Dighton Ga
4 Lysander Wk
5 Montague Ct
6 Roman Wk

Page 320
F2
1 Cherry Rd
2 Chestnut Dr
3 Meadow Rd
4 The Parade
5 River Rd
6 Streamside Rd
7 Wistaria Av

Page 324
B3
1 Broxholme Wk

M1
1 Avondown Cl
2 Caldbeck Cl
3 Easedale Cl

M2
1 Greenfield Rd
2 Westleigh Cl

M3
1 Greenfield Av
2 Greenway Dr
3 Greenway Rd
4 Kelston Gdns

M4
1 Cordwell Wk
2 Reed Cl

M6
1 Brookland Rd
2 Lansdown Ter

M8
1 Brookfield Av
2 Kersteman Rd
3 Pine Grove Pl
4 Raglan Cl

Page 326
B5
1 Crofton Av

B6
1 Draycott Rd
2 Uphill Rd

B8
1 Hopetoun Rd
2 Osborne Av
3 St Bartholomew's Rd

C2
1 Cropthorne Rd

C4
1 Austen Cl
2 Cropthorne Rd South
3 St Gregory's Wk
4 Thackeray Wk

F5
1 Ebenezer La
2 Poplar Av

F6
1 Ellbridge Cl
2 Halwyn Cl
3 Yeomans Cl

F8
1 Cook's Folly Rd

Page 325
G1
1 Dundas Cl
2 Gray's Cl
3 Henbury Rd

G4
1 Hammond Gdns

G6
1 Clifton Gv
2 Ebenezer La
3 Sunnyside

G7
1 Howecroft Gdns

H2
1 Standish Cl

H3
1 Westover Gdns

H5
1 Baileys Mead Rd
2 Heath House La
3 Little Parr Cl

H7
1 Cameron Wk

J1
1 Ellinghurst Cl
2 Fennell Gv
3 Roselarge Gdns
4 Thornmead Gv

J3
1 Elmfield Rd
2 Greystoke Gdns
3 Watkins Yd

C4
1 Cote Lea Pk
2 East Hill Eastfield Rd
3 Priory Dene
4 Southfield Cl
5 Westminster Cl
6 West Priory Cl

J6
1 Carmarthen Rd

J7
1 Alfred Rd

K1
1 Concorde Dr

Page 327
K5
1 Blandford Cl
2 Grange Cl North
3 Waterford Rd

K6
1 Fallodon Ct
2 Remenham Dr

K7
1 Ladysmith Rd
2 Palmerston Rd

K8
1 Branksome Rd
2 Iddesleigh Rd
3 The Quadrant
4 Redland Rd
5 Westmoreland Rd

G8
1 Burnside Cl
2 Keswick Wk
3 Lowther Rd
4 Mardale Cl
5 Millard Cl
6 Standon Wy
7 Twenty Acres Rd

H6
1 Danbury Wk
2 Trowbridge Wk

H7
1 Alexandra Rd
2 Falfield Wk
3 Francis Rd

H8
1 Bredon Nook Rd
2 Evelyn Rd
3 Whiteleaze
4 Woodchester Rd

L8
1 Croft Vw

H6
1 Longleat Cl
2 St Margaret's Dr
3 Tennessee Gv
4 Twickenham Rd

J4
1 Fairhaven Rd
2 Good Shepherd Cl
3 Malmesbury Cl
4 Maplemeade

J6
1 Metford Pl

J6
1 Claverham Cl
2 College Av
3 Guinea La

J7
1 Hinton Rd
2 Hockey's La

M3
1 Acton Rd
2 Ivy La
3 Justice Rd
4 Poplar Pl

K2
1 Beaufort Pl
2 Berkeley La

K4
1 Churchside

K5
1 Lanaway Rd
2 Little Hayes
3 Oldbury Court Dr

M8
1 Cunningham Gdns

K7
1 Bridges Cl
2 Chasefield La
3 Daws Ct
4 Parkhurst Av
5 Vicars Cl

K8
1 Filwood Cl
2 William St

B5
1 Bryants Cl

B6
1 Beckspool Rd

C2
1 Quarry Rd
2 Tuckett La

D2
1 Bracey Dr
2 Bridges Dr
3 Grangewood Cl
4 Shimsey Cl
5 Urfords Dr

L7
1 Pemberton Cl

L7
1 Edgeware Rd

D2
1 Eleventh Av
2 Seventh Av

D3
1 Browning Ct

D3
1 Branwhite Cl

M2
1 Bampton Dr

M3
1 Bromley Heath Rd
2 Pilgrims Wy
3 Quaker's Cl
4 Scantleberry Cl

M4
1 Cleeve Wood Rd
2 Heath Cl

M6
1 Chestnut Rd
2 Conifer Cl
3 Edmund Cl

M6
1 Christchurch Av
2 Christchurch La
3 Downend Park Rd
4 Nelson Rd
5 Tyler's La

E7
1 Croft Av
2 Rowland Av

E8
1 Chisbury St
2 Coleridge Rd
3 North Vw
4 Pendennis Av

F5
1 Bryansons Cl
2 Countess Ms
3 Princess Gdns

F6
1 Lynn Rd
2 Rockland Rd
3 Stapleton Rd

F7
1 Fry's Cl
2 Wickham Vw

Page 327
F8
1 Cloister Av
2 Herbert Crs
3 Queen St
4 Shamrock Rd

G6
1 Blackberry Av
2 Cromwells Hide
3 Frome Pl
4 Glenside Pk
5 Glebe Hay Cl
6 Lark's Fld
7 Pennyroyal Cl
8 Spires Vw

G8
1 Foxglove Cl
2 Honey Suckle La
3 Lower Grove Rd
4 Rosebay Mead

G8
1 Huyton Rd
2 Knowsley Rd
3 Marlborough Av
4 Marlborough St
5 Ridgeway Pde

H6
1 Longleat Cl
2 St Margaret's Dr
3 Tennessee Gv
4 Twickenham Rd

H7
1 Adelaide Pl
2 Albert Ter
3 Featherstone Rd
4 Langdale Rd
5 Wharf Rd

H8
1 Balaclava Rd
2 Drummond Rd
3 Halstock Av
4 Lodore Rd
5 Midland Ter
6 Stoke View Rd

J4
1 Blenman Cl
2 Probyn Cl
3 Scott Lawrence Cl
4 Stourden Cl

J6
1 Claverham Cl
2 College Av
3 Guinea La

J7
1 Hinton Rd
2 Hockey's La

K1
1 Curlew Cl
2 Lapwing Gdns
3 Ronald Rd
4 Whinchat Gdns
5 Witherlies Rd

K7
1 Bridges Cl
2 Chasefield La
3 Daws Ct
4 Parkhurst Av
5 Vicars Cl

K8
1 Filwood Cl
2 William St

B5
1 Bryants Cl

B6
1 Beckspool Rd

C2
1 Quarry Rd
2 Tuckett La

J1
1 Anglesea Pl
2 Bridges Rd
3 Highland Crs
4 Highland Sq
5 Hughenden Rd
6 Mornington Rd
7 Normanton Rd
8 Quarry Steps
9 Redland Ter
10 Richmond Dr
11 St Vincent's Hl
12 Westbury Rd
13 York Wk

L7
1 Argyle St
2 Dean St
3 Fairfield Rd
4 Kingston Rd
5 Merrywood Cl
6 Morley Rd
7 Mount Pleasant Ter
8 Murray St
9 Summer St

L8
1 Clifton St
2 Diamond St
3 Eaton St
4 Graham Rd
5 Hebron Rd
6 Kent St
7 New John St
8 Rowley St
9 St John's St
10 South Rd
11 Stanley St
12 Victoria St
13 Victor Rd
14 York St

M7
1 Alexandra Cl
2 Kensington Rd
3 North Vw
4 Pendennis Av

M8
1 Beazer Cl
2 Colston Cl
3 Leicester Sq
4 Portland Pl
5 Wesley Cl

Page 328
A8
1 Gladstone Cl
2 Gloucester Rd
3 St Stephens Cl
4 Wiltshire Pl
5 Woodchester

B2
1 Chantry La
2 Chepstow Pk
3 Coodwood Gdns
4 Havelock Cl
5 Plumpton Ct
6 Redcar Ct
7 Sedgefield Gdns
8 Wetherby Ct
9 Wincanton Cl

B3
1 Lytchet Dr
2 Rockside Gdns

B4
1 Boscombe Crs
2 Bowden Pl
3 Kimberley Cl
4 Westbourne Cl
5 Westerleigh Cl

B7
1 Bankside

C3
1 Chestnut Rd

C3
1 Meadowcroft

C5
1 Kingston Cl
2 Springfield Cl
3 Wakeford Rd

C5
1 Blackhorse Pl

C5
1 Balmoral Ct
2 Elmleigh Cl
3 Louise Av
4 Oaklands Rd
5 Westering Cl

D3
1 Youngs Ct

D4
1 Bromfield Wk
2 Cyrus Ct
3 Denton Patch
4 Howells Mead
5 Langley Mow
6 Pendock Ct

D6
1 Farm Cl
2 Harrison Cl

D6
1 Oaklands Cl
2 Shackel Hendy Ms

E5
1 Emersons Wy

E5
1 Paddock Cl

Page 335
G5
1 Bannerleigh La
2 Broad Oaks
3 Rownham Hl

G7
1 Rownham Ct

H3
1 Norland Rd

H4
1 Clifton Down Rd
2 Gloucester St
3 Westfield Pl

H5
1 Albermarle Rw
2 Cornwallis Av
3 Cumberland Rd
4 Dowry Sq
5 Freeland Pl
6 Glendale
7 Hopechapel Hl
8 Hope Sq
9 Jacob's Wells Rd
10 Joy Hl
11 North Green St
12 Oxford Pl
13 The Paragon
14 Royal York Crs
15 South Green St
16 Victoria Ter
17 Windsor Ter

J6
1 Ashton Av
2 Dock Gate La
3 Clevedon Rd
4 Oldfield Rd
5 Pembroke Rd
6 Pooles Wharf Ct
7 Rownham Mead
8 Sandford Rd

K1
1 East Shrubbery
2 Evans Rd
3 Hartington Pk
4 Luccombe Hl
5 Shrubbery Cottages
6 West Shrubbery
7 Woodland Ter

B2
1 Chantry Rd
2 Collingwood Rd
3 Cotham Gdns
4 Cotham Hl
5 Cotham Ri
6 Hampton Pk
7 Imperial Rd
8 King's Parade Av
9 Oakland Rd
10 Warwick Rd

B3
1 Alma Road Av
2 Melrose Av
3 Oakfield Pl
4 Westbourne Pl

K4
1 Berkeley Av
2 Byron Pl
3 Queen's Av
4 Queen's Rd
5 Richmond Hill Av
6 Triangle South
7 Triangle West
8 Upper Byron Pl
9 Wetherell Pl

K5
1 Bellevue Cottages
2 Cliftonwood Crs
3 Gasferry Rd
4 Glentworth Rd
5 Gorse La
6 John Carr's Ter
7 St Edward's Rd
8 Southernhay
9 Southernhay Av

K6
1 Camden Rd
2 Cafle Cl
3 Hanover Pl
4 Mardyke Ferry Rd

K7
1 Dalston Rd
2 Fairfield Pl
3 King William St
4 Phipps St

L1
1 Emleet Rd
2 Glentworth Rd

L2
1 Courtside Ms
2 Kenilworth Rd
3 Woodstock Av

L3
1 Clarence Rd
2 Highbury Vls
3 Osborne Vls
4 Southwell St
5 Tyndalls Park Ms

L4
1 Berkeley Av
2 Berkeley Rd
3 Lodge Pl
4 Lodge St
5 Old Park Hl
6 Park La
7 Park Street Av
8 Royal Fort Rd
9 There-and-back-again La

L5
1 Bigwood La
2 Brandon Steep
3 Charlotte St South
4 College Sq
5 Culver St
6 Denmark Av
7 Frogmore St
8 Gaunt's La
9 Hobb's La
10 Lower College St
11 Lower Lamb St
12 Orchard Av
13 Orchard La
14 Orchard St
15 Partition St
16 Unity St
17 Upper Wells St
18 York Pl

L6
1 West End

L7
1 Argyle St
2 Dean St
3 Fairfield Rd
4 Kingston Rd
5 Merrywood Cl
6 Morley Rd
7 Mount Pleasant Ter
8 Murray St
9 Summer St

L8
1 Clifton St
2 Diamond St
3 Eaton St
4 Graham Rd
5 Hebron Rd
6 Kent St
7 New John St
8 Rowley St
9 St John's St
10 St John's La
11 Sion Rd
12 South Rd
13 Stanley St
14 Victoria St
15 Victor Rd
16 York St

J2
1 Beaconsfield Rd
2 Downside Rd
3 King's Parade Ms

J3
1 Buckingham V
2 Clifton Pk
3 Eaton Crs
4 Worcester Ter

J4
1 Belgrave Pl
2 Boyce's Av
3 Codrington Pl
4 King's Rd
5 Richmond La

J5
1 Ambra V
2 Ambra V South
3 Ambra V West
4 Camden Ter
5 Clifton Hl
6 Clifton Vale Cl
7 Cliftonwood Rd
8 Polygon Rd
9 Royal Park

M1
1 Brookfield La
2 Brookfield Rd
3 Cotham Brow
4 Edgecumbe Rd
5 Purton Rd

M2
1 Arley Cottages
2 Arley Pk
3 Arley Hl
4 Elmgrove Pk
5 Fremantle La
6 Fremantle Rd
7 St Matthew's Rd
8 Southfield Rd
9 Victoria Gdns
10 Winsley Rd

M3
1 Barton St
2 Cherry La
3 Clevedon Te
4 Cottage P
5 Earl St
6 Henrietta S
7 Hillgrove St North
8 King Sq
9 King Square Av
10 Lower Gay St
11 Marlborough Hill F
12 Montague Hl
13 Montague Hl South
14 Montague St
15 Princess Rw
16 Spring Hl
17 Terrell St
18 Whitson St

K1
1 All Saints' St
2 Bell La
3 Blackfriars
4 Bridewell St
5 Cannon St
6 Christmas St
7 Flennes Ct
8 High St
9 Host St
10 Lewins Mead
11 Nelson St
12 Newmarket Av
13 Pithay
14 Pithay Ct
15 Quay St
16 St Stephen's St
17 Silver St
18 Union St

M5
1 All Saints' La
2 Assembly Rooms La
3 Bridge St
4 Broad Quay
5 Clare St
6 Coronation St
7 Crow La
8 High St
9 King William Av
10 Marsh St
11 Middle Av
12 Queen Square Av
13 Rackhay
14 St Stephen's Av
15 Telephone Av

M7
1 Bedminster Pde
2 Boot La
3 Brook Rd
4 Dean Cl
5 Dean Crs
6 Leicester St
7 Lombard St
8 Regent Rd
9 St Paul's Rd
10 Southville Rd
11 Whitehouse La

M7
1 Brendon Rd
2 Church La
3 Hereford St
4 Porlock Rd
5 Stafford St

Page 336
A1
1 Cheltenham La
2 Chesterfield Rd
3 Norfolk Av
4 St Andrew's Rd

A2
1 Armindale Rd
2 Barnabas St
3 Bath Buildings
4 Dalrymple Rd
5 Drummond Rd
6 Norrisville Rd
7 Woodmancote Rd

A3
1 Backfields
2 Backfields La
3 Brunswick Sq
4 Chaster St
5 Cumberland St
6 Dalton Sq
7 Gloucester St
8 Hillgrove St
9 Little Bishop St
10 Norfolk Av
11 Pembroke St
12 Portland St
13 Thomas St
14 Wilder St

A6
1 Church St
2 Ferry St
3 Long Rw
4 Narrow Pln
5 St Thomas St East
6 Three Queens' La
7 Tower St

L7
1 Colston St
2 Mede Cl
3 Phippen St
4 Portwall La East
5 Somerset Sq

A7
1 Nicholas St
2 Sargent St

B1
1 Almorah Rd
2 Newport St
3 Orwell St
4 Paultow Av

B1
1 Ashley Court Rd
2 Ashley Grove Rd
3 Ashley Rd
4 Cumberland Rd
5 Fairlawn Rd
6 Falkland Rd
7 Milverton Gdns
8 Old Ashley Hl
9 Richmond Rd
10 St Andrew's Rd
11 St Werburgh's Rd
12 Sommerville Rd South
13 South
14 York St

B2
1 Albany Rd
2 Albert Pk
3 Ashfield Wk
4 Brook La
5 Cairns' Crs
6 Corey Cl
7 Franklyn La
8 London Rd
9 Tudor Rd
10 Winkworth Pl

B3
1 Beggarswell Cl
2 Charlotte St
3 Cheapside
4 East St
5 Elton St
6 Eugene St
7 Frome St
8 Wilson Pl

B4
1 Asher La
2 David St
3 Eyer's La
4 Gloucester La
5 Hawkins St
6 Redcross St
7 St Matthias Pk
8 Tucker St
9 Waterloo St
10 Willway St

B5
1 Broad Pln
2 Louisa St
3 Midland St
4 New Kingsley Rd
5 New Thomas St
6 Providence Pl
7 Straight St

B6
1 Chatterton Sq
2 Chatterton St
3 Lower Station Approach Rd

B7
1 Bellevue Ter
2 Bushy Pk
3 Cheapside St
4 Dunmore St
5 Higham St
6 Vernon St

B8
1 Merioneth St
2 Monmouth St
3 Montgomery St
4 Nottingham St

C1
1 Boucher Pl
2 Boyce Dr
3 Cleave St
4 Dorset Gv
5 Durham Rd
6 Hereford Rd
7 John St
8 Lancaster Rd
9 Lynmouth Rd
10 Merstham Rd
11 Norman Rd
12 Ryland Pl
13 Seddon Rd
14 Stafford Rd
15 Tewkesbury Rd
16 Treefield Pl
17 Trentham Cl
18 Warminster Rd
19 Weedon Cl
20 York St

C2
1 Ashley Grove Rd
2 Baptist St
3 Barker Wk
4 Bean St
5 Blenheim St
6 Byron St
7 Conduit Pl
8 Dermot St
9 Cable Rd
10 Highett Dr
11 Kensington Pk
12 Lower Ashley Rd
13 Newfoundland Rd
14 Oxford Pl
15 Pennywell Rd
16 Rosebery Av
17 Summers Rd
18 Waverley St

C3
1 Armoury Sq
2 Ashman Cl
3 Bates Ct
4 Beaufort St
5 Beaumont St
6 Beaumont Ter
7 Clark St
8 Durbin Wk
9 Hamilton Rd
10 Harleston St
11 Perry St
12 Robinson St
13 St Gabriel's Rd
14 Webb St
15 Winsford St

C5
1 Barton V
2 Dings Wk
3 Freestone Rd
4 Queen Victoria St
5 William St

C6
1 Victoria Rd

C7
1 Angers Rd
2 Firfield St
3 Fitzroy St
4 Fredrick St
5 Highgrove St
6 Hillside St
7 Kingstree St

C8
1 Bathwell Rd
2 Clyde Ter
3 Fairfoot Rd
4 Fordell Pl
5 Goolden St
6 Knowle Rd
7 Vale St

D1
1 Chester St
2 Clare Rd
3 Robert St
4 Wood St

D2
1 Chapel Rd
2 Church Av
3 Graham Rd
4 Greenbank Av West
5 Henrietta St
6 Lawrence Av
7 Moorhill St
8 Normanby Rd
9 Northcote St
10 St Mark's Ter
11 St Nicholas Pk
12 Warwick Av
13 Warwick Rd
14 Woodborough St

D3
1 Abraham Cl
2 Adelaide Pl
3 All Hallows Rd
4 Brighton Pk
5 Cattybrook St
6 Clayton St
7 Combfactory La
8 Eastbourne Rd
9 Elmgrove Av
10 Luxton St
11 Owen St
12 Pountney Dr
13 Thomson Rd
14 Tyndall Rd
15 Vining Wk
16 Westbourne Rd
17 Windsor Gv

D4
1 Arthur Skemp Cl
2 Atchley St
3 Bright St
4 Charlton St
5 Church St
6 Earl Russell Wy
7 Ernest Barker Cl
8 Morton St
9 Payne Dr
10 Robert St
11 St Luke St
12 Strawbridge Rd
13 William Mason Cl

D5
1 Beaconsfield St
2 Bradhurst St
3 Canterbury St
4 Cookworthy Cl
5 Fripp Cl
6 Goulter St
7 Holmes St
8 Maze St
9 Napier St
10 Parkers Barton
11 Victor St

D6
1 Glass House La

D7
1 Edward Rd

D8
1 Hampden Rd

E1
1 Apsley St
2 Argyle St
3 Bay Gdns
4 Berkeley Gn
5 Boswell St
6 Caraway Gdns
7 Coombe Rd
8 Coriander Wk
9 East Park Dr
10 Fountaine Ct
11 Freeland Buildings
12 Juniper Ct
13 St Leonard's Rd

E2
1 Cartledge Rd
2 Colwyn Rd
3 Leonards Av
4 Prudham St
5 Seaton Rd

E3
1 Albion St
2 Alfred St
3 Arthur St
4 Clare St
5 Edward St
6 George St
7 Ida Rd
8 Lillian St
9 Samuel St
10 William St

E4
1 Beam St
2 Brook St
3 Brunswick St
4 Byron St
5 Cambridge St
6 Cowper St
7 Hanover St
8 Howett Rd
9 Lancaster St
10 Matthew's Rd
11 Milton Pk
12 Morse Rd
13 Osprey Rd
14 Oxford St
15 Verrier Rd
16 Weight Rd
17 Witchell Rd
18 York St

E5
1 Barton St
2 Ford St
3 Great Western La
4 Kings Park Av

E7
1 Whitby Rd

E8
1 Belmont Rd
2 Falfield Rd
3 Stirling Rd

F1
1 Berkeley Gv
2 Bridge St
3 Crabtree Wk
4 Edward St

F2
1 Camelford Rd
2 Camerton Rd
3 Turley Rd
4 Woodcroft Av

F3
1 Altringham Rd
2 Bourneville Rd
3 Charterhouse Rd
4 Congleton Rd
5 Hammersmith Rd
6 Mary St
7 Neath Rd
8 Oakleigh Av
9 Poets' Cl
10 Stretford Av
11 Tintern Av
12 Trelawney Av
13 Westminster Rd
14 Whitehall Gdns
15 Woodbine Rd

F4
1 Barnes St
2 Beaufort Cl
3 Ebenezer St
4 Gladstone St
5 Handel Av
6 Lewin St
7 Orchard St
8 Parkfield Av
9 Seneca St
10 Speedwell Av
11 Terrell Gdns
12 Weston Av
13 Worsley St

F6
1 Buckingham Rd
2 Westwood Crs

F7
1 Sandhurst Rd
2 Sandwich Rd

F8
1 Bankside Rd
2 Brook Lintons
3 Winchester Rd

Page 337
G2
1 Arley Ter
2 Bowden Rd
3 Chester Rd
4 Thurstons Barton

G3
1 Hudd's Vale Rd
2 Oakland Rd
3 Snowberry Wk

G4
1 Bennett Rd
2 Burgess Green Cl
3 Pilgrims Whf

G5
1 Holy Well Cl
2 Roegate Dr
3 Whiteway Rd

G6
1 The Beeches

H1
1 Irena Rd
2 Madeline Cl

H2
1 Dragon Wk
2 Emra Cl
3 Fernhurst Rd
4 Whitewood Rd

H3
1 Albert Gv
2 Bruton Cl
3 Orchard Rd
4 Park St

H4
1 Summerhill Ter

H5
1 Angels Gnd
2 Avonside Wy
3 Barton Cl
4 Celia Ter
5 Cousins Ms
6 Coventry Wk
7 Crew's Hole Rd
8 Elizabeths Ms
9 Quayside La
10 Riverside Wk
11 St Georges Av

H6
1 Abbey Ct
2 Chelmsford Wk
3 Davies Dr
4 Stockwood Ms

H8
1 Millbrook Av
2 St Helier Av

J1
1 Dean's Dr

J2
1 Ponting Cl
2 Thomas Pring Wk

J3
1 Kensington Rd

J4
1 Cassey Bottom La
2 Kennion Rd
3 Marling Rd
4 Parslow Barton
5 Staple Grove Crs
6 Widcombe Cl

J5
1 Dundridge Gdns
2 Gunter's Hl
3 Harcourt Av
4 Maybec Gdns
5 Petersway Gdns
6 Valma Rocks

K1
1 Forest Wk
2 Lyncombe Wk

K2
1 Beaufort Rd
2 Claymore Cresent
3 Duncombe Rd
4 Launceston Rd
5 Prospect Av

K3
1 Moniks Av
2 St Michaels Ct
3 Two Mile Ct

K4
1 Battens Rd
2 Meg Thatchers Cl
3 Sheldare Barton
4 Thatchers Cl

K5
1 Beverley Cl
2 Clyde Gdns
3 Old Farm La
4 St Aidan's St

K6
1 Bence Ct
2 Churchward Cl
3 Collett Cl
4 Gillingham Hl
5 Hawthorn Av
6 Henbury Rd
7 Lovell's Rd
8 Polly Barnes Cl
9 Vicarage Ct

K8
1 Rowan Wy
2 Sycamore Cl

L1
1 Coulson Wk
2 Henshaw Cl
3 Welton Wk
4 Wentforth Dr
5 Willow Gv
6 Woodland Cl

L2
1 Dalkeith Av
2 Lodgeside Av
3 Seymour Rd
4 Soundwell Rd

L3
1 Barcroft Cl
2 Beverstone
3 Grantham La

L4
1 Trevethin Cl

L5
1 Magpie Bottom La

L6
1 Avonlea
2 Briarfield Av
3 Creswicke Av
4 Hunters Cl
5 Laburnum Rd
6 Lower Chapel Rd
7 Martins Cl

L8
1 Hesding Cl
2 Oak Tree Cl
3 Willow Rd

M1
1 Norman Gv
2 Wellington Rd
3 Whitfield Cl
4 The Wickets
5 Woodland Av

M2
1 Brighton Pl
2 Chesham Wy
3 Gladstone St
4 Hampton St
5 Kensington Av
6 Kimberley Rd
7 Morley Ter
8 Wesley Hl
9 Worcester Rd

D3
1 Crane Cl

M3
1 Bank Rd
2 Eliesmere Rd
3 Halls Rd
4 Parklands
5 West St

M4
1 Abbotswood

M5
1 Dundry Cl
2 Woodcote
3 Woodend

M6
1 Alexandra Rd
2 Grange Ct
3 Whitefield Av
4 Whittucks Rd

M7
1 Hale Cl
2 Headington Cl

Page 338
A1
1 Blackthorn Wk
2 Deerhurst
3 Frys Hl
4 Pembroke Rd
5 Tyndale Rd

A2
1 Collingwood Av
2 Frys Hl
3 Holly Crs
4 Runnymede

A3
1 Macrae Cl
2 Staynes Crs

A4
1 Bellevue Cl
2 Berkeley Rd

A5
1 Elmfield Cl
2 Granny's La
3 High Elm
4 Kemble Cl

A6
1 Copley Ct
2 Cottington Ct
3 Cromwell Ct
4 Skippon Ct
5 Wykis Ct

B1
1 Cranham Cl
2 Elmore
3 Fairford Cl
4 Peartree La

B2
1 Burnham Cl
2 Gilpin Cl
3 Pinewood

B3
1 Barwood Cl
2 Baxter Cl
3 Dyrham Cl
4 Poplar Ter
5 Shortwood Vw
6 Taylor Cl
7 Woodstock Cl

B4
1 Brake Cl
2 Bredon Cl
3 Gee Moors
4 Kingsleigh Cl
5 Kingsleigh Gdns
6 Ladd Cl
7 Norton Cl
8 Penard Wy
9 Shilton Cl
10 Woodstock Rd

B5
1 Niblett Cl
2 Tintern Cl
3 Warner Cl
4 Worth Cl

B6
1 Davis Cl
2 Downside Close
3 Forde Cl
4 Glastonbury Cl
5 Malmesbury Cl
6 Sassoon Ct
7 Scott Ct
8 Woburn Cl

B7
1 Alwins Ct
2 Bramley Ct
3 Britten Ct
4 Drummond Ct
5 Dudley Ct
6 Frampton Ct
7 Godfrey Ct
8 Greve Ct
9 Harris Ct
10 Hicks Ct
11 Laphams Ct
12 Logus Ct
13 Lynch Ct
14 Miles Ct
15 Park Farm Ct
16 Pippin Ct
17 Press Moor Dr
18 Stibbs Ct
19 Tindell Ct
20 Turners Ct
21 Woodington Ct

B8
1 Bagworth Dr
2 Isleys Ct
3 Poyntz Ct
4 Reed Ct
5 Squires Ct

C2
1 Greenways
2 Perrott Rd

C3
1 Brook Rd
2 Charfield
3 Elberton
4 Ozleworth
5 Walnut La

C5
1 Gregory Ct
2 Horsecroft Gdns
3 Staffords Ct
4 Wentworth
5 Wilmot Ct

C6
1 Betjeman Ct
2 Churchill Cl
3 Coronation Cl
4 Dylan Thomas Ct
5 Earlstone Crs
6 Henry Williamson Ct
7 Laurie Lee Ct

C7
1 Chesters
2 Harptree Ct
3 Haskins Ct
4 Horwood Cl
5 Little Dowles
6 Marygold Leaze
7 Stokes Ct
8 Tapsters
9 The Warns

C8
1 Bakersfield
2 Beaumont Cl
3 Fairoaks
4 Penngrove
5 Redwood Cl
6 Rutherford Cl
7 Springville Cl

D5
1 Gleneagles Rd
2 Hadley Ct
3 St Pierre Dr
4 Troon Dr
5 Turnberry

D6
1 Armstrong Dr
2 Heath Ri
3 Park Cl

D7
1 California Rd
2 Cedar Cl
3 Cradock Cl

D8
1 Handford Wy
2 Rawens Wd
3 Stockton Cl

E4
1 St Barnabas Cl

E5
1 Ashbourne Cl
2 Ashcombe Cl
3 Chargrove
4 Highcroft
5 Poplar Cl

E6
1 The Dell
2 Makin Cl
3 Neads Dr

E7
1 Brendon Cl
2 Hawkins Cl

E8
1 Brookfield Wk
2 Chequers Cl
3 The Clamp
4 The Croft

F5
1 Ashcombe Crs
2 Coniston Cl
3 Haweswater Cl
4 Mitchell Wk
5 Ullswater Cl

F6
1 Hardwick Cl
2 Samuel Wright Cl
3 Summerhayes

F7
1 Batley Ct
2 Lovell Av
3 North Cft

Page 345
H6
1 Bishops Cove
2 Broadway Rd
3 Highridge Pk
4 Shuter Rd
5 Templeland Rd

J2
1 Lilton Wk

J6
1 Cornleaze
2 Gatehouse Cl
3 Goulston Wk
4 Heggard Cl
5 Innox Gdns

K1
1 Bedminster Down Rd
2 Brighton Ter
3 Churchlands Rd
4 Derry Rd
5 Hardy Rd
6 Harptree Gv
7 Hengaston St
8 Highridge Rd
9 Osborne Ter
10 South Liberty La
11 Temple St
12 Trafalgar Ter
13 Winterstoke Cl

K5
1 Hestercombe Rd
2 Pinhay Rd

K6
1 Farmwell Cl
2 Flowerwell Rd
3 Fulford Rd
4 Fulford Wk
5 Gander Cl
6 Gatehouse Ct
7 Lyveden Gdns
8 Vigor Rd
9 Whitland Av

K7
1 Binmead Gdns
2 Gullimores Gdns
3 Harnhill Cl
4 Hogues Wk
5 Honey Garston Cl
6 Lenover Gdns
7 Sallysmead Cl

K8
1 Combe Cross Wk

L1
1 Beaufort St
2 Buckingham St
3 Francis Rd
4 Stanley Ter

L2
1 Hastings Cl
2 Wimborne Rd

L7
1 Horsham Gv
2 Lasbury Gv
3 Luckley Av
4 Wymbush Gdns

L8
1 Hellier Wk
2 Pawlett Wk
3 Peterson Sq

M1
1 Sidmouth Gdns

M3
1 Camberley Rd

M4
1 Appleby Wk
2 Bratton Rd
3 Butterworth Ct
4 Corfe Rd
5 Courteney Crs
6 Cowdray Rd
7 Delius Gv
8 Langhill Av
9 Pevensey Wk
10 Purcell Wk
11 Taverner Cl

M5
1 Elgar Cl
2 Inns Court Dr
3 Stainer Cl
4 Travers Cl
5 Wilbye Gv

M6
1 Hawkfield Wy

M7
1 Pigeon House Dr
2 Rudgewood Cl
3 Wroughton Gdns

M8
1 Macey's Rd

Page 346
A1
1 Wedmore V

A2
1 Kinsale Wk

A3
1 Belfast Wk
2 Instow Wk
3 Kinvara Rd
4 Marwood Rd
5 Saunton Wk
6 Tyrone Wk

A7
1 Teyfant Wk
2 Totshill Gv

A8
1 Shortwood Wk

B1
1 Beckington Wk
2 St Agnes Cl
3 St Agnes Wk

B2
1 Silverton Ct
2 Tavistock Wk

B3
1 Barnstaple Wk
2 Corsley Wk
3 Dunster Rd
4 Hartcliffe Wk
5 Neston Wk

B4
1 Griggfield Wk
2 Pinecroft

B5
1 Haycombe

B7
1 Stockton Cl

B8
1 Bentley Cl
2 Chatterton Gn
3 Clewson Ri
4 Gooseland Cl
5 Lower Fallow Cl
6 Stratford Cl
7 Willmott Cl

C1
1 Stoneleigh Wk

C2
1 Green Wk
2 Greenwood Rd
3 Preston Wk
4 The Square
5 Teignmouth Rd

C4
1 Parsons Paddock

C6
1 Portmeirion Cl

C8
1 Beckford Gdns
2 Bridge Farm Cl
3 Churston Cl
4 Coulson's Cl
5 Glendevon Rd

D1
1 Langham Rd
2 Marston Rd
3 Merrifield Rd
4 Oakmeade Pk
5 Ryde Rd

D2
1 Newlyn Wk
2 St Martin's Gdns
3 St Martin's Wk
4 Shapcott Cl

D3
1 Allanmead Rd
2 Drayton Cl
3 Edgewood Cl

D4
1 Elderwood Rd

D6
1 Blackdown Cl
2 Copeland Dr
3 Cranleigh Rd
4 Curland Gv
5 Heart Meers
6 Otterford Cl
7 Wedgwood Cl
8 Wharnecliffe Cl
9 Winsham Cl
10 Withypool Gdns

D7
1 Foxcombe Rd

D8
1 Birch Cft

E1
1 Tozers Hl

E5
1 Honeymead
2 Whitecross Av

E6
1 Timberscombe Wk

E7
1 Bridge Cl

F1
1 Badgers Wk
2 Beeches Gv
3 Bellevue Pk
4 Bellevue Ter
5 Grove Pk
6 Wycombe Gv

F3
1 Adams Hay
2 Bartonia Gv
3 Ellesmere Rd
4 Graveney Cl
5 Hammond Cl
6 Homemead Dr
7 Prestwick Cl
8 West Town Dr

F4
1 Fontmell Ct
2 Hanford Ct
3 Morden Wk
4 Roundmoor Gdns

F5
1 Burgis Rd
2 Dutton Cl
3 Dutton Wk

F6
1 Craydon Wk
2 Gillebank Cl
3 Pensford Ct
4 Showering Cl

F7
1 Staunton Wy

Page 347
G5
1 Beale Cl
2 Cornish Gv
3 Harrington Gv
4 Harrington Wk
5 Meardon Rd
6 Puxley Cl
7 Thompson Rd

G6
1 Bagnell Cl
2 Hollway Cl
3 Pomfrett Gdns
4 Woolley Rd

J1
1 Hulbert Cl
2 Maybourne
3 Raymill
4 Regency Dr

Page 348
D1
1 Dunster Gdns
2 St Fagans Ct
3 The Tanyard
4 Warwick Rd

D2
1 Carmarthen Gv
2 Kenilworth Dr

Notes